A HISTORY OF WAR AND PEACE
1939 – 1965

The Royal Institute of International Affairs is an unofficial body which promotes the scientific study of international questions and does not express opinions of its own. The opinions expressed in this publication are the responsibility of the author.

The Institute gratefully acknowledges the comments and suggestions of the following who read the manuscript on behalf of the Research Committee: Alan Bullock, Peter Calvocoressi, and Hugh Seton-Watson.

A History of
War and Peace
1939 – 1965

WILFRID KNAPP

FELLOW AND TUTOR, ST. CATHERINE'S COLLEGE, OXFORD

Issued under the auspices of the
Royal Institute of International Affairs

OXFORD UNIVERSITY PRESS

LONDON   NEW YORK   TORONTO

1967

Oxford University Press, Ely House, London W.1

GLASGOW NEW YORK TORONTO MELBOURNE WELLINGTON
BOMBAY CALCUTTA MADRAS KARACHI LAHORE DACCA
CAPE TOWN SALISBURY NAIROBI IBADAN
KUALA LUMPUR HONG KONG TOKYO

*Printed in Great Britain
by Eyre and Spottiswoode Limited at
The Thanet Press, Margate*

TO MY PARENTS

CONTENTS

ABBREVIATIONS

American Foreign Policy, 1950–5:	US Dept of State, *American Foreign Policy, 1950–5; basic documents* (1957).
CDU:	Christlich-Demokratische Union.
CEEC:	Committee for European Economic Co-operation.
Churchill, i–vi:	W. S. Churchill, *The Second World War*, vols i–vi (1948–54).
Comecon:	Council for Mutual Economic Assistance.
Cominform:	Communist Information Bureau.
Conference of Berlin; Conferences at Cairo and Tehran; Conferences at Malta and Yalta:	US Dept of State, *Foreign Relations of the United States, Diplomatic Papers: The Conference of Berlin* . . . (1960); *The Conferences at Cairo and Tehran* (1961); *The Conferences at Malta and Yalta* (1955).
CPY:	Communist Party of Yugoslavia.
DAFR:	*Documents on American Foreign Relations.*
DGFP:	GB, Foreign Office and US Dept of State, *Documents on German Foreign Policy, 1918–45* . . . series D (1937–45).
Decade of American Foreign Policy:	US Senate, Committee on Foreign Relations of State Dept, *A Decade of American Foreign Policy; Basic Documents, 1941–9* (1950).
ECA:	European Co-operation Administration.
ECSC:	European Coal and Steel Community.
EDC:	European Defence Community.
EEC:	European Economic Community.
EMA:	European Monetary Agreement.
EPU:	European Payments Union.
Euratom:	European Atomic Energy Community.
GDR:	German Democratic Republic.
Hurewitz:	J. C. Hurewitz, *Diplomacy in the Near and Middle East* (1956).
IBRD:	International Bank for Reconstruction and Development.
IMF:	International Monetary Fund.
KPD:	Kommunistische Partei Deutschlands.
LDPD:	Liberal-Demokratische Partei Deutschlands.
MRP:	Mouvement Républicain Populaire.
OAS:	Organization of American States.

1*

OEEC:	Organization for European Economic Co-operation.
RIIA, *Documents* & *Survey*:	Royal Institute of International Affairs, *Documents* & *Survey of International Affairs*.
SED:	Sozialistische Einheitspartei Deutschlands.
SPD:	Sozialdemokratische Partei Deutschlands.
Sherwood:	R. E. Sherwood, *The White House Papers of Harry L. Hopkins* (1949).
WEU:	Western European Union.

FOREWORD

THIS BOOK owes much to many people. It is dedicated to my parents, who regarded academic life as a goal worthy of foresight and sacrifice before the welfare state made it easier of access. The help which my wife has given with the manuscript and the index is a minute part of the spiritual sustenance which she and our sons have furnished while the book was being written.

The manuscript has been read in whole or in part by Laurie Baragwanath, Alan Bullock, Peter Calvocoressi, Albert Hourani, Elizabeth Monroe, Harry Pitt, Hugh Seton-Watson, David Stairs, and Richard Storry. Their comments have greatly improved it and their help has been invaluable. My debt to Alan Bullock extends far beyond this; for a score of years the chances of academic life have brought us sufficiently close for me to benefit fully from his inspiration and example.

Miss Sheila McMeekin typed the whole intelligently and accurately; by her efficiency as my secretary she created time in which I could write. Miss Hermia Oliver has gone through the entire work, giving it the rigorous attention to detail and style with which a large number of Chatham House authors are familiar. She has also made an invaluable contribution to the book by tracing and establishing sources. The final tidying up of the manuscript was done from North Africa, and I drew heavily on the willing assistance of Mr Philip Darby and Mr Richard Mansbach, as well as Miss McMeekin and Miss Oliver.

Inevitably a book of this scope derives much from the original work done by others. In part this is evident from the bibliography, but I would acknowledge also my debt to innumerable members of my own university, and visitors to it, who have contributed in seminars, lectures, and discussions to what is written here. In a real sense this book is drawn from the life of a great university; I hope that, for all the faults that remain (and for which I alone am responsible), it will offer something in return.

W.K.

May 1966

1

FROM WAR IN EUROPE TO WORLD WAR

WAR BROKE out in Europe on 1 September 1939. In the Far East the Japanese attack on China had been in progress since 1937. But the two countries which were to emerge as the dominant powers of the post-war world were still neutral. The central themes of international affairs in the next twenty-seven months therefore were the junction of the two wars, in Europe and the Far East, and the relations between the combatants and the most important of the neutrals. These themes must be set against the course of the battles themselves – relatively slow moving in the Far East, dramatically swift in the west.

In Europe the initiative remained with Hitler. The invasion of Poland, which had been the immediate cause of the new conflict, met with resistance which was brave but ineffective. On the western front the hollowness of the last years of French foreign policy was revealed by the failure of the French army to mount any serious offensive which would bring substantial assistance to Poland by drawing off the German armies, far less by destroying them in battle. The whole framework of French policy as it had been constructed at Versailles, with its supposition that eastern Europe would be defended by a vigorous attack in the west, taking advantage of bridgeheads across the Rhine, or at least of a Rhineland demilitarized zone, had been dismantled piece by piece in the ensuing years. Within two to three weeks all effective resistance in Poland was at an end.

The success of the German armies brought into action the secret protocol attached to the Nazi-Soviet pact of August 1939, whose existence had been widely conjectured, although it was not confirmed until the Nuremberg trials after the war. The purpose of the protocol had been to draw a dividing line between Russian and German spheres in eastern Europe; and it had done so by recognizing that Finland, Estonia, Latvia, the eastern part of Poland, and Bessarabia were in the Russian sphere. As German troops were now advancing eastwards across Poland it was natural that the Russian government should act to safeguard its interests under this protocol, and on 17 September Russian troops entered Poland. The following day they met the Germans at Brest-Litovsk – the site of an earlier confrontation, less favourable to the Russians, in March 1918. Stalin's original intention appears to have been to leave a small Polish state intact, and it was presumably the presence of the German armies which led to the abandonment of this intention – accompanied by some nervousness lest fighting should break out between the two armies, particularly since in places the German armies had advanced beyond the demarcation line. In the event nothing happened, and on 28 September the two powers were able to sign a fresh treaty. Its importance lay, however, in its secret protocols rather than in the treaty itself. They modified the early treaty by transferring the greater part of Lithuania to the Soviet sphere, and by providing for the transfer of all German citizens in the Baltic states to Germany.

As might have been foreseen from the pages of *Mein Kampf*, the settlement between Russia and Germany was extremely unstable. It was immediately followed on the Russian side by the continuation of preparations against the possibility of a German attack – of which the original pact with Germany and the occupation of eastern Poland may themselves be seen as part. A brief diplomatic offensive against the Baltic states brought their representatives to Moscow, where agreements were signed between Russia and Estonia (29 September), Latvia (5 October), and Lithuania (10 October). All three treaties included agreements for mutual assistance in the event of aggression, and for the stationing of Soviet troops; while the treaties with Estonia and Latvia provided for the lease of naval and air bases to the Soviet Union.

In its relations with Finland, the Soviet Union sought to gain more, and met with more determined resistance. Russian pressure on Finland for a defensive position within that country had begun as early as 1938,[1] and had met with a negative response. It was obvious that from a Russian point of view Finland was at least as important in a defensive scheme as the more southerly Baltic states, both because of its position in relation to Leningrad, and because Germany had developed

[1] See V. Tanner, *The Winter War* (1957), pp. 1–15.

interests in Finland ever since it had assisted in the suppression of a communist revolution after the first world war. None the less Finland had endeavoured to maintain a position of absolute neutrality. It had resisted proposals for a Soviet guarantee in the spring of 1939, and the representations made by the Finnish ambassador had been one of the factors slowing up the British part in Anglo-Soviet negotiations; but it had also rejected a non-aggression pact with Germany at the same time.

The latest set of negotiations with Finland proved as abortive as previous attempts, mainly because of Finnish refusals to accede to Soviet demands on their territory. The Soviet Union attacked Finland on 29 November 1939, and a few days later set up a puppet Finnish government under the communist, Kuusinen, which accepted the Soviet demands. But three months later the Russian government having achieved limited military success, abandoned its protégé and negotiated terms with the legal government of Finland, embodied in a treaty signed on 12 March 1940. By this treaty the Karelian isthmus was ceded to Russia together with Viborg bay and its islands, and the western and northern shores of Lake Ladoga. Finland agreed to a thirty-year Russian lease of the peninsula of Hangö, and the right of transit across its territory to Norway and Sweden, together with the right to construct a railway from Kandalaksha to Kemijärvi; and to the demilitarization of its Arctic coastline. In addition, the two countries undertook obligations of non-aggression and to eschew hostile alliances.

In this way the Soviet Union succeeded in extending its defensive line from the Arctic ocean in the north to Rumania in the south. But the significance of the Finnish war went far beyond this immediate Russian achievement. The war took place after the defeat of Poland and before the attack on France, so that apart from patrol activities on the western front it constituted the only fighting of the winter. It was a war designed to protect Russia from attack via Finland, and the most likely aggressor in such an attack was Germany. But the Nazi-Soviet pact was still of sufficient importance to both powers for Germany to remain neutral in the conflict and to put up a show of disinterestedness, and for the Soviet government to keep up the same pretence. Communist propaganda showed the danger to Russia as coming from Britain and France.

This was an imputation which these two countries almost succeeded in making real. In both countries there was a strong feeling of resentment towards the Soviet Union on account of the Nazi-Soviet pact – an emotion which was probably stronger in France than in Britain, because of the large communist party which had followed the Russian lead. Anti-communism was given a respectable pretext. It also seemed almost as if those who had idly witnessed the occupation of Abyssinia and Czechoslovakia now wanted to make up for their recent inaction by going to the aid of any small country that was under attack.

No doubt this emotion would have worn itself out ineffectually had it not been that the governments of Britain and France saw a means of using the Finnish war to strike a blow at Germany. The British government in particular sought a means of stopping supplies of iron ore from Norway and Sweden from reaching Germany, and as early as November 1939 Churchill, as First Lord of the Admiralty, had been trying to persuade the cabinet to agree to minelaying in Norwegian territorial waters. If now aid were sent to Finland it would have to pass through Norway; and if the Norwegian government could be persuaded to agree to the stationing of British troops at Narvik it might be possible to use this advantage to stop the flow of Norwegian ore.

While such possibilities were under discussion the Finnish government appealed to the League of Nations under Articles 11 and 15 of the Covenant. With a speed and decisiveness which it had never managed to achieve in the face of earlier aggression, the League Assembly met, although without the attendance of the Soviet delegate, who argued that the Soviet Union was not at war with Finland and that the true government of Finland was that of Kuusinen. On 14 December, three days after the special session had opened, the Assembly unanimously adopted a resolution condemning the Soviet government, and continuing: 'in virtue of Article 16 paragraph 4 of the Covenant finds that, by its act, the USSR had placed itself outside the League of Nations. It follows that the USSR is no longer a member of the League.' In this way the Soviet Union achieved the distinction of being the only power to be expelled from the League – a fact which was to be of some importance, as we shall see, when the construction of a new post-war international organization came under discussion.

An additional fact of significance in the conduct of the war was that the Russian troops found great difficulty in dominating their opponents in the early part of the campaign. Their equipment appeared inadequate or unsuitable, and a series of attacks against the prepared Finnish positions of the Mannerheim Line were repulsed with heavy losses. Both in Germany and elsewhere the conclusion was drawn that Russian forces were weak and ill prepared for battle, and doubtless this was of marginal importance in encouraging Hitler in his later attack on the Soviet Union. Elsewhere it induced considerable pessimism, when that attack was first launched, about the possibility of prolonged Russian resistance.

But the superior weight of the Russian attack was bound to prevail in the long run, and as Norway and Sweden had been unwilling to allow the passage of allied troops or supplies to the Finns, all possibility of giving assistance collapsed – and with it the Daladier government in France, which had been heavily committed to aid to Finland. On the other hand the British cabinet at last agreed to the mining of Norwegian waters, and preparations were put in hand to carry out this operation. Throughout this period of hesitation, however, a precisely similar line of reasoning had been going on in Germany. On 3 October, four days after Churchill had drawn the cabinet's attention to the importance to Germany of Swedish ore, Admiral Räder had made a preparatory survey of the possibility of securing bases in Norway. At first Hitler had shown little interest in the idea, intent as he was on preparing for an attack on France; but as the winter postponed the feasibility of such an attack, and as British and French talk of aiding Finland made the threat to Norway seem greater, the idea appealed more strongly to him – the more so since Räder suggested that the main force of the attack could be mounted inside Norway by Quisling and other leaders of the small Norwegian Nazi party. As a result preparations were put in hand and had matured by the end of March. The threat from Britain appeared smaller now that the Finnish war was over – although in fact, as we have seen, it was for the first time becoming real – but even so the scheme was pressed ahead. Between 7 and 9 April 1940 opposing naval forces converged on Norway, the one to ensure and the other to deny supplies of iron ore to Germany; but whereas the British force was intended as a minelaying expedition, its German counterpart was a force of attack. Carrying through a well conceived operation with all the advantages of complete surprise, German forces succeeded in rapidly gaining control of the main Norwegian ports. Their fleet suffered losses proportionately more important than those they inflicted on the British; but once they had consolidated their land positions, it proved impossible for British forces to dislodge them. As a return for their naval losses the Germans had occupied Denmark and Norway, secured their iron supplies, and gained the whole northern coast of Europe for the battle of the Atlantic. Politically they had gained nothing, as both the Norwegian and Danish governments fled into exile, and the plan to establish an effective government under Quisling or his Danish counterparts with any degree of popular support collapsed entirely.

The humiliation and danger to Britain, as a sea power, of the German occupation of Norway and Denmark brought the fall of the Chamberlain government and the appointment of Winston Churchill as prime minister. On the same day, 10 May 1940, the German armies launched their main attack in the west, through Belgium, Holland, and Luxembourg and into France. Within two weeks they had broken their enemies' resistance on the continent of Europe.

In this situation Churchill's appointment was of major importance. His leadership suited ideally the needs of his nation at that moment. Protected by the Channel, supported by the Commonwealth and imbued with a natural obstinacy, the British people would have been unlikely to accept defeat unless they were crushed by invasion. But Churchill evoked qualities in his people of which they had scarcely seemed capable. As has been written of him:

In 1940 he assumed an indomitable stoutness, an unsurrendering quality on the part of his people, and carried on. If he did not represent the quintessence and epitome of what some, at any rate, of his fellow citizens feared and hoped in their hour of danger, this was because he idealised them with such intensity that in the end they approached his ideal and began to see themselves as he saw them: 'the buoyant and imperturbable temper of Britain which I had the honour to express' – it was indeed, but he had a lion's share in creating it.[2]

[2] Isaiah Berlin, *Mr Churchill in 1940* (1949), p. 26.

Thanks to the evacuation of a large part of the British expeditionary force from Dunkirk, and the refusal of the government to commit its remaining fighter strength to the battle in France, Britain was militarily able to provide for its own defence. Politically Churchill's immediate task was to try to salvage the French government, or to ensure that if it made peace Britain's interests would be protected as far as possible. The British government therefore offered to release the French from their agreement not to make a separate peace 'provided, but only provided, that the French fleet is sailed henceforth for British harbours pending negotiations'. Immediately afterwards, the British government proposed that the two nations should join in a Franco-British union, with joint organs of defence, foreign, financial, and economic policies. No favourable response to either of these proposals was forthcoming from France.

Meanwhile Italy had entered the war on the side of Germany. Mussolini saw great possibilities opening up of taking over the French empire in North Africa, but Hitler exercised a restraining hand. He asked the Duce to postpone a declaration of war until after Germany had completed the destruction of the French air force, and Mussolini then took a few extra days to regroup troops in Libya and, in so doing, to 'avoid even the slightest setback which the Allies would always exploit to the full for propaganda purposes'. The Italian declaration of war eventually came on 10 June 1940. A week later Mussolini travelled to Munich, and there Hitler made clear to him the necessity of framing a moderate armistice with France, which would induce a French government to remain in France, and would offer no incentive for the fleet to go over to Britain. Mussolini was in no position to object.

Hitler's tactics were successful. In the actual signature of the armistice with France on 22 June he subjected his defeated enemy to the maximum humiliation. The site which he chose for the occasion was the identical spot in the Forest of Compiègne where Foch had dictated terms to Germany in 1918, and the historic railway coach was brought from its museum for the purpose. But the terms imposed were such as to be acceptable to the government which had been formed under Marshal Pétain. Only the northern half of France was to be occupied; France retained its colonies, and the fleet was neither to be handed over to Germany nor sunk, only neutralized in French ports. Not only was the Pétain government willing to sign such an alliance but in doing so it had the support of those Frenchmen who saw no alternative to the acceptance of defeat on the best possible terms, as well as of the small minority who welcomed and admired their conqueror. In contrast an important and growing number were willing to continue the battle, either because they believed in the eventual victory of Britain and the Commonwealth, or because even in despair they would rather fight than capitulate. Such men found their leader in de Gaulle, who had gone to London before the armistice was signed, and, refusing to return, was condemned to death by his own government. De Gaulle's vision, however, extended far beyond that of most of his followers. For him the task was not merely to continue to fight alongside the British, but to restore the independence and sovereignty of France as a great power. As he later wrote: 'Devant le vide effrayant du renoncement général, ma mission m'apparut, d'un seul coup, claire et terrible. En ce moment, le pire de son histoire, c'était à moi d'assumer la France.'[3]

The signature of the French armistice meant that Churchill had so far failed in his initial objective of securing the French fleet to Britain. On the contrary it had passed fully armed into the reach of German hands, and the British government saw no reason to expect the Germans to honour the armistice agreement, or the French to be in a position to prevent German use of the fleet against Britain. They therefore took action against the French fleet in whatever ports it was to be found, according to the means at their disposal. In Britain this meant that the navy commandeered French ships, meeting resistance from few and welcome from some. But the most dramatic episode was at the military port of Mers el-Kebir, adjoining Oran.[4] A British naval force was dispatched under the command of Admiral Somerville, who invited his French counterpart to join with him against the Axis powers, or to sail his ships with reduced crews to British ports, or to sail them to a French port in the West Indies; but told him that if he was

[3] *L'Appel* (1954), p. 74.
[4] It is characteristic of Anglo-French misunderstanding that the episode should have bitten deeply into the emotions of Frenchmen as the episode of Mers el-Kebir, a name which few in England recognize, even though they may be aware of the Oran incident.

unwilling to accept any of these three choices, or to sink his ships, they would be sunk by the British. Whether through intention or misunderstanding,[5] Admiral Gensoul rejected the three possibilities offered to him, and the British fleet opened fire.

In this way the threat that a powerful French fleet would be added to the German and Italian navies, with the glowering threat of the Japanese in the Pacific, was eliminated. Immediately afterwards, on 5 July 1940, the French government broke off relations with Britain; on 11 July Pétain was installed as chief of state and the Third French Republic came effectively (although not legally) to an end. The British government had already declared that the French government at Bordeaux was unable to act independently and recognized the formation of a Committee of National Liberation. On 7 August an agreement was signed with this Committee, and de Gaulle recognized as 'Leader of the Free French'.

There was an obvious disparity between de Gaulle's view of himself as embodying the true France, and British recognition of him as leader of the Free French, and this disparity was matched by the practical difficulties of co-operation. The destruction of the French fleet at Oran was carried out without consultation with de Gaulle. These difficulties immediately became apparent when, at the end of August, a joint expedition to Dakar was planned with the intention of adding to the support which had already rallied to de Gaulle in French Equatorial Africa, and denying a submarine base to the Germans. The expedition was a failure, partly for military reasons, partly because the Vichy French, far from joining de Gaulle, put up vigorous and effective resistance. In the House of Commons Churchill stood firmly behind de Gaulle and reaffirmed British confidence in his leadership, but he only partly succeeded in countering the criticisms levelled at the National Committee not only in London but even more in Washington. Moreover the expedition had shown the unreliability of security amongst the Free French, and revealed the probability of bitter fighting should Vichy and Free French confront each other. As we shall see, these difficulties were to grow proportionately as British and American forces went into action in the French empire in the Middle East and in North Africa.

[5] See Churchill, ii. 209.

Map 1

Based on L. L. Snyder, THE WAR: A CONCISE HISTORY
(London, Hale, 1962)

In the summer of 1940, then, Hitler dominated the continent of Europe while Britain and its Commonwealth fought the Italians in North Africa and defended itself against attack. It was host to the governments whose lands had been overrun by invaders, and the rallying point for individuals who wished to fight on. Outside the ring stood the great neutrals, America and Russia. In the centre of the battle the German air force came within an ace of destroying the effectiveness of the British air force by attacking its airfields, before switching its targets to the cities, where civilians showed how resilient they could be under aerial bombardment − albeit on a scale which the British far surpassed in their attacks on German towns later in the war. Hitler prepared and postponed plans for an invasion of Britain, partly because of the limited success of the air offensive, but also because he was already planning an attack on the Soviet Union. In contrast, Churchill looked to the United States for the support which Britain must secure if it was to emerge victorious. He was well aware of the sympathy for Britain to be found across the Atlantic, and the isolationism which accompanied it. With great skill he sought to mobilize the one and diminish the other. He asked no more of the United States than he thought it would be willing to give; but he made clear his conviction that if Britain fell, the United States too would have suffered defeat.

Already in November 1939 Congress had modified the pre-war neutrality legislation. Following the lead given by the administration, the new act removed the embargo on the export of arms to belligerents, while still providing that they, together with war materials, should not be carried on American ships or supplied on credit. At the same time the president was empowered to declare some areas as 'combat areas', which American ships should not enter. In this way Britain and France were given an important advantage, in that they, and not Germany or Italy, were able to avail themselves of the 'cash and carry' basis of the new legislation. It was not, how-ever, until May 1940 that Anglo-American co-operation acquired momentum, for the Chamberlain government was sparing in the orders it placed in the United States and did little to enlist its support. Churchill, on taking office, resumed as prime minister his correspondence with Roosevelt, still over the signature 'Former Naval Person', and appointed Lord

Lothian to be a highly successful ambassador – as Harry Hopkins, Roosevelt's personal aide, established close relations with Churchill. Orders from Britain for the sinews of war reached a new scale, and were met with an urgent and sympathetic response in the United States. With all the grandeur of his oratory Churchill at once inspired his countrymen and linked their cause to that of the United States when he said: 'But if we fail, then the whole world, including the United States, including all that we have known and cared for, will sink into the abyss of a new Dark Age made more sinister, and perhaps more protracted, by the lights of perverted science.'[6]

Meanwhile in the Far East a decisive stage had been reached in the road that was to lead to the spread of the war into the Pacific. At the end of July 1940 a new Japanese government was formed under Konoye, with Tojo as minister of war, and Matsuoka as foreign minister. On 26 and 27 July 1940 the new cabinet considered and approved 'The Main Principles of Japan's National Policy'. The broad programme thus agreed on included in the first place a satisfactory settlement of the 'China incident', and the building of a new order in Greater East Asia. An alliance with Germany and Italy was foreseen, and a settlement of relations with the Soviet Union. While the China incident was being wound up everything would be done to restrict aid to Chiang Kai-shek and to improve Japan's own position, for example by concessions in Indo-China and the Netherlands East Indies. This would unavoidably bring Japan into a tense situation in relation to the United States. Once the China incident was settled satisfactorily, Japan would choose a favourable moment to expand southwards, and would use force to do so.

As has been said in a brilliant account of Japanese policy at this time: 'The decisions of July 26 and 27, 1940, constituted a pivotal stage in the metamorphosis of the China Incident into the Greater East Asia War'.[7] Over the next eighteen months divisions remained within the Japanese government and ruling circles, and there was persistent debate and discussion of the next moves to be made in foreign and military policy. But the minimum view of Japan's foreign requirements was that it was necessary to settle the China incident and, consequent on that,

[6] Broadcast, 18 June 1940 (*Into Battle* (1941), p. 234).
[7] R. J. C. Butow, *Tojo and the Coming of the War* (1961).

to establish a strategic position in Indo-China and make certain of oil supplies from the Netherlands East Indies. The maximum view was embodied in a policy statement approved by Konoye, Matsuoka, Tojo, and the ministry of the navy, on 4 September 1940:

The sphere to be envisaged in the course of negotiations with Germany and Italy as Japan's Sphere of Living for the construction of a Greater East Asia New Order will comprise: The Former German Islands under mandate, French Indo-China and Pacific Islands, Thailand, British Malaya, British Borneo, Dutch East Indies, Burma, Australia, New Zealand, India, etc., with Japan, Manchuria, and China as the backbone.[8]

The steps by which the realization of this programme would be achieved were affected by developments in Europe; but the mainspring of expansionism was in Japan itself, and there is plentiful evidence of the extent to which Japanese ministers lived in a fantasy world, ignorant of much of world politics, and unaware of a cause and effect relationship between their actions and the policies of the western powers which came to be ranged against them. Military needs were decisive in the formulation of national policy, and no one seriously questioned the assumption that the use of force was a normal instrument of national policy – least of all when it was justified on the practical grounds of the indispensability of obtaining oil supplies.

Events in Europe were such as to encourage Japanese ambitions. The success of Germany promised equal success to a 'dynamic' power in East Asia, while the defeat of the European colonial powers made Indo-China, the Netherlands East Indies, Malaya, and Borneo seem more vulnerable to Japanese pressure and conquest. Unfortunately for Japan, however, a deeper movement underlay these apparently promising developments, for the Nazi success in Europe reinforced the American will and determination to resist aggression and expansionism. Thus at almost the same moment that the Japanese government agreed on its national policy, Roosevelt issued orders for the control of aviation gasoline and first-class scrap. But in the eyes of the Japanese government the defensive reaction of America, Britain, China, and the Netherlands (the 'ABCD' powers) was interpreted as a strangling encirclement

[8] H. Feis, *The Road to Pearl Harbor* (1950), p. 114.

whose bonds they must burst in the legitimate pursuit of Japan's national interests. These were the emotions and the forces which underlay the diplomacy of 1940 and 1941.

The prestige gained for Germany by the Nazi armies in Europe was sufficient to enable Hitler and Ribbentrop to conclude negotiations which had gone on intermittently since before the war and to secure the signature of a tripartite pact between Germany, Italy, and Japan on 27 September 1940. Respect for Germany, compounded with resentment against the western democracies for their support of China and hostility to Japan's 'national aspirations', was given fresh encouragement by German success. Even so, the arguments used by Matsuoka in favour of the pact – for example, that a pact would encourage the German and Italian Americans to exert decisive pressure against an American war with Japan – show how far the government was removed from reality. Japan gained nothing from the pact which it did not pay for in equal coin. Germany and Italy recognized Japan's 'leadership in the establishment of a new order in Greater East Asia', in return for a reciprocal agreement in regard to Europe. More important, the three powers undertook mutual obligations in the event of attack. In the terms of Article III: 'Japan, Germany and Italy . . . further undertake to assist one another with all political, economic and military means when one of the three Contracting Parties is attacked by a power at present not involved in the European War or in the Sino-Japanese Conflict.'[9] In this way Japan was promised assistance if attacked by the United States, but only if it was willing to assume the risk of coming into conflict with America – which at this time the navy earnestly hoped to avoid – as a result of the pact. Speciously, and unrealistically, Matsuoka argued that the risk of conflict with the United States was diminished by the pact; in fact the navy had moved a step further towards the acceptance of the same policy of attack as the army, and Japan had entered a defensive alliance against America. Meanwhile the Japanese government was keeping up pressure on the Netherlands East Indies to provide an increased export of oil. All these events provoked a vigorous reaction in the United States. For many months the Roosevelt administration had been divided between those who, like Secretary Morgenthau of the Treasury,

[9] Ibid., pp. 119–20.

advocated a tough policy towards Japan, and the State Department view of Cordell Hull that moderation on the part of the
United States was the safest way to evoke moderation on the
part of Japan. But the ultimatum to the French in Indo-China
brought vigorous protest from Hull to Tokyo, and the signature
of the tripartite pact excited the secretary of state as it did the
American people – even though Hull played it down in his
public comment. In reaction to the movement of Japanese
troops into Indo-China, the president extended the control of
scrap export to all grades and thereby constituted an effective
embargo as far as Japan was concerned.

Moreover, just as appeasement grows and reinforces itself
when practised by several nations at once, so does resistance.
In July the British government had, on the demand of the
Japanese, closed the road from Burma into China by which
Chiang Kai-shek's troops were supplied. But through the
summer Churchill had negotiated with Roosevelt the exchange
of fifty old American destroyers against the right of the United
States to build bases on a ninety-nine-year lease in Newfoundland, the Bahamas, Bermuda, and the West Indies. The
agreement was concluded on 5 September. A week later the
American ambassador in Japan, who had been noted for the
sympathy with which he had interpreted Japanese policy, now
wrote home to his government in a markedly different tone:

> If the support of the British Empire in this her hour of travail is
> conceived to be in our interest . . . we must strive by every means to
> preserve the status quo in the Pacific. . . . Japan has been deterred
> from the taking of greater liberties with American interests only
> because she respects our potential power; equally . . . she has
> trampled upon our rights to an extent in exact ratio to the strength
> of her conviction that the people of the United States would not
> permit that power to be used. . . . Therefore, if by firmness we can
> preserve the status quo in the Pacific until and after Great Britain is
> successful in the European war, a situation will be faced by Japan
> which will render it impossible for the present opportunist philosophy
> to keep the upper hand.[10]

Churchill was not privy to the dispatches of United States
ambassadors, but he did not need to be, to be aware of reactions
in the administration. As soon as the destroyer agreement was
signed he took up again with the American government the

[10]US Dept of State, *Peace and War: US Foreign Policy 1931–41* (1943).

reopening of the Burma road, and hoped that this might be accompanied by an American fleet visit to Singapore; at the same time he did everything possible to encourage the government of the Netherlands East Indies and Royal Dutch Shell to persist in resisting Japanese demands for oil. The fleet visit did not materialize; but the Burma road was reopened on 18 October.

Inevitably there was uncertainty in American foreign policy at this time. There existed a common desire to limit Japanese expansion and to prepare for a possible future conflict, without by so doing precipitating war in the Far East, for which American forces were still unprepared; but the judgement of the actual danger of a Japanese attack, and of the effect of precautionary measures on Japanese policy, varied with events and between persons. More important, the president was fighting an election campaign against the effective challenge of Wendell Willkie as Republican candidate to secure the unique result of his re-election for a third term. The uncertainty of Roosevelt's position can be judged from his speeches. Addressing the Teamsters' Union Convention on 11 September he said:

I hate war, now more than ever. I have one supreme determination – to do all that I can to keep war away from these shores for all time. I stand, with my party, and outside of my party as President of all the people, on the platform . . . that was adopted in Chicago less than two months ago. It said: 'We will not participate in foreign wars, and we will not send our Army, naval or air forces to fight in foreign lands outside of the Americas, except in case of attack.'[11]

And a month later, on 12 October at Dayton, Ohio:

No combination of dictator countries of Europe and Asia will halt us in the path we see ahead for ourselves and for democracy. No combination of dictator countries of Europe and Asia will stop the help we are giving to almost the last free people now fighting to hold them at bay.[12]

These mutually conflicting assurances given to the electorate inevitably gave rise later to various and conflicting charges, that the president was cunningly and deceitfully bringing the United States into war, and that he was concealing the urgency of the situation from the electorate. (It is notable that Wendell

[11] S. I. Rosenman, ed., *The Public Papers and Addresses of Franklin D. Roosevelt*, iv (1941), p. 415.
[12] Ibid., p. 466.

Willkie went further than the president in the assurances he gave the electorate.) In fact the most accurate account of the campaign is the simplest: the uncertainty of the international situation and of American policy was reflected in the campaigning; while the uncertainty of the outcome added to the difficulties of framing an effective foreign policy.

This was no longer so after the first Tuesday in November, which brought Roosevelt's re-election and his confirmation in an office which, in times of stress, could become the most powerful in the world. Of all people, Winston Churchill was most alive to the importance of the event, and on 8 December he sent the president a letter which he described as 'one of the most important I ever wrote'.[13] He restated the theme which ran through all his references to the Anglo-American relationship when he opened his letter by saying:

As we reach the end of this year I feel you will expect me to lay before you the prospects for 1941. I do so with candour and confidence, because it seems to me that the vast majority of American citizens have recorded their conviction that the safety of the United States as well as the future of our two Democracies and the kind of civilisation for which they stand are bound up with the survival and independence of the British Commonwealth of Nations.

He went on to say that the immediate danger of Britain being overwhelmed had receded, but that it had been replaced by the 'mortal danger [of] the steady and increasing diminution of sea tonnage'. His letter was accompanied by tables of weekly losses at sea,[14] and he proposed ways in which the United States could assist by extending its responsibility for defence of the western Atlantic, by making shipping available to Britain, and by making it easier for Britain to draw on American productive resources. He concluded with the hope that 'you will regard this letter not as an appeal for aid, but as a statement of the minimum action necessary to achieve our common purpose'. In a broadcast he summarized his approach to the president in the phrase: 'Give us the tools, and we will finish the job.'

His letter had a receptive audience. The American administration, and even more the president, had been exploring means to increase the flow of aid to Britain without contraven-

---

[13] Churchill, ii. 494–501.   [14] Published ibid. pp. 638–9.

ing the constitution and without involving the United States in
war. In a press conference of 17 December Roosevelt explained
his ideas in characteristically homely language when he said:

Suppose my neighbor's home catches fire, and I have a length
of garden hose four or five hundred feet away. If he can take my
garden hose and connect it up with his hydrant, I may help him to
put out his fire. Now, what do I do? I don't say to him before that
operation, 'Neighbor, my garden hose cost me $15; you have to
pay me $15 for it'. . . . I don't want $15 – I want my garden hose
back after the fire is over.[15]

Churchill's letter served as a catalyst to Roosevelt's thinking,
and in a very short space of time his administration had drawn
up the Lend-Lease Bill – it was introduced into the House of
Representatives as HR 1776 – which was enacted and signed
by the president on 11 March 1941. Roosevelt had said in a
'fireside chat' broadcast on 29 December 1940: 'We must
become an arsenal of democracy', and the Lend-Lease Act
made this possible. Henceforth American industry would
contribute overwhelmingly, first to the war effort of Britain and
its allies, then to the common cause which America had joined,
without any precise account being kept of transfers made, and
without later payment being required. In this way the analogy
which Roosevelt had drawn proved inaccurate in the event:
in so far as aid given by the United States did resemble a
garden hose it was returned – that is to say the ships on loan
were given back – but this was a minute part of the total, and
the rest was simply absorbed in the war effort.

Lend-Lease was not the sole decisive step taken in building
the 'common law alliance' at this time. In January 1941 secret
Staff discussions were undertaken in Washington[16] which drew
up a combined world strategy, and, of more immediate
importance, made plans for the defence of the Atlantic. In
April 1941, following on these talks, the United States extended
its security zone and patrol areas to longitude west 25° and
negotiated an agreement with Greenland for the construction
of bases; in the same month the president removed the Red
Sea region from the list of areas forbidden to American shipping.

Militarily these measures were of immense importance; they

15 Rosenman, *Public Papers . . . of F. D. Roosevelt*, iv. 607.
16 There had been 'exploratory' or 'technical' discussions since July 1940, but these
had been limited in scope and commitment.

were equally so in cementing the Anglo-American alliance. To them must be added the essential driving force of mankind – ideas and ideology. On 6 January 1941 Roosevelt, as newly re-elected president, gave to Congress his annual message on the State of the Union. He then said:

> In the future days, which we seek to make secure, we look forward to a world founded upon four essential freedoms.
>
> The first is freedom of speech and expression – everywhere in the world.
>
> The second is freedom of every person to worship God in his own way – everywhere in the world.
>
> The third is freedom from want – which, translated into world terms, means economic understandings which will secure to every nation a healthy peacetime life for its inhabitants – everywhere in the world.
>
> The fourth is freedom from fear – which, translated into world terms, means a world-wide reduction of armaments to such a point and in such a thorough fashion that no nation will be in a position to commit an act of physical aggression against any neighbor – anywhere in the world.[17]

Meanwhile in the autumn and winter of 1940 the pace of events had quickened in eastern Europe. With the fall of France, Stalin, whose assumptions about the future were surely shattered as effectively as those of the western leaders, took fresh steps to secure the defensive position of the Soviet Union. In spite of the fact that the Baltic states had acceded to treaties dictated to them by the Soviet Union, they now had to suffer occupation by Soviet troops, the deportation of their leading citizenry into the interior of Russia, and incorporation into the Soviet Union. Bessarabia, which Rumania had taken from Russia after the first world war, was similarly taken over by the Soviet Union, together with northern Bukovina, which had never previously been Russian. The Hungarian government was under strong domestic pressure not to miss the opportunity offered and pressed Hungarian claims on Transylvania. Germany and Italy acted as 'mediators' and by a second Vienna award on 30 August 1940 transferred two-fifths of Rumanian Transylvania to Hungary. But transfers of territory were of minor importance beside the fact that, as Germany advanced to the south and east, these small countries would

---

[17] Rosenman, *Public Papers . . . of F. D. Roosevelt*, iv. 672.

have to choose between noble but desperate resistance and allowing themselves to be drawn along in the German wake, safeguarding such remnants of independence as they thought desirable and possible. The governments, though not necessarily the people, of both Hungary and Rumania chose the second course.

Soviet action in the Baltic states and Rumania had been carried out in agreement with Germany. Even so it was inevitable that differences would then arise between the two powers. They did so over Lithuania (since even the treaty of 28 September had left a slice of that country in the German sphere), over the influence of each in Finland, Bulgaria, and Rumania, over the nature and implications of the tripartite pact, and over the exchange of materials agreed on in the Nazi-Soviet pact.

These differences by themselves would have been unlikely to lead to a conflict, which the Soviet government was still most anxious to avoid. They were subordinate to the overriding fact that Hitler had begun to plan for an attack on the Soviet Union in the summer of 1940. He passed from the assumption that Britain would collapse with France, to half-hearted attempts at invasion, then to the assumption that once Russia was defeated (which he thought possible in a single campaign) Britain would cease to be of importance.

These were the realities which lay behind the conversations, interrupted by a British air raid, which Molotov had with Ribbentrop and Hitler in Berlin at the end of November 1940. In grandiose terms Ribbentrop sketched the areas of expansion to the south which were open to Japan, Italy, and Germany, and 'wondered whether Russia in the long run would not also turn to the south for the natural outlet to the open sea that was so important for Russia'.

The German report of this meeting continues:[18]

To a question by Molotov as to which sea the Reich Foreign Minister had meant when he had just spoken of access to the sea, the latter replied that according to German opinion great changes would take place all over the world after the war . . . whether in the long run the most advantageous access to the sea for Russia could not be found in the direction of the Persian Gulf and the Arabian Sea.

[18] *DGFP*, xi. 537.

In this way Molotov was given a clear indication of German interest in the Balkans, so vital to Russian interests. Less than a month later, on 18 December 1940, Hitler issued his directive for Operation Barbarossa, which opened: 'The Armed Forces must be prepared *to crush Soviet Russia in a quick campaign* . . . even before the conclusion of the war against England.'[19]

But it was Mussolini who by this time had broken the peace in the Balkans. It was Hitler's intention to make preparations for the attack on Russia as quietly as possible in order to avoid any additional counter-moves by the Soviet Union. But Mussolini calculated that he might score a quick success against Greece, and was piqued by the fact that Hitler had moved troops into Rumania without consulting him.

The offensive which he launched against Greece on 28 October 1940 was held by the Greek army and, as Mussolini preferred to explain it, by a 'veritable flood' and 'torrents of mud'.[20] Hitler therefore prepared to come to his aid militarily and diplomatically. To this end he pressed for the adherence of Yugoslavia to the tripartite pact, but in March 1941 the people of Yugoslavia revolted and overthrew their government rather than allow an agreement with the Axis. Hitler, unaccustomed to being thwarted in this way, ordered that Yugoslavia 'must be considered as a foe and therefore must be destroyed as quickly as possible'.[21]

German troops were thus engaged in the spring of 1941 in the Balkans (where they drew the British into action in Greece and Crete) and in North Africa. Hitler's General Staff would have liked to exploit the possibility which this offered to achieve a decisive victory in the whole area of the eastern Mediterranean and the Middle East, so decisive for British strategy and survival; but Hitler insisted on preparations for the great attack on the Soviet Union.

At this time Matsuoka visited Europe in pursuit of a utopian arrangement of world politics for the benefit of Japan's new order. Travelling to Europe across Siberia he stopped first in Moscow, where he proposed to Stalin and Molotov a non-aggression pact; from there he went on to Berlin, and stopped at Moscow a second time on his way home.

His meeting with Hitler and Ribbentrop revealed a sharp

[19] Ibid. xi. 899.   [20] Mussolini to Hitler, 22 Nov. 1940 (ibid. xi. 671).
[21] Directive of 27 Mar. 1941 (ibid. xii. 395).

2

contrast between the grand but floating ideas of the Japanese, and the much more specific intentions of the Germans. Hitler strongly urged Matsuoka to take the opportunity of a millennium and strike at once at Singapore. (In the previous autumn he had made a similar proposal to Franco and Suñer that Spain should take over Gibraltar, but the Spanish leaders were little disposed gratuitously to assist Hitler's strategy in this way.) Matsuoka, who was nothing if not anxious to please, expressed his own willingness to comply, but regretted the timidity of some members of his government. The talk ranged widely. Hitler naturally opened the discussion by forecasting the imminent collapse of Britain and the recovery of Italy from its temporary setback in North Africa, and (partly to show that he was not alarmed by the risks consequent on an attack on Singapore) said that: 'If Japan got into a conflict with the United States, Germany on her part would take the necessary steps at once. It made no difference with whom the United States first came into conflict, whether it was with Germany or with Japan.'[22] On the other hand when Russia was discussed the conversation went awry. Matsuoka explained – the date was 31 March 1941 – that he had told Stalin and Molotov that the Japanese were 'moral communists' and asked Ribbentrop whether the Führer had 'ever considered the possibility of a Russian-Japanese-German alliance'. The Germans had agreed before Matsuoka had arrived not to reveal plans for the attack on Russia, but Ribbentrop now dropped broad hints. He said, for example: 'Germany would not provoke Russia; but if the policy of Stalin was not in harmony with what the Führer considered to be right, he would crush Russia.'[23]

None the less, Matsuoka returned to Moscow eager to sign a neutrality pact with Stalin, and found his eagerness matched by Stalin's readiness to agree. Imperial sanction was sought from Tokyo and the pact signed before Matsuoka left on 13 April 1941. It provided for peaceful relations, respect for each other's territory, and for neutrality in the event of the other becoming 'the object of hostilities'. Probably both signatories would have been surprised to learn that the pact would be effective for as long as four years.

Even as Matsuoka blandly talked to Hitler and Ribbentrop about a German-Russian-Japanese alliance, Churchill in

[22] Ibid. xii. 455-6.   [23] Ibid. xii. 408.

London spotted the evidence in intelligence reports of an imminent German attack on the Soviet Union. His efforts to warn Stalin were of no avail, and the Russians continued to deliver rubber and other materials to Germany. Early in the morning of 22 June 1941 Germany declared war on Russia and the attack began. In Britain Churchill had no hesitation in embracing the Soviet Union as an ally.[24] The United States did so with greater hesitation. Neither government dared hope that Russian resistance would last long enough to give more than temporary respite to the British; but both agreed that aid should be made available to the Soviet Union – Britain from its hard pressed fighting services, America from its slowly expanding industrial potential. Stalin hoped for more and, replying on 18 July 1941 to Churchill's letter of 7 July, he said: 'The military situation of the Soviet Union, as well as of Great Britain, would be considerably improved if there could be established a front against Hitler in the West – northern France, and in the North – the Arctic.'[25] The exchange which was to continue with varying degrees of acrimony over the next two years thus began within a month of the German attack.

The invasion of Russia by Germany brought a decisive turning point in the Far East as well as Europe. In Matsuoka's view it provided the opportunity for Japan to strike northwards at Russia – with which it had so recently signed a neutrality pact; but his advice was rejected and he was manoeuvred out of office by the resignation of the whole cabinet and its immediate reconstruction, still under Konoye, without him. Instead Japanese armies moved southwards, and now occupied parts of southern Indo-China, notably the area of Saigon; operational plans were made for a further penetration to the south. To this move the governments of the United States, Britain, and the Netherlands reacted by freezing all Japanese assets. In this way positions were taken up which must inexorably lead to the extension of the war in the Far East. The Japanese government extended its plans for conquest, which were dependent on the supply of oil; the American government made it impossible for them to purchase sufficient

[24] In a broadcast on 22 June he said: 'No-one has been a more consistent opponent of Communism than I have for the last twenty-five years. I will unsay no word that I have spoken about it. But all this fades away before the spectacle which is now unfolding.'
[25] Churchill, iii. 343.

oil for their needs. From this impasse there was no way out other than the arbitrament of force.

The new turn of events in the world coincided with the first meeting between the president of the United States and the prime minister of Britain. Roosevelt had wanted such a rendezvous for some time and now at the end of July 1941 it seemed more desirable and more possible. Churchill did not hesitate to take up his invitation, and on 9 August 1941 their meeting began as Churchill left *Prince of Wales* and went aboard *Augusta* in Placentia bay, Newfoundland.

In several respects their meeting resembled others which were to take place later in the war. Stalin was not present, but Harry Hopkins had just visited him in Moscow and been given a very clear view of Russian war needs – as well as being elated and depressed by his first impression of totalitarian efficiency. Roosevelt, Churchill, and their closest advisers were occupied with immediate problems, and with post-war prospects. Roosevelt readily agreed that American patrols in the Atlantic should now extend as far as Iceland. Churchill hoped in addition to secure some firm commitment from the United States of action in the event of new Japanese moves in South East Asia, but achieved only partial success. A clear warning was to be given to Japan in the talks which were going on with Admiral Nomura, the Japanese ambassador in Washington, but the talks were to continue in order to gain time and avoid precipitating Japanese action.

It was Roosevelt's suggestion that a statement should be drawn up of the long-term policy which was shared by the two governments and their peoples – although the suggestion once made, it was the British staff who drew up the first draft. In spite of some differences, particularly over imperial preference, agreement was reached on points of detail, and the declaration issued to the press as a 'Joint Declaration by the President and the Prime Minister, August 12, 1941'. The two signatories stated that their countries sought neither aggrandizement for themselves nor territorial change against the wishes of the people concerned. They spoke of the right of all peoples to choose their own form of government, the right of free and equal access to trade and raw materials, and the 'fullest collaboration between all nations in the economic field'. They emphasized the need, 'after the final destruction of the Nazi tyranny', for security, freedom of the seas, and for disarmament, 'pending the establishment of a wider and more permanent system of general security.'

This was the Atlantic Charter. Never before had two nations, one at peace and the other at war, come so close in the expression of a common purpose. Gone were the days of the first world war, when the United States had 'associated' itself with Britain and France, after those powers had entered into a series of treaties for the disposition of territory when peace was restored. Together, Britain and America had expressed their determination to destroy Nazi tyranny, and Roosevelt had taken a first careful step towards the commitment of the United States to an international organization when the war was over.

Cordell Hull did not accompany the president on *Augusta*. Back in Washington he was engaged in conversations with Admiral Nomura – conversations which had begun on 8 March and continued until 8 December 1941. There are few examples in modern history of so much time and so many efforts being given to negotiation without result. These conversations had been undertaken in the first place as a result of the initiative of two American missionaries, who were to make a fresh attempt before the end to achieve a settlement. In September the Japanese prime minister took the extraordinary step of inviting the American ambassador to dine with him, having first sent the servants off for the evening and arranged for the ambassador to change the number-plates on his car to avoid observation. In the last days and hours before war broke out the president of the United States sought to avert disaster by a personal exchange with the emperor of Japan, but his attempt failed – possibly through sabotage by the Japanese services which should have relayed his message. There was another unique feature of the Hull–Nomura conversations: the American government had succeeded in breaking the Japanese code, and the State Department was therefore able to discover at every stage what lay behind Nomura's talk – and frequently to have a fuller knowledge of what was being said in Tokyo than Nomura himself.

In a sense a basis for the avoidance of war existed. The United States was alarmed at its own weakness in the Far East, and had Japan been willing to cut its losses in China and expand no further, it is likely that America would in the end have accepted (and even possibly recognized) Manchukuo and a position of privilege for Japan in China. But such a solution was not acceptable to the Japanese government, far less to the Japanese military who by this time were the determinant element in any decisions made in Tokyo. In their view a successful settlement of the China incident – which meant in practical terms victory over China – was a prerequisite to the survival of Japan. For this purpose the government sought a strategic position in Indo-China, and free access to the sinews of war, especially to oil. The minimum which they required from the United States was therefore more even than passive acquiescence in the conquest of China; it was a deliberate choice to do nothing to impede such conquest. This was not forthcoming, and the Japanese programme followed from that fact. Oil was necessary to maintain Japan's existing scale of operations, even if grandiose plans for a Greater East Asia were left aside; and after July 1941 oil was not available by peaceful means. The military – now including the navy, the chief consumer of oil – therefore worked out a time-scale of the depletion of oil reserves, linked to a climatic timetable for possible military operations, and the solution for their timetable proved to be an attack on the American fleet in Pearl Harbour on 7 December 1941.[26]

In retrospect it appears that the Japanese leaders might have checked their calculations when they discovered that the answer to their equation was an attack on the United States. 7 December 1941 has gone down to history as 'a date which will live in infamy', for so Roosevelt described it – partly because as a result of the office muddle which accompanies many historic occasions the Japanese message breaking off the Hull–Nomura talks was not delivered to Cordell Hull until after the attack on Pearl Harbour had begun. In retrospect it appears rather as a day of supreme folly for Japan, to pit its strength against that of the United States. As we have seen, the final decision was arrived at with a certain amount of rational calculation. The possibility of attack in South East Asia rather than on the United States was considered and ruled out, because it was assumed that the United States would enter the war anyway, and should be dealt a decisive blow from the start. The emperor and the prime minister were appalled at the

[26] For an account of the Hull–Nomura conversations, and the considerations surrounding them in Washington and Tokyo, see Feis, *Road to Pearl Harbor*; and Butow, *Tojo*.

prospect before them, and Konoye's resignation and replacement by Tojo on 16 October marked the opening of the last phase before the attack; but neither was able to provide or gain acceptance for a different policy. In the end the decision was taken by men who were incapable of a detached calculation of Japan's chances in war, and who had such a romantic view of national honour that attack was the more honourable in proportion to its recklessness. Or, as Tojo told Konoye, 'at some point in a man's lifetime he might find it necessary to jump, with his eyes closed, from the veranda of Kiyomizu-dera into the ravine below.'[27]

As the Japanese carriers prepared their aircraft for take-off to Pearl Harbour the Russian armies on 6 December launched their counter-offensive against the German invaders. They were helped by the onset of winter, and although Hitler was able by ruthless energy to hold his line intact, all his hopes of defeating Russia in one campaign disappeared. It was in this situation that the Japanese revealed to him that their negotiations with the United States were coming to an end – for they gave no longer warning of the impending attack on Pearl Harbour than Hitler had given them of the invasion of Russia. The tripartite pact imposed no obligation on Germany in these circumstances, but, consistently with what he had told Matsuoka in March, Hitler did not hesitate to declare war on the United States – scarcely realizing that the American assistance to Britain which he had been forced to witness for many months would henceforth grow to insuperable power aligned against the Axis. In London Churchill was aware of that power; 'to have the United States at our side', he later wrote, 'was to me the greatest joy.' The British government declared war on Japan. Rumania and Hungary had been drawn into the war against Russia in the wake of Germany. Conflict had broken out afresh between the Soviet Union and Finland, which was to become an ally of Germany. In Europe war thus embraced all but Sweden, Spain, Portugal, and Switzerland; beyond Europe it stretched round the world. As the mad genius of Hitler believed: 'A historical revision on a unique scale has been imposed on us by the Creator.'[28]

[27] Kiyomizu-dera is a Buddhist temple on one of the heights of Kyoto (see Butow, p. 367).
[28] See Alan Bullock, *Hitler* (1962), p. 609.

2

WARTIME DIPLOMACY BETWEEN THE
GREAT POWERS

THE ATTACK which Hitler ordered on the Soviet Union in June 1941 and the Japanese attack on Pearl Harbour in December brought an alliance which was as improbable as it was in the long run overwhelming. Their separate acts of aggression proved to be megalomaniac actions which deprived them of the advantages of limited conquest they might very well have enjoyed for many decades. But this was not apparent in 1941 and 1942. The German army in Russia and the combined forces of Japan in the Far East made swift and seemingly irresistible advances, and the alliance against them was forged in the face of overwhelming danger and in the hope of victory that was distant and uncertain. Confronted with the need to fight total and global war, the United States, Britain, and Russia sought to make an alliance that was ideological, strategic, and economic. There were certain obvious limitations on the extent to which this was possible. Differences in ideology between Russia on the one hand and Britain and the United States on the other could be overlaid by the pronouncement of anti-fascist and even democratic principles; but they would reappear as soon as the pressure of war was relaxed and national interests were at stake. Strategy could be co-ordinated between Britain and the United States to an extent and by means unprecedented in earlier wars; but the attempt to formulate overall strategy with the Soviet Union led to almost as much recrimination as co-operation (particularly since the Soviet Union was not involved in the Far Eastern war); while economic co-operation, although it too was without precedent, was restricted as far as the Soviet Union was concerned by the physical difficulties of communication. Britain and the United States co-operated in developing the atomic bomb; but Stalin only learned about their efforts through his intelligence service.

Moreover the personal relationship between Churchill and

Roosevelt was of cardinal importance. For a long time these two men were able to maintain close contact with each other and to exchange freely and openly their personal views, as well as the decisions in which they had participated with their staffs. Communication between them was further aided and enhanced by the character of Roosevelt's personal representative, Harry Hopkins. This was a fact of greater significance since Roosevelt was at the head of a government lacking the close integration which was present in Britain. Differences between the army and the navy, between the services and the administration, as well as between departments within the administration (for example between the Treasury and the State Department) meant that the fate of the country and of the alliance turned on the personality of the president, and the warmth of his relations with Churchill must be estimated in this context.

In all this the Soviet Union seemed to be cast for the role of odd man out – it was a land power, a communist country, and a neutral in the war with Japan; while Britain, on the other hand, having fought side by side with the Soviet Union since June and yet enjoying very close relationships with the United States, seemed the obvious mediator between the two continental powers. As events turned out, however, this pattern of the alliance was profoundly modified in practice by the scarcely foreseeable relationship which grew up between Russia and the United States. As early as March 1942 Roosevelt wrote to Churchill:

> I know that you will not mind my being brutally frank when I tell you that I think I can personally handle Stalin better than either your Foreign Office or my State Department. Stalin hates the guts of all your top people. He thinks he likes me better, and I hope he will continue to do so.[1]

To this feeling of communicability with Stalin was added later a sense of common purpose which balanced and sometimes outweighed the relation of kinship which joined Britain to the United States.

While Japanese aeroplanes were preparing to attack the American fleet in Pearl Harbour, the British foreign secretary, Anthony Eden, left London for talks with Stalin and Molotov

[1] 18 Mar. 1942 (Churchill, iv. 177).

in Moscow. His purpose was to end the suspicion between Russia and Britain, and to explore a common strategy and policy with which to oppose the common enemy, Germany. To this extent it was a resumption of the negotiations which had been broken off in August 1939 by the Nazi-Soviet alliance; with the important difference that Stalin now asked British recognition of the Russian borders as they were before the German attack – implying Soviet rule over the Baltic states and parts of Poland, Rumania, and Finland. In addition, Stalin proposed that East Prussia be transferred to Poland, and that Germany should be divided. But as the British government had baulked at unwanted Russian guarantees for the Baltic states in 1939, so they now refused to recognize their incorporation into Russia – albeit with Russia's alternative policy of agreement with Germany fresh in their memory. Nor could Britain offer the one single contribution to a common strategy which Stalin had sought since the earliest days of the German attack – the immediate opening of a second front in France.

Before conversations could be begun on this question the Japanese attack altered the world perspective, and Eden's visit to Moscow was eclipsed by the visit of Churchill to Washington, accompanied by chiefs of staff and Lord Beaverbrook as minister of supply, for the conference that came to be known as 'Arcadia'. The initiative for the conference came from Churchill, in consistent pursuit of his old objective of maximum American support in the dramatically new conditions created by Pearl Harbour. But the most important political outcome of the conference was the result of American preparation, and it transcended the limited sphere of Anglo-American relations.

This was the United Nations declaration, whose final details were negotiated in haste so that it could be dated 1 January 1942, and which was signed by representatives of twenty-six nations. It was a significant declaration. It marked the end of American isolationism, and Roosevelt's choice of the term 'United Nations' contrasted sharply with the 'Associated Power' of an earlier war. It expressed the hopes that wartime alliance would be transmuted into post-war international organization. Before it could be signed, however, a fundamental difficulty had to be overcome. The conference which devised the declaration derived initially from the Japanese attack on America; but the Soviet Union was not at war with Japan and was anxious to preserve its neutrality towards that country. Fortunately, careful wording made it possible to overcome this difficulty. The actual content of the declaration was more carefree: it involved simply a common subscription to the principles of the Atlantic Charter and the defence of 'life, liberty, independence and religious freedom,[2] . . . human rights and justice in their own lands as well as in other lands'.

The United States headed the list of signatories, as befitted the primacy in international affairs which it was to acquire with the full development and deployment of its resources; it was followed by Britain, then Russia, then China; and thereafter the other powers in alphabetical order. So from the very beginning of the Grand Alliance China had the courtesy title of great power bestowed upon it. But France did not sign the document. In British and American eyes there was no French *government* at war with the Axis; and when provision was made for adherence by 'appropriate authorities which are not governments' de Gaulle did not belittle the sovereign power that was France by allowing his inclusion in such a category. In the very midst of 'Arcadia', on 24 December, de Gaulle had demonstrated his own view of French sovereignty by ordering Free French forces to take over forcibly the islands of St Pierre and Miquelon from the rule of their Vichy governor against the express disapproval of the British, American, and Canadian governments. Cordell Hull's antipathy for de Gaulle was fanned to fury by this action, although it was taken less seriously by Roosevelt, and by Churchill (who had only asked de Gaulle to desist in order to meet American wishes), while the American people failed to understand the need for good relations with Vichy now that America was at war with Germany. Three years later, with victory in sight, de Gaulle would still claim that the affairs of Europe could not be settled without the participation of France; but the Potsdam declaration, like that of the United Nations, lacked a French signature.

Politically and psychologically, the Grand Alliance had thus been made. This had not been Churchill's prime purpose in proposing the conference; it was practical military co-operation

[2] Roosevelt's efforts to persuade Litvinov to propose the phrase 'religious freedom' to Stalin earned him Churchill's promise to recommend him for the See of Canterbury when it next fell vacant: but Stalin accepted without demur (see Churchill, iii. 604–5).

which he sought. He wanted to counter at once the danger that American entry into the war might lead to an actual diminution of help in Europe, if the United States either gave primacy to the Far East or concentrated all its resources on equipping the forces at home. Both these fears proved exaggerated; American troops left for Ireland before the conference ended; and Roosevelt's determination that Europe should be given priority was decisive, now and at all subsequent occasions during the war.

Of all the results of 'Arcadia', the most important and far reaching was the least foreseen and the most pragmatic in its inception. This was the setting up of the Combined Chiefs of Staff Committee, combining in a single body British and American staff chiefs. Both British and American participants in the conference had wanted to institutionalize co-operation between the armed forces of the two countries. Neither had seen the extent to which this co-operation would have to be carried if it were to be really effective; had they done so they might have thought it necessary to include at least formal representation from the lesser nations and to negotiate an arrangement with the Russians. By combining practical proposals of limited import they created the most effective instrument of military co-operation in the history of warfare. By April 1942 the combined chiefs were given authority over the entire 'strategic conduct of the war', and their weekly meetings provided an indispensable continuum to the broad strategic decisions taken at personal meetings of Roosevelt and Churchill.[3] Moreover the significance of the Committee extended beyond the war years; it added to the ties that bound America to Britain as to no other ally; and it showed the way to the close military co-operation that was later achieved in NATO.

What Churchill had failed to secure at Washington was American support for British strategy, beyond the central point of concentration on the European enemy. Essentially this strategy was that of a weak power with world-wide commitments: it consisted of the destruction of Axis positions on the periphery of Europe,[4] accompanied by aerial attacks on Ger-

[3] 'The Committee met regularly in Washington, where the British were represented by senior officers; in addition there were some 200 formal meetings during the war of which 89 took place at the conferences' (ibid. p. 608).

[4] 'The occupation of the whole coastline of Africa and of the Levant from Dakar to the Turkish frontier by British and American forces' (ibid. p. 573).

many prior to the launching of an attack on the fortress of
Europe itself. In the Far East there was to be the maximum
possible resistance to and harassment of Japanese forces, until
a countervailing Anglo-American force could be built up. Such
a strategy had no appeal to the American military leaders. If
an attack were going to be mounted by American forces across
the Atlantic it was common sense that it should be directed as
early as possible at Europe itself, not at North Africa; and they
underestimated the difficulties involved and the time required
in the build-up of such an offensive. They also attached immense importance to the necessity of relieving the pressure on
Russian forces at a time when the whole Russian front seemed
likely to collapse.

While action was still distant, it was possible to reconcile
these views. Hopkins and Marshall visited London in April
1942, and received British assent to proposals for the build-up
of American forces in Britain ('Bolero') ready for attack in
Europe in 1943 ('Roundup'). Churchill indeed expressed
enthusiasm for an attack in Europe in 1943. But in the meantime he was anxious about the Far East, wanted to press on
the attack in North Africa, and hankered after an attack in
Norway, which would permit the safe convoying of supplies to
Russia. (This latter in spite of the caution which Alan Brooke
imposed on his chief.) As a result, it now fell to Churchill to
emphasize the dangers in the Far East and the possibility of a
link up between the Japanese and the Germans. (Singapore
had fallen in mid-February 1942 and the Japanese had won
naval supremacy in the Bay of Bengal.) This was in contrast to
the American chiefs of staff, who were talking of the possibility
of mounting a limited action against Europe, known as 'Sledgehammer', in 1942. Roosevelt was less sanguine than his generals
about the possibility of such action. But he was most anxious
to offer some support to Russia; and he wanted to divert the
political pressure which Stalin was bringing on the British to
recognize their new frontiers.

This was a situation which promised to be very favourable to
Russian diplomacy. In May 1942 Molotov travelled to London
and from there, on Roosevelt's invitation, to Washington. In
London he found the British still adamant in their refusal to
recognize the existing frontier between Russia and Poland. They
were prepared to recognize Soviet rule over the Baltic states,

and Churchill had written to Stalin to this effect in March; but they were under strong pressure from the United States to admit no such abandonment of the principles of the Atlantic Charter. A telephone call to Stalin settled the matter. The demands were dropped, and on 26 May 1942 an Anglo-Soviet treaty was signed, providing mutual assistance in the war against Germany and co-operation afterwards. The two signatories abjured territorial expansion, but this concealed their disagreement about what constituted territorial expansion in eastern Europe. They also expressed their readiness to join with other states after the war 'for common action to preserve peace'.

On the question of the second front Molotov secured no promises from Churchill. But in Washington the climate was more favourable. Since Hopkins and Marshall had been in London the British generals had become increasingly dubious about the practicability of landings in Europe; their American counterparts had moved in the opposite direction. They now had the support of the president. Faced with the increasingly hopeless task of getting supplies to Murmansk in the constant daylight of an Arctic summer, sensitive to the Russian abandonment of their territorial claims, Roosevelt was extremely vulnerable to Molotov's suggestion that if the second front were not opened in 1942 it might have to be opened when all effective Russian resistance to Germany had collapsed. He asked General Marshall whether Stalin could be told that a second front was in preparation. 'Yes,' replied the General. 'The President then authorized Mr Molotov to inform Mr Stalin that we expect the formation of a Second Front this year.'[5]

The difference of view between the British and Americans was concealed from the public by a communiqué agreed between the three powers and published on 11 June which included the sentence: 'In the course of the conversations full understanding was reached with regard to the urgent tasks of creating a Second Front in Europe in 1942.'[6] The British reserved their position by presenting Molotov with an *aide-mémoire* which set out the difficulties of such an enterprise, and ended: 'We can therefore give no promise in the matter, but provided that it appears sound and sensible we shall not hesitate to put our

[5] From the record kept by the American interpreter, Professor Cross, and printed in Sherwood, ii. 667.
[6] Churchill, iv. 305.

plans into effect.'[7] But the Americans had ridden roughshod over the hesitations of the British, and a direct understanding had been established between Roosevelt and the Russians. Stalin for his part had every reason for satisfaction; he had dropped his demand for paper recognition of post-war frontiers, and received in return the promise of immediate relief, which he hoped might be worth something approaching his own target of forty divisions. But the exchange turned out to be hollow. Within two months the decision on 'Sledgehammer' had been reversed.

It would not have been easy to press ahead with invasion of Europe against the hesitation of the British, for it was recognized that they would have to provide the greater part of the forces required. But in fact the decision was reversed simply because the United Nations had not yet wrested initiative in the war from the Axis. The approach of midsummer brought heartening news from the Pacific. On 6 June American ships engaged the Japanese in the great battle of Midway, and thereby ended Japanese naval supremacy in the Pacific. But this great victory coincided with the final German assault on Sebastopol which opened the way for German troops to advance again across the plains of southern Russia. A week later came news from North Africa of Rommel's successful attack against the British lines, destroying their armoured strength and apparently rendering Egypt defenceless. By mid-July sinkings in the Atlantic had reached nearly 400,000 tons in a week, or more than twice the best possible rate of rebuilding.

These events added to the danger of the Russian resistance collapsing altogether; but at the same time they made it impossible for the British to participate in a cross-Channel invasion. They also transformed the position in the Middle East: in May the British had argued in favour of concentrating the attack against Germany in North Africa; by July it was a question of rushing tanks and bombers to the Middle East or risking the loss of the whole allied position there, with all the disastrous consequences that must follow.

In this situation the calm reflection of Roosevelt was decisive. Faced with the impossibility of mounting an offensive in Europe, the balance of view among the US chiefs of staff swung over towards a major attack in the Pacific, and on 10

[7] Ibid.

July they so recommended to the president and commander-in-chief. The president rejected their recommendation. He said to Hopkins: 'I do not believe we can wait until 1943 to strike at Germany. If we cannot strike at SLEDGEHAMMER, then we must take the second best – and that is not the Pacific.'[8] In Roosevelt's eyes the defeat of Japan would not lead to the defeat of Germany, but 'defeat of Germany means the defeat of Japan, probably without firing a shot or losing a life'.[9]

This decision led to American troops landing in North Africa in the operation originally conceived under the code name 'Gymnast' and then renamed 'Torch'. It also led to the first meeting between Stalin and Churchill. At the same time as the decision with regard to 'Torch' was being taken, one of the convoys taking supplies to Russia had been virtually annihilated, and the British had decided that no further convoys should be sent until the end of the Arctic summer and greater naval strength made them easier to defend.[10] This decision (which suspended deliveries until September) was very unwelcome to Stalin; and now that the more important question of the second front had been resolved Churchill felt it his duty to convey the news to Stalin personally. He therefore travelled to Moscow in mid-August 1942.

It was not an easy interview. Stalin alternated between conviviality and toughness, at one moment joining with Churchill in teasing Molotov, and then accusing the British and Americans of bad faith and unwillingness to take risks. Char-

---

[8] Sherwood, ii. 604; cf. W. H. McNeill: 'It was surely a fateful decision upon which the whole course of the war depended. The picture of two men deep in perplexity – the one crippled, the other chronically ill – talking things out after dinner in the White House on a hot summer evening is one which should be remembered in every history of the Second World War' (*America, Britain and Russia* (1953), p. 194 (RIIA *Survey* 1939–46)).

[9] Sherwood, ii. 606.

[10] It was symptomatic of Anglo-Russian relations that the Arctic convoys which represented such an important element in limited military co-operation should give rise to such bad feeling. The British government regarded them as a great sacrifice, both of material and of shipping, in the common cause; but they received little thanks from Stalin and the British crews and personnel on shore at Murmansk were subjected to tedious and humiliating security procedures. Stalin for his part regarded the convoys as 'an obligation assumed by the British Government . . . to the USSR which for more than two years has borne the tremendous burden of the struggle against Hitler's Germany, the common enemy of the Allies' (Stalin to Churchill, 13 Oct. 1943, USSR. Min. Foreign Affairs, *Correspondence . . . during the Great Patriotic War . . .* , i: *Correspondence with . . . Churchill and . . . Attlee* (1958), p. 171).

acteristically, Churchill told Stalin his bad news, of the postponement of the second front in Europe, first, and then went on to represent 'Torch' as the opening of a second front in a different place, and the only one which it was practicable to mount with strong hopes of striking an effective blow against the German army. Stalin handed Churchill an *aide-mémoire* reaffirming Russian belief in the possibility of a second front in Europe, and placing on record a sense of deception that the project should be postponed in spite of what had been understood at the time of Molotov's visit to London and Washington, and the Anglo-Soviet communiqué of 12 June. Churchill replied, with reference to the British *aide-mémoire* made at the time of the June agreement, 'We can therefore give no promise.' Meanwhile the military discussions between the chiefs of staff made little progress, as the Russian officers made all depend on the opening of a second front in Europe. Even so, by the time the conference was over Churchill felt that he had convinced Stalin of the value of 'Torch', and that 'now they know the worst, and having made their protest are entirely friendly; this in spite of the fact that this is their most anxious time'. He was also greatly encouraged by what he learned of the forthcoming Russian counter-attack in the Stalingrad area.

The change from 'Sledgehammer' to 'Torch' involved political complications. An attack in northern Europe would be an attack on German occupation forces. Landings in North Africa were landings in French territory where no German forces had entered. It was reasonable to hope therefore that it could be done with the co-operation rather than against the resistance of the French, and American policy was devoted to this end – beginning with the exclusion of British forces, to whom the French might be expected to be hostile after the experience of Mers el-Kebir and British attitudes towards Vichy.

But the political side of the operation was one of extreme delicacy. It was not easy to know which Frenchmen could ensure the maximum assistance to the landing. De Gaulle was excluded from the start. He was still under suspicion from the State Department and Admiral Leahy, who had been ambassador to Vichy before he became Roosevelt's personal assistant, and neither Churchill nor Roosevelt had confidence in the ability of the Free French to keep secrets. In any case, it was not thought that he would command the allegiance of the French in North Africa.

From Vichy France two candidates offered themselves, asking for supreme command of any American expedition to North Africa. They were Admiral Darlan, commander-in-chief of the French (Vichy) forces, and General Giraud, a conservative officer who had escaped from Germany to Vichy France, and whom de Gaulle had endeavoured to persuade to join the Free French.[11] The British and Americans were sceptical about these offers, and it was decided to establish contact with Giraud only, while retaining American command of the expedition. Even so, co-operation was difficult; the Americans were planning an American operation which would receive French assistance; the French conceived a French rising which would be aided by the Americans. No concession could be made to the French point of view, not least because the success of the military venture depended on the maximum degree of secrecy. The result was that Giraud only learned of the nature of the American plan six days before the attack was launched. In any case, even limited reliance on Giraud was misplaced. When American troops landed in Algiers, Oran, and Casablanca on 8 November they discovered that Giraud's following in North Africa had been greatly overrated. They also found that his authority was outclassed by the presence in Algiers of Admiral Darlan.

Once the landings had been made in the midst of bitter fighting and naval action the military situation became clear cut; French forces could not put up any effective resistance to the Americans, but it was still highly desirable to secure their co-operation so that the Germans would not have time to move in forces by air before the American position was established. The political situation was extremely confused. Many French officers welcomed the landing; but most often their superiors conceived of French 'honour' in legalistic and suicidal terms. Thus unless the Americans were willing to follow the British example at Mers el-Kebir, the only course of action was to make a deal with a superior officer exercising effective authority in North Africa. The only man who qualified for this role, and who in particular could command the French fleet, was Darlan, and General Mark Clark, acting as Eisenhower's personal

[11] Eden, *The Reckoning* (1965), p. 345.

representative, therefore negotiated with him. Darlan agreed
to order a cease-fire, and assumed complete authority in North
Africa in the name of Pétain.[12] This was followed by an agreement providing for full military co-operation between the French
in North Africa and the Americans, together with the maintenance of the existing French government and administration
in North Africa.

Inevitably the agreement was viewed differently by the two
signatories and by almost everyone else. Darlan intended that
it should be the recognition of his, and therefore Pétain's,
authority over the whole of the French empire. Clark intended
it as a temporary measure of military convenience; as such it
was accepted by his superior, Eisenhower, by Roosevelt, and
by the British government; and as a tactical measure it won the
warm support of Stalin.[13] In the long run its military value was
important but limited; it brought a cease-fire in Algeria and
Morocco, where French resistance would necessarily have
collapsed in any case; but it did not prevent German forces
disembarking at Tunis and Bizerta, with the collaboration of
the French, and putting up effective and prolonged resistance.
Meanwhile German troops occupied the whole of metropolitan
France. American public opinion was shocked by what appeared
to be a 'deal with the Axis'; the British were even more angry.
De Gaulle had welcomed the military operation in North Africa,
although his own exclusion from it amply confirmed his assessment of British and American motives and self-interest, drawn
from his experiences in the Middle East and Madagascar.
Accepting his own exclusion, he welcomed Giraud's participation, since this would sever his connexions with Vichy and
bring him *ipso facto* to the Gaullist side; but he was incensed
by and contemptuous of the understanding with Darlan.

It soon appeared therefore that the Americans had made a
temporary agreement which must become increasingly intolerable to them; but they had no serious plans for a more
permanent settlement until the French people could freely

[12] Darlan also telegraphed an order on 11 November to metropolitan France that
the French fleet should put to sea if in danger of capture by the Germans. In the
event seventy-three ships were scuttled in the harbour of Toulon.
[13] He wrote to Churchill: 'It seems to me that the Americans used Darlan not
badly in order to facilitate the occupation of Northern and Western Africa. The
military diplomacy must be able to use for military purposes not only Darlan but
"Even the Devil himself and his grandma" ' (quoted in Sherwood, ii. 647).

choose a government. From this impasse they were released by
the assassination of Darlan on 24 December. It was one of the
rare occasions when political assassination solved more problems than it created.

The following month Churchill and Roosevelt met in Casablanca. They had hoped that Stalin would join them, but he
declared himself unable to leave Russia or command of the
front. The main purpose of their meeting was to concert the
next steps in grand strategy. In retrospect, one can see that at
this time the turning-point in the war had been passed. During
the planning of 'Torch', Hopkins had pushed a note across the
table to Marshall bearing the simple legend: 'I am damned
depressed.' Since then three great battles had been won:
Stalingrad, Alamein, and the Atlantic. The Russian front would
not now collapse; Egypt was saved; radar and shipbuilding
together had defeated the submarine. But in January 1943 the
immediate objectives still eluded the Anglo-American leaders.
The Tunisian campaign bogged down, and five precious months
were to be lost until German forces in North Africa surrendered
in May 1943. The attack on northern Europe depended on the
quick conclusion of the African campaign, and as the months
wore on both Churchill and Roosevelt were reluctant to admit
that it was becoming a forlorn hope. In the Far East the holding
war of the past year was turning over to the offensive; but
Japanese resistance was still too strong for the offensive to bear
a very close relationship to the plans devised at Casablanca.

The conference was therefore important for political rather
than strategic reasons. Two political events arose directly out
of the recent events in North Africa. The first was an attempt
to tidy up the confusion which had arisen there. De Gaulle was
brought to Casablanca, following strong British pressure, and
met Giraud; but no agreement could be reached between
them. Giraud's position depended entirely on American support even though his political views and support of Vichy
legality were quite out of accord with Roosevelt's own outlook.
Nevertheless the meeting was the first step in political manoeuvring which eventually brought agreement between the two
generals on 30 May 1943, with the setting up of a French
Committee of National Liberation in Algiers. De Gaulle and
Giraud were to be joint presidents, and Giraud to be com-

mander-in-chief of the French army. Even so, neither Britain nor the United States was prepared to recognize the Committee as a government in exile, nor could they agree on the extent to which they would give recognition. In consequence different declarations were issued at the end of August, the American government stressing the limitations of the Committee's authority. However, time was on the side of de Gaulle in his relations with Giraud, who was outclassed in the infighting which the establishment of the Committee had made possible. On 9 November 1943 he resigned from the Committee; and in April from the command, which by that time had in any case become nominal, of the French army.

The second event of political importance was the announcement by Roosevelt at the concluding press conference of the principle of unconditional surrender. The enunciation of this slogan at this time was related to the outcry surrounding the agreement with Darlan; but it evoked considerable surprise. It was not mentioned in the final communiqué and Roosevelt pretended that his use of the phrase at a press conference was unpremeditated. In fact he had previously discussed the matter with Churchill. Their discussion had not reached any conclusion, and Churchill did not want the principle to extend to Italy; but he supported the president once the phrase had been expressed.[14] Stalin for his part subscribed to the principle of unconditional surrender in his order of the day of 1 May.

The significance of the principle was that the United Nations, when victorious, would impose terms on the defeated enemy. Terms of surrender there would have to be, in order to define the authority of the victorious powers within the territory of the defeated. But Germany, Italy, Japan, and their allies would not be invited to surrender in accordance with certain conditions laid down in advance, far less would it be open to them to propose the terms on which they would be prepared to surrender. Their submission would be unconditional, and the United Nations would be free to frame the detailed arrangements of surrender, unfettered by any prior undertaking. As Churchill later (22 February 1945) said in the House of Commons: 'If we are bound, we are bound by our own

[14] He later wrote: 'I would not myself have used these words but I immediately stood by the President and have frequently defended the decision' (Sherwood, ii. 693).

consciences to civilization. We are not bound to the Germans as the result of a bargain struck.'

There are obvious reasons why the formula of unconditional surrender should seem particularly important to Roosevelt. In America, even more than in other democracies, it was felt that the war should be won and military victory secured in order to provide a clean slate from which to start afresh, rather than that political considerations should influence the conduct or the ending of the war. Traditionally the United States attached greater significance to formulae as being likely to influence the course of events by their very enunciation, and as Roosevelt commented: 'Unconditional surrender means not the destruction of the German populace, nor of the Italian or Japanese populace, but does mean the destruction of a philosophy in Germany, Italy, and Japan which is based on the conquest and subjugation of other peoples.'[15]

More specifically, Roosevelt was aware that his predecessor as president in time of world war, Woodrow Wilson, had enunciated points, principles, and particulars which had been accepted by the Germans as the basis of an armistice, and that these commitments had been an embarrassment to the peace-makers and the grounds of self-vindication by later German spokesmen. He was particularly anxious to prevent a recurrence of such a situation when the nazi and fascist powers were defeated.

As the possibility of surrender came nearer, the principle of unconditional surrender was questioned, since it seemed possible that the war might be shortened if terms could be devised acceptable to the United Nations, yet sufficiently reassuring to the German, Italian, and Japanese peoples to induce them to overthrow their governments and make an earlier peace. Such considerations were most obviously relevant in the case of Italy, where the fascist government actually was overthrown, and negotiations were carried on between the new government and the British and Americans to secure the maximum advantage to both *vis-à-vis* the Germans. Even so, the principle was maintained, and was upheld with firm insistence by the Americans. As Germany approached defeat the victor powers remained unconvinced that any viable

[15] Ibid.

alternative government, acceptable to them, was likely to emerge; and *ex post facto* knowledge of the German situation supports their view. In any case, the tensions and differences in the alliance were then growing so rapidly that it may well have been impossible to secure agreement amongst the victors on what terms were acceptable to them. But it is with regard to Germany that the implementation of the principle was most questioned in subsequent years, when it was seen as leading to the division of Germany and Europe by jettisoning the possibility of a stable Germany between Russia and the west. When Japan was faced with the impossibility of continuing the war its government unsuccessfully sought conditional surrender; but although this was refused, the most important of its wishes, the maintenance of the emperor, was in fact granted.

The success of the North African campaign meant that the initiative in this sector of the war was being won by Britain and America; but every advantage had still to be wrung from the enemy with the utmost force, and there was little room for manoeuvre. It was in these circumstances that, in the spring of 1943, the British and Americans were forced to the conclusion that there could be no cross-Channel invasion of Europe in that year. This decision was taken at the 'Trident' conference in Washington in May. For the first time the Far Eastern commanders were represented at the conference, and they were able to bring strong pressure for the diversion of forces to the Pacific area; but at this juncture their arguments carried less weight than they had done ten months before. Churchill was strongly in favour of developing the offensive across the Mediterranean; exploiting the hoped-for victory in Sicily by an invasion of Italy, and extending it by bringing Turkey into the war and attacking through the Balkans. His motives were suspect to the Americans; but the impossibility of transferring forces to Britain in time for an effective cross-Channel invasion in the end forced itself on the minds of all.

The most important result of this decision was its effect on Stalin. More than any other single factor it excited his distrust of his allies, and through the summer of 1943 relations between the three great powers were at their lowest ebb. Before the decisions of 'Trident' were made known to him, Stalin had spoken in glowing terms about the success of the Tunisian campaign; the breach in Russo-Polish relations which followed the discovery of the Katyn graves[16] evoked no support of Poland from Britain or America; and on 22 May the Comintern was dissolved, presumably as a gesture of friendship on Stalin's part to his allies. A meeting between Roosevelt and Stalin was discussed.

The 'Trident' decisions changed all this. They were followed by acrimonious exchanges between Churchill and Stalin, and the withdrawal of Russian ambassadors from Washington and London. There were other, more ominous signs of possible Russian intentions. The Soviet government promoted a 'Free Germany Committee' and a 'Union of German Officers', including the Stalingrad commander, Paulus; and it issued an appeal to the German people to get rid of Hitler and form a 'real national German government with a strong democratic order'. All this seemed to point to something less than unconditional surrender, and to suggest that the Russian government might seek peace with Germany when once its territory was liberated; later evidence confirms the view that such a possibility was at least explored in Moscow at this time.[17]

Meanwhile on 25 July 1943 had begun the series of events which led to Italy's surrender. A coup d'état overthrew the government of Mussolini and brought Marshal Badoglio to power; shortly afterwards negotiations were opened for an armistice. The negotiations which followed were protracted, while in contrast Hitler acted with swift decision to achieve the rescue of Mussolini and to take over the defence of Italy. Had the British and Americans been in a position to carry out landings in Italy, no doubt a conjunction of interest between them and the new Italian authorities might have led to a rapid conclusion. But this was not the case. The Italians therefore manoeuvred for position in order to get the maximum advantage from an armistice, most of all to cover their vulnerability to German action. On the Anglo-American side discussions were hampered by differences over the nature of the agreement to be sought, the Americans wanting a swift military armistice to be

---

[16] The Polish government in exile had consistently asserted that Polish officers and men, and civilians in Russian hands had not been released. In April 1943 a note was sent to the Russian government referring to German statements that they had discovered a mass grave of Polish officers and others at Katyn near Smolensk, the implication being that they had been executed by the Russians. The Polish government asked for an inquiry by the Red Cross and the Russians broke off relations.

[17] W. Leonhard, *Child of the Revolution* (1957), pp. 256–7.

followed later by a political agreement, while the British were ready to accept the Badoglio government but thought it imperative to get the fullest possible acceptance from it of both political and military terms. In the end a military surrender was agreed on 3 September but was kept secret in the hope that American-Italian action would permit at least the landing of troops on Rome airfields and the safeguarding of the Italian government in Rome. This plan having proved abortive, Eisenhower announced the surrender on 8 September, the day after allied landings across the Messina straits into Italy. A political agreement followed on 29 September.

By this time German action had deprived the allies of any tactical military advantage which they could have hoped for beyond the surrender of Italian forces; and Badoglio's order to the Italians to fight the Germans had little practical effect. In terms of long-run strategy Hitler might well have been better advised to abandon Italy and the Balkans and to concentrate his armies in Germany, but in the short term he denied to his opponents the possibility of a swift advance up the peninsula. It was the effect on the naval balance of power that was of decisive importance. The king and Badoglio surrendered the Italian fleet, and it sailed to Malta, although it suffered losses from German attack on the way. This, together with success in North Africa, freed the Mediterranean for allied shipping and eliminated at a stroke the necessity of using the long Cape route.[18] The defeat of the first of the Axis powers was also of major psychological importance. Hitler succeeded in rescuing Mussolini from his warders in the Abruzzi by a well-directed parachute force, and a fascist government re-established itself in Northern Italy. It executed Ciano and De Bono, who had voted in the Fascist Council to deprive Mussolini of power. Even here the net advantage of the operation probably lay with the British and Americans, since it shielded the Badoglio government from charges similar to those brought against Darlan.

The Soviet government naturally took a lively and suspicious interest in these negotiations, and protested that it was not

---

[18] The advantage thus gained was enhanced by an agreement made with Portugal at the beginning of October for the use of bases in the Azores. The agreement was, as Churchill explained to the Commons, based on the treaty 'signed . . . in the year 1373 between His Majesty King Edward III and King Ferdinand and Queen Eleanor of Portugal' (Churchill, v. 146–7).

being consulted fully. It demanded the setting up of a three-power military and political commission to supervise negotiations with governments dissociating themselves from Germany. This came to nothing; but at the Moscow conference which followed these events an Advisory Council for Italy was set up, with Russian representation. It gave the Russians a formal but not an effective part in the administration of liberated territory; and this was a pattern which was to be followed, with roles reversed, in eastern Europe. In addition, the Russian government claimed a share in the surrendered Italian ships, a demand which was renewed at the peace conference of 1946. During the ensuing weeks the military situation clarified itself – in many instances tragically for Italian troops, who were caught between Germans and partisans. It moreover became clear that nothing further could be done immediately to remodel the 'Badoglio-King' government on a more liberal and democratic basis. The government was therefore pressed to declare war on Germany on 13 October 1943 and the governments of Britain, America, and the Soviet Union joined in a declaration recognizing Italy as a co-belligerent. The French Committee of National Liberation took no part in these negotiations.

By this time Stalin had abandoned whatever intention he may have had seeking a separate peace with Germany, and preparations went ahead for a meeting of foreign ministers in Moscow in October 1943. This conference proved a turning point in wartime diplomacy. It was now clear to the western powers that Stalin was intent on the final defeat of Germany; he had recovered from the suspicion engendered by the postponement of the second front and was more confident of the military power of the Soviet Union. While the foreign ministers were meeting, an acrimonious correspondence between Churchill and Stalin was brought to an end and arrangements were made to renew the Arctic convoys, which had been suspended for a second time during the summer. In consequence the conference was optimistic.

In some ways the most important single outcome of the discussions was the Declaration of the Four Nations on General Security. The declaration itself, and even more that it should be made by *four* nations, was attributable in large part to the importance which Cordell Hull attached to a committee to establish an international organization at the end of the war and to the inclusion of China as one of the founding powers. Paragraph 4 of the declaration read:

That they recognize the necessity of establishing at the earliest practicable date a general international organization, based on the principle of the sovereign equality of all peace-loving states, and open to membership by all such states, large and small, for the maintenance of international peace and security.[19]

This was rightly regarded as being the first step in the setting up of a new institution which was to replace the League of Nations, and which it was intended should have the support of the great law-keeping powers of the world. The difficulties which would arise in implementing the declaration in detail had not yet appeared, nor could it be foreseen how far short it would fall of the hopes which Cordell Hull attached to it.

The Chinese government were brought into the affair by radio, and the Chinese ambassador signed the declaration. Cordell Hull used all his powers of persuasion to induce the reluctant Molotov to accept the participation of China, and when at last he gave way the Chinese were told that they should not miss the opportunity which had opened itself to them. Eden supported Hull, although without enthusiasm. Hull alone argued the disastrous effect on Chinese morale if China were excluded, and later wrote:

I was convinced that Russian cooperation would be of great assistance to us in rehabilitating and unifying China after the war. Russia would have moral influence on the Chinese Communists, even though their type of Communism was not exactly the same as the Russians.[20]

The three foreign ministers also discussed more specific questions. Hull put forward suggestions about the treatment of Germany, embodying the general ideas of total surrender, occupation, denazification, and surrender of those who might be accused of war crimes, disarmament, and the establishment of democratic government. Molotov took Hull's proposals away to show Stalin, and brought them back the next day, 'his face radiant.'[21] The possibility of dismembering Germany was discussed inconclusively – both the British and American govern-

---

[19] L. Holborn, ed., *War and Peace Aims of the United Nations*, i. (1943), p. 8.
[20] Cordell Hull, *Memoirs* (1948), ii. 1257.
[21] Cf. Feis: 'Who has ever seen Molotov's face "radiant"? Yet Hull thought it was . . . ' (*Churchill, Roosevelt, Stalin* (1957), p. 221).

ments were divided in their opinions at this time – and at Eden's suggestion a new committee was set up, called the European Advisory Commission, to work out details of a European settlement. The conference also agreed on a declaration on German atrocities, which was issued subsequently by Roosevelt, Churchill, and Stalin, and which formed the basis of the Nuremberg trials.

Apart from the discussion of Germany, an important and precise change revealed itself in the attitude of the Soviet Union towards Austria, and this came to be embodied in a three-power declaration. In December 1941, when Eden was in Moscow, Stalin had proposed the 'restoration of Austria as an independent state'. Meeting Molotov again in October 1943, now in the company also of Hull, Eden discussed with his counterparts the wording of a declaration on Austria which would encourage the Austrians to look forward to, and by their conduct to merit, the re-establishment of an independent state. But when it came to detailed drafting in committee, Vyshinsky pressed for the insertion of a phrase which attributed to Austria 'full political and material responsibility for the war'. This was resisted by the other two; but in the end, for the sake of unity, they agreed to a modified phrase: 'Austria . . . has a responsibility which she cannot evade for participation in the war on the side of Hitlerite Germany.'[22] On this phrase, as we shall see, Russia later built its claim for reparations from Austria – a claim still not abandoned when the Austrian treaty was signed twelve years later.

Other questions were discussed, some of which derived from Cordell Hull's (and Roosevelt's) particular preoccupations with post-war reconstruction. Hull put forward ideas of trade liberalization; and spoke of the development of a trusteeship system for colonies – evoking Eden's express reservation. On the last day of the conference Hull dined with Stalin, and was greatly encouraged when Stalin told him that Russia would enter the war against Japan after the defeat of Germany. After dinner they saw a film of the 'bitter fight of Red partisans against the treacherous Japanese in Siberia during the revolutionary period of 1918'.[23] Most important, the foreign ministers had prepared

[22] Holborn, *War and Peace Aims*, i. 9.
[23] Hull, *Memoirs*, ii. 1311. Hull was so excited by Stalin's statement that he sent off a cable, half in navy and half in army code, to Roosevelt.

the way for the meeting of their principals which was to take place in Teheran at the end of 1943.

The two great conferences of the war, between Churchill, Roosevelt, and Stalin, were held at Teheran in November-December 1943 and at Yalta in February 1945; and they were followed by the Potsdam conference in July-August 1945, after the war in Europe had been won. By that time Truman had succeeded to the presidency of the United States, and a British election led to the replacement of Churchill by Attlee and Bevin in the middle of the conference. These meetings were unique in the history of modern diplomacy. They were not summoned to devise a specific treaty, but to co-ordinate policies and reach agreement on post-war settlement; and they pro-duced more tangible results than the subsequent 'summit' meeting held in Geneva a decade later.

At this time there was no other effective way of conducting diplomacy between the principal great powers. Stalin alone could speak and act for the Soviet government, and it was essential to establish direct contact with him. In the United States the State Department had been eclipsed by Roosevelt's personal conduct of diplomacy; Churchill had always had confidence in his ability as advocate in personal meetings with other leaders. The exceptional conditions of war had brought an unprecedented concentration of power in the hands of the democratic leaders, comparable to that enjoyed by Stalin, and if co-operation were to be achieved between them at all it would have to be by personal meeting. The opportunities for action if they were agreed were unprecedented too; not only were they powerful within their own nation-states, but these states themselves enjoyed unrivalled power and flexibility of action.

The conferences nevertheless were obviously subject to grave disadvantages. It often seemed more important to agree on a formula than to admit differences, and such formulae provided fertile ground for subsequent dispute. The discussions were subject to strains not present in more traditional diplomacy; work was done under pressure since time was limited; it was accompanied at Yalta by massive and fatiguing banquets. Moreover the attempt to reach a personal understanding some-times distorted the issues discussed – this was particularly true of Roosevelt's attitude to Stalin – and the feeling inevitably engendered by a closely shared participation in shaping the world's future gave an exaggerated impression of the extent of agreement on specific issues.

For all that, the wartime conferences were an improvement on anything that had happened during the first world war. When Germany sought an armistice in November 1918 little attempt had been made by the victors to arrive at agreement on the bases of a possible peace settlement. Britain and France had made secret treaties which were not recognized by the 'Associated' power, the United States; while Wilson's fourteen points had not been agreed by the 'Allied' powers. Only eighteen months had elapsed since American entry into the war, and no serious attempt had been made to arrive at a concerted policy for post-war settlement. Now such an attempt was to be undertaken, and it is worth breaking the narrative to survey the ground in more general terms.

The central problem with which the leaders of the United Nations were concerned was one which their predecessors had failed to solve, as they were constantly aware – the problem of Germany. The conclusion of the war, the common interest in future security from an expansionist Germany were the predominant considerations of mutual concern which bound them together. However, it should not be forgotten that anxiety in the face of Germany could also be a source of division between them, as was shown in the Russian reaction to the appeasement policies of Britain and France, the Nazi-Soviet pact which was associated with this reaction and which in turn accentuated British distrust of Russia, and again more recently by the mutual suspicions of the summer of 1943. As soon as the war was over, antipathy, distrust, and enmity arising out of relations with the two parts of Germany became a predominant influence in the development of the cold war. Moreover while Germany was never absent from the preoccupations of the governments of the three countries, it was often ousted from their discussions, as we shall see, by issues where, even at this time, they were divided on questions of principle.

Both with regard to Germany and in the wider perspective of the world after the war, it is relatively easy to discover the views of the western leaders. They did not intend that Germany would come to be a country divided between east and west. They thought of the division of Germany as a possible means of removing the German threat; but they then had in mind its division into a number of separate states. Such proposals, however, went by default as the difficulty of agreeing with the Russians increased; and there seems little doubt that Churchill and Roosevelt expected Germany to develop along the broad lines later laid down at the Potsdam conference. They were both aware that this would leave the Soviet Union as the dominant power on the continent of Europe; but from this realization they drew different conclusions.

Roosevelt was constantly aware of the speed with which American isolation had followed the war of 1914–18; and his own attempt to counter Congressional neutrality legislation was fresh in his memory. He therefore calculated (and stated at Yalta) that two years was the maximum time that American troops could be expected to remain in Europe after the war.[24] This being so, it was imperative that Russia should be a friendly power. It would be worth making considerable sacrifices on points of detail to achieve this result, and his optimism – that refusal to despair without which he would never have overcome the burden of polio – led him to believe that it was possible. It was not through neglect of the power of Russia but through awareness of it that he thought it so important to get on with the Russians. Conscious of America's own revolutionary past, he sought common ground with the Soviet Union in support of the rapid liquidation of colonial empires, and he foresaw the possibilities of economic assistance by the United States in the development of poor areas of the world. The evils of nazism and dictatorship had brought together the liberal and the progressive forces of the world, whatever the differences between them, and each of the great powers – Britain, China, Russia, and America – could co-operate in the maintenance of peace, each in its own quarter of the globe, while the United States would use its wealth to offer assistance in the material development of the poor areas of the world. The institutional means by which this was to be done was to be a world-wide international organization. Direct American action would necessarily be limited by the oceans surrounding the continent, and American influence on world affairs must therefore necessarily be made through an organization of this sort.

[24] At a subsequent session of the Yalta conference Roosevelt modified this statement, but it seems none the less to represent his general view. See *Conferences at Malta and Yalta*, pp. 660–1 and Feis, *Roosevelt, Churchill, Stalin*, p. 532.

Lacking the doctrinaire views of his secretary of state, Roosevelt arrived by a different route at an acceptance of the same universalism in world politics, and had no grounds for opposing the similar universalism in economics of which Cordell Hull was one of the principal exponents.

Churchill was no less visionary than Roosevelt; he was more sceptical of what the future would bring. He too was aware of the dominance which Russia would exercise on the continent of Europe once the power of Germany were removed; and it was something which could only fill him with misgiving. Assuming, as he was bound to do, that the United States would not provide a counter to Russian power, he sought the participation of France to give added weight to the west against the east. He strained every effort, with little success, to limit the area in which military victory would give Russia political power. He foresaw European union as a means of putting an end to the centuries-old conflict between France and Germany; and he attached greater hopes to the regional groupings of powers, checking and balancing each other, than to a world-wide international organization as a means of achieving peace and security.[25]

The motives and intentions of Stalin are impossible to determine with any certitude. In the absence of any documentary evidence we cannot know what his thoughts were; and any attempt to reconstruct them is made more difficult by the fact that Stalin combined Marxist beliefs with a keen awareness and eager love of power and a deep suspicion of everyone else. For all that, there can be no doubt that his prime purpose was to achieve for Russia recovery from the war and its own security. This meant that Germany should provide reparations payments; it also meant that the countries on Russia's western frontier should be dominated by Russia. It seems safe to assume too that Stalin hoped to re-establish Russia's traditional frontiers – to reclaim the national heritage to which, however Marxist he was, he had become increasingly attached since 1934.

[25] See Churchill's minute to Eden, 21 Oct. 1942: 'It would be a measureless disaster if Russian barbarism overlaid the culture and independence of the ancient States of Europe. Hard as it is to say now, I trust that the European family may act unitedly as one under a Council of Europe.' He did not insist on the view, expressed in the same minute, that 'the Chungking Government . . . would be a faggot vote on the side of the United States in any attempt to liquidate the British overseas Empire' (Churchill, iv. 504).

WARTIME DIPLOMACY BETWEEN THE GREAT POWERS 53

Beyond that it is difficult to go. Did Stalin foresee the division of Germany? Or did he, like his western counterparts, expect the partition to be temporary? If he expected a united Germany, did he nurture hopes that it would be a communist Germany? Did he expect indeed that communism would spread across western Europe, because he exaggerated either the popular support which it had won during the war or the vulnerability of the capitalist system? Or did he, by contrast, grow but slowly aware of the new strength accruing to the Soviet Union, and expect the long-awaited attack by capitalism on the socialist camp in the wake of the world war? Or should his participation in the United Nations organization be taken as proof that Marxist calculations were subordinated to the need of keeping the wartime alliance in being? To these questions the answers must be speculative; even coherence and consistency are poor tests for the validity of an explanation, in view of the frequency with which all statesmen pursue policies which are mutually conflicting.

These men were the leaders of the major powers which were to emerge victorious from the war. They crossed each other on the scale of power, as Britain exhausted the strength that had hitherto assured it a place of primacy, while the United States and the Soviet Union developed their resources to a point of supremacy unknown before. But there were others. In Europe, de Gaulle consistently acted on the assumption that France was a great power; while Britain and America as consistently left France out of their councils. In de Gaulle's eyes the weakness of France consequent on defeat in 1940 was a temporary phenomenon, and it was therefore preposterous to him that Britain and America, as maritime powers with no real stake in Europe, should settle European affairs without reference to France. On the side of Britain and America it was inevitable that in the pressing days of war, a power should be measured by the extent of its contribution to the common cause. Within the government of the United States antipathy towards de Gaulle was more positive than a mere discounting of French power. For reasons which may never be clear, Cordell Hull conceived a bitter distrust of de Gaulle, and on this point Roosevelt had no strong views which ran counter to those of his secretary of state. In the early years after American entry into the war Hull (and Roosevelt) had continued to attach importance to American relations with the Vichy government, which he believed (with some justification) could be used to advantage by the enemies of Germany; but he showed great insensitivity in expecting de Gaulle (who had been condemned to death as a mutineer) to share his cossetting of Vichy. De Gaulle never lost sight of political questions even in the heat of battle, and he was acutely sensitive to the exclusion of France from political discussions by the leaders of the three powers. This preoccupation with politics in the midst of battle was anathema to Cordell Hull, steeped as he was in American tradition. As he wrote in his *Memoirs*:

we did go as far as we could in giving him military assistance and in trying to build him up as what he should have been – a military leader and a general of the French armies who was willing to leave political considerations to a later date and to take the field and fight the Germans.[26]

With Churchill de Gaulle's relations were on a different plane. Both men had a sense of grandeur; but de Gaulle lacked the warmth and generosity which were such an important element in enabling Churchill and Roosevelt to subordinate political calculations to a sharing of effort; and while de Gaulle bore no grudge against Churchill because the interests of their two nations were bound to conflict, his 'realistic' view of their rivalry exaggerated rather than diminished it. For Stalin, who had least direct contact with de Gaulle, these considerations were of minor importance. He had denounced the Free French during the period of the Nazi-Soviet pact; but when de Gaulle welcomed Russia as an ally in June 1941 (he did so the more readily because he saw Russia as a balancer against Britain and America) Stalin gladly recognized his leadership. He did not profess to comprehend the lengths to which Cordell Hull would go to convince himself and others that de Gaulle was unrepresentative of the French people;[27] on the other hand he was not convinced of the importance of France as a great power, in spite of the fact that when Churchill declined de Gaulle's offer of troops to fight in Libya in November 1942 de Gaulle had sent for Bogomolov and transferred the offer to Russia.

[26] ii. 1193.
[27] On 12 December 1942 Hull wrote: 'according to all my information . . . some 95 per cent of the entire French people are anti-Hitler, whereas more than 95 per cent of this latter number are not de Gaullists and would not follow him' (ibid.).

It was therefore American resistance above all which delayed recognition of de Gaulle's authority. Only on 23 October 1944 was de Gaulle's committee recognized by Britain, the United States, and Russia as the provisional government of the French Republic, since it was necessary to hand over the government of a 'zone of the interior' of France to a French authority (and since it was assumed that the conditions now existed for the provisional government to make itself truly representative). Not surprisingly de Gaulle commented: 'We naturally refrained from thanking any of them for this formality performed *in extremis.*'[28]

The delay in recognizing the French government had certainly not prevented de Gaulle from working out his own clear ideas of the shape of the post-war world. For him more even than for the other leaders Germany was the central problem; and he regarded the 'abolition of a centralized Reich' as 'the first condition necessary to prevent Germany from returning to its bad ways'. Whether Germany would re-emerge as a stable and pacific power was a question for the future; the immediate step was to create a German federation, and to establish international control of the Ruhr. Compared with Germany, Russia was of minor importance. For de Gaulle no ideology was of great significance beside the dominant force of nationalism. Once Germany ceased to be a threat Russia would grow out of 'what was momentarily tyrannical and aggrandizing in the Russian régime' and 'the Russians themselves would lose all desire to exceed their own boundaries'; the more so since 'if the Kremlin persisted in its desire for domination, it would be against the will of the nations subject to its government. Yet in the long run there is no régime that can hold out against the will of nations'.[29] This being so, it would be possible to form a great association of all European states, within which France would undertake great actions and regain its place as a great power. Meanwhile it must insinuate itself into the councils of America, Britain, and Russia, while protecting French interests, particularly the French empire, from their depredations. From North Africa to Indo-China the American and British governments, in their different ways – the Americans supporting Vichy in North Africa and opposing the restoration of French rule in Indo-China, and the British siding with the

---

[28] De Gaulle, *Salvation* (1960), p. 48. [29] Ibid. p. 51.

Arabs in Syria and Lebanon – were weakening French authority. But as France regained its place in Europe it would become increasingly imperative to re-establish its relations with the colonies, not forcing them back to dependence on France, but creating an association which would add to the power of France, and turn the army of France into a colonial police force.

The greatness to which France aspired was thrust upon China. For many years past the United States had invested much moral and emotional capital in China. More recently China had acquired the prestige of being the veteran participant in the war against Japan and one of the earliest victims of aggression. In American eyes, the future China was cast for a role which could be filled by no other power, and which the American government attributed to it both because of its connexion with China and because there was no alternative. In Roosevelt's phrase, China was to be one of the four 'policemen', and to be responsible for maintaining order in the new world of the Far East. Such a view was met at first with suspicion by Churchill (who thought that China would necessarily be a pawn of the United States) and then with scepticism by him and by Stalin. The British government were well aware of the internal conflicts which the war with Japan to some extent concealed, as well as the exhaustion which the war induced. Stalin discounted, if he did not actively oppose, the possibility of the Chinese communists gaining power; and while prepared to recognize Chiang Kai-shek did not regard him as a great force in the world. As for the Chinese themselves, they had little energy to spare for the formulation of post-war plans; and while France, strong in its individual views and will for the future, was left out of account, China, constantly promoted by the United States, showed little concern for problems outside its own immediate sphere of influence.

These were the great or near-great powers – at least as they came to be defined by permanent membership of the Security Council. We should not forget that there were others, whose status and role in world affairs were to be important for their own sake, and for the effect they had on relations between their more powerful neighbours. Nor, in discussing the politics of governments, should we ignore the peoples whom the governments ruled, who were profoundly influenced and sometimes tragically affected by the war. In the post-war world their hopes and aspirations, even in an autocratic country like the Soviet Union, would help to determine the course of events. Nowhere was this more so than in those areas of Africa and Asia where the experience of war and the defeat of the old imperial powers were a most powerful factor in stimulating the growth of nationalism.

The first of the three conferences, held at Teheran, Persia, at the end of November 1943, was as important for military as for political reasons. The date for an attack in northern Europe, 'Overlord', had been fixed at the Anglo-American conference at Quebec in August, and was now agreed between the three leaders together with supporting action in the south of France. No single political decision was as important as this; it was rather in the atmosphere and alignments of the conference that its political importance was to be found. Churchill took with him a gift and token of admiration from the king to Stalin – the Stalingrad sword, in honour of that victory; but in spite of that he and Stalin were often at cross-purposes, and mutually suspicious of each other. In this situation Roosevelt was the mediator; he met Stalin privately for three discussions; and found that he agreed with Stalin at least as much as with Churchill. This was particularly so since Churchill continued to press for an offensive in the Mediterranean, for an assault on the island of Rhodes, and for pressure to bring Turkey into the war – all of which, he argued, could be attempted without detracting from 'Overlord'. Roosevelt regarded this as a distraction from the main effort in both Europe and the Far East, and as far as the European theatre was concerned he had the strong support of Stalin.

No concrete political decisions were taken at the conference, but the ground of post-war settlement was discussed in general terms. Roosevelt pressed Stalin strongly for support for a post-war international organization. He put forward the idea of 'four policemen' (the fourth was China) to ensure world order; but he made the striking and important comment that the United States would only be able to use air and naval forces, not troops, in carrying out its part in policing the world.[30] Stalin accepted the idea of a world organization, although his interest in it obviously centred on the possibilities it offered for

[30] Sherwood, ii. 781.

control of Germany, and he expressed his anxiety that Germany would start a new war in fifteen to twenty years' time. The points of view of the two leaders were thus significantly different; but they were sufficiently close for Roosevelt to be optimistic about the possibilities of Stalin's co-operation in founding a new world based on principles of law and order, provided that Stalin's point of view was taken seriously and his just claims were met.

The three leaders also discussed the post-war settlement of Germany. It was a common assumption between them that Germany would be dismembered, although they differed as to the way in which this should be done. There was much talk about the frontier of Poland, and the Russians produced maps and a telegram to show that the Curzon line was intended to leave Lvov in Russia. Both Churchill and Roosevelt accepted that Poland should move bodily westward, absorbing part of Germany in the west while the Soviet Union gained territory in the east. (The question whether the line should follow the eastern or the western Neisse did not yet arise.) Nor did they object to the inclusion of Königsberg in Russia; and Churchill gave sympathetic consideration to Stalin's statement of Russian needs for a warm water port. Stalin took up this theme when Roosevelt asked 'what could be done for Russia in the Far East'. He appears to have outlined Russian territorial aspirations, but not yet to have put forward the demands on the Chinese railway or for special concessions at Dairen, beyond the status of an international free port. These proposals met with no opposition from Roosevelt or Churchill. Finally, Stalin sought British and American support to bring the Finnish war to an end to Russia's advantage, and met with opposition from them not so much on territorial terms as on his proposal for compensation for the cost of the war.

As the war continued to turn against Germany in the months following the Teheran conference, Churchill became increasingly concerned with events in eastern Europe. At this stage he did not consider that Hungary, Rumania, or Bulgaria had any great claims on Britain or British protection, and expected that as the war ended they would come under Russian influence. But he attached great importance to the fate of Poland and to political developments in Greece. Polish independence had been the immediate cause for which Britain had gone to war; and Britain had gone to the aid of Greece against Italian and German attack long before Russia had been drawn into the war against Germany. It was also of obvious strategic importance in an area of traditional British interests.

In both countries conflict arose between Britain and Russia over the kind of government which would be established as the Germans were driven out. Churchill pressed for the return of the government in exile, which in both cases was relatively conservative, and its broadening by the inclusion of other political parties as an antecedent to the holding of elections. In Poland such an objective was countered by the support which Stalin and the Russians gave to a communist 'National Committee', which they established at Lublin, and which was amenable to their wishes. In Greece the obstacle lay in the fact that the left-wing EAM (the popular front) and ELAS (the National People's Liberation Army), which were dominated by the communists, played a more decisive role than the conservative EDES (the Greek Democratic National League), and further appeared ready to use the advantage accruing from this to take over political control.

Over developments in Greece the British government could obviously exercise considerable influence, and Churchill did not hesitate to do so. In May and again in July 1944 he bolstered up a government based on an uneasy coalition between royalists and EAM, while using British forces to oppose political activism and mutiny in the Greek armed forces. This was followed by an agreement made at Caserta on 26 September by which both left- and right-wing resistance leaders placed themselves under the orders of the Greek government, which in turn put them under the command of the British General Scobie. In December the agreement broke down. EAM ministers resigned from the government and a bid for power by EAM and ELAS seemed imminent. This brought the culmination of British intervention in Greece. The forces under Scobie's command were increased, and Churchill ordered him to stand firm in Athens.[31] On Christmas Eve 1944 Churchill and Eden flew to Athens and brought together the Greek leaders, including those of ELAS, even though fierce fighting was still going on. In the pursuit of an acceptable political

[31] His instructions to Scobie were: 'Do not hesitate to act as if you were in a conquered city where a local rebellion is in progress' (Churchill, vi. 252).

solution the king was persuaded to agree to the establishment
of a regency under Archbishop Damaskinos, and to announce
that he would not return 'unless summoned by a free and fair
expression of the national will'. A new government was established with General Plastiras as prime minister; six weeks of
fighting were brought to an end by the superiority of British
troops, and for a time peace returned to Greece.

No such possibilities of action were open to the British in
Poland, where events were entirely in the control of the Soviet
Union. In late July the Russian armies approached the city of
Warsaw, as in Germany a plot to kill Hitler came near to
success. Inspired by these events and encouraged by Moscow
radio, the leaders of the Polish underground army ordered a
rising in Warsaw, which began on 1 August. But they received
no help from the Russians. In an endeavour to meet their
desperate appeals the British and Americans flew in supplies
from Italy, though the quantities were necessarily meagre.
Churchill pressed Stalin to render assistance; and to make it
easier for Britain and America by allowing their planes to land
on Soviet airfields after flying from Italy. Stalin meanwhile
discussed post-war frontiers and the composition of a post-war
government with Mikolajczyk in Moscow; but sent no aid,
and replied through Vyshinsky to the American ambassador:

> The Soviet Government cannot of course object to English and
> American aircraft dropping arms in the region of Warsaw, since
> this is an American and British affair. But they decidedly object to
> American or British aircraft, after dropping arms in the region of
> Warsaw, landing on Soviet territory, since the Soviet Government
> do not wish to associate themselves either directly or indirectly with
> the adventure in Warsaw.[32]

In consequence, the uprising was overcome by the Germans
before the Russians arrived; and when they did, they had a free
hand to establish their own authority, without any Polish
national force being able to claim credit for the liberation of its
own territory.

In the face of these events, with the Russian armies advancing
in south as well as north-eastern Europe, with disagreements
arising at the Dumbarton Oaks conference for the establishment of a post-war international organization, Churchill

[32] Ibid. p. 118.

decided to fly to Russia to seek agreement with Stalin. He arrived in Moscow on 9 October 1944. In view of the background to the meeting and the developments in eastern Europe which were to follow, it was one of astonishing cordiality. The reason for this was that the second front was now firmly established in Europe, and its success assured. As a result Stalin wrote and talked to Churchill in terms of warm hospitality; Churchill for his part was freed from the defensiveness which he inevitably felt towards Stalin in the days of the Arctic convoys and the postponement of 'Sledgehammer'. Churchill reported to Roosevelt: 'We found an extraordinary atmosphere of good will here';[33] and in this atmosphere he and Stalin agreed on a division of interest in the Balkans, which was recorded[34] as:

Roumania:	
Russia	90%
The others	10%
Greece:	
Great Britain	90%
(in accord with USA)	
Russia	10%
Yugoslavia:	50–50%
Hungary:	50–50%
Bulgaria:	
Russia	75%
The others	25%

In this way the cards were put on the table. Churchill was well aware of the conflicts which were likely to arise as the German armies were pushed back; but he was aware too that the war was yet to be won – and that even after Germany was defeated there was still Japan. The worst that could happen in these circumstances was that civil strife would break out in the countries of eastern Europe, and that the wartime alliance would be split asunder as its members supported opposing sides in these internal conflicts. It thus seemed worth-while making quite clear to Stalin the extent to which Britain was prepared to go in each country to press its point of view, and to recognize the predominant or equal interest of the Soviet

[33] The United States was represented at these meetings by Averell Harriman, who sat as an observer.
[34] Churchill, vi. 198.

*3

Union – on the supposition that when the war was ended
Soviet troops would withdraw, and the countries of eastern
Europe would be more or less free to determine their own
destiny. Poland was notably absent from the agreement, but
the Poles were not omitted from the Moscow discussions. On
the contrary, Churchill had persuaded Mikolajczyk and his
colleagues to travel from London and meet Bierut and the
Lublin Poles. It was, as he reported to the king, 'All Poles'
Day'. The Lublin Poles showed themselves to be loyal spokesmen of the Russian point of view. Even so, Churchill pressed
the London Poles to reach an agreement on the frontier of
Poland; and to promote, both by meetings between Poles and
by hard bargaining with Stalin, a rapprochement between the
two sides so that an effective Polish government would emerge.
These efforts met with no success.

The cordiality which reigned at Moscow survived when de
Gaulle followed Churchill in visiting the Russian capital in
December. He sought the conclusion of a Franco-Soviet pact
similar to the Anglo-Soviet pact, and rejected the suggestion
that the three countries should join in a tripartite arrangement.
Churchill and Stalin each agreed that the other should sign a
treaty with de Gaulle.[35]

But the signs of future conflict were present. As Churchill
became increasingly cautious and alarmed about Russian
activity, his close understanding with Roosevelt diminished.
In November 1943 Churchill had written to Roosevelt of a
meeting between British and American staffs before they were
joined by the Russians or Chinese, and Roosevelt had replied:
'I have held all along, as I know you have, that it would be a
terrible mistake if Uncle J. thought we had ganged up on him
on military action.' This was to be a theme of increasing
importance in the future. In August 1944, when Churchill had
sought Roosevelt's support over the Warsaw rising to the extent
of sending planes to land on Russian-held airfields 'and see
what happens', the president had declined to do so, saying: 'I
do not consider it would prove advantageous to the long-
range general war prospect for me to join in the proposed

[35] Churchill wrote to Stalin on 19 December expressing his admiration of the
Russian film *Kutuzov* and said: 'I do not suppose that you showed the film to de
Gaulle, any more than I shall show him *Lady Hamilton* when he comes over here
to make a similar treaty to that which you have made with him, and we have
made together' (*Correspondence with . . . Churchill and . . . Attlee*, p. 287).

message to Stalin, but I have no objection to you sending such a message if you consider it advisable to do so.'[36] In December of the same year Roosevelt sent a sympathetic telegram to Churchill about British intervention in Greece, but one which was cautious to stay within the bounds imposed by an enraged public opinion in America – at a time when Churchill was being strongly attacked by many people in his own country.

Divergent ideas about strategy added to the distance between the two men. When the campaign in Italy had opened Churchill had pressed for the diversion of small forces to capture Rhodes, and for every effort to be made to bring Turkey into the war and open up the Balkans. Later he strongly opposed the diversion of forces to a landing in southern France, at first because it would weaken 'Overlord', and then because it deprived Alexander of success in Italy which would make it possible to drive on to Vienna. In Churchill's mind all his urgings were based on military calculation and were seen to have military advantages; but they would in addition make it possible for Britain and America to exercise a greater influence over political developments in south-eastern Europe. But as Eisenhower did not accept Churchill's views of military strategy, it was inevitable that the idea would grow up that Churchill was seeking political advantage at the expense of military objectives. In the eyes of Americans, who still regarded military victory as something necessarily distinct from and prior to political considerations, this was entirely unacceptable; the more so when the political considerations in question appeared to them to be not so much an effort to counter Soviet and communist dominance as the pursuit of British imperial interests and a Churchillian predilection for conservative and monarchist régimes.

While these events were in progress, representatives of the great powers met at Dumbarton Oaks in Washington to discuss plans for a future international organization. It was a dual conference. From 21 August to 28 September 1944 the representatives of Britain, the United States, and Russia met. Then the Russians left and the British and American delegations met the Chinese. The discussions with the Chinese, however, added nothing of great significance. The conference succeeded in laying the basis of the United Nations organization as it was

[36] Churchill, vi. 123–4.

eventually to emerge, and in defining the major problems that would endure through the ensuing discussions. Agreement was rapidly reached on the main structure of the organization – a General Assembly, a Security Council consisting primarily of the great powers, a Secretariat, and an International Court of Justice. Following Churchill's insistence, it was agreed that France should be one of the great powers with a permanent seat on the Security Council.

Beyond this differences arose. The United States proposed that the original membership of the organization should consist of the signatories of the United Nations declaration, together with eight other states, six of which were Latin American republics. This was not acceptable to the Russians who wished to confine membership to the countries at war with the Axis. As a counter to the American proposal they accordingly suggested that all sixteen republics of the Soviet Union should be represented. From this exchange no progress was made at the conference.

The second most important difference was over voting in the Security Council. Both the United States and the Soviet Union wanted to avoid a situation where one of the great powers was called on to act against its own wishes by a majority vote, and so it was agreed that the permanent members of the Security Council should exercise a veto. But the British delegation argued that even a great power should not be judge in its own cause, and consequently proposed that the veto should not be used by a power which was party to a dispute. The Soviet Union rejected this proposal and the American delegation was divided. A compromise was discussed along the lines which were eventually embodied in the Charter of the United Nations – a complete veto over decisions and enforcement action: a veto which was not available to a party to a dispute while questions were under investigation and when recommendations for settlement were made.

There were other differences between the Unites States and Russia, and behind the divergences over detail a more general conflict of view was evident. The United States saw the organization as a means whereby principles of law and justice would be introduced into international relations and would become effective in regulating the affairs of nations. Inevitably its own national interests were also present – hence the support for the

Latin American republics and, more striking, the fact that the American delegation could no longer press its views about international trusteeship since the chiefs of staff were anxious to retain control over the former Japanese mandates. But this intrusion of national interests did not invalidate the general theme of law and order. The Soviet Union in contrast was intent on keeping the wartime alliance in being. It too had its immediate national interests in eastern Europe; but the American idea of international relations based on principles of justice was meaningless to Stalin.

In retrospect, then, the post-war opposition of interest between east and west and the fundamental differences in their views of the world can be seen in formation over these months. But at the time the division was by no means clear-cut, and Churchill's attempt to limit communist influence struck a stronger note of discord with Roosevelt's liberal optimism than with Stalin's own pursuit of Russian interests. In these circumstances it appeared imperative and at the same time possible to eliminate some of the disharmony by the new conference. Only the practical difficulties caused by Stalin's active command of the army and by Roosevelt's physical weakness delayed the arrangements, and in February 1945 the meeting at last took place, at Yalta in the Crimea.

The Yalta conference was the most important of the wartime meetings, and it laid a firm basis for subsequent conflict. Victory in Europe was now assured; victory in the Far East was foreseeable, but with a high price apparently still to be paid. In these conditions the problems of peace were the more urgent, and the possibility of Russian assistance against Japan the more attractive.

The most pressing problem at Yalta was still that of Poland, and it took up most time, for the difference between Russia and the western allies proved fundamental and irremovable. The difficulty was still twofold: the composition of the Polish government, and frontiers. Stalin gave full support to the Lublin Committee to which on 31 December 1944 the Soviet government had accorded recognition as the provisional government of Poland. Churchill retained his sense of commitment to the London Poles, in spite of the fact that Mikolajczyk had now resigned from their committee because he felt trapped between the unwillingness of his colleagues to compromise with Russia and the attempts of Churchill to secure agreement on his behalf; in addition Churchill wished to resist the communizing of Poland and he was alarmed and impatient at the impossibility of British and American observers visiting Poland to find out what was going on. Roosevelt was less committed to the London Poles, but equally committed to the institution of democratic government. The problem of frontiers became more sharply defined at the conference. The western leaders accepted that Poland should move westwards, and they agreed that the eastern frontier should leave Lvov (which was important for its surrounding oil) in Russia. But Stalin now insisted that the western frontier should coincide with the Oder as far as the western Neisse, and then follow this river towards its source. Roosevelt and Churchill regarded the eastern Neisse – a different river – as an appropriate dividing line from Germany, and could not accept the inclusion of the overwhelmingly German territory between the two rivers in a new Poland. This, as Churchill said, was stuffing the Polish goose, creating either an excessive problem in transferring populations or making it impossible for Poland to assimilate its German population.

Stalin argued his case by stressing the fact that Poland was a corridor through which Germany attacked Russia; on both points he could have the last word, since the Red Army was (or soon would be) in occupation of Poland; on the other hand allied unity still meant enough for him to be willing to accept a verbal compromise for the sake of the final communiqué of the conference.[37] The formula covering frontiers eventually read:

The three Heads of Government consider that the eastern frontier of Poland should follow the Curzon Line with digressions from it in some regions of five to eight kilometres in favour of Poland. They recognize that Poland must receive substantial accessions of territory in the north and west. They feel that the opinion of the new Polish Provisional Government of National Unity should be sought in due course on the extent of these accessions and that the final delimitation of the Western frontier of Poland should thereafter await the Peace Conference.

On the question of the government the two western leaders conceded slightly more. They were persuaded to do so by

[37] *Conferences at Malta and Yalta*, pp. 968–75.

Stalin's promise that elections would be held as soon as the Germans were defeated – in about a month. They succeeded in having this written into the final agreement and, with this gained, they agreed that:

> The Provisional Government which is now functioning in Poland should therefore be reorganized on a broader democratic basis with the inclusion of democratic leaders from Poland itself and from Poles abroad. This new government should then be called the Polish Provisional Government of National Unity.

In accepting such a formula they conceded much – although the importance of the concession was in the context of the subsequent argument, rather than in any practical difference in the outcome, since their original contention had been that a new Polish government should be set up; now they had accepted Stalin's main contention that the government which Russia recognized should be broadened. It should be emphasized therefore that their agreement was given because the text also committed the reorganized Polish government:

> to the holding of free and unfettered elections as soon as possible on the basis of universal suffrage and secret ballot. In these elections all democratic and anti-Nazi parties shall have the right to take part and to put forward candidates.

In order to implement the agreement, the two western ambassadors in Moscow were to meet Molotov in a special committee.

As might be expected, it met with no rapid success. Molotov insisted that the committee could not force ministers on Poland without its consent – as expressed by the provisional government; while the western ambassadors wanted to treat this government as one of several groups of Poles out of which a new government should be set up. Their differences became more urgent when the Russians invited leaders of the home army and underground leaders to negotiate secretly with them; on accepting the invitation and arriving in Russia, fifteen of these leaders were arrested. In May Truman sent Hopkins to Moscow in a last attempt to secure agreement, and he was partially successful. The arrested Poles (whose existence had been ignored by the Russians for a month after their disappearance) were sentenced on 21 June to varying terms of imprisonment. In spite of this, agreement was reached between the Poles on the setting up of a coalition government, with a three-man presidium, of which the communist leader Bierut was chairman, and a government under Morawski, with Mikolajczyk as minister of agriculture and deputy premier. This new government was recognized by the British and Americans on 5 July 1945; but it never succeeded in holding 'free and unfettered elections', and proved a stage on the way to the setting up of a communist government.

Poland was not the only country of eastern Europe which was now being rescued from the German army. In Rumania, Bulgaria, and Hungary the Red Army was advancing victoriously; and the British and American leaders were well aware that their representatives not only had little say in the decisions which were being taken in those countries, but had no opportunity even to move about and gather information. With so much time spent on Poland it was impossible to take up this question in detail at Yalta. Instead the Americans introduced a 'Declaration on Liberated Europe', which was intended to succeed and replace Churchill's agreement with Stalin. It emphasized the principle of three-power interest in liberated countries; with the objective of instituting economic recovery, representative government, and free elections. It was accepted by Stalin without demur, and presumably without any serious intent either.

From the American point of view some of the most urgent questions for settlement at Yalta were those outstanding from the Dumbarton Oaks conference. On the two major issues – voting procedure and membership – Stalin accepted, after some argument, the American point of view. Roosevelt's proposal for voting in the Security Council was: that procedural votes should be carried by any seven of the proposed eleven members; that for decision on all other matters the concurrence of all permanent members should be necessary; but that when the Council was seeking a voluntary settlement of a dispute, a member of the Security Council which was party to the dispute (permanent member or not) should abstain. After repeating arguments about the necessity for great power unity, Stalin accepted this formula. In addition, he reduced his demand for sixteen members from the Soviet Union to three, and Stalin and Roosevelt agreed to this (though Roosevelt also reserved the right to propose three United States members as well). A further compromise was reached on the question of trusteeships – although on this issue Churchill was the odd man out. The five permanent members of the Security Council were to consult on machinery for trusteeship; but they were to be confined to the existing mandates of the League of Nations, territories taken from the present enemy, and others which might be voluntarily placed under trusteeship. The importance of this agreement was that it enabled the American government to go ahead with the organization of a conference to draw up the Charter of the United Nations organization. As we shall see, when this conference met in San Francisco it emerged that part of the agreement was not as firm as at first appeared; but great progress had been made.

This must be borne in mind when the discussions on the German question at Yalta are considered. The main outline for allied control and government of Germany after the war had been agreed in the months preceding the conference, as a result of the work of the European Advisory Commission. It had been agreed that the occupation should be by zones: that the commanding officer in each zone should have authority there, and should also be his country's representative on a Control Council, responsible for Germany as a whole. A miniature of this arrangement was duplicated for the area of Greater Berlin. Disagreement had arisen between Britain and America, both of which had wanted a northern occupation zone; but the difference had been resolved in favour of Britain.

At Yalta a significant alteration was made in this agreement: France was accorded an occupation zone in the west of Germany and of Berlin (involving no change in the border or extent of the Russian zone) and on Churchill's insistence this was accompanied by a seat on the Control Council.

Where the three leaders failed to agree was over the question of reparations. Once again there was a fundamental difference between Russia and the other two powers. Stalin's attitude was very similar to that of the French government after the first world war; he wanted to rebuild the shattered Russian economy, he thought it reasonable that German reparations should assist in this, and if this weakened Germany industrially his own security would thereby be further increased. Churchill and Roosevelt regarded the reparations experience of the inter-war years as the result of a disastrous mistake, which they should avoid repeating. They had abandoned the plan which

the secretary of the treasury, Morgenthau, had persuaded
them to accept five months previously, at Quebec, for the
'pastoralization' of Germany, and although they too wanted
to keep the level of German industry down to a reasonable
peace-time level they saw no advantage in heavy reparations.
Least of all did they want to settle a figure for reparations
payments.

The Russians on the other hand had arrived at the conference with a ready-made proposal that reparations should be
paid in kind, and should be fixed at $20 billion, one-half to go
to the Soviet Union. Churchill vigorously resisted such a
proposal, and exposed himself to taunts from Molotov suggesting that the British wanted a strong and prosperous Germany.
However, Stalin talked of the figure of $20 billion as a basis for
discussion by a Reparations Commission which all agreed
should be set up. To this manoeuvre Roosevelt, but not
Churchill, proved vulnerable.[38] It was, as a result, recorded
that the Commission should take 'as a basis for discussion the
suggestion of the Soviet Government that the total sum . . .
should be twenty billion dollars and that 50% of it should go
to the Union of Soviet Socialist Republics'.[39] The dissent of the
British government to this 'Soviet-American' proposal was also
registered.

Side by side with the three-power discussions which went on
at Yalta, Roosevelt and his delegation engaged in talks with
the Russians about a settlement in the Far East. This was the
second meeting of major importance devoted to the China–
Japan area. The first had taken place at Cairo in November
1943 and had preceded the Teheran conference. Neither
Stalin nor Molotov had participated, since Russia was not at
war with Japan, and the conference was therefore led by
Churchill, Chiang Kai-shek, and Roosevelt – although their
agreement was communicated to Stalin at Teheran, and
received his approval, before it was published. Churchill
resented the time devoted to discussions with Chiang Kai-shek
(whom he wanted to send off to visit the pyramids with Mme
Chiang) and would have preferred time for Anglo-American

<hr/>

[38] He may have been influenced by the note which Harry Hopkins passed across
the table to him saying: 'The Russians have given in so much at this conference
that I don't think we should let them down. Let the British disagree if they want
to' (Sherwood, ii. 851).
[39] *Conferences at Malta and Yalta*, p. 979.

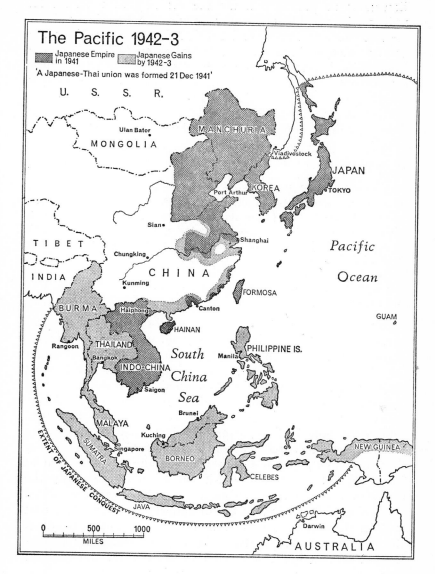

The Pacific 1942-3

Japanese Empire in 1941

Japanese Gains by 1942-3

'A Japanese-Thai union was formed 21 Dec 1941'

U. S. S. R.

Ulan Bator

MONGOLIA

MANCHURIA

Vladivostock

JAPAN

Port Arthur

KOREA

TOKYO

Sian

Shanghai

TIBET

Chungking

Pacific

INDIA

CHINA

Kunming

Ocean

FORMOSA

BURMA

Haiphong

Canton

GUAM

HAINAN

Rangoon

THAILAND

Bangkok

INDO-CHINA

Saigon

South

China

Sea

Manila

PHILIPPINE IS.

Brunei

MALAYA

Kuching

SUMATRA

Singapore

BORNEO

NEW GUINEA

CELEBES

EXTENT OF JAPANESE CONQUEST

JAVA

0   500   1000

MILES

Darwin

AUSTRALIA

Map 2

Based on W. F. Craven and J. L. Cate, Eds., ARMY AIR FORCE IN WORLD
WAR II (Chicago University Press, 1964)

discussions in preparation for the meeting with Stalin. In addition, he and his staff disagreed with the Americans about the next steps in Pacific and South Asian strategy. None the less the Cairo conference undoubtedly bolstered Chinese morale and willingness to continue the exhausting struggle against Japan. It also brought agreement on a declaration of sweeping simplicity – a simplicity which accorded ill with the complexities of Far Eastern affairs, which could scarcely be foreseen at that time. The important part of the declaration read:

The three great allies are fighting this war to restrain and punish the aggression of Japan. They covet no gain for themselves and have no thought of territorial expansion. It is their purpose that Japan shall be stripped of all the islands in the Pacific which she has seized or occupied since the beginning of the first World War in 1914, and that all the territories Japan has stolen from the Chinese, such as Manchuria, Formosa, and the Pescadores, shall be restored to the Republic of China. Japan will also be expelled from all other territories which she has taken by violence and greed. The aforesaid three great powers, mindful of the enslavement of the people of Korea, are determined that in due course Korea shall become free and independent.[40]

Far Eastern questions were also discussed at Teheran, although no full record is available; and since then Harriman, at the time of Churchill's visit to Moscow in October 1944, had talked over with Stalin the possible nature of a Far Eastern agreement. At Yalta it thus remained to tie down Stalin's undertaking to enter the war after the defeat of Germany, which he had first made to Hull at the foreign ministers' conference and had confirmed to Harriman; and also to reach a definite agreement on Russian interests in the Far East, probably along the lines which Stalin had explored at Teheran and subsequently with Harriman. Obviously the two were connected; but to suggest that Roosevelt exchanged concessions in the Far East for an undertaking on Stalin's part to enter the war against Japan is exaggerated and misleading. Roosevelt considered that Russia had just claims in the Far East. These claims might conflict with what the Chinese regarded as their national interests; but the atmosphere of wartime co-operation with Stalin, and a certain disenchantment with the divisions and inefficiencies of the Chiang régime

[40] *Conferences at Cairo and Tehran*, pp. 448–9.

were such that Roosevelt was not prepared to support China against the reasonable claims of Russia. Above all, it was indispensable to promote agreement and co-operation between Russia and China, on which the peace of the Far East depended. This seemed possible only if Russia were treated fairly in the post-war settlement rather than being left to enforce its claims in the absence either of an agreement or of effective power to prevent such action.

The result of discussions between the Russians and the Americans was a reaffirmation by Stalin that Russia would enter the war against Japan two or three months after the defeat of Germany; together with an agreement[41] – which Churchill assented to, although he had not participated in the discussions which led to it – restoring virtually intact the privileges which tsarist Russia had gained from China, and then lost to Japan. The express conditions were:

1. The *status quo* in Outer-Mongolia (The Mongolian People's Republic) shall be preserved;

2. The former rights of Russia violated by the treacherous attack of Japan in 1904 shall be restored, viz:

(a) the southern part of Sakhalin as well as all the islands adjacent to it shall be returned to the Soviet Union,

(b) the commercial port of Dairen shall be internationalized, the preeminent interests of the Soviet Union in this port being safeguarded and the lease of Port Arthur as a naval base of the USSR restored,

(c) the Chinese-Eastern Railroad and the South-Manchurian Railroad which provides an outlet to Dairen shall be jointly operated by the establishment of a joint Soviet-Chinese Company it being understood that the preeminent interests of the Soviet Union shall be safeguarded and that China shall retain full sovereignty in Manchuria;

3. The Kuril[e] islands shall be handed over to the Soviet Union.

By the standards of nineteenth-century diplomacy there was nothing remarkable about this agreement, which of course remained secret for the time being; by the professed standards of the two main signatories it is indeed striking. The gains which the Soviet Union made meant that in the Far East as in Europe there would be a close approximation to the frontiers

---

[41] *Conferences at Malta and Yalta*, p. 984.

and privileges of tsarist Russia; while Roosevelt was in the invidious position of apportioning the territory of an ally, and one which he was constantly trying to promote as a great power. The remaining paragraphs made the best of this difficulty:

It is understood that the agreement concerning Outer-Mongolia and the ports and railroads referred to above will require concurrence of Generalissimo Chiang Kai-Shek. The President will take measures in order to obtain this concurrence on advice from Marshal Stalin.

The Heads of the three Great Powers have agreed that these claims of the Soviet Union shall be unquestionably fulfilled after Japan has been defeated.

Correspondingly, Stalin gave an undertaking, which may have brought comfort to both the Americans and (later) the Kuomintang, since it implied that Russia would not support the Chinese communists in a bid for power (although the actual significance which Stalin and Roosevelt attached to this paragraph remains unknown). The relevant paragraph read:

For its part the Soviet Union expresses its readiness to conclude with the National Government of China a pact of friendship and alliance between the USSR and China in order to render assistance to China with its armed forces for the purpose of liberating China from the Japanese yoke.

The territorial settlement embodied in the agreement was enduring; for the rest its practical significance was short-lived. The explosion of the atomic bomb meant that the part played by Russia in the war was negligible; less than five years after Yalta the communists took over the government of China and Stalin abandoned to them the railway and port concessions he had regained. But the Yalta agreement had political repercussions of considerable importance, for it played a major part in the revulsion of a section of American opinion against Roosevelt's foreign policy, and what was regarded as the betrayal by the Democrats of American and Chinese interests to the communists.

As the war in Europe came to an end the frontiers of the great political divisions of the future were determined, by *force majeure*, sometimes after marginal disputes. The Russo-Polish frontier was accepted by the provisional government which the Russians had established under their control; the western frontier of Poland was determined by the fact that the Poles were given the administration of part of Germany occupied by the Russians. This was followed by the expulsion of the German population with little regard for individual suffering. Russian troops occupied Prague and Vienna, and the western allies had to use strong pressure to enforce their right to participate in the occupation and administration of the Austrian capital. On the border between Italy and Yugoslavia the rapid and decisive action of the British commander prevented the area of Trieste from being incorporated into Yugoslavia.

It was not intended that a peace conference should follow immediately on the ending of the war; this was a mistake which had been made at the conclusion of the first world war. Even so, the meeting at Potsdam might have been expected to produce more significant conclusions than in fact it did. Most of the decisions arrived at either accepted the existing state of affairs, or consisted in handing over disputes between the participants to the foreign ministers. The common military interest which had enforced cohesion between the powers during the war had greatly diminished by the time the conference began. The successful explosion of the first atomic bomb during the conference made possible the Potsdam declaration to the Japanese people inviting them to surrender; but its more important effect was to remove American and British dependence on Russian help to bring that surrender about.

In all this there was little to suggest that future relations between the victorious powers would be easy or harmonious. The most auspicious moment of all, the ending of the war in Europe, was accompanied by recrimination on the part of the Russians, who unjustifiably suspected the Americans of making an armistice in the west while leaving the Germans free to fight on in the east.

The San Francisco conference had been similarly beset with the sort of problem which has so often characterized the organization to which it gave birth,[42] as the Soviet Union sought admission for the Polish provisional government (which America had not recognized) and the United States pressed for membership on behalf of Argentina (which had departed

[42] See ch. 14 for a survey of the United Nations organization.

from its fascist leanings to make a last-minute declaration of war on Germany). Moreover the conference all but foundered on the question of voting in the Security Council,[43] which was thought to have been settled at Yalta; it was saved by the intervention of Hopkins with Stalin – Hopkins being in Moscow in pursuit of a Polish agreement, as has already been described. In Rumania the government of General Radescu was turned out by the Russians, and replaced by one in which the communists were dominant, with Groza at its head: it was no comfort to the western allies to know that the Radescu government had been one with severe limitations. In the rest of eastern Europe Russian control was being established with no reference made to the representatives of Britain and America.

On 12 April 1945 Roosevelt died. In subsequent years his successor, Harry Truman, was to make his own strong and decisive impact on the conduct of American foreign policy; but the American system of government had excluded him while vice-president from any close knowledge of events. The men who could best advise him were divided in their counsels. Hopkins, who had contributed so much to understanding between Roosevelt and Churchill, was reported as being:

skeptical about Churchill, at least in the particular of Anglo-American-Russian relationship; . . . he thought it was of vital importance that we be not manoeuvred into a position where Great Britain had us lined up with them as a bloc against Russia to implement England's European policy.[44]

Byrnes, whom Truman appointed secretary of state, was anxious to reach agreement with the Russians (and was later to be dismissed by Truman for exceeding his brief in an attempt to do so). On the other hand Harriman and General Deane, who had had most to do with negotiations with the Russians, were profoundly sceptical. The predominant view, which Truman accepted, was that there should be no 'ganging up' against the Russians. He fell in with Churchill's suggestion of a further meeting with Stalin; but he would not agree to keeping Anglo-American forces in their forward positions beyond the agreed zonal boundary with Russia to act as a

---

[43] For a fuller account see ch. 14.
[44] *The Forrestal Diaries*, ed. W. Millis (1951), p. 73. Cf. Sherwood, ii. 876 ff. and Feis, *Between War and Peace* (1960), p. 84 n.

lever in negotiations; he did not arrange for Hopkins to consult Churchill before flying to Moscow; nor would he meet Churchill himself before their joint meeting with Stalin.

This, then, was the atmosphere in which Stalin agreed to a fresh meeting, and in which the last wartime conference and the first summit conference of the peace met at Potsdam. Two further events, one of major and one of minor importance, occurred after the conference had begun. The atomic bomb was successfully exploded in New Mexico. Its full potentialities could scarcely be realized; but it was at once obvious that it would shorten the war against Japan. Russian help would no longer be so important in that conflict – although it would still (it was thought) hasten the end and save lives. The conference could therefore agree on a declaration to Japan calling for surrender with the knowledge at least in part of the new power which the bomb conferred. At the same time the Americans and British agreed that knowledge of the bomb (beyond the fact of its existence) could be shared with the Russians only after the institution of a form of international control which at this time seemed quite alien to their attitude to international affairs, possibly coupled with the institution of democratic government in Russia itself. On the other hand the time when the British and Americans felt that it strengthened their hand against the Russians was yet to come.[45]

Of minor importance in comparison was the change in government in Britain, consequent on the first election after the war in Europe. A Labour government was brought to power with an unchallengeable majority for the first time; Attlee succeeded Churchill as prime minister, and Ernest Bevin took over the Foreign Office. Although the change was from a Conservative caretaker government to a Labour government the transition was nevertheless smoother than the succession from Roosevelt to Truman, for the new leaders had participated fully in previous decisions, as members of the coalition cabinet.

The Potsdam conference opened on 17 July 1945 and lasted for sixteen days. For a venture of such importance the extent of effective agreement was small indeed; such as it was it owed

[45] Notice, however, Alanbrooke's comment: 'Now we could say, "If you insist on doing this or that, well . . . ". And then where are the Russians' (Arthur Bryant, *Triumph in the West* (1959), p. 478).

much to last-minute bargaining between Byrnes and Molotov for a 'package deal' on the main issues outstanding between them. The heads of state and their foreign ministers sat down to agree, amongst other things, on the principles which should guide their representatives in the government of Germany during the period of occupation. Given the divergences between their own systems of government, it is scarcely surprising that there should be so little common ground between them – even less than the formal wording of their agreement would suggest.

They agreed on the removal of Nazi power from Germany – on disarmament, denazification, and the bringing to trial of war criminals – and in the year after Potsdam a four-power tribunal sat in judgement on the Nazi leaders. But when they went on to the task of political reconstruction, the formulae they accepted for the re-education of the German people and the decentralization of government had quite different meanings as between the communists and the western leaders. Even the practical arrangement they came to for the participation of Germans in the administration of Germany were not implemented in practice. According to the agreement:[46]

> Certain essential central German administrative departments, headed by state secretaries, shall be established, particularly in the fields of finance, transport, communications, foreign trade and industry. Such departments will act under the direction of the Central Council.

In the event it was the absent member of the four-power occupation – France – that prevented the implementation of this section; but in any case the consensus to make it work did not exist.

The three powers also agreed that the economic power of Germany should be limited, and its power to make war removed. But just as the destruction of political power produces rivalry to take advantage of the vacuum thus created, so the removal of economic resources was fraught with disagreement. The Russians still wanted to make certain of the delivery of reparations from Germany to Russia; the British and Americans insisted that Germany should not be so mulcted that it could not pay its own way – a divergence of view even wider than at first appears, if account is taken of the different standards of living in the United States and the Soviet Union. The Russians wanted to draw to the maximum extent on the economic resources of Germany as a whole, without sacrificing control over their own zone; the western powers intended that Germany should be united economically, but did not want to have the worst of both worlds, unable to control what went on in the east yet committed to supply reparations from their own zones to the Russians.

From these conflicting purposes the agreement that eventually emerged gave neither side all that it wanted, and provided ample ground for dissent in the future. It was stated that: 'During the period of occupation Germany shall be treated as a single economic unit', and furthermore: 'Payment of Reparations should leave enough resources to enable the German people to subsist without external assistance'. But while economic unity was thus reaffirmed in one section, the next settled reparations on a zonal basis, and nothing was now said about payments to be made out of future German production.

1. Reparations claims of the USSR shall be met by removals from the zone of Germany occupied by the USSR and from appropriate German external assets.

4. In addition to the reparations to be taken by the USSR from its own zone of occupation, the USSR shall receive additionally from the Western zones:

(*a*) 15 per cent of such usable and complete industrial capital equipment . . . as is unnecessary for the German peace economy, and should be removed from the Western zones of Germany, in exchange for an equivalent value of food, coal, potash, zinc (etc.) . . .

(*b*) 10 per cent of such industrial capital equipment . . . to be transferred to the Soviet Government . . . without payment or exchange of any kind in return.

From this agreement the Russians had got less than they had hoped for; in particular they had secured no pledge of deliveries from the production of the Ruhr; and they were dependent on the goodwill of the western powers even for delivery of 25 per cent of an unspecified amount.

In contrast, they gained almost all that they wanted with regard to Poland. The final report of the conference took note 'with pleasure' of the agreement on the government of Poland. In addition, Stalin and Molotov sought recognition of the frontiers of Poland. This the British and Americans would not agree to, even though they were faced with the impossibility of making any actual change in the frontier. But the formula which they eventually accepted as part of the bargain with the Russians read:

The three heads of Government agree that, pending the final determination of Poland's western frontier, the former German territories east of a line running along the Oder River to the confluence of the western Neisse River and along the western Neisse to the Czechoslovak frontier shall be under the administration of the Polish state and for such purposes should not be considered as part of the Soviet zone of occupation in Germany.[47]

In this way they avoided committing themselves on paper; but it would need much optimism to imagine that the separation of this area from Germany would soon be reversed.

For the rest of eastern Europe, the Americans with British support pressed for the implementation of the Yalta declaration, and they secured the inclusion in the final report of a statement of principle about the tripartite nature of the control commissions in Rumania, Bulgaria, and Hungary, for what it was worth. Austria was still a question at issue between them and the Russians. They were still pressing for admission to occupation zones in Vienna, for themselves and for France; and they were distrustful (needlessly, as events proved) of the provisional government which the Russians had set up under Karl Renner. Again the question of reparations was one of importance. The Russians had insisted at the foreign ministers' conference in October 1943 that Austria should take some responsibility for the war, while the British and Americans wanted Austria to be treated as a liberated country. Under British and American pressure the Russians met their wishes to the extent of including in the protocol of proceedings the statement that 'reparations should not be exacted from Austria'. The practical effect of this undertaking was, however, negligible, for three reasons. The most important was that the Russians exercised control over their zone of occupation; the second was that they insisted that the Austrian government should not be told about this section of the protocol (and it was omitted from the published report); and the third reason was that the Soviet government did not abandon its claim to

[47] *Conference of Berlin, 1945*, ii. 1509.

German enterprises in its zone of Austria – and this gave it a very free hand.[48]

When the conference was over much work would remain to be done, requiring agreement between the major powers, to settle European questions outside Germany. For this purpose the three powers agreed to set up a Council of Foreign Ministers. Even on this point agreement was not immediate. The United States proposed that the composition of the Council should be the same as the permanent membership of the Security Council; but the Soviet Union opposed the participation of China and France. As a compromise, all five were formally included in the Council; but when it was engaged in its first task of making peace treaties with the German satellites it was to consist only of those states 'which were signatory to the terms of surrender imposed upon the enemy State concerned' (thereby excluding China and France) except that 'for the purpose of the peace settlement with Italy, France shall be regarded as a signatory to the terms of surrender for Italy'.[49] In addition, one long and complex chapter of the final report embodied at least in verbal form the views of the American government on the future of the former German satellites. It was agreed that a peace treaty with Italy: 'Will make it possible for the three Governments to fulfil their desire to support an application from Italy for membership of the United Nations'.[50] Less conclusive formulae were used to stress the need for the setting up of democratic governments in eastern Europe and for freedom of press reporting. It was envisaged that these states could 'work their passage' and qualify for admission to the United Nations; but the three governments managed to agree on a warning in another direction saying: '[they] feel bound . . . to make it clear that they . . . would not favour any application for membership put forward by the present Spanish Government'.[51]

In many respects the Potsdam agreement, as we have seen, consisted in the enunciation of principles which had little effect on the actual course of events. Where substantial

[48] Section 9 of the chapter on German reparations in the published report read: 'The Governments of the UK and the USA renounce their claims in respect of reparations to shares of German enterprises which are located in the Eastern zone of occupation in Germany, as well as to German foreign assets in Bulgaria, Finland, Hungary, Rumania and eastern Austria'.
[49] *Conference of Berlin, 1945,* ii. 1500.   [50] Ibid. p. 1509.   [51] Ibid. p. 1510.

questions were at issue, formulae were worked out which represented a compromise between opposite points of view, with the result that in subsequent months each party could insist on an interpretation of the agreement most in accord with its own intentions. An additional factor also supervened to render implementation more difficult – the participation of France in the occupation and control of Germany, without its having been party to the Potsdam agreement. In any event meetings between the leaders of the great powers seemed now to have served their purpose; ten years elapsed before the next summit meeting, in Geneva in 1955.

3

FROM WAR TO COLD WAR

THE CENTRE of politics in the years immediately following
the war continued to be Germany. This was inevitable from
the fact that here the representatives of the great powers met
most closely and were responsible for the government and
control of the defeated country. Not only that, but for the
western powers at least failure to agree with Russia over
Germany had far deeper consequences than misunderstanding
anywhere else in the world. Disagreement with Russia with
its accompanying tension and even the possibility of conflict
was something no one wanted to accept so soon after the
conclusion of a world war; but disagreement over Germany
seemed to negate the very success of that war. What indeed
was the use of defeating Germany if the failure of the victors
to agree on how to control Germany made it possible for
Germany to rise again? Twenty years later the irony of the
situation is apparent; their very disagreement ended in the
division of Germany into two parts, each closely integrated
into the half of Europe to which it was joined. This was a
settlement so daring in its simplicity and so contrary to the
wishes of the defeated nation that it could never have been
brought about by agreement – only by disagreement.

There can be no doubt that this was an outcome contrary to
the intentions of British and American statesmen. By the time
the war ended, the ideas which they had conceived for the
dismemberment of Germany, which had been talked about
at Teheran and Yalta, and by Churchill in Moscow in October
1944, had gone by default. Their intention was to see that over
an indeterminate period of years Germany should be reconstructed as a democratic country. In this they at first disagreed
with the French, who continued to look for the break-up of
Germany into a number of separate states, four-power control
of the Ruhr, and particularly for the detachment of the
Rhineland and the Saar from Germany. In their economic
policies Britain and America had gone through a similar

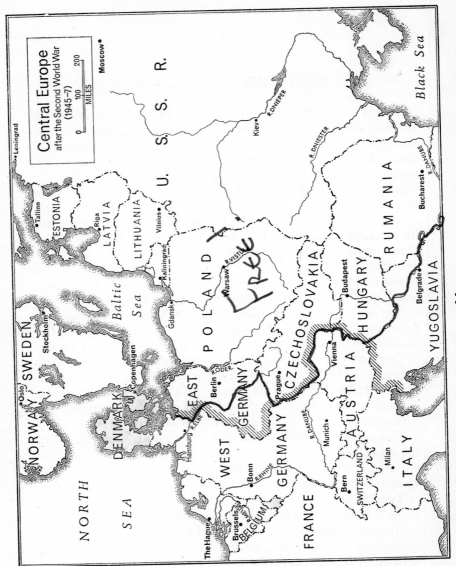

Central Europe
after the Second World War
(1945–7)

0   100   200
MILES

Map 3

revision of ideas as the actual occupation of Germany grew nearer, and the maintenance of a viable Germany came to be as important as the reduction of its industrial capacity to a safe level; and here again the French government continued to lay greater stress on reparations payments.

About Stalin's attitude only two things can be said with certainty: that he sought to recover the maximum reparation for damage to the Soviet Union in the minimum time, and that he was determined to counter the threat which he saw renewing itself in Germany in fifteen to twenty years' time. The optimum means to securing these ends would obviously be Russian control of the whole of Germany, through the mechanisms offered by a satellite communist state. It may be that Stalin supposed that there was a real possibility of achieving such a state of affairs, especially in view of Roosevelt's suggestions that the Americans would not remain in Europe, and the hopes which the Russians entertained of a post-war slump in the capitalist west. Meanwhile, as Russia did not yet control the whole of Germany, there were two ways open to achieve the maximum advantage, which were bound to conflict with each other: one was to retain complete control of the Russian zone and brook no western interference, the other to work for the greatest possible Russian influence in the direction of Germany as a whole. So for example in the matter of reparations, Russia could have a free hand in removals from its own zone; but the great industrial complex of the Ruhr was in the west, and Russia could only mulct it for reparations and guard against its threat to security by participating in four-power control. Obviously, however, there was no reason to suppose that the western powers would readily accord to the Soviet Union the double advantage of unfettered control over its own zone and full participation in the direction of Germany as a whole, unless for some reason they were reduced to a position of weakness or lost interest in the German question. Not only that, but it is reasonable to suppose that the wartime alliance was still for Stalin a possible means of countering the German threat unless Germany came to be subordinate to Russia.

Reasoning of this sort must remain speculative. What is certain is that the government of the Soviet Union did not wait for the effective setting up of four-power control before taking decisive steps, for which advance preparation had long been

4

made, in its own zone and in Berlin. Politically this was to be
done through an 'anti-fascist bloc', which was an attempt to
enlist the support of the German people, and provide a net-
work of volunteers and committees through which the occupation could function. A month after surrender, on 10 June 1945,
the basis of the anti-fascist bloc was changed with the creation
of four political parties – Christian Democrats (CDU), Liberal
Democrats (LDPD), Social Democrats (SPD), and Communists (KPD) – which participated in an anti-fascist coalition. At
the same time social groups, of which the trade union organization was the most important, were constituted, and these
appeared to serve the same purpose as the political organization,
namely to provide a chain of command and control between
the occupiers and the German people.

This rapid establishment of effective government was most
notable in Berlin, not only because of its efficiency, but because
it covered the whole of Berlin before western troops arrived,
and because Berlin was treated as a capital city. The men
responsible for this operation were Germans who had been
living in Moscow, led by Ulbricht.[1] They left Moscow on
30 April, and rapidly set up an efficient administration by
seeking out men to be mayors of districts who were of a political
complexion appropriate to their area, and placing communists
as their deputies and as holders of effective office under them.
At the same time a German government for the city as a whole
was set up (the *Magistrat*), which began organizing such vital
aspects of the citizens' lives as the direction of labour and
rationing: and a German police force was established under
Russian direction.

The result was a remarkable achievement in the restoration
of order in the chaos that followed the end of fighting. But it
also meant that by the time the four-power *Kommandatura* was
established on 7 July 1945 a Russian-directed government for
the whole city was functioning – and the first act of the *Kommandatura* was to confirm all the orders made by the Soviet
commander and the *Magistrat* up to that time. The city was
run by the Russians as the capital of the Soviet zone, just as
in the next three months a 'German Central Administration
for the Soviet Zone' was set up, consisting of twelve depart-

---

[1] Wolfgang Leonhard, who was a member of this group, has described these events
in *Child of the Revolution*. See also Philip Windsor, *City on Leave* (1963), ch. 2.

ments under presidents drawn from the four parties already created. In this way the German administration envisaged under Potsdam came into existence in the east, at a time when no counterpart existed in even draft form in the west. A powerful apparatus had been created which, it might be thought, could at least retain Berlin as a capital for the Soviet zone and reduce the western position there to a dwindling formality, and would even be able to extend Russian control to Germany as a whole. How realizable such possibilities appeared in the minds of the Soviet leaders is a matter for conjecture; in the end they were not achieved, as we shall see, because of the opposition of the people of Berlin and Germany working in conjunction with the western powers.

2) Meanwhile, just as political and administrative organization had been put in hand without waiting for four-power control, so had the collection of reparations. However, reparations policy was directed from Moscow, where four different organs of government had differing authority. As a result the dismantling agencies, which arrived with the second echelon of the army of occupation, were independent both of the Red Army and of the German central administration, and could call on their services. They immediately set about dismantling not only factories but telephone exchanges, railway workshops, even a university laboratory, and they also began both to take reparations out of current production and to organize German labour for reparations purposes. In doing so they cut across the activity of the German central administration, which was achieving some success in re-establishing a productive economy (but one which was dependent on precisely those items which the reparations agencies were removing). They also made the political objective of working with the Germans through the 'anti-fascist coalition' more difficult.

The speed and extent of Russian organization of the eastern zone and of Berlin (even allowing for the conflict of authority and purpose in the matter of reparations) provided the background for the activities of the four powers in their joint administration of Germany. Superficially the institutional arrangements for their activities had every appearance of adequacy. Each zone was administered by its commander-in-chief; and the four commanders met in the Allied Control Council, while Berlin was administered by a four-power

Kommandatura, subordinate to the Control Council. When the Allied Control Council was unable to reach unanimous agreement, questions were referred to national governments, and this meant in effect the Council of Foreign Ministers.

In practice there was very little that the Control Council was able to settle by itself; and although the foreign ministers met three times in 1946 and twice in 1947 to discuss the German question, they made little further progress.[2] The immediate problems before the Control Council were to establish an effective administration of Germany and to make provision for reparations payments, and the reduction of German industry to a peace-time level. These problems were obviously bound together. The economy could hardly be run on a normal footing until the question of reparations and dismantling had been cleared out of the way, but the level of reparations could not be determined until the productive capacity of the country as a whole was established.

On neither topic did rapid progress prove possible. The speedy establishment of reparations and economic administrations in the Soviet zone had been accompanied by the sealing of that zone to the west, and whether or not the Russians had thought of this as a means of extending their own control to the whole of Germany, they were certainly not willing to open their zone either to outside control or to trade with the rest of Germany. Nor was there unity amongst the western powers. The French government resisted all moves which tended towards the unification of Germany as prejudicial to their own policy of dismemberment. Thus when it was proposed in October 1945 that the central German administrative agencies envisaged in the Potsdam agreement should be set up (a step which may well have given great advantage to the Russians, in view of their own preparedness in this field), the French representative on the Control Council refused to agree, and nothing could be done. After this, disagreement between Russia and the western powers, coupled with the continued seclusion of the Soviet zone, made such a move even less possible.

Meanwhile steps had been taken to determine the level of industry which should be allowed in accordance with the

[2] In contrast, the International Military Tribunal at Nuremberg succeeded in reaching agreed verdicts on the charges brought against the Nazi leaders, and the Tribunal proceedings produced a stream of evidence of Nazi tyranny.

Potsdam formula – a level which, once settled, would permit a determination of the extent of removals in the form of reparations. An inter-allied Level of Industry Committee was set up in September 1945 to arrive at appropriate figures. Their work bore little relation to the actual state of the German economy, where the immediate problem was not to determine at what level the economy of Germany should operate, but how it could most rapidly be made to work at all. They therefore based their calculations on forecasts of the future potentiality and productivity of German industry, and these were forecasts which could only be roughly made. The precision of the figures which they eventually produced is consequently attributable to political bargaining between the participants and not to statistical excellence. The British allowed the highest level, and the Russians pitched their starting figure lowest, while the Americans were divided amongst themselves.[3]

The key figure was that for steel production. By January 1946 agreement was reached in the Control Council that productive capacity should be reduced to 7.5 million tons, although actual annual production should be fixed at 5.8 million (pre-war production had been over 19 million tons). Once this had been settled the remainder of the plan was more straightforward, and it was agreed in the Control Council on 26 March 1946. It provided for the prohibition of fourteen industries and limitation of a further twelve; the surplus plant thus created should in any case be dismantled and would be available for reparations payments.

In accordance with the Potsdam agreement the Russians had been removing equipment from their zone in advance of the Level of Industry agreement, thereby taking delivery of reparations 'on account'. Under the same principle, the western commanders had arranged for the transfer of equipment from their zones to the east. But the Russian government insisted on the right to take not only capital equipment, but also goods currently being produced in their own zone. This claim they derived from the figure of $10 billion of reparations which they insisted had been accepted at Yalta. The governments of Britain and America contested this claim on the

[3] The State Department proposed the lowest figure of all for steel production – 3·5 m. tons, compared to the British 9 m., French 7 m., and Russian 4·9 m. (see L. du B. Clay, *Decision in Germany* (1950), p. 108).

grounds that the Potsdam agreement provided that payment for imports must come first. They argued their case with a vigour which is easily explained by the fact that they found themselves having to subsidize western Germany in order to prevent its people from starving, since industrial production and exports from their zones were much too low to pay for imports of food and materials. What they wanted was a flow of food and raw materials from the Russian zone into their own and the sale of surplus goods from the Russian zone as exports, so that the people in the whole of Germany could be kept at a roughly equal, adequate standard of living, with the minimum burden on their own economies.

Yet nothing the British or Americans could do altered the conduct of the Russians in their own zone; the only means of action open to them lay in the administration of their own (British and American) zones. To these means General Clay resorted; and on 3 May 1946 he announced that the delivery of reparations from the American zone would be suspended. This was a decision of cardinal importance. It did not deflect Russian policy in its own zone, but its implication was the abandonment at least for the time being of the economic unity of Germany, and the acceptance of an independent western policy *faute de mieux*. Yet it came only five weeks after the Level of Industry agreement.

Clay's decision was shortly followed by further significant developments. On 11 July the Secretary of State, Byrnes, offered to merge the United States zone with any other for the purposes of economic administration, and the offer was accepted by the British. The two governments agreed to share the cost of the combined zone in equal proportions (an advantage to the British, whose zone was more thickly populated). They proceeded to set up German administrative agencies of the kind that had been foreseen at Potsdam for Germany as a whole. Equally significant was a speech which Byrnes made at Stuttgart in September 1946 explaining his government's action. In so doing he went beyond a justification of the formation of Bizonia:

Germany must be given a chance to export goods in order to import enough to make her economy self sustaining. Germany is part of Europe, and European recovery, particularly in Belgium, the Netherlands and other adjoining states will be slow indeed if

Germany with her great resources of iron and coal is turned into a poor house.[4]

This was fundamentally different from the policy which the victors had adopted towards the defeated enemy. It indicated a common interest in the task of European recovery; and from this it would be but a small step to common European progress and growth.

Yet nothing which the British or Americans had so far done in Germany was intended as an irrevocable step towards the division of the country. Byrnes's original offer of zonal fusion had been made in the Council of Foreign Ministers, and the German agencies set up in Bizonia were regarded as prototypes for extension to the whole of Germany. In spite of this a momentum was established which it was difficult to break, and nothing that the Russian government offered provided any inducement to halt the development which had been set in motion. When the foreign ministers met in Moscow in March 1947 Molotov had two principal demands to make: they were recognition of the Russian claim to $10 billion reparations, and four-power control of the Ruhr; and he coupled these with insistence on the setting up of a German central government. Bevin and Marshall now insisted that economic unity of Germany must first be achieved; and events in Germany and the rest of Europe made the possibility of four-power control of the Ruhr singularly unattractive to Britain and America. In December 1947 the foreign ministers met again in London; but by that time events outside Germany, especially the Russian rejection of the Marshall offer of June 1947, provided an added deterrent to agreement, and the conference adjourned *sine die.*

Between the British and American administration of their occupation zones there were considerable differences of detail; but in their basic approach to the problem of Germany their views were very similar. This was not true of the French government. Churchill had pressed for France to participate in the occupation in order to strengthen his own position in Europe; but in the event the French position sometimes corresponded more closely to the Russian than to the British and American. As we have seen, the events of the war years in

[4] J. F. Byrnes, *Speaking Frankly* (1947), p. 189.

no way presaged an automatic alliance between France and the other occupiers of western Germany as long as de Gaulle was in command, and there was no immediate change in the policy of France when he suddenly resigned in January 1946 and Bidault took over control of foreign policy.[5] Moreover it should be remembered that the Communist party was the largest in the French Chamber, and was correspondingly represented in the government.

What bound Russia and France together was a long history of rivalry with the dominant power of central Europe. Nor could the French government readily accept the revised basis of Anglo-American policy, that Germany was part of Europe. In French eyes Germany was still the conquered power who should pay tribute to the rest of Europe. It was in accord with long-standing foreign policy that France should be ready to accept the new eastern frontier with Poland which the Anglo-Americans still refused to recognize. As the Russians did, the French took reparations from their zone out of current production; their zone was itself the most closed of the western zones, not only to the rest of Germany but (as far as Germans were concerned) to the outside world. The French government joined with the Russian in demanding 'international nationalization' of the Ruhr industries; they differed from Britain and America in insisting on maintaining coal exports from Germany to supplement the inadequate supplies of other European countries, rather than leaving the coal to feed German industries and thereby increase other exports.

This similarity of view between traditional allies was evident as late as the Moscow conference of March 1947, but it was far from being an identity. The Russian demand that a strong central government be created in Germany was one from which the French dissented even more vigorously than the British and Americans. They did not only seek to detach the Rhineland from Germany but to incorporate the Saar in France, at least economically. The detachment of the Rhineland won no support with the other powers; but as differences with Russia widened, the British and Americans found the absorption of the Saar into the French economy a small price to pay for the closer relationship with France over Germany. Meanwhile the

[5] The differences that had arisen between Britain and France in the Middle East during the war rose to a crescendo in 1946. See ch. 5.

widening gulf between the west and Russia was paralleled
within France by growing conflict between the communists
on the one hand and the socialists and moderate Catholic
party, the MRP, with whom they formed a government, on
the other. In May 1947 the communists were ousted from the
government, and Ramadier reconstructed it without them.
This was followed by French acceptance of the Marshall offer,
and communist policy designed to thwart its purpose. It was
under these conditions that the traditional policy towards
Germany became anachronistic; the French zone was merged
with Bizonia, and the three western powers now pursued a
common policy. As we shall see, however, this was to be a
temporary phase. The French government now accepted that
Germany was part of Europe. A few years later they gave a
fuller development to the same thesis by proposing the first
steps towards a united Europe—too radical a departure for
their British allies to follow.

In this makeshift way the three western powers, albeit with
France lagging at first behind the other two, were taking the
first steps towards the integration of western Germany into
western Europe and an Atlantic alliance. Not surprisingly, a
similar course was being followed in the east. As we have seen,
Russian reparations policy ran counter to other aspects of zonal
administration and was institutionally independent of it. Moreover the appropriation and removal of German industrial
equipment by rival Soviet agencies in Germany was often
chaotic in the extreme; it was, as one Russian has said, 'like
the Klondike during the Gold Rush'.[6] In the spring of 1946 the
policy of removal was accordingly modified. Dismantling continued, but at the same time east German industry was
organized for the production of goods valuable to the Soviet
Union, not only for the Russians' consumption but for exchange
with other eastern European countries under the control of
Mikoyan and the ministry of foreign trade. It was this policy
which provoked the objection of the western statesmen to the
absorption of east German 'current production' as reparations.
Soviet-owned corporations were established in the eastern
zone, and key industries taken over by them.

In short, the policy of the Soviet Union was now following,

[6] Vladimir Rudolph, in R. Slusser ed., *Soviet Economic Policy in Postwar Germany*
(1953).

4*

mutatis mutandis, the same evolution as that of the western powers. Germany was no longer regarded as a prey or a potential foe, but as part of Europe; the difference being that the Russians meant eastern Europe, in which the interests of the Soviet Union should predominate.

Meanwhile the four occupying powers had permitted the organization of German political parties. As we have seen, the Russians did not in the first instance inhibit the growth of non-communist parties, any more than they did in the rest of eastern Europe, although the communists were given the advantage of prior registration and organization shortly before the other parties, and were obviously favoured by the Russians. Thus it was in the French zone rather than the Russian that progress was slowest, since the French authorities insisted on acceptance of their own view of the federalization of Germany. The Germans themselves naturally regarded the occupation as a temporary and artificial imposition on their own affairs, and therefore organized on a national rather than a zonal basis, as far as communications and the attitude of the occupying powers would permit.

This came to an end, however, in the spring of 1946, when the SPD in the Soviet zone fused with the KPD. The movement for fusion had been started by the Russians and the KPD in the autumn of 1945. Within the SPD it had the support of Grotewohl, chairman of the party in Berlin (whose motives remain obscure) but it was vigorously opposed by the rank and file. Similarly, Russian attempts to prepare the way for fusion through the trade union organization and a newly founded youth organization met with little success in terms of numbers. But where the Russians were in control, and where they could find a handful of men ready to work with them within the SPD, it was impossible to prevent fusion taking place, just as it was in the other countries of eastern Europe, and by February 1946 the Socialist Unity party (SED) was a well-established project. But in the western zones, and even more in Berlin, where the social democrats were strong and where the conflict was most intense, the rank and file could maintain their opposition and make it effective.

As they did so they brought about a change in the attitude of the British and Americans to German politics. Until this time they had hesitated to interfere in German party politics.

Now they moved to protect the SPD against the manoeuvres of the Russians and the KPD. In March the SPD in Berlin organized a referendum on fusion in Berlin; they were protected from intimidation by the western powers, and when polling took place on 31 March the booths were open in the western sectors, but not the eastern.[7] The result was an overwhelming majority of a 75 per cent poll against fusion.

All the same, in the eastern zone fusion proceeded. The SPD ceased to be recognized by the Russians, but was recognized in the western zones of Germany. Once again the meeting point was Berlin. There the new-born alliance between the western powers and the SPD held firm, and the former fought their point through the *Kommandatura* and the Control Council. As a result both SED and SPD could organize in Berlin; and when elections were held in October 1946 they came into open competition. As in Austria in the previous year the result was disastrous from the Russian point of view. The SED won only 20 per cent of the votes compared to nearly 50 per cent won by the SPD.

Popular resistance to communism in the German capital was thus amply demonstrated; but the significance of this series of events was even greater than that. Had the Russians and the KPD succeeded in carrying through fusion without causing any commotion or arousing effective opposition, they would have been in a position to dominate the government of Berlin. Instead of this they had brought the issues out into the open and evoked western support for the anti-communist German parties. They had not only lost the round in the battle for Berlin but had created the alliance which was to rob them of victory in the future.[8]

By the summer of 1947, then, the German problem had thus assumed a form totally different from the expectations of the western leaders, and probably of the Russians too. However, it was not the only problem which now divided east from west, and although it remained the central preoccupation of the former allies, the policies which they adopted towards each other in Germany were in part determined by what was happening in the rest of the world.

---

[7] The Russians opened booths, but quickly closed them again.
[8] Cf. Windsor, *City on Leave*, ch. 3.

From the western point of view, it was the action of the Soviet Union in occupation of the countries of eastern Europe which was of first importance in arousing their distrust and opposition. The motives for Stalin's action in this area, and the extent to which his actions followed a prearranged pattern have been the subject of much discussion, in the absence of any evidence to provide a decisive conclusion. It has been suggested that a genuine misunderstanding existed between Stalin and the western leaders as a result of their wartime discussions, in the sense that Stalin supposed an agreement to have been made on spheres of interest by which he would not provoke communist coups in western Europe, and would in return have a free hand in the east. If this were the case, he would naturally regard the refusal of the western countries to disinterest themselves in eastern Europe as further evidence of capitalist hypocrisy and aggressiveness. The grounds for accepting such a view are, however, slight. It is true that Stalin refrained from pressing the communist parties of France, Italy, and China forward to revolution at a time when they enjoyed an unprecedented popularity and strategic advantage; but there was nothing new in such a policy, which was entirely consistent with the inveterate caution which Stalin showed towards the possibility of communist revolutions outside his immediate control. It is true too that Molotov expressed indignation at the 'interference' of the west in the affairs of Rumania and eastern Europe[9] and would not be convinced that the Americans wanted governments that were both democratic and friendly to the Soviet Union; but his remarks should not be taken entirely at their face value.

It has also been suggested, with good reason, that Stalin attached more importance to Poland and Rumania than to any of the other countries of eastern Europe, because of Russian territorial claims and even more because of Russian dependence on these two countries for its security. During the war the western leaders had been sensitive to Russian feelings on this point, and it is possible to imagine a degree of Russian control in Poland and Rumania which would not have excited their alarm and hostility. Such a relationship came to exist between Russia and Finland, where the government enjoyed genuine independence as long as it accepted Russian bases and did not

[9] Byrnes, *Speaking Frankly*, p. A.

pursue a policy directly prejudicial to Russian security. But whatever the motives behind Stalin's Finnish policy there is no evidence that it was attempted in Poland and Rumania: and it would in any case have required a degree of sophistication and tolerance which was alien to Stalin's character and quite out of accord with the history of Russian relations with Poland and Rumania.

The simplest explanation of Russian and Stalinist policy in eastern Europe is therefore probably the most accurate: that Stalin prepared the means, by the training of communist leaders and cadres, for the establishment of communist rule should the opportunity occur; that the border states had a particular importance in his strategy, both as a defensive barrier and as a possible starting-point for future expansion, and when the Red Army established control further west there was no reason to withdraw and no pressure to do so. On the contrary, power, economic advantage, and belief in the historical inevitability of communism provided every inducement to stay. This being so, it was inevitable that as long as Stalin lived the degree of coercion and control exercised from the Kremlin would be as great as the personal power which Stalin wielded in Russia itself.

In spite of this the Russians did not at once establish monolithic dictatorships in all the countries of eastern Europe. Except in Bulgaria and Yugoslavia none of these countries had anything approaching a majority of communists and communist sympathizers, and opposition to the communists was strong and persevering. The Russians met this situation by well-established communist methods. They tried to split the peasant parties by allying with a 'left' wing, as Lenin had split the social revolutionaries in 1918; they endeavoured to bring about, or manipulated a 'fusion' of socialist parties with the communists, fusion always being followed by the subjection of the socialists. Where coalition governments were formed communists occupied key positions, controlling the police, food, and sometimes justice, and using land reform for political purposes to build up a clientele of communist supporters.

Ultimately this process reached approximately the same end in all Russian-occupied countries, and was extended to Czecho-slovakia. The pace at which it proceeded varied. Thus Hungary (and Austria, which was partly occupied by the Russians) enjoyed approximately free elections in November 1945, and genuine coalition governments were established as a result. But in Poland, although the government was remodelled to meet the insistent pressure of the British and Americans, the communists never shared real power; in Rumania the communists took over effective control in February 1945, and had little difficulty in staving off a gallant rearguard action by King Michael; in Bulgaria the Russians were traditionally popular, and this made their control easier. In all these cases the façade of coalition government was maintained; but it was no more than a façade. In Yugoslavia and Albania no pretence was made.[10]

The western powers were well aware of the way in which the countries of eastern Europe were administered; they were represented on the control commissions of these countries, even though they were unable to affect policy towards them. Through the control commissions, and more importantly in the Council of Foreign Ministers, they pressed continuously for a 'reconstruction' of these governments, and for the holding of free elections. But their pressure was necessarily verbal, and therefore of limited effect.

To some extent it was possible to bargain with the Russians; for if the west wanted to broaden the base of eastern European governments, the Russians wanted western recognition of them. Moreover on the other side of the world the United States was establishing a monopoly of control over Japan, so that here too it was possible to envisage an exchange of concessions.

This possibility was indeed taken up at a meeting of British, Russian, and American foreign ministers in Moscow in December 1945. The American secretary of state, Byrnes, there proposed an eleven-member Far Eastern Commission to sit in Washington, and Russian participation in the Allied Control Council in Tokyo;[11] in return the Russians agreed to give 'friendly advice' to the Bulgarian government, and to permit supervision of the broadening of the Rumanian government, followed by free elections. In the latter instance appearances were kept up sufficiently for Britain and America to give recog-

[10] For a full analysis of this development see H. Seton-Watson, *The East European Revolution* (1956) and *The Pattern of Communist Revolution* (1953).
[11] See pp. 179ff.

nition to the Rumanian government in February 1946;[12] but in fact the communists had sacrificed none of the realities of power; nor, in the Far East, did the Commission or the Council exercise any control over General McArthur, who was not in any case an easy man to control.

The western powers wished not only to modify the occupation régimes in eastern Europe but to conclude peace treaties with the former German satellites and with Italy. The Potsdam agreement had assigned this task to the Council of Foreign Ministers, and it appeared an obvious step towards the re-establishment of normal conditions in eastern Europe. It might, it was hoped, lead to the ending of the Russian occupation, and this in turn would permit the withdrawal of the United States from active participation in European affairs, outside Germany.

Inevitably the negotiation of such treaties was beset with difficulty. The Russians argued that the decisive work of preparing the treaties should be confined to the three great powers, as signatories of the armistices. At Moscow in December 1945 their contention was accepted by the British and Americans, in return for agreement on the summoning of a peace conference of twenty-one countries. Four months later, in April 1946, the Council of Foreign Ministers met in Paris, and Molotov then withdrew his government's opposition to the participation of France; by the end of the conference a date for the full peace conference in the summer had been fixed.

The substantial issues were equally contentious. The most important of them were: the disposal of the Italian colonies (particularly in view of the Russian suggestion that it should participate in a trusteeship over Tripolitania); Italian reparations; the Italo-Yugoslav frontier and the status of Trieste; and the economic clauses of the treaties with the eastern European countries. As a result the process of reaching agreement seemed interminable. It dragged on through the preparation of drafts by the Council of Foreign Ministers in the autumn and spring of 1945–6; it continued through the peace conference of twenty-one powers which occupied the whole of a long Paris summer, from 29 July to 15 October 1946; it was resumed when the Council of Foreign Ministers met again in New York in November 1946 to consider the amendments made by the peace

[12] The Bulgarian government was recognized after the signature of the peace treaty in 1947; by Great Britain in February and by the United States in October.

conference. Throughout this period the British and American governments still pursued a compromise with the Russians. But they soon passed the point where any concession was preferable to a breakdown of negotiation on these issues, and at the beginning of December 1946 Byrnes suggested to Molotov that there was no further point in seeking agreement. The Russians on the other hand stood to gain much from the success of the negotiations, which would free eastern Europe from western interference and bring the withdrawal of American troops from Italy. As a result concessions were made on both sides in the course of the year-long negotiations. A satisfactory borderline between Yugoslavia and Italy was found, ar.d an international régime proposed for Trieste;[13] the British and Americans agreed to the figure of $100 million as reparations from Italy; and the Russians agreed to the transfer of the Dodecanese islands to Greece. In the face of the danger that no agreement would be reached Molotov also accepted, in December 1946, a large number of amendments of minor importance which had won a two-thirds majority at the full conference in the summer. The final texts of treaties with Finland, Rumania, Bulgaria, Hungary, and Italy were thereby agreed, and signed in February 1947.

Yet the discussion of the treaties had never given the appearance of genuine negotiations. Throughout the Paris peace conference the Soviet Union, the Ukraine, Byelorussia, Yugoslavia, Poland, and Czechoslovakia invariably voted together, and thereby proclaimed to the world the fact of Russian dominance over eastern Europe. Even when agreements were reached they rarely gave the impression of honest attempts to achieve a common purpose; the *nyet* of Molotov became a music-hall joke. Even when concessions were made – as when Molotov inexplicably reversed the Russian position on the Dodecanese islands – little credit was gained for the Soviet Union.

Yet in the immediate practical results the advantage went wholly to Russia. The Control Commissions came to an end, so that a chink in the iron curtain could be closed. British and American troops were to be withdrawn from Italy; but Russian troops remained in eastern Europe to safeguard communications to Austria and Germany. The treaty with Finland confirmed the cession of Petsamo to Russia and the leasing of a

[13] See below, pp. 313–17 for subsequent developments in the Trieste question.

naval base at Porkkala, as well as the payment of large reparations which had been agreed in the armistice. Similarly the treaty with Rumania confirmed the cession of Bessarabia and northern Bukovina.[14] Hungary was restored to its 1920 frontiers, except for an additional adjustment of the frontier with Czechoslovakia to the latter's advantage. Hungary, Rumania, and Bulgaria were to make substantial reparations payments. No doubt it was to secure these practical advantages that Molotov made the concessions he did. The treaties made provision for civil liberties; but there was no means of enforcement and therefore no practical obstacle to continued Russian control and domination of eastern Europe.

Meanwhile the experience of Austria had been quite different from that of either Germany or its satellites. As we have seen, Austria was from the first regarded as a liberated rather than an occupied territory — although the Russians had insisted on placing responsibility for the war on Austrian shoulders, in order to secure reparations. In any case, occupation of Austria was necessary when the Germans were expelled, in order to re-establish an independent Austrian government (although it was reasonable to expect that such occupation would be short-lived). Detailed arrangements for this had been handed over to the European Advisory Commission. There it was originally proposed that occupation of Austria should be linked to occupation of Germany, so that in the west the power occupying southern Germany should also occupy western Austria, while the Soviet Union occupied the eastern part. The result was that as both Britain and the United States wanted the northern zone of occupation in Germany, neither wanted to assume responsibilities in Austria. By the spring of 1945, however, this had changed. The experience of the Soviet occupation of the countries of eastern Europe was such as to indicate the necessity for western participation in the occupation of Austria if western influence was to be safeguarded. The differences between Britain and America over the disposition of their occupation zones in Germany had been resolved; France had joined the European Advisory Commission and had been accorded participation in Austrian as in German affairs. The outcome was a

[14] At the same time southern Dobruja went to Bulgaria, but northern Transylvania was restored by Hungary to Rumania.

four-power occupation of Austria. The only remaining differences in the proposed division of Austria lay in the Russian
demand for that part of upper Austria which was north of the
Danube, and the Styrian part of the province of Burgenland;
and to this demand the other powers acceded. In so doing, they
left within the Soviet zone the whole of the frontier of Austria
with Czechoslovakia and that with Hungary.

Meanwhile the Soviet Union had co-operated with Britain
and America in maintaining the territorial integrity of Austria.
As German resistance in northern Italy collapsed, Yugoslav
partisans followed the British in occupation of the Klagenfurt
area, to which Yugoslavia made claims based on its Slovene
population. The British government and the provisional Austrian government then sought the help of the Soviet Union in
persuading or ordering Tito's forces to withdraw, and such help
was forthcoming, so that Yugoslav forces left Austria.

But dispute between the four powers arose over the occupation of Vienna. The Russians, both in the European Advisory
Commission and through their government, proposed and insisted on a very restricted boundary for Vienna; the Americans
and the British pressed for a larger area, and one which would
allow freedom of movement and provision for an airport within
each occupation sector. The dispute was made more acute by
the fact that the western missions were not at this time admitted to Vienna at all. In the end the Soviet government gave
way, and at the beginning of July agreement was reached. At
the same time the machinery for the administration of Austria
was established. It was similar to that in Germany in that each
commander-in-chief had authority in his own zone, while
supreme authority over Austria as a whole was vested in an
Allied Council (not, as in Germany, a 'Control Council').
Amongst the tasks assigned to the Council were the establishment of a central Austrian administrative machine and of a
freely elected Austrian government. Shortly after this agreement
was reached, economic policy towards Austria was discussed at
Potsdam, with the conclusion which we have already noted – no
reparations, but an implicit recognition of Soviet rights over
German assets in its sector.

Of even greater importance, in contrast with Germany, was
that a central Austrian government was quickly established and
immediately achieved real independence, although with some

limitations. The Russian army, as it advanced into east Austria, brought out of retirement Karl Renner, the socialist who had been first chancellor of the Austrian Republic after the first world war,[15] and placed him at the head of a provisional government. The British and Americans were at first reluctant to recognize Renner, not only because of their doubts of his independence, but because of their dispute with Russia over Vienna. However, by October 1945 the Allied Council agreed to recommend to their governments the extension of the authority of the Renner government to the country as a whole, and its recognition as a provisional government. It was also agreed that elections should be held before the end of the year.

The elections took place on 25 November 1945. The poll was very heavy, 94 per cent of the electorate; the votes were divided: 50 per cent to the right-wing People's party, 45 per cent to the socialists, and 5 per cent to the communists. The People's party leader, Figl, consequently formed a coalition government, in which the communists were given the newly created ministry of power and electrification.

The establishment of such a government opened the way for a revision of the Control agreement. Disagreement between the occupying powers delayed revision until the end of June 1946, but when it was finally accepted in the Council it gave the Austrian government virtual independence. Hitherto its laws had required the approval of the Council. Under the new agreement all laws other than constitutional laws came into force unless they were disallowed by the Allied Commission within thirty-one days. The effect of this arrangement was to give the Austrian government the benefit of the veto – the positive step which the occupying powers had to take was to disallow a law, so that only by unanimity could they stop an Austrian law coming into force. At the same time the competence of the government was extended, so that only demilitarization, control of the property of United Nations nationals, and various other matters were left to the occupying powers.

It is impossible to know whether the situation thus created in Austria came about as the result or in spite of Russian policy.

[15] The story of the incident is told in Karl Renner, *Denkschrift über die Geschichte der Unabhängigkeitserklärung Österreichs* (1945). See also RIIA *Survey: Four-Power Control in Germany and Austria* (1956), p. 299.

It had been suggested that the Russians expected a very much higher communist vote in the November elections – perhaps of the order of 30 per cent, and that their moderation and their choice of Renner as the head of a provisional government were designed to win popular support. As it was the Austrian communists were relegated to a position of minimal importance, and Soviet influence was further diminished by the revision of the Control agreement.[16]

For whatever reasons nothing now interfered with the political development of Austria. But the Soviet Union clung to the claims it had made to the economic resources of Austria, and its exaction of these claims followed a similar pattern to that in Germany. At first German assets were removed to the Soviet Union, with similar accompanying disorder; then, starting in 1946, they were put to work under Soviet ownership in Austria. No doubt this was one reason why the Soviet Union was reluctant to agree to a peace treaty with Austria; for while it was true that Austria enjoyed virtual independence from 1946, a peace treaty providing for the withdrawal of occupation troops was not signed until 1955.

Developments in eastern Europe were increasingly interpreted by western leaders and people as evidence of Russian expansionism. Their convictions were strengthened by events on the other borders of the Soviet Union. The most important of these occurred in Iran. In 1942 British and Russian troops had occupied Iran to forestall a possible nazi coup, with an agreement that they would withdraw six months after the end of the war. At the Council of Foreign Ministers in September 1945, Bevin and Molotov had interpreted this date as not later than 2 March 1946. But in the winter of 1945–6 it appeared that Russian troops in Iran were being reinforced, and that a separatist government was being set up under their auspices in Azerbaijan. In January the Iranian government brought the question before the Security Council, charging the Russians with interference in its internal affairs. The 2nd of March came and went, without the withdrawal of Russian troops. Conversations, however, had begun between the governments of

[16] Soviet action in the Council during the subsequent months has been interpreted as an attempt to re-establish their authority, as if they had failed to realize the full significance of the revision when they agreed to it.

Russia and Iran, and led to a successful conclusion. The Iranian prime minister, Qavam as-Saltaneh, was not only an able negotiator but a man whose behaviour and policies at the time made the Russians suppose he would be an instrument for their purposes. Their agreement included the grant of an oil concession to the Russians, to be ratified by the Iranian parliament. This achieved, and under such pressure as the Security Council could bring to bear, Russian troops were withdrawn in May, although they left behind a communist-dominated government in Azerbaijan.

This sequence of events proved a severe setback for the Soviet Union. Qavam, liberated from the presence of Russian troops and in response to internal conditions in Iran, completely changed his position. A new parliament was elected which rejected the oil concession to Russia, so that it never took effect. Thereafter the Iranian government systematically and over a long period carried out an effective purge of communist infiltrators in the army; and in December 1946 the Azerbaijan government was easily removed. The communist Tudeh party remained an important element in Iranian politics; but the Soviet government could claim no positive achievements as the result of its action.

Yet while it lasted the Russian presence in Iran had caused grave anxiety. This was the more so since it was associated with pressure on Turkey and Greece. There were reports of troop movements in Iran towards the Turkish border. When the powers negotiated with Turkey for a revision of the Montreux convention governing the Straits of the Dardanelles, the Russian government pressed for the right to station troops along the straits for their protection. The Russian press, as if inspired by ghosts from the past, pressed for the cession by Turkey to Russia of the frontier provinces of Kars and Ardahan.

Meanwhile in the Far East it seemed for a brief time as if the Iranian pattern might be repeated, as Russian troops delayed their withdrawal from Manchuria. But withdrawal was carried out in April 1946, and although the occupation had given an advantage to the Chinese communists, the Russians continued to give legal support to the government of Chiang Kai-shek.

Over all these issues the differences between Russia and the western powers were brought sharply before the eyes of the public. Stalin and Molotov did not hesitate to counter the charges brought against them with charges of their own. Reproached with the failure of Russian troops to withdraw from Iran and Manchuria they attacked the presence of British and French troops in the Middle East, and British troops in Greece and Indonesia, and these attacks evoked strong echoes from left-wing parties in the European democracies. It became increasingly difficult to believe at all in the idea of a common purpose in the post-war world. The very citadel of post-war co-operation was stormed, when the first meetings of the Security Council took place in London from January 1946 onwards. The Soviet use of the veto over Syria and Lebanon, where its interests were in no way concerned, over Greece and the admission of new members, the use of countercharges to meet criticisms of Soviet action, all indicated that the rivalry between the former victors would find a field of combat rather than a conciliation chamber in the United Nations. Equally significant, particularly in the formation of American opinion, was the Russian rejection of the Baruch plan for the control of atomic energy.

Yet in spite of these events throughout the year 1946 the statesmen, at least of the non-communist world, and even more their peoples, were reluctant to accept the conclusion that the growing gulf between Russia and the west was unbridgeable. This can be easily understood, for how can men be expected readily to accept the inadequacy of their reward after so sacrificial a struggle? As differences with the Russians multiplied, they resorted to two causes for hope. They took courage from the fact that conversations with the Russians went on, however acrimonious they became, and they drew hope from the very necessity of reconstruction in the world. As Smuts said on 7 October 1946:

There is no fundamental dividing line between East and West. This is largely the aftermath of the war-time enemy propaganda. There is place and space and function for all of us in this wide world. There are no differences which cannot be reconciled, no divisions which cannot be bridged. The misfortune is that in the Press and propaganda undue stress is laid on these differences because they are more exciting to the public and have greater news value. Ideologies on both sides are propagated *ad nauseam* until people believe there is nothing else in the world so important as our particular brand of ideology.

I wish the veto could be imposed on the ideologies and the world just be allowed to settle down to its real business. For in what is really wanted we are all agreed. People want to be fed and housed and clothed, to be secured against unemployment and sickness and all the other miseries of our daily life – to be secured against these fears and this fear of war. In all this there is no East or West and no ideologies. There is just simple stark humanity.[17]

Most indicative of the mood of these months was the speech which Winston Churchill made at Fulton, Missouri, on 5 March 1946. There, in the presence of President Truman, he first developed publicly the idea of the 'iron curtain'. He said:

From Stettin in the Baltic to Trieste in the Adriatic, an iron curtain has descended across the Continent. . . . All these famous cities and the populations around them lie in what I must call the Soviet sphere, and all are subject in one form or another, not only to Soviet influence but to a very high and, in many cases, increasing measure of control from Moscow.[18]

But *The Times* (6 March 1946) was critical, and commented in its leader:

Mr Churchill was perhaps less happy in the passages in his speech in which he appeared to contrast 'western democracy' and 'Communism'. . . . While western democracy and Communism are in many respects opposed they have much to learn from each other, Communism in the working of political institutions and in the establishment of individual rights, western democracy in the development of economic and social planning.

As 1946 passed popular attitudes were increasingly determined by alarm for the future rather than allowance for supposed injuries and insults to Russia in the past. American opinion, both governmental and public, moved through a much greater distance than British, because it had farther to go. Attlee and Bevin had had experience of the Russians throughout the war; it came new to Truman. But it was not in Truman's nature either to truckle to an aggressive rival, or to make specious compromises to preserve the semblance of agreement. He resented the deals which Byrnes made with the Russians at the foreign ministers' conference of December 1945, the more so as Byrnes did not consult him in advance. Moreover the grounds which had made Roosevelt suspicious of British

[17] *The Times*, 8 Oct. 1946. [18] *The Sinews of Peace* (1948), p. 100.

imperial designs began to disappear as the Labour government pressed ahead with plans for independence in India. In Greece the March elections took place under the supervision of an international mission which the United States sponsored and participated in but which the Soviet Union refused to join.[19] Thereafter British support of a conservative Greek government against the communist guerrillas could no longer be dismissed as the pursuit of traditional British interests.

In this way the divergences between British and American attitudes disappeared. The hardening of Truman's attitude was made clear in September 1946 by his dismissal of Wallace as Secretary of Commerce after Wallace had spoken publicly in favour of more conciliatory policies towards the Russians. But this change was to have its most practical and far-reaching results in the spring of 1947, as the result of a financial crisis in Britain.

Eighteen months of peace had done nothing to remove the basic difficulties of Britain's economic position. The aftermath of the war called for more extended commitments in Europe and the rest of the world than at any other period in its peace-time history; and the initial stages of decolonization added to the burden in the short run. In consequence the government, and particularly its foreign secretary, were under constant pressure from Dalton, as chancellor of the exchequer, to reduce expenditure; and the most obvious target for reduction was overseas military spending.

In February 1947 Bevin at last gave in to this pressure, and on 24 February the American government was informed that Britain could no longer afford to give assistance of any kind to Greece; in consequence its troops there would have to be withdrawn. The reaction of President Truman to this news was that the United States must step in to offer aid to Greece and Turkey, and in the next two weeks of consultation with his administration and with Congress he did not depart from this initial resolution. On 12 March 1947 he addressed Congress

[19] 'The Mission reported that the elections were "on the whole free and fair, and that the general outcome represents a true and valid verdict of the Greek people". The Populists and other royalist parties won an overwhelming majority, but on a poll of only 49 per cent. The EAM and Communists boycotted the elections and then claimed the abstainers as their supporters' (B. Sweet-Escott. *Greece* (1954), pp. 51–52).

to recommend the giving of immediate aid to both Greece and Turkey in a speech whose import was immediately described as the 'Truman doctrine'. His speech received overwhelming support from the Congress; and by the end of May Congressional legislation had enacted financial aid to Greece and Turkey.

It is hardly possible to exaggerate the importance of the Truman doctrine in the development of American foreign policy. As so often in the affairs of men, its immediate cause, namely the financial difficulties of Great Britain, appears as an irrelevant side issue beside the magnitude of the event. The more basic cause from the American viewpoint was the continuing pressure which the Soviet Union was exercising round its borders, seen in the context of its domination of eastern Europe. But whatever the cause it meant an abandonment of American isolation from Europe, and in the shorter term it meant a complete reversal of the attitude of disapproval which the United States had shown only fifteen months earlier when British troops first established a conservative government in Greece. In a sense the commitment undertaken was a limited one, since it consisted only of financial and economic aid; but President Truman was well aware of the historic nature of the occasion and the Truman doctrine went far beyond its immediate implementation. He said:

Our way of life is based upon the will of the majority and is distinguished by free institutions, representative government, free elections, guarantees of individual liberty, freedom of speech and religion, and freedom from political oppression.

The second way of life is based upon the will of a minority forcibly imposed upon the majority. It relies upon terror and oppression, a controlled press and radio, fixed elections, and the suppression of personal freedoms.

I believe that it must be the policy of the United States to support free people who are resisting attempted subjugation by armed minorities or by outside pressures.

I believe that our help should be primarily through economic and financial aid which is essential to economic stability and orderly political processes.

The seeds of totalitarian régimes are nurtured by misery and want. They spread and grow in the evil soil of poverty and strife. They reach their full growth when the hope of a people for a better life has died.

We must keep that hope alive.

The free peoples of the world look to us for support in maintaining their freedom.

If we falter in our leadership, we may endanger the peace of the world – and we shall surely endanger the welfare of our own Nation.[20]

The practical commitment was thus limited to Greece and Turkey, where it took the form of economic aid; the verbal commitment was world wide, and its form was that of political leadership. The significance of this could hardly be lost on the Soviet government. The days were past when President Roosevelt had sketched an international association based on the assumption that America would withdraw increasingly within its own borders. More than that the area in which the new American policy was first taking shape was the area of the eastern Mediterranean, which for nearly 200 years had been the most sensitive point of Russia's relations with the outside world. And Stalin, as we have seen, was very much the inheritor of this tradition.

American support of Greece and Turkey met the needs of an immediate crisis. It did little to remedy the overall economic weakness of western Europe. There the task of reconstruction went on falteringly, hindered by the harsh winter of 1946–7, to be followed by severe drought in the summer. Trade was disrupted by the political upheaval in central Europe and the diversion of east European agricultural products to Russia. Without essential imports of food and raw materials the industrial countries of western Europe could sustain neither their industries nor their peoples; without exports of industrial products they could not purchase supplies. In order to save foreign exchange they imposed severe restrictions on imports from the United States and also from each other, even though they were aware of the effects on the exporting countries.

In this situation of emergency only one substantial move towards closer economic co-operation had been made by the countries of western Europe. In September 1944 a customs union agreement had been signed between the governments of Belgium, Luxembourg, and the Netherlands. The agreement was revised in March 1947 and was due to come into operation the following year. It was seen as an example which might be

[20] *Decade of American Foreign Policy*, pp. 1256–7.

followed; but not so potent a one as to form the core of a greater customs union movement – least of all at a time of such economic stress.

The United States had made important contributions to the alleviation of economic crisis. It had provided three-quarters of the income of UNRRA; it had sold surplus supplies at low prices and lend-lease surplus on easy credit; it had made loans to Britain, France, Holland, and Belgium;[21] to these were now added the proposed support to Greece and Turkey. By thus trying to plug the holes and stave off immediate collapse in different areas the United States had become the financial provider of Europe; but 'Europe' had no shape; it remained a conglomeration of small political units, each with its own balance-of-payments problem, each with its own limited reconstruction policy. In retrospect this appears clearly; what is remarkable is that it was seen with equal clarity at the time by the American administration, particularly by the policy planning staff which Secretary of State Marshall[22] had established in the State Department under the chairmanship of George Kennan. Together with his advisers Truman reached the conclusion that the problem of European recovery must be met by additional United States aid, but that this could only be used with the maximum effect if it were met on the European side by joint planning for the recovery of trade and investment.

Seeking a platform from which to announce this momentous development in United States policy Marshall chose the commencement ceremony at Harvard University. There on 5 June he said:

Aside from the demoralizing effect on the world at large and the possibilities of disturbances arising as a result of the desperation of the people concerned, the consequences to the economy of the United States should be apparent to all. It is logical that the United States should do whatever it is able to do to assist in the return of normal economic health in the world, without which there can be no political stability and no assured peace. Our policy is directed not against any country or doctrine but against hunger, poverty, desperation and chaos. Its purpose should be the revival of a working economy in the world so as to permit the emergence of

---

[21] Britain $3,750 m., France $1,200 m., Holland $400 m., Belgium $100 m. (RIIA *Survey 1947–8*, p. 68).
[22] Marshall had succeeded Byrnes on 21 Jan. 1947.

political and social conditions in which free institutions can exist. Such assistance, I am convinced, must not be on a piecemeal basis as various crises develop. Any assistance that this Government may render in the future should provide a cure rather than a mere palliative. Any government that is willing to assist in the task of recovery will find full co-operation, I am sure, on the part of the United States Government. Any government which manoeuvers to block the recovery of other countries cannot expect help from us. Furthermore, governments, political parties, or groups which seek to perpetuate human misery in order to profit therefrom politically or otherwise will encounter the opposition of the United States.[23]

The 'Marshall offer' came as a complete surprise to the rest of the world. The British embassy in Washington took so little account of it that it prepared to send its report in the ordinary diplomatic bag. The result was that in Britain Ernest Bevin first heard of the proposal on the BBC's early morning news. He responded immediately, for the plan fitted so closely to his own view of the needs of Europe that it could almost have been devised by him for American implementation. It corresponded to his own views of the need for practical European co-operation in economic affairs; and it brought the United States clearly and firmly into the European framework. It was thus Bevin who was the first European statesman to see the full possibilities of the offer and lead the European reaction to it.

If the British were surprised by the Marshall offer, the Russians must surely have been so. The offer was made to the whole of Europe, not only to its western part. This was a paradoxical decision since the supposition behind it was that the economic instability and shortage of food and consumer goods made conditions favourable to the spread of communism, and there could be no doubt about the reference of the last two sentences quoted above from Marshall's speech. But the administration was aware of the grudges which the Soviet Union nursed against the United States over the ending of lend-lease and the failure to negotiate an American loan in 1946. They were aware too that the offer was intended to help primarily countries such as France and Italy where, although the communists had left the government in the previous month, they still had the support of a quarter of the voting population. They ran risks in making the offer open to Russian sabotage; but

23 *Decade of American Foreign Policy*, p. 1269.

they calculated that it was unlikely the Russians would participate. And although the Marshall plan eventually proved to be
the forerunner of large plans for American aid to the rest of the
world, at the time it was conceived as a final settlement of the
cost of the war and its aftermath, a once-for-all programme
which it was therefore easier to offer to the Soviet Union as well.

Up to this time events in Europe had seemed to confirm the
hopes which any Marxist-Leninist might reasonably entertain
that the capitalist economy would collapse under the strain of
war and its aftermath. Soviet economists had themselves pre- *Intro*
dicted a slump, not only in Europe but in America as well.
Instead of this, the United States was taking the initiative in
planning recovery and offering its wealth to Europe. In March
the Truman doctrine had drawn a sharp line between democracies and dictatorships and offered support to one against the
other; now economic aid was offered on equal terms to both.
It was a confusing situation in which the Soviet government
had to make up its mind; and its difficulty in doing so is seen
in the fact that, in order to miss no opportunity, Molotov
attended a preliminary meeting in Paris with Bevin and
Bidault. But to accept the Marshall offer in any real sense
would have meant a more fundamental change in Soviet policy
even than in American. The essence of the offer as it was made
and as it was interpreted by Bevin and Bidault was that a
recovery programme should be based in the first place on the
production resources of the European countries, and in the
second on possible external aid. No communist government, *footnote*
least of all a Stalinist one, could accept the inquiry into its own
industrial resources which this implied; and there was therefore
no possibility of their acceptance on these terms.

Even as the preliminary discussions on the implementation
of the Marshall offer began, Britain and the United States were
protesting vigorously to the Soviet Union against its action in
Hungary where a government crisis had been caused by the
resignation of Ferenc Nagy while on holiday in Switzerland.
This was rightly seen in the west as a move towards stricter
communist control in Hungary, and the British and American
governments took advantage of the last days of the armistice
agreements to press their rights as members of the Control
Commission to be informed of all that had passed between the
Soviet and Hungarian governments.

The unlikelihood that the Soviet Union would participate in any arrangement of the sort envisaged by Marshall and accepted by Bevin and Bidault became increasingly apparent. On 16 June *Pravda* commented:

Mr Marshall's plan, announced in his speech of 4 June at Harvard, is, notwithstanding its apparent 'novelty', only a repetition of the Truman plan for political pressure with the help of dollars, a plan for interference in the domestic affairs of other countries. As soon as any country, like Hungary, purges its Government bodies of conspirators convicted by a court there resounds the bossy shout of the United States. Why then deliberately obscure the phraseology of Mr Marshall's presentation of the Truman doctrine to the world ?[24]

Meanwhile Molotov argued that European countries should be invited to make known their individual needs for credits and goods, and that these should be examined without any interference in their national sovereignty. There were, he said, two possible ways of economic recovery: interchange between equal states, and co-operation with great powers by states under their domination; the Soviet Union proposed the former, the United States the latter. On 27 June Molotov met Bevin and Bidault in Paris for preliminary discussions, but the disagreement between them persisted. Molotov insisted that the Soviet Union believed in economic co-operation and mutual respect between countries, and that the British and French plans could only be implemented by interference in the internal affairs of others. As a result this preliminary meeting broke down without agreement being reached.

But the time was long past when Bevin or Bidault would sacrifice the opportunity offered in order to secure Russian agreement. They were more than ready to go ahead without the Russians, and Anglo-French invitations were sent on 4 July to twenty-two European countries (Spain was not included) to set up a committee of co-operation.

In spite of Molotov, it was obvious that such invitations opened up tempting prospects to the states of eastern Europe. Jan Masaryk had welcomed the original Marshall offer, and on 7 July the Czechoslovak government accepted the Anglo-French invitation. On 9 July it was reported that Cyrankiewicz, the prime minister of Poland, had announced his government's acceptance while in Prague; the Hungarian government was

[24] Quoted by *The Times*, 17 June 1947.

reported as 'hoping to be represented'. Finland refused 'for political and geographical reasons'; Rumania refused after initial hesitation; Yugoslavia rejected the invitation with verbal violence. However, the weight of Soviet pressure quickly made itself felt, and both Poland and Hungary sent their refusals. More significantly the Czech government, whose prime minister and foreign minister were in Moscow, withdrew its acceptance. This news was given in an announcement which said:

It has been decided that the countries of central and eastern Europe, with which Czechoslovakia has close economic and political ties based on treaty obligations, will not participate in the Paris conference. In these circumstances the participation of Czechoslovakia might be interpreted as a blow to the friendly relations between her and the Soviet Union and her other allies. For this reason the government decided unanimously not to take part in the conference.[25]

In this way the Marshall offer was converted into a western European recovery programme and the line drawn down the continent of Europe deepened. It was of great importance in the formation of western opinion that the Soviet Union not only rejected the Marshall offer, but forced this rejection on countries which more and more came to be seen as its satellites; and that it had been able to do so even in the case of Czechoslovakia, where communists still participated in a genuine coalition government with other parties. It was also a grievous omen for the future that as a line was drawn in Europe, Czechoslovakia was seen to be on the east of it.

The stage was now set for the intensification of the cold war. As we shall see, it may be supposed that Stalinist control within Russia and over the Soviet bloc would have become tighter from this time even without the development of the cold war. But it is also reasonable to assume that the Russian government, having rejected the possibility of joining the Marshall plan — whether to make it work for the sake of the aid it promised, or to cause the maximum havoc from within — now prepared to wreck the effective working of the plan from without by a switch to a policy of violence on the part of the communist parties of the world, especially of Europe. The United States and western Europe for their part adopted the policy which George Kennan identified as the containment of the Soviet Union.

[25] H. Ripka, *Le Coup de Prague* (1949), p. 55.

4

CONFRONTATION

WITHIN two years of the end of the war international relations had thus assumed a form hitherto unknown. This was a condition which was neither peace nor war, in which actual fighting was limited in scope and objectives, but nevertheless fitted into a pattern of world-wide struggle in which every other weapon was used. In this conflict the western powers were always on the defensive, and with few debatable exceptions they were bound to be so. The conditions of freedom which in varying degrees characterized non-communist countries enabled a communist offensive to take advantage of opportunities for propaganda and electoral activity as well as infiltration and subversion. Within the communist world, in contrast, totalitarian control was based on highly developed techniques of coercion. As long as this was so it could only be broken by well-armed and well-prepared revolution; even though it might be modified (as we shall see) in reaction to a more modest revolt. Equally important, the western powers, however much they might want to diminish Russian power in Europe, could only do so by a frontal attack, with all the risks which that involved.

One of the most surprising features of the development of the cold war is that it evoked unprecedented and unsurpassed talent among the leaders of the principal democratic powers. In each of these countries a radical departure from traditional foreign policy was called for by the needs of the situation, and each produced leaders who were capable of bringing this about. In the United States Harry Truman acquired fresh authority when he was elected to the office of president in 1948, thereby confounding the pollsters and showing political ability to match the chance which had first brought him to that office on Roosevelt's death. By that time he had already shown an awareness that the first and outstanding duty which fell to him as president was that of making decisions, and not letting events shape themselves or go by default. He had also shown ability in the choice of men, appointing Marshall as secretary of state, to be

116

followed in 1948 by Dean Acheson. The leadership which he
and his administration – with the cross-party support of
Senator Vandenberg – exercised was to bring the United States
out of isolation.

Eleven years after the Congress amended the pre-war neutrality legislation Truman appointed an American supreme commander in Europe; in doing so and in the other acts of his
administration he went far beyond involving the United States
in European affairs – he also made it possible for America to
give leadership to Europe. However much European countries
might chafe under the dominant role of the United States in
world affairs, this was a leadership which no one of them could
have given itself and which profoundly altered their destinies.
Not that Truman was without opposition in his own country.
Two of the many occasions on which he showed his ability to
act decisively were when he secured the resignation of Henry
Wallace and when he dismissed General MacArthur. Each of
these men underestimated the difficulties of the international
situation and miscalculated the nature of the cold war; the
one in neglecting the necessity of a position of power in relations
with the Soviet Union, the other in supposing that military
victory in the Far East would solve political problems. Even so
it may be argued that the dismissal of MacArthur was a far
easier step than the creation and maintenance of popular
support for a policy of containment. It was not only that an
electorate is commonly loath to accept the burden of high
defence spending and continued tension; even those who favoured military expenditure found much that was attractive in
the idea of 'fortress America', and the reservation of American
strength within the continent of the United States.

The part played by Ernest Bevin as foreign secretary in the
first majority Labour government was no less significant. As a
trade union leader, then a minister who had never been in
opposition or sat as a private member of parliament, he had
been confirmed in his natural disposition to see politics in
terms of power. Yet he belonged to a party of which a large
section had long hankered after a reform of society or of human
nature which rendered questions of power irrelevant. His first
success, therefore, in building a position of strength in relation
to the Soviet Union was in circumventing and then overcoming
opposition within his own party. This was a victory of which
5

the most decisive battle was fought in the conference of the trades union congress in 1948. But his difficulties were greater than that, since he and his government came to power at a time when Britain was on the brink of bankruptcy. For the first time in its history the country was forced to abandon positions of strength through sheer financial necessity. In spite of this Britain had to play the part of a great power. Dependent in fact on the United States for financial support, forced thereby to jeopardize further its economy by accepting too quickly a return to convertibility, it nevertheless must, in Bevin's view, pursue an independent policy and achieve an understanding or alliance with the United States on terms of equality. This Bevin achieved, and the most important single act of originality which stands out in his doing so was his acceptance of the Marshall offer of June 1947, and his realization of its full possibilities for Britain and for Europe.

In France no single statesman stands out to the same extent, and the political system of the Fourth Republic fell into disrepute for the inadequacies of its policies. Nevertheless the change in its foreign policy in the conditions of the cold war was no less fundamental and no less imaginative. For France more than any other western country in 1945 the control of Germany was the *sine qua non* of peace and security, and the means by which such control might be exercised were drawn from the history books. By 1948 events had overtaken any such policy and France was in danger of standing isolated while western Germany was reconstructed as part of Europe. Instead of this the French foreign minister, Robert Schuman, supported by the creative intelligence of Jean Monnet in the civil service, effected a complete revaluation of foreign policy, leading eventually to the construction of a new political and economic unit in which Germany and France became close if competitive partners. Such a revision of policy could not have brought success had it not been for the response it received from Adenauer in Germany and De Gasperi in Italy. It was nevertheless a breath-taking change of course which, because of the relatively minor part played by France in the early occupation policies, too often passes unnoticed.

On any calculation the achievement of Stalin in statesmanship compares poorly with those of his democratic counterparts. This is not to say that he was unsuccessful; he restored to Russia

the frontiers it had enjoyed under the tsars, and he brought
the countries in eastern Europe under communist rule and his
own direction. But there was nothing original in the demands
he made, as his monarchic predecessors had done, for control
of the Dardanelles and the cession of Kars and Ardahan. As if
to make the similarity complete he suggested that Russia might
be given a trusteeship over Libya, as Alexander I had offered
the services of the Russian fleet in the Mediterranean to
suppress the Barbary pirates. The gains which he made were
achieved by conquest and the techniques of totalitarian control;
where statesmanship was needed he sacrificed his gains, as
happened when Tito was driven out of the Cominform. He
destroyed the goodwill towards Russia which had been built
up in the democracies during the war. He played a greater part
even than Bevin, Schuman, and Truman in the revolution in
foreign policy in their respective countries, and the consequent
peacetime alliance which was built against him. In all this
Stalin was perhaps not disappointed. Just as he had succeeded
in creating within the Soviet Union the very exploitation of
labour and enslavement of the intelligence which Marx had
condemned as the inevitable characteristic of capitalist society,
so the cold war most closely resembled the conditions of tension
and conflict which Stalin regarded as the natural relationship
between 'socialist' and 'imperialist' states.

While Soviet policy may be seen as initiating the cold war,
it should not be presumed to have followed a planned and
foreseen line of development undeterred and unaffected by
western action. The western policy of containment inevitably
brought its own reaction from the Russian side. In the short
run this was quite different from what Kennan foresaw as the
ultimate outcome of containment. In his view it would bring

the break-up or the gradual mellowing of Soviet power. For no
mystical, Messianic movement – and particularly not that of the
Kremlin – can face frustration indefinitely without eventually
adjusting itself in one way or another to the logic of that state
of affairs.[1]

It remains to be seen how justified Kennan was in this long
view, but one would expect to find (if one had access to the
records of Russian policy) that the immediate effect of western

[1] 'The Sources of Soviet Conduct', *Foreign Affairs*, July 1947, p. 582.

reaction to Soviet moves was to increase the momentum of the cold war, and that the precise course which Stalin's policy followed, within the general framework of communist expansion, was determined in part as a reaction to western moves.

But there were also problems within the new Soviet empire which of themselves led to a hardening of Russian policy during and after 1947. In the Soviet Union itself there can be little doubt that the historical pattern of the impact of war on Russian society was repeating itself. All the wars of the nineteenth and early twentieth centuries had produced alarming repercussions for the tsarist system of government, and had been followed by reform and revolution or both. These forces were equally at work in communist Russia. Under the necessities of war the military had naturally acquired a position of pre-eminence and Stalin's carefully constructed system of party control had been seriously loosened. As in the previous century the closed society of Russia – more closed under Stalin than at any previous time – was prized open by contact with the west. Intellectuals like Wolfgang Leonhard[2] looked forward in exactly the same way as their counterparts in the west, to a new departure from the old abuses of the pre-war days. Such a state of affairs could not remain static; it must lead to an opening up of the régime, or the restoration of rigid control of the old kind. It was evident from Stalin's character which he would choose.

Conditions in the countries of eastern Europe also invited a change in policy. The ease with which the Red Army had established control in this area, and the withdrawal of the western powers after the signature of the Paris peace treaties was an obvious asset which Stalin may not have hoped to acquire so quickly. But from his point of view political conditions were chaotic. No proletarian revolution had occurred outside Yugoslavia, and the formula of 'people's democracies' had been evolved to meet this non-Marxist pattern. But this again was a temporary phase, and as the importance which communists attach to an ideological interpretation of a particular stage of historical development has an exaggerated rigidity only because it is so shortlived, there was nothing to delay development to a more monolithic form of organization. The communist parties of eastern Europe themselves invited such a develop-

[2] See above, p. 86 n.

ment. They were a motley crew, including intellectuals attracted to a progressive and even liberal image of the party as well as the tough inner core of the party; there were those who had been in Spain, those who had been in Moscow, and those who had stayed at home. This was a heterogeneity which Stalin, who had purged his own party a decade previously, was unlikely to allow to continue.

There were thus internal reasons for a tougher line from Moscow. They were greatly reinforced by the development of western policy. It was necessary to close the gaps in the political systems of eastern Europe; to assert more rigid discipline, and engage in more positive political indoctrination. This was obvious in the speeches which Stalin and Zdhanov made on the occasion of the twenty-ninth anniversary of the Bolshevik revolution, on 7 November 1946, the theme of which was the increasing split of the world into socialist and imperialist camps, and the consequent need for militancy within the Soviet bloc.

The Marshall plan provided a further impetus to this development, from two points of view. It implied an economic reorganization of the west which finally dispelled the hopeful expectation of collapse built up by the economist Varga, and invited a counter-offensive from the communist side. But it also showed the need for discipline within the Soviet bloc. The leaders of the communist parties of Poland, Czechoslovakia, and Rumania had been ready to accept the Marshall offer, and they thereby showed a degree of independence which it was as important to check as it was to defeat the purposes of the plan itself. There were other indications of excessive 'domesticism' as national communist parties sought solutions to their own political and economic problems, sometimes in co-operation with a neighbour, as was the case with Poland and Czechoslovakia. If such domesticism should flourish there was an obvious danger of its running counter to Soviet objectives in eastern Europe.

It was this situation which lay behind the establishment in September 1947 of a 'Communist Information Bureau' at a meeting of communist parties summoned in Warsaw. The members of this new 'Cominform' were the communist parties of those countries of eastern Europe which had acquired power in their own states, but excluding Albania, together with the largest parties of western Europe (who may or may not have been thought to be within reach of power), from France and Italy. The purpose of the organization was to provide the institutional framework and even more the cover behind which eastern Europe could be forced into a concentrated mould. Communists, especially in power, have always regarded education and agitation as an essential part of government and politics,[3] and they have never relied solely on coercion and terror. The Cominform provided the resources of which the most important was its journal, *For a lasting peace, for a people's democracy*, for this kind of activity. No one could be in any doubt as to where the directing organ of the Cominform lay. But the Russian communists had always used other communist parties as agents in disciplining each other, and the Cominform provided the medium for this, while creating the fiction that control was centred in Belgrade rather than Moscow.

In the west the establishment of the Cominform was taken as evidence that Russia was returning to its old ways. More important in provoking the hostility of the west was the process by which individual communist parties intensified their control over their own countries. Except in Poland and east Germany this involved the humdrum task of installing communists in key positions throughout the state machine, particularly in the police. But it also meant destroying the power and the leadership of the opposition parties. This was done by coercion and terror against the peasants' parties, and by 'fusion' between the communists and the social democrats, so arranged that the former swallowed the latter. In consequence the year 1947 was punctuated by a succession of arrests of those leaders who did not manage to escape. In February 1947 Béla Kovács, secretary-general of the Hungarian Smallholders' party (himself a peasant) was arrested, and disappeared for several years; in May the leader of the party and premier of Hungary, Ferenc Nagy,[4] went on holiday in Switzerland, and while he was away was 'implicated' in the Kovács affair and replaced as premier. He decided to remain abroad. In June Iuliu Maniu, leader of the Rumanian National Peasant party, was arrested, submitted in the same month to a trial which was a travesty of justice, and was sent to prison where he died some years later. In October Mikolajczyk, who for two years had kept up an unremitting

---

[3] See A. B. Ulam, *Titoism and the Cominform* (1952).
[4] Not to be confused with the communist Imre Nagy.

rearguard action against communist pressure and terror directed against the Polish Peasants' party, fled from Poland secretly
in order to avoid arrest.

But the greatest advance in the consolidation of communist
power came in Czechoslovakia in February 1948. There is no
means of knowing how far ahead this was foreseen or planned
by Stalin. After the war Russian troops had withdrawn from
Czechoslovakia; but free elections had given the communist
party by far the largest vote (38 per cent). A coalition government was formed under the communist Gottwald, who gave
the ministries of the interior, finance, agriculture, and information to members of his own party. But the government had
functioned as a genuine coalition, and although abuses occurred,
the opposition took advantage of their freedom to expose them.
In this way Czechoslovakia came to be seen as a bridge between
east and west – a role in which many Czechs were very happy
to be cast, the more so as they were confident that Czech
communists were Czechs before they were communists.

As the world divided into two it was evident to any keen
observer that this state of affairs could not continue. As we
have seen, the Czech government was ready to accept the
Marshall offer, but a delegation including Gottwald, Jan
Masaryk (who was foreign minister), and Drtina (the National
Socialist minister of justice) in Moscow at the time were given
a clear choice in the form of an ultimatum between retaining
the 'friendship' of the Soviet Union or accepting the Marshall
offer. Even so the western powers hoped that the elections
which were to be held in May 1948 would bring Czechoslovakia
into the western camp. There was clear evidence that support
for the communists had declined, and it was hoped that Czechoslovakia would eventually go the way of France and Italy,
retaining its large communist party but with government in
the hands of the non-communists.

The communists did not allow this to happen, but the crisis
which brought them to power was provoked by the non-
communist members of the government. On 21 February the
ministers belonging to the Czech People's, National Socialist,
and Slovak Democrat parties, but not the social democrats,
resigned from the government in protest against the way in
which Nosek, the minister of the interior, with the support of
the premier, was packing the police force with communists.

But they obviously did not foresee that this would mean a showdown with the communists; and when it did, they were at every disadvantage. They relied on constitutional methods; but they did not form a solid block with the social democrats, where the pro-communist Fierlinger took over control of the party. The government itself having broken up, the power of initiative passed to President Beneš, who was now a sick man. In the election of their presidents republics seldom foresee the moment when their whole future will turn on the decision of a man whose office normally required him to be a figurehead, and Beneš failed, as Lebrun had failed in France and Hindenburg in Germany.

The communists were thus in a strong position constitutionally; they reinforced their position by unconstitutional acts, parading armed detachments of factory workers, taking over physically the ministries whose heads had resigned, setting up action committees in local government and universities, claiming to replace the properly appointed or elected authorities, whom they declared to be defunct. In all this they may have been directed by the Soviet deputy minister, Zorin, former ambassador to Prague, who was in the capital on a trade mission at the time; they certainly derived some assurance from the fact that the country was surrounded on three sides by Soviet troops. In contrast there was virtually no possibility of western troops taking any action, and the morale of the Czechs had never recovered from their desertion by Britain and France ten years before.

So the communists brought pressure to bear on Beneš, who on 25 February consented to appoint a government consisting of communists, left-wing social democrats, and a few representatives of other parties chosen by the communists themselves. Jan Masaryk remained foreign minister, presumably to save something, and some people, from the wreck. The communists pretended that there had been no real change in the character of the government. But no one was deceived; and when Jan Masaryk's dead body was found in the courtyard of the foreign ministry on 10 March, his death made tragic and bitter the loss of Czechoslovakia to the west. The communists for their part soon abandoned the pretence that nothing had happened, and Stalin could congratulate himself on his success, for whether he regarded it as an advance towards the west or the consolidation of a gain half achieved in 1945, he had stopped up a vulnerable gap in the system of eastern Europe. As long as Czechoslovakia was free it formed a deep salient into the Soviet empire. As a communist country it took on a vital role of its own in the cold war. Industrially developed, with a talented and educated people, it added to the resources of eastern Europe; having very distinctive characteristics which marked it off from the Soviet Union, it was to play an in-dispensable part in the economic and cultural offensive of the Soviet bloc. Under these conditions its people were to enjoy greater prosperity, more sophistication, and readier avail-ability of western literature than was the case in the other satellites; and for this the majority would pay the price of docility which was exacted from them.

The consolidation of power in Czechoslovakia was the more important in view of the conflict which was beginning to develop between Stalin and the communist ruler of Yugoslavia, Tito. In a way the conflict was paradoxical; but it was a paradox that was not new in the Soviet system. Stalin was now pursuing the intensity of communist rule which Tito had advocated in 1945; and as a result Tito was forced out of the Stalinist empire, to become the representative of the dissident communists.

Up to this time the Yugoslav experience had been unique: communist rule had been established through the efforts of a native Yugoslav partisan army, receiving some aid from the Russians, but more from the British. Moreover the objectives of Tito's campaign had always been the establishment of a communist state; the Communist party of Yugoslavia (CPY) had prepared for armed uprising to this end before the war, and the war gave them their opportunity. Battle with the Germans added nationalist fervour to their communist enthusiasm; but not to the extent of compromising their objectives or detracting from their antagonism towards their rival, Mihailović. Equally they saw no need for compromise when the war was won. They established a communist state on the Russian model and spurned the 'people's democracy' which, for ideological and practical reasons, the Russians sponsored in the countries they occupied.

The Soviet government repeatedly urged moderation on Tito. They wanted him to create a 'broad national front' rather than a communist partisan movement; they counselled him to

5*

recognize his legal obligation to the royal Yugoslav government; and they discouraged his enthusiasm for the 'Fatherland of Socialism' rather than for the Grand Alliance. As the war ended Tito failed to receive the support he hoped for from the Soviet Union which would enable him to take and hold Trieste. All this was incomprehensible to Tito and his immediate followers; but they explained it in terms of the necessity imposed on Russia by its dependence on allies, and they did not allow it to diminish their fervour for the cause for which they saw themselves and the Soviet Union as the vanguard.

The post-war years brought a further conflict in the policies of Russia and Yugoslavia. From 1944 to 1948 Tito pursued the objective of a Balkan federation, primarily with Bulgaria. Negotiations were carried on to this end with Dimitrov in Sofia and then Moscow. Then in January 1948 the whole project was dropped by the Russians, for reasons which have never emerged, and it was evident that Yugoslav interests (as well as those of Bulgaria) had been sacrificed to the dominance of the Soviet Union. More serious from Tito's point of view was the accumulating evidence of Soviet infiltration into the Communist party of Yugoslavia and the Yugoslav army. In the spring of 1948 the Soviet government began to bring pressure on Tito by withdrawing its advisers and to accuse the Yugoslavs of unpardonable deviations from Marxist-Leninist conduct and of an unfriendly attitude towards the Soviet Union.

There is no reason to suppose that in doing this Stalin was singling Yugoslavia out for special treatment. If he maintained police supervision over the Soviet Communist party there was every reason why he should do so over the CPY, regardless of the fact that it formed the government of the country. There were several aspects of the Yugoslav régime which were unattractive to Stalin; but of these none was so important as the fact that Tito was no longer his creature. It was accordingly natural that he should seek to bring Tito to submission. There was a well-established way of so doing: it was to subvert the party with men who could identify their own ambition with loyalty to Stalin rather than to Tito: to promote an alternative leader who would forward Stalin's policies (in this case Hebrang); and by a series of charges discredit Tito until he either reduced himself by submission or could be purged by a new leader. It is in this context that the actual charges brought against the CPY must be seen. The party was charged with being organized in a dictatorial manner, and it was accused of hiding behind the 'people's front'.[5] It was further accused of ignoring the Marxist-Leninist doctrine of classes and class struggle in their application to the countryside, 'contrary to the well-known Lenin thesis that small individual farming gives birth to capitalism and the bourgeoisie continually, daily, hourly, spontaneously and on a mass scale'.[6] And it was accused of harbouring Vladimir Velebit and 'other spies', and in a variety of ways showing unfriendliness to the Soviet Union.

There was, of course, substance in these charges; but to say this is only to say that Stalin made careful choice of the ground on which to conduct his campaign. How much and how little substance is most evident from the fact that although private property in land was still to be found in Yugoslavia, Tito had pressed ahead with collectivization much faster than the tactics of gradualism had allowed in the other states of eastern Europe.

But Stalin made the mistake of underestimating the strength of his opponent. Tito was not the leader of a minority party struggling for power, and depending for support on the Soviet Union. To sever relations with the Soviet Union was admittedly all but inconceivable, but at least the resources of the Yugoslav state were at his command if he did so; and he had behind him a party of his own creation, made up of young communists who had risen under his leadership through a campaign of which they were proud. To such a party, Stalin, and whoever else hid behind the title of the Central Committee of the CPSU, should not have written contemptuously that they 'became arrogant and now feel that the depth of the sea reaches only up to their knees . . . intoxicated by their successes, which are not so very great'.[7] For Tito to break with the Soviet Union meant taking a stand in a friendless world; there was no reason to ask or hope for support from the capitalist world.

---

[5] 'We are amazed by the fact that the CPY, which is the leading party, is still not completely legalized and still has a semi-legal status. Decisions of the Party organs are never published in the press, neither are the reports of Party assemblies' (Letter from the CPSU to the CPY, 27 Mar. 1948, RIIA, *The Soviet-Yugoslav Dispute* (1948), p. 15). See also the letter of 4 May 1948: 'there is no democracy in the Party; there is no system of elections; there is no criticism or self-criticism, . . . the CPY Central Committee is not composed of elected persons but of co-opted persons.'
[6] Cominform communiqué, 28 June 1948 (ibid. p. 63).   [7] Ibid. p. 50.

But he was too old a communist not to know the worse alternative which faced him, for he had himself achieved the leadership of the Yugoslav party as a result of the purge of 1936–7 and the elimination of his predecessor, Milan Gorkić. It was not offered to him to discuss the organization and policies of the CPY on terms of equality; and he well knew that whatever the risks involved in resisting Stalinist pressure the result could not be worse than the political and probably physical extinction which would follow submission. In any case Tito was not known to flinch easily.

The refusal of Tito to bow to Stalin's demand led to the formal expulsion of Yugoslavia from the Cominform and the severance of economic links with the Soviet bloc – an operation conducted through Comecon. 'Titoism' henceforth became a deviation from the communist line no less heinous than Trotskyism, and figured largely in the charges brought against other east European communists whom Stalin wished to remove from power. Little justification as there usually was for such charges, Tito's experiment of a socialist state following a different policy from that of the Soviet Union and demonstrating its independence from Stalinism became a source of attraction for the left in western Europe. Moreover as the number of countries independent of the two sides in the cold war increased, so Yugoslavia came to enjoy eminence as a leader of neutralism.

It was in Germany that the most immediate confrontation of the two power blocs took place. Dismantling continued at the same time as steps were taken to reconstruct the economy, and the Germans were brought in to work with the occupying powers in the latter task, thereby leading directly to the development of embryonic political institutions.

In the west the process was complicated by the fact that there were three occupying powers, the more so since agreement between the French on the one hand and the British and the Americans on the other was difficult to achieve, because of lingering differences on the political treatment of Germany and because of practical questions about the supply of coal and its distribution between Germany and the occupying powers. And a new framework for the reintegration of west Germany into western Europe had been created as a result of the Marshall offer of June 1947.

Following the establishment of the Anglo-American bizone, with effect from the beginning of 1947, an Economic Council was set up, consisting of fifty-four members chosen by *Länder* parliaments. At the beginning of 1948 its membership was doubled, it was given increased powers and a second chamber, the *Länderrat*, was created, so that a further step was taken towards establishing a German government. More important, the failure of the four-power foreign ministers' conference in December 1947 was followed by a conference of the three western powers, joined within a few days by the Benelux countries. This was significant, for it indicated that the problem of western Germany was now one that concerned western Europe, a departure from the principle that Germany as a whole was the concern of the occupying powers. It marked a far closer agreement between the French and the Anglo-Americans, not only on the specific question of the Ruhr, but on the more fundamental topic of currency reform for the whole of the western zone. The French zone was at the same time invited to adhere to the OEEC, where the bizone was already represented by the Economic Council.

Similar developments had taken place in the east. In June 1947 a German Economic Council was established. In December of the same year a German People's Congress for Unity and a Just Peace assembled in Berlin – coincident with the foreign ministers' conference in London – and met again in March, with over 1,000 delegates from the Russian zone and 500 from the west.

At the same time the Russians protested against the measures being taken in the west. The foreign ministers of Czechoslovakia, Poland, and Yugoslavia were brought together to register such a protest in February 1948; criticisms of western action in the Control Council became more virulent and propaganda attacks more strident. Literature from the west was confiscated in Berlin and the Soviet zone, and Soviet inspectors claimed the right to board military trains to Berlin and check the identity of individual passengers. It was at this time that Clay 'felt instinctively that a definite change in the attitude of the Russians in Berlin had occurred and that something was about to happen. From Sokolovsky down there was a new attitude, faintly contemptuous, slightly arrogant, and certainly assured'. Clay accordingly made a report to Bradley as chief of staff in which he expressed his growing concern about Soviet intentions. As he later wrote:

I pointed out that I had no confirming intelligence of a positive nature, but that I did sense a change in the Soviet position which I was certain portended some Soviet action in Germany. I did not predict what course this action would take, though I did state that I was no longer adhering to my previous position that war was impossible and felt that we could no longer preclude such a possibility.[8]

The tempo of the crisis quickened when Sokolovsky demanded, in the Control Council, to be informed of the agreements reached between the western powers at their London conference in February and March. When this was refused the whole Soviet delegation walked out of the Control Council on 20 March. Quadripartite government of Germany had come to an end, and immediately afterwards restrictions and interference with road and rail communications with Berlin were increased. However, Russian action was unlikely at this stage to break the unity between the western powers. Not only had they drawn closer together over Germany, but the coup d'état in Czechoslovakia had been followed by the signature of the Brussels pact on 17 March 1948. In these circumstances Russian action confirmed the western powers in the course they had adopted, rather than deterring them from it. In April the six-power conference resumed, and proceeded to discuss the preparation of an occupation statute regulating the relations between the three western powers and their zone of occupation in Germany, and of a constitution for western Germany. At the same time Britain, France, and the United States concluded that nothing was to be gained by continuing with the attempt to secure Russian agreement to a scheme for currency reform, without which economic recovery was impossible, and decided to introduce measures for currency reform into their own zones forthwith, leaving open the question of currency in Berlin.

Such a decision could only threaten still further the attainment by the Russians of the objectives which they seem to have pursued since the end of the war. Strong as they were in their own zone, they were no nearer to control over the whole of

[8] *Decision in Germany,* p. 354.

Germany, or to participation in the control of the Ruhr. And
Berlin, which might have been expected to become part of the
eastern zone, with the withdrawal of American troops from
Germany and western Europe, was rapidly developing as an
outpost of capitalist democracy within a communist state. Yet
the existence of Berlin as a separate entity derived in law from
post-war agreements between the conquering powers providing
four-power control, and in practice from the fact that Berlin
could be supplied and garrisoned from the west along routes
which had never received written sanction. The first of these
two guarantees the Russians had already denounced when they
withdrew from the Control Council, saying that western action
had destroyed the basis of four-power control in Germany. The
second they now set about breaking.

On 18 June the western government issued the first of the
decrees necessary for currency reform, and informed the
Russian military governor. On that evening all passenger trains
between the Russian and western zones were stopped, and so
was traffic on the Berlin–Helmstedt road. The new western
currency had not yet been introduced into west Berlin. The
Russians insisted that the Berlin currency should be the same
as that in the eastern zone; and this the western powers
accepted; but with the proviso that it should be subject to
four-power control. This the Russians would not accept; on
23 June they carried out their own currency reform in their
zone, and made it applicable to the whole of Berlin. The
western powers then introduced their own new currency to
west Berlin, where it rapidly gained a premium on the eastern
marks. This was on 23 June, and on the same day rail traffic
of every kind between Berlin and the west was stopped. Road
and water traffic was similarly stopped in the course of the next
few weeks, and the blockade of Berlin made complete – except
by air.

Few people imagined at this point that it would be possible
to supply Berlin by air alone. The question had not been
seriously considered, in spite of the slowly increasing harassment
of communications, and when the blockade was established no
plans were ready for alternative means of supply. It thus looked
to the governments in Washington, Paris, and London as if
they might be faced with the choice between using force to
stay in Berlin, or retreating from the city altogether. This

choice was one they did not want to face; they endeavoured to gain time for negotiation by supplementing Berlin's stocks of food and fuel by airlift.

On 28 June President Truman expressed his own view of this choice when he said: 'We are going to stay. Period.' But no one could be unaware of how serious it would be to use force in Germany, and the British and American governments, with the support of the French, therefore hoped to bring in sufficient supplies to augment stocks in Berlin while negotiations with the Russians proceeded. Notes were exchanged in July, and these were followed in August by ambassadorial meetings with Stalin and Molotov. These resulted in an agreed directive to the military governors for a settlement of the currency question; but in September the attempt of the military governors to implement a directive that glossed over the crucial differences broke down. Meanwhile the Russians were bringing considerable pressure to bear on the government and population of Berlin, in an effort to undermine the government and to destroy public morale. But as they did so the airlift began to acquire its own momentum. The daily average throughout August approximated 4,000 tons, and plans were afoot for increasing this in the following month. Within Berlin Russian pressure only served to increase the determination of the population, led by the mayor, Reuter, to withstand the blockade. The western powers imposed a counter-blockade on goods going into the eastern zone of Germany; and they sought to mobilize world opinion on their side by taking the Berlin question to the Security Council of the United Nations (on 29 September) as a threat to the peace under Article VII of the Charter.

As a result confidence began to grow in the west. Russian action in Berlin was now rapidly moving towards the division of the city into two, as non-communists were eliminated from government positions in east Berlin, and the city Assembly was prevented from meeting in the city hall in the eastern sector. The Assembly announced its intention of proceeding to fresh elections, as required every two years by the provisional Berlin constitution; but the Russians refused to allow preparation for them to take place in their sector. At the end of November, a week before the elections were due, a communist sponsored meeting in east Berlin declared the city government deposed, and a new *Magistrat* was elected in its place, with Fritz Ebert (son of the Weimar Republic's first president) as mayor. In west Berlin on 5 December elections showed a very heavy poll. Some 84 per cent of the possible votes were shared between the three democratic parties, amongst which the SPD increased its majority.

This made it evident that the goal of four-power control of Berlin's currency was one scarcely worth pursuing; and as the airlift began to pass the test of the heavier requirements and tougher conditions imposed by winter the western powers became less ready to sacrifice any part of their position in negotiation. The American administration had acquired added confidence by the election of Truman as president in his own right in November 1948; the western alliance was taking shape as negotiations for the North Atlantic pact proceeded; and western Europe, including western Germany, was seeing the first fruits of industrial recovery under the impetus of the Marshall plan. A 'Parliamentary Council' consisting of west German states had met in Bonn in September 1948 to draw up a constitution for Germany, and the western powers paralleled this with the preparation of an occupation statute to govern their relations with a west German government when it should come into being.

In January 1949 Stalin discussed the Berlin blockade with an American journalist. When the interview was published Acheson and Truman noticed that it contained no reference to the currency question, and they therefore instructed the American delegate at the United Nations to inquire of the Russian delegate what significance should be attached to this fact. One month later came the reply that the omission was 'not accidental'. In this way negotiations for the ending of the blockade were begun. Before they were complete the airlift had established an Easter Day record of nearly 13,000 tons of supplies in 24 hours. On 4 May the four governments announced from the four capitals that Russian restrictions on transport to Berlin, and western restrictions on transport to the Russian zone, would be ended on 12 May. It was also stated that 'on 23rd May, 1949, a meeting of the Council of Foreign Ministers will be convened in Paris to consider questions relating to Germany and problems arising out of the situation in Berlin, including the question of currency in Berlin'.[9]

[9] Cmd. 7729.

This was an admission of failure on the part of the Russians. When the blockade started, it appeared that they could not lose. A determined action offered excellent promise of driving the western powers out of Berlin, thereby preparing the ground for a further onslaught on the western position in Germany. In the mind of General Clay there was no doubt how much the Russians stood to gain from a success in Berlin. In a tele-type conference of 16 April he said: 'When Berlin falls, western Germany will be next. . . . If we withdraw, our position in Europe is threatened. If America does not understand this now, does not know that the issue is cast, then it never will and communism will run rampant.'[10] With the benefit of hind-sight, one may suppose that Clay exaggerated the dangers, since it would have been incomparably more difficult to under-mine the western position in the rest of Germany than to take over Berlin. But Stalin could scarcely have foreseen the extent of possible failure. Not only did the western powers secure a great reinforcement of their own morale, but the blockade cemented the alliance which had already taken shape between the west Berliners and the west Germans on the one hand and the western powers on the other. It produced a readiness on the German side to work closely with their former opponents and on the part of the western powers a great acceleration in the process of reintegrating western Germany into western Europe.

The status of Berlin was indeed changed as a consequence of the blockade, but not as the Russians had intended. As we have seen, two governments came into existence during the blockade. Both east and west Berlin retained a special status in relation to the corresponding parts of Germany. In 1956 east Berlin was incorporated into the German Democratic Republic as its capital. West Berlin remained a *Land* of western Germany, with certain special features of its own (its representa-tives sit in the Reichstag, but do not vote) and the capital of the German Federal Republic remained at Bonn. At the same time the legal fiction of the four-power occupation of Berlin was preserved, and continued to be the basis for the claim of the western powers to maintain troops in west Berlin, while the inhabitants of Berlin remained free, until 1961, to travel between west and east in a way that was impossible between the two Germanies.

[10] *Decision in Germany*, p. 361.

In accordance with the agreement by which the blockade was brought to an end the foreign ministers of the four powers met throughout May and June 1949 to discuss the German problem. But their meeting was eclipsed by the fact that agreement had been reached on the establishment of a west German government, paralleled by arrangements for a German government in the Russian zone. The discussions which had begun between the western powers in 1948 were continued through the blockade. The German Parliamentary Council which came into being as a result drafted a basic law (which was in fact a constitution) while the occupying powers drew up an occupation statute. Agreement was reached by April, and on 23 May – the day that the four-power conference opened – the basic law was signed. The two documents together defined a German constitution and the relationship between Germany and the western occupying powers. Under these provisions a west German parliament was elected in August, and on 7 September 1949 Theodor Heuss was elected president and Konrad Adenauer chancellor. Still under occupation, west Germany had yet to gain its full sovereignty; but a new era in German and European politics had begun.

Similarly a German Democratic Republic came into existence in the east in October 1949. Formally it was a two-chamber government, of which the lower should be popularly elected. In practice elections were contrived in a familiar communist pattern. Non-communist parties remained in existence, but they were absorbed into a common front, dominated by the SED, presenting a single list to the electorate. In practice power rested with the apparatus of the SED, and in particular in the hands of its first secretary, Walter Ulbricht, who was to enjoy exceptional longevity amongst the communist leaders of eastern Europe, but who none the less remained dependent on the Russian forces of occupation.

The experience of the Berlin blockade was of wider significance outside developments in Germany. Each of the important moves which Stalin had made since 1947 had strengthened those forces in America and western Europe which supported a vigorous policy of containment. The coup d'état in Czechoslovakia destroyed the arguments of those who claimed that Stalin merely sought security in eastern Europe and had no expansionist aims; the break with Tito discredited those who would make common cause with Stalin because he was, after all, a socialist; the Berlin blockade confirmed the view that a policy of strength was the one most likely to bring results in the cold war. All this was important, for in the next year the scene of action was to move to the Far East, even though its implications were of greatest moment in Europe; and the reaction of the United States, the west European, and other countries to war in Korea might well have been different had it not been for the experience of these years.

In the face of these developments the western powers had found themselves singularly unprepared, militarily and politically. As soon as the war ended Britain and America began to withdraw their troops from Europe and to disarm. When Germany surrendered, the American forces in Europe numbered 3·1 million men; a year later 391,000; British forces in Europe were reduced from 1·3 million to less than half a million. In contrast the Soviet Union had neither reduced its occupation strength nor disarmed. Western Europe and America had placed their hopes for the security of the Continent and the world on the United Nations organization and on four-power control of Germany. Now that these seemed inadequate they found themselves disorganized, divided into small political units in the face of the apparently monolithic power of the Soviet Union, to which could be added the organized strength of the new satellites.

It is not surprising, therefore, that the common theme of statesmen on both sides of the Atlantic was the necessity of organization for defence, and the repeated evidence of Soviet pressure gave these proposals an impetus they would otherwise have lacked. Already in 1947 the British government had sought to counter the mistakes of previous decades by signing an alliance with France – symbolically called the treaty of Dunkirk. This was a treaty guaranteeing assistance in the event of a renewed attack by Germany, and both governments had taken care to keep the Soviet Union informed of the negotiations, and allay Soviet anxieties as to its nature. Then on 22 January 1948, in a speech of historic importance, the British foreign secretary, Bevin, proposed the extension of the treaty with France to other countries of western Europe. As he made clear in his speech the context in which his proposals were made had quite changed. The hopes placed in the

United Nations and four-power agreement had not been
realized; the Soviet Union dominated eastern Europe, and it
was impossible to reach agreement on Germany; while the
whole tone in which negotiations with the Soviet Union were
conducted was determined by the abuse which was levelled at
western statesmen at the conference table and in the columns
of *Pravda*. The United States had made the offer of economic
aid to Europe, but it was declined by the Russians, and under
pressure from them by the countries of eastern Europe. In
these circumstances, said the foreign secretary: 'I believe the
time is ripe for the consolidation of Western Europe.'[11]

Ernest Bevin had in mind a series of bilateral treaties with
the Benelux powers, comparable to that with France. Beyond
this nucleus of western Europe they could then be extended
to include such countries as Italy. The foreign secretary's
vision went beyond the confines of his own continent. Europe
had already, he said, spread overseas; now the time had come
to plan seriously for the development of these overseas territories 'to establish particularly out of our capital production
year by year, and also out of our production of consumption
goods, a proper proportion in the right order of priorities to
assist this development . . . '.[12]

The leadership which the British government thus offered to
western Europe was warmly welcomed by the governments to
which it was particularly addressed. Exactly a month later
came the communist coup d'état in Czechoslovakia, and with
the sense of urgency which this provoked representatives of the
Benelux countries, France, and Britain met in Brussels to
negotiate a treaty of mutual assistance. From their deliberations
emerged the Brussels treaty – an instrument more novel and
more far reaching than the series of bilateral treaties which
Bevin had proposed in January.

In its text the Brussels treaty[13] indicates the turning-point
which had been reached in the affairs of Europe. The only
power named as a possible aggressor was Germany, and the
text explicitly provided for the 'event of a renewal by Germany
of a policy of aggression'; yet it was clear that it was Russia not
Germany that the signatories had in mind when they agreed
in Article IV that:

[11] RIIA, *Documents 1947–8*, p. 211.   [12] Ibid. p. 213.   [13] Ibid. p. 225.

If any of the High Contracting Parties should be the object of an armed attack in Europe, the other High Contracting Parties, will, in accordance with the provisions of Article 51 of the Charter of the United Nations, afford the Party so attacked all the military and other aid and assistance in their power.

The significance of the treaty, however, lay also in the provision it made for continuous consultation through a Consultative Council. In this way the western European powers accepted the principle of collective defence, which went far beyond the terms of a traditional alliance, and was to be given full realization in the North Atlantic treaty a year later.

This development in Europe accorded exactly with the hopes and intentions of American foreign policy. The president and the State Department were committed to the defence of western Europe, and they were ready to extend military aid for its assistance. But, as with economic aid, they required the European countries to take the initiative in organizing themselves for purposes of defence. When they did so, President Truman immediately told Congress: 'I am sure that the determination of the free countries of Europe to protect themselves will be matched by an equal determination on our part to help them.'

The Brussels treaty was signed on 17 March 1948; within a week Berlin was blockaded and the whole air strength of the United States as well as Britain was being bent to the preservation of the status of the beleaguered city. In these circumstances the president and the State Department won the ready agreement of Congress to a policy of support to Europe. This policy was embodied in a resolution which bears the name of the man most responsible for mobilizing Congress and particularly the Republican party in bipartisan support for the radical departures which the administration made in its policy towards Europe – Senator Vandenberg, chairman of the Foreign Affairs Committee of the Senate. The Vandenberg resolution of 11 June 1948 advised the president:

of the sense of the Senate that this Government, by constitutional process, should particularly pursue the following objectives within the United Nations Charter: . . . (3) Association of the United States, by constitutional process, with such regional and other collective arrangements as are based on continuous and effective self-help and mutual aid, and as affect its national security.[14]

14 RIIA, *Documents 1947-8*, p. 234.

Shortly after the Vandenberg resolution, on 6 July, discussions were begun in Washington between the Brussels treaty powers, the United States, and Canada, for the negotiation of a larger treaty to provide security in the whole North Atlantic area. From the point of view of the powers participating in these discussions it was obviously desirable to associate as many of the North Atlantic powers as possible with them, apart from Spain, whose ideology they found repugnant. Not all the countries of western Europe were equally enthusiastic about associating themselves with the new organization. The Irish Republic did not join and neither did Sweden. The Norwegian and Danish governments explored the possibilities both of joining a North Atlantic alliance and forming a separate Scandinavian pact; but the neutrality of Sweden was unacceptable to them, and their move towards the North Atlantic powers was accelerated when in February 1948 Russian pressure on Norway had the opposite effect to that intended. Negotiations proceeded through March, and on 4 April 1949 the North Atlantic treaty[15] was signed by representatives of the United States and Canada, the Brussels treaty powers, Norway, Denmark, and Iceland, Italy, and Portugal.

The core of the alliance lay in the obligation which members undertook towards each other in Article 5:

The Parties agree that an armed attack against one or more of them in Europe or North America shall be considered an attack against them all; and consequently they agree that, if such an armed attack occurs, each of them in exercise of the right of individual or collective self-defence recognized by Article 51 of the Charter of the United Nations, will assist the Party or Parties so attacked by taking forthwith, individually and in concert with the other Parties, such action as it deems necessary, including the use of armed force, to restore and maintain the security of the North Atlantic area.

Any such armed attack and all measures taken as a result thereof shall immediately be reported to the Security Council. Such measures shall be terminated when the Security Council has taken the measures necessary to restore and maintain international peace and security.

Yet the intentions of the founders of the alliance went far beyond a traditional military pact. The treaty laid strong emphasis, as this article indicates, on the 'purposes and prin-

[15] RIIA, *Documents, 1949–50*, p. 257.

ciples of the Charter of the United Nations'. At the same time it sought to create some sort of Atlantic community based on free institutions and the elimination of conflict in international economic policies. It sought to base defensive strength on 'continuous and effective self-help and mutual aid', and to this end it established a council, which should set up appropriate subsidiary bodies to implement the principles of collective defence and mutual aid.

The impetus which had produced the North Atlantic treaty did not disappear with its signature. It was followed by the implementation of the principle of 'mutual aid' at a time when this could mean only one thing in practice – the supplying of the alliance by the United States. As soon as the treaty had been ratified by the United States Congress, President Truman initiated the Mutual Assistance Defense Bill, which became law in October. It made provision for military assistance throughout the world, with the major emphasis on the North Atlantic area. The first year of the programme allotted $1 billion to the European members of the alliance. At the same time the organization envisaged in the alliance took shape; a Council came into being, consisting of foreign ministers, with subordinate defence and financial and economic committees. In this way the framework of a totally new form of international organization was created. The experience of the first year revealed its inadequacies, and the shock of the Korean war provoked a new sense of urgency in the development of the institutions of the alliance; but such was the novelty of the organization that it could only be evolved by trial and error.

5

PALESTINE, ISRAEL, AND THE ARAB STATES

THE AREA of the world which is bounded by Persia in the north and the Arabian coast in the south, which stretches from the borders of Pakistan to the coast of North Africa, has a distinctive and unique character of its own. To the western world it is known as the Middle East, a name which indicates the importance it has always assumed for Europe as part of the route to the east. With the opening up of Africa this importance increased, as the Middle East was now on the route from western Europe and from Russia to Africa, even though aeroplanes were now added to land and sea transport. More striking is the contribution which the Middle East has made to the thought and religion, and to the material welfare of the world.

It is perhaps characteristic that a contribution of such magnitude should give rise to conflict and tension more than to harmony. It is an astonishing fact that the Christian, Jewish, and Islamic religions should have their origins in so small an area; as a result, the history of the Middle Ages was pre-occupied by the Crusades, while in the period with which this work is concerned the single most obdurate problem was that created by the political offshoot (some would say perversion) of Judaism – Zionism and the creation of a Jewish state. Similarly, Islam created a sense of unity amongst all the peoples of the Middle East, and this was reinforced in modern times by pan-Arabism, the counterpart of the pan movements of Europe at the end of the nineteenth century. But western intervention in the affairs of the Middle East at the end of the first world war created artificial divisions between Arab states which proved, for whatever reason, a physical barrier to Arab unity. As for the material contribution, in modern times this has been in the form of an abundant supply of oil; but for the exploitation of these resources the Arabs have been dependent on capital and skills brought from the outside.

The two powers, Britain and France, which before 1939 had

intervened most actively in Middle Eastern affairs had brought political, social, and cultural influence with them in addition to the capital they had invested. This was especially true of French education and culture in Egypt, Syria, and Lebanon; but the British had established Victoria College in Alexandria, had trained Arab army officers, and had introduced ideals and practices of good government. Politically, their intervention was distinguished by the fact that here more than in any other part of the world their statesmen seem wilfully to have sown dragon's teeth. During the first world war the British government fostered Arab nationalism in revolt against the Turks while at the same time giving undertakings to the Jews of an ambiguous kind; but as soon as the war was over the archaic overlordship of the Turks was replaced by British and French variants of imperial rule and influence, over Arab states divided by artificial boundaries.

Despite this, the British succeeded in the 1920s in establishing a high degree of co-operation with the rulers of Transjordan and Iraq, whom they had established in power. In Egypt they were constantly harassed by nationalist agitation and violence; but they did not meet with the open revolt which led the French to shell and bomb Damascus. Iraq (which had been placed under British mandate) became virtually independent, linked to Britain by defence treaties which provided for the maintenance of bases. Egypt acquired nominal independence in 1922, although Britain retained a decisive influence over defence and foreign policy, and even some aspects of domestic sovereignty. The relations between the two countries were not put on a formal basis until the alarm excited by the Italian invasion of Abyssinia led to the signing of an Anglo-Egyptian treaty in 1936. In Syria the revolt of 1925-7 delayed the development of a realistic settlement with France as the mandatory power, and a fresh attempt in 1936 was aborted in the French parliament. In the same year a similar treaty was signed with Lebanon, which thus maintained the division between the two countries.

Although Italian intrusion south of the Arab states facilitated the conclusion of the Anglo-Egyptian treaty a new phase in the opposition of Arab nationalism to foreign influence can be seen beginning by the time war broke out in 1939. But it was in Palestine that the tension was rising towards imminent crisis. In 1917 the Balfour declaration had promised the establishment of a National Home for the Jews in Palestine, and this had been underwritten in the terms of the British mandate over Palestine. Within twenty-five years of its formation the Zionist movement had secured the first of its objectives, in public recognition of the right of the Jews to establish their home in Palestine. In the ensuing years the movement encouraged and developed Jewish immigration, until the British government could no longer escape from the question of the extent of political power which it would give to the Jewish community; while the Arabs in Palestine rose in revolt against the increasing numbers of Jewish immigrants and against any proposal for the partition of Palestine. At the beginning of 1939 the best way out of the dilemma appeared to the British government to be to limit the number of Jewish immigrants, and then to establish, within ten years, an independent Palestine state 'in which Jews and Arabs share in government in such a way as to ensure that the essential interests of each community are safeguarded'.[1]

The outbreak of war in Europe and its early course had a profound effect on the Middle East. It became of vital importance to Britain to safeguard its lines of communication and the supply of oil from the Middle East. With the fall of France the danger was immeasurably increased as Germany was free to turn all its strength to the Balkans and the Mediterranean. Seen from the Middle East the success of Germany and Italy was overestimated; the shah of Persia had long been impressed by the German example, and the mufti of Jerusalem was dazzled by the possibilities of an alliance with Hitler. In Egypt Faruq entered into correspondence with Germany and Italy; the common people were equally affected.

Egyptian peasants in the delta held meetings to decide how to parcel out the land when Hitler came, and Palestinian Jews desperately discussed whether the flower of their young people should die in a last-ditch battle or withdraw with the British towards India in order that a nucleus might survive for another Return.[2]

But the number of Arabs or Persians who wished to carry their sympathy with the Axis powers to the point of revolt

[1] *Palestine Statement of Policy* (The Palestine White Paper), May 1939 (Hurewitz, ii. 218).
[2] Elizabeth Monroe, *Britain's Moment in the Middle East* (1963), pp. 89–90.

were few, while the Jews could not side with Hitler. There
were no hesitations on the part of the Hashimite rulers of
Transjordan and Iraq, or Ibn Saud. Where the British considered it necessary to act in defence of their own security they
did so decisively and effectively; but the French were unable to
join them, as the local authorities in Syria and the Lebanon
supported Vichy, while the Free French had but limited forces
in the area. It was inevitable, therefore, that long-standing
rivalry between the British and French in the Middle East
should be revived in its most acute form.

Amongst the most dramatic occasions for the assertion of
British power was that which started in Iraq and led on to
Syria. In the inter-war years British relations with Iraq had
been on the whole harmonious; personal connexions were more
easily established on terms of equality between British and
Iraqis than between British and Egyptians, while the most
outstanding and powerful of Iraqi politicians, Nuri al-Said,
belonged to the group of older Arab leaders who were ready
to advance their own cause in co-operation with the British.
On the outbreak of war the Iraqi government had behaved
correctly according to the terms of the Anglo-Iraqi treaty, and
broken off diplomatic relations with Germany. But it was
natural that extreme nationalists should hope to take advantage
of the war to press their cause against the British, and they saw
no reason to exclude the possibility of assistance from Germany. The most assertive of the nationalist politicians was
Rashid Ali, a man descended from an ancient and noble
family but knowing little of the world outside Iraq.

Rashid Ali became premier in March 1940, relying on the
support of Nuri al-Said who seems to have thought him safer
in office than out. When Italy entered the war Rashid Ali's
government did not break off relations, so that, in Churchill's
view, 'the Italian Legation in Baghdad became the chief centre
for Axis propaganda and for fomenting anti-British feeling'.[3]
With the fall of France a German armistice commission arrived
in Syria, and a working alliance between Iraqi nationalists and
the Axis seemed an obvious possibility. The British government
therefore brought pressure to bear on the regent and Nuri to
secure Rashid Ali's resignation. This was achieved, and he
resigned on 31 January 1941. Outmanoeuvred and lacking

¹Churchill, iii. 224.

wide political support, he allied himself with a group of nationalist army officers (the 'Golden Square'), who on the night of 1 April staged a military demonstration, forced the premier's resignation, and brought Rashid Ali back to power. Rashid Ali then immediately declared his adherence to the Anglo-Iraqi pact; but the British government was not convinced, the more so since the Iraqi government still refused to break off relations with Italy.

These events occurred at a time when British forces in the Mediterranean were hard pressed. Rommel was advancing across Cyrenaica, and the Germans were attacking in Yugoslavia and Greece. The possibility of an alliance between Iraq and the Axis therefore presented grave dangers to the British government. Churchill's reaction was: 'The situation in Iraq has turned sour. We must make sure of Basra, as the Americans are increasingly keen on a great air assembling base being formed there.'[4] As a result, a brigade was moved from India, and this precipitated conflict with the Iraqi government. Iraqi forces surrounded the British air base at Habbaniya in the north, and appeared strong enough to wipe it out; but they were defeated. The British brought the few reinforcements which could be spared and transported from Palestine and Transjordan; the Iraqis received the assistance of about 120 German aeroplanes, which they were unable to use effectively. Once Habbaniya was relieved, Iraqi resistance collapsed and Rashid Ali and his supporters fled to Persia and to Turkey.

Churchill may have exaggerated the threat to the British position; but it should be remembered that the next step in German strategy might well have been to encircle the British Middle East position and clear up the whole eastern Mediterranean, rather than embark on the Russian campaign. As it was, the confrontation between Britain and Arab nationalism, and even more the natural acceleration of events, chastened both sides. The Iraqi government declared war on the Axis on 16 January 1943, and under the predominant influence of Nuri al-Said sought to achieve the objectives of Arab nationalism in co-operation with the British, while the British government took far more seriously the sensitivity of Arab nationalism, and its own dependence on friendly relations with the Arab states.

⁴ Ibid. p. 225.

The Rashid Ali affair, however, had immediate repercussions in the neighbouring French mandated territories of the Levant. When France fell in June 1940 the local administration in Syria refused to join de Gaulle and remained loyal to Vichy. The danger to Britain, particularly at the time of the Iraq coup d'état, that Germany would be able to take over the area at almost no cost, was obvious. There was little military force which the British could spare to prevent such action, but as Churchill wrote to Wavell: 'if the Germans can pick up Syria and Iraq with petty air forces, tourists, and local revolts we must not shrink from running equal small scale military risks.'[5] The most effective assistance that Germany could give to Iraq was in air power; but the aeroplanes would have to stage their flight in Syria. The French gave their agreement to this on 21 May, as well as to the sharing of intelligence about British military forces in the Middle East, in the hope of improving the terms on which they would collaborate with the Germans in metropolitan France. The agreement, and its implementation when German aircraft landed in Syria, brought a strong reaction from the British and the Free French. The airfields were bombed, and as soon as a force of Commonwealth and Free French troops could be gathered it invaded Syria. The Vichy French commander, General Dentz, in communication with his government explored the possibilities of German assistance; but this was something which the French were for obvious reasons reluctant to resort to. In the end none was requested or given, and the Vichy French gave in to the British, signing an agreement with them at St Jean d'Acre on 14 July 1941.

In this way a further German threat to the British position in the Middle East was removed; but at the same time a fertile ground was opened up for differences between Britain and the Free French. The French had long been highly suspicious of British designs in the Middle East; a century of history had taught them to be so, and no one was more jealous of French interests than de Gaulle. The area in which their rivalry could now shape itself was in their relationship with the Arabs in Syria and Lebanon.

Commonwealth and Free French troops acted together against the Vichy forces in Syria, but there was direct opposi-

[5] 21 May 1941 (ibid. p. 290).

tion of view between those who commanded them. Churchill wanted the forces engaged to be British in the first instance, not Free French, 'whose intervention would be bitterly resented'; de Gaulle had already foreseen that he must assert his influence at Beirut or Damascus, since otherwise France would be driven out either by the Germans or by the British. Behind this difference lay conflicts of interest of a more fundamental kind. De Gaulle's position was one of extreme delicacy. He was well aware that he lacked the force to succeed in a direct confrontation with Arab nationalism: on the other hand his political position as leader of the Free French was too vulnerable for him to be able to surrender French sovereignty in one of the first areas of the French overseas dependencies to come under his control. Nor is it likely that de Gaulle wished at this time to give independence to Syria and Lebanon, in spite of the importance which he attached to nationalism as the dominant force in international affairs when he later wrote his memoirs.

The declaration which accompanied the Free French entry into Syria and Lebanon should be read in this context. The Arabs were told 'your sovereign and independent status will be guaranteed by a treaty, which will transform our mutual relations'. At the same time de Gaulle placed the Free French forces under British military command. But he expected that the British would work with the Arabs to eliminate the French from the Middle East. As he wrote after the event:

Their game, – settled in London by firmly established services, carried out on the spot by a team without scruples but not without resources, accepted by the Foreign Office, which sometimes sighed over it but never disavowed it, and supported by the Prime Minister, whose ambiguous promises and calculated emotions camouflaged what was intended, aimed at establishing British 'leadership' in the whole Middle East. British policy would therefore endeavour, sometimes stealthily and sometimes harshly, to replace French at Damascus and at Beirut.

The procedure to be employed by this policy would be that of going one better – letting it be thought that every concession granted by us to Syria and the Lebanon was granted thanks to England's good offices, egging the local rulers on to formulate increasing demands and, lastly, supporting the acts of provocation to which it was bound to lead them.[6]

[6] *The Call to Honour* (1955), p. 188.

In one respect de Gaulle exaggerated: there was no Machiavellian plot in London. But the British representative in Syria, General Spears, was undoubtedly strongly motivated by suspicion of France and support of the Arabs. In any case events seemed to confirm de Gaulle's fears in every detail. The British insisted on accompanying the Free French promise of independence with a guarantee of their own, against the express protest of de Gaulle, who denied that they had any right to pronounce on the transfer of sovereignty from France. The St Jean d'Acre convention appeared to end the German threat in Syria (in fact the threat was more decisively averted by Hitler's decision to attack Russia rather than to drive Britain out of the Middle East), but it was unacceptable to de Gaulle because it transferred authority in Syria and Lebanon to the British, and made no mention of the rights of France.[7] In a tough interview with Oliver Lyttelton, de Gaulle threatened to remove French forces in the Middle East from British command, and succeeded in extracting important concessions, particularly about the return of Vichy troops to France.

In addition, the British government emphasized its disinterestedness in a note which Lyttelton sent to de Gaulle, which said:

I am happy to repeat to you the assurance that Great Britain has no interest in Syria or the Lebanon except to win the war. . . . Both Free France and Great Britain are pledged to the independence of Syria and the Lebanon. When this essential step has been taken, and without prejudice to it, we freely admit that France should have the predominant position in Syria and the Lebanon over any other European Power.[8]

But this was unconvincing. In French eyes it was clear and evident that the British maintained their own position with the utmost firmness in the Arab states under their own influence, while expressing support for Arab nationalism and aspirations to unity. The only way they could reconcile these diverse positions was by stimulating the Syrians and Lebanese against

---

[7] When de Gaulle learned that the British intended excluding him from the armistice negotiations he decided that: 'My only means of limiting the damage was to gain space and height, to reach some cloud and from there swoop down upon a convention which would not bind me, and which I would tear up as far as I could. The cloud was Brazzaville. I stayed there, while at Saint John of Acre the act was drawn up, whose substance and form went beyond my worst fears' (ibid. p. 194).
[8] Hurewitz, ii. 232.

the French. In May 1941 Anthony Eden gave fresh evidence of the British view when he said:

This country has a long tradition of friendship with the Arabs, a friendship that has been proved by deeds, not words alone. ... Many Arab thinkers desire for the Arab peoples a greater degree of unity than they now enjoy. In reaching out towards this unity they hope for our support. No such appeal from our friends should go un-answered. It seems to me both natural and right that the cultural and economic ties between the Arab countries, and the political ties too, should be strengthened. His Majesty's government for their part will give their full support to any scheme that commands general approval.[9]

It is not surprising that the conflict over Syria and the Leba-non continued through the war. In both countries elections were held in the summer of 1943. In Syria the Nationalist Bloc was virtually unopposed, while in Lebanon the pro-French party was successful only in Beirut. As a result governments under Quwatli in Syria and al-Khuri in Lebanon came into existence with the full authority of a popular mandate to support them. In contrast the Free French, who claimed tutelary rights in Syria and Lebanon, were in exile from their own country and had no recognized authority. The French National Committee, which had recently established itself in Algiers, was dependent on its allies for the liberation of France, and was neither inter-nationally recognized nor democratically elected.

A more serious difficulty facing the French in the negotiation of a new position in the Levant was that the predominant force in the area was not French but British; and as long as the war lasted, even if only in the Far East, the British were determined that the Middle East should remain tranquil. This tranquillity they thought could only be achieved by agreement between the French and the Arabs, and while urging moderation on the Syrians and Lebanese they brought pressure to bear on the French to make concessions. Such pressure was at times direct and forthright; as when the French delegate-general in Nov-ember 1943 dismissed and arrested the Lebanese government, and the British government told the French that the Lebanese ministers must be released and reinstated, and that if this were not done 'they will be set free by the British troops'. From this error of judgement de Gaulle and his delegate in the Levant,

[9] *The Times*, 30 May 1941, quoted by Monroe, *Britain's Moment*, p.   .

6

General Catroux, quickly retreated, removing the local officials from office. In seeking a settlement with the Syrians and the Lebanese, however, they looked for men who would be dependent on French support rather than on Arab nationalism.

In the end an agreement was negotiated which, from 1 January 1944, gave the governments of Syria and Lebanon virtual independence, with the exception that the French retained control over the 'services of social assistance, education and culture' and – more important – kept their command over the local troops. Thereafter the two governments began to receive international recognition. In February 1945 Churchill and Eden conferred with the Syrian president on their way back from Yalta. At the end of the month Syria and Lebanon declared war on the Axis, and thereby earned for themselves membership of the San Francisco conference (with the compliance of France).

Understandably the new states were not prepared to accept the limitation on their independence which French command of local troops represented; and their governments recognized that they would be weaker *vis-à-vis* the French once the British left. The conflict came to a head as the war ended. The French prepared for negotiations by dispatching fresh troops to the Levant; but these inevitably provoked further the nationalist feeling in the two countries. The Syrian and Lebanese governments were naturally anxious to control such demonstrations, in order to give no pretext for intervention by the French. But at the end of May, as rioting spread in the principal towns of Syria and Lebanon, they were no longer able to do so. The French troops then resorted to heavier military measures, which included the shelling of Homs, Hama, and Damascus.

The situation of November 1943 thus repeated itself in a more serious form, and the British government, maintained by its own military supremacy, acted to restore order. The British requested de Gaulle to order a cease-fire and withdraw French troops to their barracks, while the local French army commander was told: 'You no longer have any authority, except the disciplinary authority over your own troops in their barracks.' The conflict was brought before the Security Council in February 1946, and in the following month agreement was reached for the withdrawal of both British and French troops, and the complete independence of both Syria and Lebanon by the end of the year.

British action in Iraq and intervention in Syria had been a potent force in stimulating Anglo-French differences. In Persia similar dangers to the campaign against Hitler seemed to arise as German troops advanced across the Caucasus. The ruler of Persia, Riza Shah, had always enjoyed good relations with the Germans. Through trade, technical services, and a very successful *Deutsches Haus*[10] in Teheran, Germany had achieved an effective penetration of the country which was free of the pressure to which Persians had been accustomed from the Russians and the British. However, faced with the possible prospect of German forces finding a 'neutral' ready to provide a supporting base or a route to India when they arrived at the Persian frontier, Britain and Russia, who had signed an entente in tsarist days dividing Persia into spheres of influence, now invaded by agreement, and with American consent, from the south and from the north.[11] Riza Shah abdicated and the Persians, unable to act otherwise, signed a non-military alliance with Britain and Russia, so that the threat from Germany was countered and a supply route into Russia from the south was assured. The treaty signed with Persia provided for the withdrawal of Russian and British troops as soon as the war ended.

Of all the countries of the Middle East Egypt was affected most directly by the war. Its territory was invaded, although not so deeply as to affect the populated area; Alexandria suffered aerial bombardment, although not heavy enough to cause serious damage or casualties. It was thus not so much by the direct attack of the Axis powers that Egyptian life was transformed through its involvement in the war; the reason was rather that it was at the very centre of British resistance to Italy and Germany, a vital base and centre of communications which Britain would defend at all costs. The desert fringe was the scene of actual battle; but the chief cities were under virtual occupation by the British, who established their Middle East Supply Centre in Cairo and attracted many Egyptians

[10] Monroe, *Britain's Moment*, p. 90.
[11] It is questionable whether the British had exhausted the possibilities of securing a route through Persia by diplomatic means before resorting to the extreme measure of invading a neutral country, and agreeing to the Russians doing so too.

into their service as civilian labour. Inevitably the effect of this was to create inflation and shortages in the Egyptian economy. Had the British been responsible for the government of the country they would have made every effort to counter rising prices and disruption of trade; as it was the economy suffered all the disruption of war, with little of the control that would normally be exercised.

Where the British did exercise control in Egypt it was to ensure that the government in power would provide a reliable and effective support to them in their war effort. But in 1940, with France defeated and Germany and Italy apparently triumphant in Europe, it was difficult for Egyptians – as for others – to believe that British strength would long survive. So although relations were broken off, first with Italy and then with Germany, the government of Ali Mahir and the king kept the lines open to the Axis as reinsurance against the complete collapse of Britain. In June 1940 the British government therefore brought pressure to bear on the king, and on 23 June 1940 Ali Mahir resigned and was succeeded by Hasan Sabri.

The new government fufilled the terms of the 1936 treaty in the support they gave to the British. Some few Egyptians argued that Egypt should declare war, to enhance its prestige and bargaining power when the war was over, but they were an uninfluential minority. Alternatively it was argued that Egyptian interests could most effectively be pursued by a bargain with the Axis; and as the arrival of Rommel in the desert added to the surging tide of war against the British, while the Egyptian people suffered from shortage and speculation, it was inevitable that such a policy should recommend itself.

Opposition naturally centred on Ali Mahir, and when in February 1942 a combination of pressure on the king and student demonstrations in the streets brought the dismissal of Sabri, he appeared the obvious successor. However, this was a development which the British could not countenance, and the British ambassador insisted that the king should appoint Nahas Pasha, leader of the Wafd party, to form a new government. At first the king declined to do so; whereupon the British ambassador visited him at 9.0 p.m. on 4 February accompanied by the GOC British troops in Egypt and three light tanks. An hour later Nahas was appointed prime minister.

The incident was important in clarifying the relationship

between the two governments for the remainder of the war. The British had shown their readiness and ability to act to counter any threat to their position in Egypt; and they were in part successful because the Wafd remained loyal to the alliance with them. Within a year victory at El Alamein marked the turning point of the Middle Eastern war, and the British position was not challenged again. But the experience of February 1942 made a deep impact on young nationalists, especially young army officers, who would nurture the passionate desire to free their country from all foreign control and influence.

For the remainder of the war the Egyptians continued to chafe under the restraints which British occupation represented. They resented too the first moves which the British government made towards the independence of the Sudan, where the Egyptian government hoped to transform its share of the Anglo-Egyptian condominium into more effective control; but such emotion availed little against the reality of the British military presence. As the war drew to its end, the Egyptian government was suddenly made aware that its future membership of the post-war international organization would depend initially on its participation in the war, which thus for the first time presented itself as a matter of Egyptian national interest. This persuaded the government, led since October 1944 by Ahmad Mahir, to propose a declaration of war; but even then feeling ran sufficiently high for the prime minister to be assassinated on his way from the Chamber of Deputies to the Senate, although his intentions were carried into effect by his successor.

However, it was in Palestine that the changes which would have the most far-reaching consequences on the Middle East were centred. As we have seen, the war was immediately preceded by a British White Paper limiting the numbers of Jewish immigrants into Palestine. If such a policy were carried out effectively, it would thwart the central purpose of the Zionists, whose object was to increase overwhelmingly the number of Jews in Palestine. They therefore refused to accept limitation, and supported illegal immigration into Palestine. This would necessarily bring them into conflict with the mandatory power, but they were in any case prepared to accept such a conflict. From 1917 until 1939 the Zionists had gained most from working with Great Britain, whose policies had permitted the establishment of sufficient Jews in Palestine for it to become *de facto* a partly Jewish country, and as late as 1936–7 it appeared that Britain might opt for partition. But the 1939 policy ruled out such a possibility. It did so just at the time when the Jews and Britain were under attack from the common enemy – Nazi Germany – and it was their common interest to do nothing which would prejudice the outcome of that conflict. But the Zionists also realized that if Germany were defeated, they would be presented with a unique opportunity for the realization of their objectives. They were sufficiently strong in Palestine, they had won widespread sympathy amongst Gentiles, and, as the holocaust of war died down, the governments of the world would accept a redrawing of frontiers and the creation of a new state as they would in no other circumstances. An arrangement as temporary as the British mandate over Palestine must come to an end at some time, and they should be in a position to assert their claim when it did.

The dilemma in which the Zionists were placed was resolved in Ben-Gurion's advice: 'Fight the White Paper as if there were no Hitler and Hitler as if there were no White Paper.' But such a formula was easier to frame in words than to implement in practice and the Jews in Palestine were divided as to which course of action was the more profitable for their cause. However, the most important organized group of the Jews in Palestine, Haganah, co-operated with the British in the maintenance of order, as they had done since the beginning of the Arab revolt in 1937. The British were equally uncertain in the early years of the war as to the extent to which co-operation with the Jews was advisable. They were in no position to spurn any ally; on the other hand they were aware of the extent to which the Jews could improve their position *vis-à-vis* the Arabs by an alliance with Britain. Outside Palestine it was thus in 'special activities' in the Balkans and in Libya that co-operation was at first most practical.

By 1943 the Zionist dilemma began to resolve itself. On the one hand the victories at El Alamein and Stalingrad showed that the tide of war had changed; on the other the news from Germany provided devastating evidence that the Nazi attack on the Jews was a wholesale and planned attempt at extermination rather than merely persecution and cruelty. As a result

Haganah took to the organization of illegal immigration into Palestine in order to build up Jewish strength there, feeling free to act in Zionist interests even though by doing so they created difficulties for the British. None the less the British government, influenced by Churchill's long-standing sympathy for the Zionist cause, had now recruited Jews for military service overseas and in September 1944 a Jewish brigade was created and fought in Italy under its own flag, later the flag of Israel.

Meanwhile Zionist political activity outside Palestine was redeployed. Until 1940 it had been centred in London, since it was most profitable to work through the mandatory power; but from 1940 an intensive campaign was developed in the United States. An American Zionist Emergency Council was created to act as an agent of the World Zionist organization in co-ordinating the activities of the American Zionist groups, and as the war proceeded increasing pressure and propaganda were brought to bear on every part of American political life. The reasons for this reorientation of effort are easy to understand. If the Zionists were going to enter into open conflict with Britain, it would strengthen their position to have the friendly support of an American ally; and when the United States entered the war it would obviously have a predominant voice in decisions affecting the future of a Jewish state.

The most important single manifestation of the new Zionist policy in the early years of the war was the meeting organized by the American Zionist Emergency Council at the Biltmore Hotel in New York in May 1942. The conference marked the emergence of Ben-Gurion as the pre-eminent Zionist leader, the successor of Chaim Weizmann. In addition it passed a resolution, later called the Biltmore programme, which urged that:

the gates of Palestine be opened; that the Jewish Agency be vested with control of immigration into Palestine and with the necessary authority for the upbuilding of the country, including the development of its unoccupied and uncultivated lands; and that Palestine be established as a Jewish Commonwealth integrated into the structure of the new democratic world.[12]

It should be remembered that the acceptance of such a

[12] Hurewitz, ii. 235.

resolution was an important step within American Jewry, for American Jews were traditionally assimilationist. In the United States, as in Britain, the Zionists succeeded in prevailing over their Jewish opponents (represented by the American Council for Judaism) by their greater militancy. But it was equally important in providing a formula which could be promoted unceasingly for the rest of the war in American political life, so that it would be accepted by Labour unions and Congressional committees; most important, it was adopted by both political parties in the presidential elections of 1944.

It is easy to see, then, that the Zionists had established a very strong position as the war drew to a close. They had established a governmental and military organization which enjoyed the advantages of both legality and illegality, receiving arms from the British, but not hesitating to acquire them by illegal purchase as well. In this way the foundation was laid for a unique military force, which became literally a nation in arms. The Zionists could draw on the widespread sympathy felt for the Jews as a result of their persecution by Hitler, and they had built up an extremely effective pressure group organization in both Britain and America which could outflank those departments of government – the Foreign Office and the State Department – which were most concerned about good relations with the Arabs. In Palestine itself terrorist organizations, whose relationship with the Zionist leadership remains indeterminate, rendered the task of government increasingly difficult, even though they forfeited support by their extremism.

Outside Palestine it might have appeared at the end of the war that Britain had reached the apogee of its power in the Middle East and was unchallenged by any rival. The interventions which Britain had made during the war in the Arab states had demonstrated British power over the area as a whole; and Britain had succeeded in conducting the war in the Middle East with freedom of communication and movement. The Middle East Supply Centre emphasized still further the freedom with which resources could be mobilized and distributed through an area over which Britain exercised no direct governmental control.

Of the traditional rivals of Britain in the Middle East France had been severely weakened and had forfeited its military bases.

The Soviet Union had followed tsarist precedent in establishing itself in northern Persia, but as later events showed it had failed to secure a permanent hold there. Its pressure on Turkey and the Straits brought no reward. The United States had spread its military and economic activities throughout the Middle East as elsewhere in the world; air bases had been established in Arabia, lend-lease agreements signed with Turkey, Iraq, Arabia, and Persia. But although Roosevelt had visited the Middle East and talked with Arab leaders, there was no reason to expect that America would play an important part in the diplomatic activity of the post-war period. Only the anti-imperialism of the United States and, more ominously, its support for Zionism, appeared to endanger the British position.

However, the appearance of British power was illusory. Britain retained responsibilities, legally in the mandate for Palestine, and more extensively in the self-imposed task of 'policing' an area where order and stability were regarded as essential to the preservation of British interests. But throughout the world its power to meet its responsibilities, real or imaginary, was grievously attenuated. The sterling balances – Britain's unpaid debts to Middle Eastern countries – were a striking indication of a changed relationship. In the years immediately after the war the two new great powers, America and Russia, would be slow to take an active part in Middle Eastern politics, in spite of the dramatic entry of the United States into the eastern Mediterranean consequent on British withdrawal from Greece. But sooner or later the conditions of the cold war would be such that the Middle East would be too vital an area in international affairs to remain the only concern of a declining power.

Moreover British power in the Middle East had always rested on a realization of mutual advantage between Britain and the Arab states, or at least the Arab rulers. Only because of this had the limited action taken in Iraq and Egypt been successful. This mutual advantage was now breaking down. Traditionally British dominance had been based on a claim to defend Arab states from domination by other foreign powers; but in the early part of the war British power seemed no longer invincible, and when the enemy was beaten the Arabs no longer felt any external danger. After 1948 new dangers appeared, but they

6*

affected Britain and the Arab states differently; for while to
Britain the direct threat was from Russia, for the Arabs it was
from Israel, which Britain had allowed to come into existence.
The United Nations organization did little to add to the
security of the area; but it did provide a new framework where
the Arab states could make display of their independence, and
where the attributes of statehood were control over defence
and foreign policy – precisely those areas where British influence had been most important.

The British connexion had brought other benefits to the
Arab states; but these were even less apparent now than they
had been previously. In a few years the Aswan dam was to
become the symbol of Egyptian economic development; it was
called the 'High Dam' to distinguish it from that which the
British had built in 1902. But in the post-war period these
economic advantages were limited by British financial weakness. In a decade when international aid programmes were to
become increasingly fashionable, British resources were inadequate to provide substantial subsidies in the Middle East.
In the past, membership of the sterling area had given Egypt,
Iraq, and Transjordan a stable currency and secure reserves.
Now these states were creditors of Britain, but Britain was
unable to offer them the free convertibility of their sterling
balances. As long as the Arab states in general had enjoyed
advantages at British hands, they had accrued most obviously
to the established ruling classes. For them the British connexion
meant the maintenance of law and order, and therefore protection to their political and social position; it had meant
greater prosperity, from which they benefited. British advisers
naturally maintained the interests of their own country; but
they did so with an integrity and reliability which was not
always found in indigenous politicians or administrators. But in
the post-war period the traditional rulers belonged to a
generation that was passing, and one which was increasingly
challenged by a new intellectual élite or by young army officers
who sought national self-respect in independence from all
outside interference. In many respects post-war conditions were
similar to those which had existed in Russia after the Napoleonic wars, when they had produced the prototype of the intelligentsia; and then, as now in the Middle East, the intelligentsia
was frequently to be found in the army. The new classes opposed

the old both for their dominance of national politics and for their alliance with foreign powers. In so doing they could draw on a political force which had grown in importance during the war – ordinary people who were open to propaganda emanating from the radio, and who, first in Egypt and later elsewhere, were pushed into the towns by rural overpopulation, there to form volatile masses.

For all these reasons British influence in the Middle East would inevitably have declined in the period after the war. In addition, Britain now reaped the harvest of the seeds sown in 1917. In 1948 a Jewish state came into existence, and the British could not free themselves in the eyes of the Arabs from responsibility for the admission of this alien intruder, representative of western imperialism.

Even so, these factors might have been of less importance were it not for the strength of emotional feeling amongst the Arabs in their striving for independence and unity. These emotions are usually referred to as 'Arab nationalism', a term which is deceptively simple. The Arabs passionately desired independence, in the sense of complete freedom from outside influence, and complete control over their own government in all its aspects. This was a demand to which statesmen and people in Britain were often insensitive. They were genuinely convinced that states like Iraq and Egypt were independent, and had signed treaties with Britain with the same freedom as Britain enjoyed in signing treaties with its European neighbours; they were unable to appreciate Arab feelings of hostility and resentment towards an influence which was no less pervasive and no less powerful because it was indirect. Or, more crudely, they regarded the British position in the Middle East as an absolute which must not be challenged – an attitude which was especially widespread towards Egypt.

Yet while wishing for such independence Arabs were necessarily aware of their actual dependence on outside help for the realization of their national identity and prosperity. The more sophisticated recognized the conflict between their desire for independence and their hopes of external aid to raise their prosperity and impart to them dignity in the eyes of the world as countries whose whole population enjoyed a reasonable standard of living.

Similarly the Arab search for unity was often a source of

division rather than a unifying force. There was not even a remote possibility that the political process of federation which the Americans had achieved after the war of independence would be repeated in the Middle East, where tolerance and restraint, the give and take of democratic politics, had not been achieved on a national scale. Unity would only come through the dominating force of one man or one country; yet the appearance of any such force was inevitably a source of rivalry elsewhere, and there was no obvious means of reconciling different ambitions to be the dominant partner in a union. Not only that, but the very concept of union differed from one country to another. Egypt had its own national tradition and sense of unity, and was content with its frontiers; its leaders thus sought Arab unity in the sense of co-operation between Arab states, especially against the foreigner. To some extent Iraqis and Lebanese shared this feeling of the importance of their own nation. But in Syria and for some Jordanians the demand for Arab unity was one which ignored frontiers, and emanated from a desire to find a political unit with which the individual could identify himself simply because of the insufficiency or the inadequacy of his own artificially created state.

Even the question of Israel was a divisive force amongst the Arabs; for while none would admit one iota of the Jewish case, the actual cost of opposition to the Jews was unequally divided, and if ever the state of Israel should be overthrown, the Arabs would necessarily be divided amongst themselves on the distribution of the spoils.

These sources of difference amongst the Arabs were insufficiently obvious to the outside world. All too often westerners either underrated or exaggerated the force of Arab nationalism, while remaining unaware of the differences between Arabs, and the tensions to which their conflicts, even conflicts between individuals and personal perplexities, gave rise. Meanwhile the Arabs themselves found their aspirations to independence, unity, and economic progress constantly inhibited by their own political differences, in spite of the tolerance and restraint sometimes achieved, for example in Lebanon.

Economically the Middle East in the post-war years found undreamed-of wealth in the exploitation of its one great natural resource – oil. Since the beginning of history there had been evidence of oil deposits in the region, but in 1939 the

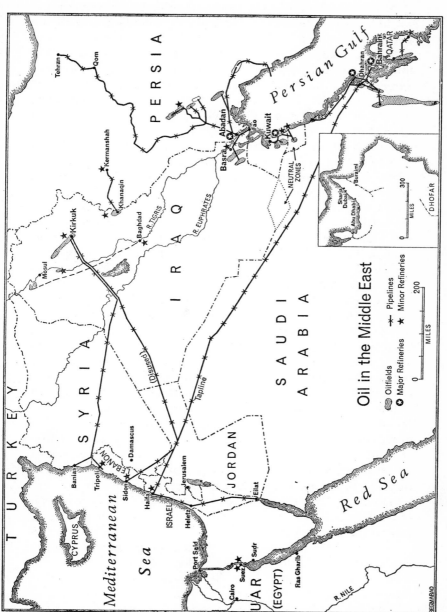

Oil in the Middle East

Oilfields
Major Refineries
Pipelines
Minor Refineries

Map 4.

total output of its oil was less than 16 million long tons out of a world total of 278, and of that amount 9½ millions came from Persia.[13] Twenty years later, in 1959, Middle Eastern output had risen to 227·2 million long tons out of a world total of 964 million, representing an increase from less than 6 to more than 24 per cent of the world's output. Persia remained an important contributor; but it was almost equalled by the second most important producer of 1939 days, Iraq, while both had been overtaken first by Saudi Arabia, where only exploration had taken place before the war, and then by the small shaikhdom of Kuwait. By 1959 the production from Kuwait alone, having begun in 1946, was 68·4 million long tons, or four times the output of the whole Middle East in 1939.

Yet the development of great natural wealth was accompanied by its own problems. It emphasized the dependence of the Arab states on outside resources of capital, skill, and technical and scientific knowledge, without which the mineral remained useless under the sand. Foreign exploitation appeared deceptively simple. Fruitless searches left no evidence of their wasted expenditure; and even an established oil well or a pipeline gave little indication of the resources necessary to bring it into being. Oil in the Middle East is unevenly distributed; in 1965 Egypt, Syria, Lebanon, Jordan, and Israel had scarcely any known sources, while certain shaikhdoms of the Persian or Arabian Gulf can provide their few inhabitants with an income per head far surpassing that in European states. But it does not follow automatically that the discovery of oil will benefit the population as a whole, and the extent to which wealth has been distributed beyond the pockets of the rulers has varied greatly. In Iraq a chemical and fertilizer industry was financed out of oil revenues, and a similar development began in Iran; but in the Gulf kingdoms there was little secondary industry. Egypt remained in 1959 the most advanced industrially of the Arab states, while the economic development of Israel depended on capital from quite different sources.

We see, then, that during the war little progress had been made either in fulfilling the aspirations of the Arabs towards their own unity, or by the British in re-establishing their traditional alliance with Arab nationalism on a more modern footing. In December 1942 Nuri al-Said had proposed a partial

[13] See S. H. Longrigg, *Oil in the Middle East* (1954).

union of Arab states, consisting essentially of the 'Fertile Crescent' – Iraq, Lebanon, Syria, Transjordan, and Palestine – with semi-autonomy for the Jews in Palestine. Such partial union was obviously disadvantageous to those left out, particularly Saudi Arabia and Egypt. It was therefore not pursued. Instead a general conference of Arab states was held in the autumn of 1944, and this resulted in the formation of the Arab League, established by the signature of a pact on 22 March 1945. The League provided for a Council sitting in Cairo, and various commissions on cultural and economic affairs. It received the support and encouragement of the British government. But the core of the pact lay in the anxieties of the Arab states over the Jewish question and the eruption of that problem after the war limited the effectiveness of the League and handicapped British relations with it.

With the advent to power of a Labour government, British policy underwent no fundamental change as, on the evidence available, might have been expected. Before and during the war the Labour party had shown itself a strong supporter of the Zionist cause, and had been severely critical of the limitation of Jewish immigration into Palestine. In power, the Labour party was divided on the Palestine question, but the foreign policy which emerged from cabinet discussions under the dominant influence of Attlee and Bevin did not envisage the establishment of a Jewish state against the opposition of the Arabs – an operation thought to be too costly in terms both of military resources and Arab goodwill. Moreover a Labour government might be expected to give more importance to economic development and less to questions of defence. Such would indeed have been Bevin's policy of choice; but the scope for the development of such a new approach was severely limited. In the first place Britain's financial resources made substantial aid impossible and inhibited Bevin's deep-felt desire to provide the means for capital development. Secondly, the importance of the Middle East for British defence increased rather than diminished. The end of the war was followed not by a peace generated by the United Nations, but by the cold war. This conflict was on a global scale: yet at the very same time Britain sacrificed the lynchpin of a century-old system of global defence – India. For 100 years India had provided and been the base for a British strategic reserve which could be moved east or west as need required. As India was given independence this base was sacrificed, and the need for a defence establishment in the Middle East became of increased importance.

As a result the policy of the Labour government remained in its essence, and especially as it appeared to the Arabs themselves, a continuation of a traditional policy towards the eastern Mediterranean and the Middle East that had a century's history behind it. This was to provide for British influence in the area, and especially for the security of British interests, by agreement with local governments, to the mutual advantage of them and Britain. The policy was revised in detail to make room for the growth of Arab nationalism; but events were to show that it was a policy unacceptable in its fundamentals.

In pre-war years Britain had signed treaties with the three Arab states which had been in its immediate sphere of influence: Egypt (1936), Iraq (1930), and Transjordan (1928).[14] Seen from Britain, these treaties seemed susceptible of revision in such a way as to meet the demands of Arab nationalism, and to make British influence less obvious. This would be achieved, for example, if new agreements could be reached providing for the withdrawal of British forces from the area and for the 'reactivation' of bases in the event of emergency. Seen from the Arab states such revision of the old order carried no sufficient change of principle. Their basic supposition was an alignment of their foreign and defence policies with those of a European power. In the old world this had been relatively unexceptionable, since defence and foreign policies had not meant very much; in the new world, particularly as it was to develop over the next decade, with the focus of world attention centred on new states, questions of defence and foreign affairs seemed to be at the very heart of national sovereignty – as they were indeed for European states. In addition, the most important specific question of external affairs and national security was that of Palestine and Israel, where Arab interests diverged from those of Britain.

These obstacles towards fresh agreements were immediately evident when the British government sought to negotiate a fresh treaty with Egypt to replace that of 1936. The 1936 treaty

[14] Although a treaty was signed with the ruler of Transjordan, it was not a sovereign state.

had a duration of twenty years from its signature, the Egyptian demand for its revision was insistent, and the British government was ready to recognize the changed conditions since that time. As a result the two governments succeeded in negotiating an agreement in October 1946, which was signed by Bevin and Sidqi Pasha, the Egyptian prime minister. It provided for the staged evacuation of British troops from Egypt, to be completed by 1949; a joint defence board was to be set up, and consultation with Britain for the maintenance of security in the area to be provided for. It was an agreement which held some promise for the future; but it provided no solution for the future of the Sudan, and on this obstacle it aborted.

The problem of the Sudan continued to bedevil Anglo-Egyptian relations until 1953. In the nineteenth century the Sudan had been part of Egypt and Egypt had been part of the Ottoman empire. But as the sultan of Turkey had no effective control over the khedive of Egypt, so the khedive for his part was too weak to suppress the revolt of the Mahdi in the Sudan, and the task of reconquest was undertaken in 1898 by Kitchener. Thereupon an Anglo-Egyptian condominium was established – and although the British retained the dominant role they claimed to be acting in support of Egypt. But the predominant British interest in the Sudan had always been to keep it out of the control of any other power, and after 1922 this policy was extended to Egypt. Having, up to this time, protected the Sudan ostensibly on behalf of Egypt, they now felt it incumbent on them to defend it against Egyptian encroachment. For the Egyptians, however, the 'unity of the Nile valley' had a great emotional appeal; for the king the title 'King of Egypt and the Sudan' had an obvious attraction; and few believed that the British were sufficiently trustworthy to give independence to the Sudan, or that the Sudanese were so perverse as to prefer it to union with Egypt. However near the two countries came to solving the general problems of a new treaty, therefore, the particular problem of the Sudan would prove an obstacle.

An attempt to negotiate a fresh agreement with Iraq was similarly thwarted by the opposition of Iraqi nationalism. Geographically close to the Soviet Union, the Iraqi government was susceptible to the British plea that the two countries had a common interest in defence. Politically it was not by nature stable, but its rival parties and groups were kept in flexible rein by the master of Middle East politics, Nuri al-Said. The development of its oil resources made it a comparatively wealthy country; and the British government was able to extend limited convertibility. As a result a new treaty to replace that of 1930 was drafted, and signed at a luncheon on board HMS *Victory* in January 1948. This treaty of Portsmouth provided for the continuance of the British air bases in Iraq, which were described as 'an essential element in the defence of Iraq itself and of international security and as a link in the essential communications of both parties'. But the treaty was stillborn. It was one thing to sign it in Portsmouth, and another to secure ratification in Baghdad. The government took insufficient care to secure political support and had to face hostile nationalist demonstrations, which derived much of their force from communist agitation. So the new treaty lapsed, and the old one remained in force until the negotiation of the Baghdad pact.

Only with Transjordan did it prove possible for the British government to negotiate a treaty along entirely traditional lines. Certain obvious differences distinguished it politically from both Egypt and Iraq. Transjordan was scarcely viable as an independent state; and its needs were sufficiently limited for Britain to be able to make a substantial contribution to its finances. The British had helped organize the Arab Legion and were willing to go on doing so; this was attractive to Abdullah, who looked for greater security against the Jews. The politics of Transjordan, inhabited largely by Beduin tribes, were simpler than in Egypt, and the ruler enjoyed a firm hold over his country. In these circumstances a new treaty with Transjordan in 1946, giving independence and providing for British financial aid and military advice in return for the right to station troops. A revised treaty, parallel to the abortive treaty with Iraq, was signed in 1948. Even here, however, political stability was gravely threatened when Transjordan absorbed part of Palestine, thereby becoming the state of Jordan, and was faced with the task of integrating a Palestinian Arab population, as well as that of assimilating Arab refugees.

The British hope that their own interests would correspond with those of the Arab states was thus largely unfulfilled. They were even more thwarted in their attempt to limit or control the force of Zionism. We have already seen the

political skill and unwavering determination with which
the Zionists pursued their objective of a Jewish state. When this
was joined to the urgent demand of the Jewish people for
justice and redress, and to the mingled feelings of guilt and
sympathy evoked in the western world by the Nazi murder
of some five million Jews, it produced a force difficult if not
impossible to resist. But such resistance the Arabs would offer;
for even to the extent that they were aware of the Jewish case,
it was inadmissible to them that it should be met by the
establishment of Jewish rule over Arab lands.

In retrospect it is possible to see that the Palestinian situation
at the end of the war was such that it could only be settled by
the arbitrament of force. The decisive force could in theory
have been relatively impartial force from outside – whether
from Britain, or the United States, or the United Nations; or
it could be, as it in fact was, the superior force of one of the
contestants on the spot. But this fact was one which the statesmen concerned found it hard to accept, or if they did, they
were not willing to accept its consequences. The acting secretary of state, Joseph Grew, provided President Truman with a
memorandum on Palestine in which he stated:

The Arabs, not only in Palestine but throughout the whole Near
East, have made no secret of their hostility to Zionism and their
Governments say that it would be impossible to restrain them from
rallying with arms, in defense of what they consider to be an Arab
country. We know that President Roosevelt understood this clearly,
for as recently as March 3, after his trip to the Near East, he told an
officer of the Department that, in his opinion, a Jewish state in
Palestine (the ultimate Zionist aim) could be established and maintained only by military force.[15]

Yet the only alternative to fighting it out between Jews and
Arabs was to provide a blanket of force from the outside, under
which a settlement could be imposed. This the British had done
inadequately under the mandate; they had neither the will
nor the resources to continue doing so, far less to enlarge
their operation; and no one else was ready to replace them.

Seeking assistance in the discharge of its duties under the
mandate, the British government at the end of 1945 proposed,
and the American government agreed, the setting up of an

[15] H. Truman, *Memoirs* (1955–6), ii. 133.

Anglo-American Committee of Inquiry. There appeared obvious advantages in sharing responsibility for such an intractable problem; but it was a novel step to invite the Americans into a closed area of British interest, the more so in view of the extent of the commitment of the American political parties and the sympathy which Truman had shown for the Zionist cause. It may be that Bevin supposed that if the American government were more closely associated with the problem it would be better aware of the consequences of acceding to the Zionist demand for the admission of 100,000 Jews to Palestine; it may be also that the British government overestimated the strength of the State Department view, anxious as it was about American relations with the Arab states.

In any case there were obvious differences of emphasis between the two governments in the setting up of the Committee. A message of 5 October from Attlee to Truman made it clear that the British government sought a general approach to the Jewish problem, and that of Palestine. It did not accept the Zionist view of these issues, but insisted 'that Jews should be enabled to play an active part in building up the life of the countries from which they came, in common with other nationals of these countries'.[16] It also referred to the possibility of resettling Jews in other countries outside Europe. In this way the Committee would approach the general problem of the Jews as it had been created by the war, visiting Europe first in order to do so, and then go on to consider the specific problem of Palestine. Truman was suspicious of such a general approach to a problem which he considered to have a simple urgency. He had already in August pressed Attlee to extend immigration into Palestine, and argued that 'the granting of an additional one hundred thousand . . . certificates would contribute greatly to a sound solution . . . '.[17] In accepting the Committee of Inquiry, he clung to his point of view. As he later said: 'I did not want the United States to become a party to any dilatory tactics.'[18]

The Committee reported on 30 April 1946, having succeeded in reaching unanimity; but its report was one which would inevitably create rather than resolve difficulties. It contained one practical proposal, susceptible of immediate implementation – the admission of a further 100,000 Jews into Palestine. But

[16] Ibid. ii. p. 141.   [17] Ibid. p. 139.   [18] Ibid. p. 142.

for the political problem of Palestine, and the difficulties which such immigration could only exaggerate, its recommendations were unrealizable in practice, however estimable they may have been in themselves. They were:

I That Jew shall not dominate Arab and Arab shall not dominate Jew in Palestine.

II That Palestine shall be neither a Jewish state nor an Arab state.[19]

Bevin had undertaken to implement the Committee's report provided that it was unanimous; but the report with which they were presented merely stated the problem in the guise of recommendations. Truman, on the other hand, found his support for the proposed immigration of the 100,000 endorsed. Other factors weighed with the British government. The negotiations which would lead up to the Bevin-Sidqi agreement were in train; while in Palestine the Jews presented themselves, not as the victims of persecution, but as the instigators of violence and terrorism.

The result was that both governments accepted the need for speedy consultation with Jews and Arabs to secure a practical implementation of the report, but Truman did not wait to advocate the immediate issuing of immigration certificates to the 100,000, and the two governments viewed each other with suspicion and distrust.

The next nine months were taken up with abortive attempts to reach a solution. The British government proposed a plan for provincial autonomy; but it was rejected by the United States. Jews and Arabs refused to sit down together to seek an agreed solution; and since their minimum requirements were fundamentally incompatible one with the other, it would have been a waste of time to do so. From the point of view of its own interests the British government was torn between the cost of being responsible for Palestine, and the possibilities of establishing a Middle East base there if the immediate problems could be overcome – a question which was obviously important as long as it seemed possible that British troops would be withdrawn from Egypt under the Bevin–Sidqi agreement.

The failure of direct negotiation in February 1947 led the British government to place the question of Palestine before the

[19] Hurewitz, ii. 265.

United Nations, seeking advice on how to execute its task. In doing so it obviously wished to bring to world notice the difficulties that beset the solution of a problem which it regarded as of international importance, but for which it had so far borne almost entire responsibility. Further than that it is difficult to see what useful outcome could be expected, since the government continued to oppose any plan which would not be acceptable to both Jews and Arabs.[20] A special session of the General Assembly was called, which set up a Special Committee on Palestine. In September the Committee produced a majority and a minority report. The majority report had the support of Canada, Czechoslovakia, Guatemala, India, Iran, the Netherlands, Peru, Sweden, and Uruguay. It advocated the partition of Palestine into an Arab and a Jewish state, with an international régime for Jerusalem. Britain was to continue to be responsible for the administration of the country, under the United Nations, until 1 September 1947, when both countries would become fully independent.

These recommendations never had the support of the British government. Its delegation at the United Nations spoke against the plan and persuaded friendly delegations not to vote for it; they insisted that Britain would not undertake the task of imposing a policy on Palestine by force of arms. But the Committee's recommendations in a slightly modified form won a majority in the General Assembly, which on 29 November 1947 recommended 'to the United Kingdom, as the mandatory Power for Palestine, and to all other Members of the United Nations the adoption and implementation . . . of the Plan of Partition with Economic Union'.[21] It also requested the Security Council to take the necessary measures to implement the plan. The British delegation abstained from voting.

Faced with this decision, the British government immediately defined its own responsibilities. It declared that the mandate would end on 15 May 1948, and that until that time it would not share its authority with any other body. The two sides in Palestine were thus given five months to prepare to fill the vacuum. This they did, the Arabs with some assistance (although surprisingly little in view of the size of the stakes) from

[20] Unless, as has been suggested, the British government hoped for a renewed trusteeship, giving it a free hand in Palestine.
[21] Hurewitz, ii. 281.

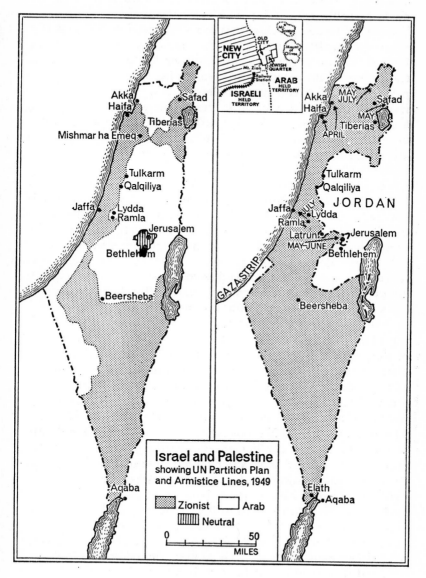

Map 5.

Based on John Marlowe, THE CITY OF PILOT
(London, Cresset Press, 1959)

across the borders. Violence inevitably spread and there was no foreseeable conclusion save the success of one side, or a balance of forces. In this situation the American government proposed on 19 March 1948 that action to implement the United Nations partition plan be suspended, and the mandate transformed into a temporary trusteeship. However, the proposal was abortive; and understandably neither side in Palestine paid any attention to the Security Council's order of a general truce on 17 April. British forces continued to withdraw, the circumstances of their withdrawal in each individual area inevitably giving an advantage to one side or the other in the battle which was to follow.

The day before the ending of the British mandate, on 14 May, the Jews proclaimed the existence of the state of Israel; and within a quarter of an hour it received recognition from the United States. Such diplomatic support was the more impressive because of the caution which the United States habitually showed in its recognition policy. But the actual survival of the new state was due to the success of its military forces in the inevitable war which ensued. Inferior in numbers, but superior in every other military asset – equipment, generalship, and will to win – the Israelis quickly established a military supremacy of which the eventual reward was the occupation of an area of Palestine larger than that envisaged in the United Nations partition plan. The fighting was interrupted at the end of May in response to a Security Council resolution; renewed and ended again in July, when the Security Council's resolution actually spoke of sanctions under Article VI of the Charter. The United Nations had appointed Count Bernadotte as mediator in the conflict as soon as the state of Israel was proclaimed; and by September he felt able to make proposals for a general armistice. He was then assassinated; but the fighting had now established a balance of forces between the two sides. The Arabs had suffered defeat, and defeat was followed by recrimination between those who had borne the brunt of the fighting and those who had not. The Israelis were realistic enough to leave well alone; the British having announced that they might have to invoke the 1936 treaty with Egypt because of incidents in Sinai, and the United States being obviously ready to modify the support it had so far given. From February 1949 armistice agreements were therefore signed between Israel and Egypt, Lebanon, Transjordan, and Syria. In this way an armistice line was drawn between Israel and its neighbours, following the arbitrary division along which the fighting had ended, frequently splitting a village in two or leaving houses on one side and their land on the other. The remainder of Palestine was annexed in part – the Gaza strip – to Egypt, and the rest to Transjordan, which thereby became Jordan.

The issue had thus been settled by force, as it inevitably must have been. It might have been settled by superior force from outside; but it is easy to see why this did not happen. The British were well aware of the scale of force that would be necessary to effect a settlement of the Palestine problem, and by the end of the mandate over 80,000 troops were inadequate to maintain order. This was a commitment which the British government was more anxious to escape from than to add to. The government of the United States from an early date decided that it could not use force to effect a settlement. In May 1946 the joint chiefs of staff recommended to Truman that 'no action should be taken that would cause repercussions in Palestine which would be beyond the capabilities of British troops to control'.[22] As the problem prolonged itself, the attention of Britain and the United States became increasingly concentrated on the development of the cold war. In February 1948 Warren Austin, United States delegate to the United Nations, made the enigmatic statement that the United States was prepared to consider the use of force to restore peace, but not to enforce partition. But this was the month of the Czecho-slovak coup d'état, and it was clear that if American forces were sent anywhere it would be to Europe and not to the Middle East.

It was impossible for the United Nations to use force, since none was available. It is interesting to speculate on the value of a United Nations force, had it existed in strength in 1945–6. At that time there was no deep division between the Soviet Union and the United States over the Palestine question – the Soviet Union voted for the partition plan (as had Czecho-slovakia in committee); there were no great power interests directly opposed to each other and no great powers in the area. If a strong United Nations force were to operate anywhere,

[22] Truman, *Memoirs*, ii. 149.

and create conditions for peaceful change under the blanket of its own overwhelming forces, it might have been in Palestine; but such speculations are of purely academic interest.

The policies of Britain and the United States were thus strictly irresponsible – the British avowedly so, the American implicitly. The British again and again expressed their unwillingness to use force to achieve a settlement; and finally withdrew altogether. The United States pressed for large Jewish immigration, although it was not prepared to take responsibility for the political consequences of such action; it supported the plan for partition, although it was not prepared to carry it through by force; and it recognized the state of Israel, although it was not prepared to send its own armies to its defence. That such policies did not end in complete disaster was the result solely of the success of the Israeli army. One may well question what action the United States might have taken, and how its subsequent policy would have differed, had the fortunes of the Arab–Israeli war gone the other way. The reasons for such irresponsibility are difficult to judge on the evidence available. It is possible that Bevin and the British government were affected by events in India, where the seemingly irreconcilable differences between Hindus and Muslims resolved themselves sufficiently for partition to be achieved, once the British made clear that they intended to hand over responsibility whatever the consequences. Truman has stated in his *Memoirs* that 'I was of the opinion that the proposed partition of Palestine could open the way for peaceful collaboration between the Arabs and the Jews'. Optimism of this sort may have been spontaneous; it may have been induced by the unacceptability of the alternative view. In any case, the Palestinian problem was only one problem with which these governments were concerned. Had times been more peaceful, their attitude might have been different; but it was never of overriding importance during the years of growing tension between Russia and the west; and if, in 1947 and 1948, it gave cause for anxiety, it could hardly compete with the growing danger which they saw of Russian expansion in Europe.

However that may be, the creation of the state of Israel had profound consequences in the future development of the Middle East. It created in an especially acute form the common international problem of tension resulting from the radically different viewpoints from within and without. From within Israel, the new state seemed immensely vulnerable. Not an inch of its land frontier was even neutral, let alone friendly; at its narrowest point the territory was nine miles wide, and every airfield was within artillery range from across the frontier, where the opposing forces outnumbered the Israelis beyond all hope of equalization. Its military leaders could only conclude therefore that the military readiness achieved by this nation in arms must be maintained; furthermore that the only war which Israel could fight was a pre-emptive war – all was lost if the enemy were allowed to choose the place and time of attack. From outside Israel the situation looked totally different. Israel appeared inevitably expansive – as more immigrants entered the country, the impulse to expand must be overwhelming, and the expansion could then come in any or every direction. It was not only people but money which flowed into Israel from outside, and while the Arabs struggled with their poor resources, Israel would be built up by outside aid until it was too powerful to be resisted.

In these circumstances tension round the borders was inevitable; it was only increased by the arbitrary nature of the armistice line. The armistice was broken by raids across the frontier of varying scale; Egypt refused to allow the passage of Israeli ships through the Suez canal; and there was no trade between Israel and the Arab states. The western powers sought to reduce the inflammability of the situation by limiting the import of arms into the area. On 25 May 1950 they issued a tripartite declaration in which they said that applications for arms would be considered only 'in the light of legitimate self defence and defence of the area as a whole'; and they undertook to take action both within and outside the United Nations should there be any threat to the agreed armistice lines.

The defeat of the Arab armies added to the tension within Arab states. Some Arab nationalists later convinced themselves that their armies were held back by the intervention of the great powers; but officers who had taken part in the campaign were well aware of the inefficiency and corruption which had been so large a source of weakness. Egyptian officers whose patriotism had been stirred and inflamed by British tanks entering the palace courtyard in May 1942 and enforcing the foreigners' will on the king were now humiliated by the performance of their own army; and their peace of mind was not enhanced by the fact that the one successful Arab army in the campaign was the British-trained and officered Arab Legion. Emotions of this sort were directly responsible for the officers' rising which succeeded in Egypt in 1952; they also lay behind a military coup d'état in Syria in 1949. The state whose stability was most threatened by the result of the war was Jordan; because it was the recipient of the largest number of refugees, and because the addition of Palestinian territory brought about a deep division in Jordanian society between the Beduin tribes of the old Transjordan and the Palestinian Arabs, more settled in their lives, but full of bitterness in their attitudes.

Finally, the whole diplomacy of the area was changed. Henceforth there would be an irremovable difference between the Arab states, especially those contiguous with Israel, and the western powers; for the interest of the former would be the expulsion of Israel, which the western powers were unwilling to permit. In contrast the Soviet Union, although for some years playing little part in Middle Eastern affairs, would be under no similar restraint. This would make hard ground for the western powers to hoe when they sought the support of the Arab states in defence against Russia. Moreover the creation of the Jewish state of Israel had destroyed the Arab state of Palestine. The Arab refugees were not political refugees from a despotic régime who could easily be assimilated into other Arab lands. Quite apart from their number – some 570,000 compared with a total Jordanian population (1965) of approximately 1,850,000 – they were a people, in many respects one of the most advanced in the Arab world, who were now torn from their lands and their homeland and denied any possibility of achieving statehood.

6

CHINA, JAPAN, AND DECOLONIZATION
IN ASIA

THE RAPID development of the cold war in the quinquennium following allied victory had its central nexus in Europe, where the confrontation of the two emerging blocs was most immediate. But developments in the Far East in this period were no less striking or significant. Asian countries achieved their independence sometimes through the speedy and willing transfer of power by the imperial government, sometimes through bitter conflict, in which internal disputes played a part equal in importance to that of the war against the imperial power. This formed part of a world-wide political process which had begun in Europe in the early nineteenth century, had spread to the Middle East and Asia, and reached its climax in the mid-twentieth century. In addition, the pattern of politics in the Far East was determined by two distinctive events: the success of the Chinese communists in winning power in the most heavily populated and one of the largest countries in the world, and the transformation of Japan from a defeated and occupied country to an ally of its principal former enemy.

The United States had played the predominant part in the war against Japan, and it was the intention of its government, when war ended, to maintain the controlling voice in policy towards the defeated country. In general the western allies of the United States in the Far Eastern war accepted this situation, although sometimes under protest. Then, as occupation policies in Japan (as in western Germany) were modified in the direction of reconstruction rather than retribution and control, they began to voice anxieties proportionate to their own degree of rivalry with Japan. The Soviet Union, in contrast, differed vigorously from the United States on nearly all questions of occupation policy; but it now had to pay the price for its late entry into the Far Eastern war. There was little or nothing it could do to enforce the acceptance of its views in international negotiation. Within Japan it maintained no occupation troops and the Communist party was weak. As a result it lacked the levers to manipulate events from the inside.

The circumstances of surrender were different in Japan from those in Germany. Although surrender was unconditional, there existed a fundamental element of agreement between victors and vanquished. In August 1945 the Japanese government faced inexorable defeat. Two atomic bombs had been dropped, one on Hiroshima on 6 August, and one on Nagasaki on 9 August; the Soviet Union had entered the war on 8 August. Following the leadership of the emperor, they therefore decided to accept surrender on the basis of the Potsdam declaration; but on condition that it did not comprise 'any demand which prejudices the prerogatives of His Majesty as a Sovereign Ruler'. To go farther, in the eyes of some members of the government, meant a fate for Japan worse than the slaughter of its people or military subjugation. The American government would accept no such conditions. But at the same time the United States and its allies thought it necessary and desirable to keep the emperor system in being, and supposed that their task in Japan would be very much easier to accomplish if they could, during the occupation, exercise authority through the emperor and a Japanese government rather than by attempting to rule directly. They therefore replied to the initial Japanese proposal of surrender, in a note drafted by Secretary of State Byrnes, that from the moment of surrender 'the authority of the Emperor and the Japanese government to rule the state shall be subject to the Supreme Commander of the Allied powers who will take such steps as he deems proper to effectuate the surrender terms', and that the ultimate form of government of Japan would be established 'by the freely expressed will of the people'.[1] After much heart-searching and long debate, the Japanese government, once again following the lead offered by the emperor, decided to surrender in spite of the absence of the safeguards they had considered essential. The United States government was notified and the emperor took the unprecedented step of broadcasting to his people to explain the instrument of surrender, saying:

---

[1] Byrnes, *Speaking Frankly*, pp. 209–10.

Indeed, we declared war on America and Britain out of our sincere desire to ensure Japan's self-preservation and the stabilization of East Asia, it being far from our thought either to infringe upon the sovereignty of other nations or to embark upon territorial aggrandizement.

But now the war has lasted for nearly four years. Despite the best that has been done by everyone – the gallant fighting of the military and naval forces, the diligence and assiduity of our servants of the State and the devoted service of our one hundred million people – the war situation has developed not necessarily to Japan's advantage, while the general trends of the world have all turned against her interest . . . .

We are keenly aware of the inmost feelings of all you, our subjects. However, it is according to the dictates of the time and fate that we have resolved to pave the way for a grand peace for all the generations to come by enduring the unendurable and suffering what is insufferable. Having been able to save and maintain the structure of the Imperial State, we are always with you, our good and loyal subjects, relying upon your sincerity and integrity.[2]

The instrument of surrender was signed on 2 September 1945 by representatives of the Japanese government, General Mac-Arthur as supreme commander, allied powers, and representatives of nine of the allies. Japan undertook to carry out the Potsdam declaration, and surrendered unconditionally. Shortly afterwards the emperor issued a proclamation in which he accepted the instrument of surrender himself and commanded his people to do likewise. In this way the counsel of the emperor and the political sense of the United States and its allies brought about the surrender of a country where patriotism was a religion, and which had not previously experienced defeat. The transition from war to occupation was thus achieved with a minimum of suffering and conflict – a pattern which was to continue during the occupation period.

While the arrangements for the formal surrender of Japan were going forward, the United States had proposed to its allies the setting up of a Far Eastern Advisory Commission, consisting of the ten nations which had been at war with Japan. As its title suggested it was to be advisory only; and as such it was unacceptable to the British, as well as to the Australians and New Zealanders, although Russia and China were ready to agree. The following month a modified proposal won the

[2] RIIA, *Survey: The Far East, 1942–6*, p. 497.

acceptance of the British, but lost that of the Russians. Only at the foreign ministers' conference of December 1945 was an agreeable formula arrived at. This was for the setting up of a Far Eastern Commission, sitting in Washington, composed of eleven nations with Far Eastern interests (the United States, the Soviet Union, Australia, New Zealand, Canada, India, Britain, France, the Netherlands, China, and the Philippines). The functions of the Commission were to 'formulate the policies, principles, and standards in conformity with which the fulfilment by Japan of its obligations under the Terms of Surrender may be accomplished'.[3] It was excluded from making recommendations with regard to the conduct of military operations or territorial adjustments; and in practice its powers were more seriously limited by the procedure laid down for it to follow. An affirmative vote in the Commission required a majority, including the votes of the four major powers, Britain, the United States, the Soviet Union, and China. Moreover the United States government could issue interim directives to the supreme commander. The combination of these two provisions obviously made it easy for the United States and the supreme commander to act independently of the Commission when the Commission itself was not agreed on the American point of view. It is not surprising that the Commission soon lapsed into a body of negligible importance.

It was to be accompanied by an Allied Council sitting in Tokyo, consisting of the supreme commander, as American member and also chairman, a Soviet and a Chinese member, and another member representing jointly the United Kingdom, Australia, New Zealand, and India. This Council, however, was also to be advisory. The supreme commander was to 'consult and advise with the Council in advance of the issuance of orders on matters of substance, the exigencies of the situation permitting. His decisions on these matters shall be controlling'. The only limitation placed on his action was on questions 'concerning a change in the regime of control, fundamental changes in the Japanese constitutional structure, and a change in the Japanese Government as a whole'.[4]

Similarly, although the United States government in 1945 was willing and eager to share the burden of occupation with its allies, its invitation to them to do so assumed that their

³ Ibid. p. 529.   ⁴ Ibid. p. 531.

forces would be under General MacArthur's command. This the Soviet Union refused to accept, and their refusal meant, in practice, that they took no part in the occupation. The Chinese were in no position to offer troops, and it was therefore left to the British Commonwealth to share in the occupation, under an agreement reached in January 1946. A corps of Australian, New Zealand, and British-Indian troops, with naval and air force units, garrisoned a small area of Japan under the command of an Australian general, subordinate to MacArthur. Their function was solely that of an occupation force, and they took no part in military government, which rested with the Americans.

Meanwhile the occupation had since the surrender been under the direction of MacArthur, who was responsible only to the American government. The policy of this government was moreover made clear in an initial statement approved by the president and distributed to the supreme commander and appropriate United States agencies. It stated:

Although every effort will be made, by consultation and by constitution of appropriate advisory bodies, to establish policies for the conduct of the occupation and control of Japan which will satisfy the principal Allied powers, in the event of any differences of opinion among them, the policies of the United States will govern.[5]

Even when the Commission and the Council came into existence, any supreme commander would have found great power and discretion resting in his own hands, and this was the more so as a result of the character of MacArthur and the relationship which he and his command had established with the Japanese. As has been said, 'MacArthur revealed himself as that rare figure, the American version of the traditional British grandee.'[6] Yet paradoxically the supreme commander and his command – which became the more difficult to distinguish when both were referred to indifferently as SCAP – were genuinely concerned to bring about the establishment of democratic government in Japan. Fortunately their directives and their reforms had a more enduring effect on Japanese political life than the example of aloof remoteness which the supreme commander set. That this was so can obviously only be explained by the fact that SCAP succeeded in releasing a

[5] Ibid. p. 501.   [6] G. R. Storry, *A History of Modern Japan* (1962), p. 240.

7

pent-up desire for reform amongst many sections of Japanese society; and that whatever its shortcomings its basic integrity and overall efficiency evoked the admiration of the Japanese, at least in the first year and a half of the occupation.

In some respects the initial tasks of the occupation were similar to those in Germany. National leaders were tried before an International Military Tribunal between 1946 and 1948. They were sentenced variously to death or terms of imprisonment up to life; although with some dissent from the French and Dutch members of the tribunal, and a recommendation from the Indian representative that all be acquitted, as war was not a crime in international law. This was accompanied by trials of 'minor' war criminals charged with cruelty towards prisoners and natives of occupied countries, and by a series of purges from local and national office, conducted by SCAP, of all those held responsible for supporting aggression. As the definition of this class was very wide it was inevitable that a very large number of persons (about 200,000) should be affected; and equally inevitable that they should return to public life, as they did, when the first severities of the occupation had passed.

The punishment and purging of individuals was accompanied by institutional reform designed to ensure 'that Japan will not again become a menace to the peace and security of the world' and 'to bring about the eventual establishment of a peaceful and responsible government'. A new constitution was devised by SCAP, more democratic than that which the Japanese government proposed itself, and the mystical authority of the emperor transmuted into the utilitarian functions of a constitutional monarch. The constitution also included a unique dedication to pacifism, which with the rapid changes of the next few years was to become an embarrassment to the Americans and a focus of political debate within Japan. This was in Chapter II of the constitution, consisting solely of Article 9, which read:

> Aspiring sincerely to an international peace based on justice and order, the Japanese people forever renounce war as a sovereign right of the nation and the threat or use of force as means of settling international disputes.
>
> In order to accomplish the aim of the preceding paragraph, land, sea, and air forces, as well as other war potential, will never be

maintained. The right of belligerency of the state will not be recognized.[7]

Political democratization was accompanied by land reform; its effect was enhanced by the inflation which enabled debtors to free themselves more easily. A serious attempt was made to break up the large family industries, to which were attributed a large share of responsibility for the promotion of aggressive policies, and the organization of trade unions was allowed and encouraged. The latter measure, coupled with the release of political prisoners, made it possible for the Communist party to reorganize itself and exercise some influence. But the equally rapid organization of social democratic forces left no vacuum for it to fill; it was hampered by the decisiveness of SCAP in controlling strikes, and the fact that this was not generally resented by the Japanese; and it was further handicapped by divided leadership and by obvious direction from Moscow.

As in Germany, some decision was called for with regard to reparations. United States policy on reparations, as shown in the Potsdam agreement and its own policy statement, was that Japanese industry should be kept at a level sufficient to sustain the Japanese economy and make reparations payments, which were thought desirable to assist the victims of Japanese aggression in the task of reconstruction. Such payments were to be made in part by the transfer of Japanese property abroad; although, in the event, the biggest collection of such property, in Manchuria, was taken over by the Russians as 'war booty' which should not, they asserted, be included in their share of reparations. Transfers from Japan itself depended on a decision as to the appropriate level of industry to which Japan should be reduced. This the Far Eastern Commission fixed at the level prevailing in 1930–4; but as the actual level of production in 1946–7 rose only from 30 to 40 per cent of the 1930–4 level, this decision was of no great importance. Although plans for transfers, especially from army and navy arsenals and synthetic rubber plants, were made, no transfers actually took place before the end of 1947.

By that time the initial period of occupation was coming to an end. It was indeed the opinion of MacArthur that the time had come when a peace treaty should be signed and the

[7] RIIA, *Far East*, pp. 547–8.

occupation terminated. Consequently, in July 1947, the United States government proposed to the other ten members of the Far Eastern Commission that a conference be held, consisting of members of the Commission, to discuss terms of a peace treaty. The proposal came to nothing, however, because both the Russian and the Chinese governments rejected a proposal which would deprive them of a veto in the peace settlement. Then, as the cold war sharpened in intensity in Europe and the communists advanced in China, the United States decided not to press for a treaty which might make it more difficult for it to maintain its troops in Japan and influence its policies.

But although the occupation lasted its character changed. The guiding principles of the first years had been retribution and reform, that of the subsequent period was reconstruction. Japanese trade had been severely hampered by the disruption caused by war and defeat; and production was hindered by the continuing uncertainty over reparations payments. This meant a drain on United States funds amounting in 1947 to $400 million to cover Japan's adverse balance of trade; and it ran counter to the whole American policy of promoting industrial prosperity as a safeguard against the spread of communism. As a result, reparations were dropped, the dissolution of the large family combines was left unfinished, private international trade was encouraged, and measures of wage and price stability were introduced by the government on the advice of SCAP. Recovery began to take shape, and as China was lost to the communists, the United States inevitably came to regard a predominantly conservative and relatively stable Japan as a substitute for the peace-loving great power which Roosevelt had hoped for in China. All these developments – economic recovery and political independence as an ally of the United States, as well as rearmament – received their strongest impulse from the great accelerative force of 1950: the Korean war. Before going on to this later period we must, however, survey the course of events which brought the communists to power in China.

At the Yalta conference in February 1945 the United States had reached an agreement with the Soviet Union, approved by the British, which gave the Soviet Union substantial advantages in the Far East. The agreement was to have the concurrence of Chiang Kai-shek, and Roosevelt undertook to see that this was forthcoming. In July direct negotiations were opened between the Chinese and Russian governments, which terminated in an agreement on 14 August 1945, substantially confirming that of Yalta. The Soviet Union secured its interpretation of the Yalta accord as it affected Outer Mongolia, thereby retaining its virtual control over that country. Russia regained a decisive share in the running of the Chinese Eastern and South Manchurian Railways; however, the security of the railways now became a Chinese responsibility, and did not rest with the Russians, as had been the case before the Japanese took over ownership. This gave the Russians an important economic interest in Manchuria, particularly since the railways operated a variety of subsidiary enterprises such as coal mines and forest enterprises, a large part of which, under the terms of the agreement, came under joint Russo-Chinese management. The military port of Port Arthur was to be shared by the Russians and the Chinese, and controlled by a commission in which the Russians had three representatives and the Chinese two; while the adjacent commercial port of Dairen was to be a free port, in which Russian interests would be preserved by the leasing of docks and warehouses.

The motives of the United States government in signing the Yalta agreement and supporting the Sino-Soviet agreement can easily be surmised. Within the American administration different evaluations were made of Russian intentions in the Far East as well as of the desirability of the Russian participation in the war. In the period between the Yalta agreement and the Sino-Soviet agreement these evaluations had changed. Russian participation in the war attained a brief moment of actuality as Japan sought an armistice and as events in Europe evoked growing suspicion of the Soviet Union. In the same period Truman had replaced Roosevelt as president. In spite of these differences and developments we may assume, however, that the American presidents and their administrations were in part convinced of the justice of the Russian case, and in part impressed by the *force majeure* which Russia could bring to bear if no agreement was reached. In these circumstances, the counterpart to the concessions they made was that Russia accepted and recognized the Nationalist government of China. This was counted a substantial gain. Recognition of the

Nationalist government was made more explicit in an exchange of notes relative to the Sino-Soviet treaty against renewed Japanese aggression, in which the Soviet government undertook moral support and military aid 'to be entirely given to the National Government as the central government of China'. There can be no doubt that these considerations weighed equally strongly with the government of China, which was even more aware of the pressure which the Soviet government could exercise once its troops had entered Manchuria at the end of the Far Eastern war.

The motives of Russian policy are always more difficult to establish with any degree of certainty; but the broad outlines of that policy are clear. The Soviet Union was in a strong position in the Far East, both as a great power with traditional interests in the area, and as a communist country. In the arena of great power politics its major enemy, its victorious adversary of 1905, was now defeated and prostrate. On the ideological plane, it could if it wished look to an ally of growing strength in the Chinese Communist party, mobilized as a military force, brilliantly led, and exercising actual control over a substantial part of Chinese territory.

It was open to Stalin to press his advantage in both these spheres of conflict; but he appears to have given predominant importance to Russia's interests as a great power. We may assume that George Kennan made an accurate assessment of Soviet aims when he telegraphed to Washington on 23 April 1945:

Actually I am persuaded that in the future Soviet policy respecting China will continue what it has been in the recent past: a fluid resilient policy directed at the achievement of maximum power with minimum responsibility on portions of the Asiatic continent lying beyond the Soviet border. This will involve the exertion of pressure on various areas in direct proportion to their strategic importance and their proximity to the Soviet frontier. I am sure that within the framework of this policy Moscow will aim specifically at : (1) Reacquiring in substance, if not in form, all the diplomatic and territorial assets previously possessed on the mainland of Asia by Russia under the Czars. (2) Domination of the provinces of China in central Asia contiguous to the Soviet frontier. Such action is dictated by the strategic necessity of protecting in depth the industrial core of the USSR. (3) Acquiring sufficient control in all areas of north China now dominated by the Japanese to prevent other foreign powers from repeating the Japanese incursion. This means, to the Russian mind, the maximum possible exclusion of penetration in that area by outside powers including America and Britain.[8]

Whatever the accuracy of Kennan's analysis, Stalin regained almost intact the position which Russia had held under the tsars. The careful provision which had been made for Chinese participation in the administration of Dairen and Port Arthur was nugatory. There, as in Manchuria, the Russian army and administration ruled unfettered. Whether Stalin nurtured long-term plans for the establishment of Russian dominance must remain uncertain. In the short run he secured an immediate economic advantage for the Soviet Union by removing Japanese industrial equipment as 'war booty', and laid the basis for the subsequent development of economic interests. Russian troops both safeguarded and concealed from the world the depredation of Manchuria.

At the same time Russian occupation of Manchuria prevented the deployment of Chinese Nationalist forces, and thereby made it easier for the communists to take over when the Russians withdrew in 1946. Apart from this, Stalin did nothing to help the Chinese communists take power. He did not apparently consider them strong enough to win in a conflict with the Nationalists at this time. Neither did the communists suppose that victory was attainable in the near future, but this did not modify their actions, since they were a revolutionary organization striving for power, however distant their objective might appear. Whether Stalin would have acted differently had he believed in the imminent victory of the Chinese communists is unknown and unknowable. It would be in keeping with his attitude to foreign communists to view with alarm the emergence of so strong a rival as an independent Chinese communist government. As things were, it was certainly consistent with Stalinist policies in the rest of the world that no encouragement, far less material assistance, should be given to the Chinese communists to take power. Stalin's policies always had a monolithic character, and for general reasons of foreign policy communist parties all over the world were pursuing a policy of restraint and co-operation, under his direction, at this time.

[8] US State Dept, *United States Relations with China* (1949), p. 97.

It was not in Stalin's character to take risks in foreign policy, and he may well have calculated that it was dangerous for Russia to be involved in the Chinese civil war, quite apart from the risk that this might bring about a similar intervention on the part of the United States.

If Stalin did not think the communists strong enough to take power, no more did the American government think that the Kuomintang was strong enough to secure military victory over the communists, or that this would be a wise policy to pursue. A decision of this sort inevitably depended greatly on the judgement of men on the spot; and such men were by no means unanimous in the advice they gave. Already in 1944 Roosevelt had sent General Hurley to China to bring about agreement between the Kuomintang and the Chinese communists. He failed to do so, and felt that he was constantly undermined by American officials whose evaluation of the rival forces in China favoured the communists by exaggerating their independence from Moscow and supposing that their interests and those of the United States might coincide.

As we have seen, the American government at this stage hoped that the Chinese communists would follow the Russian lead and that Russian recognition of the Nationalist government would encourage the communists to join a coalition with the Nationalists. At the same time the supreme commander, General MacArthur, endeavoured to strengthen the position of the Nationalists by ordering, in his first General Order, that the surrender of Japanese troops in China be made to Nationalist commanders alone (except in Manchuria, where the surrender was to be made to the Russians). In practice, however, the Nationalists did not control large areas of northern China where the surrender was to be made, and the American government had therefore to decide on the extent to which it would intervene to assist the Nationalist government to take advantage of the opportunity offered by MacArthur's order. In this situation it was decided to furnish air and sea transport for the movement north of Nationalist troops, and also to land some 50,000 United States marines in north China to assist the Nationalists in keeping control and in supervising the surrender and repatriation of the Japanese. The Nationalists thereby secured a great advantage, since they were able to occupy key points such as Shanghai, Nanking, and Peiping.

Even so the communists in the interior greatly extended the area under their control, and succeeded in capturing large amounts of Japanese material, and there is no reason why they should have hesitated to fill the vacuum left by the Japanese if they had not been forestalled by the Nationalists and Americans.

But it remained the desire and intention of the Truman administration to secure agreement between the Kuomintang and the communists. General Hurley was too discouraged and disillusioned to be willing to return to China, and Truman therefore sent instead General George Marshall as his personal representative. At this time the United States sought to avoid a situation where its own troops would be drawn into conflict; United States marines were there to supervise the surrender, and 'incidental effects of US assistance upon dissident Chinese elements will be avoided in so far as is possible'. It was thought that the interests of the Nationalist government and the United States could best be served by a cessation of hostilities, followed by a national conference of representatives of the major political elements. In this way a genuinely representative government could be formed, and autonomous armies eliminated.

Subsequently the Truman administration was charged with having been soft towards the communists, and allowing China to fall to them by default, by misunderstanding the true nature of Chinese communism – misunderstanding which was fostered by communists and fellow-travellers in the State Department and the Foreign Service. In fact this was not the case. It is true that some members of the Foreign Service were excessively optimistic about the policies which might be adopted by the communists, just as in Britain many people accepted Lord Lindsay's view of them as 'agrarian reformers'. But neither Roosevelt nor Truman shared this judgement. In the early years after the war Truman underestimated the possible time in which the communists could take power in China – as did the Russians and the Chinese communists themselves. Moreover he had no great respect for the Kuomintang, whose reputation did not stand high in any respect, whether with regard to political freedom, efficient government, or military organization. The best hope for a stable democratic China seemed, therefore, to be first in the achievement of peace, then in reconstruction and economic progress, which would weaken the communists or at least keep them out of power. In Europe such a programme proved successful, and the coalition governments of France and Italy proved able at first to contain the communists, then to govern without them.

Such reasoning did not commend itself to Chiang Kai-shek and the Kuomintang. Chiang was no doubt right in his profound suspicion of the communists; but he appears to have made two serious miscalculations. One was to exaggerate his own strength; the other was to suppose that, although the Americans wanted to avoid a conflict, they would not fail to support him if such a conflict did in fact occur. In contrast, the communists at first seem to have favoured a political agreement. Truman reported that it was Marshall's impression that 'the Communists were more ready to take their chances in a struggle conducted in the political arena than were the Nationalists'.[9] But as time passed their military strength increased relative to the Nationalists, as Russian connivance increased their supplies of captured Japanese arms and the Nationalists involved themselves in ill-conceived adventures. The more the military balance turned in their favour, the less attractive did a political agreement appear.

The result was that in the long run General Marshall achieved no greater success than Hurley had done. A temporary settlement was arranged in the first two months of his mission. An agreement signed on 10 January 1946 provided for the cessation of hostilities, movement of government troops into Manchuria, and a political consultative conference which immediately set about making plans for reconstitution of the government. A military executive headquarters was set up headed by one communist, one Nationalist, and one American, and truce teams similarly composed were established to supervise the truce in the field.

This was an auspicious start, but it foundered when put into practice, especially in Manchuria. Relations between the Soviet government and that of Chiang Kai-shek had deteriorated rapidly since the surrender of Japan, as a result of Soviet action in Manchuria. In the absence of Nationalist troops to take over from the Japanese, the Russians had made it easy for the communists to do so, and to appropriate Japanese arms

[9] *Memoirs*, ii. 73.

left behind. When Nationalist troops did come north the Soviet troops would not allow them to land at the port of Dairen, on the grounds that it was a commercial port, so that they had to fight their way in past the communists. The conflict had wider repercussions in the growing tension between the United States and the Soviet Union in the Far East. An attempt was made to reduce this tension at the foreign ministers' conference in December 1945, when machinery to supervise the occupation of Japan was set up; but the agreement on Japan was little more than a reaffirmation on the part of the Soviet Union of its support for a national government. It was therefore of little comfort to Chiang Kai-shek, who remained convinced that the Russians were assisting the communists to take control of Manchuria.

In these circumstances it is not surprising that the truce arrangements made in January broke down when the attempt was made to apply them to Manchuria. Fundamentally there was no chance of a truce while either side thought that some substantial gain could be made by military action. When in April the Soviet troops at last left Manchuria – very rapidly once they began to withdraw – the advantages open to the communists were even greater if they could move in as the Russians moved out. This they did, and fighting intensified, particularly round Changchun, between communist and Nationalist troops who had moved north to prevent the loss of Manchuria to the government. Once more, in June, Marshall managed to negotiate a temporary truce; but it lasted only three months before hostilities broke out again. By this time Marshall despaired of the possibility of success of his mission, although he remained in China for the rest of the year, returning to Washington in January 1947 to replace Byrnes as secretary of state.

This meant that the United States government accepted the fact that civil war was continuing in China, and it had to face in an ever more pressing form the question of whether to extend substantial aid to one side in that conflict. This question had already provoked debate in the United States and called forth vigorous attacks from the Chinese communists and the Soviet government during 1946. The United States had supplied the Chinese Nationalist government during the war, and these supplies had not come to an end with Japanese surrender. Nor at that time was there any reason why they should, since the Nationalists were recognized as the government of China, and it was the intention of the American government to promote stability in China. The continuance of aid on this basis depended, however, on the success of Marshall's mission, for unless political agreement were reached between the two sides in China, American supplies would go, not to a united government, but to one side in a civil war – a war in which the Americans were at the same time trying ineffectively to act as mediators. Obviously there was a case for continuing aid on this basis, namely to assist Chiang Kai-shek defeat the communists; but this would be quite different from the earlier intentions of the American government.

Meanwhile the Chinese government continued to receive aid, directly and indirectly, from the United States. Supplies were sent by UNRRA and loans made by the Export-Import Bank: the United States made possible the purchase on credit of Lease-Lend equipment contracted for but not delivered during the war, and for the purchase of ancillary military supplies, but not including munitions. By limiting its aid in this way the administration kept to its policy of restraint on Chiang Kai-shek. It was attacked on the one hand by those who argued that it prejudiced Marshall's work of mediation and on the other by those who wanted full-scale support to the Nationalists. Meanwhile the remnants of American troops remained in China, and gave added substance to the propaganda attacks which the communists made against the Americans.

As the possibilities of truce disappeared at the end of 1946 the reaction of the American government was to withdraw farther from China, by evacuating the remaining troops, now numbering about 12,000 and reducing aid to a minimum, but in the spring and summer of 1947 this was the opposite course to that followed in Europe, where the Truman doctrine and the Marshall plan were greatly adding to American commitments. It was inevitable that those sections of opinion in the country and in Congress which were most favourable to the Chinese Nationalists, and which did not share the critical pessimism with which the administration viewed Chiang Kai-shek, should now demand the extension of the Truman doctrine to China. Instead the president sent a fresh representative to China, not this time to mediate but to advise on possibilities of action. This time his representative was General Wedemeyer, who had served in China during the war, and who now returned there in July 1947 for a stay of a month. He was sharply critical of the Kuomintang, and disappointed them by the uninhibited way in which he offered his criticisms to them. On his return to Washington he neverthelesss advised the administration to provide financial, material, and advisory aid to the Chinese government in return for commitments from China to implement reforms, but his report was not published at the time; nor was it acted upon. In February 1948 the administration did introduce a China Aid Bill into Congress, in part to assist the Nationalist government to meet its most pressing financial and economic problems, but also to meet the mounting demands of what came to be known as the 'China lobby' in Washington. Nevertheless the president and the secretary of state remained profoundly sceptical of the capabilities of the Kuomintang, and were impressed by the way in which their corruption and inefficiency persuaded non-Marxists to join the communist ranks. Moreover the administration felt itself forced to make a choice, as its predecessors had done before and during the war, between Europe and the Far East. Neither Truman nor Marshall hesitated in opting for Europe. As Marshall said:

We cannot afford, economically or militarily, to take over the continued failures of the present Chinese Government to the dissipation of our strength in more vital regions where we now have a reasonable opportunity of successfully meeting or thwarting the Communist threat, that is, in the vital industrial areas of Western Europe with its traditions of free institutions.[10]

In the autumn of 1948 the Kuomintang armies suffered their most decisive defeat, as a result of which they forfeited control of the whole of Manchuria and lost some 300,000 of their best troops. It was now for the first time that the communists realized that victory was imminent, and that in the immediate future they would constitute the government. In January 1949 the Nationalist government appealed to the four powers – Britain, France, the United States, and Russia – to act as mediators between itself and the communists; but each in turn declined. The United States government was under increasingly strong

[10] *US Relations with China*, p. 383.

pressure to assist the Nationalists, but it held firm to its insistence that the large-scale military and economic aid given already had availed little, and that more aid now would avail even less. In China Chiang Kai-shek resigned formally and temporarily from the presidency in January in an abortive attempt to negotiate. But the Nationalist position continued to crumble. On 1 October the communists announced their victory by proclaiming the People's Republic of China. Six weeks later the Nationalist government moved to Formosa.

This brought to a head the question which Britain and the United States had been discussing for some months: that of recognition of a Chinese communist government should it come into existence. Once the question became actual it produced a division between the two governments. Their interests were different, in that British trade and the position of Hong Kong meant that recognition would bring advantages to Britain. Moreover it was generally accepted in Britain, by government, opposition, and public, that recognition should follow on the facts of the situation, without implying approval or disapproval of the régime that had come into existence; while in the United States the increasingly vocal forces which had demanded aid to the Nationalists rendered impolitic any swift recognition of the government that had replaced them. Not only had the British generally been as critical of the Nationalists as the American administration, but their contacts with Chiang Kai-shek had been more remote, and British shipping had suffered from the Nationalists more directly than from the communists. There was a further important factor determining the British attitude, and that was the urgency which the Indian government attached to recognition, in the belief that this would lead to good relations between the two countries and strengthen Chinese independence of Russia. On 30 December the Indian government announced its recognition of the new Chinese government, and it was followed by Pakistan. On 5 January the British government took the same step, as did Ceylon and Norway, and they were followed within two weeks by Denmark, Israel, Finland, Afghanistan, Sweden, and Switzerland.

The hopes which were attached to recognition in Britain were not realized. The Chinese government then proposed opening negotiations for the establishment of diplomatic representation. This the British had supposed would follow automatically; in fact it became the subject of increasingly difficult argument, in which the Chinese government reproached the British for their continuing *de facto* recognition of Nationalist rule in Formosa, for their failure to support the communists' claim to China's seat in the Security Council, and for their failure to hand over Chinese aircraft flown to Hong Kong. This was an argument which made recognition seem even less attractive to the United States government, whose initial reaction of suspended judgement was to harden through the spring of 1950. Meanwhile the French government refused recognition because of the Chinese communists' recognition of Ho Chi Minh's government in Indo-China and the efforts of Trygve Lie to change this attitude fell short of success when the outbreak of the Korean war postponed French recognition until 1964.

Recognition or non-recognition of the new government was of more than formal importance. Not only did it raise questions of prestige, but recognition would normally be accompanied by the exchange of diplomatic missions and the consequent establishment of centres of Chinese communist influence. Even so, the question of recognition was irrelevant to the actual achievement of the communists in establishing their control over the whole of China. They succeeded where the Nationalists had failed in bringing about the unity of China. First by military victory, then by the development of a peculiarly Chinese form of totalitarian control they brought the whole of the mainland under a single political authority which was quickly anchored into every city and village. They added to the aggregate strength of the communist world while opening up fresh possibilities of conflict and division within it. They restored China as a potentially great power of first-class importance.

But the actual boundaries of China remained a matter of dispute and disagreement in the world. This became evident in the year after the communist victory as Chinese armies advanced into Tibet. They did so claiming that Tibet was an integral part of China. Their claim was resisted by the Tibetan government, and by the Indian government, which supported it. An earlier Chinese revolution, that which overthrew the Manchu dynasty in 1911, had in fact enabled the Tibetans to establish their independence of China. In the inter-war years the Nationalists had sought to reimpose Chinese authority, but had been too preoccupied, both with the war against Japan and with their own civil war, to do so effectively. The British government meanwhile continued to accept Chinese claims to suzerainty (as late as August 1943) provided it was coupled with Tibetan autonomy.

Within Tibet both spiritual and temporal authority was exercised by the Dalai Lama. Unfortunately his spiritual authority was rivalled by that of the Panchen Lama, and in 1944 the Chinese Nationalists had discovered the latest rein-carnation of the Panchen Lama in northern China. Five years later the support which they gave to this young boy's claims was taken over by the communists, with the result that as soon as the Dalai Lama (who himself was only 14 in 1949) was freed from the pretensions of the Chinese Nationalists, he was faced with a challenge which he was unable to resist. The Chinese now set up a provisional government of Tibet in the Chinghai province of China in February 1950 and this was followed by the Chinese invasion of Tibet in October 1950.

Outside the fastnesses of the Himalayas there was compara-tively little reaction to these important developments. In the west the question of Tibet was of less importance than that of Korea. There were some doubts about the justice of Chinese claims of suzerainty over Tibet, and there was no possibility of safeguarding Tibetan independence by intervention. A Tibetan appeal to the United Nations was buried in a resolution of the General Committee to postpone the matter *sine die*. The Indian government deplored Chinese action and strongly criticized the use of force; but it had not questioned Chinese suzerainty and had no intention of using force to resist force.

Chinese forces did none the less meet a formidable obstacle in the climate, the altitude, and the terrain in which they were operating. Moreover the Chinese government too now had to meet the more pressing demands of the war in Korea. As a result a compromise agreement was reached in 1951 between Tibetan representatives and the Chinese government. While this placed Tibetan foreign relations under the authority of the Chinese government, it left Tibetan civil society intact for the time being. The Dalai Lama and the Panchen Lama each retained his respective authority and dignity, and the monasteries kept their independence. On the other hand a Sino-Tibetan commission was set up to supervise the agreement, and the Chinese government soon used the advantage they had gained to achieve a full military domination of Tibet. As we shall see, this led in a few years to revolt in Tibet and conflict with India.

At least as important for the future was the question of the island territory of Formosa (Taiwan), to which Chiang Kai-shek and his Nationalist government had retreated. China's allies during the war regarded Formosa as an essential part of China, and at the Cairo conference of November 1943 had agreed that 'Manchuria, Formosa and the Pescadores should be restored to the Republic of China'. The Chinese communists saw no reason to reinterpret this declaration now that they governed the mainland of China, and prepared a fleet for the invasion of Formosa.

Nor did American foreign policy immediately spring to the defence of Formosa. On 31 December 1949 it was reported that Truman and the National Security Council had agreed that the strategic importance of Formosa was not sufficient to justify the risk of 'another Spanish situation', with the Soviet Union giving support to the Chinese communists. On 12 January 1950 Acheson spoke to the National Press Club at a luncheon in New York, and gave a careful definition of the United States own defensive perimeter, which excluded both Formosa and South Korea. He asserted that the Soviet Union was 'detaching' territory from China and 'attaching' it to the Soviet Union – a process that was 'complete in Outer Mongolia, nearly complete in Manchuria, progressing swiftly in Inner Mongolia and Sinkiang'. Soviet action was likely therefore to draw Chinese anger, and the United States would be foolish to take any action which would divert that anger to itself.

Turning to the defensive policies of the United States, Acheson confirmed that the defensive perimeter running from the Ryukyu islands and the Aleutians to the Philippines would continue to be held. Elsewhere the United States would only be able to help when the conditions were ripe for help to be effective – as (he argued) they had not been in China, where the defeat of the Nationalist government was due to its failure to provide a positive policy for the Chinese people, to inspire their loyalty and leadership, and to do something about their basic needs. Should an attack occur outside the defensive perimeter of the United States therefore:

initial reliance must be on the people attacked to resist it and then upon the commitments of the entire civilized world under the Charter of the United Nations which so far has not proved a weak reed to lean on by any people who are determined to protect their independence against outside aggression.[11]

The administration's policy was vigorously attacked by a group of Republican Senators who came to be known as the 'China lobby' – Bridges of New Hampshire, Knowland of California, and Brewster of Maine. They fought a bitter battle on the floor of the Senate and forced Connally (as chairman) to invite the military commanders to appear before the Foreign Relations Committee. A bill giving aid to South Korea was narrowly defeated in the House, because it did not provide for aid to Formosa as well. Fear and frenzy intruded into the debate; for on 21 January Alger Hiss, a former assistant to the assistant secretary of state, was found guilty of perjury at the end of a long judicial process that had started in December 1948; while in England Klaus Fuchs, a scientist who had been at the centre of British nuclear research, was arrested and convicted of spying for the Russians. Responding to the news of the conviction of Hiss, Acheson said: 'I do not intend to turn my back on Alger Hiss'; and thereby offered himself as a target for the venom which fear of communist infiltration generated.

In the next few months, however, the administration's policy began quickly to change in reaction to Chinese moves. The Sino-Soviet alliance of February 1950 tied China to the power which the United States had recently confronted in Europe in the Berlin blockade. Malik, the Soviet representative at the United Nations, had already walked out of the Security Council on 10 January, in protest against its refusal to exclude the Chinese Nationalist representative. The Chinese communists denounced 'America's aggressive policy', seized United States consular offices, and laid claim not only to Formosa but to the Ryukyu islands, which the United States occupied as a United Nations trust territory following the Japanese defeat. Tension between the United States and China grew accordingly.

[11] RIIA, *Documents, 1949–50*, pp. 103–4.

Even so it seems possible that had the Chinese communists been free to play their cards with sufficient care – and had shown the skill to do so – they could have achieved the conquest of Formosa without American intervention. This possibility disappeared in June 1950 when North Korean troops invaded southwards, and Truman ordered the Seventh Fleet to the Formosa straits.

Meanwhile the Soviet government had experienced no difficulties comparable to those of the western powers over the question of the recognition of communist China. Stalin had not rushed to act on the assumption of communist victory: but when the People's Republic was proclaimed the Soviet bloc gave immediate recognition, on 2 October 1949.

It was to be expected that the relations between the two largest communist powers would go beyond formal recognition, and this proved to be the case. On 14 February 1950 a new Sino-Soviet treaty of friendship, alliance, and mutual assistance was signed in Moscow, together with an agreement on the Chinese Changchun Railway and another providing Russian long-term credits to China. The new treaty was designed to prevent a repetition of aggression on the part not only of Japan, but 'of any other state which should unite in any form with Japan in acts of aggression'. To this end the treaty included a formal military alliance, expressed thus:

> In the event of one of the High Contracting Parties being attacked by Japan or States allied with it, and thus being involved in a state of war, the other High Contracting Party will immediately render military and other assistance with all the means at its disposal.

At the same time the two powers agreed not to conclude a separate peace with Japan, but to 'strive for the earliest conclusion of a peace treaty with Japan, jointly with the other Powers which were allies during the Second World War'.[12]

The most striking departure in the new agreements, however, referred to the concessions which had been made to the Soviet Union in Manchuria. Here the Soviet Union renounced its rights over the Manchurian Railways and Port Arthur, although the agreement was not to take effect until 1952 or the conclusion of a peace treaty with Japan, whichever was earlier. The position at Dairen was left for review after the

[12] Ibid. p. 542.

peace treaty, but the property on lease to the Soviet Union was to return to China by the end of 1950. Further, under a third agreement the Soviet Union extended credits to China, although the amount agreed – $300 million – was comparatively small compared to the credits which had been extended to Russia's European satellites (for example, $450 million to Poland).

The signature of these agreements gave rise to considerable speculation in the non-communist world. It appeared to belie Acheson's references to the attempt of the Soviet Union to 'detach' Chinese territory; but it was reported in addition that the Soviet government had pressed China for the use of seven of its northern ports, and for a large Chinese labour force to work in Siberia. It was noted that Mao Tse-tung had been in Moscow since 16 December, and that representatives of Sinkiang had been invited in the course of his visit; and it was concluded that Mao had been resisting adamantly the more extravagant Soviet demands. Again, the publication of the agreement seemed to belie this argument, and the preamble to the agreement on the Changchun Railway outlined the changes which had come about in China, making possible friendship and co-operation with Russia.

The facts are not yet available to provide the answer to contemporary speculation of this sort; but it is evident that the relations between Russia and China were not as smooth as the phraseology of the agreement would suggest. The Chinese communists only decided to sign an agreement with the Soviet Union after long discussion and debate. Stalin was far from treating Mao Tse-tung as an equal or giving him the eminence in Moscow which he felt he deserved. The credits extended to China were far from generous – and were loans not grants; while advice by Russian technicians contained the seeds of future conflict.

In the spring of 1950, however, it appeared that Sino-Soviet relations were growing steadily closer. Further agreements were signed at the end of March, providing for the establishment of Sino-Soviet joint-stock companies for the exploitation of oil and non-ferrous metals in Hsinchiang, and for the setting up of a Sino-Soviet aviation company. The Soviet Union gave diplomatic support to China, and after his initial walk-out on 10 January 1950, Malik announced that he would not participate in the work of the Security Council until the Kuomintang delegate had been replaced. The Soviet delegates thereupon withdrew from all United Nations bodies of which China was a member. It was in this way that when the outbreak of the Korean war brought the hasty summoning of the Security Council, the Russian delegate was absent.

Before the outbreak of war in 1939 nearly the whole of South and South East Asia had been under colonial rule. The war rendered the reimposition of this rule impossible, at least in its earlier form. The European powers and the United States had suffered defeat and had been expelled from the greater part of their possessions by the Japanese, so that they had failed in their first claim of providing peace and protection. Of all South East Asian countries Thailand, an independent state, had suffered least. Moreover the Japanese had given nominal independence to the countries they had occupied, and in many areas local administration had been left in the hands of the Asian population, while the Europeans were interned. The Asians were therefore not convinced by arguments that they were unable to rule themselves.

In consequence movements for national independence acquired much greater strength and self-confidence than they had ever had before. In some countries they acquired two further assets of great value: they had the organization and the armament of resistance units at their disposal; and in Indo-China and Indonesia they were able to form governments exercising at least elementary control of the country in the hiatus between the surrender of the Japanese and the arrival of the Europeans.

In these circumstances the continent of India, Burma, Ceylon, and the Philippines achieved their independence in agreement with their former rulers. For the first three a decisive change had been made when the Labour party was successful in the British general election of 1945. The Labour party had constantly pressed for greater concessions to Indian self government while they had been in opposition; Labour leaders had always sought friendly relations with the leaders of the Indian Congress; and the independence of India formed part of the party's election programme.

But the transfer of power in India was no simple problem. Nationalism had first developed there in opposition to British rule; then, as the British provided increasing opportunities for

Indians to participate in their own government, rivalry and hostility emerged between different racial and religious communities, of which the most important were between Muslims and Hindus. A turning point had been passed before the second world war, when Mohammed Ali Jinnah returned from London to resume leadership of the Muslim League. Three years after his return, when the 1937 provincial elections convinced him that the Congress party would not recognize the independent interests of the Muslims, he transformed the League into a mass opposition party, which by 1940 took up the idea of Pakistan – a separate Muslim state.[13] Thereafter he rejected British proposals for the independence of India, both that of the Cripps mission in 1943 and that of the Cabinet mission of 1946. By then the strength of the League was such that the Congress could no longer claim to be the sole representative of the people of India, so that the transfer of power by Britain would have to meet the demands of the League.

It was to be expected then that the League and the Congress alike would manoeuvre to secure as much of their demands as possible in negotiations for the transfer of power. As they did so large areas of India dissolved into unprecedented violence and savagery which seldom stopped short of murder and arson. The restraints of civilized society and the normal companionship of village life broke down as Hindus and Sikhs set upon Muslims, and vice versa. Town and countryside through the northern half of the subcontinent, from Afghanistan to Burma, were submerged in communal slaughter. The partition of India became inevitable.

The British government's reaction was that independence must be achieved as quickly as possible. On 20 February 1947 it announced its intention to hand over power in India not later than June 1948. The viceroy, Lord Wavell, retired, to be replaced by Lord Mountbatten; in March the timetable for independence was speeded up; in June the India Independence Act was passed in the British parliament, setting up two independent dominions, India and Pakistan, from 15 August 1947.

[13] The name Pakistan was created by a young Muslim at Cambridge, Choudri Rahmat Ali, who later explained: 'Pakistan is both a Persian and an Urdu word, composed of letters taken from the names of our homelands: that is, Punjab, Afghania (NW Frontier Province), Kashmir, Iran, Sindh, Tukhuristan, Afghanistan, and Baluchistan. It means the land of the Paks, the spiritually pure and clean' (Ian Stephens, *Pakistan* (1963), p. 9).

Partition had been preceded by civil war; it was accompanied by massive movements of Hindus and Sikhs into India and of Muslims to Pakistan – although those in the southern half of the continent remained, to constitute, in India, the largest Muslim minority in any state. A deep fund of bitterness remained. There was also a residue of disputed territorial claims. The British government had claimed no right to determine the future of the princely states of India, in which they had exercised paramountcy. It was for them to decide whether to join India or Pakistan, or to remain independent. Inevitably there was a struggle between the two new governments for control of three of these states, which might be expected to go either way – Hyderabad, Junagadh, and Kashmir. By forceful action India established its rule over the first two, where a Hindu population had been governed by Muslim rulers. In Kashmir by contrast a predominantly Muslim population was ruled by a Hindu prince. Into this beautiful though poor kingdom Muslim tribesmen entered, encouraged and assisted by Pakistan. Thereupon the prince declared the accession of Kashmir to India, and Indian troops occupied the greater part of the kingdom. On 1 January 1948 the government of India took the Kashmir dispute to the Security Council, claiming that Pakistani action in Kashmir was tantamount to aggression against India. The Security Council proceeded to set up a United Nations Commission for India and Pakistan under the chairmanship of Sir Owen Dixon. The Commission organized a cease-fire from 1 January 1949, which left the actual division of Kashmir between the two countries as it was. In addition, both India and Pakistan agreed to accept two Security Council resolutions, providing respectively for the demilitarization of Kashmir and the holding of a plebiscite.

The Security Council endeavoured to secure the implementation of its resolutions from 1949 to 1953, and resumed discussion of Kashmir in January 1957, when Hr. Jarring took over the unrewarding task previously attempted by Sir Owen Dixon. In the meantime, however, relations between the two contenders had hardened. Pakistan insisted on the holding of a plebiscite; India insisted with equal force that Pakistani troops must first be withdrawn from western Kashmir. The Indian-controlled territory had become part of India, and when elections were held there the Indian government claimed that they were as good as a plebiscite. By this time too other differences had grown between the two powers as Pakistan joined in alliance with America – and so acquired arms, which the Indians regarded as a threat to themselves. In September 1960 a lesser dispute than Kashmir was settled when the two governments reached an agreement on the use of the Indus waters; but Kashmir remained as a focus of this secondary cold war, which was to erupt, in 1965, into renewed violence.

The independence of India was a fact of immense importance in the future development of international affairs. It set the pattern for further changes in Asia, where it was the more difficult to delay the granting of independence once it had been achieved on the Indian subcontinent. It initiated those changes in the British Commonwealth which transformed it from a close grouping of settlers of European, predominantly English descent, into a much larger but looser grouping in which Europeans were outnumbered, and the epithet 'British' ceased to be appropriate and was only rarely used. It had a direct and profound influence on Britain's position as a world power, and brought to an end a period when the Indian army and the British army in India formed a strategic reserve which could be moved east or west as occasion required. This was particularly important, as we have seen, in its repercussions on Middle Eastern policy.

In almost every respect the history of India ran counter to that of Pakistan. While Nehru survived as the leader of his people until 1964, Jinnah (who had become governor-general on independence) died from tuberculosis in September 1948, and the first prime minister, Liaqat Ali Khan, was assassinated in October 1951. India pursued the ideal of a secular multiracial state – an ideal which sometimes called force to its aid, as in the government's resistance to the Nagas' demands for autonomy and the seizure of Goa from the Portuguese in 1961. Pakistan in contrast was a Muslim state. In its foreign policy India sought to give a new direction to the conduct of international relations, inspired by its Gandhian tradition and the assumption that a state neutral between opponents in the cold war had an important mediating role to play in world affairs; while Pakistan, until the 1960s, followed a policy closely aligned to that of the United States, and joined both the Baghdad and the Manila pacts.

Ceylon and Burma could not easily be kept under British rule when India became independent. Ceylon moved quietly to independence in December 1947, its communal conflict muted for several years to come. From the outside the case for an interim government in Burma, as the British originally proposed, appeared a strong one in view of the disruption which had occurred during the war, the persisting economic chaos, and the internal conflicts between Burmese and Karens. But the British government had neither the intention nor the resources to offer prolonged resistance to the demands of nationalist leaders, and Burma became independent on 4 January 1949. In contrast to its neighbours, it chose complete independence, and did not join the Commonwealth.

The independence of the Philippines had been provided for in the Philippines Independence Act of 1934, after a transitional period of ten years; and these provisions were implemented in 1946. Like Burma, the Philippines had suffered grievously from the war which had been fought across its territory and had to reconstruct both its physical resources and the trade on which its economic livelihood depended. The grant of independence was accompanied by an economic agreement with the United States, which was severely criticized in the Philippines as tying the country's economy to that of the United States, making the Philippines the suppliers of raw materials to an American market whose whims would affect the prosperity and livelihood of the islands. In addition, the new government of the Philippines was faced with a severe threat from a well organized resistance movement, the Hukbalahaps, which had deep roots in agrarian discontent, particularly in central Luzon, but was dominated by communists. For these reasons it was obvious that the task of any government of a newly independent Philippines would not be an easy one; but the United States did not suppose that this was a reason for delaying the fulfilment of promises made in 1934.

In Indonesia the transition to independence was less smooth. Under MacArthur's General Order No. 1, Japanese troops in Indonesia were to surrender to the South East Asia Command, under Admiral Louis Mountbatten. But in the interval between the Japanese first offer of surrender on 10 August 1945 and the surrender itself on 2 September, the Indonesians, encouraged by the Japanese, realized the plans which they had prepared since April 1942, also under the auspices of the Japanese, and set up a republic, becoming the unitary state of Indonesia, under the presidency of Dr Sukarno. This republic was not recognized by the Dutch government, which, while realizing that the pre-war relationship with its colonial empire could not be restored, looked forward instead to some sort of Commonwealth in which the component parts of the Netherlands Indies would enjoy less than full sovereignty. British troops under the command of General Christison, who expected merely to arrange the repatriation of Japanese and the release of internees, thus found their task unexpectedly complicated. The capital, Batavia, was called Djakarta by the republicans. To know which government to work with was more difficult. The British forces had no choice but to recognize the control which the republic exercised over the island if they were to accomplish their mission although to do so meant incurring obvious criticism from the Dutch. At the same time they strove to mediate between the Dutch and the Indonesians and produce a satisfactory agreement. Meanwhile the Republican government sought international support for its cause. There was fertile ground in which to do so, and the Ukrainian delegate to the Security Council in January 1946 very readily brought a complaint against the presence of British troops in Indonesia, as a counter to the charges made against the Soviet Union of keeping its troops in Azerbaijan. From the Indonesian point of view, however, this was limited success, for they had only succeeded in becoming part of a propaganda battle. Negotiations between the Indonesians and the Dutch continued throughout 1946, interrupted by a communist attempt to carry out a coup d'état, and a more orderly change of government in Holland following on elections. Finally on 15 November 1946 an agreement was initialed by both sides at the town of Linggadjati, from which it took its name. By this time Dutch troops had replaced British in many areas, and the agreement allowed the remainder of the British to leave, without any deep feeling of regret.

The Linggadjati agreement was a compromise. It recognized the Republic as the *de facto* government in Java, Madura, and Sumatra. On the other hand the Indonesians had conceded a formula which foresaw a federal system rather than a unitary

Indonesian state, and a 'Netherlands-Indonesian Union' with its own agencies for defence and foreign affairs.

But the agreement needed filling out in detail, and in the succeeding months this proved impossible to achieve. Indeed the distance between the two sides widened, as the agreement was attacked both in Holland and Java as being too moderate and making too many concessions to the other side. Meanwhile economic conditions deteriorated drastically and sporadic fighting went on between Dutch and Indonesian troops. Impatient with this costly situation, the Dutch government in July 1947 decided to launch a 'police action' in order to secure a dominant military position and so improve the chances of agreement on its own terms

This brought the issue once again before the Security Council, the Indian and Australian governments taking the initiative independently of each other. The Dutch government claimed that the question was one of domestic jurisdiction and therefore outside the province of the Security Council, but this was a limitation which the members were unwilling to accept, even though some, such as Britain, had much sympathy for the Dutch point of view. The Security Council therefore passed two resolutions, calling for a cease-fire and the submission of the dispute to arbitration or settlement by other peaceful means, and they set up a Committee of Good Offices to make this possible. As a result of prolonged negotiations in which the Committee acted as mediator, a further agreement was signed, this time on board the American ship *Renville*.

The Renville agreement, however, did not differ in its essentials from that of Linggadjati, and went no further to settle the real issues in dispute between the two sides. Fundamentally the problem was a simple one: there had existed in Indonesia since 1945 an independent republic exercising effective control over part of the territory, side by side with the civil and military power of Holland in Indonesia. Between these two there were all the differences of a European colonial power, with the mixture of conservatism and liberal paternalism which that implies, and a vigorous, nationalist, new Asian country. It was inevitable that there should be a struggle for power, the Indonesian government aspiring to complete independence and control of the whole of Indonesia, and the Dutch seeking to maintain a strong and decisive influence both to safeguard its considerable investments and commercial interests, its own nationals, and its international position; and with the genuine intention of protecting the interests of the constituent regions of this vast territory. In this struggle the Indonesians were weakened by the absence of a strong economic or military base from which to operate and by the divisions within their own ranks; the Dutch by the fact that they were a small nation recovering from the destruction of war in their own continent, and trying to conduct a colonial operation against a hostile or apathetic population on the other side of the world.

The result was that the Renville agreement presented the same difficulties of detailed application as that of Linggadjati, and the pattern of 1947 repeated itself with depressing similarity through 1948, the end-piece being a second Dutch 'police action' in December, and the imprisonment of the Republican leaders.

But although the Indonesian pattern repeated itself to this extent, it was set against a very changed background in the rest of the world. The importance of Indian self-government had already made itself felt in 1947 when India had brought the Indonesian case before the Security Council, and through 1948 its importance both as an example and as a willing advocate of the Indonesian cause steadily increased. Within the Commonwealth it was vigorously supported by the Australian government, to the extent that the Indonesian Republic chose Australia to represent it on the Committee of Good Offices. On 25 January 1949 a conference of representatives of Asian and African countries, as well as Australia, met in Delhi at Nehru's invitation, and ended by condemning Dutch action and urging the Security Council to bring about the release of the Indonesian prisoners and the restitution of their full freedom of action. The importance of the increasingly effective support which the Indonesians received was shown by the British attitude in the United Nations. Between July 1947 and December 1948 the British government had become more closely tied to the Dutch through the development of the cold war in Europe and the signature of the Brussels pact; in spite of this the British delegation at the United Nations attached much less importance on the second occasion to the question of domestic jurisdiction, and supported the Security Council resolution calling for an immediate cessation of hostilities and the release of the Republican prisoners.

Another change which had come in this year was in the complex relationship of the colonial conflict to the cold war, and the changed policy, under Russian direction, of Asian communist parties. On the whole these developments worked to the advantage of the Indonesians. Communists played an important part in all the nationalist movements of South East Asia. Their local strength varied considerably, but their organization and training, the genuine aspirations of some and the ambition for power of others, together with the international support which the Soviet Union gave to the cause of anti-imperialism, put them in a very favourable position to acquire power within a national independence movement.

In the spring of 1948, however, the changed policy of the Soviet Union in response to the Marshall plan spread to Asia. At the Calcutta conference of the World Federation of Democratic Youth directives were conveyed to Asian communist parties for an intensification of communist activity unbound by the restraints of a popular front policy, or of the adoption of violent methods to seize power. The result in Indonesia was that the communists now attacked President Sukarno as the tool of American imperialism, seized the town of Madiun, set up a communist government, and broadcast an appeal for full-scale revolt. This was met by decisive action on the part of the Indonesian government. Dutch offers of help were refused, and the revolt was quickly and successfully suppressed by Indonesian forces. Inevitably this caused a hiatus in negotiations with the Dutch. But it strengthened the self-confidence of the Indonesian republicans, and it enhanced their prestige with those western governments and sections of opinion which believed that the best defence against communism in Asia lay in support for non-communist nationalist forces. It was in this atmosphere that the second 'police action' was carried out.

Within Holland the importance given to these developments inevitably varied considerably between different political parties; but the Dutch government could not be insensitive to them, or to the continuing cost of the Indonesian operation. For its part the Indonesian Republic wanted to restore order. Meanwhile the Security Council put pressure on both sides to end the use of force, and set time-limits for the establishment of an interim government, to be followed by a constituent assembly and a transfer of sovereignty by July 1950. The Security Council also turned its Committee of Good Offices into a United Nations Commission for Indonesia. From this moment negotiations moved forward slowly but effectively towards agreement. It took six months for discussions to proceed sufficiently for Dutch troops to withdraw from Djakarta, the republican capital, and nine months for a round-table conference to be arranged at The Hague. But the conference reached a threefold agreement. The first part provided for the transfer of sovereignty to a new sovereign republic of federal form. The second part was a statute of union between the Netherlands and Indonesia, which was to be voluntary and egalitarian, recognizing the queen as its head, and including arrangements for a ministerial conference, a permanent secretariat, and a court of arbitration. The third part was a transitional agreement, of which the most sensitive clause was an agreement that the disputed territory of Western New Guinea should remain under Dutch sovereignty for a further year.

To some extent the terms of the agreement were valuable for the support they won in the Dutch parliament rather than for what they achieved. In Holland ratification was won by a bare majority, while in Indonesia it was naturally welcomed with acclaim. Once in control, the Indonesian government transformed the federal state into a unitary one; and although the union with Holland functioned as planned at first, in the long run it had no more importance than one would expect from an attempt to join two so disparate countries across the breadth of the world. As with most of the new countries, independence brought as many problems to the new government as it solved. It was easier to legislate for a unitary state than to establish effective government over an area almost as large as Europe. Separatist movements, Muslim enthusiasts, and communists, together with a Dutch adventurer, Captain Westerling, who achieved some temporary notoriety, remained a serious obstacle to effective government in the first year. Economic difficulties were also obvious, the more so since the new republic could claim, in the island of Java, one of the most densely populated areas in the world. In spite of this President Sukarno saw an important future for Indonesia as a leader of Asian opinion. He invented a new formula, if not a new form of government, when he called the quasi-dictatorial rule which he established 'guided democracy'. He brought fame and prestige to Indonesia when in 1955 the conference of African and Asian states was held in Bandung. Even so, few people in Europe or America had yet become aware of the potentiality of this new Asian power: stretching some 2,500 miles across the ocean between Australia in the south and Malaya and the Philippines in the north; heavily populated, abundantly fertile, receiving American aid, and soon to be copiously armed by the Soviet Union.

The attempt made by the Dutch government to restore its position in the East Indies, albeit on a basis of partnership rather than colonial rule, had thus led to four years of sporadic fighting before agreement was reached. A similar attempt on the part of France in Indo-China led to seven years of warfare, growing in intensity and ending in the almost complete withdrawal of the French. This must be explained in part by the numerous disadvantages under which French policy laboured in this particular example of decolonization. They lacked the established tradition of imperial devolution enjoyed by the British. For when the British gave independence to their Asian colonies and dominions, they merely extended a policy which had its origins in the Durham report of 1839 and had been developed in the grant of responsible government and independence to such countries as Canada, Australia, and New Zealand. In France the imperial tradition had been quite different and had formed round a consistently centralizing ideal, whether in the form of assimilation or of federation. Whereas in Britain the liberal view of empire had been to grant complete self-government as soon as possible, the radical and socialist view in France had been to bring colonies to the point of civilization where they could be most closely associated with France, or most closely integrated into the French system of government. In the early years after the war even the French communists did not advocate the separation of Indo-China from France, and although account must be taken of the advantages of such an arrangement in permitting close connexions between the French and Indo-Chinese communist parties, it was also characteristic of a dominant French point of view. This view of empire always had a hollow centre, for it never posed the question of the position of France within such an empire when equal political rights were given to all its citizens, and those overseas greatly outnumbered the French themselves. In addition, it proved to be out of accord with the aspirations of the Africans and Asians living in the empire who for the most part, gallicized as they were, wished to acquire full independence, and retain only loose ties, advantageous to themselves, with France. In the context of Indo-China, the French concept of empire opened a gap between French presuppositions, based on the genuine and justified belief that the policy of the resistance and of the Fourth Republic towards Indo-China was much more liberal than that existing before the war, and Annamite desire for a full measure of sovereignty.

Before the war the French empire in Indo-China had been made up of four protectorates – Laos, Cambodia, Tongking, and Annam; and one colony, Cochin-China. Of these Laos and Cambodia now presented little problem. French rule had borne lightly on the peoples of these countries, and French 'protectorate' had real meaning. Both had lost territory to their traditional enemy, Siam, during the war, and therefore welcomed French support for its recovery. Both Cambodia and Laos moreover had good reason to regard Annam as their traditional rival, and only a small section of the Laotian nationalist movement was willing to make common cause with its neighbours in opposition to France. In consequence the French government was able to make agreements with Cambodia in January and Laos in August 1946, whereby they became autonomous states within the Indo-Chinese Federation of the French Union. When the French Union took shape under the constitution of 1946, their position as Associated States, with the right to send representatives to the Assembly and Council of the French Union in Paris was confirmed. Further treaties with France were signed in 1949 and 1953 and complete independence secured without bloodshed. But as we shall see, the war against the Vietminh in the remainder of Indo-China had its overspill in Laos (and to a minor extent in Cambodia). Independence was not accompanied by political unity, and the government of Laos was left with the enduring problem of integrating the Pathet Lao, allies of and sympathizers with the Vietminh, into its political life.

It was the future of the other two protectorates, Annam and

Tongking, and of Cochin-China, which gave rise to the deepest and most chronic conflict. Like the Dutch, the French were unable to re-enter Indo-China as soon as the Japanese surrendered; but the arrangements for surrender put them at a far greater disadvantage. During the war the French administration in Indo-China, which was loyal to Vichy, had continued to operate by favour of the Japanese, but in the spring of 1945 the Japanese brought this to an end, disarmed and interned the French, and set up instead a pro-Japanese Annamite administration under the emperor Bao Dai.[14] Then in August 1945, while the surrender was being negotiated, this government was in turn overthrown by a nationalist and communist organization under the leadership of Nguyen Ai Quoc – better known by his pseudonym Ho Chi Minh – who became president. Under MacArthur's orders, however, the Japanese north of latitude 16° surrendered to the Chinese; to the south of that line to South East Asia Command, which meant the British. As in Indonesia, the British were only too ready to carry out the immediate essential tasks and then hand over, and this they had done by March 1946. This was less true of the Chinese. In February 1946 an agreement was negotiated by the French and the Chinese by which the French abandoned extra-territoriality in China and gave customs advantages to the Chinese at Haiphong. In addition, all Chinese forces were to withdraw by 31 May. They did so, although not without shots being exchanged as the Chinese left and the French arrived; but in the meantime the government of Ho Chi Minh had been able to establish itself in Tongking. Elections to a national assembly had been held, and as well as establishing the authority of his government, Ho Chi Minh had been able to ensure the supremacy of his own party, the Vietminh, over other, non-communist, nationalist parties.

Fundamental differences then arose between the Republic of Vietnam under Ho Chi Minh, and the French. The former wanted independence; the latter envisaged a liberal settlement, but one which continued French participation in an Indo-Chinese federation, and French control over defence and foreign policy. Ho Chi Minh insisted that Vietnam included Cochin-China as well as Tongking and Annam – a claim which was expressed in the formula 'the unity of the three Kys'

[14] They acted similarly in Laos and Cambodia.

8

– whereas the French talked of consulting the people and envisaged a separate status for their former colony.

At the beginning of 1946 it was possible to conceal these differences in a form of words; and this was done in an agreement signed between the Republic of Vietnam and the French High Commissioner in March. But real agreement was made more difficult when the French High Commissioner pressed ahead with the formation of governmental institutions in Cochin-China. In April Ho Chi Minh left Indo-China for France, and entered into conference with the French government at Fontainebleau. While he and his deputation were there, however, the French High Commissioner in Indo-China, Admiral d'Argenlieu, announced on 1 June the formation of a provisional government of Cochin-China; and in July arranged for a conference to take place at Dalat of representatives of Cochin-China, Laos, and Cambodia, but not Vietnam, to discuss the constitution of the Federation of Indo-China. In these circumstances the Vietnamese delegates withdrew from the Fontainebleau talks. Even so, before returning to Indo-China, Ho Chi Minh signed an agreement with the French embodying a *modus vivendi* to govern French property and financial and cultural matters, as well as an undertaking to cease 'all acts of violence'; the whole to be supervised under joint commissions.

The next stage in the Indo-China question was opened by the Vietminh. On 19 December 1946 their forces, numbering some 30,000 men launched a prepared attack on the town of Hanoi. The reaction of the French government to this news was inevitably that the first task must now be to restore order; and the possibility of negotiation became slender indeed.

But the French government did not imagine that it could or should subject Indo-China to French rule. What it sought to do was to build up a political and military force of Vietnamese which would be an effective counter to the Vietminh. At first an attempt to do this was made in Cochin-China; but it suffered a severe setback when the president committed suicide to escape from the impossible position in which he found himself. The second possibility lay in the leadership of Bao Dai, and the French government devoted its energies to this possibility from December 1947 onwards. The operation had two stages. First it was necessary to persuade Bao Dai to assume the role of national leader opposed to the Vietminh. It was not an attractive one, least of all for a man who enjoyed life as much as Bao Dai, and who was intelligent enough to know that his support in Vietnam was limited. Nevertheless in March 1949 an agreement was signed, and ratified two months later, between Bao Dai and the French government. As three years had passed since the Fontainebleau conference, the French naturally found themselves making to Bao Dai the concessions which a more left-wing government had refused to make to Ho Chi Minh with regard to Cochin-China, defence, and foreign policy. As a result, on 14 June 1949 the new state of Vietnam was inaugurated with Bao Dai as its head, retaining the title of emperor. With some difficulty he formed a government, and nominated a provisional assembly until conditions made elections possible.

It was now possible to pass to the second stage – the victory of Bao Dai over Ho Chi Minh. But by this time the whole character of the Indo-Chinese war was changing. The most important fact was that the Chinese communists were rapidly advancing towards the border with Indo-China. Once contact was established between the Chinese and the Vietminh the task of building up a successful Vietnamese army, and even the military task of the French army, became immeasurably more difficult. The second factor was that what had begun as a colonial war had now become part of the cold war. The government of Bao Dai had been recognized by the British and American governments, as well as many of the other western powers. In January 1950 the government of Ho Chi Minh was recognized by the Chinese and Russian governments – a fact the significance of which was not confined to the ideological alignment it indicated, for Stalin was notoriously slow to back horses that might not win. In consequence the American government began to take an increasing interest in the success of France and Vietnam, and in May 1950 economic and military aid began to flow to Indo-China. Once again it was the outbreak of the Korean war which accelerated this process; even though its success was in the end limited.

Nowhere had the collapse of western rule been more dramatic or more complete than in the Malayan peninsula, where British forces surrendered to the Japanese on 15 February 1942 after a brief campaign of some ten weeks. As the war drew to an end, British and Indian troops prepared to return to embark for a counter-invasion, when the atomic bombs dropped on Japan rendered further military action unnecessary. The task then confronting the British government was considerable. It had no wish to reimpose colonial rule; and was reluctant to devote resources to so doing. On the other hand the Malayan people, while tired of foreign occupation, were ill organized to pass quickly to self-government.

The population of mainland Malaya was not an easy one within which to achieve political unity. It was made up of three distinct communities – Malays, Indians, and Chinese. There were divisions within at least the first two of these communities: Malay aristocrats were suspicious of the nationalism and reformism of some of their people; while the divisions in China between Kuomintang and communists were duplicated amongst the Malayan Chinese. Before the war, the British had not governed Malaya as a unit; they had brought some, but not all of the Malayan states into a federation, and governed through the Malay rulers; while Singapore, together with Penang and Malacca, had remained a separate colony known as the Straits Settlements.

As soon as something approaching normal government had been re-established after the war, the British government sought agreement with the Malay rulers which would establish political unity and be a first step towards self-government. In doing so, they deliberately separated the political development of the mainland from that of Singapore – a decision which was consistent with the general policy of seeking support in the first place from the Malay rather than the Chinese community.[15] A new federation covering the whole peninsula (but excluding Singapore) was established, and federal legislative and executive councils established. Formally, the latter were purely appointive; in practice the appointments were made after careful consultation of political interests and organizations, so that they were effective representational bodies.

The most decisive event in the post-war history of Malaya, however, had its origins (as far as is known) in Moscow. We have already seen that the Soviet government, having decided

[15] For a reference to wartime discussions of the possible separation of Singapore see Victor Purcell, 'Malayan Politics', in Saul Rose, ed., *Politics in Southern Asia* (1963), p. 218.

against entering the Marshall plan, tried to use the world communist movement to bring about its defeat by a policy of violence. In Malaya in 1946 and 1947 the Malayan communist party, under rather uncertain leadership, had sought to infiltrate the labour movement and political bodies. Then in February 1948 they received instructions from Moscow, through the communist-led youth conference in Calcutta, to resort to open revolt. The resources were available to them to do so. They could invoke afresh the spirit of the resistance movement against the Japanese, and uncover the arms which the British had sent to them in those days, and which had subsequently been cached in the jungle. They could organize the Chinese squatters on the fringe of the jungle as sources of food and supply. Above all, they could exploit the possibilities of dense jungle, where men may pass within a few feet of each other without being seen. Using these resources, they set out to dislocate the Malayan economy and then, following the Chinese example, to establish areas under their own effective government, which would be linked up to complete the conquest of the country.

The first dramatic action of this campaign was the murder of three European managers of rubber plantations in June 1948; for the next ten years guerrilla war was waged to the point of exhaustion; only on 31 July 1960 was the 'Emergency' officially declared to be over – and by that time Malaya had acquired its independence. The success of the operations against the terrorists[16] was of outstanding importance, since it was at the time and has remained one of the very few examples of victory over a guerrilla movement. The expenditure of resources to achieve this result was very great, especially in comparison with the opposition. The number of terrorists remained roughly constant at 4,000–5,000 men. Until 1954 their losses were made good by new recruits. Thereafter they maintained a depleted and despairing resistance to the security forces. Against them were deployed, at the height of the campaign, some 40,000 regular soldiers, and 70,000 police, together with village home guards, aircraft, artillery, and naval vessels (in so far as they could be used in this type of warfare).[17] New methods

---

[16] The word 'terrorist' slips easily into common parlance, and did so particularly in this context. It is, however, accurately used, in the sense that the communist guerrillas ensured support from civilians by terrorizing them.

[17] J. M. Gullick, *Malaya* (1963), p. 97.

of counteraction against the terrorists were developed. The necessity of protecting the civilian population from terrorism, and thereby breaking the guerrilla supply lines, led by the spring of 1950 to the resettlement of Chinese squatters in villages which could be effectively defended. This had the double effect of demonstrating to the population that the government could provide for their security, and of denying food and other supplies to the terrorists. In this way, and by the development of skills in jungle warfare, the strength of the communist movement was broken, and complete victory eventually secured.

By that time Malaya had achieved its independence. The British government had been very ready to ally itself with a nationalist movement, and it had the support of the Malays against the communists, who were almost exclusively Chinese (a factor of decisive importance in the guerrilla war). The most rewarding political development came in 1952–3 when the leading Malay and Chinese parties – the United Malay National Organization under Tunku Abdul Rahman and the Malayan Chinese Association founded by Tan Cheng Lock – formed an alliance, formalized into an Alliance party, which went far in transcending Sino-Malayan conflicts. It was thus able to press for early elections, and the British government was more confident in moving quickly towards independence. Federal Council elections were held in July 1955 and an Alliance government took office under Tunku Abdul Rahman. Two years later, in August 1957, Malaya became independent, maintaining its membership of the Commonwealth.

The politics of Singapore were in important respects different from those of Malaya. The population was predominantly Chinese, there being only 20 per cent Malays. The Malays took little part in politics, although from time to time they erupted in outbursts of violence. Singapore had escaped the 'Emergency' which had sapped the energies of Malaya since 1948; the communists did not enjoy open legal existence as a political party but were a constant irritant on the fringe of politics. Finally, the British interest in Singapore was greater than in Malaya, because of the importance of the naval base spread across the island territory.

After civil government was restored to Singapore in 1946, steps were taken by the British government to provide first for popular representation in the administration of the territory, then for the setting up of responsible government as a move towards independence. These developments followed the familiar pattern of preparation for independence, with the addition of the special consideration which was given to British defence interests. In spite of the turbulence of Singapore politics there eventually emerged in 1954 a left-wing People's Action party under the leadership of Lee Kuan Yew which in May 1959 was able to win a decisive victory in elections for a new legislative assembly. Immediately afterwards (at midnight on 2–3 June 1959) the self-governing state of Singapore came into existence.

There was none the less a considerable anomaly in the position of this new state, separated politically from the mainland of Malaya and dominated physically by the British naval base. Within a short time both of these problems began to assume a new perspective. Malay political leaders had resisted the idea of union with Singapore because of the decisive effect which it would have on the balance between the two largest communities in Malaya. In 1961, however, Tunku Abdul Rahman sought a solution to this problem in the concept of a Greater Malaysia, which would include Malaya, Singapore, and the British territories in Borneo. The proposal for federation met with no opposition, either in Britain or in Singapore, and it remained only to reach agreement on detailed terms. The Tunku urged that this should be done as speedily as possible, so that the Federation did not fall prey to communist imperialism. In the event the greatest danger which the Federation had to face when it came into existence in 1963 was from the open hostility of Indonesia. This in turn made it possible to settle the question of the Singapore base, since Britain and Malaysia now had common defence interests, which were embodied in a treaty between the two states. At least for some years these common interests would provide a firm basis for the British position in Singapore and give it durability and security of a sort which had not been enjoyed by British bases elsewhere in the world. In return for the retention of the base the British entered into a commitment to the defence of Malaya which would certainly involve the retention of active military forces in South East Asia, a commitment which might in the future assume alarming proportions.

The future of China and South East Asia had been a matter of continuing concern to the western powers during the war. In the heat of the battle they had spared little time to consider the fate of Korea. This peninsula, occupying a key position in the old nineteenth-century rivalries of the Far East, had been brought under Japanese protectorate after the defeat of Russia in 1905, and annexed to Japan in 1910. Japanese rule depended entirely on police and military control and was met with continuous resistance in whatever form possible by Korean nationalists. It was natural, therefore, that the opponents of Japan in the second world war should plan for the independence of Korea, although, because its political development had been suppressed, this was foreseen as coming 'in due course'. Such was the phraseology of the Cairo conference of November 1943 between Roosevelt, Churchill, and Chiang Kai-shek.

The future of Korea could not but be of interest to Stalin, sensitive as he was to Russian national interests. He accepted the possibility of Russian participation in a four-power trusteeship arrangement and then in 1945 pressed for a Soviet trusteeship of Korea, as of Libya. It was not however these discussions which determined the régime actually instituted in Korea when the war ended. This followed from the arrangements which MacArthur made, as supreme commander, for the surrender of Japanese forces. Under these provisions the Russian commander accepted the Japanese surrender north of the 38th parallel, the American commander to the south.

The Americans scarcely expected that this arrangement would give so permanent a form to the division of Korea. Stalin's expectations are, as always, more difficult to reconstruct. When the foreign ministers met in Moscow in December 1945 it was Molotov's proposal which was taken up in their agreement to establish as soon as possible a 'provisional Korean democratic government'; and to provide for a conference between Russian and American zonal commanders to handle urgent and immediate problems and prepare the way to self-government. It may have been that Stalin hoped that the Korean government thus established would come under communist control once American troops had left, even as the Americans looked for a genuinely democratic régime.

Such expectations were, however, disappointed. It rapidly became apparent that there was no political consensus in

Korea, but that the Korean community was torn between extremists of right and left, in whose midst a few moderates struggled precariously. In the north the Russians supported the communists, while in the south the Americans enjoyed an uneasy alliance with the right wing under Syngman Rhee, in default of any viable political force of a more moderate anticommunist kind. Meanwhile it was impossible to reach agreement in the joint Russo-American Commission on the next moves towards self-government, with the result that north and south became separate communities almost closed one to the other.

In these circumstances the United States government brought the Korean question before the General Assembly of the United Nations in September 1947. There it was able to dominate proceedings and override the opposition of the Soviet Union and its eastern European satellites. The outcome was the setting up of a Temporary Commission on Korea which would travel, observe, and consult throughout Korea, and then supervise the election of an all Korean national assembly.

But while the American government could win votes in the United Nations it could do nothing to force a way for the Commission into North Korea, and the division of the country now became permanent. Elections to a national assembly were held in South Korea, leading to the setting up of a government under Syngman Rhee, while in the north a communist government was established at Pyongyang, making a spurious claim to be based on representation from the country as a whole. The government of South Korea enjoyed the advantage of having been elected under the supervision of the United Nations Commission, from which it had won a favourable report, qualified by the fact that a small team could only cover a limited number of polling stations. When this was confirmed by the General Assembly, the United States and Britain recognized the government of the Republic of Korea under Syngman Rhee in January 1949, and the Soviet Union replied by similar recognition of the Pyongyang government under Kim Il Sung. The United Nations Temporary Commission on Korea was replaced by one which was no longer called temporary, and so could be more euphoniously abbreviated as UNCOK.

By this time the Soviet Union claimed to have withdrawn its

troops from North Korea, and although it was impossible to verify this claim, it was probably justified. In doing so, however, the Russians had left a formidable military force in a well armed and equipped North Korean army under the direction of a government which they had created. Through 1949 the United States also withdrew its forces from South Korea; but its attitude to the government of Syngman Rhee was one of nervous caution. While Syngman Rhee was warmly supported by a section of American opinion, of which MacArthur was the most outstanding representative, the administration could only be alarmed at the apparently reckless way in which the government of South Korea sought unification of the peninsula. The growing success of the communists in China in 1949 had not yet had the effect of winning over a majority of the American people to a policy of toughness in the Far East, so that at the beginning of 1950 the administration had actively to persuade the Congress to enact economic aid for Korea. All this was to change dramatically at midsummer.

7

THE FAR EAST : KOREA AND AFTER

ON THE morning of 25 June 1950 North Korean troops invaded
South Korea. At that time President Truman was at home in
Independence, Missouri, where it was still 24 June. Soon after
10 in the evening he received a telephone call from Acheson in
Washington giving him news of the attack, and the two men
agreed that an immediate appeal should be made to the
Security Council. This was done in New York at 3 a.m. the
next morning. Following a second telephone call from Acheson,
Truman left for Washington at 2 p.m. on 25 June. By the time
he arrived the Security Council had met in New York. The
United Nations had received news independently from its
Commission in Korea of the North Korean attack, and the
Security Council, by a 9–0–1 vote (Yugoslavia abstaining),
accepted an American resolution calling for a cessation of
fighting and withdrawal of troops, and requesting all members
to help in executing the resolution. Later on the same evening
Truman and his advisers rapidly agreed on orders to Mac-
Arthur (as supreme commander in the Far East) to supply the
South Korean army by airdrop, and for the Seventh Fleet to
move north into the Formosa straits.

Prompt as this action was, it did not immediately redress the
balance of force in Korea, where the superior forces of North
Korea were rapidly advancing down the peninsula. On the
following day, therefore, Truman again met his advisers, and
orders were telephoned to MacArthur to use air and naval
forces in support of South Korea. At the same time the order
to move the Seventh Fleet into the Formosa straits was confirmed, with the intention of preventing the conflict spreading
as a result of attacks either way between the mainland and
Formosa – the danger of sorties from Formosa being considered
as great as a communist attack on Chiang Kai-shek's island.
Next day, 27 June, the measures taken to assist South Korea
were reported to the Security Council, which proceeded to
adopt a further resolution recommending that members should

224

Map 6.

give such assistance as was necessary to repel the North Korean attack.[1] On 7 July the Security Council, on British initiative, voted for the setting up of a unified command in Korea, under an American commander, flying the United Nations flag. A British force was dispatched to Korea at the end of July; this was joined by contingents from Turkey and France, as well as other states, to a total of sixteen in all. Forty-five states gave aid of some sort.

Thus in a very brief period of time a series of events of vast significance had occurred. The origins of the war were naturally a matter of dispute between the communist world and their opponents. The Soviet government and its communist supporters throughout the world denied that North Korea had committed an act of aggression, and placed responsibility for the war on the government of South Korea. In so doing they had little difficulty in pointing to warlike utterances on the part of Syngman Rhee, the president of South Korea, who had never concealed his view that Korea should be unified, if necessary by force. They also attached great importance to a visit which Dulles had made to South Korea,[2] when he had referred to the division between North and South Korea as the 'front'. For all that, the evidence of South Korean responsibility for the war was unconvincing outside the communist bloc, as the voting in the United Nations showed. The relative strengths and preparedness of the two armies, the course of the fighting, and the rapid initial success of the North Koreans were all witnessed not only by observers friendly to the south, but also by the United Nations Commission, which reported directly to its parent body.

But the western powers and the opponents of North Korea generally went a step farther in attributing the North Korean attack not to local initiative, but to the Soviet Union. The British and American governments both appealed to the Soviet government to end the fighting – little expecting that their appeals would have effect. They also determined their action on the assumption that the attack was the successor in

---

[1] The voting on this resolution was 7–1–2. Yugoslavia opposed; Egypt and India abstained, waiting for instructions; on 29 June the Indian delegate reported his government's support for the two resolutions.
[2] John Foster Dulles was at this time working for the State Department preparing the Japanese peace treaty.

Soviet strategy to the Czech coup d'état and the Berlin blockade, and that if it succeeded it would prove to be the prelude
to aggression on a larger scale. For this assumption there was
and is no direct supporting evidence. There is indeed counter
evidence in the fact that the Soviet Union still boycotted the
United Nations, because China was represented by the Nationalist government, and by thus waiving its veto, made possible the
smooth and speedy working of the Security Council. Moreover
the attack was neither preceded nor immediately accompanied
by the propaganda which normally surrounded Soviet action.

In the circumstances of the time, however, it was inevitable
that Soviet intentions should be assumed. The world had grown
accustomed to the uniformity of speech and behaviour which
characterized the Stalinist world, and it was difficult to believe
that if Czechoslovakia, even before the coup d'état, could not
go against Soviet wishes by accepting Marshall aid, North
Korea could embark on a venture which might have incalculable consequences for the Soviet Union without a directive
from Stalin. It was known and recognized that Stalin was a
cautious man who, except in Finland, had avoided military
conflict until it was forced on him; but the invasion of South
Korea seemed at once the extension of a pattern which had
built up in all the Soviet forward moves since 1945, and a
convenient way of testing western reaction by involving an
expendable satellite rather than Russian forces themselves.

The evidence which would settle the question of possible
Russian direction of the attack is still unavailable. Even more
difficult is it to judge the part which the Korean war played in
Soviet strategy, supposing it had any part at all. In retrospect
it appears unlikely that it was the prelude to further aggression
in the way in which Hitler's moves against the Rhineland
proved to be; but if the attack had met with no more than verbal
protests it would have been encouragement to Stalin, whatever
his initial role, to extend his probing into the non-communist
world.

Whatever conclusion one chooses to reach in this form of
historical speculation there can be no doubt about the impact
of the Korean war on the western policy of containment. Acting
on the assumption that the best one could do was to prepare
against further communist aggression, fortified in the belief
that, even in face of the new type of challenge which commun-

ism represented, it was still necessary to develop military strength, the western powers pressed ahead with the development of NATO; accepted (albeit with hesitation on the part of some) the need for German rearmament, and increased their efforts to surround Russia with a ring of security pacts, so that no area should be left in a state of naked unpreparedness and thus offer an invitation to the next round of Soviet probing.

In spite of the fact that the Korean war acted as a general tocsin for the western powers, the conflict itself remained limited. Whatever calculations or miscalculations Stalin had made he did not meet the support of the United Nations for South Korea with corresponding help to North Korea, and the danger of escalation was thus avoided. The United States for its part extended its diplomatic activity to the Soviet Union by addressing appeals to Stalin, but restricted its military activity to the local conflict – initially even to the area south of the 38th parallel. It dispatched the Seventh Fleet to the Formosa straits, but this was done, as we have seen, in full awareness that the war was as likely to be spread by Nationalist attacks against the mainland as by communist attacks on Formosa. Equally significant was the fact that Truman declined the offer made by Chiang Kai-shek for some 33,000 Nationalist troops to be made available for the war in Korea. Whatever military doubts there may have been about the value of such troops, particularly since they would have to be equipped, and would be taken away from their more obvious role of defending Formosa against possible attack, they none the less were soldiers immediately available in the area, and it was the political argument against their use which swayed the balance.

The desire of the American government and its allies to limit the war obviously stemmed in the first place from its awareness of the consequences of a general conflict – indeed the presupposition of resistance in Korea was that by fighting a small war in immediate response to an act of aggression one could avoid the need to fight a general war later. To this view the western powers adhered, in spite of extremist demands in the United States for some kind of 'victory' against communism, which could only be won by a general offensive – demands which increased after China joined in the fighting. They were reinforced in this view by the fact that the war was fought on behalf, not of national governments, but of the United Nations, under the United Nations flag. As we shall see, the degree of control which the United Nations could exercise over the conduct of operations, whether military or political, was severely limited, and member states obviously remained free to take action, as the Americans did by moving the Seventh Fleet, outside the range of United Nations direction. None the less, the responsibility to an international organization, and the need to justify action in its Assembly remained. At the same time the circumstances in which action had been initiated by the United Nations had their effect on the development of that institution itself. It was recognized that the unique success which the organization achieved derived from fortunate circumstances – the absence of the Soviet Union from the Security Council, the presence of United Nations representatives in Korea, and the availability of American forces in the region of the conflict. In the future these chance advantages might not be present, and it would be wise therefore to make institutional and procedural arrangements to guard against frustration, deadlock, and impotence in the future.[3]

The course of the Korean conflict, from the initial attack on 24 June (or 25 June local date) to the signature of an armistice on 27 July 1953, falls easily into five distinct periods. The first phase was that of rapid North Korean success, until the South Koreans, with the slender support which could be rushed to them, were reduced to the tip of the peninsula. On 15 September American forces were landed at the beachhead of Inchon, and the conflict entered its second period, that of equally rapid United Nations success; the 38th parallel was crossed at the beginning of October and North Korean resistance virtually overcome by the end of the same month. But far from this being the end of the war, it was now enlarged by the arrival of Chinese troops coming to the assistance of the North Koreans – their presence as an effective, organized force being recognized by General MacArthur in a special report to the United Nations on 5 November. The third and fourth periods of the conflict resembled in some respects the first and second. The immediate impact of Chinese intervention was to bring the retreat of the United Nations south of the parallel; but by April 1951 the new onslaught was being held, and in the fourth brief period of continuous violent fighting the United Nations regained the

[3] See below, p. 534 ff.

initiative and their former ascendancy. The fifth and final period then opened, in June 1951, with the beginning of armistice negotiations. It dragged on for two years before an agreement was finally signed in July 1953.

While the general lines of the conflict can thus be sketched very rapidly, the actual course of the war and the negotiations which ended it provoked as many questions of political importance as did the initial outbreak. The most enduring of these, in its various forms, was the extent to which the battle should be carried into the enemy's camp. As we have seen, Truman's original orders to MacArthur were to give assistance to the South Korean forces south of the 38th parallel; while the recommendations which the United Nations made to its members had been to give aid, without specifying where or how. But as the Inchon landing was prepared, and the American government could safely predict an advance northwards, the question of how far it should advance became critical. Truman's intention was to limit the extent of the war; to allow it to spread into a world-wide conflict would defeat the aims of the operation. On the other hand military victory had to be secured. His orders were therefore to cross the parallel, unless there were evidence of substantial Russian or Chinese intervention. In the United Nations, the Russians had resumed their place at the beginning of August, when it was Malik's turn to take the chair in the Security Council. Whether he used the chair or the veto, Malik was able to obstruct decisions in the Security Council, and any possibility that there might previously have been of developing an executive authority to give clear directives to United Nations forces disappeared. However, the United Nations had since 1947 been committed to the unity of Korea. On 7 October it confirmed this commitment by a resolution passed in the Assembly stating that the aim of its action was to establish a 'unified, independent and democratic Government of Korea'.

By this time South Korean forces had already crossed the parallel; American forces followed them a day after the Assembly resolution. The Chinese government had made statements which might be interpreted as bluff, or might be ominous warnings. At the end of September Chou En-lai had said that the Chinese would not 'supinely tolerate their neighbours being savagely invaded by imperialists'. He had also summoned the

Indian ambassador to Peking, Pannikar, and told him that if United Nations forces crossed the parallel China would intervene with its own troops – suggesting that they would not do so if South Koreans alone crossed.

The decision to cross the parallel was taken in full awareness of these indications of possible Chinese intervention. It appeared that there was no other way of achieving lasting military victory – quite apart from the further objective of bringing about the unity of Korea – and as the North Koreans, trained and equipped by the Russians, had all but overwhelmed the south in the initial phase of the war, the northward advance could not be left to South Koreans alone. Moreover the supreme commander attached very little importance to the possibility of Chinese intervention. On 15 October (local time) Truman met MacArthur on Wake island to discuss the future of the campaign, and of Pacific politics. At this meeting MacArthur told the president that the possibility of Chinese – or Russian – intervention was slight, and that if it occurred it would be on such a scale that it could easily be overwhelmed, particularly through the United Nations supremacy in air power. He expected that resistance in North and South Korea would collapse by Thanksgiving Day (i.e. before the middle of November) and that the Eighth Army could be withdrawn to Japan by Christmas, leaving two divisions for a further month or two to supervise elections.

MacArthur proved to be entirely mistaken in his judgement of the future: the Chinese intervened, and did so with such force that the United Nations advance was first halted and then turned into a retreat. Their intervention opened up entirely new possibilities for the outcome of the war. It was possible that the United Nations would have to sue for peace – although they would do so through lack of will rather than lack of long-term military strength. More important was the possibility that the United States would aim for victory in the war through the use of more destructive weapons, or by an attack on China itself. A further possibility was that, just as the risk taken in crossing the 38th parallel had resulted in Chinese intervention in support of the North Koreans, so the fighting against China would involve the Soviet Union in war, however much the United Nations might hope to avoid such escalation.

Alive to these possibilities, the Truman administration

remained steadfast in its original policy of securing victory in a limited war in Korea, avoiding the spread of the war into a general conflict. It did so against a background of strongly rising emotion among important sections of American opinion. The involvement of the United States in world affairs had subjected its public to a series of psychological blows of which the conflict in Korea seemed the culmination. In Europe the new commitments meant that American troops were stationed abroad for an indefinite period; in Korea it meant that they were in combat and suffering heavy casualties. In the cold war with the Soviet Union the United States was dealing with a power with which it had had comparatively little contact before 1941, and which it had for a generation accepted as a communist country; in Korea it was at war with China, with which it had long and close contacts involving a large number of individual American citizens, from which a strong sentimental attachment had developed. The effect of the communist revolution was therefore to evoke resentment that America's ideal in the Far East should be so betrayed, together with a strong feeling of solidarity with those Chinese whom the new régime proscribed. Under this sense of shock, Americans, who more than most peoples tend to ascribe something which has gone wrong to an identifiable failing on the part of some individual, looked for the cause of the spread of communism into their sphere of predilection in the Far East; some of them found it in the 'sell-out' to the communists at Yalta, and the failure of the Truman administration to give adequate aid to Chiang Kai-shek in the civil war. This surge of alarm at the communist menace, and criticism of the administration for being too soft in dealing with it, was amply fed by the Hiss trial.[4]

The difficulties of this situation were increased by the fact that the supreme commander, less emotional than many of the administration's critics, none the less shared some of their views; and, more important, he expressed them openly. From the beginning of the war MacArthur had wanted to make use of Chinese Nationalist troops from Formosa, discounting the political difficulties which were argued against such a course. Now that communist China had entered the war he sought authority for an extension of the United Nations offensive beyond the limits of Korea, involving the bombardment and

[4] See above, p. 198.

blockade of China itself, and he argued that if this were not done it would be impossible to achieve limited victory in Korea. He went further than arguing his case with the joint chiefs of staff, for he made his views publicly known. His statements about the course of the war, for example when he announced (as late as 24 November 1950) a 'general offensive . . . to end the war', had provoked Truman into issuing an order that no statement or press release concerning foreign policy should be published until it had been cleared by the State Department. But in March 1951, at the time when Truman was preparing a statement on American foreign policy for which he carefully sought the agreement of other United Nations governments involved in the war, MacArthur issued his own statement, expressing his readiness 'to confer in the field with the commander-in-chief of the enemy forces', suggesting the possibility of the extension of the war to the mainland of China. This evoked a reprimand from the joint chiefs of staff, acting on Truman's instruction; and Truman decided that MacArthur must be relieved of his command. His dismissal was precipitated when on 5 April Representative Joseph W. Martin read to the House a letter he had received from MacArthur, in which the commander not only made clear that his views differed from those of his administration, but implied scorn for those who failed to 'realize that here in Asia is where the Communist conspirators have elected to make their play for global conquest', continuing: 'here we fight Europe's war with arms while the diplomats there still fight it with words. . . . There is no substitute for victory.'[5]

There was no alternative to Truman's course of action – in spite of the dire warnings (exaggerated in the event) of the trouble it would involve. On 11 April MacArthur was relieved of his command, and General Ridgway was appointed to succeed him. Announcing the change at a special press conference at 1 a.m., Truman said:

Full and vigorous debate on matters of national policy is a vital element in the constitutional system of our free democracy. It is fundamental, however, that military commanders must be governed by the policies and directives issued to them in the manner provided by our laws and Constitution. In time of crisis the consideration is particularly compelling.[6]

<hr />

[5] Truman, *Memoirs*, ii. 381, 383, 440, 445–6.   [6] Ibid. p. 449.

Whatever the pressure from some sections of opinion in the United States, Truman was equally aware that the allies of the United States in Korea, and the United Nations generally, were extremely alarmed by the possibility of an extension of the war. Such alarm became particularly strong when Truman was asked, at a press conference on 30 November 1950, whether he contemplated the use of the atomic bomb, and he replied that the use of the bomb had been considered, to the extent that 'consideration of the use of any weapon is always implicit in the very possession of that weapon'.[7] His statement created a sensation in Europe, particularly in Britain, where the prime minister, Attlee, announced that he would fly to the United States to confer with Truman. They met in the first week of December, and rehearsed the differences of policy between the American administration and the Labour government in Britain. Attlee urged that China was 'potentially Titoist', and should be seated in the United Nations; he pressed for the earliest possible negotiations with the Chinese, to avoid the risk of general war.

The outcome of their conversations was to allay Attlee's anxieties about American intentions. For his part he expressed warm support for the continuance of a limited war as long as it was possible. Even so, the difference between American and British policy in the Far East persisted, and was liable to be exploited and exaggerated at any time. In part the difference derived from the fact that for the first time America and Britain were involved in a common conflict, but that Britain was not regarded as an equal partner, although this was scarcely surprising in view of the disproportionate contribution which each country made to the conflict. Thus there were occasions when action was taken without the British being consulted (one of the most important being the bombing of the Suiho power station, on the Yalu river in June 1952). This pleased neither the left, who were nervous about the extension of the war, nor the right, who were unwilling to accept a subordinate position for Britain; and a general anxiety that the country would be drawn into a crisis or a conflict not of its making was felt generally throughout the country.

There were more fundamental differences of view. Lacking the emotional ties of some Americans with China, the British were

[7] Ibid. p. 396.

inclined to see some justification for Chinese intervention in the war, on grounds of self-defence. Thus while the United States wanted the United Nations to 'brand' China as an aggressor, British opinion supposed that it would be easier to treat reasonably with communist China if it were given a seat in the United Nations. The American view prevailed. A deputation from Peking visited the United Nations to argue its case, but such a short visit was scarcely likely to vindicate the British point of view. The American delegation, after weeks of discussion with other governments, introduced a more moderate resolution into the General Assembly than the one they had originally considered, and a reluctant Britain was counted among the forty-four member states that supported it.[8] Equally reluctant were some of Britain's Commonwealth partners, and their views were an additional factor in making for a more moderate policy towards China than that of the United States. Conscious of the attitude taken by the Indian government towards China – aware that it had acted as intermediary in conveying warnings from the Chinese of their proposed intervention if the parallel were crossed – the British government sought to avoid a division growing between themselves and the Asian nations, and were the more sensitive to efforts of a nascent Afro-Asian group in the United Nations to secure a cease-fire.

By the spring of 1951 the American persistence in a policy of limited war began to be fully justified. The Chinese advance was held – as a result partly of the use of the napalm bomb, scarcely less terrifying than the atomic weapon itself. But by this time the objectives of the war on the United Nations side had become still more limited, and at the beginning of June Acheson took up a theme already promoted by the Canadian foreign minister and the secretary-general of the United Nations, that the purposes of United Nations action would be fulfilled if aggression ceased – that is to say if North Koreans and Chinese stayed north of the 38th parallel. On 23 June Malik stated – almost as an aside in a United Nations broadcast – that the Russian government believed a solution could be found to the problem of the

---

[8] The resolution (498(V)) read: '*The General Assembly* (1) ... *Finds* that the Central People's Government of the People's Republic of China . . . by engaging in hostilities against United Nations forces has itself engaged in aggression in Korea ... (6) *Requests* a Committee composed of the members of the Collective Measures Committee as a matter of urgency to consider additional measures to be employed to meet this aggression . . . '. It was passed by 44–7–9.

Korean war, and that negotiations should begin for a cease-fire and withdrawal from the parallel.

This was the starting-point for armistice negotiations, but it was two years before they came to fruition. In most respects the armistice agreement which was signed on 27 July 1953 was of the simplest kind. It provided for a cease-fire line, which corresponded to the positions occupied by the opposing armies, and a narrow demilitarized zone along it. It carried provisions for the stabilization of armaments on each side which were disregarded, and it looked forward to a political conference which was never held. One might well suppose that an armistice of so simple a nature could be negotiated in less than two years. The stumbling block in the way of speedy agreement lay in the question of the exchange of prisoners of war. At an early stage in the negotiations the United Nations provided a list of prisoners in their care, and demanded a similar list in return – being sceptical of communist intentions to declare and offer for exchange all the prisoners in their hands (a scepticism which was justified by the small list which the communists first offered). They also insisted that no prisoners on either side should be repatriated against their wishes; and when they had questioned all their prisoners they announced that of 96,000 North Korean prisoners 65,000 chose repatriation, and of 21,000 Chinese, only 5,000.

The deadlock in the negotiations resulted from the combination of these two factors. The United Nations could not risk the forfeit of its own men by quietly releasing those of its prisoners who did not want repatriation, particularly since it had provided a list of them. But there were fundamental difficulties in the way of agreement on voluntary repatriation. The United States and its allies were genuinely opposed to the forcible return of prisoners: on grounds of free choice, and because prisoners who had once stated their hostility to the communist governments in their own country could expect rough treatment if they returned home. They also wanted to show that refugee-prisoners would be respected and well-treated, to encourage desertion in any future conflict. The communists for their part were unwilling to let it be seen that any large number of their men preferred capitalism to communism – particularly in the case of the Chinese, in view of the large proportion of their soldiers involved, and their traditional reluctance to lose face.

While the deadlock in negotiation persisted fighting had become desultory, except for occasional flares, such as the bombing of the Suiho power station. But the cold war continued with unabated intensity, and was stimulated by accusations brought by the Chinese, with support from the Russians, that the United States had carried on 'germ warfare' in Korea. The charges were first made in May 1951, but were then dropped until February 1952, when a massive propaganda campaign was launched to back them up. The charges were not very specific, since they claimed that a range of illnesses were being spread by a range of carriers, from fleas to rats. But they were supported by the 'evidence' of villagers who claimed to have seen American planes dropping containers, by photographs, and by the reports of international bodies of lawyers and scientists, all of them favourably disposed towards the communist powers, who were invited to China to see for themselves. Finally, the Chinese began to broadcast 'confessions' coming from American officers of having engaged in bacteriological warfare. The only evidence not available was that of an impartial body. When the American government proposed that the International Red Cross be invited to investigate, the Chinese government said it would not be admitted, and the Soviet Union used its veto in the Security Council to prevent discussion or decision going forward.

The precise objective which the communists aimed at in this campaign is difficult to establish. To some extent it rebounded against them, for the prisoners who had 'confessed' were eventually released with the others and could testify to torturing and 'brainwashing' at the hands of the Chinese which had broken down their resistance and reduced them to a state of supine acceptance of their tormentors' wishes. Whatever else was intended, the campaign built up a large reserve of bitter hostility in the United States to the evils of communism which it would be hard to dissipate.

The break in the deadlock began to appear in the spring of 1953. It came as a result of concession from the communist side, and to that extent must be attributed to a change of communist policy. At the end of February the possibility opened up that the communists would agree to the exchange of sick and wounded prisoners; and on 28 March the communist command in Korea accepted the principle of such an exchange, adding that it should lead to a smooth settlement of the prisoner question. Between these two dates Stalin died, on 5 March, and it is impossible to know whether the new approach was initiated by him before his death, or was the work of his successors. It may have been in reaction to the advent of the new administration in the United States, which may have prompted anxiety about the possible renewal and extension of the war; the more so since Eisenhower, in his first State of the Union message on 2 February 1953, announced that the American Seventh Fleet would no longer shield the mainland of China from Nationalist attacks from Formosa. On the other hand it may be correct to trace the change in communist policy back to the previous autumn, with the issue of Stalin's *Economic Problems of Socialism* and Malenkov's speech to the 19th party congress.

Whatever the reasons for the change it was sufficient to bring a settlement. On 8 June an agreement was signed providing for the submission of prisoners who did not wish for repatriation to a Neutral Nations Repatriation Commission, consisting of a representative from each of the five countries, Sweden, Switzerland, Poland, Czechoslovakia, and India, with India providing the troops and personnel necessary to safeguard and conduct the operation.

The negotiations had been conducted throughout between representatives of the opposing sides in Korea, at the previously unknown village of Panmunjon[9] and they had increasingly become a contest between the United States on the one hand and Russia and China on the other. Concurrently with the negotiations in Korea discussion had persisted in the United Nations; but effective as that body had been in initiating resistance to the North Korean attack, it was quite ineffective in bringing the war to an end. The organization lacked representatives from either communist China or Korea; even if such representatives had been present it is unlikely that they would have added substantially to the contributions of the Soviet Union. The forum of the Assembly enabled nations which were more or less neutral to put forward plans designed to hasten an armistice, and this was done by Poland, Mexico, and India in the autumn of 1952. But progress was dependent on decisions taken by governments which were at most marginally affected by the climate of opinion in the United Nations.

Even within each bargaining side, it appeared on the one

[9] Negotiations were begun at the equally obscure village of Kaesong, but transferred to Panmunjon after a series of disputes about violation of the truce zone.

hand that the Soviet Union rather than China set the pace, while on the other the United States was dominant. The first possibility of serious armistice negotiations had been opened up by Malik, and the change of policy on the prisoners-of-war question may have come from Moscow. On the side of the United Nations the leading role naturally fell to the United States, while its allies, particularly Great Britain, were alarmed at the possibilities of lack of consultation.

It is difficult to assess the independence of North Korea *vis-à-vis* its more powerful allies in the conduct of negotiations. South Korea, under the presidency of Syngman Rhee, was powerfully placed to play an independent part, and President Rhee tried to make the most of his position. He rejected the United Nations view that their objectives would be achieved if they had driven back aggression, and would have liked to involve his allies in a continuing war until victory was won and Korea united. He was thus singularly unimpressed by the fact that an agreement was made for the exchange of prisoners, and took independent action to undermine it by giving orders to the South Korean guards that prisoners should be released. The communists took the maximum advantage of this event to deride their opponents. The United Nations denied that they had any complicity with Rhee's action; but thereby only opened themselves to the charge of being unable to control their ally. However, the war was not renewed, and the fact that the communists still persisted in negotiations was an indication of their wish to end the conflict. Even so, Rhee was able to negotiate a defence pact with the United States.

It is difficult to exaggerate the importance of the Korean war in the development of post-war international relations. We have already examined its impact on western policy in Europe and the development of NATO. It brought an important change in the structure and nature of the United Nations organization, marked by the Uniting for Peace resolution, and it led to the hounding of Trygve Lie and his subsequent resignation from the secretary-generalship. It disrupted European economies just as they were recovering from the world war, both by increasing raw material prices and by imposing a sudden burden of rearmament – and on the other hand it gave a temporary boost to the economies of primary producers. In Japan the orders given for supplies of every kind, and for repairs and services for the United Nations

forces gave the Japanese economy a decisive injection of prosperity and started the boom which has continued virtually un-
interrupted until the present.

The war gave great prominence to the new nations of Asia, and
in particular it established India as a would-be mediator between
the two sides in the cold war – a role which impressed the British
as it aroused the suspicion of the Americans. Between the western
and the communist blocs the conflict brought a bitterness of
relations to deepen the enmity of the early cold war, and dug a
deep gulf between America and China. As we have seen, it provided a fresh moral crisis for the American people. George
Kennan has commented on the general tendency of democracies,
particularly evident in America, to be slow to enter armed conflict, but when they do so to seek total victory for a moral crusade.
In Korea the United States suffered heavy casualties for the
sophisticated objective of resisting aggression, without achieving
'victory' in any normal sense.

This sense of frustration was scarcely evident in Britain, where
there was a widespread feeling of relief that the war had been
fought to a successful conclusion without growing into a general
conflict. The difference of attitude was reflected in the preparatory moves toward a political settlement of Korea, which was
foreseen in the armistice. The American government wanted to
continue negotiations between the two 'sides' in the dispute, and
to make clear that it regarded Russia as the mainspring of the
original aggression in Korea. The British government looked
rather for a round-table conference which would seek a general
settlement in the Far East. As far as Korea was concerned these
differences were relatively unimportant, as negotiations were
short and abortive. They were initiated in the United Nations
and in the foreign ministers' conference in 1954; but they led
nowhere. They were far more important, however, in the settlement of the next major climax in the Far East, the crisis in the
war in Indo-China. Before examining this in detail it will be
advisable to survey the developments in the area generally since
the outbreak of the Korean war.

The pattern of international relations had changed as rapidly
in the Far East as in Europe in the five years since the war. There
had been similar transition from anxiety about the wartime
enemy, in this case Japan, to anxiety about a communist threat;

but in this instance the transition was sharpened by the immense gain to the communist world of China. The old imperial powers had either given up their colonial possessions or were involved in wars to determine their future; and there had emerged a collection of newly independent Asian states. Of the three imperial powers Britain was the freest to manoeuvre and at least attempt to create a new policy to meet changed circumstances. Holland had virtually abandoned its interest in the area, except for its continued rule over Dutch New Guinea and its property and rights in Indonesia; and France was tied down by the war in Indo-China. In this new situation Britain attached great importance to maintaining the respect and co-operation of Asian governments, particularly India. Although intent on bringing the Malayan war to a successful conclusion, it was aware of the limits on its own resources in the area, and expected that its influence and policies could only be upheld through the goodwill of Asian countries. The importance of this appeared that much greater as a result of the drawing together of some of these countries, as well as with the established countries of the Commonwealth, at the Colombo conference in 1951, which set up the Colombo plan.[10]

For the United States a more fundamental revision had taken place. Before the war American political commitment on the mainland of east Asia was minimal. But in a rapid series of events after the war the United States had been faced with the threat of expanding communism; Roosevelt had not expected America's long-term commitment in the Far East to be appreciably greater after the war than before, and had therefore looked to China as a great power which would ensure stability, and the maintenance of American interests in the area. Now China was a second communist power, no less alarming because its potential was incalculable. The construction of positions of strength as a safeguard to communist expansion in the Far East posed problems which did not exist in Europe, and the sense of alarm at the possibility of further successful civil wars as in China, or of infiltration across jungle borders was only heightened by the fluid nature of a threat with which it was difficult to come to grips. All these questions were given fresh consideration when the Eisenhower administration succeeded that of Truman in January 1953.

[10] See below, p. 598 f.

Before the outbreak of the Korean war the United States had begun intensified efforts to achieve the signature of a peace treaty with Japan. Responsibility for this task had been taken by John Foster Dulles, soon after his appointment as special consultant to the State Department, to provide liaison between the administration and the Republican party. The onset of the Korean war made the task more urgent as the United States did not want to incur the odium of keeping troops in Japan as an occupation force; and it made Russian concurrence even less important in American eyes. By September 1951 the objective of a peace treaty was achieved, and this represented a considerable success for American diplomacy. The aims of United States policy were to regularize its relations with Japan, which it had ceased to regard as an enemy nation; to avoid the imposition of heavy economic burdens; and to provide for the continuance of Japanese participation in an American security system. These objectives were not shared by other countries interested in the future of Japan. Not only were they opposed by the Soviet Union, but Australia, New Zealand, and the Philippines hoped for reparations payments to facilitate their economic development or merely to help balance the budget. A further difficulty arose from the different attitudes taken by the American and British governments towards China; for while the United States had no intention of recognizing communist China, the British regarded it as essential that the Japanese peace treaty should be negotiated and signed by the communist government. Their view was shared by the governments of India and Burma. The Indian government went further in condemning the subordination of the honour and interests of Japan to the needs of American security. It declined an invitation to the San Francisco conference; so did the Burmese government, dissatisfied with the provision for reparations.

The American government could more easily allay the fears of those who saw their own security threatened by Japan. It gave a guarantee to the Philippines, Australia, and New Zealand by signing a pact with the former in August, and a tripartite pact with Australia and New Zealand in July 1951. Although the peace treaty with Japan made no specific provision for reparations, it did recognize that Japan should negotiate compensatory settlements with the countries it had overrun in the Pacific war. But apart from this the American government pressed forward to the conclusion of a treaty embodying its own objectives. This was done by conducting all the negotiations through formal diplomatic channels before the summoning of a conference. When the conference met in San Francisco at the beginning of September 1951 it thus had before it a draft treaty, and the chairmanship of Acheson and the promotion of the treaty by Dulles secured its acceptance. The Soviet Union had accepted an invitation to the conference, but was unable to make any serious impact on the proceedings or on the treaty. It neither bid for Japanese support by proposing a much more favourable treaty, nor sought to exploit the anxieties of Japan's former enemies, and it was out-manoeuvred in the conference itself. The United States felt little need to bow to the wishes of a power which had scarcely joined in the war against Japan, and which was no longer in any sense an ally.

The treaty followed the lines foreseen at Potsdam, reducing the territory of Japan to its four main islands. It foresaw a United Nations mandate, with the United States as the sole administering authority, over the southern Ryukyu islands, and recognized the right of the United States to administer them in the meantime. It was followed immediately after its signature by a security pact signed between the United States and Japan, providing for the maintenance of American forces in Japan. Meanwhile the Japanese government had itself, during the year 1951, strengthened its 'National Police Reserve', a force of 75,000 men trained by American instructors and equipped with light artillery. Understandably the Soviet Union, Czechoslovakia, and Poland did not sign the Japanese peace treaty.

By the beginning of 1954 the United States had thus built an imposing political and military arsenal to contain communism in the Far East. The treaty signed with Syngman Rhee did everything possible to restrain South Korea from action which would provoke a fresh conflict; and at the same time indicated the readiness of the United States to intervene again if South Korea were threatened. Formosa was an essential part of the strategic line, and was safeguarded by American-trained Chinese troops and American bases. Between Formosa and the mainland the Chinese Nationalists still held Quemoy, Matsu, and the Tachen and Nanchi islands.[11] To the south there were the security provisions of the pacts with the Philippines, Australia, and New

---

[11] The Tachen and Nanchi islands were evacuated by the Nationalists in February 1955 under cover of the US Seventh Fleet.

Zealand. The communist government of China was not recognized by the United States nor seated in the United Nations, and the United States had succeeded in gaining acceptance amongst its allies for its own policy of embargo on trade with China. In this way much was done to provide for a rapid response to any infringement of the line, which although not as clear-cut as in Europe, was nevertheless by now evident in the Far East. Moreover in January 1954 Dulles suggested that American strategy would not rely solely on meeting limited attacks in the area where they were made. Speaking to the Council on Foreign Relations on 12 January 1954, he said that the National Security Council had decided 'to depend primarily upon a greater capacity to retaliate, instantly, by means and at places of our own choosing'. [12]

This position of strength which the United States had taken up, first under the Truman administration and then with the changed style of Dulles's conduct of foreign policy, was only partially supported by its allies. As we have seen, the Korean war had not convinced the British Labour government of the justice of the American case with regard to China. It continued to believe that communist China should be seated in the United Nations, and to be suspicious of American support for Chiang Kai-shek. It began by favouring the return of Formosa to China, and then put forward a policy of 'two Chinas' – in contrast to the American supposition that the government of Chiang Kai-shek was still the lawful government of China as a whole. The Labour government had insisted in the negotiations for the Japanese peace treaty that Japan should remain free, when its full sovereignty had been restored, to choose with which Chinese government it would establish relations; but in January 1952 a letter from the Japanese prime minister, Yoshida, to Dulles revealed that he had given an undertaking that Japan would establish relations with Taipeh and not with Peking, and the change of government which had occurred in Britain in the interim made little difference to the criticism which this provoked. The British government had at first resisted the idea of an embargo on trade with China, and wished to confine restrictions to strategic imports; at the same time it received with bad grace a Japanese peace treaty which seemed to expose British trade once again to the full force of Japanese competition. The anxiety which had prompted Attlee to fly to Washington in December

[12] *American Foreign Policy, 1950–5*, i. 83.

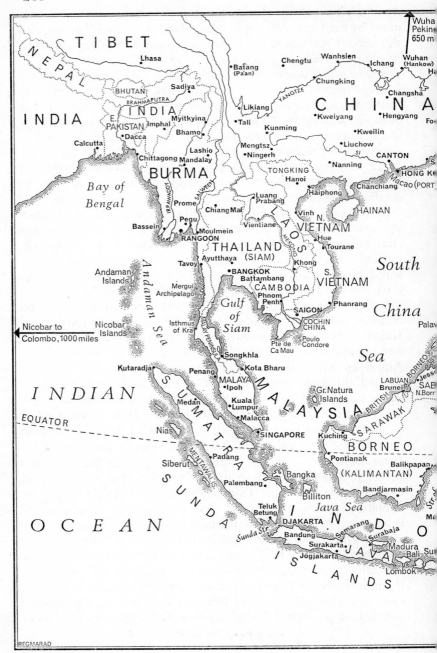

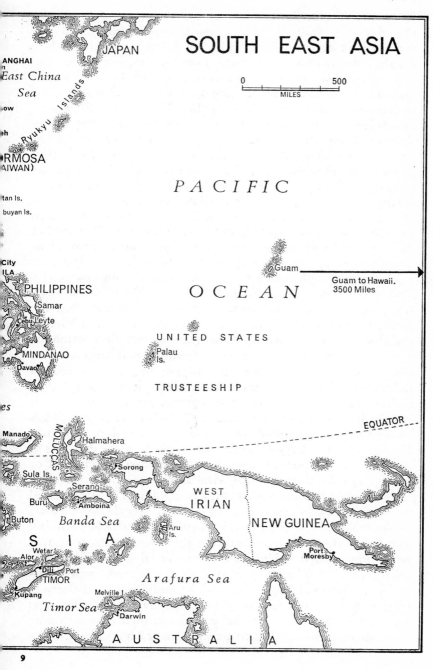

SOUTH EAST ASIA

0   500
MILES

ANGHAI

East China
Sea

ow

eh

Ryukyu Islands

RMOSA
AIWAN)

tan Is.

buyan Is.

PACIFIC

City
ILA

PHILIPPINES

Samar

Cebu Leyte

OCEAN

Guam

Guam to Hawaii.
3500 Miles

UNITED   STATES

Palau
Is.

MINDANAO

Davao

TRUSTEESHIP

es

EQUATOR

Manado

MOLUCCAS

Halmahera

Sula Is.

Sorong

Serang

WEST
IRIAN

Buru

Amboina

Buton

Banda Sea

Aru
Is.

NEW GUINEA

S I A

Wetar

Alor

Dili   Port
TIMOR

Kupang

Port
Moresby

Arafura Sea

Melville I.

Timor Sea

Darwin

A U S T R A L I A

9

1950 after Truman's mention of the atomic bomb was only redoubled by Dulles's talk of 'massive retaliation' and the explosion of an American hydrogen bomb in March 1954. Finally, the British government attached importance to the attitude of India and other Asian countries to the Far Eastern question, while Dulles at this time did not conceal his antipathy to the neutralism of Indian foreign policy. These actual differences in foreign policy between the two countries were only made sharper by the fact that each government was under attack from an extremist wing. In the United States Senator McCarthy prodded the administration with accusations of harbouring communists; in Britian the Bevanites resisted proposals for German rearmament and questioned the whole assumption of the policy of strength. In each country these manifestations of extremism in the other were exaggerated, and it was thought in Britain that the day must soon come when McCarthy would be president and (in America) that Bevan would soon be prime minister.

There remained, however, one area which was not covered by a security organization – that of South East Asia; and the gap was more striking since it was precisely in this area that the greatest immediate military threat existed. French and Vietnamese forces had been unable to win a victory over the communist Vietminh. They suffered from lack of political will, both amongst the Vietnamese and in the French government thousands of miles away. France clung tenaciously to winning the war, but its government failed to adopt the rigorous measures which this required. No conscripts were sent to Indo-China; French forces included German members of the foreign legion. Similarly France accepted large-scale American aid to meet the costs of the war, but had no wish to see the conflict 'internationalized' or to acquaint the United States with the course of the campaign.

To these factors was added at the beginning of 1954 a classical military mistake of great magnitude. The French commander, General Navarre, decided that it was necessary to hold Vietminh forces away from Laos and prevent their movement westwards by occupying and holding the village of Dien Bien Phu. The village was 300 kilometres away from the nearest French positions, and although there were no Vietminh forces in the area to offer resistance, it could only be taken by paratroopers, and supplied from the air – first by parachute, then from a rapidly constructed airstrip. The village was in a valley, surrounded by

hills on all sides so that everything depended on the French retaining complete freedom to fly in supplies and equipment, and
on the Vietminh being prevented, by the surrounding terrain, by
their lack of heavy weapons, and by aerial interdiction from
attacking the position with a heavy concentration of fire power,
particularly artillery. Unfortunately these conditions were not
fulfilled, and Dien Bien Phu immediately passed from being a
striking example of the supremacy of air power to being the most
vulnerable position which had ever been occupied voluntarily in
modern warfare. The Vietminh forces proved to be equipped
with long-range artillery with which they had been supplied
from China; by using brute force and sheer human determination
they moved themselves and their equipment through the hills,
mainly at night, in order to take up position; and they succeeded
in installing their artillery under clever camouflage on the down-
ward slope of the surrounding hills, scorning a safer but less
effective position on the reverse side. Once this had been done it
was no longer possible for the French to maintain supplies from
the air, there was no scope for generalship, however skilled, and
bravery was of no avail. The newly constructed fortress was lost
in advance, at the cost of some of the best units in the French
army; and that in turn meant that instead of being in a position
to launch a successful offensive in the main sector of the war, the
French and Vietnamese forces were themselves open to defeat by
the Vietminh.

By this time there had been much talk between the United
States, Britain, and France about the possibility of organizing a
defence pact in the South East Asia area. The idea had been put
forward to the Truman administration by the French in 1952;
it was welcomed by the British, who were eager for support in the
war they were fighting in Malaya. But such long-term plans did
not meet the needs of the immediate situation. On the one hand
the conduct of the war in Indo-China had reached a decisive
turning-point; on the other it had been agreed at the abortive
Berlin conference that a further foreign ministers' conference
should be held to discuss the Far East, and that it should convene
at Geneva on 26 April 1954. This conjunction of circumstances
meant that the way was open to a radical change in the situation
in South East Asia, either by military means or by negotiation.

The origins of the Geneva conference were themselves complex
and tortuous. The first proposal at Berlin had been for a con-

ference to discuss the Korean question. On United States initiative the scope of the conference was then widened to cover the problem of Indo-China. But this exchange raised the question of China's status and participation. The Soviet Union sought to take advantage of the American wish for the conference to take place to secure acceptance of communist China as a great power on equal terms with the others – and this attempt was resisted with equal force by the American government. Only very shortly before the conference was due to meet was a compromise arrived at which provided for equal participation of China at the conference, but agreed that 'neither the invitation to, nor the holding of, the above-mentioned conference shall be deemed to imply diplomatic recognition in any case where it has not already been accorded'.[13]

In so far as the conference was concerned with the problems of Korea, it was abortive. The actual aims of each side were irreconcilable, since the Russians supported the North Koreans in pressing for reunification without internationally supervised free elections, followed by the withdrawal of foreign troops; while the west wanted supervised free elections in the whole of Korea, which they were confident would lead to the emergence of a non-communist government.[14] Since the war itself had shown that neither side could achieve its objective without running the risk of general war, and since the division of Korea as it had emerged from the war was as good a second best as was to be found, it is not surprising that no general settlement was arrived at, either at the Geneva conferences or later.

The British view of the Indo-China problem was that it was essentially similar to that of Korea. Total victory was only open to either side at the risk of general war; while the only negotiated settlement which could be envisaged was one which provided for a balance of forces, either in the form of a coalition government including the communists, or partition – and of these two the latter was clearly preferable to the British government. Once partition had been secured, it would be guaranteed both by undertakings from the parties to the agreement, and by the development of a South East Asia security organization follow-

---

[13] RIIA, *Documents, 1954*, p. 78.
[14] The South Korean government did not want elections in the whole of Korea, need to be view that the elections already held in the South in May 1954 did not taking the repeated so soon after the event.

ing the pattern of NATO. For the United States in contrast the first problem was the defence of South East Asia. Immediately before the opening of the conference Dulles, in consultation with Bidault and Eden, had explored the possibility of American intervention in the war itself. It was recognized that it was too late to save the fortress of Dien Bien Phu, but both Dulles and Admiral Radford, representing the joint chiefs of staff, pressed for the maximum use of American forces consistent with the president's constitutional power, together with immediate support from the British forces in the area. It has been suggested that in separate discussions with the French government Dulles went so far as to offer nuclear weapons to the French. However, these proposals for American and British intervention came to nothing. They were dependent in the first place on French willingness to prosecute the war vigorously, in order to achieve military victory, followed by independence for Indo-China. Although at first Bidault appeared to welcome the offer of direct military aid (it should be remembered that the United States was already bearing a substantial part of the cost of the war), his government, under Joseph Laniel, lacked the authority to pursue a course so attendant with risk. The British government for its part made clear that it was opposed to the extension of the conflict. Even on the American side, it is reasonable to suppose that when the possibilities of intervention were examined in detail it would appear exceedingly difficult to intervene successfully in the type of warfare which was already going on in Indo-China, particularly if American forces had to be integrated with those of France and Vietnam – while the use of atomic and nuclear weapons was not only fraught with dangers of all kinds, but was scarcely adapted to the strategy or tactics of this kind of warfare.

The conduct of these discussions between the three western powers was by no means tidy and clear-cut. They appeared to have proved abortive by the time the conference opened on 26 April. But on 4 May Dulles returned from Geneva to Washington, handing over United States representation at the conference to Bedell Smith. The other members of the conference continued to be represented by foreign ministers and the conference was the focal point of their diplomacy; but the United States government had reduced its commitment to a conference which appeared likely to result in recognition, and possibly even guarantee, of communist conquest. Moreover in Washington Dulles was able to continue diplomacy on the sidelines of the conference itself. He pursued the possibility of establishing a security organization, somewhat to the alarm of the British, who wanted first to settle Indo-China. On 15 May this alarm was greatly increased when Eden read in the Swiss press of Franco-American discussions on the possibility of direct American military intervention, and Bedell Smith's explanation that the American government had merely contemplated training Vietnamese troops mitigated but did not allay Eden's anxiety.

Of the other members of the conference, the Soviet Union appeared the most anxious to reach a settlement; and Eden soon came to think that he and Molotov were working towards the same ends, against the constant tendency on the part of the United States to produce a hardening of attitudes on both sides. The Chinese and the Vietminh, and the Vietnamese, appeared less ready to make concessions than their allies; but the Vietnamese were clearly dependent on the French, and the Chinese and Vietminh seemed to be receptive to Russian pressure or persuasion. Moreover although Chou En-lai had given a vigorous demonstration of the new role which China might play in world affairs by flying off to visit Nehru in Delhi and U Nu in Rangoon in the early days of the conference, and visiting Ho Chi Minh on his way back to Peking, the communiqués which resulted from these meetings reaffirmed the 'five principles' of peaceful coexistence.

By mid-June the conference had made some progress; but the most decisive change came not at Geneva but in Paris. On 12 June the Laniel government fell, and a new government was formed under Pierre Mendès France. On 17 June he announced that he would seek an honourable cease-fire to be concluded within four weeks, and if no settlement was reached by 20 July he would resign. Thereupon the conference agreed to hand over detailed armistice negotiations to bilateral military committees, leaving the principal delegates free for a period of twenty-one days.

Diplomacy was thus dispersed between France, Switzerland, Britain, and the United States. Such diplomacy was effective because the great powers whose interests were directly concerned were in agreement that a settlement was preferable to a resumption of the conflict. British attention was devoted to gaining the support of the United States for an agreement, but had little success in bridging the gulf between the views of Dulles and those of the principal negotiators. The extent of this difference was evident when Eden, shortly before going with Churchill to Washington, spoke of the possibility of a reciprocal agreement similar to Locarno – implying that communist states could be accepted as equal partners in an inclusive treaty of guarantee. The American government in contrast would not give its approval to any agreement which placed Vietnamese under communist rule – although it could offer no alternative solution to the problem. Only with reluctance did the government decide that Bedell Smith should return to Geneva for the final phase of the conference, and although the two governments expressed their common intention to press forward with plans for collective defence, wide differences between them remained.

Eden and Mendès France flew back to Geneva on 14 July, only six days before the deadline which Mendès France had himself set for agreement. Final agreement was signed on 21 July. It divided Vietnam along the 17th parallel (the French having first insisted on the 18th, and the Vietminh having started from the 13th), thus leaving Hanoi and the Red river delta in the communist sector, but retaining the greater part of what the French had hoped for. No fresh troops or equipment were to be introduced into either zone or new military bases established, and the signatories were to ensure that the zones assigned to them did not adhere to any military alliance. The arrangement so made was intended to be temporary, and the agreement provided for elections to be held in the whole of Vietnam in July 1956. A tripartite commission (provided by Canada, Poland, and India) was set up to supervise the armistice arrangements and elections.

Separate armistice agreements were concluded for Laos and Cambodia. Cambodia, which had been relatively little involved in the fighting, was fully safeguarded. All foreign troops were to be withdrawn and the local insurgents to be demobilized and integrated into the political life of the country. Moreover the country was to be 'neutralized' although the wording of this part of the agreement left much room for interpretation. The agreement on Laos was less favourable to the government; the members of the Pathet Lao pro-Vietminh forces were given the choice between demobilizing or regrouping themselves in the two north eastern provinces of Phongsaly and Samneua; and in return the French High Command was allowed to retain 1,500 officers to train the Laotian army. Apart from this, all French and Vietminh forces were to be withdrawn and an election was provided for in 1955. As in Vietnam the settlement was to be supervised by a joint commission from the two high commands, and also by a tripartite commission from the same three powers.

The separate armistice agreements were embodied in a final declaration of the conference. This declaration was not signed by either the Vietnamese or the United States delegation. The former refused to accept the surrender to the Vietminh of territory occupied by Vietnamese troops and protested against the intrusion of the French high command into political matters. The United States refused to accept the agreement, and made its position clear in the special message read to the conference by Bedell Smith, in which he stated that the United States would refrain from the threat or use of force to disturb the armistice agreements, and would 'view any renewal of the aggression in violation of the aforesaid agreements with grave concern and as seriously threatening international peace and security'.[15]

An eight-year-old war was thus brought to an end. The settlement which had been agreed on was, however, precarious. In Vietnam both north and south sought the unity of the whole, but it was unlikely that either would be successful except by military force. Certainly there was no incentive for the holding of free elections once the pressure of outside force was removed (although, in contrast to Germany, it was the communist side which accused the south of putting off elections *sine die*). In the north the Vietminh lost no time in developing forces which could offer assistance to their supporters in the south in fighting a fresh guerrilla war. Against such infiltration the best defence which the new state of south Vietnam could offer was an efficient, democratic, and reforming state; but this the government of Ngo Dinh Diem (which had come into power during the Geneva conference) never succeeded in establishing.

In Laos the settlement also proved to be precarious. The country had escaped partition, but the Pathet Lao were firmly established in Phongsaly and Samneua under the leadership of Prince Souphannouvong. It therefore seemed difficult if not impossible to achieve the political unity of the country. Sporadic

[15] *DAFR, 1954*, p. 316.

fighting between Pathet Lao and government forces went on throughout 1955. In August of that year agreement was reached at Vientiane between the government of Souvanna Phouma, formed after elections of the preceding March, and the Pathet Lao. From then until 1958 Souvanna Phouma sought to follow a reformist policy at home and a neutralist foreign policy – although dependent on American aid, particularly to the army. In this endeavour he failed, at least in the short run. The Pathet Lao had, under the Vientiane agreement, formed a political party called the Lao Patriotic Front, which was a stronger force than any that Souvanna Phouma could command; in opposition to them right-wing forces, with the support of the army, formed a Committee for the Defence of National Interests. The latter grouping had the support of the United States, and between the two opposing forces it became increasingly difficult for Souvanna Phouma to survive. In August 1958 he was succeeded by Phoui Sananikone, who formed a government including four members of the Committee for the Defence of National Interests. In the spring of 1959 this government sought to complete the integration of the Pathet Lao forces into the national army, but the attempt was resisted by one battalion, and the gap between government and Pathet Lao once again widened.

The question of Laos now became once more of international importance. In March 1958 the International Control Commission set up at Geneva had dissolved, against the opposition of the Polish member, on the grounds that its work was done. The communist powers sought its reconvention without success. Then, at the beginning of 1959, charges of North Vietnamese intervention were made to the secretary-general of the United Nations, and countered by the communist powers. Britain and the Soviet Union, as co-chairmen of the Geneva conference, were unable to agree on terms for the reconvention of the Control Commission. In September 1959 the government of Laos asked the United Nations to dispatch an emergency force to resist aggression from North Vietnam. Instead a fact-finding commission was dispatched, which reported in November. Its report confirmed the provision of arms, supplies, and political advice to the Pathet Lao by the government of North Vietnam, but did not assert that there had been crossings of the frontier by regular North Vietnamese troops. This was followed during

9*

the same month by a visit on the part of Hammarskjöld to Laos. His report recommended a policy of neutralism for Laos, supported by United Nations aid.

Whatever possibilities such recommendations might have opened up were pushed aside when on 9 August 1960 Captain Kong Le, at the head of a small force of paratroopers, seized power in Vientiane. The exact political character of Kong Le was not easy to determine, even in Laotian terms. His coup won the approval of the communist powers, but he was not obviously a communist, and won the support of the neutralist Souvanna Phouma. Only at the last moment did he accept the support of the Pathet Lao army. He was, however, sufficiently on the left to provoke the establishment of a counter force of the right led by Boun Oum and Phoumi Nosavan at Savannakhet. By the end of 1960 this force had regained the capital and established a government there, without being strong enough to suppress or absorb their opponents. Inevitably the sporadic civil war now being fought increased the interest shown by the major contenders in the cold wars, minor and major, which raged outside Laos. China and the Democratic Republic of Vietnam maintained their assistance to Pathet Lao and the Soviet Union flew in support for Kong Le, while the weight of the United States was put behind Boun Oum. It was therefore a matter of major importance to Laos that the success of the Savannakhet forces in regaining the capital in December 1960 coincided approximately with the election of a new administration in Washington. President Kennedy proved sensitive to the advantages which a fresh attempt to establish a neutralist government might promise, and although a further eighteen months of civil war and international tension were to pass, a coalition government was formed in June 1962, and a neutral status for Laos agreed at a fourteen-nation conference at Geneva during July.

The settlement of Cambodia proved more stable than that of Laos. Vietminh forces were withdrawn and the integrity of the country was maintained. At first King Norodom Sihanouk resisted the neutralization of his country and looked for western support. But in 1955 he became aware of the possibilities of assuming fully the political role which he could not altogether avoid. He abdicated in favour of his father and then, as Prince Norodom Sihanouk, led a coalition movement widely based on Khmer nationalism and socialism. In foreign policy this meant that while he readily accepted aid from the United States, he also established close relations with the communist countries, and became the leading exponent of neutralism in South East Asia.

The Geneva conference and its concluding agreement had put into practice a distinctive approach to the problems of the area. Agreement involving concessions by both sides had been achieved, while both the concept of 'neutralization' and the institution of international commissions implied a continuing minimum of co-operation. At the same time it left the way clear, on the non-communist side for the negotiation of a collective defence treaty. The early negotiations to this end between the United States, Britain, France, Australia, and New Zealand had been taken further by an Anglo-American committee set up after the Churchill–Eden visit to Washington in June. The British government insisted that the new countries of South Asia be invited to participate in the discussions, since it attached great importance to the contacts which it had maintained with them throughout the Geneva conference. However, the invitation received a cool welcome from all except Pakistan. As a result the conference which met at Manila at the beginning of September was attended by only three Asian states – Thailand, the Philippines, and Pakistan, together with the United States, Britain, France, Australia, and New Zealand.

The treaty which they devised was known as the South-East Asia Collective Defence Treaty,[16] and was signed at Manila on 8 September 1954. The wording of the treaty itself and the documents which accompanied it brought out clearly both the political difficulties which surrounded it, and the divergent interests of the signatories. The core of the treaty was in Article IV, of which the first two paragraphs read:

1. Each Party recognizes that aggression by means of armed attack in the treaty area against any of the Parties or against any State or territory which the Parties by unanimous agreement may hereafter designate, would endanger its own peace and safety, and agrees that it will in that event act to meet the common danger in accordance with its constitutional processes. Measures taken under this paragraph shall be immediately reported to the Security Council of the United Nations.

[16] RIIA, *Documents, 1954*, p. 154.

2. If, in the opinion of any of the Parties, the inviolability or the integrity of the territory or the sovereignty or political independence of any Party in the treaty area or of any other State or territory to which the provisions of paragraph 1 of this Article from time to time apply is threatened in any way other than by armed attack or is affected or threatened by any fact or situation which might endanger the peace of the area, the Parties shall consult immediately in order to agree on the measures which should be taken for the common defence.

These two paragraphs, providing for 'action' in the event of aggression and 'consultation' in the event of an apparent threat to security were supplemented by a definition of the 'treaty area', which was contained in Article VIII, supplemented by a Protocol. The definition in Article VIII was 'the general area of South-East Asia, including also the entire territories of the Asian Parties, and the general area of the South-West Pacific not including the Pacific area north of 21 degrees 30 minutes north latitude'. This carefully defined latitude runs just south of the island of Formosa, which was thus excluded from the operation of the treaty. The Protocol[17] on the other hand extended the treaty area, to include: 'the States of Cambodia and Laos and the free territory under the jurisdiction of the State of Vietnam.' The treaty was thus carefully defined in extent. A further limitation was placed on its action by the United States, and the treaty included as part of its text an 'understanding of the United States of America' which read:

The United States of America in executing the present Treaty does so with the understanding that its recognition of the effect of aggression and armed attack and its agreement with reference thereto in Article IV, paragraph 1, apply only to Communist aggression, but affirms that in the event of other aggression or armed attack it will consult under the provisions of Article IV, paragraph 2.

It will be seen from this that the treaty was a carefully worded document. Nevertheless it might appear to smack of colonialism. It was therefore accompanied by a further declaration, known as the Pacific Charter,[18] which expressed important principles and intentions. The signatories declared their acceptance of the

[17] This Protocol followed from Art. VIII, which provided for the possibility of unanimous amendment to redefine the treaty area.
[18] RIIA, *Documents, 1954*, p. 157.

provisions of the United Nations Charter and the principle of equal rights and self-determination of peoples, and they undertook to co-operate in the political, economic, social, and cultural spheres to promote self-government and material advancement.

It is evident from the text of the treaty that it was very different from the North Atlantic treaty, to which it might seem to bear a superficial resemblance. The differences are even more apparent on closer examination. It was signed by only three Asian nations, and so was attacked by the others as a treaty more likely to create conflict than to allay the possibility of it. This charge was made particularly strongly by India, which was opposed altogether to a policy of 'blocs'. Moreover the Indian government had an additional reason for opposition to the treaty, in that it seemed to reinforce still further its neighbour, Pakistan, and it not unnaturally concluded that Pakistan sought strength and support to be better equipped for the Kashmir dispute rather than against the Soviet Union or China. Burma and Cambodia felt similar anxieties in their relations with Thailand. Thus while it was possible to talk about and aim towards an 'Atlantic community' (albeit with very little success), nothing comparable could be envisaged in South East Asia. Even the western members of SEATO were not unanimous in their attitude towards it. The French contribution to the alliance was always very small, and the French government did not hesitate to criticize publicly the military exercise in which the organization engaged, urging the greater importance of economic and cultural activities. This detachment from the alliance increased sharply with de Gaulle's advent to power, and once his government was free of the incubus of the Algerian problem, he began to urge a policy of neutralization of South East Asia which at that time ran counter to the attitudes of the other western powers.

Like NATO, SEATO set up its own organization, and appointed a secretary-general in September 1957. (He was Pote Saratin, a former foreign minister of Thailand.) It organized joint military exercises; but effective military co-operation between powers of such disparate strength dispersed over so wide an area was difficult to achieve. Nor has the SEATO Council engaged in political consultation with a broad purview, even to the extent that NATO has succeeded in doing.

In contrast to NATO, which has not yet been called on to face an actual conflict of arms, SEATO has been concerned with war

in Laos and with the possibility of large-scale Vietminh invasion
of that country in support of the Pathet Lao. It has also been
confronted with the problem of war in Vietnam. But the war
in Laos was a civil, guerrilla war against which conventional
warfare could achieve only limited success. Assistance from
across the border was even more difficult to counter. The
obvious means for SEATO to assist Laos would be by the use of
Thai troops: but this could have been no more welcome to Laos
in 1960 than, say, Hungarian assistance to Yugoslavia in the
1930s. The war in Vietnam brought a deep rift in the alliance:
when the Council met in May 1965 France did not attend
and Pakistan would not sign the communiqué.

The United States has played an independent role outside
SEATO, as well as being a full member. Initially it appeared that
the American government would limit its commitment to
SEATO; it decided that it would not commit forces of its own to
the South East Asia area. The greatest danger at this time seemed
to be that of Chinese aggression, and Dulles reaffirmed his earlier
policy of replying to such aggression, should it occur, at the place
of America's choosing. Thus at the first meeting of the SEATO
Council Dulles was reported as saying that the areas most vital
to the security of South East Asia lay outside the area itself, and
that the defence of the area must be conducted from South
Korea, Japan, and Formosa; and on 8 March 1955 he said in a
broadcast that he had 'pointed out at Bangkok that, for military
purposes, the Chinese Communist front should be regarded as
an entirety because if the Chinese Communists engage in open
armed aggression this would probably mean that they have
decided on general war in Asia'.[19]

At the same time the United States government had entered on
a programme of aid to the countries of South East Asia, and
assumed an independent role, often at variance with the views of
its SEATO allies. Aid to South Vietnam grew into the involvement of the United States in war against the Vietminh and
North Vietnam. Before that the proportion of such independent
American activity in relation to SEATO itself is indicated by
the fact that the United States Information Office in Thailand
had a budget and staff larger than that of SEATO.[20] American
aid had begun in 1950, and was increased when Laos, Cambodia,

[19] RIIA, *Collective Defence in South East Asia* (1956), pp. 121–2.
[20] George Modelski, ed., *SEATO* (1962), p. 18.

and Vietnam emerged as independent states after the Geneva agreement. As we have seen, the kingdom of Cambodia welcomed American aid while successfully pursuing a neutralist foreign policy – a change of direction from the decisively pro-western stand of the Geneva conference. In Laos the United States gave copious military aid, and sustained the whole of the Laotian military budget. But by so doing it did not make it possible for the government to achieve either the elimination of the independent Pathet Lao army or the political unification of the country; instead it created in the army a new and disruptive force in Laotian politics. It sought to maintain a stable anti-communist government in power, but from 1958 to 1960 achieved at best the reluctant agreement of its allies in the support which it offered to the right-wing anti-communists rather than to the neutral Souvanna Phouma.

For all that, SEATO represented a combination of Asian and 'western' countries united in opposition to communism. At the same time a quite different grouping appeared to be coming into existence. In January 1954 the prime ministers of Ceylon and Indonesia[21] agreed on the desirability of a meeting of the Colombo powers, with the possibility of wide participation on the part of African and Asian countries. The idea was pursued further at a meeting of the Colombo powers at Bogor in December 1954, and invitations were sent to a wide but by no means comprehensive assortment of African and Asian countries to attend a conference at Bandung in April 1955.[22] The purpose of the conference was entirely general, and so was its outcome. The interests of its participants were obviously of great diversity. Some states which might be thought of as African or Asian, notably South Africa and Israel, had been left out for obvious political reasons; even so the range of ideology and outlook on foreign affairs was very great. For some 'imperialism' had its old-fashioned meaning of the rule by European powers of Asians and Africans; for Kotelawala of Ceylon it included Russian domination over eastern Europe. The general tone of the conference was

---

[21] Sir John Kotelawala and Dr Sastroamidjojo.
[22] The Colombo powers (see below, p. 598f) sponsoring the conference were Burma, Ceylon, India, Indonesia, and Pakistan; those invited were Afghanistan, Cambodia, the Central African Federation, China, Egypt, Ethiopia, the Gold Coast, Iraq, Japan, Jordan, Laos, Lebanon, Liberia, Libya, Nepal, Persia, the Philippines, Saudi Arabia, Siam, the Sudan, Syria, Turkey, both North and South Vietnam, the Yemen. All accepted except the Central African Federation.

one of neutralism; but its membership included both China and members of SEATO, both North and South Vietnam. It was inevitable that the outcome of the conference should be wordy. A long communiqué[23] was produced, which expressed support for those grievances of individual members which did not cut across the interests of others – the Arab states against Israel, Indonesia against Holland over West Irian, and the Yemen against Aden. It pressed for the elimination of nuclear weapons under international control, and it enunciated ten principles of political conduct. Some of these were simple enough in their wording – 'respect for the sovereignty and territorial integrity of all nations; recognition of the equality of all races and of the equality of all nations large and small'.

The importance of the Bandung conference should not however be judged by the terms of its communiqué alone. It provided a meeting ground for small nations which previously had had little or nothing in common with each other, but which could now think of themselves as a force in international affairs. Leaders who until this time had felt themselves to be on the horns of a dilemma, desiring complete independence yet aware of their economic dependence on the west, now became aware that they could profitably seek aid and support from west and east while offering allegiance to neither – this was especially true of Sihanouk of Cambodia and Nasser of Egypt. Bandung above all marked the watershed between neutralism as a negative refusal to take sides and a positive policy. Henceforth neutralism would rapidly acquire respectability in international politics and emotional support at home – for very often 'neutralism' was a new word to evoke the old force of nationalism.

Neutralism was not new at Bandung. Under the form of 'non-alignment' it had characterized Indian foreign policy since independence. Inheriting a Gandhian tradition and inspired by Nehru, the Indian government and Indian political leaders demonstrated that Asia had suffered historically from European conflicts fought across its territory, in which it had no interest. These wars represented a moral decline in the west from which Asia, whatever its other failings, had been free – the great exception of Japanese conquest proved the rule, since the fault of Japan had been its emulation of the west. The cold war which had developed between Russia and the west was a successor to these conflicts, with the difference that India and other Asian countries had achieved their independence and become a force in international affairs. They should therefore remain true to their inheritance and maintain their moral standards. They should not be drawn into either power bloc and they should not commit themselves to either side. They should act as mediators while the conflict continued and stand ready as it diminished – for diminish it would, following the pattern of earlier struggles – to bring the two sides together in harmony.

Critics of Indian foreign policy argued that India was merely following its own national interest, taking advantage of a balance of power which provided an umbrella for Indian independence but which only persisted because the Atlantic powers pursued just those policies which India so readily condemned as immoral. They saw little sign of higher standards in Indian handling of the Kashmir dispute or, later, the Indian invasion of Goa. For others the test of Indian foreign policy was in its relations with China, and as we shall see, comparatively little time was to pass before the Indian government was urgently seeking support to ward off Chinese invasion.

However that may be, neutralism was a force of growing attractiveness for newly independent states – and others. It took varying forms, depending on the geographical, historical, and political position of each state. The neutralism of Yugoslavia had obvious roots in the conflict with Stalin, while that of Sweden, Finland, and Austria had a closer affinity with the traditional neutrality of Switzerland. In the hands of a clever politician like Nasser, neutralism had less of the moral overtone which Nehru gave to it and was more a weapon of great potentiality to gain the maximum advantage from each side in the cold war, with a minimum commitment. For some of the new African states 'positive neutralism' included a large element of anti-colonialism and implied a contrived policy of seeking aid from the east to square the circle of emotional independence coupled with actual dependence on outside aid – which was readily forthcoming from the west. In this important and luxurious growth Bandung played a key part. It was followed six years later by the Belgrade 'neutralist summit' conference of September 1961.[24]

[24] For an essay on neutralism see the book under that title by Peter Lyon, Leicester University Press, 1963.

The Geneva and Bandung conferences left no doubt about the importance of the role which China was likely to play in future international politics, but the precise nature of Chinese foreign policy was extremely difficult to forecast. To many, China appeared as a potential great power; but it was impossible to predict how soon this potentiality would be realized. The rapidly growing population of China, which might one day become a major source of strength (and which undoubtedly contributed to the general sense of alarm which was often felt towards China), was an obstacle to economic development in the short run, in spite of the intelligent use which the Chinese made of their prolific labour supply as a substitute for capital.

In this respect the Chinese view of themselves was equally a factor of real importance. They had never thought of themselves as a country in the 'Far East'. On the contrary, China was the centre of the world, and all other nations were barbarians. The isolation to which China was subjected by the refusal of the United States (and other governments) to recognize the communist government and its exclusion from the United Nations encouraged rather than limited this feeling of natural superiority.

A similar dichotomy appeared when China was considered as a communist power. During the civil war, and in the early days of the communist government, many people, particularly in Britain, were willing to see the Chinese communists as 'agrarian reformers'. This concept soon disappeared; but the exact nature of Chinese communism was difficult to determine; and certainly China was regarded as being in varying ways a communist country second to the Soviet Union. The Chinese view of themselves once again rapidly came to differ fundamentally from this. It came naturally to the country which under the T'ang dynasty had regarded itself as the centre of the world, the upholder of civilization against the barbarians, to assume in a more modern period the role of defender of the faith, the depository of the revolutionary ideal, a modern version of the 'lawgiver to the barbarians'.[25]

There were other reasons for doubt concerning the part which China could be expected to play in Asian affairs. China was now laying claim to be the true inspiratory centre of world revolution. But in its day it had been a great empire. Would it then behave,

[25] This view of China is one that has consistently been put forward by C. P. Fitz-Gerald. See for example his Chatham House Essay, *The Chinese View of Their Place in the World* (1964).

not as a revolutionary communist power, but in the pursuit of traditional objectives and historical boundaries? Moreover its people had emigrated from China, and were now to be found in large numbers, particularly in the countries of South East Asia. Would these important groups act as an advance guard for a Chinese communist revolution – playing the part that they had done in Malaya? Or would Chinese support of its minorities, regardless of their political allegiance, create diplomatic difficulties with China's neighbours – as seemed to be the case in Indonesia? Whatever the answers to these questions, there was little doubt that the overseas Chinese themselves looked to China, making no change in their attitude now that it was a communist country, as a homeland, to which they sent remittances, and from which they expected the maintenance of national greatness. So much was this so that even the Chinese on Formosa supported the claims which the communist government made against India.

One further difficulty in interpreting and forecasting China's foreign policy lay in the fact that it seemed possible for China to develop and exploit its position in Asia, by wooing those nations which were naturally hypersensitive to imperialism and by building up a clientèle of states whose aspirations were in the first place nationalist and not communist; while on the other hand it appeared equally possible for China to assert its primacy by a policy of toughness and force. It was the first of these possibilities which characterized the early years of the new régime, and was extended into the conciliatory policies of the Bandung conference; it was best defined in the 'five principles' which China seemed ready to agree with all its Asian neighbours, and was developed still further by aid which it could ill afford to such countries as Guinea. On the other hand the Chinese government had early established what it regarded as its hereditary rights over Tibet; and as we shall see, when these were challenged by a revolution among the Khampa tribes it exhibited unrestrained ferocity in reaffirming its rule.

In the midst of this uncertainty one element of Chinese foreign policy was clear, and that was its hostility to the United States. It was the United States which defended not only Formosa but the offshore islands of Quemoy and Matsu; and however much foreigners might question China's claims in other parts of the world, it remained convinced that its claim to Formosa was unquestionable, the more so since Britain and the United States (and Chiang Kai-shek) had recognized it as part of China in the Cairo declaration of 1943. The United States had intervened in Korea and supported the French in Indo-China; the United States was the most effective and resolute power preventing Chinese admission to the United Nations, and had sponsored a motion there to 'brand China as an aggressor'; while Dulles had made clear the intention of his administration to take massive action against the mainland of China in pursuit of the policy of containment.

The conflict between the two powers was most intense in 1958, when China made her most determined effort to wrest the off-shore islands of Quemoy and Matsu from the Nationalists. In their defence of the islands the Nationalists had the full support of the United States. Indeed the readiness of Dulles to go to the brink of war to aid the defence of islands just off the coast of China was one of the aspects of his foreign policy which had excited the maximum alarm and opposition amongst his allies. But by providing the Nationalist forces with modern weapons the American government made possible the successful defence of a position which was otherwise quite untenable. It is easy to understand that if American policy caused disquiet among its allies, Russian restraint should cause a major rift between the two communist powers. Chinese aircraft were shot down by American sidewinder missiles, and China had access to no comparable (or superior) weapons with which to reply. Not only that but Russia positively refused to support China with more than words; and Khrushchev prepared to visit the United States and talk with Eisenhower at Camp David. As has been shown elsewhere, the growing rift between Russia and China owed most to the refusal of the Soviet Union to share its nuclear knowledge or weapons with China; the failure to provide actual and armed support in the pursuit of what China regarded as its most legitimate claims against its most irreconcilable enemy, and the readiness of Russia to enter into friendly negotiations with that enemy, only intensified Chinese feelings of bitterness. For the first time in its history China had an ally, and one to which it might expect to be linked by more than national interest; but the conduct of its ally seemed to confirm the Chinese in their harshest judgement of the perfidy of foreigners.[26]

[26] Cf. FitzGerald, *The Chinese View*, pp. 51 ff.

8

ATLANTIC ALLIANCE AND
EUROPEAN UNION

THE NORTH Atlantic treaty was a new kind of alliance, and was set in unprecedented conditions of international politics. Hitherto peacetime alliances between democratic countries had been rare, and the few that had been signed had been intended to maintain the existing state of affairs against possible revisionism on the part of an opponent. This was not true of the North Atlantic treaty; ideally the signatories would have liked to change fundamentally the political framework of Europe. As events turned out they were unable to do so; but the desire to alter the existing political system brought criticism of NATO from two opposing sides: from those who asserted that it was not doing enough to effect change in Europe; and from those who insisted that the existence of NATO meant the sacrifice of any possible chance of achieving revision by negotiation.

None of the signatories wanted to accept as permanent the Russian occupation of eastern Europe. There were no obvious means, short of massive frontal attack, by which the withdrawal of Russian troops could be secured; but this did not stop politicians and public from hankering after such a possibility from time to time. This was particularly true during the election campaign in the United States in 1952, when the future secretary of state, Dulles, spoke of the inadequacy of a holding operation, which stopped short of the 'liberation' of eastern Europe, and expressed a hope which was not readily abandoned by those who had lived through communist rule – some of them in the United States, where immigrants from eastern Europe were a constant reminder to politicians.

Germany formed a special case. The attitude of public and governments to eastern Germany was more complicated, and subject to many variations. On the one hand Germany was still regarded as the defeated enemy; on the other it had lost territory to communist Poland, and eastern Germany was under communist rule. Attitudes varied, therefore, according to the importance attached to each of these considerations. But more important was the fact that Germany was divided. The natural German desire for reunification evoked some sympathy in the west – the more as the distance from the earlier experience of the use Germany had made of unity increased. In addition, the view was widely held that there could not be peace in Europe while Germany was divided. Different reasons were given for holding this view; they all stemmed from the feeling that there was something unnatural about such a division, and that it was an open invitation to the wrecking force of German nationalism. It was argued that if the east Germans rose in revolt against Russian rule, the west Germans could not prevent themselves going to their aid; that the west Germans would, when they were sufficiently recovered and under new leaders, spontaneously seek reunification by force, or the recovery of the lost provinces; or alternatively that they would 'do a deal with the Russians' to secure reunification. The conclusion to be drawn from such arguments was obviously that the most important objective of policy must be the reunification of Germany, in order to remove the most pressing danger to peace, and to forestall a Russian attempt to buy Germany by offering reunification. To the extent that NATO inhibited diplomacy to this end it was opposed and criticized.

There were other grounds for opposition to NATO, which derived from a different interpretation of national interest. On the continent of Europe the most important political force of this kind was that of the neutralists. Their policy was essentially one of seeking security in weakness; they argued that as they were not strong enough to defend themselves, they should stand aside from any possible conflict altogether; if they succumbed to it, they could not fare worse than if they had accepted the weight and implications of an alliance. This view was particularly strong and widespread in France, where the experience of the last war led people to believe that France could not by any efforts avoid being overrun, and that it would be better advised to save money and avoid provocation by remaining weak. While in most of Europe neutralism found its political home amongst the left, in France it was in addition represented by the prominent daily, *Le Monde*, which was widely read in business and professional circles.

A similar form of neutralism appeared in Germany, particularly in reaction to the proposal that Germany should rearm. It was described by the phrase 'ohne mich', and was a local variant of the desire to contract out of a possible future war. Similar emotions and ideas were expressed, particularly by left-wing socialists, in Italy and Britain. The local variation which was most prominent in Britain laid considerable stress on the argument that the communist threat was economic and social rather than military – a view that was put forward repeatedly by Aneurin Bevan and his followers in the Labour party.

Whatever the local variation, neutralism of this kind appeared more attractive when it claimed to represent a 'third force' in world politics. The phrase was taken from French politics, where the confrontation of communists and Gaullists, after the government's break with the communists in April 1947 and the creation of the *Rassemblement du peuple français*, encouraged a certain degree of cohesion and solidarity amongst the middle parties, since by this alone could parliamentary majorities be achieved. The transference of the phrase to international affairs was, however, misleading; for within France the third force was unmistakably anti-communist, and by remaining in office it commanded the coercive power of the state. In international politics, by contrast, neutralism was less decisive in its attitude to the Soviet Union; and Europe without America was at this time so weak that the word 'force' was a misnomer. Another decade was to pass before General de Gaulle embarked on his attempt to create a third force in the full sense of the term.

In the United States neutralism had its equivalent in a new form of isolationism, but it was an isolationism of strength. No one supposed that a world conflict could bypass the United States, or sought refuge in weakness; while the theme that military expenditure inhibited negotiation and limited defence on the economic front had only a few adherents after the resignation of Wallace. Thus in the American context the alternative policy to NATO was the strengthening of the United States alone for the defence of the North American continent. The signature and the implementation of the North Atlantic treaty meant that within five years of the time when Roosevelt supposed that American troops would leave Europe altogether soon after the end of the war, it appeared probable that they would remain there, in strength, indefinitely. It was inevitable that this would provoke

major controversy, and the occasion for the intensification of the
discussion was Truman's decision to reinforce American troops
in Europe in response to the threat implied by the war in Korea.
This launched what was known as the 'Great Debate' in American
politics. As in many other similar debates, the arguments were
often framed in constitutional terms, and isolationists like Senator
Bricker of Ohio sought to limit the independence of the president
in foreign affairs, and the scope of his power as commander-in-
chief. Essentially the debate was over foreign policy and strategy;
the degree of American commitment to Europe, and whether
American security could be best achieved by the holding of a
line in Europe, or withdrawal behind the oceanic borders of the
United States. As might be expected, such views found their
strongest expression in the Republican party.

Opposition to NATO was the more persuasive since the nature
of the threat from the Soviet Union was ill defined in 1949. It
was easy to trace the events which had led to the signature of the
alliance – the Russian domination of eastern Europe, the Berlin
blockade, the Czechoslovak coup d'état; but it was equally easy
to point out that only the second of these could have been met by
military means, short of a frontal attack. True, the North
Atlantic treaty did not confine itself to military measures.
Article 2 of the treaty reads:

The Parties will contribute toward the further development of
peaceful friendly international relations by strengthening their free
institutions, by bringing about a better understanding of the principles upon which these institutions are founded, and by promoting
conditions of stability and well-being. They will seek to eliminate
conflict in their international economic policies and will encourage
economic collaboration between any or all of them.

In practice, however, the work of the alliance in this field was
very limited, and economic co-operation was left to OEEC. In
any case, the first objective was to build up armed strength, and
this meant expenditure which could otherwise have been diverted
to economic and social welfare – the area in which, according to
some, the main battle with communism should be fought and
won.

The strength of arguments of this kind naturally varied with
events. They were diminished by the attack on South Korea; but
they were given a particularly sharp edge when 'military

strength' came to embrace the possibility of German rearmament; they acquired conviction with the death of Stalin and the apparent possibility of a new start in international relations. Economic arguments were especially strong in Britain, where the burden of NATO fell most heavily on the balance of payments, because British troops were stationed in Germany. The 'miracle' of German recovery, coupled with recurrent financial crises in Britain, meant that it was increasingly difficult for Britain to finance its commitment to NATO – unlike other European countries, whose main contribution was made on their own soil and therefore in their own currencies. The attitude of successive British governments to their NATO obligations was inevitably coloured by this fact; it also gave a more convincing background to the arguments of Bevanites and others who opposed German rearmament and advocated economic and social rather than military policies.

The Soviet Union was well aware of the nature and strength of this natural resistance to rearmament and alliances. It was very easy for communists to refer to NATO as a 'military alliance', and this phrase caught on amongst many who had little sympathy with communism. The Soviet Union encouraged, both by direct diplomacy and through the intermediary of the east German government, the idea that German reunification could be achieved – although obviously at the sacrifice of German participation in a western alliance. It also developed propaganda in favour of 'peace'. A conference of intellectuals was held in Wroclaw in the autumn of 1948, and this was followed by the setting up of a World Peace Council which met in Berlin in February of the next year. A further meeting took place in Vienna in November. Such gatherings no doubt provided opportunities for the transmission of information and directives amongst communists; but they also served to provide a sounding board for the amplification of opposition to the policy of 'military alliances'.

In spite of opposition to the alliance, from its internal critics and from the Soviet Union, it became an established institution, although it never acquired the degree of cohesion, unity, or stability which its warmest supporters hoped for. In none of the member countries did there occur a major electoral defeat which prejudiced the future of the alliance. The success of the Christian Democrats in Germany, in 1953, the choice of Eisenhower as

Republican candidate for the presidency in 1952, and the impotence of the left wing of the British Labour party, in opposition after 1951, assured the continued existence of the alliance. Moreover it gained in strength in 1951, by the admission of Greece and Turkey to membership. The application which the governments of these two countries made for admission to NATO had been received with some hesitation by member governments, for the understandable reason that a slight accretion of strength was balanced by a greater weight of commitment. The addition of Turkey appeared particularly hazardous, since it could be seen as a provocation to the neighbouring Soviet Union, and Turkey was difficult to defend against actual attack. But these hesitations were overruled, and a protocol to the North Atlantic treaty, signed on 22 October 1951, provided for Greece and Turkey to become full members of the alliance. It thereafter became even more difficult to justify the title of the alliance; but its strategic strength was increased by the inclusion of these Mediterranean states.

During the first five years of its existence, the alliance undertook unprecedented steps to build up military strength and political cohesion. It started from little more than nothing. The Brussels Treaty Organization had begun a certain amount of military planning, including the provision of 'infrastructure' for defence which NATO was able to take over; but it amounted to little. Britain and the United States had troops stationed in Europe, a fact of cardinal importance, since it was so much easier to strengthen such forces once they were there. But while the political importance of this fact cannot be exaggerated, the military strength of such forces was small indeed; not only were they limited in size, but they were organized as an army of occupation, and were in every way vulnerable as a defence force against the Soviet Union. It was necessary to reverse the postwar trend, to rearm and re-equip, and to do so along lines agreed by the whole alliance, with a fair sharing of the burden.

On the military side, in addition to the straightforward strengthening of military forces, the problems may be summarized as the need to agree on a strategy, to set up a command structure, to integrate national forces, and to provide a military infrastructure common to the whole alliance. In political terms the problem was to set up a suitable civilian administrative structure and to devise a machinery for taking policy decisions. This applied particularly to the economic and financial aspects of rearmament, which would bear some relation to the capabilities of member countries, but which would at the same time draw out from them a greater effort than they might make if left to themselves, or if the natural tendency to let someone else take the burden should be allowed to prevail. In addition, the alliance was presented within the first year of its existence with a political problem of the first magnitude which no one had foreseen when it was signed – the rearmament of western Germany. This followed as a direct result of the attack on South Korea and the sense of urgency and alarm which it provoked. But as soon as this problem was posed, the French reluctance to see a German army, even within the framework of NATO, led to the proposal that German troops should be raised as part of a European army. In this way German rearmament became intimately bound up with the question of European unification, and it is in this context that it will be discussed. The speed with which these problems were tackled naturally varied. In 1949 a relatively slow start was made; in 1950 and 1951 the Korean war brought frantic haste; as the immediate urgency subsided the pace settled down to a long haul.

It was agreed that the grand strategy of the alliance should be one of forward defence, as near to the eastern border of western Europe as possible. A decisive step was then taken in December 1950, when General Eisenhower was appointed as supreme commander in Europe – a post which he held until May 1952 when he resigned in order to campaign for the presidency.[1] He immediately organized a supreme headquarters in Paris, and set up four subordinate commands, to cover northern, central, and southern Europe and the Mediterranean. At the same time as Eisenhower's appointment the NATO Council agreed to set up a supreme command for the Atlantic. The implementation of this decision took longer (until January 1952) as a result of the opposition of Winston Churchill, both as leader of the opposition and later as prime minister, to the appointment of an American to a command which he thought should fall to a British officer.[2]

---

[1] His successors were Generals Ridgway, May 1952 to July 1953; Gruenther, 1953–6; Norstad 1956–62; and Lemnitzer, 1962—.
[2] For a time his compatriots pretended that they could not pronounce the name of the American admiral proposed for the command (Fechteler). Admiral Lynde McCormick (USA) was finally appointed.

The special problems of the Channel area were covered by a Channel Committee, consisting of the chiefs of naval staffs of Belgium, France, the Netherlands, and the United Kingdom.[3] A Canada–United States planning committee was also established, responsible among other things for a warning system for North American defence.

Under the commanders, headquarters were set up which were genuinely international; French and English were adopted as the languages of the alliance, and as officers of different nationalities worked together on a NATO staff they acquired NATO loyalties and a certain measure of *esprit de corps*. Integration was not attempted except at staff level. National forces were placed under NATO command; they were either assigned to NATO, or earmarked to come under NATO either at some future date or in the event of attack. (In addition, some member countries, Britain and France as well as the United States, retained some of their forces under national control.) The proposal for German rearmament at first evoked the suggestion that international military units should be formed, in which the Germans would be 'lost'; but this came to nothing, and there were no other advantages to be gained from breaking up national commands, subordinate to the appropriate NATO commander. At the same time all NATO forces benefited from the NATO infrastructure of airfields, pipelines, and communications systems. A certain amount of standardization of communications and armaments was introduced, and above all NATO manoeuvres gave practice in fully co-ordinated operations.

The civilian side of the organization provided more complex problems, and they were amongst the many sent to a Temporary Council Committee[4] in September 1951. The report of the committee made the next meeting of the Council, at Lisbon in February 1952, one of the most important in the development of the alliance. It provided a guarantee (abortive in the event) of the European Defence Community. It also reorganized the Council, which now became a body in permanent session. Ministerial meetings were to take place three times a year; but throughout the year the Council would meet in the persons of permanent representatives, and it would be charged overall with

---

[3] There was a sixteenth-century precedent for this arrangement (see Ismay, *NATO* (1957)).
[4] Averell Harriman, Edwin (later Lord) Plowden, and Jean Monnet.

questions not only of defence but of financial and economic policy. The Council would be served by a secretariat, under a secretary-general, who in the first place was Lord Ismay, chief staff officer to Churchill (as minister of defence) during the war.[5] Furthermore, the Council instituted as permanent practice the procedure which the TCC had devised in the preceding six months, and which became known as the Annual Review. It consisted essentially of an analysis of defence requirements, followed by an exhaustive examination of the defence and financial programmes of member governments in order to see how these requirements could be met.

The goals which this meeting of the Council actually set – including fifty divisions in Europe – were never in fact reached. But the obvious way in which to work towards such a target was for each member country to devise a plan of 'ways and means', and for this to be reconciled (usually, it must be admitted, by scaling down the targets) with defence needs. This process, which very quickly acquired a continuous pattern covering each defence year, was in many ways similar to the estimates and budget procedure of a single country; the difference was that it was an international organization which drew up the estimates, and national governments which were asked to meet them.

The military side of the alliance structure continued to be headed by a Military Committee, made up of the chief of staff of each member country, and a continuously active body (since chiefs of staff could meet only rarely), the Military Representatives Committee. To expedite planning and to provide a more manageable committee a smaller body, known as the Standing Group, had also been established, consisting of representatives of the three powers whose forces were of greatest importance – Britain, France, and the United States. As the alliance was an intergovernmental organization, depending on the affirmative vote of all its members, the Standing Group had no independent power; but its influence and directing role could at times be of great importance.

The military committees of the alliance were located in Washington, while the Council had its headquarters in Paris. This gave the military men the advantage of greater independence from the political delegations concentrated in Paris, and

<hr/>

[5] He was succeeded in 1957 by Henri Spaak, who was followed in 1961 by Dirk Stikker.

made it easier for them to think of military objectives for the alliance as a whole to the maximum extent compatible with their status as national representatives. In order to connect the two sides a Standing Group Liaison Officer (later called Representative) was appointed and given a staff and office in Paris.

The work which had so far been done in planning and organization would have been of little practical use had not the alliance been given the means to implement its plans. In its early years these resources were afforded in large measure by the United States. The signature of the treaty was followed within a short time by the passage of a Mutual Defense Assistance Act, which provided military assistance to the value of a billion dollars in the next fiscal year – this being a separate programme from that already in existence under Marshall aid. In October 1951 economic and military aid were brought together under the United States Mutual Security Act, and as European recovery was now well under way the proportion of military assistance increased. Some of this aid took the form of 'offshore procurement' – an inexplicable piece of jargon which referred to the practice whereby the United States paid for military supplies produced in a European country and gave them to that country for NATO purposes. This was often cheaper than if they had been produced in the United States, and it enlarged the productive base of the European countries. On a smaller scale the Canadian government contributed to the equipping of European defence forces. In principle there was nothing exceptional about aid of this sort; Article 3 of the treaty itself provided that:

In order more effectively to achieve the objectives of this Treaty, the Parties, separately and jointly, by means of continuous and effective self-help and mutual aid, will maintain and develop their individual and collective capacity to resist armed attack.

In practice the transatlantic traffic was one way.

By 1954 immense progress had been made in establishing the organization, and giving it both permanence and an institutional character of its own. But the question of what precisely it was supposed to do remained one to which a blurred answer was usually given. In these early years the Council generally aimed at defence targets which were outside the capabilities and/or the will of member countries, and which, even if they had been achieved, would still have appeared meagre and inadequate compared with estimated Soviet strength in Europe, which in 1951 was placed at 175 divisions. The balancing force on which the western powers, therefore, relied was the atomic bomb; but only the United States at this time possessed atomic capability, and, in the hands of the Strategic Air Force, it was outside NATO control. It was, of course, intended that the atomic bomb should act as a deterrent; but no one was in serious doubt that if the Soviet bloc made a massive attack in Europe, the atomic bomb would have to be used in defence as well. As a result United States foreign and defence policy was directed towards the construction of a series of air bases from which the Strategic Air Force could operate, parallel to but outside the development of NATO. In this situation there was one compelling reason for the maintenance of adequate NATO forces in Europe, namely that they countered the possibility of a limited Soviet attack in Europe. If such an attack were made and there were no substantial conventional forces with which to offer resistance, the United States would be faced with the choice of doing nothing, or using atomic weapons, and this was a predicament to be avoided. It was in addition argued by some people in European countries that NATO was a means of keeping United States troops in Europe, so that an attack would involve the United States. In this way NATO forces would act as a 'tripwire'. These arguments, especially the former of the two, were of permanent importance throughout the many developments in atomic and nuclear weapons, and the changing strength and relationship between the United States and Europe. But it was much more difficult to give precise answers to the consequent questions, such as how strong the NATO forces needed to be for this purpose, and what part the NATO Council and the command structure would play in the event of an actual attack, given that the United States alone held the most powerful weapon.

The intergovernmental structure of the alliance and the achievement of very close co-operation without any element of supranationality followed closely the lines which the British would have liked to have laid down for European union. The NATO Council worked in many respects like a British cabinet, in that problems were talked out until agreement was reached, and votes were thereby avoided. The first secretary-general was British, and obviously drew on the experience of the cabinet secretariat. The near-revolutionary change in the relationship between governments, whereby they submitted their defence proposals to NATO examination and criticism, without accepting any supranational direction, accorded well with British practice, and even more with the exchange of information and discussion between Commonwealth countries. Moreover in NATO, as in the other movements towards integration at this time, the British applied a brake on any movement beyond intergovernmental co-operation.

None the less the British considered themselves as having gone far in abandoning their traditional isolation from Europe and avoidance of peacetime alliance. They were helped in so doing by the fact that there was always an element within NATO of a special Anglo-American relationship. In a sense the close military co-operation of NATO had grown out of the wartime joint chiefs of staff; certainly many British people failed to draw any distinction between the wartime SHAEF and the new SHAPE[6] – the more so since Eisenhower commanded both – and their view of European countries in relation to Britain and America was coloured by this. In these early years the actual contribution of Britain to the defence of Europe, at a time when France was far more deeply involved in war in Indo-China, the fact that Britain and France alone were members with America of the Standing Group, and that France was going through a period of internal political weakness, all helped to strengthen the special Anglo-American relationship, at least until Dulles took over as secretary of state.

NATO, like OEEC, had been created in response to an immediate practical necessity and both had achieved a degree of co-operation which would have been inconceivable before 1939. In addition, there existed on the continent of Europe a spontaneous movement towards the creation of a new community transcending national frontiers. The institutional developments to which this gave rise were closely linked with NATO and OEEC, and they also were stimulated by military and economic necessity. But the movement had its origins in the second world war, and derived its strength from positive hopes for the future as well as from the needs of the moment.

Hitler's invasion of the countries of western Europe had broken down established frontiers, and in so doing had shown nation

---

[6] SHAEF: Supreme Headquarters Allied Expeditionary Force; SHAPE: Supreme Headquarters Allied Powers Europe.

states to be inadequate in the first and fundamental purpose of their existence, the maintenance of security and the defence of their citizens. By driving governments into exile it had broken the natural ties which normally exist, to a greater or lesser degree, between a people and its government; for however ardently a government in exile strove to keep in touch with its homeland, its experiences of the war could not but be fundamentally different from those of a population suffering under the burden of occupation. In France the problem had been more acute, since ordinary Frenchmen had been called on to choose between two rival governments, and soldiers to decide which orders to obey. In Germany and Italy the people were called on to disown completely their pre-war governments.

In this way the framework of nation states, and the common acceptance of nation states as the obvious unit of government, had been weakened, particularly amongst those who were in a position to influence and determine the course of events. Such people were able to find a new political unit worthy of their aspirations in 'Europe', and there began to develop an enthusiasm for the unity of the continent and for the means to achieve union between the countries of which it was composed. This new loyalty was evoked partly by the sudden awareness of Europe, distinct from communist Russia and the United States. There was strong feeling in continental Europe that Europe had a tradition, history, and ideals which distinguished it sharply from both Russia and America; and to this was added a realization that in terms of power no individual European country could compete with the two new super-states, while combined they might.

The European tradition to which the enthusiasts for European union felt themselves heir could not be given a simple definition; different men conceived this tradition differently. For Catholics the European tradition derived from the Middle Ages, and was essentially one of Catholic unity; socialists saw Europe as the birthplace of their ideas and looked back a shorter distance to the internationalism of the socialist movement; liberals for their part were inspired by the common theme of the value of the individual and the restraint of governmental power which they regarded as the essential contribution of western Europe to the ideas and institutions of society. But diversity of this sort did not affect the strength of enthusiasm for the new idea; just as different men could be equally patriotic towards their individual countries, while nurturing totally different ideal visions of their homeland, so could the ideal of Europe be variegated, but no less strong for that. Indeed, the strength of the appeal of the new allegiance lay partly in the fact that it transcended domestic political conflicts. For while Catholics and socialists continued to differ in the objectives they sought to realize, they at least started from a new point of departure, uncomplicated by past conflicts which had lost their rationale but retained their divisive force. Similarly European union was sought by socialists who aspired to a greater arena for socialist planning, and liberals who looked forward to larger scope for the free play of economic forces. In the event this was to prove in part a false antithesis; and the new economic unit of Europe provided the ground where new concepts of planning could be evolved.

There was a particular sense in which the impulse to achieve the union of Europe emerged from the experience of the war. Men living on the continent of Europe could not but be aware that the suffering of Europe in two world wars had been the direct result of the struggle for mastery in Europe, and that this struggle had been fought primarily between France and Germany. For seventy years since the unification of Germany no solution had been found to this problem, and it was natural therefore that they should seek to make a new start, and to end the conflict by establishing a new framework within which the two powers would be equal partners, working for the construction of a new political unit. This desire to achieve the reconciliation of France and Germany through European union was the stronger because both the rivals were now less strong, and each was conscious of a graver threat than that presented by its traditional rival. But the impulse to reconciliation through a larger union was prior to the realization of the Russian danger, and it is significant that it found its strongest expression in France amongst some of those who had been most actively engaged in the resistance movement, and who had come most closely into contact with the Germans as enemies.

These aspirations towards European union were most strongly felt in those countries which between them dominated western Europe, although in none of the three largest did the supporters of a European policy constitute an overwhelming majority. In France the European ideal found many protagonists amongst

Catholics, and the MRP as a party gave consistent support to the union of Europe. But French Catholicism had a proud and distinctive tradition of its own, with strongly nationalist overtones, and in this tradition many Catholics, some of them supporters of de Gaulle, viewed with reluctance and apprehension the abandonment of French sovereignty. The socialists rallied to the support of Europe, although there was considerable division about the part the new unit should play in the cold war; while that most French of political parties, the Radical party, was divided. In outright opposition were the communists, who represented a quarter of the population. The attitude of Germans was complicated by the unique position in which they found themselves. For some there were strong and compelling reasons for supporting European union. It was seen as a way for Germany to regain its place in the international community and escape from the stigma of nazism; while Germany was divided it was a way of strengthening western Germany, and securing the full commitment of western Europe on the side of Germany against Russia; for those bereft of a national ideal, who sought a means of reconciliation with France or who sought a return to Catholic universalism, Europe offered itself as the obvious ideal. This was the political outlook of Konrad Adenauer, and with perseverance and determination he led western Germany along this path. But for others the union of Germany with western Europe meant a sacrifice of the union of Germany itself. Paradoxically it was the socialists, under the leadership of Schumacher, who advocated this opposite point of view. Impressed by the vulnerability of the Weimar socialists through their failure to respond to the nationalist ideal, they put the unification of Germany as the first point in their programme; and they argued that every step towards the integration of western Europe as a bastion against Russia would make it more difficult to secure concessions, and free east Germany to reunite with the west.

Italy provided, proportionately, the strongest body of adherents to the European cause. It also had the highest percentage of communist voters, but their strength evoked a stronger commitment to Europe amongst their opponents. The European Union of Federalists had nearly 200 members amongst Italian members of Parliament, a number far exceeding any other country; the Christian Democratic party, which has remained the largest single party, was oriented towards Europe, and was less affected by a nationalist tradition than its counterpart in France. The right-wing socialists were also supporters of European unification. In Belgium considerable divisions presented themselves, partly on religious grounds, partly within the Socialist party itself. In Holland the loss of Indonesia made for readier acceptance of the European ideal, although with strong reservations which derived from Dutch Protestantism, lingering anti-Germanism, and strong emotional ties with Great Britain. In Luxembourg the European movement had strong support from all but the communists.

Outside this central part of western Europe the movement towards unification was weak. The Iberian peninsula had for centuries been remote from the main line of European development and tradition, and this was the more so as a result of the war; moreover the governments of Spain and Portugal were so organized as to be unacceptable to many people in western Europe, and were based on political ideals which they rejected. Scandinavia had a Protestant liberal tradition not to be found in strength in the main part of the continent, and was geographically remote; while Greece, the founder and home of much that the Europeans claimed as their spiritual inheritance, was also separated by religious tradition and by distance from the centre.

The position of Britain was especially important. Historically Britain had been linked to Europe by warfare more than anything else. It had in the sixteenth century broken away from the Church of Rome and established its own national church, later giving birth to other Protestant groups which had little in common with Continental Protestantism; it had a continuous political history composed of a succession of practical expedients and little affected by abstract thought. Its prosperity was founded on trade with the world rather than with Europe and its citizens had emigrated to found a Commonwealth overseas. Above all, its experience in most recent years separated it from continental Europe. It had not known defeat; on the contrary it had stood alone in Europe at a dramatic moment in its history, supported only by the members of the Commonwealth. Its soldiers had returned to the continent of Europe as part of an army of liberation; but their one great hope and ambition was to return to their own land, and whether as victors or as liberators they enjoyed an almost unreal relationship with European peoples, in which few permanent links were forged. As a result the number of people in

Britain who were prepared to make any real sacrifice of sovereignty to a European union was very small indeed.

And yet the individual who above all others gave inspiration to the European movement was Winston Churchill. He shared the outlook of many people in continental Europe. He was impressed by the size and power of the United States and Russia, and saw little future for Europe if it remained weak and disunited. As his life had been dominated by the Franco-German conflict he sought eagerly for the resolution of this conflict within the framework of Europe. He was a man of large ideas, able to express them in moving terms. During the war he had already, both in the cabinet and publicly, talked of plans for European Union; but it was at Zurich on 19 September 1946 that he made an historic speech which became the very core of inspiration for the European movement. He then said:

> We must build a kind of United States of Europe . . . .
> The first step in the re-creation of the European family must be a partnership between France and Germany . . . .
> I must now sum up the propositions which are before you. Our constant aim must be to build and fortify the strength of UNO. Under and within that world concept we must re-create the European family in a regional structure called, it may be, the United States of Europe. The first practical step is to form a Council of Europe. . . . In all this urgent work, France and Germany must take the lead together. Great Britain, the British Commonwealth of Nations, mighty America, and I trust Soviet Russia – for then indeed all would be well – must be the friends and sponsors of the new Europe and must champion its right to live and shine.[7]

His words were received the more avidly because Europeans at this time looked to Britain for leadership. They had not yet recovered from the disruption of economic life, the suppression of political activity, the loss of life, and the deep social divisions which the war had caused, and they therefore looked for leadership to the one country which had remained intact. Up to a point the British were willing to give such a lead, for if there were few people prepared to join a federal Europe, there were no more who wished to return to the isolation of the inter-war years. But the government saw the first area of its activity as being in Britain itself. This was a Labour government, which had come

[7] *The Sinews of Peace* (1948), pp. 198–202.

to power with a majority nearly half a century after the party had been formed, and which was intent on realizing its programme within its own frontiers. It saw the inseparability of some of its problems from those of Europe; but it looked for the solution of those problems in strictly practical ways, and fought shy of rash political ventures. In opposition Conservative leaders in contrast found the European climate one in which they could flourish, and, Churchill first amongst them, they played a decisive part in the development of the European movement. They found a release for the energies which were frustrated by opposition at home, a receptive audience for the airing of large ideas which seemed inappropriate to the measured hardship of Britain, and a stick of righteousness with which to beat their own government.

While the Conservative party in Britain and some Continental parties took up the cause of European union, the distinctive character of the movement came from the *ad hoc* bodies established in its support. These voluntary organizations acted as pressure groups of a novel kind. Their objective was a reformation of society, rather than some limited end of their own. They made little or no effort to popularize their cause, but confined their propaganda and proselytizing to a limited number of informed and influential people. But they included an important proportion of politicians and members of governments, who pursued their objectives with equal vigour in voluntary organizations and their own governmental institutions. Only in Great Britain did a conflict between the two arise, when the Labour party not only expressed its strong disapproval of the movement, but tried to prevent individual members taking part in it, arguing that the issues involved were too important to be left to the discretion of individuals.

The movement gained momentum in the spring of 1948 with the meeting of a Congress of the European Movement at The Hague from 7 to 10 May. The Congress owed much to the inspiration of Churchill and the leadership of Duncan Sandys, who became chairman of the movement's International Executive.

The Hague Congress was a great success in stimulating enthusiasm amongst its participants and propagating the idea of European union. Many different opinions were represented, but the common purpose of promoting union, whether it be federalist or not, liberal or conservative, predominated over possible divisions. Since European politicians and ministers were so strongly represented, it was comparatively easy to move to the next step of persuading governments and parliaments to arrange for the convocation of a European assembly.

It fell to the French government to take the lead, and on 20 July 1948 Bidault proposed to the Consultative Council of the Brussels powers the creation of a federal parliament of Europe and a European customs and economic union. The next day the French government fell. This was a sequence of events which confirmed the British government in its doubts about plans for European union, and while French governments continued to show the instability which had characterized the inter-war years the British saw little useful purpose in joining with them in the creation of a new political organization which they expected to be even less effective.

But this was to underestimate the strength on the continent of Europe of the demand for an assembly. The foreign affairs commission of the French Assembly voted overwhelmingly for the convening of such a body, and the new French government took up where its predecessor had left off. In reply the British government rejected the idea of an assembly, and proposed instead a ministerial council, supplemented by an inter-governmental conference of delegates, who would vote in blocks according to their briefs. By January 1949, however, the British government was forced to admit the strength of the opposite point of view, and on 28 January the Consultative Council of the Brussels powers agreed on plans for the creation of a Council of Europe, which would consist of a Consultative Assembly and a Committee of Ministers.

On 5 May the five Brussels powers, together with Italy, Norway, Sweden, Denmark, and Ireland, signed the statute of the Council of Europe, which embodied these proposals. As a result of the position taken up by Britain, which had the support of the Scandinavian countries, the Committee of Ministers was given important powers over the conduct of the Assembly's business, so that the Assembly could only discuss matters referred to it by the Committee, or which the Committee agreed should be included in its agenda.[8] Moreover the statute of the Council excluded questions of defence from its competence – a restriction

[8] This was amended in 1951, but not in such a way as to increase substantially the Assembly's power.

which obviously accorded well with the British position, but was in any case widely accepted, as it cleared the Council from any charge of being a military alliance.

The first meeting of the Council of Europe took place on 10 August 1949, at Strasbourg, where it was located by its Statute. As might be expected, the great majority of participants spoke with enthusiasm of the occasion as one of historic importance. The outstanding exceptions were to be found on the Labour side of the British delegation, where the mood expressed was one of down-to-earth caution and practicability. Thus Herbert Morrison warned the Assembly:

> We must keep the vision of a new and better Europe always before us, as our guide and our inspiration. At the same time, we should be false to ourselves and our peoples if we pretended that the practical difficulties were insignificant .... We must set our faces against slogan-mongering and get down instead to hard objective study of the realities, with a view to the formulation of really practical proposals for the benefit of the peoples to whom we are responsible. . . . New ideas do not frighten me. I just want to know . . . what the new ideas are and what they mean.[9]

However, the delegates included an important proportion for whom the Assembly was excessively restricted by statute, and was in any case only a step on the way to federalism in Europe. They therefore pressed for an extension of its powers and its competence. But this was not to have any decisive effect on the course of events. The great issues before Europe at this time were economic recovery, defence, and the position of Germany. For the first, two international organizations, OEEC and NATO, existed; the third was under discussion by national governments. As a result the Assembly took issue with the Committee of Ministers on the preparation of a Convention on Human Rights (the Committee at first rejected a proposal that the Assembly should undertake this, and later reversed its decision), and it undertook general debates on such topics as a European nationality and passport and international programmes of public works. But by the time its first session came to an end at the beginning of September it could claim as its greatest achievement to have come into existence, rather than anything it had done.

[9] Council of Europe, Consult. Ass., 1st sess., 10 Aug.–8 Sept. 1949, *Agendas, Minutes* (1949), p. 124.

As we have seen, one of the motives behind European unification was the desire to provide a framework for Franco-German reconciliation, and Germans had taken an active part in the voluntary organizations for union. The creation of the Council of Europe inevitably posed the question of the participation of Germany, and this in turn raised a further question which was to recur throughout the development of European institutions, until it was finally settled in 1956 – the question of the Saar. The Committee of Ministers which had competence over questions of membership proposed the admission of Germany as an associate member, but there was some hesitation in the Federal Republic over the acceptance of such status (which carried representation in the Assembly but not the Committee of Ministers). There was further opposition of views over the Saar between the French government, which sought simultaneous or prior admission of the Saar, and the German government, which wished to avoid any decision on the Saar which would prejudge the peace settlement. But by the spring of 1950 agreement had been reached on both these points, and Germany and the Saar were invited to become associate members and to send observers to the Committee of Ministers. A year later, in May 1951, Germany became a full member. At the same time a representative of the Saar was admitted to the Committee of Ministers as an observer.

Up to this time the European movement had included many different shades of opinion about the steps to be taken in achieving a union of Europe. In order to achieve at least the setting up of an Assembly every effort had been made to secure the widest possible support, and the minimum of division. In the spring of 1950, however, three factors gave a very definite direction to the development of European unification.

The first of these was the continuing coolness of the British government towards European union. In continental western Europe (but only amongst a minority in Britain) the federalists had always been a strong force – their objective being the rapid establishment either of political institutions which would be the groundwork for a federal government of Europe, or the setting up of a supranational authority within a limited sector of government. It was well known that this federalist approach received little support in Britain, and there were some men, for example Spaak, who were ready to proceed more slowly in the hope that they could draw the British along. But they received no encourage-

10*

ment from the British government, and the impulse to proceed more rapidly towards federalism without Britain was therefore the stronger.

The other two considerations affected French policy in the first place, and they derived from the experience of Jean Monnet as head of the commissariat for planned reconstruction in France. The commissariat's task included the reconstruction of the French part of the industrial complex which stretched across political frontiers into Belgium, Luxembourg, and Germany. From this vantage point it was obvious how much was to be gained if economic reconstruction through government planning could transcend the artificial barriers of national frontiers.

This was the more so in view of the imperative need, from a French point of view, to control the reconstruction of German industry. French policy at the conclusion of the war was a repetition of that of an earlier victory, and relied on close control of Germany by the victorious powers so that it should not again be a threat to peace. This policy had been overtaken by events and by the willingness of Britain and America to press ahead with the economic rehabilitation of Germany, partly to relieve the burden which a weak Germany imposed on their own economies. Apparently faced with the choice between the vain pursuit of old objectives or the relinquishment of any control over German industry, the French government, and more particularly Monnet, had the imagination to conceive a third possibility, that of supranational control of the German coal and steel industries, with Germany itself making a contribution to the governing institutions.

It was these ideas which lay behind the proposals (known as the Schuman plan) which the French foreign minister, Schuman, made on 9 May 1950, namely:

> To place Franco-German production of coal and steel as a whole under a common higher authority, within the framework of an organization open to the participation of other countries of Europe. The pooling of coal and steel production should immediately provide for the setting up of common foundations for economic development as a first step in the federation of Europe, and will change the destinies of those regions which have long been devoted to the manufacture of munitions of war, of which they have been the most constant victims . . . .
>
> Europe, with new means at her disposal, will be able to pursue

the realization of one of her essential tasks, the development of the African continent . . . .

By pooling basic production and by instituting a new higher authority, whose decisions will bind France, Germany and other member countries, these proposals will lay the first concrete foundation of a European federation which is indispensable to the preservation of peace.[10]

This was a great and imaginative new departure in French foreign policy. It would have remained barren if it had not met with response from Germany; but Adenauer had already in October 1949 spoken of the desirability of Franco-German collaboration in the steel industry as a means to Franco-German understanding, and he was prepared to lead western Germany in this direction. His task may have appeared easier than that confronting the French government; but the acceptance of a western policy seemed to many Germans to mean the sacrifice of the possibility of reunification. It also meant that the question of the Saar would be revived, and as France was still in a strong position in relation to Germany it meant that Germany could accept the proposal only by forgoing some of its demands for the Saar.

The French initiative was also accepted by Italy, Belgium and Luxembourg, and by Holland, with some reservations resulting from anxiety about the impact of the proposed supranational authority on its new steel industry. A year after the original French proposal, on 18 April 1951, the treaty setting up a European Coal and Steel Community was signed by France and by June 1952 it had been ratified by all the signatories, the German Federal Republic, Italy, and the Benelux countries.

It is impossible to exaggerate the importance of this initiative on the part of France, and its subsequent success. Its significance in the history of Europe is immediately obvious, in the sense that it set up the first of the organizations which, by incorporating a certain element of supranationality in their constitutions, made revolutionary progress not only in removing economic barriers but in preparing the way for the political integration of Europe. There were other respects, less immediately obvious, in which these steps were important. The Schuman plan cut through the academic discussions which had gone on amongst supporters of the European movement about the extent and the pattern of

[10] RIIA, *Documents, 1949–50*, pp. 315–16.

288

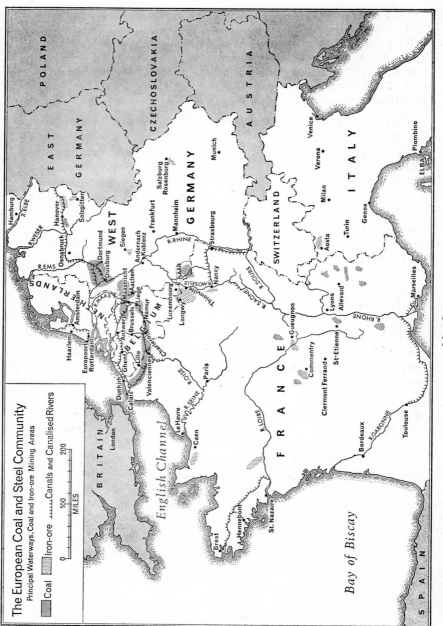

The European Coal and Steel Community

Principal Waterways, Coal and Iron-ore Mining Areas

Coal ▨ Iron-ore ▦ Canals and Canalised Rivers

MILES

0   100   200

Map 8

federalism, and straightforwardly adopted what was commonly known as the sector approach. The original French communiqué read: 'L'Europe ne se fera pas d'un coup ni dans une construction d'ensemble; elle se fera par des réalisations concrètes créant d'abord une solidarité de fait.'[11] The physical character of the coal and steel industry in this great industrial concentration of northern Europe, coupled with the need (from the French point of view) to control German industry made this particular sector an ideal one for the first realization of a *solidarité de fait*.

The second notable characteristic of the plan was that it was a governmental act. It emanated from one of the most creative civil servants of modern times, and was proposed to the rest of Europe without any prior consultation amongst 'interested parties'. Once such parties became aware of what was proposed, considerable alarm was immediately expressed on almost every side. Monnet's vision of the plan was that it would expand production of both coal and steel by removing restriction and discrimination; but individual producers were afraid of the effect of the removal of restrictions which protected their own particular section of the industry. This anxiety manifested itself in France, Belgium, and Italy. French producers were pleased to expect good supplies of German coke, but as a result of their pressure the ratification by the Assembly was accompanied by a number of resolutions designed to safeguard French industrial interests. Italian industrialists were relatively ineffective in opposition, but only because of the strong political and ideological commitment of the Christian Democratic party to European union; and while it might be supposed that Belgium above all would welcome a large market in these commodities, even there anxiety over increased competition was strongly felt. To this was added political opposition of the kind already mentioned, socialist anxieties that the new community would favour cartels and capitalism, and the hesitation of some, particularly the Dutch, to accept the principle of supranationality. In spite of this opposition the treaty secured ratification by overwhelming majorities in the Benelux countries, by a large majority in Italy, and easily in France and Germany. In this way economic interests were forced by political decision into a framework which benefited them far more than they were aware. And the treaty demonstrated a political fact of great importance in the ensuing years:

[11] RIIA, *Documents, 1949-50*, p. 315.

that although there was considerable opposition to the development of European union, there was no coherent political force to oppose itself to the movement towards federalism.

The most important of the ancillary factors in the setting up of ECSC was the fact that it was done without British participation. Britain was one of the three important steel producers which did not join; but the other two were Norway and Sweden, and as they were marginal to Europe their self-exclusion had relatively little importance in political development. The British government for its part declined the invitation of the French to participate in the initial discussions, on the grounds that the French government insisted that they should be undertaken on the understanding that the principle of supranationality was accepted. In this they were undoubtedly right, as the background to the Schuman plan indicates, and as is shown in the correspondence exchanged by the two governments. But they found their position difficult to defend for two reasons. The first was that their attitude to European unification over the past few years had been one which was curiously insensitive to the strength of European feeling; while the antipathy of some members of the Labour party (but not the government) derived from reasons which were intellectually scarcely tenable. This would not have been so evident at the time were it not that on the very same day that the Labour government published a White Paper setting out its correspondence with the French, the Labour party published a pamphlet on *European Unity*. The pamphlet put forward sound views on Britain's relationship with the United States, and the consequent difficulties of joining Europe; but it also rehearsed old arguments to the effect that as Britain had a Labour government it could only join a Europe that was socialist.

The second reason why the government had difficulty in defending its position was of a more fundamental nature. Britain was placed on the horns of a dilemma, although this fact was scarcely realized at the time. But in the House of Commons on 26 June 1950 Eden led the attack on the government, arguing that it should have gone into the negotiations, expressing reservations similar to those of the Dutch government.[12] In doing

[12] He quoted: 'it wishes to reserve its freedom to go back on the acceptance of these general proposals during the negotiations if, contrary to what it hoped, it should prove in the future that the application of these principles raises serious objections in practice' (H. C. Deb., 26 June 1950).

so he said: 'If the Schuman proposals were not to succeed, nobody denies that this would be a calamity for peace. If they were to succeed without us, there would be real dangers for us, I think, political as well as economic.' The danger to peace which Eden spoke of was still primarily that which might arise from Germany, but the essence of his dictum was essentially true. It was in the interests of Britain that this revolutionary development in Europe should succeed, and that Britain should participate in that success; but the only terms on which Britain was asked to participate involved the abandonment of at least some part of national sovereignty, and at this time few people in the country were prepared to accept so drastic a step. Eden and his fellow Conservatives could press a strong case against the government on the stand it took, and as they were in opposition they could argue that a middle road was open to Britain; but in fact it was not.

In the long run the Schuman plan set the basis for more fundamental developments in Europe; but immediately after it was proposed the outbreak of the Korean war initiated events in Europe which threatened to disrupt the whole movement towards European unification. The Korean war posed the question of western European defence in an acute and urgent way. The similarities between Korea and Germany were startling: both were countries which it was intended (at least by the western powers) should be unified; both were divided into a communist and a non-communist half, and each therefore included a Russian satellite. Moreover the history of Europe up to this time suggested the possibility of increasing aggressiveness in Russian pressure against the west, and it was easy to believe that if the Korean attack succeeded against only a nominal resistance, the blow would fall next in Germany.

Western rearmament had made very little progress up to this point. Although NATO was in existence, there had been neither the time nor the sense of urgency for it to proceed very far. Moreover western Germany had only a police force, of a relatively small size. There could be little doubt that western Europe was unprepared to resist a Russian attack on the ground, and the threat seen in Korea therefore called for a straightforward strengthening of western armaments. This in turn raised the question of what contribution Germany could and should make to her own defence, and to the joint defence of western Europe.

Up to this time the western governments had repeatedly re-affirmed their intention to 'demilitarize' Germany, and had denied rumours (for example at the time of their meeting in Germany in November 1949) that they were considering the creation of a German army. As late as 21 June 1950 (four days before the Korean invasion) the western High Commissioners turned down a request from Bonn for an increase in the strength of the west German police force. On the other hand the possibility of a contribution by Germany to a European army had been mentioned by a number of eminent westerners, including Rey-naud and Churchill.

The belief that an attack in Europe was a real possibility changed all that; for in the simplest terms it seemed absurd that if there should be an actual defence of western Europe, including western Germany, the Germans should have no part in it. In the Council of Europe Winston Churchill framed the problem in broader terms. Casting aside the statute's prohibition on defence questions, he spoke of the need to organize the defence of western Europe, and referred to Germany as a nation which would 'share our peril and augment our strength'. His speech was warmly received, and his proposal sent to committee; when it was reported back the Assembly voted by an overwhelming majority for the creation of a European army under a European defence minister.

Meanwhile the government of the United States was con-cerned with the possibility of securing the maximum increment to western strength in the shortest time; and it reached the decision that this could only be done with the participation of Germany. Such a decision was easier for it to reach than for its European allies; not having experienced invasion, scarcely touched by the first world war, enjoying the security of a wide ocean, it had none of the emotional anxieties about German rearmament which were so deeply felt in Europe. Once the decision had been taken, it had to be put before Britain and France and the other allies. This was first done in a meeting of the three foreign ministers, Acheson, Bevin, and Schuman, in New York before the NATO Council meeting of September 1950; the subject was taken up again at the Council, and dis-cussions between the three continued afterwards. It was not possible to reach immediate agreement. Bevin was susceptible to Acheson's arguments and he had less anxiety about a German army than Schuman. Moreover the NATO Council had agreed on the creation of an integrated army under a supreme commander, who would be American. From Bevin's point of view this was a great gain, since it achieved one of the overriding objectives of his foreign policy, the maintenance of the American commitment in Europe. For this it was worth trading acceptance of German rearmament.

Schuman would enter into no commitment before he left New York. But on his return to Paris the French government produced a plan under which German troops would be integrated into the armies of other European states to form a European army under a European minister of defence (while these states kept their own military establishments intact, in addition to their contribution to the European army). It was a bad plan and won little support inside or outside France, although it was approved by the National Assembly. It was particularly unattractive to Germany, for although the German government wanted to provide for its own defence and also to increase the support it would receive from the United States, the rearming of Germany met with fierce opposition from the Socialist party and weary inertia from the population; and it was therefore unlikely that it would accept rearmament under conditions of such evident inequality.

However, as the months passed the pressure to move ahead with defence became the more urgent. After the initial success of the United Nations armies in Korea they had advanced towards the frontier with Manchuria, and then been driven back down the peninsula by Chinese intervention. By the end of the year the French government accepted in principle the creation of German armed units, of a size to be determined by military considerations, without waiting for the establishment of a European army – even though their agreement was hedged round with safeguards for the superior strength of the French armed forces. As a result, two sets of conferences were begun at the beginning of 1951. The three High Commissioners for Germany began to discuss with Adenauer the extent and nature of a German military contribution, together with the necessary revision of the occupation status which should accompany this; while in Paris the six powers already linked by the Schuman plan began discussions on the creation of a European army.[13]

[13] Invitations were sent to all the European members of NATO, but only the six ECSC powers attended as full members.

The second of these conferences produced agreement by the end of July 1951, and when further details had been settled this was embodied in the treaty of the European Defence Community, which was signed (but not ratified) in Paris on 27 May 1952. In its essential features the Community was similar to the ECSC. It provided for a European army, composed of national groups roughly equal in size to a division. Air, but not naval, forces would also be integrated. The integrated forces would be under the control of a Board of Commissioners, while a Council of Ministers would harmonize the activities of the Board with the policies of the six governments. There would also be an Assembly, which could by an adverse vote, bring about the resignation of the Board of Commissioners.[14]

In spite of this similarity, the EDC was stillborn, while the ECSC became one of the most successful European institutions. It is obvious in retrospect that the attempt to create a European army imposed an intolerable strain on the still weak community of Europe. The ECSC embodied the best possibilities for European union, since the industrial complex clustering round the Rhine and Moselle rivers was an obvious economic unity, artificially severed by political frontiers. In contrast, the EDC required that European nations, particularly a nation such as France – with its long tradition of nationalism, embodying a succession of glorious victories, royalist, republican, and Napoleonic – should abandon what is usually regarded as the first function and prerogative of a nation state, and the most persistent symbol of national independence – the army. There was another way in which the EDC would differ from the ECSC. As we have seen, the latter was proposed as a way of controlling German industries which were already in existence, and which did not appear as an immediate and obvious threat to the peace of Europe (even though they were recognized by governments as providing the sinews of war). EDC in contrast proposed the creation of a German army, with all the emotions which that evoked in Europe.

Moreover the French government had already made concessions in order to arrive at the EDC treaty. It had originally spoken of the battalion as the national unit; René Pleven (who

---

[14] The Assembly was the same as that of ECSC, with the addition of three extra members each from France, Germany and Italy. The Community was also to share the Court of ECSC.

had succeeded Bidault as premier), in response to appeals from the Americans, agreed on a larger national unit of 5,000–6,000 men; and when the treaty was signed the final level was left undetermined between the 12,000 for which the Germans argued and the 10,000 which was now the French maximum. The French government had furthermore argued that a European army should first be created, and a German contingent then added to it. On this point too it gave way, so that a German army would come into existence at the same time as the European.

In the interval between the American proposal for German rearmament and the signature of the EDC treaty elections occurred in both France and Britain, which did nothing to diminish the difficulties. In France the election of 17 June 1951 had greatly reduced (by electoral arrangements) the number of communist seats in the National Assembly; but this was quite outweighed by the return of 120 Gaullist deputies, representative of conservative nationalism, and a greatly increased representation of the old Radical party of the Third Republic. These gains were at the expense of the Catholic MRP, the most reliably European of the French political parties.

In Britain the general election of 25 October 1951 brought a Conservative majority in the House of Commons (even though the Labour party polled more votes). It might have been expected that this would produce a markedly more European policy on the part of Britain, now that the great inspiratory force of European union, Winston Churchill, was prime minister. This was indeed the expectation of many people on the continent of Europe who most wanted that movement to succeed. But their hopes were ill founded, as would have been evident to them had they made a cool appraisal of Conservative attitudes to Europe in the preceding period. The outstanding fact confronting the new government was that the federal current in Europe was now in full flow, and this was one with which British Conservatives had never been prepared to swim. They therefore sought association with the European institutions which were coming into existence; but at the end of November Maxwell Fyfe at Strasbourg – where he had but recently chaired the Committee on Human Rights – made clear that Britain would not enter any European federal organization. This detachment of Britain from Europe was to be of signal importance in the ensuing months.

While every western European power nurtured anxieties in

varying degrees about the implications of German rearmament, it was not immediately attractive to the majority of Germans. Yet Chancellor Adenauer adopted the policy of rearmament in the European framework, both to provide for German defence and to further the cause of European union. At this time no other western statesman succeeded to such an outstanding degree in forming a clear view of the direction his country should take, imposing his will on national politics, and securing popular support for his actions.

He was strongly opposed by the SPD, under the leadership first of Schumacher and then of Ollenhauer. The social democrats expressed a unique form of nationalism, which derived in part from regret at their failures in the early 1930s, in part from a sense of national self-justification in that they had suffered as much as anyone in opposition to the nazis (they were bitterly resentful that the British Labour government failed to give any recognition to this fact during the early years of the occupation), and in part from opposition to the particular kind of Europe, Catholic and Conservative, which they thought was coming into existence. They therefore steadily opposed the policies of the chancellor. They argued against the integration of western Germany into western Europe, and insisted that this would be done at the price of possible German unification. They saw German rearmament as making negotiations with east Germany or with Russia more difficult, and they accused the government of neglecting opportunities to arrive at a settlement with the communists. As we shall see, both Russians and east Germans directed their diplomacy to give plausibility to these views; and they appeared the more convincing as a result.

Even so, Chancellor Adenauer was convinced that western Germany should seek integration with western Europe, through the ratification of the Paris and Bonn treaties, before seeking reunification. He believed it essential that Germany should achieve the closest possible co-operation with the United States, in order to keep American troops in Germany and to avoid a settlement between Russia and America at the price of Germany. He was not hopeful of the outcome of negotiations with the Russians, and would not compromise the essential principles of free elections throughout Germany as a way to reunification and subsequent freedom in defence and foreign policy; and he believed that if these objectives could be achieved at all, it would be

ATLANTIC ALLIANCE AND EUROPEAN UNION

through strength – that is to say, that Germany would gain, not lose, if it signed the Paris agreements before negotiations with the Russians.

Adenauer won a majority for his policy both in the German parliament and from the German people. The SPD, unable to defeat the EDC agreements in the parliament, challenged their constitutionality in the Federal Supreme Court, and Adenauer followed their example by seeking a favourable verdict from the Court. In both cases the Court decided that it had no competence to rule on the constitutionality of a measure before it had been enacted. By the end of 1953, however, the possible verdict of the Court became unimportant. In the September elections the CDU won the highest percentage of votes ever cast for one party in Germany (45.2 per cent). With the alliance of the Free Democrat and German parties the government was able to command the two-thirds majority in both houses necessary to enact the agreements by means of constitutional revision.

Italy did not face the same difficulties as western Germany in considering the EDC treaty. It was opposed by the left-wing socialists under Nenni, as well as by the communists; but this did not prevent the formation of a majority in favour. But there was reluctance to ratify before France did so; and while Germany and France were concerned about the Saar, Italy had its own immediate problem in Trieste, where it was reasonable to hope some advantage might be secured in return for ratification of EDC. In June 1953 an election reduced the majority of the Christian Democrat party and shortly afterwards De Gasperi resigned. However, the future of the treaty was never in serious danger; and ratification only waited for the French vote.

The Benelux countries had no reason to welcome the rearmament of a country from which they had suffered more than any of their western partners in the recent war; but they accepted what they felt unable to oppose, particularly since it was a further step in the direction of united Europe.

It was therefore in France that the future of the EDC was decided; and it was so only after a long period of indecision and hesitation. Successive French governments, realizing how doubtful it was that a majority would be found for ratification in the Assembly, postponed submitting the treaty to that body. Instead, French diplomacy was directed to securing a modification to the treaty which would safeguard French national interests, and to achieving the maximum possible association of Britain with the Community. These objectives were particularly sought after by the National Assembly, and gained in importance when Bidault succeeded Schuman as foreign minister in January 1953.

It might have been supposed that the new balance of power in Europe, and the system of alliances first created in the Brussels treaty and then extended in NATO would have allayed traditional French anxieties about Germany. But in fact the proposed EDC treaty appeared to resuscitate these fears, and to renew the French dependence on British support which had so weakened French foreign policy in the 1930s. In 1947 Britain had belatedly attempted to repair its pre-war isolation by signing the Dunkirk treaty promising support to France in the case of renewed German aggression. The Brussels treaty renewed this guarantee, although the treaty was directed primarily against Russia. The North Atlantic treaty provided mutual guarantees against attack in Europe or North America; and in September 1950 the foreign ministers of Britain, France, and the United States declared that they would regard an attack on western Germany and western Berlin as an attack on themselves. By the time the EDC treaty was signed, therefore, there already existed an intermingling of guarantees against the old danger and the new. The actual signature of the treaty was accompanied by three additional guarantees, of varying strength. Promises of military assistance were exchanged between the Defence Community and the North Atlantic Council; Britain and the Defence Community entered into a guarantee of mutual assistance, to last as long as Britain was a member of the North Atlantic alliance; and the British and American governments stated that they would regard a threat to the integrity or unity of the Community as a threat to themselves, and would keep on the continent of Europe 'such forces as they deem necessary and appropriate to contribute to the joint defence of the North Atlantic area'.

These were substantial guarantees; but they did not allay French anxiety. Basically this anxiety derived from the fear that the EDC would provide a cover for German rearmament, and that when German forces were strong enough they would leave the Community. Other eventualities which it seemed necessary to guard against were that Germany would be reunited, and no longer be bound by the treaty; or that the British guarantees would lapse when the twenty-year North Atlantic treaty came to

an end and EDC still had over thirty years to run. On the political plane too the French were alarmed at the possibility of being
outvoted in EDC, and they therefore looked for a full British
participation and political commitment in addition to guarantees of mutual assistance.

This debate did not go on in a vacuum; but political developments outside France served only to worsen the French position.
The death of Stalin and the subsequent negotiations over Germany made the Russian threat appear less urgent to some
sections of French opinion, and the recovery of Germany made it
appear a more unwelcome rival, so that the Bundestag vote and
the subsequent election did nothing to encourage, as Adenauer
had hoped, similar support in France. But while the recovery of
Germany appeared a threat to France, Adenauer's consistent
support of the western alliance, the stability of his government,
and the country's growing economic prestige meant that
Germany appeared to some, particularly in the United States, a
more valuable ally than France. This was the more so since
French prestige was at its lowest ebb. It appeared to the outside
world that when government stability was achieved it was only
at the price of *immobilisme*. The war in Indo-China dragged on,
as a succession of promises of victory were unfulfilled. It appeared
discreditable that the French government should become entirely
dependent on American financial aid for the war, and yet lack
the political strength to draft conscripts to fight in Indo-China;
it was even more discreditable that the war was associated with
two major scandals of a classical type – the one involving
speculation in Indo-Chinese currency and the other a major
leakage of staff plans. Connoisseurs of European politics noticed
that the question of the Saar continued to be a bone of contention
between France and Germany, and only the more convinced
Francophiles felt able to give wholehearted support to the way in
which France sought to maintain its position there.

The American government saw its hopes of European development thwarted by the long drawn out hesitations over the
ratification of the EDC treaty. It had not favoured the European
army in 1950, since, less sensitive to the German danger than its
European allies, it would have preferred the rearmament of
Germany as a member of NATO. On the other hand it appeared
from across the Atlantic that European union was the only and
obvious way to strength, and it therefore favoured EDC as part

of that development. The failure of the French government to secure the ratification of the treaty prevented any development towards European union; it prevented the ratification of the Bonn agreements with Germany; and it delayed the provision of German troops as a contribution to NATO defence. As a result ratification of EDC came to be the basis on which the United States hoped to construct its policy towards Europe, and this was especially true when the Republican administration took office in January 1953. But it was clear that if France should fail to ratify the EDC treaty, American defence policy, and American policy towards Europe, might have to be substantially revised. Secretary Dulles did not hesitate to make this clear in private discussions with British and French statesmen. Then, at the opening session of the NATO Council on 14 December 1953, he made it appear that American defence and economic support for Europe was dependent on the achievement of European unification. In a public speech that contributed markedly to French resentment towards the United States he said:

The United States is primarily concerned that European civilization should survive and prosper. This cannot be without a European community in which will be combined, indissolubly, the interests and capacities of two great nations at the heart of Europe, France and Germany. It would be difficult for me to exaggerate the anxiety with which our people await the consummation of this historic act. . . . Our concern has been demonstrated through . . . vast material contributions for economic aid, and the stationing in Europe of substantial ground and air forces, with strong naval support. . . . But decisive steps remain to be taken. . . . Mere promises for the future are not enough to bury a past replete with bitter memories. The need is for Europe to move onward to more complete and organic forms of union. . . .

If, however, the European Defense Community should not become effective; if France and Germany remain apart, so that they would again be potential enemies, then indeed there would be grave doubt whether Continental Europe could be made a place of safety. That would compel an agonizing reappraisal of basic United States policy.[15]

Meanwhile nothing that had occurred was likely to persuade the British government to enter fully into the EDC. As we have seen, the accession to power of the Conservative government had brought no substantial change in the British attitude to federal institutions; but the new government did seek the means to associate closely with the new political organizations in Europe – and this was an initiative that was warmly welcomed by some of the European federalists, particularly Jean Monnet, who wished to minimize the isolation of Britain. A British mission was sent to Luxembourg as soon as the High Authority of the ECSC was established, and initiated informal discussions through a joint committee until a formal agreement of association was concluded in December 1954. At the same time the foreign secretary, Eden, proposed a plan which was dubbed with his name whereby the ECSC, and the EDC when it came into existence, would be closely linked with the Council of Europe – in Eden's words 'should draw on the facilities existing here in the Council of Europe'. The terms in which Julian Amery thought it best to recommend the plan to the Consultative Assembly indicate the reaction it evoked amongst some of them – he said that it was not 'some Machiavellian device to secure the harlot's privilege of power without responsibility'. In the end the Eden plan reduced itself to little more than an annual joint meeting of the Assembly of ECSC with the Assembly of the Council of Europe. The European federalists had other plans to integrate ECSC with EDC, and in March 1953 these took shape in a draft treaty setting up a European Political Community of which an important part would be a European Parliament elected by universal suffrage. This showed clearly the difference which existed between their objectives and even the most pro-European of British parliamentarians; but it was also far ahead of French opinion. The draft treaty languished while EDC awaited ratification, and the two projects eventually died together.

In April 1954 the British government went to the furthest lengths it felt able in support of the EDC treaty. A convention was signed on 13 April 1954 – one which had been worked out previously, but kept until what was thought to be a favourable moment to secure ratification. It included a provision whereby Britain would appoint a representative of ministerial rank to attend the meeting of the Council of Ministers of the EDC, whenever problems of co-operation with the United Kingdom were discussed, and would appoint a representative to the board of commissioners in order to establish close and continuous liaison with the Board. In a separate declaration Great Britain undertook to maintain forces on the Continent as long as there was a threat to western Europe and EDC; and undertook further that if the supreme commander so decided British army formations and air force units would be included in European formations and vice versa. The convention also provided for close military co-operation. At the same time the United States made a declaration to the effect that the United States would continue to keep armed forces in Europe, and would consult the EDC about the level of its forces, and would integrate its forces as closely as possible with those of EDC.

However, the defence committee of the French National Assembly and the Council of the Republic had in February appointed as rapporteurs on the EDC treaty Jules Moch and General Koenig respectively – both known opponents of the treaty and a decisive counterbalance to any support which the Laniel government might receive from across the Channel and the Atlantic. Moreover the government was increasingly pre-occupied with events in the Far East. On 13 March the Vietminh had launched a massive attack on the fortress of Dien Bien Phu, and thereby opened the decisive battle of the Indo-China war; at the end of April delegates began to gather in Geneva for the Far Eastern conference. On 9 June the National Assembly was in the middle of a major debate on Indo-China; but at the same time the Foreign Affairs Committee adopted by a small majority a report of Jules Moch recommending the rejection of the EDC treaty. On 12 June on the question of Indo-China, the Assembly passed a vote of no confidence in the Laniel government, and it resigned. On 17 June Pierre Mendès France became prime minister.

His advent to power seemed to give a new character to French politics. He was an outsider from the game of politics as practised in France. He had once before held office; but at other times he had preferred the integrity of opposition to the ineffective hold-ing of a portfolio. Becoming prime minister, he made it clear that he did not intend to fall into the traditional ways of his pre-decessors; he would choose his ministers rather than allow them to be imposed on him by a majority in the Assembly. He thus succeeded in imposing himself as a man who would resolve the questions left outstanding by his predecessors, even if not on the best terms – above all a solution of some sort should no longer be postponed. First and foremost he committed himself and his government to reaching a solution of the Indo-China crisis within four weeks, in default of which he would resign.

This new style in a prime minister was a source of strength but also of weakness. Although a member of the Radical Socialist party, which of all French parties was most associated with the political habits of the Third Republic, he created a sense of renewal, which won him popularity especially among the young and the intellectuals. It also won him approval abroad, particularly in Britain where for once the name of the French prime minister was a familiar word. But Mendès France inevitably evoked distrust amongst the old hands of the political game, including those in his own party. Similar distrust was felt in the governments of Germany and the United States, where a certain degree of acquaintance had been built up with the panel of *ministrables* to which Mendès France did not belong and he was under suspicion as a defeatist and an opponent of EDC. He incurred the odium of the bearer of bad news, for when he said that there was no majority in the Assembly for ratification of EDC he was either disbelieved or held responsbile for what he merely reported. He was closely identified with the weekly newspaper *L'Express* and its editor Servan-Schreiber, even though, while sharing some of its policies and much of its style, he was severely critical of many of its views and had no control over them. Undoubtedly *L'Express* had contributed to his popularity amongst an intelligent public; but he was unable to convince his critics, including Adenauer, of his independence from it. This was particularly important since *L'Express* was strongly neutralist, while Mendès France never doubted the importance of the Atlantic alliance.

Mendès France had never been a partisan of EDC; he had always been critical of a devotion to a European ideal which he saw as a form of escapism from problems which were essentially French and had to be solved within the framework of French politics. He was moreover convinced that the majority necessary to ratify EDC did not exist in the Assembly. On the other hand the problem could not be postponed indefinitely; and he was aware of the dangers of the isolation of France, particularly from the United States, if it should be rejected. He therefore sought a compromise which would be acceptable to a majority of the Assembly, and also to the other five signatories of the treaty. Such a compromise he succeeded in persuading his cabinet to accept, at the price of the resignation of three Gaullist members. It included the alignment of the EDC treaty with the North Atlantic treaty, so that one could not exist without the other; the possibility of negotiation should the North Atlantic treaty come to an end, American troops withdraw from Europe, or Germany be reunified. The supranational clauses were to be suspended for eight years and the integration of forces limited to German territory.

This compromise he took to a conference of the EDC powers in Brussels. He did so with little optimism, and it soon appeared that there was no chance of his success. The other five signatories had waited patiently for France to accede to the treaty it had done so much to originate, and there was little incentive to them, now that France appeared isolated, to agree to amendments which would alter the whole character of the treaty, and which would also discriminate openly against Germany. The only reason which might have persuaded them to adopt such a course was the belief that nothing else was possible; but it was hard to convince themselves that the Assembly would actually reject the treaty, and its supporters in France understandably did all they could to encourage the other five powers to stand firm, believing that then Mendès France would be forced to put the weight of his government behind securing ratification.

Defeated at Brussels, Mendès France flew to England, where he talked with Churchill and Eden before going back to Paris. He was still convinced the treaty would not be ratified, and he wished to guard against a possible alliance of Britain, the United States, and Germany which would exclude France. He therefore indicated that he was ready to accept German political sovereignty without EDC, together with German admission to NATO. Churchill and Eden for their part were unattracted by an alliance which excluded France; but they did not let Mendès France know this, and left the threat hanging over him. Mendès France then returned to Paris. On 30 August a vote was carried in the National Assembly rejecting the EDC treaty by 319 to 264. The government had refused to make it a vote of confidence, and itself abstained.

There could be no doubt that the opposition vote embraced those who were not prepared to see German rearmament, including communists, socialists, and Radicals; and those who rejected supranationalism, particularly the Gaullists and the right. Supranationalism which destroyed the army was particularly unacceptable; but there were also those who voted against the EDC as a rearguard action against integration, with the threat it seemed to imply to their industrial interests, because they had failed to defeat the ECSC treaty. Of all the French parties, only the MRP gave massive support to the treaty.

It was one thing to reject the EDC treaty – and with it the hopes which had been built up round the project for a European Political Community; but it was impossible to put the clock back to the days before 1950. This was especially true with regard to Germany, which awaited the ratification of EDC in order to secure the sovereignty promised under the Bonn agreements, and which now appeared as the well-behaved state of Europe, in contrast to its neighbour. It remained to be seen whether a device could be constructed which would halve the opposition to EDC by abandoning either supranationalism or German rearmament – and it was obvious that in this political configuration it would have to be supranationalism.

For this new development the initiative came from Britain. For the first time since 1947 Britain was in a position to play a decisive role in Europe, by patching together the remnants which were left after the vote in the French Assembly. Eden therefore planned a meeting to include Britain and the United States as soon as it could be arranged. Then, according to his memoirs, as he took his bath on the morning of 5 September 1954 it occurred to him that the means by which German rearmament and membership of NATO might be brought about was the Brussels treaty, if it could be widened to include Germany and Italy; and that to bring this about it would be worth visiting the EDC capitals – leaving Paris until the last – in advance of the conference.

His progress was smooth as far as Paris; the Benelux countries, Germany, and Italy welcomed a solution which combined the advantages of Germany sovereignty and rearmament together with the full and equal participation of Britain. Up to this point Eden's main cause for anxiety therefore came not from his immediate negotiations, but from the unexpected news which he received in Rome on 15 September that Dulles was going to fly to Europe and visit Bonn and London but not Paris. The purpose of the visit was not altogether clear, and Eden could not but be concerned at so open and unexpected a reproach directed at the

French defaulters. In Paris it was more difficult to win acceptance of his views; Mendès France at first appeared sceptical of
securing acceptance by the Assembly of German admission to
NATO in any form. But Eden had reason to suppose that he had
convinced him of the dangers for France of isolation.

Dulles's mission for its part appears to have been useful in
enabling him to form a better judgement of the situation without
imposing his own view of it. As we have seen, the American
administration was increasingly committed to a supranational
community in Europe, and appears to have seen this as a
necessary step to the reduction of the American commitment
overseas. A number of resolutions in Congress had pressed
strongly for European integration; the most important of them
being an amendment to the Foreign Aid Bill proposed by Con-
gressman James P. Richards in July 1953, by which one-half of
American military aid to Europe was to be made available to the
Defence Community and not to individual countries (unless the
president recommended and the Congress authorized otherwise). But however susceptible Dulles was to Congressional
pressure of this kind he was forced to admit that the motive force
of supranationalism in defence was not strong enough to carry
the day. He moreover gave unstinted praise to Eden's initiative,
in spite of the differences which had arisen between them at
Geneva a few months previously.

On 18 September 1954 the British government sent out invitations to eight countries – Canada and the United States in
addition to the six European partners, and the conference met
in Paris ten days later. On all sides it was recognized that the
future of the western alliance was at stake, and this provided
sufficient incentive to reach agreement. As it had been accepted
that no supranational organization would be created, there were
three necessary contributions to such an agreement; one was an
American and British commitment to Europe, the second was
acceptance by France of German admission to NATO, the third
was acceptance by the other powers, including Germany, of
limitations on German armaments which would inhibit the
development of any potential German threat to Europe.

The framework within which these contributions were made
was the enlarged Brussels Treaty Organization, reconstructed to
admit Germany and Italy, and renamed Western European
Union. Like the Brussels Treaty Organization, it had a Council

of Ministers (in which decisions were taken by unanimity or simple majority, depending on the nature of the question); and to this was now added an Assembly, composed of the representatives of the Brussels treaty powers to the Assembly of the Council of Europe. The support of the United States was held out as an inducement by Dulles at the beginning of the London conference; and on 10 March 1955 Eisenhower wrote to the prime ministers of the WEU countries and substantially transferred to WEU the undertakings which had been offered to EDC in April 1954. The British commitment was more formal, and was included in the Paris agreements themselves. It was to the effect that the United Kingdom would:

continue to maintain on the mainland of Europe, including Germany, the effective strength of the United Kingdom forces now assigned to SACEUR [the Supreme Allied Commander, Europe] – four divisions and the Tactical Air Force or whatever SACEUR regards as equivalent fighting capacity.[16]

At first sight this was a change of revolutionary importance. Unlike the United States, the British government had not been under any constitutional limitation against giving such a guarantee earlier in its history, but this might almost have been the case, so contrary was it to the fundamental assumptions of British foreign policy. In practice, however, the new decisive departure had already been made by the practice of keeping troops in Germany, and the importance of this part of the agreements was largely political. Very flexible safeguards were written into the agreements; for while the British government undertook not to withdraw these forces 'against the wishes of the majority of the Brussels Treaty Powers', exception was made in the event of 'an acute overseas emergency', and provision was also included for review of the 'financial conditions on which the [United Kingdom] formations are maintained' in the event of 'a heavy strain on the external finances of the United Kingdom'. As events turned out, only three years were to pass before the United Kingdom revalued its whole defence policy and for that reason withdrew some of its troops from Europe; with the grudging agreement of the other WEU powers.

The third of the necessary preconditions of agreement, the limitation of armaments, with Germany particularly in mind but without creating conditions of obvious inequality for Ger-

16 Cmnd. 9289, p. 18.

many, was achieved by agreement and by the setting up of an agency. All the signatories accepted a maximum level for their armed forces on the continent of Europe (the level for Britain was in this way made both a maximum and minimum). In addition, the Federal German Republic accepted a limitation which it did not share with any other signatory, not to manufacture on its territory any atomic, biological, or chemical – ABC – weapons, long-range and guided missiles, influence mines, warships, or bomber aircraft. In order that these limitations should be observed, an agency for the control of armaments was set up under a director and responsible to the Council, with rights of inspection and the right to receive reports from members about ABC and major conventional weapons.

Further safeguards surrounding Germany's admission to NATO were made by the way in which WEU was accepted into the alliance. It was agreed that all armed forces in Europe would come under the authority of the supreme commander (except for overseas and police forces) and that no forces might be re-deployed in this area without his consent. This clarified the position of the existing members of NATO with regard to re-deployment[17] but not with regard to withdrawal. Since Germany had no overseas territories, and was entirely within SACEUR's command, the independent action of its forces was effectively limited by this undertaking.

These were the essential features of the Paris agreements as far as they concerned defence. They made possible the conclusion of a further agreement which modified the Bonn conventions of 1952 and restored sovereignty to west Germany. They were accompanied by an agreement between France and Germany providing for a 'European' settlement of the Saar question. They were accepted with little opposition in Britain and the Benelux countries; in Germany they were met with continuing strong opposition from the social democrats. In France ratification could only be secured by a political battle in which the rancours left over from the debate on EDC were an important factor. German rearmament in any form still found its opponents in the communists, amongst some of the socialists, radicals, and inde-pendents, and a group of the Gaullists round Soustelle. This meant that the MRP occupied a decisive position, and this party

[17] Italian action over Trieste in 1953 was an example of national redeployment without SACEUR's approval; but such cases were likely to be rare.

of all others was animated by a certain vindictiveness and personal animosity towards Mendès France, who was a scapegoat for the failure of policies they had pursued in Indo-China and Europe. On the first vote on WEU they added their massive opposition to a negative vote which otherwise (except for the communists) was made up of a small contribution from each of the main political groupings, and this resulted in the defeat of the first article of the bill of ratification. To many within and outside France the effect of such a vote seemed catastrophic; but procedural devices made it possible to take the vote again. This time the obvious dangers implicit in rejections of the agreements, the influence which Adenauer tried to bring to bear on his friends in the MRP, and the fact that Mendès France made the vote one of confidence secured a majority on 29 December. The next month the ratification procedure was completed in the Council of the Republic.

The importance of the Paris agreements lay in the fact that they permitted the re-emergence of western Germany as a sovereign state. Although the WEU treaty expressed hopes and intentions about further integration, the institutions it established were of little future importance; and in the following year a meeting of foreign ministers of the ECSC powers at Messina restarted European developments along federal lines, which were still unacceptable to Britain. In the military sphere there was little room for WEU to act. The level of armies on the continent of Europe never presented a problem of too great size, and their integration, training and deployment were carried out by NATO and not by WEU. In western Germany material progress was accepted as a preferable alternative to old fashioned militarism, and the balance of power in Europe was a more effective safeguard against German aggression than anything written in a treaty. In the last resort the western alliance rested on the acceptance of a basic minimum of commitments on the part of its members; the essence of WEU was that it permitted a reaffirmation of that fact, and that western Germany was accepted as a nearly equal partner.

It was hoped that the part of the Paris agreements which concerned the Saar would bring to an end a difference between Germany and France which had continued intermittently since the end of the first world war. Under the Versailles settlement

11

the Saar had been placed under League of Nations control until a plebisicite was held in 1935, when the Saarlanders chose to return to Germany. With the end of the war in 1945, the Saar fell in the French zone of occupation. In a comparatively short time, however, the French government saw the possibility of special treatment for the Saar which would be far more beneficial to French interests than the policy of control and dismantling which they supported in Germany as a whole. On 20 December 1946 General Költz announced in the Control Council that his government would proclaim a customs union between the Saar and France – a statement which met with protest, but no effective opposition from the other three occupying powers. Consequent on this the French government developed the political autonomy of the Saar and its economic attachment to France, so that its resources, especially its supply of coal, were available for the reconstruction of French industry.

In the autumn of 1947 this arrangement was given formal status. Elections to a Saar *Landtag* were held, and a constitution was agreed by the *Landtag* which united the Saar to France economically and financially, and provided for political autonomy, subject to French control over defence and foreign relations, and to the power of a representative of the French government to disallow legislation which endangered the constitution or the customs union between France and the Saar. French currency was introduced, and a *Régie des Mines de la Sarre*, under majority French control was established.

Such an arrangement brought obvious advantages for the Saarlanders as long as Germany was treated as a defeated country; and French policy had no serious critics, for German interests were not yet given expression and France's western allies were willing to accept French policy in the Saar in return for the greater unity to be achieved between the three western powers on the question of Germany as a whole. These circumstances changed after 1949. The establishment of a government in west Germany meant that there were now spokesmen for Germany's interests; and as German economic recovery proceeded apace in the 1950s, the traditional attachment of the Saarlanders to Germany was increased by the possibility of material advantage.

This being so, the French government sought to achieve a *fait accompli* in the Saar before German political and economic rehabilitation had gone very far. They did so particularly in the Franco-Saar conventions of 3 March 1950, which included provision for the exchange of diplomatic missions between France and the Saar. The conventions evoked strong opposition in Germany, where the Adenauer government protested that there must be no definitive settlement of the Saar before the conclusion of a peace treaty, and argued that French action prejudiced the issue in advance – as was indeed the intention of the French government. Nevertheless, at the end of March 1950 the Council of Ministers invited both western Germany and the Saar to join the Council of Europe as associate members; and after considerable debate the German government accepted – thereby agreeing implicitly to the Saar's separate status. With the conclusion of the treaty setting up the Schuman plan, France signed for the Saar, and Schuman and Adenauer exchanged letters agreeing that the status of the Saar was unaffected by the treaty. The Saar was, however, given three representatives in the Assembly of the Community.

The establishment of the ECSC might have been expected to mitigate or remove altogether the economic problem of the Saar by creating a common market in these basic products, so vital to French industry. It also seemed reasonable to expect that in the atmosphere of European union, national rivalries over the Saar question would be attenuated, and that a solution to the political problem would be found within the framework of European union. Certain steps were taken in this direction. In 1952 elections were held in the Saar which resulted in a victory for the Catholic People's party under Hoffmann – which won 55 per cent of the votes cast. Just before the ballot the French government had announced its intention of revising the 1950 conventions, and this was indeed done in May 1953, in a sense favourable to the Saar. Hoffmann's policy was known and declared to be to develop the Saar towards partnership as a seventh member of the Europe of the Six; while within the European Community a plan was devised, bearing the name of its author, van Naters, for conferring a European status on the territory.

These promising developments were, however, accompanied by evident discord and strong opposition. Within the Saar Hoffmann's success in the 1952 election was marred by the fact that the pro-German parties were not allowed to stand –

having failed to convince the minister of the interior that they were loyal to the constitution of 1947 – with the result that 24·4 per cent of the ballots were spoiled. The revised Franco-Saar agreement met with severe criticism from the Saarlanders; at the same time the governments of both France and Germany were vigorously attacked by the opposition in their own country accusing them of sacrificing national interest – a charge which Adenauer had especial difficulty in combating at a time when his whole western European policy was under fire from the SPD in the election of 1953. Outside the Europe of the Six those who were alert to European politics, particularly in Britain, were sceptical of the strength of a European movement which was apparently unable to absorb so longstanding but comparatively small a problem as that of the Saar.

The establishment of a European status for the Saar – a modified version of the van Naters plan – did, however, provide the basis for the agreement of 1954 between Adenauer and Mendès France. With the acceptance of the London and Paris agreements, the recognition of the sovereignty of the German Federal Republic, and the acceptance by France and Germany of the Saar statute, the course appeared to be set fair for the final elimination of an enduring problem. In fact there was a final act still to be played. In the course of 1954 the Saarlanders themselves had become less and less enamoured of the European status which was proposed for them. The growing prosperity of Germany was increasingly attractive, and stood out in strong contrast to the apparent instability of the French economy. French prestige was low in the Saar as elsewhere in the world as the war in Indo-China and hesitations over EDC appeared interminable; the eventual defeat of EDC in the French parliament made the future of European union appear a very unreliable basis on which to build. The result was that in October 1955, when the Saar statute was put to the Saarlanders for their approval by referendum, they rejected it by 423,434 votes to 201,973.

No alternative was offered in the referendum: but there remained only one possible course to follow – that of political reunion with Germany. The French government had the wisdom to recognize that it could not hope to command majority support in the territory; the German government was prepared to use its economic prosperity to facilitate a settlement. In

October 1956, a year after the rejection of the statute, a series of agreements between France and Germany provided for the incorporation of the Saar into Germany as an eleventh *Land* from 1 January 1957. At the same time a settlement was reached for the remaining contentious issues of the ownership and production of the coal and steel industry to safeguard French interests. Most important for its impact on the development of French industry, an agreement was reached with Germany for the canalization of the Moselle from Thionville to the junction with the Rhine at Coblenz, so that this beautiful, viniferous, but winding river would in the future give direct access from the industry of eastern France to the great waterway of northern Europe.

The hopes of 1954 for a settlement of the Saar question had thus been held in suspense before their final fulfilment; but that same year had seen the liquidation of another of Europe's historic problems – that of Trieste. This port, and the area of Venezia Giulia surrounding it, had been the outstanding Italian irredentist claim against Austria-Hungary before the outbreak of war in 1914 – a claim which was met by the peace treaty of 1919. At the same time, however, the state of Yugoslavia came into existence, and when the second world war ended Yugoslavia was in a position to assert its claims to Trieste, while Italy was prostrate as Allied troops drove out the Germans. The result was that as the German army collapsed, Yugoslav partisans and New Zealand troops raced for Trieste. By the time they met, the Yugoslavs were in occupation of Trieste, but the New Zealanders were the stronger force; and from this balance of power the two commanders, Morgan and Jovanović, worked out an agreement on 21 June 1945 for the partial withdrawal of Yugoslav troops to a line known (at least in the west) as the Morgan line. This division, which acquired an unforeseen permanence, ran roughly north-south down to Koper (Capodistria), leaving a Zone A, including the city of Trieste, to the west, under British-American administration, the remainder (Zone B) being under Yugoslav administration.

The diplomatic position of Yugoslavia was at this time complex. Tito had received far greater support in his battle for the liberation of Yugoslavia from Britain than from the Soviet Union; in any case Britain and the Soviet Union had reached

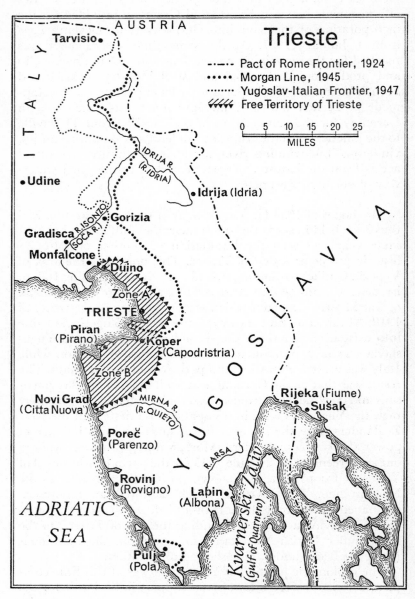

AUSTRIA

Tarvisio•

Trieste

-··-·· Pact of Rome Frontier, 1924
••••• Morgan Line, 1945
······· Yugoslav-Italian Frontier, 1947
〰〰 Free Territory of Trieste

0   5   10   15   20   25
MILES

ITALY

IDRIJA R.
(R.IDRIA)

•Udine

Idrija (Idria)•

R.ISONZO
(SOČA R.)
•Gorizia

Gradisca•
Monfalcone•

•Duino

Zone A

TRIESTE•

Piran
(Pirano)
•Koper
(Capodristria)

YUGOSLAVIA

Zone B

Novi Grad
(Citta Nuova)
MIRNA R.
(R. QUIETO)

Rijeka (Fiume)•
•Sušak

Poreč•
(Parenzo)

R.ARSA

Rovinj•
(Rovigno)

Labin•
(Albona)

ADRIATIC
SEA

Kvarnerski Zaliv
(Gulf of Quarnero)

Pulj•
(Pola)

Map 9

agreement in December 1943 in the encouragement of Tito to co-operate with the royal Yugoslav government. By the end of the war it had become evident that such co-operation was impossible, and Tito looked to the Soviet Union as a communist ally, although it was evident at the time, and has become even more so with the publication of Djilas's memoirs, that differences between the two had begun to arise.

When the Council of Foreign Ministers met in the autumn of 1945 Molotov proposed that the whole of Venezia Giulia should be transferred to Yugoslavia under the Italian peace treaty, at the same time as he demanded reparations from Italy and suggested that Russia administer Tripolitania as a trust territory. The west accepted reparations and rejected the trusteeship proposal; Trieste fell in the middle, and to the chagrin of the Yugoslavs a compromise was agreed, whereby Trieste was to be internationalized and placed under a governor to be appointed by the Security Council. The Italian peace treaty embodying this compromise, it will be remembered, was signed in February 1947.

No practical change resulted in Trieste, however, because by this time it was impossible for the Security Council to agree on a governor. Candidates were proposed from Czechoslovakia, Sweden, Norway, Switzerland, France, Spain, and South Africa; all to no avail. But while Trieste remained unchanged, the politics of Europe underwent fundamental revision with the beginning of the cold war, and Trieste seemed to occupy a position of cardinal importance. By the spring of 1948 Russian control had been established over eastern Europe and the coup in Czechoslovakia had brought that country under communist rule. In May 1948 elections were to take place in Italy, and there was widespread anxiety in the west lest the communists should achieve a victory which would place Italy too within their grasp.

In these circumstances Bidault visited Turin – the first time that a French statesman had made an official visit to Italy since 1935; while there he announced on 20 March 1948 that the three western governments would 'recommend the return of the Free Territory of Trieste to Italian sovereignty as the best solution to meet the democratic aspirations of the people'.[18]

[18] RIIA, *Documents, 1947–8*, p. 256.

The impact of such a pronouncement on something so beset with irrationality as an election is impossible to determine; but the result brought victory to the Christian Democrats and a government under De Gasperi which would lead Italy along the path to western European union.

But these events were immediately followed by the split between Russia and Yugoslavia. As a result the western powers found themselves hoist with their own petard. They now wanted a settlement of the Trieste question even more strongly because it constituted a weak link in the growing chain of western defence; but they also wanted to draw Yugoslavia away from Russia, and were unable to use Trieste for this purpose because of the commitment to Italy – a commitment which the Italians lost no opportunity to reiterate. Meanwhile the Soviet Union could only profit from the absence of a settlement; it no longer had an interest in supporting Yugoslav claims and could make propaganda advantage of the force of British and American troops held uselessly in occupation of one zone of Trieste. In Trieste and Venezia Giulia itself the Yugoslavs were in full control of their zone and held elections there in 1950 – won by the Titoists; in the other zone the Italians chafed increasingly under foreign military occupation, until they burst out in riots against the British in 1952.

Unable to find a solution, the British and American governments decided in 1953 that they must force the issue. Secretary Dulles announced that the declaration of March 1948 should not be regarded as 'the law of the Medes and the Persians'. Then, on 8 October 1953 the two governments, without prior consultation with the Italian or Yugoslav governments, announced that they would withdraw their troops from Trieste. The immediate result was one of alarums and excursions: Italian troops replaced British and American troops in Zone A, as the Italian government asserted its right to the whole area; while Yugoslav troops moved into Zone B and prepared to resist attack. In fact, however, neither side was prepared seriously to go to war with the other; troops were withdrawn from positions of immediate confrontation, and a conference was summoned. It took nine months, until 5 October 1954, to produce an agreement which was not called by that name but was known as a 'Memorandum of Understanding'. The basis of the understanding was a minor change in the existing position, with the transfer of some nine square kilo-metres from the Italian zone (Zone A) to the Yugoslav.

So in an atmosphere of bathos this small vignette of European history was finally etched in. It was a problem of traditional character in the old Europe, for the difficulty of reconciling Italian and Yugoslav claims lay largely in the fact that the town of Trieste was inhabited by Italians, but situated in a pre-dominantly Slav province. Trieste had once been of some economic importance, but the new political divisions after 1945, quite apart from the unsettled state of Trieste itself, had greatly diminished its usefulness as a port. Yet the political importance, the prestige involved, the commitments under-taken were sufficient to keep the issue alive in all the changing circumstances of the post-war world – as Italy changed from a defeated Axis power to a member of NATO, and Yugoslavia changed from being a partisan ally of the British to a communist enemy and finally to a recipient of American aid. Character-istically too the dispute was kept alive by public statements and proclamations; it was settled by old-fashioned secret diplomacy.

318

Map 10. Based on R. N. Taaffe and R. C. Kingsbury, A

319

THE SOVIET BLOC
At the time of the Geneva Conference,1955

::::: Soviet Gains made since 1939

/// Warsaw Pact   ▓ NATO or CENTO

0   500
MILES

ingrad

MOSCOW•   U   S   S   R

THENIA
N
KOVINA   U K R A I N E

Caspian Sea

Black Sea

Istanbul   T U R K E Y   I R A Q
Ankara

LAS OF SOVIET AFFAIRS (London, Methuen, 1965)

9

THE SOVIET WORLD AND ITS
EXTERNAL RELATIONS

By 1939 Stalin had established a firm direction over the communist parties of the world which was never effectively challenged, and which gave dissidents little choice but to abandon the communist movement. Although it is in some respects surprising that he could dominate and direct men of different nationalities half-way across the world, in countries of which he knew nothing (and probably cared little), it is obvious that he had immense resources at his command to achieve this centralization. He directed the state apparatus of the Soviet Union, including its financial resources; he was the effective head of the Communist party of the Soviet Union, whose politburo had a highly developed international section; and he commanded the pervasive force of the secret police. These institutional assets were reinforced by the ideological unity of the communist movement, and by the indisputable success of the Communist party of the Soviet Union in gaining and retaining power in its own country.

The Comintern was one of the instruments which Stalin had used to enforce his will. Meetings of the Comintern had provided a means of communication by which directives could be passed from the leadership in Moscow to the militants in every country. Under its aegis training could be provided for agents, and authority conferred on them without the directing power ever passing out of Russian hands. In May 1943 the Comintern was dissolved, and this caused a certain amount of confusion and disruption of a kind to which trained communists had to accustom themselves.[1] But in the conditions of the war it had no fundamental effect on Stalinist rule in the communist world. Many communists had taken refuge in Moscow and were undergoing training there for the tasks that

[1] See Leonhard, *Child of the Revolution*, for an account of how the dissolution affected him.

would await them after the war; others were beyond the reach of communication from Moscow, with or without the Comintern.

After the war the Comintern was not re-established; in the immediate aftermath of the war it would have gone counter to Russian policies to excite the distrust of western governments and dissipate the goodwill of non-communists by returning to the institution which had been the most potent cause of suspicion in pre-war days. Instead it was the front organization which received the fullest development. This device owed its origin to the enigmatic personality of Willi Münzenberg in the inter-war years.[2] Its essential characteristic was to embrace all political parties and present a front which was almost non-political (although always 'progressive' and opposed to 'fascism') while communists, by their greater energy, efficiency, and discipline, placed themselves in positions of power from which they could lever the whole cumbrous organization in the direction they wished. From 1945 there was a proliferation of organizations of this sort; in the liberated countries of western Europe the movements based on memories and groupings of the resistance provided the most fertile ground. Internationally the trade union movement, student and youth movements offered obvious opportunities. Within a few years the communists overplayed their hand in almost every case; their tactics became obvious, and the division of the world with the beginning of the cold war was accompanied by a division in the front organizations, leaving the communists controlling a minority body which was recognized to be under their control. Even so, they performed a useful function as one of the channels of communication within the communist world, by which directives could be transmitted and control exercised.

More significant than this, however, was the fact that the conditions under which the unity of communism must be achieved had changed in the part of the world closest to the Soviet Union. To meet these new conditions two new institutions were created: the Cominform in September 1947, and the Council for Mutual Economic Assistance (abbreviated either as Comecon or CEMA) in January 1949. Neither of these bodies achieved any substantial importance under Stalin.

[2] See N. Carew Hunt, 'Willi Muenzenberg', in D. Footman, ed. *International Communism* (1960; St Antony's Papers no. 9).

Instead the national communist parties in eastern Europe took over and bent to their own purpose the institutions of their own state, in accordance with directives from Moscow. It was thus national state organization and the relationship with the Soviet Union that predominated, while the Cominform played a subsidiary role and Comecon one of even less importance.

We have already seen, in the context of the development of the cold war, how Stalin's attempts to bring Tito under his control led to his withdrawal from the communist bloc. In the rest of eastern Europe the communist parties, having gained power as a result of the Russian presence, were subjected to violent purges, at the end of which the men controlling the newly acquired state machines were Stalin's men. The charges brought against those who were purged were similar to those made in Russia in the 1930s, the victims were accused of being agents of the American or the Yugoslav intelligence services, or of being Gestapo agents.

A new element was added, in that Jews were purged as being 'Zionist infiltrators'. In this way László Rajk was executed in Hungary in October 1949, followed by Traïcho Kostov in Bulgaria. In 1950–1 the executions were extended to Czechoslovakia, where Slánský and Clementis were the main victims, but where the purge itself removed some fifty out of ninety-seven members of the central committee of the communist party, and was marked both by its intensity and its anti-semitism. Rumania, Poland, and east Germany were dealt with similarly; except that in Poland the principal target, Gomulka, was first only expelled from the party and, when arrested in 1951, was neither tried nor executed. This was possibly the result of a strong instinct of self preservation in the Polish communist party, which had been dissolved by Stalin before the war. The trials themselves produced a series of confessions following the pattern of the 1930s; in Bulgaria Kostov created a sensation by withdrawing his confession (although his accusers said he withdrew his withdrawal before being executed).

There was no common political outlook amongst the purged; some, like Gomulka, were moderate, others were more radical than was Stalinist policy at this time. But the result of their elimination was that the old units of cohesion – dating from the

Spanish civil war, or from exile in London or Moscow or some other common experience – were broken down; and in contrast those who remained were in no doubt that their survival depended on Stalin.

In these circumstances it is not surprising that the formal arrangements between and with the eastern European states, including the Cominform itself, became of little importance. Stalin dealt directly and bilaterally with men who now, following the Soviet pattern, headed both party and state in their own countries, and who depended on him as much as any party secretary in the Soviet Union. There was indeed a double dependence on Stalin, both to counter rival aspirants to power in their own party, and to maintain the party in power against the anti-communist forces which formed a majority amongst their own countrymen. Like party officials, they felt that their success and their survival depended not so much on doing what they were told, but on guessing correctly what they would be told if they did not do it first. As one writer has said:

between 1949 and 1953 many (but certainly not all) of the most radical decisions were made [by eastern European communists] not on the basis of direct orders from Stalin but through the application of the principle of 'anticipated reaction' – by attempting to do what Stalin might wish done.[3]

While it was important that the leadership of the east European communist parties should fit the Stalinist pattern, it was equally important that the parties themselves should be effective instruments of control. To this end the membership of the parties was increased in number up to about the end of 1949; then there was some reduction, associated with the purges, followed by numerical stability.[4] This increase made possible the development of the party as an instrument of communist rule, as party controls extended into every sphere of political, economic, and social activity. At the same time the purges gave added coercive powers to the police, as had been the case in the Soviet Union – although in this case Russian police were active as well as national police. In this way the political framework of each state came to resemble closely the Soviet pattern. Moreover the political structure was used to

[3] Z. Brzezinski, *The Soviet Bloc* (1960), p. 112.
[4] For figures of party membership see ibid. p. 86.

develop the economy along Stalinist lines. Industrialization was pressed forward and many workers thereby transformed into an industrial proletariat, amenable to controls and industrial organization. Equally important, collectivization was adopted in all the countries of Soviet eastern Europe in 1948–9, except in eastern Germany, and was pushed ahead with greater speed in the following year. As in the Soviet Union in the 1930s this could only be done with considerable coercion, and its success was proportionate to the coercion used. In no country did collectivization proceed with either the speed or the inhumanity which had been seen in Russia before the war, but it was most developed in Bulgaria, least in Poland.

In all this, the development of eastern Germany was a special case. As the western powers developed western Germany politically, giving more and more control to the Germans themselves, so the Soviet Union followed suit in east Germany. But at the same time the Russians continued to emphasize the need for German unity, and to seek a means of bringing this about. As a result, non-communist parties were kept in existence, collectivization was not immediately adopted, and the government of the 'German Democratic Republic' played an ostensibly independent part in making overtures to the government of western Germany to bring about unification.

The principal political institution set up in eastern Germany was at first the 'People's Congress for Unity and a Just Peace'.[5] The Congress met through 1948 and into the spring and summer of 1949, and being a large organization it set up a smaller People's Council. Its purpose was largely one of propaganda. It sought to bring pressure on meetings of the foreign ministers to promote German unity – or at least to make a display of the fact that east Germans were doing this, and meeting with resistance from the western leaders. It also tried to sponsor its own elections in the western zones (which were not allowed) and claimed a certain number of representatives from across the zonal border.

The east German leaders were undoubtedly aware of the risks they would run if their proposals were taken up. In the event of a free vote the communists would have been in a

---

[5] It had been preceded in June 1947 by an Economic Council, following that which had been set up in the western zone.

minority, while the leaders of the non-communist parties (Nushke of the CDU and Kastner of the LDPD) in the eastern zone would have met with short shrift if their parties had been merged with those in the west.

The failure of the Berlin blockade and the setting up of the west German government brought a new development, and the People's Congress again proved useful in very quickly producing an east German constitution and a German government in October 1949. Grotewohl became prime minister and Pieck head of state. A year later elections were held to a new People's Council. In the interim period the CDU and the LDPD were emasculated and the SED purged. The election was run on a single list of candidates. Even so, the CDU and the LDPD continued to be formally represented in the new government. Thus from October 1949 a German Democratic Republic had come into existence east of the Elbe. Inevitably the western powers refused to recognize it or to regard the People's Council as in any way legally or politically representative. It was recognized by the eastern European governments and by that of Soviet Russia – the government of Poland doing so after the GDR had recognized the Oder-Neisse line as its frontier. However, none of this formal development had impeded the consolidation of the communist party (under the guise of the SED) as the effective instrument of government, under Soviet direction. In July 1950 Ulbricht, who had returned to Germany with the Russian occupation forces as the instrument of Stalin's policies, became secretary-general of the SED, thus furthering a career whose political longevity rivalled that of Stalin within the Soviet system.

The development of eastern Germany was more complex than that of the other satellite states, since it was at once a part of the Soviet empire, and an advanced post in the cold war. In so far as Stalin had cherished plans for Soviet control over the whole of Germany it meant settling for part rather than a whole; and the more fully developed the east German state system became, the more difficult it might be to prevent the establishment of an independent west Germany. On the other hand the existence of the German Democratic Republic made it possible for its leaders to make direct appeals to the government of west Germany, at the same time as the Soviet Union kept up a diplomatic offensive aimed at the western powers.

These attempts were barren of success; while at the same time the aggressive actions of the Soviet Union did more than anything else to accelerate the reconstruction by the western powers of western Germany in partnership with themselves. The Berlin blockade had a direct impact on this development, and by May 1950 the European powers were prepared, some of them to join, others to accept, the reconstruction of the west German economy within the framework of the Schuman plan. The following month the Soviet government (we may assume) initiated the war in Korea. Everything suggests that in doing so it expected a quick victory for the North Koreans which would outweigh any possible repercussions elsewhere in the world – although whether Stalin saw it as a prelude to further predatory raids, or merely as closing a gap in the perimeter, is uncertain. As events turned out no advantage was secured in Korea, while in Europe the effect of the attack was to provide an even greater stimulus to the development of a western alliance including western Germany, even to the extent of rearmament.

From the end of 1950, therefore, the Russian attempt to delay the rearmament of Germany and the greater integration of the west was intensified – no less so because it was in fact an attempt to reverse the consequences of the action over Berlin and in Korea. On 30 November 1950 Grotewohl opened a new round in the exchange with west Germany by a letter to Adenauer proposing the convening of an all-German council to discuss ways and means of unifying Germany. In spite of the distrust which Russian action over Berlin and in Korea excited, and in spite of the practical difficulties in the way of achieving German unity on any other than communist terms, this was an appeal which retained its unique attractiveness to some sections of west German opinion – the more so since the west German SDP under the leadership of Schumacher had become the protagonist of German national unity, and based its opposition to association with the west, and rearmament, on the grounds that it meant abandoning real possibilities of reunification. On the other hand the Adenauer government, with the support of the western High Commissioners and their governments, could safely reply that free elections throughout Germany, internationally supervised, were an indispensable condition to unification, since the east Germans could never agree to this with any intention of putting it into practice. It could also attack the east German government at another of its weak points, namely its acceptance of the Oder-Neisse line as the eastern frontier of Germany; but (in part because of dependence on the western powers) it refrained from exploiting this essentially nationalist line of attack.

The western powers gave support to the Adenauer government to the extent of taking the question of all-German elections to the United Nations in November 1951. It was discussed in the Political Committee, the two parts of the country were asked to send representatives to explain their views, and a vote was actually taken supporting the western position in December. The debate had no practical effect, and there was in fact no means of reconciling the two positions. Only the details of the exchanges between the western and the eastern governments varied; the Adenauer government made other conditions in addition to free elections, such as the establishment of independent courts, the release of political prisoners, and the disbandment of the secret police. Grotewohl was flexible in the detailed suggestions he made for a constituent council from the two sides to prepare unification, and he even spoke about 'general free, equal and direct elections for the whole of Germany'; but he rejected any proposal for international supervision as subjecting Germany to a humiliating form of colonialism; and he brushed aside a practical proposal by Ernst Reuter, mayor of Berlin, for 'pilot' elections in the city.

The exchange between the two governments was accompanied by exchanges between the Soviet Union and the west. Inevitably the Soviet government, and the eastern European governments, had protested against the western powers' decision of September 1950 on German rearmament; then in November 1950 the Soviet Union proposed a conference of foreign ministers on Germany, with particular reference to rearmament and reunification. The western powers replied that if they were going to meet in a conference they would want to discuss other topics as well, and after an exchange of notes sufficient agreement was reached to permit the calling of a preparatory conference. Its purpose was to provide an agenda for a foreign ministers' conference, which met in Paris, at the Palais Rose, from 5 March to 21 June 1951.

The Soviet view at this conference was that the world's troubles came from the actions of the United States and its servile allies – from the division of Germany and rearmament, and from American alliances and bases; the western view was that there were genuine international problems, exacerbated by Russian action, to which their own policies had reacted. There was no real meeting ground between these views, and the conference went on as long as it did only because each side wanted the other to be responsible for breaking it up – the western representatives being particularly anxious that it should not break up before the elections in France, which were held on 17 June. In a sense the negotiations were then merely transferred to the other side of the world, where in Korea the negotiations for an armistice began the following month – negotiations which were even more protracted, although they did at last arrive at a conclusion.

The exchange between the two German governments and Soviet diplomatic efforts were set against a background of vigorous propaganda in favour of 'peace'. In August 1948 a conference of 'intellectuals' had been organized in Wroclaw; it elected a committee, and this committee in turn organized meetings in various capitals in the succeeding year. The most important was the World Congress of the Partisans of Peace, held in Paris in April 1949, and widely advertised by posters carrying a drawing by Picasso of a dove. Neither this congress nor any other in the series was intended for any sort of genuine discussion; rather it was a sounding board and amplifier for the main lines of communist peace propaganda, opposed to the North Atlantic alliance (signed in the same month as the Paris congress), rearmament, and the atomic bomb. The Paris congress in turn elected a World Committee for Peace, which planned further meetings. The third of these took place in Stockholm in March 1950, and produced a document known as the Peace Appeal, for which the adherents to the movement then sought signatures all over the world. The campaign was successful in that it amassed a vast number of signatures – although this is not surprising since the signatures of communist countries could be taken as given, while in other countries there were not lacking signatories to 'demand unconditional prohibition of the atomic weapon as a weapon of aggression and mass annihilation of the people, and that strict international control for the implementation of this decision be established'.[6] The World Committee for Peace organized a second congress in 1950, which should have been held in Sheffield, England; but the British government, while not banning the congress, refused visas to its organizers and participants coming from abroad, so that it had to be transferred to Warsaw. This congress handed on the torch to a World Peace Council, which held meetings in 1951, including one in Berlin and another in Vienna in November – the second producing an appeal for a five-power pact for which a vast number of signatures was again collected (supposedly one-quarter of the inhabitants of the world). The whole peace campaign was obviously organized by communists, and the resolutions which its various congresses and councils adopted were closely related to the demands being made at the time by the Soviet Union in its diplomatic negotiations and the proposals it put forward for disarmament. At the beginning, particularly at the Wroclaw congress, many non-communists had also participated in a genuine desire to find common ground or to counter the growth of international tension. But the number of such people diminished very rapidly as the movement became markedly militant, and as the Soviet government tried to run it in harness with the Berlin blockade and the Korean war. Its effect in the long run was probably very small. At first it acquired some respectability from the support of eminent men who were known to be non-communists (and who thus fitted a well-established communist tactic); but after a relatively short time the process was reversed, and those who maintained the association were discredited in the eyes of all but a few outside the communist world. However, the effort put into the campaign, including the organization of vast congresses and the actual collection of signatures in non-communist countries, was very considerable.

An offshoot of the campaign may have been the more specific charges which were brought against the American government by the North Korean government, shortly afterwards supported by the Russians and the Chinese. The peace movement had always included bacteriological warfare as one of its targets, and in May 1951 the government of North Korea claimed that

[6] D. H. McLachlan, 'The Partisans of Peace', *International Affairs*, Jan. 1951, p. 12.

the Americans were distributing smallpox germs. In February 1952 these charges were repeated by the three communist governments, and were extended to cover typhus and other diseases. The American government denied the charges and proposed inspection by the International Red Cross. But although the Russian delegate took the question to the Disarmament Commission of the United Nations, the American proposal was never acted upon. It was never clear whether the charges were intended as solace for troops who had actually contracted these diseases, or whether the purpose was solely one of propaganda.

The 'failure' of the Palais Rose conference did not end the exchange between east and west on the subject of Germany.[7] On the contrary, the spring of 1952 brought the most striking of the notes which the Soviet Union had so far prepared on this subject. By this time the integration and strengthening of the western world seemed to be making definite and very positive advances, particularly since the Lisbon conference of the NATO Council had been held in February and proposals for a new status for western Germany, including rearmament, appeared virtually complete. In the face of this development Stalin addressed a note to the western powers on 10 March 1952 – the anniversary of his pre-war speech which presaged the conclusion of the Nazi-Soviet pact. The importance of this note was that it abandoned the previous Soviet insistence on German disarmament. It proposed four-power discussions for a German peace treaty, the unification of Germany, and the withdrawal of foreign troops; it insisted on the neutrality of Germany, but accepted a German national army – provided that Germany did not join an alliance directed against any state which had been an enemy of Germany in the last war. An additional incentive for Germany was the possibility of the opening up of eastern markets to German trade.

The note had no positive effects in the long run. The western powers in their reply deplored the proposed concession to Germany of control over its own armed forces, and the restric-

[7] To speak of the failure of a conference such as this is as deceptive as to speak of the 'success' of some revolutions. Since neither a conference nor a revolution can have aims of its own, distinct from those of its participants, neither can strictly be said to succeed or fail. Without knowing more precisely what the Russian objectives were one cannot judge how successful the conference was, at any rate from the Russian side. Cf. J. P. Plamenatz, *The Revolutionary Movement in France* (London, 1952), p. x.

tion on its foreign policy if it had to remain neutral; and at the same time they returned to the question of the frontier of Germany, and above all to the possibility of free elections and of a United Nations commission entering the Soviet zone. Thus the only positive result of the exchange was to give the social democrats an additional lever with which to attack Adenauer's foreign policy – the more so since many of them were convinced that there was a real possibility of negotiation on the basis of the note of 10 March.

The diplomacy of the Soviet Union in these years may well have followed from its internal needs. Totalitarian systems depend for their stability on the maintenance of stress and tension, and Stalin had been adept at creating the impression that Russia was surrounded by enemies. It was appropriate that a war-weary people, now more than ever, should be told that the Soviet Union was the great protagonist of peace, while the tension of external threats was maintained undiminished.

However that may be, in western Europe Soviet diplomacy gained no real success, while its propaganda had lost both party members and sympathizers.[8] It is understandable that in the first decade after the war which had ended with Hiroshima and Nagasaki, peace propaganda should have a strong appeal. But it needed to be more subtle to counter the impact of Russian action in Czechoslovakia, Berlin, and Korea; while the attempt to draw on anti-fascist feelings was inevitably less successful while it was coupled with the cult of Stalin's personality, which was the central theme not only of propaganda but of every speech, article, and news item within the communist world. In the Far East the pattern was the same. The United States had proceeded with the conclusion of a peace treaty with Japan, and the Soviet Union had failed to make any impact on the course of the negotiations. It could not prevent the signature of the treaty, and it could do nothing to make communist China a participant in the negotiations.

By the autumn of 1952 it appeared that the Stalinist line was undergoing a fundamental revision. A congress of the

[8] Since 1947 party membership had fallen in Britain from 45,000 to 33,000; in France from 907,000 to 506,000; in Denmark and Norway the fall was far more marked – from 45,000 to 16,000 and from 40,000 to 7,000 respectively (see J. M. Mackintosh, *Strategy and Tactics of Soviet Foreign Policy*, 1962).

communist party of the Soviet Union was called for 5 October
1952 – the first since March 1939, although the party rules
provided for one every three years. In the month before it met
Stalin published a pamphlet he had written earlier in the year,
entitled *Economic Problems of Socialism*. This, and the key speech
of the congress – the report of the central committee, delivered
by Malenkov – had the same central theme. It was a denial of
the suggestion that the conflict between the capitalist and the
socialist powers was the most imminent at the present time;
on the contrary, at the present stage of historical development
the most probable immediate conflict was between the capitalist
powers. Malenkov said:

> The contradictions between the USA and Britain and between
> the USA and France are growing more acute and will continue to
> grow more acute as American capitalism penetrates the economies
> of Britain, France and Italy and seizes raw materials and markets
> in the British and French colonies by granting loans under a fanfare
> of 'aid'. First Britain and, following her, France and the other
> capitalist countries are trying to wrest themselves from subjection
> to the USA in order to win an independent status and high profits.
> A stubborn struggle by the capitalists of Britain against American
> domination in international trade is already unfolding.[9]

One can only suppose that this was the directive for a change
in the policy and direction of the whole communist movement.
How far such a change would have gone, how successful Stalin
would have been in carrying it through, is impossible to judge.
It was accompanied by structural changes in the communist
party of the Soviet Union, which enlarged the central committee and replaced the old politburo and orgburo by a
presidium and secretariat, which were also enlarged. In eastern
Europe the purges had continued throughout 1952, especially
in Czechoslovakia and Rumania, and they were characterized
by their anti-semitism. In January 1953 Jewish doctors were
accused of having murdered prominent Soviet leaders, including Zhdanov, and of being engaged in plotting the death of
others. All these developments pointed the way to an imminent
purge within the Soviet Union itself, and later evidence,
including Khrushchev's speech at the 20th party congress,
confirms that such a purge was indeed under way when Stalin
died. Was this, in the Stalinist scheme of things, a necessary

[9] L. Gruliow, ed., *Current Soviet Policies* (1953), p. 101.

concomitant of a change of party line? And if it was, how successfully could Stalin, now an old man, showing ever increasing signs of madness, have carried it through?

Only speculative answers can be given to these questions, for Stalin died on 5 March 1953, just five months after the 19th party congress. At his death the whole of Soviet foreign policy stood in need of revaluation. The channels and contacts by which national and communist interest could be furthered were seriously clogged, or in the fast developing areas outside Europe had scarcely been constructed. Negotiations over Germany were at a stalemate; and defence policy, one may assume, still followed from Stalin's search for security from a traditional form of attack, at a time when atomic and nuclear weapons – which the Soviet Union had been developing for a number of years – had rendered all the old concepts of warfare out of date.

On balance it is highly doubtful whether Stalin, had he lived, could have revitalized a foreign policy which had gone dead on his hands. However, the first impact of his death was such that no one else could either. The Stalinist system was sufficiently personal for it to be impossible for anyone to succeed directly to the dead dictator; and it had been accompanied by elements of inefficiency and rigidity which no one would want to continue. More important was the fact that there was almost bound to be a struggle for power of some sort as men who held one or two of the directing reins of the Soviet system – the party, the state machine, the police, and the army – manoeuvred between themselves.

The western reaction to the death of Stalin was generally one of relief, accompanied by a great deal of caution. But it was inevitable that someone should raise the question of the possibility of fresh negotiations with Russia as a result of the change of leadership. The question was most directly put by Winston Churchill, as prime minister of Britain – the sole survivor from the days of the wartime triumvirate, and a man who of all men could not be accused of appeasement. On 20 April he spoke of the possibility of a conference at the highest level unimpeded by an agenda; on 11 May he developed the idea further, and referred to the 1925 Locarno treaty as a model which might be followed in the present search for security. Ten days later he proposed a three-power meeting in May in

Bermuda to prepare for a conference with the Russians. From the Russian side there were various indications that made it appear realistic to hope for some form of negotiation. The Soviet government had withdrawn its opposition to the appointment of Dag Hammarskjöld as secretary-general of the United Nations; it renewed diplomatic relations with Israel (which had been broken off at the time of the 'doctors' plot'), and meanwhile the propaganda attack on Yugoslavia had begun to diminish. On 28 March a decisive step was taken to further the repatriation of Korean prisoners of war – and therefore towards an armistice in Korea;[10] and in April *Pravda* reported a speech by Eisenhower accurately, not only without denunciation, but actually with favourable comment. This was particularly significant since Eisenhower had called on the new Soviet leaders to give tangible evidence of a desire for peace.

In the light of later knowledge it seems possible that there was a move in the Soviet leadership for a decisive step towards an international *détente*, particularly over Germany. This policy was associated with Beria. The leadership in east Germany was pressed to adopt a 'new course' in economic and political policies – to increase the production of consumer goods, to show more tolerance politically, and to be more restrained towards western Germany. There is evidence that a change of leadership was prepared, and that there was talk of the party going underground in the event of a settlement with the west of the German question – a policy which the existing leadership could not be expected to accept voluntarily.

It is impossible to know under what circumstances Churchill and Beria might have effected a fundamental change in the European situation. In the event Churchill's initiative led to no decisive result. His proposals had been coolly received in Washington and Bonn, although the French government and Assembly welcomed any suggestion that might offer a way out of the impasse of the moment. In America the new administration had just taken office after a tough anti-communist electoral campaign, and it would have been quite out of character for Dulles to begin his period as secretary of state by optimistically embarking on negotiations with the Russians. There were

[10] See above, p. 236.

marked differences of opinion between the British and American governments about trade with communist China, and Senator McCarthy was beginning to whip these up into violent denunciations of Britain; while the newly elected Congress was suspicious of the personal diplomacy of the Old World statesman. Similar feelings were prevalent in Bonn, and the foundations of a special relationship between America and Germany were being laid. The Adenauer government had just won a round of the political battle for the acceptance of the EDC treaty, and was preparing for elections in September.

The possibilities of negotiation initiated from the west were moreover now minimized by the temporary removal from the political scene of the men most interested in them. In Britain Anthony Eden underwent an operation for gallstones, from which he did not fully recover, and in June went to Boston for a further operation. At the same time Churchill suffered a stroke and was rendered inactive for several weeks. On 21 May the French government suffered a defeat in the Assembly, and a month passed before another government could be formed. The Bermuda conference therefore did not take place until December. In the meantime Lord Salisbury (acting foreign secretary) and Bidault conferred with Dulles in Washington and then again in London. As a result of their Washington meeting, in July, an invitation was sent to the Soviet government for a foreign ministers' conference, and after an exchange of notes this was finally settled for January 1954.

But the decisive events affecting the possibility of serious negotiation came from the Soviet side. The 'new course' was announced in east Germany on 9 June 1953; however, as we have seen, it was a Russian-inspired change which did not have the support of the east German government, and it may have been for this reason that it was accompanied a few days later by the introduction of tougher norms for factory workers. The combination of leniency and toughness brought crowds into the streets in protest on 16 June, and the next day these developed into full-scale riots in east Berlin and several other east German cities. Government buildings were set on fire and Russian flags torn down. The east German communists immediately demanded the intervention of Russian troops. These were at first withheld, but as the riots spread and some of the east German police refused to take action against the crowds, Soviet tanks were called in and the riots collapsed. In spite of this the policy of economic concessions was continued. The decisive change connected with the riots came rather in the Soviet Union itself, for at some time between 10 and 25 June Beria was overthrown; on 10 July *Pravda* reported that he had been relieved of all party functions 'as an enemy of the Communist Party and the Soviet people'. He then disappeared from view until December, when he was tried and executed along with other members of the security service.

It appears certain that the decisive reason for Beria's fall was that his rivals in the government wished to curtail the power of the police, and may have feared a bid for complete power from Beria himself. But the events in east Germany may well have had a part in causing his overthrow; in any case the riots put a practical end to any possibility of negotiation – if such had ever existed – which would open the way to further demonstrations on the part of the east Germans. Beria's elimination from the party leadership was followed by a small but significant purge in the east German party, the victims of which were accused of following Beria in a policy of compromise which would have sacrificed the achievements of communist Germany. It was perhaps of equal significance that a purge was carried out in the North Korean communist party, suggesting that Beria had been ready to seek some compromise with the west in Korea as well as in eastern Germany.[11]

Whether or not there had been the possibility of some major settlement in Korea the negotiations did move forward to the conclusion of an armistice on 27 July 1953. The Berlin foreign ministers' conference on Germany of 25 January – 18 February 1954 in contrast was completely without result. Britain, America, and France continued to press for free elections in the whole of Germany, which would produce a German government, with which a peace treaty could be negotiated. The Russians, represented by Molotov, proposed proceeding in the reverse order, setting up a German government by a merger of the existing governments, followed by a peace conference and then free elections. They also wanted a neutral Germany which would not be a member of NATO. The foreign ministers then turned to Austria, but here again no

[11] Leonhard, *Kremlin since Stalin* (1960), p. 75.

basis of agreement could be found. In fact the conference produced only one item of agreement; this was that a fresh conference should be held to consider the questions of Korea and Indo-China.

As a result of this second foreign ministers' conference, held in Geneva from 26 April until 20 July, the war in Indo-China was brought to an end, and the communist state of North Vietnam came into existence. It remains unclear at what stage the Soviet government, presumably in conjunction with the Chinese, reached the conclusion that they would bring the war to an end and settle for a part of Indo-China as a communist country, but one must assume that this represented the maximum gain which they calculated possible without the risk of defeat by strengthened French forces or by American military intervention.[12] However that may be, the net result was that the Soviet Union had liquidated the two conflicts in the Far East. In Korea the *status quo* had been restored; in Indo-China a gain of vital significance had been made. But in Europe nothing was achieved. Not only was there no settlement on Germany and Austria, but in the remaining months of the year the Soviet government failed to prevent the decision to rearm Germany being taken, or west Germany being given its sovereignty. Inevitably the defeat of EDC was warmly acclaimed in the Soviet Union; but it was rapidly followed by Eden's initiative and the diplomacy which led to the conclusion of the London and Paris agreements. In the face of this the Soviet government made frantic efforts first to persuade the western governments to participate in a new four-power conference, then to organize a twenty-three-nation conference on European security. Threats were added to cajoling, when Molotov said that if the agreements were signed the peace-loving European states would have to give thought to new measures to guarantee their security. These and other threats were not taken seriously by the western governments, and events following the signature and ratification of the London and Paris agreements indicated that they were right. In 1955 the Soviet Union initiated a new treaty with the countries of

[12] It has sometimes been suggested that Malenkov hoped, by reaching an agreement with Mendès France on Indo-China, to secure the defeat of EDC, but it seems unlikely that such reasoning could have been decisive. See pp. 247 ff. for an account of the conference and the settlement.

eastern Europe, the Warsaw treaty. Its signature did not alter the forces which the western powers faced in Europe, nor did it indicate any change of policy or strategy. The treaty was formally drawn in accordance with the UN Charter, and made reference to Article 51. It provided for consultation between the signatories, and for mutual assistance in the event of attack; it included agreement on the establishment of a joint command for their armed forces. Article 9 stated that the treaty was 'open to be acceded to by other states– irrespective of their social and state systems'.

Although the Warsaw treaty did not substantially alter the military challenge which the western powers faced, it was important in providing a legal and institutional framework for the development of Soviet policy in eastern Europe. It was signed the day before the signature of the Austrian treaty, and therefore afforded justification for the maintenance of Soviet troops in Hungary and Rumania once the pretext of safe-guarding communications to the Soviet zone of Austria had gone. It provided a useful counter in international negotiations since it could be pretended that NATO and the Warsaw pact were equipollent security systems. It also offered a means whereby the relationship of the eastern European states to the Soviet Union could be reframed. Henceforth membership of the Warsaw pact and acceptance of the foreign policy of the Soviet Union would remain *de rigeur* in the Soviet bloc, while an attempt was made to establish a framework of voluntary co-operation, permitting some diversity of detail, between communist governments.

This experimentation with new forms coincided with the growing dominance of Khrushchev. Until February 1955 the most outstanding figure in Soviet politics since the fall of Beria had appeared to be Malenkov; but Malenkov never succeeded in establishing a supremacy over his closest colleagues in the presidium, with whom he had important and substantial differences. In foreign and domestic policy he was to some extent an heir of Stalin, and this was reinforced in foreign policy by the decisive role which Molotov continued to play. On the other hand he tried to make new departures from the Stalinist legacy, most of all in economic policy in the Soviet Union and the eastern bloc, by giving greater priority to the production of consumer goods. It was in this sphere that he was most heavily criticized, and his policies obviously could not produce quick results. The result was that he lost ground in the fierce competition for leadership, and on 8 February 1955 he asked to be allowed to resign.[13]

Malenkov was succeeded as chairman of the Council of Ministers by Bulganin; but his successor had no impact on the course of events. The important change was that Malenkov had withdrawn before the first secretary of the party, Khrushchev. His resignation presumably gave the impulse for the return of Rákosi to power in Hungary, in place of Nagy, who had been responsible for the policy of the 'new course' since 1953. Here too the importance of the change in persons was evident, since Rákosi was not allowed by Khrushchev to return to the policies of Stalinist days.

Khrushchev was twenty-three when the communist revolution occurred in October 1917: he joined the Bolshevik party the following year and had had a continuous career in the party from that time. He became Moscow first party secretary in December 1949, as well as a member of the politburo and of the central committee secretariat. A few days after Stalin's death he took over the secretaryship of the party when it was relinquished by Malenkov. His whole adult life had thus been spent in intimate association with the growing power and success of the Soviet Union; it had also been passed under the dominance of Stalin, with whom he worked and whom he had praised, but of whom he had lived in constant fear. He lacked Stalin's conspiratorial past and even more his conspiratorial nature. He enjoyed immense physical vigour, although after a few years the strain of Soviet leadership and politics seriously threatened his health; he was invigorated by contact with others, and sought their support by the success of his policies and the cleverness of his politics.

He was also a leader who expressed the revulsion which was so widely felt against the whole Stalinist period. In every sphere of Soviet life there was an obvious need to open up the Stalinist system, to break down its rigidities and explore the possibilities of new ideas; and behind these practical needs lay a

---

[13] This was itself a new form in Soviet politics. Malenkov admitted no political or ideological errors, but merely pleaded inexperience (see Leonhard, *Kremlin since Stalin*, pp. 92–93).

pressing demand for emotional release from the terror of the Stalinist system and the perversion of human personality which it induced. At the same time the Soviet system of government, like any successful dictatorship, depended on the retention of power in the hands of a small ruling group, if not of one man. To initiate changes while adhering to the single overriding objective of a dictatorship – to remain in power – would require great political skill.

Malenkov's resignation on 5 February 1955 was neither the beginning nor the end of rivalry with Khrushchev. This dated back at least to the war years, and the struggle for power continued until June 1957. The battle was partly fought over real issues of economics, foreign policy, and defence; it was also a struggle for power between two men who operated or could command important levers in the Soviet system. In a conflict of this sort nothing succeeds like success – success both in the choice and implementation of certain policies, and in winning each round in the struggle. We have already seen how the actual failure of Malenkov's 'new course' told against him. Similarly Khrushchev's appointment as first secretary of the central committee (a promotion from being merely one of the secretaries) was the most decisive factor in ensuring that the central committee would support him against his rivals in June 1957. This political manoeuvring followed from the fact that the succession crisis involved a change in the structure of government as well as its dominant personality. Stalin's dictatorship was one of the harshest and most totalitarian the world has known. Once it was removed, those who aspired to the succession manipulated the power groups in the Soviet system – the police, the party, the economic bureaucracy – as each tried to gain an advantage over the others. The struggle by itself loosened the system, and neither Malenkov nor Khrushchev wanted to restore it to its full Stalinist rigidity. Equally, they were anxious that the system should not slip out of their control. Events proved that the acute sensitivity to power which had ensured their personal survival also ensured the continuance of communist dictatorship, even though the old leader and his system had disappeared.

This background must be borne in mind when the outstanding events of the years 1955–7 are examined. In the first half of this period the Soviet Union negotiated a treaty with Austria, withdrew from military bases in Finland and at Port Arthur, put forward important new proposals on disarmament, initiated a reconciliation with Yugoslavia, participated in the summit conference at Geneva, and sold arms to Egypt.

The first of this series of developments in external affairs must obviously be linked to general questions of defence. It is reasonable to assume that in matters of defence the Stalinist system stood as much in need of reappraisal as in everything else. Soviet strategy at the end of the war had been entirely conventional and traditional, and Stalin had sought defence in depth, with a belt of satellite states to act as a substantial fender before a blow could be struck against Russian territory itself. The development of atomic and nuclear capability by the United States rendered this concept out of date. At the same time the Soviet Union had itself developed atomic and nuclear weapons, while research was well advanced towards the development of a rocket force which would make the traditional concentration on territory as a means of defence even more anachronistic.

There is no means of knowing how far the implications of new weapons had been explored before Stalin's death; but there is plentiful evidence, in Soviet military journals, of the debate which broke out in the immediately succeeding years. The terms of the debate were very similar to those found in the west at varying times since the emergence of the new weapons. Military men and political leaders sought to calculate the deterrent effect of nuclear weapons, as against the need to build up a retaliatory system; they weighed the relative importance of nuclear weapons against conventional forces – although the latter always had a greater importance to Russia as a land power than to Britain or the United States; and they tried to assess the economic cost of building a modern weapons system.

In this debate it appears that Malenkov, as premier, had argued that nuclear weapons were so much of a deterrent that war was no longer possible; while Khrushchev pressed for the development of a retaliatory force on the grounds that a communist state could survive nuclear war, and a capitalist state could not. There was an obvious consistency in Malenkov's position, since he wanted to build up consumer goods industries. It may also be relevant that Khrushchev at this

12

Movie of K.

time enjoyed the support of the army in his struggle for power with Malenkov – and continued to do so until the last round of this particular series of bouts had been won, in June 1957. Shortly thereafter, in October 1957, Marshal Zhukov, who had been made minister of defence after Malenkov's resignation in February 1955, paid the penalty exacted by the Soviet system for his support of the winner, and was relieved of his office. This was the clearest single indication that the decisive role which the army had played in politics over the last few years had temporarily come to an end; it was accompanied by a re-establishment of political control over the army itself.

The precise connexion between this internal struggle for power and defence and foreign policy is impossible to establish. The events show, however, that a revaluation of defence policy made possible the liquidation of advanced posts held by Soviet forces, which had ceased to have great military value, and could therefore be traded for political goodwill and the re-establishment of political contacts with the west. The most important of these withdrawals was from Austria. As we have seen, the Soviet Union had effectively prevented the conclusion of a treaty with Austria since 1946. Once the Soviet government decided to negotiate seriously, agreement was arrived at with great speed. The Austrian chancellor visited Moscow in April 1955; on 15 May the foreign ministers of the four powers met in Vienna for the signature of the treaty, which provided a commutation of the economic advantages which Russia had secured by the Potsdam agreement. From a military point of view the importance of the treaty was that it meant the withdrawal of Russian troops – in fact a small force of two divisions – in exchange for the withdrawal of an even less important force of western troops and the guarantee of Austrian neutrality (together with curiously archaic safeguards made by the old anti-Comintern pact powers against Austrian purchase of armaments). In so far as this withdrawal had an effect on the military balance in Europe, it was to the advantage of the Russians. Originally the occupation of eastern Austria had provided a legal justification for the maintenance of troops to safeguard lines of communication in Hungary and Rumania; but now the Warsaw pact provided the framework within which the governments of these two countries could request the continued maintenance of the Russian garrisons. On the western side, however, the neutrality of Austria provided an important break in the north–south line of NATO and, together with the neutrality of Switzerland, provided an effective barrier to land communications between the German Federal Republic and Italy. From a political point of view the Austrian treaty improved the image of the Soviet Union and appeared a very conciliatory move; it may also have been intended to assist the reconciliation with Yugoslavia, where Tito had always been nervous about Russian troops in Austria.[14]

The treaty recognized the re-establishment of Austria as a sovereign, independent, and democratic state with the frontiers of 1 January 1938. It had been a condition of Soviet willingness to sign a treaty that Austria should not rejoin Germany and should remain a neutral state; the former condition was provided for in Article 4 which prohibited *Anschluss*; the latter was the subject of Austrian legislation when on 26 October the parliament passed a constitutional law 'declaring of her own free will her perpetual neutrality'. At the same time the Soviet Union received a commutation of the benefits which it gave up by returning the appropriated German assets to Austria, accepting payment of $150 million in Austrian goods.

Article 31 laid down that navigation on the Danube should be free and open for the nationals, vessels of commerce, and goods of all states, on a footing of equality in regard to port and navigation charges and conditions for merchant shipping.

The Austrian state treaty liquidated one of the most obdurate of the issues between east and west since the end of the war. No less striking was the fact that in September 1955 the Soviet Union renounced the rights which it had been accorded by the peace treaty with Finland to maintain and supply a naval base at Porkkalla. The base itself had ceased to be of military advantage; it was none the less remarkable that it should be surrendered without any *quid pro quo* being demanded – for although Finland was invited to join the Warsaw pact, it was not pressed against its wishes, and a treaty of friendship was signed despite its refusal to do so.

A few days before the signature of the Austrian treaty, on 10

---

[14] See Mackintosh, *Strategy and Tactics*, p. 106 n.

May 1955, the Soviet Union made a fresh proposal on disarmament to the UN General Assembly, in which it not only abandoned its earlier insistence on nuclear disarmament as a prelude to general reduction of forces but put forward plans for phased disarmament which were virtually the same as those previously suggested in an Anglo-French plan. As we shall see, this proposal fell to the ground as a result of the unwillingness of the United States to pursue disarmament by this means.

The *détente* which made these events possible also opened the way for a meeting of the heads of the four governments – the American, Russian, French, and British – in Geneva in the summer of 1955. Eisenhower and Bulganin expressed their readiness for such a meeting, and on 10 May the three western powers proposed a conference in Switzerland. The next month the four powers agreed 18 July as the date for the opening of the conference, and Geneva as its place.

This was the first meeting between Russian leaders and their western counterparts since the wartime conferences of the big three. The circumstances of the meeting were obviously totally different. During the war the big three enjoyed unrivalled power to remodel the world – a power which they enjoyed because the war had disrupted the established frontiers and political alignments of the world at the same time as it had given unprecedented powers to the democratic leaders. Moreover, Stalin, Roosevelt, and Churchill, whatever their differences, were bound by a common sense of purpose in the defeat of Germany. The meetings necessarily were arranged and took place in secret, and the communiqués issued afterwards disclosed only a small part of the discussions which had actually proceeded.

In 1955 all this was quite different. There was admittedly a small element of common purpose between the Soviet leaders and those from the west; each side wanted to inform itself better about the other. The diplomacy of the cold war was normally conducted through the established machinery of diplomacy – or by the megaphone of public speeches and newspaper articles. Neither side wished to embark on an actual war, and it was natural that the men who took responsibility for the conduct of the cold war should wish for direct contact with their counterparts on the other side.

The summoning of a conference inevitably aroused the hopes

of ordinary people. It was natural that those who had such free access to news and information as was available to people in western countries – and indeed to educated people all over the world – should suppose that a 'summit' meeting must produce some results. They rarely analysed their feelings or formulated their ideas precisely; but they were profoundly aware of the bonds of humanity which bound them to ordinary people in the Soviet Union and elsewhere. It was natural, therefore, that they should imagine that the problems of the cold war were to some extent the product of the machinery and the artificial atmosphere of international relations, so that if their leaders met with those of the Soviet Union they too would find sufficient common humanity to break down the divisions and the suspicions engendered by international tension. They hoped that a summit meeting would escalate into world peace.

To some extent the leaders and members of governments on the western side shared this hope. They nurtured little optimism that they would be able to negotiate a radical change in European politics or in the cold war itself, but they genuinely wished for a relaxation of tension which would in the long run lead to a gradual dismantling of the conflict between east and west. After the conference, Eden for one was convinced that it had 'damped the explosive force' of the Chinese offshore islands.[15] They were not prepared – as the British and French leaders had been before 1939 – to make substantial sacrifices either of their own positions or of their objective for a freer Europe in order to achieve this relaxation of tension; nevertheless, within these limitations, it was an objective worth pursuing for its own sake. Moreover they were aware of the public opinion which pressed them to have discussions with the new Soviet leaders. (In contrast to the secrecy which necessarily preceded the war-time conferences.) They could not ignore the pressure of a public which yearned for relief from the tension of the cold war and the threat of nuclear weapons, or disregard the effect on the uncommitted nations of the world if they appeared wilfully to disregard the possibilities of negotiation – even though they were aware that participation in a summit conference had its own attendant dangers. Since the

[15] *Full Circle* (1960), pp. 308–9. During the spring of 1955 it had appeared possible that armed conflict might develop between the Chinese communists and Chiang Kai-shek's forces, supported by the United States.

secrecy of Teheran and Yalta had given way to the open
diplomacy of Geneva, their meeting would be the focus and
centre of the attention of the world, and this was a situation
which the Soviet government, more unscrupulous, and having
a total control of propaganda, could be expected to exploit
more fully than they could themselves.

The Soviet leaders shared the western outlook to the extent
that they too wished to establish contact. They too wished to
avoid general war (the more so in view of their nuclear inferior-
ity) and saw the conference as one means of averting war by
miscalculation. One must assume that they were less interested
in a relaxation of tension for its own sake, since within the
Soviet Union the communist system has always thrived on
tension, and at other times the Soviet government has deliberately provoked international crises to suit the purposes of the
moment. They were certainly not prepared to abandon any of
their established positions, and they made this clear in agreeing
to meet the western leaders. They made it a condition of the
meeting that it should not discuss eastern Europe or international communism. To this extent the conference took place
on their terms – and even so the western leaders thought it
worth while if they could initiate discussions on some of the
outstanding topics. But Khrushchev and Bulganin – and it was
obviously Khrushchev who was the decisive figure – had more
positive reasons for seeking a relaxation of tension. It would
facilitate their diplomatic activity in Europe if they could at
least improve their speaking terms with western governments;
and it would also help them to dismantle the Stalinist image of
Russia as an autocratic, secretive, and closed society. This
would make it easier to penetrate the Asian and African
world; it would also provide an additional resource in their
European diplomacy if the Soviet Union could once again
appear to the world as a reasonable power with genuine
grievances and legitimate claims.

The first two items on the agenda which the conference
agreed when it met were the future of Germany and European
security – and they were discussed together at the Soviet
request. It was logical that they should be so coupled, and at the
same time inevitable that the real connexion between these two
questions should always be referred to obliquely. The facts of
the situation were that if Germany were united, and if a united

Germany were to be allied to one side in the cold war, that side would be immeasurably strengthened. It was easy to obscure the issue by pretending that Germany was an exceptionally dangerous state with a bad record of aggression; but while it was true that the division of Germany derived from its last aggressive war, this was now a consideration of historical importance. Any state of similar industrial and military potential, similarly situated and divided, would have presented the same problems. True, the German war was history through which the participants at the conference had lived – Khrushchev and Bulganin had vivid memories and deeply felt emotions of the German invasion. There were also anxieties on the Russian side lest a reunited Germany on the side of NATO might give the alliance a quality of rashness and uncontrollability which at present it lacked. But fundamentally the problem was one of balance of power in the cold war.

In all the discussions of Germany the western leaders were at an advantage. Western Germany was stronger and much more populous than eastern Germany; and Khrushchev was under no illusion that the population of east Germany would choose a communist government. Moreover the Soviet attitude to the German question, as to so much else, was undergoing revision since Stalin's death. Whatever the old dictator's hopes for Germany might have been, it was obvious that west Germany could not be brought into the Soviet camp in the foreseeable future, either directly or by subterfuge. More than that, the German Federal Republic, government and people alike, had resisted the pressures and the lures by which the Soviet Union had hoped to persuade it to reject full membership of the western alliance because of the enticement of unity. The actual objective of German unification had therefore become valueless for the time being, since such a Germany could not be communist; and the propaganda line of unity had exhausted much of its usefulness. The alternative policy was to accept that the division of Germany could not be changed, to derive the best advantage from this by promoting and supporting east Germany – and to depict the great irritant of Berlin as an 'anomaly' to be cleared away. This alternative policy had already been evident before the Geneva conference when the Soviet government invited Adenauer to Moscow to talks designed to establish diplomatic relations with the German

Federal Republic as a separate state. The new policy was not, however, expressed in a clear-cut manner at Geneva since it would go against the 'Geneva spirit' which Khrushchev and Bulganin were anxious to create to oppose directly the idea of German unification based on the consent of the German people. But whatever line they followed they were at a disadvantage in an argument with the west, which could only gain by German freedom and reunification.

The western powers accordingly argued that the division of Germany was the greatest threat to European security, and they suggested that reunification should be achieved first, followed by a European security pact in which the reunited Germany should participate. Eden in addition proposed (with the approval of the other western leaders) a plan for joint inspection of forces in the zone along each side of the borderline dividing east from west Europe. The Russians on the other hand placed the question of European security first, and proposed a non-aggression treaty between the member states of NATO and the Warsaw pact; while in discussions over the actual directive which should be given to the foreign ministers, and the agenda which they should follow, they argued that security and disarmament should come first, so that Germany would take third place. In the end a formula was agreed. The two questions of security and Germany were joined under a single head – in that order. The directive read:

1. *European Security and Germany.* For the purpose of establishing European security with due regard to the legitimate interests of all nations and their inherent right to individual and collective self-defence, the Ministers are instructed to consider various proposals to this end, including the following: A security pact for Europe or for a part of Europe, including provisions for the assumption by member nations of an obligation not to resort to force and to deny assistance to an aggressor; limitation, control, and inspection in regard to armed forces and armaments; establishment between East and West of a zone in which the disposition of armed forces will be subject to mutual agreement; and also to consider other possible proposals pertaining to the solution of this problem.

The Heads of Government, recognizing their common responsibility for the settlement of the German question and the reunification of Germany, have agreed that the settlement of the German question and the reunification of Germany by means of free elections shall be carried out in conformity with the national interests of the German people and the interests of European security.[16]

The Soviet leaders thus went a long way in adhering publicly to the idea of free elections in Germany – so far that they could later be reproached for departing from the Geneva agreement in this respect. A careful reader of the directive, however, could see how the Soviet position was safeguarded in the phrase 'in conformity with the national interests of the German people'; and the point was made more explicit when Khrushchev made a speech in east Berlin on his way back to Moscow in which he said: 'We are convinced that the workers in the German Democratic Republic will not agree to a solution which puts the interests of the Western groupings ahead of the interests of the German Democratic Republic.'[17]

The other major topics which the conference discussed were disarmament and the improvement of contacts between east and west. Under disarmament there was no shortage of proposals. The Soviet leaders had made their main contribution to this subject in their note of 10 May. Eden's proposal for an everyman's zone along the iron curtain we have already mentioned. Eisenhower surprised the other leaders – western as well as Russian – by suggesting that the four powers should provide each other with blueprints of their military installations, and should each permit aerial surveys over its own territory. This novel means of inspection, which was designed to provide a safeguard against surprise attack, received a scornful reception from the Russians, and did not have much future. The proposal, together with the Russian plan, was handed over to a sub-committee of the UN Disarmament Commission. On the subject of east-west exchange there was little disagreement because there was little commitment; the agreement on this topic as it was expressed in the directive was that the foreign ministers were to examine the progressive elimination of barriers to free communications and peaceful trade, and also 'such free contacts and exchanges as are to the mutual advantage of the countries and peoples concerned' – an escape clause which allowed for such banning and jamming as each government thought appropriate.

[16] RIIA, *Documents, 1955*, p. 48.
[17] *Pravda*, 27 July 1955 (quoted by Mackintosh, *Strategy and Tactics*, p. 112).
12*

The limitations of the agreements reached at this first conference were seen when the foreign ministers of the four powers
met, also in Geneva, at the beginning of October. Their task
was to implement the directive which they had received from
the heads of government. The new spirit was already diluted
by the fact that the Soviet Union was represented by the familiar figure of Molotov, and the caveats which the Soviet leaders
had entered in the summer took on their full importance.
Moreover, in the interval since July, Adenauer had responded
to the invitation to visit Moscow and engaged in frustrating
talks with the Russian leaders, in which he failed to gain any
satisfactory responses to his demand for the return of German
prisoners in Russia prior to the establishment of diplomatic
relations. Diplomatic relations were none the less established.
His visit was followed by that of a delegation from east Germany
to conclude a treaty by which the Soviet Union recognized
the sovereignty of the GDR, including its right to establish its
own diplomatic relations with other states.

It was not surprising, therefore, that when the foreign
ministers met, Molotov should have made it clear that the Soviet
Union would not consent to free elections in Germany. Forced
to give serious attention to the question of German unity,
Molotov insisted on referring to the two Germanies, and
proposed that unification should be achieved through meetings
of representatives of the two parliaments, from west and east,
and the setting up by them of an all-German council. This
first stage would be accompanied by the beginning of the
withdrawal of foreign troops and limitations on the German
army. The question of real elections he disposed of in familiar
communist language, saying that:

such a plan ignores the real conditions in Germany, inasmuch
as the question of holding such elections had not yet matured. Such
a mechanical merging of the two parts of Germany through so-called
free elections, held, moreover, in the presence of foreign troops as
envisaged in the Eden plan, might result in the violation of the
vital interests of the working people of the German Democratic
Republic, and we cannot agree to that.[18]

It was this apparent withdrawal from the principle of free
elections which led westerners to charge the Soviet leaders

[18] *Pravda*, 9 Nov. 1955 (quoted ibid, p. 114).

with bad faith; in fact it was merely a reaffirmation of a consistently held position. On disarmament no progress was made – nor had there been any in the United Nations subcommittee. On the extension of east–west contacts detailed discussion again served to highlight differences, for the western leaders looked for improved means of unofficial contacts and visits (they had prepared a list of seventeen ways of facilitating movement through the iron curtain) while Molotov spoke only of official visits, and once again revived memories of the Stalinist era by describing some of the western proposals (for example the way he denounced proposed reading-rooms as 'centres of espionage').

For all that, the relaxed atmosphere which the summer conference between heads of governments had produced brought considerable relief to the peoples of the world. It was an achievement for the Soviet leaders in that it created a favourable image – Bulganin excelled Eisenhower as a grandfather figure as he drove round Geneva in an open car. It made possible the visit of Khrushchev and Bulganin to Britain in the spring of 1956, where they were generally met with non-committal silence – except by Oxford undergraduates, who sang 'Poor old Joe', and by the Labour party, which pressed for news about social democrats who had disappeared behind the iron curtain.

The greatest importance of the new image was, however, outside Europe, where it opened the way for Soviet penetration of the Middle East, Asia, and Africa. There was a precedent for the initiative which Khrushchev undertook in this area of the world. From the earliest days of communist Russia Lenin had stressed the needs and the possibilities of supporting colonial revolutions and turning the flank of the imperialist powers by the penetration of Asia. But Stalin had devoted little attention to regions of which he knew little It should be remembered that Stalin was far less travelled than other early revolutionaries, like Lenin and Trotsky, and once in power his intensely personal dictatorship and the reign of terror with which it came to be associated meant that it was an event for him to go outside the Kremlin, let alone travel abroad. He appears to have judged the possibilities of communist development in Asian and African countries by the strength of their proletariat and their communist parties; and there is no reason to suppose that he had any real wish to see successful communist revolutions in countries remote from the Soviet Union's land frontier. Moreover it seems certain that scholarly knowledge of Asia and Africa in the Soviet Union was limited, and obscured more than in some other areas by the Marxist goggles through which these lands were seen. It was not only that Stalin had not travelled abroad – no more had other Russians, except for limited foreign service and security personnel. It was no doubt for these reasons that Stalin had entirely neglected the possibility of developing and cultivating relations with the new states, so that they might act as allies in the cold war and provide echoes to the main Soviet themes in international propaganda. For the new countries history began again with independence from imperial rule – this was the great and overwhelming event in their national consciousness; but for the Stalinists it was merely a transition from rule by a foreign imperialistic bourgeoisie to a compromise between (for example) the Indian bourgeoisie and the imperialists, to the betrayal of the Indian people.

This barren policy began to disappear immediately after Stalin's death. India was the first country to enjoy new favours from the Soviet Union. In September 1953 the Soviet Union signed a five-year trade agreement with the Indian government and cultural exchanges were arranged. The new government also made an offer of a steel plant to India, and when the offer was accepted in February 1955 it became one of the most famous examples of Russian economic aid to developing countries. In June 1955 Nehru visited Moscow, and in November Khrushchev and Bulganin visited India and Burma. The exchange was accompanied by the maximum amount of fanfare and speechmaking. For Khrushchev and Bulganin the experience must have been overwhelming. Nehru's visit to Moscow was unlike anything that had happened in Stalin's time; even more the natural exuberance of Khrushchev must have been overwhelming when he himself went to India. Only three years before he had still been living under the shadow of Stalinist terror; now he glowed and swelled in the warmth of Indian hospitality, and for the first time felt the eager curiosity and spontaneous interest of vast crowds of people who came to see the Russian visitors. It is scarcely surprising that he misjudged the mood of his hosts and was carried away with his own enthusiasm. For both in India and Burma Khrushchev and Bulganin made vigorous speeches denouncing the imperialists of Britain and the west. They thereby forfeited a certain amount of the limited goodwill they had established in the west at Geneva; more important, they misjudged the sophisticated ideas of 'non-alignment' held by educated Indians, and were insensitive to the high regard in which many of them held England, even though they found much less occasion to give expression to these sentiments rather than to those of nationalism.

The visits were accompanied by further trade agreements. In the long run the offers made to India did not all come up to expectation. But the proposals which the Soviet leaders made to exchange industrial equipment and machinery for Indian agricultural and industrial produce, created a great impression as India struggled to meet the targets of the second five-year plan. In July 1955 a trade agreement was signed with Burma under which the Soviet Union undertook to buy 200,000 tons of Burmese rice. Premier U Nu visited Moscow in November 1955, and this was followed by more proposals for industrial and technical aid, for which Burma would pay with its rice crop. In the spring of 1956 Mikoyan visited India and Burma. Nearly as important as these practical steps was the fact that they were accompanied by a complete revision of the Soviet attitude to the newly independent countries. Encyclopedias and histories were re-written in the Soviet Union, and brave words calculated to enhance national pride replaced the sneering jibes about bourgeois and right-wing socialists in league with the old imperialists.

In South East Asia Indonesia was the most fertile ground for communist activity. Its political complexion was different from that of India in that its communist party was far larger. Since 1952 particularly its numbers had grown very rapidly, so that it looked as if the party might be preparing to take power. It did not in fact do so; but it maintained its strength in succeeding years and became, with the army, an indispensable prop of government. In 1954 relations between the Soviet and Indonesian governments were developed, embassies being established in Moscow and Djakarta. Sukarno visited Moscow in 1956 and signed a trade agreement. Nevertheless the actual amount of Soviet aid going at this time to Indonesia was considerably less than to India and Burma. Laos and Cambodia were also brought on to the Soviet Union's books; the Cambodian crown prince and premier joined the list of visitors to Moscow in the summer of 1956, and accepted the offer of Soviet economic and technical assistance.

However, of all the moves to extend Soviet influence into Asia and Africa the most dramatic was that taken in the summer of 1955 to sell arms to Egypt – even though the arms were actually supplied from Czechoslovakia. The general course of Soviet policy in the Middle East was exactly similar to that in Asia at this time. A parallel revaluation had taken place after Stalin's death. By 1955 and even more in 1956 invitations were being offered and visits welcomed; in February 1956 there was a Soviet-Egyptian agreement on atomic power; Syria appeared to be moving quickly into the Soviet sphere as the respective legations were raised to embassies and the Soviet government offered economic and technical aid. All this was similar to what was happening elsewhere, but the sale of arms to Egypt and Syria was unique at this time, and particularly striking since the communist party was illegal in Egypt. The bargain was in part the result of western diplomacy, and especially the formation of the Baghdad pact. Nasser – in contrast to Nehru and U Nu – wanted a supply of arms more than anything else. The Soviet Union could supply from stock more easily than it could meet some of its other promises, while the western powers were restricted by the Tripartite Declaration. At a single stroke the Soviet Union established itself in the Middle East, and by supporting Egypt against Iraq took a stand against western interests – careless meanwhile of the tension it added to Arab-Israeli relations. Longer-term Russian intentions are more difficult to assess. When Britain and France attacked Suez the Soviet technicians went south and the Soviet aeroplanes were flown to safety. The military effect of the deal was thus minimal compared with its very great political importance. Whether it was the hope and intention of the Soviet government to build a base in agreement with a friendly Egyptian government appears doubtful, unless the new Soviet leaders were unduly optimistic in the judgement of existing and possible future governments of Egypt.

In these ways the Soviet Union, where Khrushchev was now

the most important single directing force (even though he had not yet established the dominance he was to enjoy later), was opening up new avenues in external affairs. More important than this, however, was the revision which Khrushchev sought to effect within the socialist bloc – including Yugoslavia which now, for the first time since 1948, was once again described as a socialist country.

On 14 May 1955 it was announced that a Soviet delegation would go to Belgrade. This fact itself was an indication of how the strength of the Yugoslav position had increased since Stalin had talked of 'shaking his little finger'. Tito no longer led an isolated country whose very survival appeared threatened. In the seven years which had ensued since the break with the Cominform he had demonstrated his ability to ensure his country's survival and development with the help of aid from the west, without any sacrifice of independence. Immediately after the break the United States had provided financial aid and Britain had signed a trade agreement. The drought of 1950 was alleviated by American shipments of food — acknowledged and publicized by the Yugoslavs, as American observers watched its distribution. The Cominform's blockade redirected Yugoslav trade towards the west, and Britain, France, and the United States financed the consequent deficit in Yugoslavia's balance of payments. In 1951 food was followed by arms, and a military aid agreement was signed with the United States at the end of the year. Relations with near-neighbours in the western alliance changed similarly. In February 1953 a treaty of friendship and co-operation was signed with Greece and Turkey in Ankara, and a military alliance, called the Balkan alliance, in August 1954.

Only an imminent military threat would persuade Tito to go farther in alignment with the west; on the contrary, the political position of Yugoslavia made it eminently suited to offer leadership in the neutralist world, as was evident when Tito visited India and Burma before going to the Bandung conference in April 1955. Both limited alignment with the west and the possibilities of neutralism had the same effect of making Yugoslavia of first-class importance for Soviet diplomacy once the rigidity of Stalinism was abandoned – quite apart from the motive of Khrushchev's new policy towards the satellites. It appears certain that in the discussions before the proposed Russian visit, Tito exploited the strength of his position to force acceptance of his terms – that the Russians should come to Belgrade, and that they should come with an apology for the split of 1948.

In any circumstances reconciliation with Tito could be expected to produce upheaval rather than stability. Many people in the Soviet Union, and even more in the countries of eastern Europe, owed their positions and lives to the fact either that they had supported Stalin against Tito, or that they had been the beneficiaries in a struggle for power in which alleged Titoism had been the main ground of denunciation; and there were others who admired and envied both the Yugoslav road to socialism and Tito's independence in following it, who would find fresh respite and fresh incentive if Tito once again became *persona grata* with Moscow. In terms of doctrine and personalities the effects of a move towards Yugoslavia were therefore likely to be far-reaching.

The visit to Belgrade began at the end of May 1955. Six months previously, in November 1954, a significant preparatory step had been taken in the release of the American Noel Field, who had been arrested in 1948 and had been a key figure in the prosecution's case that 'Titoists' in the eastern European countries had links with the American secret service. When the Soviet delegation arrived in Belgrade Khrushchev, in his speech at the airport, placed the blame for the break with Tito on the Soviet Union – even though Beria and other 'agents of imperialism' were used as scapegoats. But the visit was only a limited success. In the concluding declaration an immense concession was made from the Stalinist position, for it was stated that 'differences in practical forms of socialism are exclusively the affair of individual countries'. But the declaration was signed by President Tito and Premier Bulganin – not by Khrushchev, who was first secretary of the party. It was thus an agreement between governments, not between the communist parties of the two countries; it was the latter which Khrushchev had wished to achieve, and which Tito had rejected.

The visit to Belgrade was followed by discussion with the Rumanian, Hungarian, and Czech party leaders in Bucharest, and then by further meetings, particularly of the central committee, in the Soviet Union. These meetings were necessary to revise the substance of Stalin's eastern European policy. This had involved the subordination of the economies of the satellites, both in what they produced and in the actual direction of them, to the Soviet Union – an arrangement in which the device of mixed companies played a key part. However, such an arrangement had all the drawbacks of extreme centralization, and as this was now called into question in the Soviet Union itself, it was inevitable that it should be in the eastern bloc as well. But the importance of the meetings was also that they formed the arena where Khrushchev fought for the continuance of his new policies against Molotov; and when *Kommunist* published a statement of self-criticism by Molotov on 16 September 1955 it was clear that Khrushchev was still in the ascendancy. Meanwhile he laid the foundation for future success by steadily filling the posts of provincial party secretaries with men of his own who two years later would play a decisive part in keeping him in office.

In February 1956 there took place the 20th congress of the communist party of the Soviet Union. It was the first since Stalin's death; it was also the first for many years to be summoned within the time laid down by the party statutes. It met in a fundamentally different atmosphere from Stalinist days. The ubiquitous police cordons were gone from Moscow; the portraits of Stalin were missing from the meeting hall. These changes, however, paled into insignificance beside the report which Khrushchev made to the congress, in which he denounced Stalin and the practices by which he had ruled. The report was given in secret session, and it has never been published in the Soviet Union; but it was made public by the United States government, following a highly successful coup on the part of its intelligence services, in June. The theme of the speech was 'how the Stalin cult gradually grew, the cult which became at a certain specific stage the source of a whole series of exceedingly serious and grave perversions of Party principles, of Party democracy, of revolutionary legality'.[19] The condemnation of Stalin began with documentary evidence of his rudeness to Lenin's wife, and proceeded to a report of the way in which charges which were 'absurd, wild and contrary to common sense' were brought against the majority of participants at the

---

[19] Gruliow, *Current Soviet Policies*, II (1957), p. 172.

17th party congress. Khrushchev indicated that the murder
of Kirov, at the end of 1934, which had been the signal for the
great purges, was almost certainly done with the complicity of
the police and therefore of Stalin – as critics outside the Soviet
Union, both non-communists and communists who had defected, had often alleged. Even the prowess which Stalin had
claimed for his leadership and command of the Soviet armies
during the war was thrust aside by specific examples of disastrous decisions he had taken; and this was followed by a
condemnation of his handling of the Yugoslav affair, which,
Khrushchev said, 'contained no problem that could not have
been solved through party discussions among comrades' – he
went on to say that the 'abnormal situation' which Stalin's
actions had produced had been liquidated in the interest of the
whole camp of socialism.

It followed from the reconciliation with Yugoslavia that there
could be 'different roads to socialism', and this theme was
stressed by all the chief speakers at the congress. It was admitted
that there could be different ways of achieving power and different ways of using such power to achieve socialism. It was
even said that socialism could be achieved by parliamentary
means, and that revolution was not an indispensable preliminary. To non-communists in the west this idea was unconvincing, as the Soviet leaders could give no recognizable
example of where this had occurred; its importance was rather
for communists in countries like France and Italy, in the lengths
to which it went in admitting variations from the Russian
pattern of achieving power. Taken in conjunction with the
condemnation of Stalin it went far to destroy the idea of a
single central authority for the communist world. It provided
a basis for the idea of polycentrism.

The congress saw a further ideological revision of major
importance. In addition to 'different roads to socialism'
speakers stressed the equally new theme of 'coexistence' – not
as a temporary tactic, which it had always been before in the
communist armoury, but as a necessary result of the destructive
power of nuclear war. Khrushchev himself said that there
were social and political forces sufficiently strong to prevent the
imperialists fighting a new war. These forces were to be found
in the new states of Asia and Africa, and in the 'workers' movement'. While rejecting revision which went so far as to suggest

that there was no conflict with the west, he condemned the
theory of the inevitability of war.

These changes in party doctrine were of very great importance. They were accompanied by a rewriting of party history
and by a rehabilitation of those communists, alive and dead,
who had suffered under Stalin. At the congress itself old and
well-known Bolsheviks who had been condemned in the past
and executed, or who had simply disappeared, were now
declared innocent of the charges which had been brought
against them. One of the most important examples was the
Polish communist party, which had been dissolved by the
Comintern in January 1938. This action was now condemned,
and in addition the action taken by Gomulka in refounding the
party in 1942 was praised in the press – the first move towards
his rehabilitation. The whole process of rehabilitation was continued and extended after the congress in articles in the press,
and an impressive range of old communists, from Bela Kun
(executed in 1938) to Vavilov (purged in disgrace because of
his opposition to Lysenko), became once more praiseworthy
members of the party. There were obvious consequences for
Soviet foreign policy. In addition to the new accord with
Yugoslavia a close relationship with China and the other bloc
countries should be developed. At the same time friendship
should be developed with the 'countries which stand for peace
[and] refuse to be involved in military blocs'.[20]

Khrushchev's secret speech had nevertheless been a carefully
controlled speech. He had denounced Stalin above all for his
cult of personality, for substituting his own dictatorship for the
leadership of the party, and for crimes which he committed in
pursuit of this end. Not all of Stalin's opponents were vindicated; for example, nothing was said to rehabilitate Trotsky
and his followers, although their physical annihilation was
condemned. In so far as denunciations were extended from
Stalin to his followers, their direction was carefully planned. It
could not be otherwise, because the new leadership of the
Soviet Union was associated with all that Stalin had done.
Within that leadership Khrushchev was still manoeuvring for
pre-eminence; it followed that the most radical denunciation of
Stalin must be directed to the promotion of Khrushchev and

[20] Ibid, p. 38.

not his rivals, for the speech was part of a campaign to break the hold of the Stalinists within the party and to consolidate Khrushchev's following in support of the new policies. As it was intended that the speech should remain secret, those who actually heard it – and who knew enough to recognize the validity of what was said – would feel that they had been taken into the confidence of the leadership and formed the élite of the new régime; thereafter suitable versions of the speech would be disseminated in a controlled manner throughout the communist world. This process was begun after the congress; and control continued to be exercised within the Soviet Union; but outside the Soviet bloc and in the satellite countries control was shattered by the American publication of the speech.

The cumulative effect of all that had happened since Stalin's death was enormous. There had been first the abortive 'new course' of Malenkov; this had been followed by the attempted reconciliation with Yugoslavia, the accepted implication that there could be different roads to socialism, and the necessary accompanying rehabilitation of 'Titoists'; then came the culmination of the denunciation of Stalin. Within the Soviet Union this must have caused upheaval and questioning, but it was a process that was still largely under control by the new leadership which had succeeded Stalin. In eastern Europe – and beyond – this was not so; there had been few changes of leadership and the men in power were themselves Stalin's creatures, faced now with the choice of joining in denunciation of themselves or running counter to the line of the new Soviet leaders. In the Soviet Union Khrushchev had not entirely succeeded in keeping the denunciation of Stalin as a domestic matter within the communist party – the crimes with which he charged Stalin had touched too many people for that – but at least the party was an established institution dominating and penetrating every aspect of Soviet life. In the satellite countries it was still an unpopular and fragile institution which a moment's freedom would sweep away altogether. Outside the Soviet bloc communist leaders were freer to make their own adjustment to the new situation – many of them had enjoyed a political longevity equal to that of Stalin, and recognized the enhanced prestige and importance which they could derive from the new ideology. Thus it was Togliatti who developed the theme of 'polycentrism', and went farther than Khruschchev in condemning the centralized system of the Stalinist world rather than particular errors within it.

Although it was obvious that the crescendo of shocks to which the communist world was exposed must begin to produce unforeseen effects, the process was continued in the early summer of 1956. In April the Cominform was dissolved, and this was the prelude to a visit by the Yugoslav leaders to Moscow followed by a triumphal tour of the Soviet Union. The visit by itself reasserted the idea of different roads to socialism, which was further reaffirmed by a declaration signed at the end of it. Thereafter it began to appear that within the Soviet Union the leadership was attempting to put brakes on the movement for reform, and to backpedal for the time being on criticism of Stalin.

But in eastern Europe it was impossible to maintain this sort of sophisticated control. Above all in Poland and in Hungary events had begun to move forward towards the immense upheavals that took place in those two countries in October 1956.

On 28 June 1956 the workers in a large engineering factory in the Polish town of Poznán went on strike against their low wages and the refusal of the government to make what they regarded as adequate concessions. The workers were joined by the citizens of Poznán, and a riot quickly developed in which some forty-four demonstrators were killed. Industrial and popular unrest, evoked by changing economic policies and the general political ferment of the Soviet empire, coincided with changes in the party leadership. The Stalinist leader, Bierut, had died in March and was succeeded by Ochab, while Gomulka and others were released from prison. Throughout the summer it was known that a struggle for power was going on within the party. Although Gomulka was not readmitted to the party until the beginning of August his prestige was great, and the reformists he led gained ground. Both his release and restored authority derived from Khrushchev's denunciation of Stalin, though it was known that the Russians wanted to keep control of the Polish party. But the reformists had Yugoslav support and drew courage from similar developments taking place in Hungary. There too intellectual unrest accompanied changes in party leadership. Gerö replaced

Rákosi as first secretary and the 'Titoist' Rajk was rehabilitated – posthumously.

The direction in which events were moving in Poland was evident in the treatment of the rioters who had initiated the upheaval. At first they were denounced in the usual communist terms; but soon afterwards the prime minister referred to foreign agents who had exploited undeniably real grounds of grievance. In September the accused were brought to trial, but there was no violent denunciation, no reference to a foreign plot, and only a few convictions to minor sentences. The climax occurred in mid-October, when the central committee of the communist party met to elect a new presidium. Gomulka was known to hold a strong hand. No fresh uprisings had occurred. His group controlled the police and security forces. It appeared that he could only be shaken by direct Russian intervention.

Dramatically such intervention now occurred. Ochab opened the meeting of the central committee on 19 October by announcing that the leading members of the Soviet government – Khrushchev, Mikoyan, Kaganovich, and Molotov – had arrived in Warsaw that morning. At the same time it was known that Soviet troops in eastern Poland were on the move. But the Poles stood firm. They rejected the Russian demands, and said that they would break off negotiations if Russian troops advanced farther. The Soviet leaders were forced to recognize that intervention had solidified the Polish party behind Gomulka so that he enjoyed the same position of strength as Tito. The population supported Gomulka against the Russians – whatever their views of communism. Marshal Rokossovski – a Soviet officer of Polish birth and, since 1944, a Polish citizen – reported that the Polish army would not act against the people. The Russian leaders recognized Gomulka's strength – and were reassured that the Polish government was firmly communist. They returned to Moscow. The next day the membership of the new politburo was announced. Gomulka became first secretary and Marshal Rokossovski lost his seat, as did the Stalinists opposed to Gomulka. On 23 October Khrushchev telephoned that the Soviet Union 'saw no obstacles to developing relations between the two countries'.

Khrushchev's decision in Warsaw was taken in the face of

growing popular pressure in Hungary. At the same time the success of reformism in Poland obviously encouraged the Hungarians. Pressure for change turned into revolt in accordance with a classical nineteenth-century pattern, for the originators of it were students dissatisfied with university conditions and their lack of freedom, and factory workers demanding higher wages. On 23 October the people of Budapest came out in a mass demonstration in support of these two groups. The government appeared at a loss to know how to act; but when Gerö, just returned from Belgrade, broadcast in the evening it was clear that it intended little concession. At about this time orders must have been given to Soviet troops on the border of Hungary and in Rumania to move in towards Budapest. There the crowd grew more violent, and at 9.30 p.m. succeeded in overturning the massive statue of Stalin which had been built in the centre of the city. However, this symbolic triumph was a prelude to tragedy. Shortly afterwards the Hungarian security police opened fire on the crowd. Inevitably the crowd backed away; but its size went on increasing. Then in the small hours of the morning of 24 October the first Soviet tanks and troops began to arrive. However, the people of Budapest did not give up at the sight of tanks, and it soon appeared that they could successfully improvise resistance to the Russians – many of whom were half-hearted in their unwelcome task.

The revolution had thus acquired strong momentum. The government was aware that its own resources for keeping it in check, being virtually limited to the security police, were inadequate, and had (as it announced at 9 a.m. on 24 October) sought Russian aid. The question now was whether the uprising could be stemmed by changes in leadership, or by concessions to the demands of the insurgents. Rákosi's replacement by Gerö had been of no substantial importance – indeed his uncompromising speech of 23 October had fanned the flames of revolution – even though it had been accompanied by changes in the central committee, including the appointment of Janos Kadar, widely regarded as a revisionist. The demand of the intellectuals (whose Petöfi circle had been a focus of discontent through the summer) and the insurgents was for Imre Nagy who, in disgrace under Stalin, had re-emerged to take over the government from July 1953 until April 1955, and who had introduced substantial reforms as well as releasing alleged Titoists, including Kadar, from prison.

During the day of 24 October Gerö yielded to these demands and it became known that a new government had been formed under the premiership of Nagy – although Nagy was a virtual prisoner in party headquarters. The next day Mikoyan and Suslov arrived in Budapest and took the change of leadership a step farther by ousting Gerö and replacing him as first secretary by Kadar. Nagy regained his freedom of movement and formed a new government. Meanwhile the revolution had spread across the whole country.

It seems probable that the Soviet government was prepared to make a settlement with Nagy, as it had with Gomulka. But in contrast to Poland, where the framework of government had remained intact and under the direction of the communist leadership, in Hungary the supports on which an unpopular régime had rested were being broken down by revolt. The Soviet government therefore staged a tactical withdrawal of its forces from their exposed position in Budapest. Their withdrawal was announced by Nagy. But at the same time the Russians deployed fresh troops in eastern Hungary. Meanwhile the revolution proceeded with such speed that the old political parties came back into existence and spontaneous popular councils – the parallel of the soviets of 1917 – took over the work of government in the localities.

The Hungarian leaders were thus confronted with two opposing forces, neither of which they could control – the revolution of their own people, and the gathering Soviet armies. There was no available position between these alternatives; they had to choose. At some time in the first days of November Kadar, who had been closely associated with Nagy up to this time, chose the Soviet armies, and made his way to the headquarters of the commander-in-chief; Nagy chose the side of his own countrymen, and the revolution. On 30 October the one-party system of government was abolished, and coalition along the lines of the 1945 government announced – it included the names of Kovács and Tildy, the leaders of the former Smallholders' party, and other non-communists, as well as dissident communists. On 1 November a telegram was sent to the secretary-general of the United Nations announcing this and requesting the help of the four great powers in defending Hungary's neutrality.

A cool-headed combination of threats and diplomacy on the part of the western governments might have been capable of exploiting the breach made by the Hungarian revolution, to the extent of achieving by negotiation the establishment of a neutral belt of states in central and eastern Europe. In the event the western governments were in no position either to bring pressure or to negotiate. At no time was neutralism a goal which Secretary Dulles was likely to pursue; and at this particular moment his government was preoccupied with the Suez question and sharply divided from the British and French. The Security Council could debate the appeal it had received from Nagy, but could take no effective action against the Soviet veto. Within Hungary there was no united political force on which Nagy could rely; and Nagy himself was incapable of evoking the national cohesion which might have welded together all the Hungarian parties, communist and anti-communist alike, behind his leadership. Even if he could have done so, the extent to which the revolution had now gone would have made him unacceptable to the Soviet leadership, and he could command no coercive force to match their armies.

The Soviet government was now in a very much stronger position. It had found in Kadar a Hungarian communist whom it could put in power and who would re-establish communist rule with its help. Khrushchev had the support of the Chinese communists, who had supported Gomulka in Poland and urged restraint on the Russians in dealing with him, but who now advocated repressive action against the 'reactionaries' in Hungary (an intervention in European affairs which was taken as an indication of the growth of Chinese authority within the communist bloc). It appears certain that on the night of 3–4 November Tito was also consulted, and agreed to Soviet action in support of Kadar against the revolution.[21] On 4 November Soviet troops and armour opened a fresh attack on Budapest in an operation which, in contrast to the improvisation of the first intervention, was planned with care and rigorously carried out. It was met with tragic heroism on the part of the Hungarians, which tortured the consciences and moved the hearts of people in the western world; but to no

[21] R. Lowenthal, *World Communism* (1964), pp. 83 ff.

avail. The revolt was crushed, Nagy sought refuge in the Yugoslav embassy,[22] and the Kadar government was established in his place.

In the west emotion was deepened by the belief which some people held that the Russians found themselves morally and strategically freer to act because of the Suez expedition. There is no evidence for such a view. Whether the British and French expedition to Egypt affected the course of events remains open to speculation therefore only in the sense that the Soviet government might have acted otherwise in Hungary if the western powers had been able and willing to offer effective counter-action. Similarly it might be argued that the Soviet leaders for their part would have been able to exploit the Middle Eastern crisis more effectively had they not been occupied in Hungary. As will be seen, it was not until 5 November that Bulganin threatened Britain and France with rocketry. As might be expected, the result of his doing so was to bring American support for its allies – as well as to make at least some Arabs shiver with alarm at the extent to which they had become involved in the cold war. Again, with the benefit of hindsight, it seems probable that even without Hungary the Soviet government would have drawn the maximum advantage by watching the discomfiture of the western alliance rather than becoming involved itself in the crisis.

Within the Soviet Union the Hungarian revolt was never fully reported. In the Asian and African world the Suez expedition, which was imagined to be simply a return to imperialism, made a deeper impact than the suppression of the Hungarian revolt. The United Nations, which was so actively involved in the Middle East, could only act verbally on Hungary. In seeking to establish the facts of the case it was denied the co-operation of the Hungarian government, and its report was published long after the two crises of 1956 had been liquidated.

In western Europe and in the United States the impact of the Hungarian revolt and its suppression was most deeply felt. It shattered the atmosphere of thaw which had prevailed since

---

[22] The Yugoslavs gave Nagy asylum in their embassy; he left there under promise of safe conduct later in the month, but was arrested by the Russians. His trial and execution were announced by the Hungarian government (with no date given) in June 1957.

Geneva and put an end to the growing programme of exchanges between Russia and the west – those who came through the iron curtain from the east were not now the temporary visitors of the Bolshoi ballet company but a stream of refugees from Hungary who sought a new life in the western world. Amongst non-communists it recreated universal distrust of and antipathy towards the Soviet Union; amongst left-wing sympathizers it went far to destroy the image of the Soviet Union as a power which was, in spite of everything, on the side of the underdog. For communist parties outside the communist bloc it meant the loss of many members, particularly intellectuals, who were at last no longer able to reconcile Soviet behaviour with their idealism.

The communist world could never be the same again after the events of 1955 to 1956. In Poland it soon became clear that there would no no reversion to the orthodox mould which had been broken in the brave days of October. The immediate effect of the affirmation of partial independence was an emotional stimulus which produced a great outburst of free expression. By the spring of 1957 Gomulka had consolidated his power and began to use it to construct the 'Polish way to socialism'. This meant a limitation of the freedom which had been secured since October and a restoration of party control; it also meant a restriction on the power and activities of the Catholic Church, which had very rapidly taken advantage of the cracks in the régime. The machinery of communist rule had been shaken but not broken, and Gomulka's own position, as well as his ideological convictions, rested on his retaining control of and controlling the country through the party apparatus and the security forces, while making sure of the loyalty and reliability of the army. At the same time the Polish communists were profoundly aware of the power across the border of the Soviet Union, both in the sense that without the Soviet Union there would not be a communist government in Poland at all and in the sense that it was dangerous to deviate too far from Soviet practice. The direction which they must pursue was therefore defined by the need to avoid conflict with the Soviet Union, and at the same time to retain the popularity and national cohesion which were their only source of strength when they differed from their powerful neighbour.

In these circumstances the Polish road to communism had

unique characteristics. One most important feature was that collectivization was abandoned; with the result that agriculture prospered, and the free peasants were the citizens whose standard of living most obviously improved. Poland was more receptive than any other country to Yugoslav ideas, and experimented to some extent with the device of workers' councils. In spite of the retrogression which began in 1957, there was more political freedom than in other east European countries. Where there were differences between Polish and Soviet practice the Poles took care not to avoid any formulation of ideological differences which would invite Soviet denunciation.

In external affairs the Polish government followed the same policy as its Soviet partner and was able to argue that its own national interests with regard to Germany were identical to those of the Soviet Union, especially since the Federal Republic had not abandoned its claim to the 'lost provinces'. It may have taken an independent step, as we shall see, in proposing the Rapaćki plan; but it was one fully in accord with current Russian policy, and was in no way comparable to the independent foreign policy of Yugoslavia.

In Hungary it took many months for Kadar to establish the power of his government and for the people to find a new adjustment to the fact of communist rule. By the end of the 1950s, when this had been achieved, it began to appear that there would be a 'Hungarian road to socialism'. Kadar's role during the revolution had always been problematical; he had been anathematized in the west as the lackey of the Russians, but it should be remembered that until the crucial days at the beginning of November he was a close associate of Nagy and had been imprisoned as a Titoist. Once he had grasped power and restored the authority of his government, he was able to introduce measures of liberalization and showed as much independence from the Soviet Union in his handling of internal affairs as Gomulka in Poland.

In the Soviet Union Khrushchev was able in 1957 to consolidate his own position and concentrate power in his own hands. In June he was outvoted in the presidium, but outmanoeuvred his opponents by summoning the central committee and reversing the presidium vote. Thereafter his rivals –

Malenkov and Molotov – as well as those on whose support he had relied, including Zhukov – were removed from power; although they were not tried, imprisoned, or executed as they would have been in Stalinist days, but were given subordinate positions. In a position of strength in his own country and basking in the prestige of the first Sputnik, Khrushchev sought to use the occasion of the fortieth anniversary of the Russian revolution to reassert the unity of the communist world. Meetings were held in Moscow in November 1957 and a declaration was devised and signed by twelve ruling communist parties. It referred to 'the invincible camp of socialist countries headed by the Soviet Union', and condemned revisionism, whose dangers Khrushchev claimed (in a speech of 6 November) were exemplified by the careers of Djilas[23] and Nagy. At the same time Comecon, which had been ineffective during Stalin's lifetime, was revived and became extremely active. Representatives from China, North Korea, North Vietnam, and Outer Mongolia attended as observers, but the work of the Council and its commissions was essentially that of planning the production of eastern Europe as a whole. Its object was to escape from the autarkism which had characterized the Stalinist era and instead to co-ordinate investment, to develop and share technical knowledge, and achieve a division of labour between the member countries according to their available resources and skills.

It was not the intention of either the twelve-party declaration or Comecon to restore the inflexible and wasteful unity which Stalin had enforced. But once that rigid unity was abandoned it was unlikely that all the major communist parties would agree to accept the same point on the scale of polycentrism. The condemnation of revisionism could not reverse the acceptance of ideological diversity implicit in the Belgrade visit of May 1955 or re-establish the authority of Moscow intact as if the 20th party congress had never happened; nor could the subservience of foreign communists to the Soviet leadership be restored without a revival of the Stalinist apparatus of police rule. In eastern Europe the dependence of communist parties

---

[23] Milovan Djilas, a close collaborator of Tito who became increasingly critical first of the Soviet Union, then of communist society, publishing his views in *The New Class*. He was imprisoned, but conditionally released in 1961, when he wrote *Conversations with Stalin*, leading to his arrest and imprisonment again.

on the Soviet Union remained; but it was a diminished dependence, as the example of Poland and later Hungary and Rumania showed. Outside the satellite states, communist parties could choose a fuller independence from the direction of Moscow than had previously been known, as was evident in Italy, where Togliatti welcomed the possibilities opened up by the 20th party congress, which he would not lightly forego. This was even more true of the Yugoslav and Chinese parties.

Significantly Tito did not go to Moscow for the conference of November 1957 and Yugoslavia did not sign the twelve-party declaration. Before the conference Tito had gone far in reconciliation with the Soviet Union, abandoning neutralism and aligning his foreign policy with that of the Soviet government to the extent of recognizing the GDR. He possibly did so in the expectation that he could have a decisive voice in the councils of the communist bloc, equal with the Russians and the Chinese.[24] But Khrushchev, confident of his own position, was not satisfied with anything less than the subordination of Yugoslavia. In exchanges between the Russian and Yugoslav leaders before the conference it was made clear to Tito that he must accept the same conditions as the other eastern European governments, including membership of the Warsaw pact, or be condemned as a revisionist.

It was this demand which decided Tito not to go to Moscow, and a new phase in the Soviet-Yugoslav split was thereby opened. In March 1958 the Yugoslavs published a draft of their own new party programme, with invitations to all communist parties to attend a congress in Ljubljana. The draft was condemned by the Soviet government, which saw it as a counter to the twelve-party declaration of the previous November; when the congress met the Yugoslav Ranković spoke of people who were 'sharpening the old rusty weapons of the Cominform', and the representatives of all the communist countries except Poland walked out. Nor was the disapproval of orthodox communists surprising. The programme was entirely revisionist in character and severely critical of the fact that Moscow and its satellites made no attempt to evaluate the developments which had taken place in capitalist countries towards control of private capital, or the contribution which

[24] See Lowenthal, *World Communism*, pp. 134 ff.

trade unions, national revolutionary movements, and social democratic parties made to socialism. Thereafter Yugoslavia continued to receive aid from the west, particularly from the United States, and was one of the leading neutralist powers.

The case of China was different. As we have seen, the Chinese leaders actively encouraged Khrushchev both in the compromise he made with Gomulka and in the repression of the Hungarian revolution. When the Moscow conference met in November 1957 they continued to give their full support to the Russians; indeed it was Mao Tse-tung who insisted that recognition be given to the leadership of the Soviet Union in the declaration of the twelve ruling parties, arguing the indisputable superiority of Soviet industry and power.

Support of this kind the Chinese were ready to give the Soviet Union in pursuit of a common policy. Nothing in the experience of the two countries before 1956 suggested, however, that such a common policy would be easy to achieve. The Chinese communists had come to power by ignoring the advice of Stalin; they had devised their own strategy for taking power and, being Marxists and intellectuals, they were prepared to give an ideological interpretation of it – one which conflicted with the Soviet version of Marxism. Their view of international politics was basically different from that of the Soviet Union and the national interests of the two powers were likely to conflict. From the amalgamation of these factors there would develop a division between the two major communist powers of far greater importance than the Soviet-Yugoslav split.

In external affairs the new initiative which had been taken in 1956 to extend Soviet influence in the Asian and African states was not seriously affected by the Hungarian revolt. The growing productivity of Soviet industry made possible the extension of trade agreements, credit arrangements, and technical aid; and in the autumn of 1957 the success of the Soviet Union in putting the first artificial satellite into orbit greatly increased its prestige amongst those who saw Russian industrial progress as a model for their own countries. In the Far East the state of war with Japan was brought to an end by the signature (at the end of 1956) not of a peace treaty, but of an agreement and a trade protocol. Throughout the previous year the Russians had refused to yield to Japanese territorial claims; but now the Japanese accepted what they could get – including a promise of the return of 1,000 (out of 10,000, according to a Red Cross estimate) detainees from the Soviet Union. However, comparatively little positive achievement was made in the area where it might be supposed the greatest opportunities existed for the spread of communist influence – the Middle East.

At the beginning of 1957 it looked as if the Soviet Union might establish an invaluable foothold in Syria. In July a military delegation from Syria travelled to Moscow and Prague, and this was followed by the announcement of an agreement in principle for extensive economic co-operation between the two countries and the suggestion of a military agreement as well. As we shall see, this brought a flurry of American activity in the Middle East, as Loy Henderson was sent to Ankara[25] and Eisenhower expressed the view that Syria was approaching communist domination within the terms of the Eisenhower doctrine.

Khrushchev made the most of the atmosphere of crisis which this provoked. He gave an in interview on 7 October to the *New York Times* and supported Syria against Turkey in the United Nations. He made the most of the new role of the Soviet Union as protector of Middle Eastern states: allegations and proud statements were made, and Rokossovski was given command on the Turkish-Persian frontier. Under cover of these alarums and excursions Zhukov, on whom Khrushchev had depended in all his battles for political leadership, was dismissed.

However, the growing Soviet position in Syria was cut back not by the intervention of the western powers but by the Arabs themselves. At the height of the crisis Egyptian troops had been landed at Latakia, on the authority of the joint command which had been established before the Suez invasion. As soon as the crisis was over the pro-Egyptian party in Syria regained the ascendancy and in November 1957 succeeded in carrying through union with Egypt, so that on 1 February 1958 the United Arab Republic was officially proclaimed. The Syrian pro-communists as a result were removed from commanding positions, the communist party (like other political parties) was suppressed and henceforward suffered the same restriction as its counterpart in Egypt; its leader, Khalid Baqdash, fled to eastern Europe.

Similarly it looked as if the coup in Iraq in July 1958 must be to the advantage of the Soviet Union. In a sense it was, since it meant the complete overthrow of the Baghdad pact – but this had been virtually achieved anyway, as a result of the Anglo-French attack on Suez. The communist party regained its freedom in Iraq under the new régime; but for a number of years Kassem was able to use the communists as a supporting political force without becoming dependent on them.[26] Once again the British and Americans showed that they could intervene with impunity in the Middle East by sending troops to Jordan and the Lebanon; while the Soviet Union protested in the Security Council – but without securing a majority for its own resolution – and pressed for a summit meeting to discuss the Middle Eastern situation.

As the Soviet Union sought to re-establish its control over eastern Europe after the upheaval of 1956, so in the Atlantic world intensive efforts were made to regain the strength of the alliance after the divisions of Suez and to keep it up to date with improvements in weapons systems. Khrushchev naturally tried to prevent this happening; he also, through 1957 and 1958, tried to re-establish contact with the west, and to secure some outstanding diplomatic success. He was in a stronger position in some respects after the successful launching of the Sputnik on 4 October 1957. Thereafter the Soviet Union gave increasing importance in its diplomatic statements and its propaganda to the summoning of a fresh summit meeting.

The theme of a new summit meeting was one that was easy to develop, since large sections of public opinion, once they had recovered from the shock of Hungary, thought it possible to achieve some sort of valuable discussion with the Russians. In October 1957 the Polish foreign minister, Rapacki, put forward a suggestion at the General Assembly for the creation of an atom-free zone in Germany and Poland, and the suggestion was taken up by Czechoslovakia. This was an attractive idea to those in the west who pursued 'disengagement' and seemed an additional reason for an exploratory meeting with the Russians.

[26] When it appeared that he could no longer do so he was overthrown by a further coup d'état in February 1963.

13

Khrushchev's own reasons for pursuing a summit conference must remain obscure. It may be that he shared the desire of western rulers – and people – to loosen up the situation in Europe. Alternatively it may be that his main preoccupation was with industrial decentralization and the problem of agriculture, that the development of a rocket system was still in progress, and that in any case it was not easy to alter the European situation to the advantage of the Soviet Union, any more than it could be altered in a reverse way from the west. In that case a summit meeting would be a substitute for actual change. Khrushchev may have calculated that as Dulles's health declined, Eisenhower would be vulnerable and gullible if he could be brought to a meeting.

The campaign for a summit conference achieved some success in improving the Soviet image in the western world; the more so when in December 1957 and January 1958, the Soviet government took up Polish proposals for an atom-free zone in central Europe, spoke soothingly about disarmament, and on 31 March 1958 announced the unilateral suspension of nuclear tests. But it did not prevent the consolidation of the Atlantic alliance, and above all the installation of American intermediate-range rocket bases in the territory of its allies; and although there was pressure to accede to the Russian proposals for a summit meeting, Dulles could steadfastly maintain that such a meeting must be properly prepared so that it would not be a mere empty show. In the summer of 1958, moreover, it seemed that the Soviet Union could no longer play an entirely free hand in the conduct of this sort of diplomacy. During the crisis in the Middle East, provoked by the coup in Iraq and British and American intervention in Jordan and the Lebanon, Khrushchev made a dramatic call for a summit meeting. Macmillan countered with the suggestion that this should be held within the framework of the Security Council. Khrushchev at first accepted this, but almost immediately afterwards withdrew and talked instead of an enlarged conference within the United Nations. Then on 31 July he flew to Peking, and on his return suggested an extraordinary session of the General Assembly.

It can be assumed that Khrushchev's acceptance of Macmillan's proposal had to be reversed because of Chinese opposition, stemming from the fact that the Security Council meeting would include Nationalist China. Moreover, as soon as the Middle East crisis was over, new tension showed itself in the Far East as China began a fresh attack on the islands of Quemoy and Matsu. As Khrushchev had been accompanied on his visit to Peking by Malinovsky as defence minister, the impending attack had presumably been discussed with the Chinese; but it is impossible to know how far it fitted in with Khrushchev's own tactics at this time. In the end the attack was a failure; all parties (except possibly the Nationalist Chinese) were anxious to avoid the outbreak of a major war, and the trick seems to have been won by the Nationalist Chinese because the United States provided them with Sidewinder missiles, and the Russians were unable or unwilling to provide their Chinese allies with a higher trump. Certainly the conflict between China and the Soviet Union was now entering on a new and more open phase.

10

ABADAN, SUEZ, AND THE COLD WAR
IN THE MIDDLE EAST

ON 28 May 1901 Muzaffar al-Din Shah granted a concession
for the exploitation of Persian oil to W. K. D'Arcy. Almost
exactly fifty years later, on 1 May 1951, the Iranian government
under the premiership of Musaddiq, nationalized the oil
industry. In the intervening period it had been built up by the
Anglo-Iranian Oil Company, which had taken over the concession in 1909, and of which the British government owned
51 per cent of the shares. The immediate complaint of the
Musaddiq government was that Iran received insufficient
revenue from the industry; yet its action is only explicable as
a nationalist move against foreign exploitation and against the
old order in Persia with which it was associated.

Musaddiq had himself come to power two months previously
as a result of the assassination of his predecessor, General
Razmara. He was personally wealthy, and came from an old
ruling family of Persia. He was in no way a social reformer;
but he owed his power to popular appeal. He aroused
the suspicion and antipathy of many of his own class, and
alarmed the shah and the army; yet they did not feel strong
enough to act against him, and were afraid of the nationalist
bands who kept him in power. Forced to resign by opposition
from the shah in July 1952, he was reinstated by agitation in
the streets. Excitable and unbalanced, he in the end over-
reached himself and was ousted from power by his own
countrymen; but in the meantime he had occupied the centre
of the world's stage; as often as not in bed, as he indulged his
hypochondria.

Events showed that, in contrast to Colonel Nasser some five
years later, he had chosen a weak position from which to make
his attack on foreign imperialism. The AIOC was a typical
Middle Eastern enterprise. It owned one of the largest tanker

fleets, and its refinery at Abadan was the largest in the world; yet it existed in a country whose other resources were scarcely developed, and whose economic and social backwardness accorded ill with a proud and cultured past. The company was a vast enterprise which negotiated with the Iranian government almost as a sovereign power; it made large profits from the sale of oil; yet the fact that the British government was both a shareholder and a taxing authority meant that more money flowed into the British than the Persian treasury. In 1949 the company had proposed a new but complicated agreement with the Persian government which would have given a greater share of the profits; but although accepted by Razmara, it was defeated in the Majlis, where Musaddiq at this time chaired the oil commission. Just before nationalization a further proposal for a simpler 50–50 sharing of net profits was ignored by Musaddiq, so great was his resentment against the enterprise as a whole, and his hope of securing complete ownership.

Yet the industry was indispensable to the Iranian economy; while the world could, with little hardship, go without Persian oil. In the best year before nationalization the company supplied 30 per cent of Iran's national revenue and 60 per cent of its foreign exchange. In the world market the company was an important supplier; in 1950 its output was still greater than that of any other Middle East country, and accounted for 16 per cent of the world total. Nevertheless the output of other wells and refineries could be increased to replace that of Iran; and it was possible not only to dispense with Iranian oil but to prevent its transport and sale.

The company was a commercial concern in which the British government had an important interest as a shareholder. But this was far outweighed by the political importance of nationalization. It fell in the first place to the Labour government to decide what action to take. Then in the autumn the dispute with Persia became one of the rare issues of foreign policy to be of some importance in an election. Domestic politics, however, loomed larger, and when a Conservative victory led to the replacement of Herbert Morrison by Anthony Eden at the Foreign Office, there was no marked change of policy.

From the first the British government was extremely chary of the use of force. It made a demonstration of force, and undertook preparations to safeguard its nationals if this should be

necessary. But there was no clearly defined objective which
force might achieve; and both Labour and Conservative
governments were understandably reluctant to disturb the
delicate balance of the Middle East by armed intervention.
They therefore sought negotiation and international arbitration. However, neither one nor the other brought any tangible
results. There was in fact little scope for negotiation, since the
starting points of the two governments were so far apart. The
British government argued that the nationalization was a
breach of contract, for which compensation must be paid over
and above compensation for nationalized property; and they
insisted that the amount of compensation must be fixed by
agreement between the two governments, or the Persian
government and the oil company, with the assistance of an
international arbitrator. The Persian government rejected both
these contentions. The British government instituted proceedings against the Iranian at the International Court of Justice;
and a few weeks later, when the Iranian government ordered
all British staff to leave the country within a week, took the
dispute to the Security Council. But the Security Council
delayed acting on the complaint until the Court pronounced
judgment; and the Court in July 1952 ruled that it was not
competent.

Meanwhile the Persians lacked any means of transporting
and selling their product. When a few independent tankers
loaded oil the company, in a series of court actions round the
world, succeeded in establishing its legal ownership. The
refinery remained idle and produced no revenue.

Although the affair was one primarily for the British government, the government of the United States had taken a sharp
interest from the start, and its view differed substantially from
that of the British. While making every effort to arrive at a
settlement, the British were prepared to wait, convinced that
they would sacrifice too much if they made a bad agreement,
and hopeful that in the end Musaddiq would have to see
reason, or would be replaced by more moderate men. For them
the issues at stake included the whole range of foreign enterprises in the Middle East, which would be vulnerable to
similar nationalization once the first act had proved successful.
The American government on the other hand supposed that the
only possible replacement for Musaddiq was a communist

government, and they therefore did everything possible to bring the two sides in the dispute together. Musaddiq took the obvious course of exploiting American fear of a possible communist coup, supported from Russia (particularly as the Korean war was still being fought). But he exaggerated the extent of the difference between Britain and America and the degree to which he could use it to his own advantage. He went to New York at the beginning of the crisis to lead his country's delegation to the United States and was entertained to lunch by Truman, but no positive results followed,[1] although the United States maintained its financial aid to Iran as a safeguard against economic collapse and against any temptation to seek aid from the Soviet Union. In April 1952 'Point Four' pacts were signed providing for some $811 million of aid, and at the same time it was announced that military aid would be renewed. Moreover Musaddiq alienated support abroad as he did in his own country. The difficulties in the way of negotiating with him were made most evident in the summer of 1952. In August the British and American governments proposed compensation to the International Court; in the meantime the company would discuss ways and means of getting the oil to flow again, the British government would lift its economic pressure, and the American government would provide interim aid to the extent of $10 million. It was reported that the proposal was based on Musaddiq's own suggestions of a possible basis for settlement, but the offer was declined, in interviews with the two ambassadors conducted in terms of characteristic threatening rudeness. This was followed by the breaking off of diplomatic relations with Britain.

In January 1953 the new administration took office in the United States. Eisenhower and Dulles were if anything even more eager than their predecessors to reach an agreement. Yet the fact was that Musaddiq was incapable of negotiating any kind of settlement which would be acceptable; while his behaviour suggested that however favourable an agreement he might make, it would soon be overthrown. Moreover his quest for complete power within Iran alienated more and more of his supporters. His dictatorship was for obvious reasons unattractive to the shah; he provoked the hostility of the army,

[1] During his stay he occupied the presidential suite at the Walter Reed Army Hospital in order to take advantage of American medical advice.

by seeking to bring it under his own control; his domination of
the Majlis brought him into conflict with the mullah Kashani,
its president, and turned the nationalist leagues against him.
He could call on the Teheran mob to undermine the power
of his rivals, but it was of no use for the attainment of positive
political objectives.

The dénouement came in the second half of August. A first
attempt by the shah to replace Musaddiq by General Zahedi
failed, and the shah fled to Baghdad, then to Rome, accompanied only by the queen and one officer, shunned by his
ambassadors in the two capitals. Musaddiq thereupon dissolved
the Majlis. Two days later the power of the shah and the army,
supported, it is generally supposed, by the United States
through its Central Intelligence Agency, returned victorious.
The change has been described:

> The Shah's dismantled statues still lay beside their plinths, in the
> main squares and streets of Teheran and of other cities, when
> suddenly the Army appeared; not, as a day or two before, in the
> shape of groups of nervous and uncertain soldiers who had in the
> end either gone with the mob or made themselves scarce, but as
> a well-disciplined force, under firm command.[2]

General Zahedi took over control, Musaddiq was arrested, his
house destroyed, and the shah returned to his throne.

By this time it was imperative for Iran to find a solution to
the problem of the oil industry, in order to recover the revenue
from it. With the help of the American ambassador, Loy
Henderson, and with the Swiss government acting as an intermediary, diplomatic relations were restored between Britain
and Iran, and successful negotiations quickly followed. They
led to an agreement being signed between the Persian government, the National Iranian Oil Company, and a consortium of
eight American, British, and French oil companies. It left the
Persian nationalization decree untouched, and the Iranian Oil
Company continued to operate two small refineries and the
distribution of oil products in Iran. Moreover the whole industry remained nationalized in principle; but under a twenty-five
year agreement (renewable up to a further fifteen years) the
operations of the AIOC were taken over by a new consortium.

[2] Peter Avery, *Modern Iran* (1965), p. 439.

The capital of the new consortium was held, 40 per cent by AIOC (soon renamed British Petroleum Company), 40 per cent by five American companies, 14 per cent by Royal Dutch Shell, and 6 per cent by the Compagnie Française des Pétroles. The consortium set up two operating companies, one to produce and explore for oil in Iran, the other to run the refinery; and the Iranian government appointed two out of the seven directors of each of these companies. The AIOC for its part received £25 million compensation (payable over ten years) together with payment from the other oil companies for their share in the consortium, which amounted to £214 million. Profits for all oil operations in Persia were to be shared in equal parts between the consortium and the Persian government.

The agreement was eminently satisfactory. It was tender towards Iranian susceptibilities; it provided compensation to the AIOC, and removed some of the stigma which had attached to the company (in spite of the fact that the conditions which it had created for its labour force were vastly superior to common standards in Persia). And both Iran and the world benefited once again from the production and refining of oil. The policy of the British government since the opening of the crisis was vindicated – although this scarcely made up for its earlier shortsightedness and that of the AIOC; Musaddiq had been replaced as a result of the opposition of his own countrymen; the long-standing antipathy of Persians towards Russia had safeguarded the country against the communist infiltration which the United States so much feared; and as a result an agreement was possible, both more advantageous and more stable than could possibly have been made with Musaddiq. The American government for its part had been more anxious to do something than to allow the situation to develop by its own momentum; but the Truman administration had shown restraint in its dealings with the British government, as did its successor in the short period before a settlement was reached.

Even so, the Abadan crisis had lasted more than two years. When it began in 1951 it was not easy to see the outcome, and its immediate effect was to act as a blow to British prestige in the Middle East. This was particularly important in Egypt. It was in the summer of that year that the British government proposed a 'new approach' to the problem of the 1936 treaty. This new approach consisted essentially of a proposal for a Middle East Defence Organization, to include Britain, France, the United States, Turkey, and Egypt. From the point of view of great power politics the proposal had some novelty in that it emanated from a joint Anglo-American initiative, in an area of traditional British and French pre-eminence. However, the Turkish government insisted on membership of NATO before being incorporated in a new organization, and this was not agreed by the NATO powers until the Council meeting in September. In the meantime the Egyptian government was incurring considerable criticism in the Security Council as a result of its refusal to allow Israeli shipping to pass through the Suez canal. The debate ended on 1 September with a resolution calling on Egypt to end its embargo on shipping bound for Israel – a vote on which the Russian delegate abstained.

From the point of view of the Egyptian government the novelty in the proposal for a defence organization was unconvincing. Essentially the plan was for the British to hand over their base to Egypt – on condition that it immediately became a MEDO base. This practical aspect of the plan was of more importance to the Egyptians than the theoretical equality of Egypt with Britain, France, and the United States in the new organization. The prime minister, Nahas Pasha, had different ideas, and two days after the MEDO proposal was put to the Egyptian government the parliament enacted laws abrogating the 1936 treaty and the 1899 condominium over the Sudan. The MEDO proposal was rejected.

There then followed a period in which the Egyptian government encouraged attacks of a guerrilla kind on the British base in the canal zone, and forced the British GOC to take increasingly tough measures to safeguard his troops and their supplies, especially water. But the more energetically they defended their military position, the more openly did they expose their political flanks. Overwhelmingly strong if called on to fight a war against Egypt, they were vulnerable to sniping and sabotage, and any counteraction which they might take provided admirable material for nationalist propaganda. Events proved, however, that the Egyptian government was itself too insecure to incite unrest in its own country even against a foreign occupant.[3] The Wafd party, which had cemented Egyptian politics in the past by combining nationalism with practical readiness to come to terms with the British, was materially enriched but politically bankrupt. It was discredited by its notorious corruption, and sacrificed the advantage of collaborating with the British without being able thereby to seize the leadership of the new forces of nationalism. The king for his part had forfeited his credit by succumbing to fleshly pleasures and courtly blandishments.

This became evident in January 1952 when the fever generated by the activities of the 'liberation army' against the British erupted in Cairo itself in riots the responsibility for which is difficult to establish. On 25 January 1952 British troops at Ismailia, seeking to disarm auxiliary Egyptian police who had shown active sympathy for their guerrilla compatriots, engaged in armed conflict with them. On the 26th the violent reaction which this provoked spread to the capital. There the rioting was at first condoned by some of the Wafdist ministers; it was enlarged by organized bands, whether Muslim enthusiasts or supporters of the king against the Wafd, and finally taken over by the mob. The police, incensed by the killing of their comrades at Ismailia, took no action until it was too late for them to do so. The king was entertaining army officers to lunch in the palace, and was too doubtful of the loyalty of the army to order it into action until the afternoon – although in fact the army showed itself intent on maintaining order, and had no use for mob action. In all some 700 premises were burned and looted on this 'black Saturday'. British residents who were at the Turf Club were pushed back into the fire by the mob and incinerated.

In one way or another mob violence of this sort represents a threat to any but stable and strong government, and so it proved in Egypt. The king dismissed Nahas Pasha, and appointed Ali Mahir (who had been kept out of office by British tanks in 1942) to succeed him. But this was the first of several

---

[3] The harassment of British troops continued after the change of régime. As Nasser said: 'Not formal war. That would be suicidal. It will be a guerilla war. Grenades will be thrown in the night. British soldiers will be stabbed stealthily. There will be such terror that, we hope, it will become far too expensive for the British to maintain their citizens in occupation of our country' (interview with Marguerite Higgins, *New York Herald Tribune*, 21 Nov. 1952, quoted by Monroe, *Britain's Moment*, p. 173).

makeshift expedients which were brought to an end on the night of 22–23 July by a coup d'état, carried through quietly and with a minimum of bloodshed, by a group of majors and colonels. General Nagib became president of the Council and a year later president of the Republic with Colonel Nasser as vice-president, but the latter's dominance steadily increased until in November 1954 Nagib was deprived of his presidency and placed under house arrest.

The origins of the revolt can be traced back to the period before the war; its immediate planning was skilled and discreet. Its key leader, Gamal Abdel Nasser, was the son of a fellah from Upper Egypt who had become a post office employee. He had entered the army in 1936, when the Anglo-Egyptian treaty and reforms carried out by the Wafd had opened the army to men from the lower ranks of society. In this Nasser was typical of many other young officers, in Egypt and the Middle East. The experience of the army was doubly important to him. It opened horizons which would have been closed elsewhere, since in no other occupation would he have been likely to rise so high in the social scale; while the knowledge he acquired in the army – especially during the war – extended and enlarged his view of the world. At the same time he often found his experiences humiliating. Senior officers had for the most part abandoned whatever military virtue they might have had; and younger officers were naturally ready to condemn the shortcomings of their superiors and to attribute them to the influence of the British, whose interest it was to prevent the development of a strong Egyptian army. He was sensitive to the interference of the British in Egyptian affairs, particularly the humiliation of 4 February 1942; and above all he had fought bravely in the Palestine war, only to see the Arab armies defeated as a result of inadequate supplies, bad generalship, and insufficient support at home. All this, in the mind of Nasser and his fellow Free Officers, provided an obvious background to an ardent reforming nationalism. They were ashamed of much that they saw in their country; and the cause of their shame they attributed to corrupt politicians, the palace, and British interference. It was their aim to rid Egypt of these. Beyond this Nasser, in common with most of his colleagues, had few coherent political ideas. As young officers they had come into contact with fascistic organizations as well as with the Muslim Brotherhood; but they had embraced no coherent political creed beyond a simple nationalism. What Nasser lacked in political ideas he amply compensated for in political ability.

Outside Egypt there were few who regretted the passing of the Faruq régime. Moreover the revolt was well managed, the king went quietly after signing his own abdication, and foreign lives and property were in no danger. The differences between Nagib and Nasser on the other hand raised doubts about the stability of the new régime. In consequence both the British and American governments waited with guarded optimism on the development of events.

Over the question of the Sudan, negotiations did in fact follow a smooth path and reach a successful conclusion. The abdication of the monarch removed the vexed question of the royal title. Nagib was half Sudanese and better aware of Sudanese feeling than many Egyptians. Under his influence the new government was willing to accept the principle of independence for the Sudan rather than unity with Egypt. It supposed that the continued use of propaganda and financial support would persuade the Sudanese to choose union for themselves. In any case it was worth taking the risk in order get the British out. The British for their part were genuinely anxious to hand over self government, and were under pressure from the United States to reach a settlement with Egypt; they were also concerned that the transitional arrangements should be fair, and that the rights of the southern Sudanese, who were less evolved politically, should be safeguarded.

In May 1952 a Sudanese Commission, under the presidency of a British judge, had drawn up a self-government statute, which had been submitted to Britain and Egypt as co-domini for approval. This the British government gave in October 1952, but the new Egyptian government, after consultation with Sudanese political leaders, made reservations. In January 1953 they strengthened their position when Saleh Salim and Shaikh Bakhuri toured the Sudan on behalf of the government, and secured the agreement of the leaders of all the Sudanese political parties to certain principles, particularly relating to the transitional period leading to independence. As a result, an agreement was signed between Britain and Egypt on 12 February which provided a novel framework for the political changes which it envisaged. The governor-general was to retain important powers in the transitional period, but he was to exercise his powers with the aid of a commission of five, of whom two were Sudanese, one British, one Egyptian, and one Pakistani, as chairman. Two other international commissions were also appointed, the one to supervise elections and the other to supervise the sudanization of the administrative service. The transitional period was to last not more than three years, and on its termination all British and Egyptian troops were to leave. The agreement worked well. Elections were held in the Sudan in November-December 1953, and the National Unionist party (pro-Egyptian) succeeded in winning a majority. An incident occurred when Nagib attended the opening of the Sudanese Parliament in March 1954, and there was a more serious revolt in the south in 1955; but on the whole the transitional arrangements went smoothly, and on 1 January the Sudan became independent, being admitted to the Arab League the same month and to the United Nations in November.

By this time the movement for union with Egypt had dwindled, partly because of the character of the Egyptian government, and partly because the Sudanese enjoyed managing their own affairs, so that the country remained independent. On the other hand when the Suez crisis occurred in October 1956, not only had the Sudan ceased to be a station for British troops, but the government closed their airports to British and French military planes and supported Egypt as a member of the Afro-Asian bloc.

Both Britain and Egypt thus improved their position by the settlement of the Sudan question, and the way to a revision of the 1936 treaty was to that extent made smoother. But it seemed in 1953 that the two governments had moved steadily farther apart in their attitude to the treaty since 1936. The Egyptians wished to be rid of the whole encumbrance, troops, treaty, and all; but for the British the Egyptian base had become even more important, since its object was not only to defend the canal and safeguard the transit of oil, but to provide for the defence of the whole Middle Eastern area. Not only that, but governments in both countries were under great pressure from their own public. In Egypt it was easy to outbid any government in nationalism. In Britain the Egyptian base acquired increasing importance as other bases were given up;

and Egypt was a subject already charged with emotion, especially on Conservative back benches.

The British government was under pressure from its Arab allies, Jordan and Iraq, to achieve a settlement: the attitude of the American government was less clear. When Anthony Eden discussed Egypt directly with President Eisenhower or Secretary Dulles he had no difficulty in securing agreement to his general proposition that the canal was necessary for Britain's defence, and in the interests of the alliance, for Britain to maintain a base in Egypt, and that the best arrangement likely to be acceptable was that the base should be evacuated, with arrangements made for rapid re-entry in the event of war in the Middle East. On the other hand the American government, including the secretary of state, tended to regard the Egyptian question as an imperial dispute, in which they were on the side of Egypt. This ambivalence was made evident when Dulles and Stassen (as director of Mutual Security) visited Cairo in May 1953. Dulles disappointed the Egyptians when he said:

We came to the conclusion that there should be a solution consistent with full Egyptian sovereignty, with a phased withdrawal of foreign troops – all to be arranged, however so that the important base in the canal area, with depots, supplies and a system of technical supervision should remain in good working order and be available for immediate use on behalf of the free world in the event of future hostilities.[4]

On the other hand he startled his hosts by presenting Nagib with an automatic pistol bearing on the butt plate a silver plaque inscribed: 'To Gen. Mohammed Naguib from his friend Dwight D. Eisenhower'.[5] At the same time the American ambassador to Cairo, Jefferson Caffery, acted on the assumption that the Americans understood (in a way the British could not be expected to) the attitude of revolutionaries who had liquidated an *ancien régime*. To this extent therefore there was pressure on the British to reach a settlement with Egypt, even though, when the question was put directly, the American

---

[4] *New York Herald Tribune*, 12 May 1953.
[5] 'A witness of the presentation ceremony said General Naguib betrayed momentary surprise when the United States secretary of state opened the diplomatic conference by placing the weapon on the table in front of him. "This is for keeping the peace, not for war", Mr Dulles said. "I know", said General Naguib' (*New York Times*, 12 May 1953).

government saw an identity of interest with the British in the maintenance of a base; while the Egyptian government was never sure how far it could rely on support from the United States in its dialogue with Great Britain.

Suddenly, however, the whole datum of the Egyptian question changed, for a simple reason of strategy. In 1953 the Soviet Union exploded a nuclear device and soon afterwards the British government reached the conclusion that the development of atomic and nuclear weapons made the Egyptian base of little value. As Anthony Eden later wrote:

The tangled mass of workshops and railways in an area the size of Wales was cumbersome and dependent on Egyptian labour. It did not seem likely that in this nuclear age we should ever need a base on the past scale. Smaller bases, redeployment and dispersal would serve our purpose better. . . . Service in the canal zone was also a poor recruiting agent.[6]

It was this single change of military policy more than anything else which made possible the negotiation of an agreement, which was signed on 19 October 1954. It provided for the evacuation of British troops, to be completed over a period of twenty months; for the maintenance of the base by civilian labour; and for the reactivation of the base should Egypt be attacked. The signatories also undertook to uphold the 1888 convention guaranteeing freedom of navigation of the canal.

The agreement seemed to put an end to a decade and more of strained relations between Britain and Egypt. Yet, like many international agreements, it looked different to different people. For the Egyptians it meant that the British had at last agreed to end an iniquitous infringement of Egyptian sovereignty. Nasser went further in interpreting the agreement as an expression of willingness on the part of the British government to pursue its Middle Eastern policy through Egypt – a fact which was to be of great importance a year later, when, instead, Britain joined the Baghdad pact. For Anthony Eden it was an undertaking which involved risks, but was justified by the promise it held that the British Middle Eastern position would be re-established on a sounder basis of equality and understanding. In his eyes the risk was increased by the fact

---

[6] *Full Circle*, p. 260.

that since negotiations had begun, Nasser had ousted General Nagib from the presidency, and this was taken to be a move towards military dictatorship and away from the restoration of parliamentary democracy. For some members of his party it was an abandonment of British rights, and a further step in the policy of scuttle to which the Conservative government, no less than its Labour predecessor, now seemed to be party. The most important asset which Eden regarded himself as leaving outside the immediate safeguard of British troops was the freedom of the Suez canal, and it was for this reason that the 1888 convention was reiterated; it was unfortunate, however, that at this very time the Egyptian government still prevented the passage of Israeli ships through the canal – a breach which Nasser might reasonably suppose had been condoned, since it was not mentioned in the negotiations. All these factors were to be of great importance two years later.

The signature of the Anglo-Egyptian agreement removed one of the most obdurate of the political problems of the Middle East. But this one piece of successful diplomacy was outweighed by a number of other factors which were leading to the progressive disintegration of stability. These factors constituted a situation of common occurrence in international politics, of which the component parts are rivalry between states within an area, coupled with divergent or opposing interests of external great powers.

Middle Eastern rivalries were long standing, and at least as important a political force as the more diffuse emotion of Arab nationalism or the desire for Arab unity. In the mid-1950s they were made more intense by the fact that three countries, Iraq, Egypt, and Saudi Arabia, became strong enough to make their rivalry more active. On the surface Iraq was in a particularly strong position. Its oil production was increasing, and in 1951 a new and more profitable agreement had been negotiated with the Iraq Petroleum Company and its subsidiaries; on the basis of this a development board was set up to use the oil revenues for the progressive advancement of the economy. The development plan was one which would make the rich richer before it had any marked effect on the general standard of living; and in so far as it caused inflation would make the poor poorer in the short run; and it enhanced rather than diminished the corruption and manipulation which characterized Iraqi politics. This meant that the strength of Iraq depended to a large degree on the success of Nuri al-Said in remaining in power and riding the storm of discontent which the economic and political condition of the country promoted. The further Nuri went in co-operating with the western powers in the promotion of their defence policies, the greater his difficulties would become; but as long as he retained control, Iraq was a wealthy and powerful contender for leadership.

Egypt lacked the advantage of substantial oil resources, and when the new government came to power in 1952 its first task was to restore the economic equilibrium of the country after the confusion of the moribund monarchy. But by its population, its industry, its education, and its propaganda resources Egypt had always been a leading power in the Middle East. When Nasser and Nagib took over the government in 1952 two things changed. One was that Egypt now acquired political strength from the authority of its government; the other was that it was drawn into a position of leadership in the Arab world. Traditionally Egypt had been the least Arab of the Middle Eastern countries (and continued to participate in African politics in a way the Asian-Arab countries did not). But Nasser's attitude to western imperialism, his burning desire to rid Egypt of British troops, only made sense if extended beyond the borders of Egypt. The gain to Egypt of liberating itself from the presence of foreign troops would be immeasurably reduced if they were still present in other countries, interfering in their politics and bringing pressure to bear on their foreign and defence policies. It was natural, therefore, that Nasser should seek to bind the Arab states in a united policy towards the outside world. Moreover this was a leadership which won a ready response from Arabs in other countries, who were attracted in different ways by the image of Nasser as it was projected to them by the press and radio of Cairo, or by Egyptian schoolmasters throughout the Middle East; and the response came especially from army officers, intellectuals, and ordinary people who made up the forces of opposition to a régime like that of Nuri al-Said.

The third party in this rivalry was the most backward of all, and the country which has for the longest time survived any attempt at a reforming revolution – Saudi Arabia. Its rivalry with the Hashimite dynasty which ruled in Iraq and Jordan was one of the oldest of the Middle Eastern conflicts. It was now enhanced by the growing wealth of Arabia, derived from the oil concession made to Aramco. Royal expenditure on Cadillacs, palaces, and pleasure was suitably exploited by the world's cartoonists.[7] But oil revenues also made it easier to pursue old-fashioned methods of intrigue, stirring up trouble, and recruiting soldiers on the borders of a neighbouring country like Jordan. Anthony Eden described the situation colourfully and tendentiously when he wrote: 'The agents of King Saud, their pockets bulging with gold, were co-operating everywhere with the Communists against Western interests'.[8]

These, then, were the three states able to take a most active part in the Middle Eastern rivalry. The common antipathies of Egypt and Saudi Arabia made possible a working alliance between them, even though the internal revolution which Nasser had effected was anathema to King Saud. Between the three there were two states which were the objectives of their rivalry – Jordan and Syria. Of all the Middle Eastern states Jordan was the most vulnerable, having minimal economic resources and so being dependent on outside aid, while harbouring the most concentrated force of resentment in the Palestinian Arabs and the refugees, and held together by kings who were obvious targets for assassins' bullets.[9] Syria was the greatest prize, and was the decisive factor in the rivalry between Iraq and Egypt. It was the vital connecting link in the Fertile Crescent plan which had always been the centre of the Hashimites' plans for Middle Eastern leadership; while a link between Syria and Egypt would give Egypt the key to Arab Asia. To add to the complexity of the situation, it was in Syria that was found in the Baath socialist party the strongest and most thoughtful group of people who aspired to the kind of Arab unity that would transcend national boundaries.

In this setting the interests and policies of the United States and Russia were now added to the long-standing participation

---

[7] The British public were scarcely aware of the death of Ibn Saud on 9 November 1953 and his succession by Saud.

[8] *Full Circle*, p. 342.

[9] King Abdullah was assassinated on 20 July 1951; he was succeeded by Talal, who surrendered the throne in August 1952 because of illness; he was succeeded in turn by Husain.

of the British. Increased United States interest in Middle Eastern politics can be explained in part by the involvement of that country in the cold war. American forces held the line in Europe, and had fought in Korea; the war in Indo-China had been largely financed in its last years by the United States, and had been followed by the Manila pact. It was to be expected, therefore, that the Middle East would also be considered in a policy of defence against the Soviet Union. This was the more so when Dulles became secretary of state; for Dulles was the defender in the first place of American interests, and it would not come easily to him to leave the Middle East as an area of British dominance.

As we have already seen, American policy was at first ambivalent, and Anglo-American co-operation was not easy. Elsewhere in Asia the relation between the United States and its Asian allies was very similar to that between Britain and its allied Arab states; and yet the United States was reluctant to accept the British position because of its imperialist background. There were smaller, but sometimes no less important, causes of difference between the two countries. The one Arab state with which America had a direct relationship was Saudi Arabia. During the war the two governments had signed a contract for the construction of an American air base at Dhahran. This was completed in 1946, and in 1951 a new five-year lease was signed which confirmed that the airfield was Saudi property and available for the aircraft of other nations, but also the special rights of American aircraft. In addition an American company, Aramco,[10] in December 1950 had negotiated a fresh agreement with the Saudi government, which was the first Middle Eastern 50–50 agreement, giving the Saudi government a half share in net income. By 1956 this half share amounted to about £100 million a year. As we have seen, this revenue made it easier for the Saudi government to conduct an independent foreign policy which sometimes ran counter to British interests. The American government regarded the oil arrangements as purely commercial; but it became a source of growing irritation to Eden that an American company should provide the finance for opposition to his policies.

[10] Participants: Standard Oil Company of California, Texas Company, Standard Oil Company (New Jersey), holding 30 per cent each, Socony Mobil Oil Company 10 per cent.

It would have been easier to overcome these differences if the persons whose chief responsibility they were had found each other more congenial. Eden and Dulles suffered from different kinds of vanity, and were basically antipathetic; their most important diplomatic encounter up to this time had been in and around the Geneva conference on the Far East, which had given neither cause to respect the other.

That the Soviet Union should enter Middle Eastern politics at this time is less surprising than that it should have shown so little interest hitherto. It has been suggested that Stalin avoided involvement in the Middle East in order not to attract American intervention; but it seems hardly likely that this alone explains the lack of attention which the area received. It was obviously inhospitable to communist penetration of a Stalinist kind. Arab rulers had generally been drawn from a privileged class anxious to preserve its privileges intact and hostile to any Russian or communist interference, while the material for the development of an orthodox communist party, based on an industrial pro- letariat, was extremely small. In Iran in 1946 Stalin had been outwitted, and he may have feared that if Arab nationalism were set alight it might send dangerous sparks into the six Muslim republics of the Soviet Union.

Whatever the reason, the Middle East was a neglected area in Stalinist Russia. There was little investigation into Middle Eastern problems and Arabic was little taught or known. Inevitably the Soviet Union had participated in Middle Eastern diplomacy in the United Nations. It had voted, as was to be expected, in support of Syria and Lebanon on the question of the presence of British and French troops in those two countries in the spring of 1946; but it also voted for the partition plan for Palestine and proposed the resolution calling on the Security Council to enforce it. Since then, as we have seen, it had moved over to support of the Arab states in the question of Israeli rights in the Suez canal.

The emergence of Khrushchev to leadership in the Soviet Union brought a revaluation of some aspects of Soviet foreign policy, which was beginning to take shape in 1955. This re- appraisal had as two of its aspects a loosening up of the Soviet system in Europe; and a new attitude towards the emerging states of Asia and Africa. Khrushchev, seeking in this as in other things a return to true Leninism as he conceived it, saw the possibilities of developing Soviet influence among the nations which were neutralist in their foreign policy; and where Soviet prestige and economic resources might make up for the weakness of local communist parties. This positive change of policy in the Soviet Union coincided with the growing American interest in the Middle East, which might in any case have forced the Soviet Union to be more actively involved; moreover some of the Middle Eastern states, above all Egypt, were placed in a position where Soviet support seemed most attractive. The combination of these three factors – a change of Soviet policy, the entry of the United States into Middle Eastern affairs, and Egyptian receptivity to Soviet approaches – meant that increased Russian participation in the Middle East came with alarming and threatening suddenness.

These developments reached their first crescendo in the negotiations for the Baghdad pact. This pact came to be of outstanding importance in the emotionalism of Middle Eastern politics; and the British government attached great importance to it as the key to its Middle East policy. Yet its growth was curiously haphazard. The first part of the structure was a pact signed by Turkey and Pakistan in April 1954. The basis for their agreement was obvious. These were two neighbours of the Soviet Union, the one a Muslim state, the other having a predominantly Muslim population, both strongly hostile to the Soviet Union. The pact moreover fitted in well with American policy. The failure of the British plan for a Middle Eastern Defence Organization had induced Dulles to seek other more limited means of achieving security in the area, and he saw that this could be done by building up an alliance of the 'northern tier' states. In consequence the United States strongly encouraged the signature of the pact, and signed military aid pacts with both Turkey and Pakistan.

In broad terms the 'northern tier' pacts might seem to accord well with the British wish to provide for the defence of its interests, and to offer a shield for the whole of the Middle East. But it was insufficient to meet the needs of British policy, which depended on agreements with the Arab states; and it excited the alarm of Nuri al-Said, who feared that Iraq would be bypassed in the flow of arms and defence from America to the Middle East. The alternative for Nuri was to find some means of associating Iraq with the northern tier without thereby endangering the connexion with Britain, and also in such a way as to remain a pivotal point in Middle Eastern politics.

Such an arrangement was unacceptable to Nasser. It ran counter to the ideology of Arab nationalism and to his wish to free the Middle East from foreign bases and foreign troops, and it threatened to do so by giving pre-eminence to Egypt's rival, Iraq. Nasser and his colleague Salah Salim therefore bent all their efforts to persuading Nuri to abandon his own plans in favour of a purely Arab defence pact. But their efforts failed. Menderes of Turkey visited Baghdad in January 1955 and he and Nuri al-Said announced their intention of signing a mutual co-operation pact, open to other interested powers. The agreement was duly signed on 24 February 1955.

The alignment of Iraq, an Arab state, with Turkey, a near-European member of NATO, was obviously a move of more far-reaching significance than the pact between Turkey and Pakistan. To the British government it appeared to offer great possibilities. As Eden said: 'It was possible that the pact could grow into a NATO for the Middle East'.[11] It was particularly attractive in that it offered a means of renegotiating the Anglo-Iraqi treaty of 1930, following the abortive attempt of the 1948 treaty of Portsmouth. In this way the feelings of the Suez group would be assuaged, and it would be possible to retain the RAF bases, whose importance on the eastern flank of NATO and on the route to the east had increased in air ministry strategy (in contrast to the diminished importance of the Suez base). The possibility of British association with the pact was attractive too to Nuri al-Said, caught as he was between the nationalist feeling in his own country and the desire to maintain relations with Britain. The United States welcomed the junction of Iraq to the northern tier and encouraged the British government to add its weight to the pact. The British government therefore took the decisive step of joining the Turco-Iraqi pact on 4 April 1955, thereby converting it to the Baghdad pact. In September the pact was joined by Pakistan and in October by Iran.

It is easy to see why the foreign secretary, Eden, regarded the pact as a great achievement; it seemed to provide security for a frontier stretching 'from the Mediterranean to the Himalayas', at the same time as it solved the old problem of

[11] *Full Circle,* p. 222.

Britain's bilateral treaties with Arab states. In retrospect, however, it can be seen as adding to all the disintegrating forces in Middle Eastern politics at this time. It gave greater incentive to the Soviet Union to be active in the area. It accentuated the differences between Britain and the United States, as a result of ambiguous policy of Secretary Dulles. Not least important, by widening the gap between Egypt and Iraq it intensified Egyptian hostility towards Britain, at a time when the British foreign secretary from his side was becoming increasingly alarmed about the dictatorial character of the Egyptian régime and its objectives in the Arab world. Nasser as well as Nuri was aware of the military weakness of his country, and did not at this time suppose that it could be removed except by arrangement with the west. Such an arrangement he would in the long run probably have been willing to make. But in the meantime he regarded the maintenance of British bases, guaranteed by a new treaty rather than by a vestige of the old order, as a surrender of the very independence which arms were designed to protect.

More than that, he considered the pact to be a breach of the understanding which he believed to have been reached in the 1954 agreement, in that Britain had adopted a Middle Eastern policy which ran directly counter to Egypt's own interests in the area. Instead, Iraq would now be in a position to move ahead in the Arab race for armaments.

It soon became evident that there was much popular opposition throughout the Arab lands to the policy of the Baghdad pact – not least in Iraq itself. But the key to the success of Iraqi or Egyptian policy lay, as always, in Syria. There, in February 1954, the benevolent despotism of the Shishakli dictatorship had been overthrown, and the way left open to neutralism and nationalism, at the very moment when Nasser's appeal to Arab feeling was gaining strength. In consequence Nasser and Salah Salim, having failed in their earlier attempt to wean Iraq away from a non-Arab alliance, were successful in their fresh diplomatic offensive in Syria and also in Saudi Arabia. In March 1955 an Egyptian-Syrian-Saudi alliance was signed which was of no military value, but which constituted a diplomatic victory for Nasser and a defeat for British policy – the more important since it exaggerated the suspicion and distrust which Eden now felt towards the Egyptian leader.

There were other events which added to the crisis in the Middle East. The first was a re-emergence in an acute form of the problem of Israel. As Nasser knew, Israel had succeeded in purchasing arms secretly from France in 1954. Ben-Gurion returned to office (after living in a kibbutz) as defence minister. Immediately afterwards, in February 1955, the Israeli army carried out a great reprisal raid into the part of Palestine which had been acquired by Egypt, the Gaza strip. Its purpose was to counter the raids made by Egyptain *fedayeen*,[12] which had resulted in murders as far as the outskirts of Tel Aviv, and to deliver a warning blow against Egypt now that the British had left.

The importance of the Gaza raid derived from the fact that once the Palestine question was reopened it still, as in 1948, could only be settled by force.

The tripartite declaration of 1950 was intended to provide a deterrent to fresh outbreaks of violence and a limitation on the supply of arms to the area. But the guarantee it offered was far from adequate to reassure the powers involved, and the limitation on the import of arms into the area was inadequate. In addition to the French government supply of arms to Israel the Syrian government had made a less important purchase 'for a song' from the Czechoslovak government of a number of German tanks left behind in Prague.[13] In consequence any increase in tension was likely to escalate to the point of a fresh showdown between Israel and the Arab states. Both Israel and Egypt looked abroad for the means to strengthen their armed forces. Meanwhile at the end of April 1955 – the month in which the Baghdad pact came into being – Nasser left the Middle East and journeyed across the world to the Bandung conference. There new perspectives opened before him. Astute politician that he was, he saw the possibilities of neutralism. Trapped until this moment by a desire for independence, coupled with a realistic assessment of Egypt's dependence on more advanced countries, he saw that he could make a virtue out of necessity by pursuing a policy of 'positive neutra-

---

[12] The ancient meaning of *fedayeen* was persons ready to give their lives for their religion or for a cause. The common modern translation by Arabs is 'commandos', while the Israelis have made the word synonymous with marauders and murderers. The *fedayeen* captured and killed by the Israelis at this time were all Palestinian refugees; see Lt.Gen. E.L.M. Burns, *Between Arab and Israeli* (1962), pp. 85–86.

[13] See Patrick Seale, *The Struggle for Syria* (1965).

lism'. Taking by right a position of eminence amongst the leading neutralists, Nehru, U Nu, and Sukarno, he could at the same time explore the practical possibilities of selling cotton to China and voice his difficulties over the purchase of arms.

The conjunction of circumstances in the summer of 1955 was, then, that Nasser sought arms as a safeguard against rising tension with Israel, and to increase the prestige of his régime, and that he became aware of the advantages of neutralism at a time when the Soviet Union was extending the area of its active foreign policy to embrace the Arab and Asian states, with a particularly strong incentive to counter the position taken up by Britain and America along its southern borders. Meanwhile both Britain and the United States found their hands tied when Nasser sought to buy arms from them, as he did at this time. They were tied by the tripartite declaration, with its object of maintaining rough parity of arms between Israel and the Arabs; the Americans were prevented by the Mutual Security Act from giving arms to Nasser and by domestic interests from accepting cotton in payment.

In these circumstances Nasser negotiated the purchase of arms from Czechoslovakia. In announcing the deal which had been made on 27 September 1955 he made the most of the resistance he had encountered from the west. He said:

> France always bargained with us. She bargained with us over North Africa. She says to us: 'We will give you arms on the condition that you should not criticize our position in North Africa, and on condition that you relinquish your "Arabism", that you relinquish your humanitarianism . . . .
>
> I'll tell you the story of America . . . The promise was a promise circumscribed with conditions. We would get arms if we signed a mutual security pact. We would get arms if we would sign some form of alliance . . . .
>
> England provided us with a quantity of arms which was not sufficient to achieve the goals of this Revolution . . . .[14]
>
> We received a reply from Czechoslovakia saying that she was prepared to supply arms in accordance with our needs and those of Egypt's army on a commercial basis, the transaction to be considered like any other commercial transaction. We agreed and last

[14] The British government at this time sold Egypt two destroyers (balanced by two sold to Israel), 32 centurion tanks, and surplus material from the Suez base.

week Egypt signed a commercial agreement with Czechoslovakia to supply us arms.'[15]

There was, as we know from the testimony of Salah Salim, an additional reason for Nasser's readiness to make a deal with the Soviet Union: the Soviet ambassador had expressed his government's willingness to help with the finance of the Aswan dam.[16] Even so, the decision to purchase arms from the communist countries was only taken when other sources failed. Once that decision had been taken, its political importance was immense. The freedom from Soviet action which the western powers had enjoyed in their Middle Eastern manoeuvring was a thing of the past. The tripartite declaration, which they had taken seriously for five years, was undermined. Nasser had immeasurably increased his prestige in the Arab world, and if he had access to a supply of modern arms, would be in a position to strike at Israel. Israel therefore in turn looked for additional support from the west, and the Israeli General Staff would argue that the conditions had been created when Israel must make a pre-emptive strike against the enemy. In France and Britain the danger which governments and many of the people alike had begun to attribute to Egyptian nationalism assumed a new proportion with the possibility of Egypt serving as a Russian base, staffed by technicians in peacetime and made ready for a large-scale Russian incursion in time of crisis. The repercussions of this last factor went far beyond the tensions of the Middle East, since the arms deal gave the impression that the 'Geneva spirit' cultivated by the Russians at the summit conference was merely a façade behind which an expansionist and trouble-making policy in Asia and the Middle East could be developed. Finally, the arrangement had its importance even in so far as it was commercial, since the cost of the purchase (which was to be paid for out of Egypt's only major export, cotton) would make any other large-scale loan, notably that for a proposed Aswan dam, a very dubious business proposition.

In this situation the attitude of the French government alone amongst the western powers was straightforward. It had lost its political and military base in the Middle East in Syria and Lebanon. Like Britain its interest in the free passage

---

[15] Hurewitz, ii. 404. [16] See Seale, *Struggle for Syria*, p. 235.

through the canal had increased as a result of the growing importance of oil. Moreover it sought to regain a position in the Middle East, and was willing to cultivate an alliance with Israel to this end. At the other end of the Mediterranean it was at war with the nationalists in Algeria, who received support and encouragement from the Arab states of the Middle East. Such support was marginal in its effect on the course of the Algerian revolt, but as the French government denied that the revolt had a broad popular base, it was easy to attribute its success to outside support, and to make Nasser the scapegoat for their ills. In all these ways France came to have an interest in the overthrow or at least the humiliation of Nasser.

The British position was more complicated. Eden, who had succeeded Churchill as prime minister in April 1955, would have liked to stabilize the situation around Israel. In November 1955 he used the occasion of the prime minister's annual speech at the Guildhall to propose that Israel and the Arab states come to some arrangement about their boundaries, after which the United States and Britain, and possibly other powers, would give a formal guarantee of them. As Israel had succeeded in extending its frontiers beyond those of the United Nations plan, a proposal for readjustment was biased on the Arab side; but it was in any case difficult to imagine that Arabs and Israelis at this stage would succeed in reconciling their differences, merely in the disinterested service of world peace. There was little response to his speech. In February 1956 he went to Washington for discussions with the president and the secretary of state, which covered the Middle East and the Far East particularly. He sought American support for a reaffirmation in stronger terms of the tripartite declaration; but the Americans were not prepared to go this far. The background of differences over the Baghdad pact inhibited useful discussion. To this was added an incident of the previous autumn which was characteristic of Anglo-American relations in the Middle East at this time. In October 1955 British officers had led a small force which had reoccupied the oasis of Buraimi on behalf of the sultan of Muscat and the shaikh of Abu Dhabi. The oasis of Buraimi was a small area over which sovereignty was claimed by Saudi Arabia, and which tribal forces under its control had occupied in 1952. Like many other places in the area it had acquired importance because of the discovery of oil. But while the British took so decisive a part in asserting the sovereignty of the sultan and the shaikh, the American government supported Saudi Arabia; and regarded the British action as an act of aggression.[17]

Meanwhile the rivalry between Britain and Egypt came to be focused on Jordan. It was to be expected, therefore, that the British government should try to bring its ally Jordan into the Baghdad pact; and they were strongly encouraged to do so by the Turks. But the attempt was disastrous. In December 1955 General Templer was sent to Amman to discuss the possibility of Jordan joining the pact (in which the accession of Pakistan and Persia only increased the isolation of Iraq, the one Arab state). His mission provoked rioting and the collapse of the cabinet. Then in March 1956 King Husain felt compelled to dismiss General Glubb and his fellow officers, who had been responsible for training the Arab Legion and making it into the only truly effective Arab army. He did so in order to assuage nationalist feeling, and to open army appointments to Jordanians. But his action had a strong emotional impact in Britain – no less because Selwyn Lloyd, who was now foreign minister, was meeting Nasser in Cairo when the news came through. For many British people, the prime minister chief amongst them, General Glubb symbolized what they regarded as the rightful relationship between Britain and the Arabs. Glubb had rendered loyal service to Jordan, and given to the Jordanian army qualities which the Arabs admired but could not achieve by themselves. In return, it was thought that Husain was a loyal ally of Britain. It was a gentlemanly arrangement which had been brought to an end in an ungentlemanly way. The British government and public regarded the manner of Glubb's dismissal as uncharacteristic of Husain; and they made the mistake of attributing too much to the sinister machinations of Nasser and too little to the spontaneous nationalism which had spread through the Arab world, and to the concentrated bitterness of the Palestinian Arabs in Jordan.

The greatest crisis in the Middle East was precipitated by the American government, when it withdrew the offer it had

[17] The dispute had been submitted to an arbitration tribunal; but in September 1955 the British withdrew from arbitration on the grounds that the Saudi government was subverting the tribunal.

previously made to give financial support to the building of the High Dam at Aswan. The proposal to build such a dam appeared to offer great advantages for Egypt. It would make possible continual storage of the Nile water (the existing low dam provided for an equal supply through one water year, not from one year to another); it would feed a very large irrigation area, and it would provide electricity for the development of industry. On the other hand it was very expensive and it would take ten to fifteen years to build, The decision to assist in financing such an operation therefore involved a certain element of gamble from a technical point of view, since calculations about such a large project must to some extent be guesswork; it also meant a political gamble on the future of Egypt; and expenditure on a single large project of this kind must be at the sacrifice of smaller developments with more immediate reward. From the Egyptian point of view the dam had the attraction that it would give immense prestige. In October 1958, when an agreement with Russia for finance for the dam had been made, Nasser wrote:

For thousands of years the Great Pyramids of Egypt were foremost among the engineering marvels of the world. They ensured life after death for the Pharaohs. Tomorrow the gigantic High Dam, more significant and seventeen times greater than the Pyramids, will provide a higher standard of living to all Egyptians.[18]

By 1956 the technical difficulties were beginning to resolve themselves. Surveys were made of the project, and a plan devised whereby support would be offered in the form of a loan from the World Bank of $200 million, conditional on British and American support to the extent of $200 million, and Egyptian participation, in the form of services and materials, equivalent to $900 million. But this time the political difficulties had increased. The Egyptian government had accepted the offer of arms from the Soviet bloc, and it was known that the cotton crop was mortgaged to pay for them. Nasser let it be rumoured that the Soviet Union would finance the dam (apparently without any supporting evidence). The result was that Britain and America had good reason to doubt Egypt's ability to repay loans. Nasser's recognition of commu-

---

[18] *Egyptian Political and Economic Review*, Oct. 1958, quoted in *The World Today*, Feb. 1960, p. 59. The quantitative comparison with the Pyramids is by weight.

nist China in May 1956 would arouse the hostility of Congress. The British were made particularly aware of the political difficulties by Nuri al-Said, who pointed out that Britain's friends in the Middle East seemed to fare less well than its rivals. But neither of the western governments wanted the Soviet Union to finance the project, provide technicians, and increase their foothold in Egypt.

Eden's solution was to prolong the negotiations in the hope of finding some way out. Dulles in contrast decided that Egypt was too unreliable a debtor. He was also reluctant to commit as much money as Congress was likely to approve for a number of years to a single project, thus depriving the administration of manoeuvrability *vis-à-vis* Russia when Egypt sought other credits. The Egyptians pressed for a decision and Dulles, having informed but not consulted the British, told their ambassador that his government would not proceed with the loan. Nasser heard the news on 19 July on his way back from a neutralist meeting with Tito and Nehru at Brioni in Yugoslavia.

On 26 July 1956 Nasser announced in a public speech at Alexandria that the Suez canal had been nationalized. It is impossible to know whether this action had been planned in advance, and the refusal of money for the Aswan dam used as a pretext, or whether it was a brilliantly improvised response to the humiliating news which had been received at Brioni. In either case, it was a risky step to take, but one which placed Egypt in an extremely advantageous position.

The canal was the one great foreign asset in Egypt. It had been built and at first operated under a concession originally granted to Ferdinand de Lesseps, and then taken over by the Suez Maritime Company, which was to run for 99 years from the date of the opening of the canal; thereafter the canal was to revert to the Egyptian government. The canal was opened for navigation in 1869. Dues were paid for its use to the company, which divided its receipts between a reserve fund for maintenance and improvement of the canal, and dividends to the shareholders. This was of no benefit to Egypt because the khedive had sold his own and Egypt's shares in 1875 and 1880. Only from 1937 was a regular annual sum of £300,000 paid to the Egyptian government. In 1949 a new agreement allocated 7 per cent of the profits to Egypt – amounting to about £1

million per year. Thus the canal was not as valuable an asset
as oil wells and a refinery; but it was one which was more
easily appropriated. The canal remained part of Egypt;
sovereignty over the territory through which it ran had never
been surrendered, as it had in Panama,[19] and there was a
primitive sense in which the canal formed part of the land in
which it was dug. It was irreplaceable and immovable; no
other canal would serve the same purpose, and it could not be
dismantled and re-erected somewhere else; it was also easy
to run – even though those responsible for running it were able
to pretend that it was not. The attraction to Egypt of possession
of this asset was therefore obvious. It would enable Egypt to
receive the whole of the payment which foreign ships were
willing to pay for the convenience of passing through Egyptian
territory, thereby making Egypt less dependent on grants and
loans which foreign governments, out of charity and political
interest, might care to make. From a legal point of view it could
be argued that to end the concession before its expiry was to
break a contract; it could on the other hand be maintained that
Egypt was exercising its sovereign rights in nationalizing an
Egyptian company (the fact that most of the shareholders
were foreign being irrelevant); and to this argument there could
be no final answer.

But the reaction of the principal western governments to the
nationalization was one of alarm, protest, and preparation for
action. Western Europe was especially dependent on communications through the canal. In the previous year nearly
15,000 ships had passed through it. Of these three-quarters
belonged to countries of the North Atlantic alliance, and nearly
one-third to Britain. Moreover nearly two-thirds of these
ships had been carrying oil. In other words, western Europe
had become far more dependent on the canal than when it was
first dug; not only because of the increase in the number of
ships, but because it was an indispensable line along which oil
was carried.[20] The British government was also, thanks to

[19] The American government in 1903 had leased in perpetuity a ten-mile strip of
land from the government of Panama, which had granted authority therein to the
American government for the construction of the canal as if it were sovereign.
The interpretation of this provision was a matter of dispute between the American
and Panamanian governments.
[20] Tanker tonnage passing through the canal as a percentage of the total traffic
was in 1938 17·3, in 1955 64·0 (RIIA, *The Middle East* (1958), p. 546).

Disraeli, the holder of 44 per cent of the shares in the Suez Maritime Company; but its property rights were to be of minimal importance compared with the dependence which it shared with other countries on free passage through the canal. Perhaps most important of all, the Suez canal zone had burnt itself into the experience of thousands of British soldiers who had served there and acquired a proprietary interest in it. Twenty years earlier the Rhineland and Czechoslovakia were indeed remote and unknown; in 1956 every bus queue in the land had something near to a first-hand account of Suez.[21]

Nothing had been stipulated about passage through the canal in the original concession; but in 1888 a convention had been signed at Constantinople between the great powers of the time, including the Ottoman empire, of which Egypt then formed part. The convention opened with a preamble, which linked it to the original concession; and its first article read: 'The Suez Canal shall always be free and open, in time of war as in time of peace, to every vessel of commerce or of war without distinction of flag.' The convention had been re-affirmed in the Anglo-Egyptian treaty of 1954; even though at that time the Egyptian government was preventing the passage of Israeli ships through the canal.

Both the Egyptian nationalization law and Nasser's speech announcing it presupposed that the canal would remain open. The law provided a framework for the operation of the canal, and Nasser spoke of Egypt's use of the revenues, which could only accrue as long as ships used the canal. But the character and tone of this speech, and the provisions of the law, inevitably increased the shock felt outside Egypt. The occasion of the announcement of nationalization was the anniversary of the 1952 revolution (26 July 1956), and it therefore came at the end of a long speech, which was full of fiery enthusiasm for the cause of Arab nationalism. Nasser said:

Arab nationalism has been set on fire from the Atlantic Ocean to the Persian Gulf. . . . We can never say that the battle of Algeria is not our battle. Nor can we say that Jordan's December battle was not our battle. And we also cannot say that battles of alliances are not our battles. . . . My fate in Egypt is linked with that of my

[21] Similarly, while Eden gives to his chapter on Abadan the unemotional heading 'Oil', his chapter on the nationalization of the Suez Canal is entitled: 'Theft' (*Full Circle*).

14

brother in Jordan, in the Lebanon, Syria and in every country, and also in the Sudan. Our fates are linked.[22]

Western governments were accustomed to the inflammatory nature of Arab rhetoric, but now as in later years Nasser underestimated the effect of his words on a foreign audience. He went on to speak of the appropriation by the Egyptian government of the revenue from the canal, and its use to build the High Dam. He exaggerated the revenue from the canal and minimized the cost of the dam; and no one with interests at stake could fail to see that the revenue could not easily be spread to cover both compensation to shareholders and finance for such a large project. The terms of the act were moreover brutal in two respects: they made payment of compensation dependent on 'all the assets of the nationalized company' being 'fully handed over to the State'; and at the same time froze all the funds of the company. They also compelled the officials and employees of the company to remain at their jobs, under pain of imprisonment and loss of all rights to gratuity or compensation.

This would have placed any western government in a difficult position. At the least, the nationalization of the canal was a blow to prestige and a threat to any other property in the Middle East (or elsewhere) which might appear to the indigenous government to be ripe for nationalization. On the other hand the only grave threat to security, the closing of the canal, was a threat that was potential, not actual; and Nasser, more temperate as the crisis went on, constantly affirmed that he would keep the canal open. The question of control over the canal was not in fact affected by nationalization. Even while British troops were in the canal zone Egypt hindered free passage through the canal; by withdrawing their troops the British government abandoned effective physical control to the Egyptians. In any case the concession was due to expire in 1968, and the canal would then normally revert to the control of the Egyptian government – a fact which Eden overlooked in taking his stand on legal principles, saying:

No arrangements for the future of this great international waterway could be acceptable to Her Majesty's Government which would leave it in the unfettered control of a single power which could, as recent events have shown, exploit it purely for purposes of national policy.[23]

[22] RIIA, *Documents, 1956,* p. 89.   [23] *Full Circle,* p. 434.

The American government, less dependent on the canal than its allies, could make a more detached calculation, of the issues. Even so, its initial reaction was to state that nationalization had far-reaching implications and that it was urgently consulting the governments concerned.

The response of the British and French governments was of an entirely different order. For them nationalization was set in the context of Nasser's propaganda in the Middle East and the extravagant nationalism of his speech. For Guy Mollet, the French prime minister, Nasser was the supporter of the Algerian revolt; for Eden he was the man who had made an agreement in 1954 and had now broken it. In Article 8 of that agreement Britain and Egypt not only reaffirmed the Constantinople Convention but also recognized 'that the Suez Maritime Canal, which is an integral part of Egypt, is a waterway economically, commercially, and strategically of international importance'.[24]

Whatever the legal aspects of nationalization it appeared political folly to Eden to regard Nasser as a man 'who would keep his word' — as Chamberlain had judged Hitler. The British and French saw accumulating evidence of Egyptian and Syrian connexions with the Soviet Union. For them nationalization was not a question to be taken solely on its merits. It was at once clinching evidence of the danger of Nasser and the issue, which justified the use of any means to bring him down. As Eden said in a broadcast on 8 August: 'We all know this is how fascist governments behave and we all remember only too well what the cost can be of giving in to fascism. With dictators you always have to pay a higher price later on, for their appetite grows with feeding.'[25]

But the possibilities of action relevant to the nationalization of the canal were limited, and it was this which put Nasser in such a strong position. It was open to the western powers to negotiate; but there was no pressure which they could bring to bear in negotiation. They could use economic sanctions, but the most obvious form of pressure — boycott of the canal — would harm them more than Nasser, who could probably draw on Soviet aid in any case. They could use military force; but none was immediately available. After the event Eden wrote that immediate military action would have been contrary to

---

[24] RIIA, *Documents, 1954*, p. 250.   [25] Ibid. 1956, p. 89.

the United Nations Charter; but the decisive factor at the time (which he also refers to) was the state of preparedness which required at least ten days' mobilization to launch any form of attack, and even longer to mount a seaborne attack in support of landings from the air. The logic of the 1954 agreement with Egypt would have been the construction of a base in Cyprus to replace that of Suez (from where the last troops were embarked in June 1956); moreover many of the pronouncements of the British government in defence of their position in Cyprus presupposed that such a base existed. In fact Cyprus had no natural large harbour and was therefore inadequate to mount a seaborne invasion.

However discouraging the military prospects appeared, other pressures offered no better prospect for success. The only alternative to military action was to argue that the security of western Europe now depended on a community of interest with the Arab Middle East in the exploitation of oil and in free passage through the canal. The implications of such an assumption were to accept nationalization with the best possible grace, merely insisting on compensation and the maintenance of free passage. Such a policy would have demanded great resources of political courage and sophistication. It was not the policy of the American government and would have been far more difficult to carry out in countries like Britain and France, where the emotions evoked by declining power and status in the world ran so strong.

Nasser had secured his tit for tat for the blow to his prestige which he had received on his way back from Brioni; the news of the nationalization was brought to Eden while the king of Iraq and Nuri al-Said were dining with him at 10 Downing Street. Nuri, it is thought, urged Eden to immediate action which would humiliate if not destroy their common rival. Although the American secretary of state was in Peru, conversations were begun between the British and French governments on 29 July and Dulles arrived in London on 1 August. The British and French governments both wanted to take urgent and decisive action; but there was little they could do. They therefore retaliated against Nasser by freezing Egyptian sterling balances.

Superficially the American position at this meeting appeared similar to the British and French. Dulles impressed Eden by saying that 'A way had to be found to make Nasser disgorge what he was attempting to swallow', and stated it as his view that 'it was intolerable that the canal should be under the domination of any single country without international control'. But these words were misleading. It was his mission to prevent the British and French resorting to force. He (in common with Nasser) thought that the passage of time would make action politically impossible; while the British and French were forced to accept delay in order to mobilize.

Meanwhile the issue which might have divided Britain from France – the question of Israel – was for the moment sufficiently quiet to be left on one side. Eden later wrote correctly, but in the long term misleadingly, when he said: 'to associate Israel's problems with those arising from the nationalization of the canal would, at this time, have tangled them to Nasser's advantage. If we were to get action, we had to keep the issues crisp.'[26]

The conclusion of the meeting was to summon a conference in London of the powers signatory to the Constantinople convention (as Dulles insisted that it should have a legal basis). Russia was thereby included – although times had changed since 'His Majesty the Emperor of the Russias' had sent his plenipotentiary to the Ottoman capital – but the lands which in 1888 had been ruled by 'His Majesty the Emperor of Austria, King of Bohemia, etc., and Apostolic King of Hungary' were not represented. In addition, the sixteen most important users of the canal who were not signatories were invited. All except Egypt and Greece accepted the three governments' invitation; the meeting was called for 16 August.

Dulles returned to Washington and made a broadcast speech which condemned the nationalization of the canal, but which also expressed a careless optimism about the outcome of negotiation. He said that to permit President Nasser's decision to exploit the Suez canal to go unchallenged

would be to encourage a breakdown of the international fabric upon which the security and well-being of all peoples depend . . . It is inadmissible that a waterway internationalized by treaty, which is required for the livelihood of a score of nations, should be exploited by one country for highly selfish purposes. And that the operating

[26] *Full Circle*, p. 436.

agency which has done so well in handling the Suez Canal in accordance with the 1888 treaty should be struck down by a national act of vengefulness.

We have given no commitments at any time as to what the United States would do in that unhappy contingency [of the failure of the London conference]. We assume . . . that the conference will not fail but will succeed . . .

I believe . . . that out of this conference there will come a judgment of such moral force that we can be confident that the Suez Canal will go on . . . to serve in peace the interests of mankind.[27]

At this time too Dulles spoke of taking the question to the United Nations. American diplomatic activity was directed to securing the maximum support for the London conference; and plans were initiated to provide alternative oil supplies for western Europe should those from the Middle East be cut. But he gave no indication of how a successful outcome might be achieved if the diplomatic pressure proved no more effective than it had done in securing the passage of Israeli ships through the canal.

This was in strong contrast to the preparations made by the British and French governments. Their military leaders conferred together in London from 7 to 9 August. Some reservists were called up, naval forces in the Mediterranean were reinforced, and small striking forces built up in Cyprus and Algeria.

At the same time divisions began to appear within the Commonwealth. The Australian government played a strong supporting role to Great Britain. The prime minister, Menzies, was in the United States when the nationalization occurred; he cancelled his plans, and accepted Eden's invitation to London. There he gave a vigorous interpretation of his nation's interests, situated at the other terminal of the route through Suez. He conferred with Eden, participated in the London conference, and became its emissary. In contrast the Asian members of the Commonwealth showed evident sympathy for Nasser. This was particularly true of India, which actually conveyed to London Egypt's rejection of the invitation to the London conference. In this way the cross-currents in the Commonwealth began to gather force. They were evident for all to see, and when the time for action came the British government decided it knew its supporters and opponents without

[27] DAFR, 1956, pp. 297-9.

further consultation. Nehru and Dulles, who took very different views about the cold war, were united in suspicion of British imperialism, from which their countries had been freed; Menzies, in contrast, was amongst Eden's strongest supporters. The other party to the dispute, Egypt, had been not a colony, but part of the 'unofficial' British empire; but the intensity of Eden's feelings derived not only from lingering imperialism but also from a feeling of betrayed trust, and a supposition that Egypt would play the role of Britain's erstwhile European rival, Germany.

The Middle East also showed a complex reaction to events. Arab states were bound to adopt a posture in support of Egypt, and did so in varying degrees. The Political Committee of the Arab League met on 6 August; the Libyan government denied to Britain the use of the British base on its territory against Egypt. Nasser began to acquire heroic stature; but there were some Arabs who were torn between support for the Egyptian cause and anxiety lest Nasser should acquire overweening power. Most important, Nuri al-Said was discomfited by the growth in prestige of his rival for Arab leadership and would have welcomed a surgical blow, delivered without help from France, far less Israel, from which his own relations with both Britain and the Arab states would emerge unscathed. Meanwhile the Israeli government made its own calculations about the immediate future, with an eventual outcome which we shall presently observe; and no Arab government was likely to ignore the risk of a new phase in the conflict with Israel which any major disturbance in the Middle East would provoke.

The London conference met from 16 to 23 August 1956. It opened a period of five weeks in which the powers who used the canal, although having some difficulty in reaching agreement in detail amongst themselves, devised plans to secure their own interests, and endeavoured to persuade the Egyptian government to accept them, without having sufficient unity or resolution to reinforce diplomacy with effective pressure. During this time the Egyptian government pursued a moderate course with regard to the operation of the canal, and followed its own diplomatic course, with the constructive support of India, and the less responsible backing of the Soviet Union.

The first of the users' plans was agreed by eighteen of the

twenty-two nations that attended the first London conference. It stressed the principles of the 1888 convention and the principle of the 'insulation of the operation of the canal from the influence of the politics of any nation'; and it proposed the setting up of a Suez Canal Board, on which Egypt would be represented, to be responsible for the running of the canal. It also provided for 'effective sanctions for any violation of the Convention by any party to it'. The conference agreed that the representatives of five powers, headed by Menzies, should present the proposals to Nasser and secure his acceptance of them.

The proposals, however, offered no advantage to Nasser, save that they would enable him to escape any worse consequences of the nationalization. But these consequences did not appear very serious to him. It was true that the British and French governments intended, should the Menzies mission fail, to take the question to the Security Council, in preparation for their own use of force. As the Menzies mission travelled to Egypt French troops moved to Cyprus – thereby adding to the growing opposition in Britain to the government's policy, because of the link it made between the issues of Algeria, Cyprus, and Egypt. But in Washington Dulles and Eisenhower gave press conferences in which the former said 'the Suez Canal is not a primary concern to the United States' and the latter 'we are committed to a peaceful settlement of this dispute, nothing else'. Nor did the American government at this time take steps to prevent American shipowners from paying canal dues to the nationalized company, as Britain and France had done.

By this time preparations for military action against Egypt were nearing completion – disembarkation was planned for 15 or 16 September. The French government considered the moment to act was approaching. Negotiation had served its purpose of demonstrating good intentions, and had failed to produce results. The British were under stronger political pressures, from both within and outside the government. Both were prepared to go to the United Nations; the French to complete the necessary if useless diplomatic formalities, the British through a firmer commitment to the principles of the organization.

Dulles knew that time was running out, and he sought means to prolong it. He saw that an Anglo-French resolution before the Security Council would be a prelude to military action, and sought a more effective way of keeping people talking. The ambiguities of his diplomacy were ascribed at the time and subsequently to the demands of a presidential campaign, which gained momentum in September. In fact the election made little difference. It was reasonable for the American government to hope that by talking, by supporting now one side now the other, it would so confuse the issues of 'sovereignty, dignity, grandeur and East versus West'[28] that the practical question of ships going through the canal would predominate – especially since the British and French were not given to reckless and expensive aggression.

On 4 September Dulles produced a new plan by which the users of the canal could secure their own interests. This involved the setting up of a Suez Canal Users' Association, whose precise function and purpose would be agreed by a further conference. It was intended that the Association would co-operate with Egypt, as far as possible, in such practical matters as pilotage and signalling. Failing Egyptian co-operation it would operate from ships stationed at each end of the canal, collecting dues to cover the expenses of the Association. At the same time Dulles spoke of increasing pressure on Egypt by financial measures (in which his government lagged behind those of Britain and France) and of developing alternative routes round the Cape to diminish European dependence on the canal.

There was no reason to expect Nasser to agree to the SCUA proposal; it offered no satisfaction to the British and French demands for international control of the canal – far less did it help them towards their objective of unseating Nasser – and it was not backed up by any provision for enforcement. None the less Eden took up the idea in the hope of improving the British and French position *vis-à-vis* the United States. He was corresponding with Eisenhower, urging the threat to the American as well as the British position in the Middle East, stressing the link between the Soviet Union and Nasser, and emphasizing the similarity of the thirties – but receiving only dissuasion from the use of force in reply. He had difficulty in persuading some of his ministers that SCUA was worthwhile, and even more in convincing the French. They were certain that nothing was to be gained from Dulles, whose sole object was procrastina-

[28] Dulles's words (Eisenhower, *Waging Peace* (1965), p. 674).

14*

tion designed to undermine the British and French will. In
London on 11 September Pineau, in company with Mollet, said
that the ships should already have put to sea; but they were
unable to act without the British, and agreed to postpone military action. Eden later described the decision to take up the
SCUA proposal as 'the most crucial we had to face during the
whole Suez crisis. Its consequences were far reaching.' So they
were, although not for the reasons Eden gave: the delay which
followed permitted a new combination to emerge between Britain, France, and Israel.

The Menzies mission finally reached deadlock in Cairo, after
six days of discussion, on 9 September. Nor did Nasser take long
to denounce the Users' Association on the 15th. By that time
the position of Egypt had improved steadily. The essential
fact was that shipping was still passing through the canal with
no greater let or hindrance than before nationalization. The
staff and particularly the pilots of the old company had been
pressed to stay by the company, itself under pressure from the
British government; but on 11 September they were finally
given permission to leave, and the Egyptian government, notwithstanding the provisions of the nationalization law, did not
stop them. In spite of this, the Egyptian authorities were able
to keep the canal open and working, with the help of Egyptian
and Greek pilots who remained, and others recruited over the
world. Nor had the economic sanctions which the British and
French governments had imposed caused any serious difficulty.
From this strong position the Egyptian government was able
to be unyielding on the central question of its full sovereignty
over the canal, and moderate in everything else.

Partly as a result, support for the stern measures which Britain and France sought to organize dwindled throughout the
world. The anti-colonial powers were strengthened in their
natural sense of alliance with Nasser and the smaller users were
content to use the canal without being disturbed by the fact
that it had been nationalized. To this extent Dulles's tactics of
preventing military action by delay appeared to be bringing
success.

But in fact preparations were under way which would bring
the crisis to a head. The French had kept the Israeli government informed of the military plans they had formed with the
British. The more hesitant the British appeared and the more

successful American delaying tactics became, the more urgent
and the closer grew Franco-Israeli co-operation. In Ben-Gurion's
judgement the Gaza raid had achieved only part of Israel's objectives – it had not destroyed the *fedayeen* base, far less had it
opened the Gulf of Aqaba. Moreover if Nasser should now
succeed unchecked, his prestige would stand higher than ever,
and the way would be open for him, possibly with Russian help,
to threaten the existence of the state of Israel. But for Israel
to take pre-emptive action alone involved the risk of its cities
and armies in the desert being bombed by the Egyptian air
force. The aeroplanes it had acquired from France did not
equal Egypt's Russian bombers. For Israel therefore Anglo-
French action was the best guarantee of success in war; to the
French government it began to look as if Israeli action would
be necessary to precipitate the war.

On 19 September a fresh conference met in London to work
out the details of SCUA. Only with great verbal skill was a
façade of unity maintained between fifteen of the eighteen
nations which had agreed together at the first London conference. On 23 September the British and French governments
announced that they would bring the nationalization question
before the Security Council.

This open diplomacy coincided with an increase in the pace
of secret diplomacy. Contacts between the Israelis and the
French became closer in the third week of September, and by
that time the Israeli general staff was examining plans based
on the assumption of an association with other forces operating
against Egypt. Visits were exchanged too, on 23 and 25 September, between London and Paris. Knowing or guessing at least
half of what was going on, Dulles dissociated himself from Britain and France – in a manner scarcely consistent with his
intention of making the Suez question a practical matter, free
of confusing issues. At a press conference on 2 October he denied
that SCUA was ever intended to have any teeth in it and spoke
of 'the shift from colonialism to independence' saying:

I suspect that the United States will find that its role . . . will be
to aid that process, without identifying itself 100 percent either
with the so-called colonial powers or with the powers that are
primarily and uniquely concerned with the problem of getting their
independence as rapidly as possible. I think we have a special role
to play, and that perhaps makes it impractical for us . . . in every

respect to identify our policies with those of other countries on whichever side of that problem they find their interest.[29]

Even as he spoke, agreement between Britain, France, and Israel had gone far enough for Eden, on 3 October, to tell his cabinet of a proposed Israeli attack which would provide the opportunity to launch the long-delayed Anglo-French expedition. By the time the Security Council met on 5 October the prospects for compromise were therefore slender indeed. Britain and France submitted a resolution calling for support for the eighteen-nation proposals of the first London conference and for Egyptian co-operation with SCUA. On 9 October Dulles addressed the Council and spoke warmly in support of Britain and France, commending the fact that the nations which had been 'deeply aggrieved and endangered' by the nationalization of the canal had made no forcible response.   The Security Council went into secret session and private, informal meetings were also arranged by Hammarskjöld. From these meetings a new compromise emerged, in the shape of six principles, which were accepted by Britain, France, and Egypt. They provided for free and open transit through the canal, respect for Egyptian sovereignty, the insulation of the canal from the politics of any country, agreement between Egypt and the users on the fixing of tolls and charges, the allotment of a fair proportion of dues to development, and arbitration in the event of a dispute between Egypt and the users. Embodied in a resolution, these principles were unanimously endorsed by the Security Council on 13 October; although the second part of the resolution, stating that the eighteen-nation proposals accorded with these principles, was defeated by a Soviet veto (supported by Yugoslavia's vote).

But while the British and French foreign ministers negotiated in New York, their governments had moved closer to a working alliance with Israel. Lloyd returned to London with the fruits of his open diplomacy on 16 October. His papers were brushed aside and he immediately went to Paris with Eden. Writing later of this meeting Eden gave a veiled reference to the discussions when he explained the dilemma if Israel were to attack Jordan, and continued:

If Israel were to break out against Egypt and not against Jordan,

[29] US Dept of State, *American Foreign Policy; Current Documents 1956*, pp. 41-42.

this dilemma would not arise. For this reason, if there were to be a break-out it was better from our point of view that it should be against Egypt. On the other hand, if the break-out were against Egypt, then there would be other worries, for example the safety of the canal. We discussed these matters in all their political and military aspects.[30]

His account did scant justice to the exchanges which took place – there now existed a co-ordinated Franco-Israeli strategy, which the British agreed to join. But the dilemma was real enough. For the French a working arrangement with the Israelis was only an extension of the policy initiated by the supply of arms to Israel in 1954. For the British it represented a fundamental departure of foreign policy. The contradictions of their old commitments and the new adventure in which they were involving themselves had been brought home when the Israelis made diversionary skirmishes on the Jordanian frontier, including a fierce raid on the frontier post of Qalqilya on 10 October. Husain sought help under the Anglo-Jordanian treaty. Eden gave a formal warning to Israel and British planes were on the point of taking off. Important as the treaty with Jordan was, it was less so than that with Iraq – the solid, oil-producing core of British Middle East policy, centre of the Baghdad pact.

The British would have preferred to keep their commitments vague and unwritten; but for Ben-Gurion the traditions of British foreign policy were those of *perfide Albion*, and the Jordan incident was the latest episode in his long experience of the British. On 22 October he flew to France and met Mollet and Pineau at Sèvres, outside Paris. They were joined later by a British representative, and a written agreement was prepared which tied the British down. It was signed (according to Pineau) by British, French, and Israeli representatives. The agreement was accompanied by a vow to secrecy; but Pineau talked privately to the Americans ten days later and publicly after ten years.

On 29 October Israeli forces attacked Egypt. They were supported by patrols of the British and French air forces, by a French airdrop of supplies, and French naval protection of the Israeli coast (involving the crippling of an Egyptian des-

[30] *Full Circle*, p. 513.

troyer). The French ministers flew to London. Communication
with Washington had ceased to the extent that the British sent
their new ambassador to Washington by sea at this time. Eisenhower and Dulles told the British chargé d'affaires that they
would go to the Security Council in the morning of the next
day. On the afternoon of 30 October the British and French
governments dispatched an ultimatum to the governments of
Israel and Egypt, which, on the grounds that freedom of navigation through the canal was threatened, called for a cease-fire,
the withdrawal of Israeli and Egyptian troops ten miles from
the canal, and the acceptance by Egypt of the temporary occupation by the Anglo-French forces of Port Said, Ismailia, and
Suez. The recipients were given twelve hours in which to comply; the United States ambassador was informed of the ultimatum shortly after it had been delivered. Before the expiry of
the ultimatum the Security Council had met and voted on a
resolution moved by the United States, calling for a general
cease-fire. Seven members voted for the resolution; it was
vetoed by Britain and France, with Australia and Belgium
abstaining.

The Israeli government accepted the ultimatum; its forces
were ordered to push on towards the line indicated by the
ultimatum in order to make it convincing. The Egyptian
government rejected the ultimatum, and Anglo-French bombing operations against Egypt began. This was on 31 October.
Only on 5 November did British and French troops land,
since the supporting force could not (if the pretence of independent action were to be kept up) leave Malta before the
Israeli attack. Much was to happen in those six days. In the
United Nations the British and French veto of the Security
Council resolution brought into action for the first time the
'uniting for peace' procedure of November 1950. The General
Assembly was called into emergency session, and Dulles
on 1 November introduced a resolution[31] which referred to
the breaches of the armistice by Egypt and Israel and the
military operations being conducted by Britain and France,
and then urged an immediate cease-fire. In the early morning

---

[31] He said: 'I doubt that any delegate ever spoke from this forum with as heavy a
heart as I have brought here tonight' (Dept of State, *United States Policy in the
Middle East, September 1956 – June 1957* (1957), p. 151).

of 2 November this resolution was accepted by 64 votes to 5 (Australia and New Zealand voting with Britain, France, and Israel). The next night Dulles was taken ill, and early in the morning of 3 November underwent surgery for cancer. In London Eden learned that the Canadian government intended to propose the setting up of a United Nations force to keep the peace in the Middle East and announced in the House of Commons that Britain would withdraw if United Nations troops were provided. But the Suez crisis was not the only matter of urgency before the United Nations. In Hungary the Nagy government was struggling vainly for survival, as Russian troops re-entered the country. At 2.15 a.m. in the morning of 4 November the General Assembly voted by 57 votes to none, with 19 abstentions, a resolution calling on the secretary-general to produce within forty-eight hours a plan for setting up 'an emergency international United Nations force to secure and supervise the cessation of hostilities'. Three hours later the Security Council voted on a resolution censuring the Russian attack on Hungary – which was vetoed by the Soviet Union. Meanwhile the British air attack convinced Nasser of the reality of the Israeli-Anglo-French alliance, and he withdrew his forces from Sinai to defend Cairo. The consequent Israeli success, coupled with the pressure of open diplomacy, threatened to make an Anglo-French landing militarily implausible and politically indefensible. But the Israelis delayed their cease-fire until after their allies landed paratroopers in Egypt. Nasser gave orders for the canal to be blocked by the sinking of ships, and the Syrian army blew up two pumping stations on the pipeline from Iraq. At this point too the Russians intervened verbally by sending messages to the governments of Britain, France, and Israel, all phrased in a tone similar to that addressed to Britain:

In what situation would Britain find herself if she were attacked by stronger states possessing all types of modern destructive weapons? And such countries could at the present time refrain from sending naval or air forces to the shores of Britain and use other means – for instance, rocket weapons.[32]

Bulganin also suggested to Eisenhower that they act together in the Middle East to end the conflict.

Very soon after forces had landed it was announced that Egyptian forces in Port Said had surrendered: but fighting was

[32] RIIA, *Documents, 1956*, p. 289.

resumed, and an advance pressed on towards Ismailia and Suez. However, while the advance was still short of this objective, at 6.0 p.m. on 6 November, the British prime minister announced that a cease-fire would be ordered from midnight. The bald announcement followed from a cabinet decision which the French were left no choice but to accept and which supporters and critics of the expedition alike found incomprehensible.

The objective of the Anglo-French expedition had never been fully and clearly stated. Both the British and French governments wanted to destroy Nasser's power not only over the canal but over Egypt and the Middle East as well. Their initial estimate was that this purpose could be achieved expeditiously and cheaply, and that a minor operation would suffice to topple Nasser – while American intelligence made a more realistic estimate of Nasser's strength. Eden and Mollet avoided public discussion of the issue as they saw it; the British ministers denied to the House of Commons that there was any collusion with Israel – and were believed. They concealed the concerted nature of their action behind the claim that it was a 'police action' to separate Israelis and Egyptians and prevent a 'brush fire' from spreading in the Middle East.

The British and French alike were dominated by their memories of Rhineland and Munich. Those in Britain who most favoured the use of force – Macmillan and Eden – had in their different ways rejected Chamberlain's appeasement; while their French counterparts, Mollet, Pineau, and the defence minister, Bourgès-Maunoury, shared a common experience in the resistance. The excitement engendered by these emotions concealed a deeper anxiety. For two centuries the political development of the Middle East had been largely determined by the foreign policies of Britain and France in the pursuit of their own national interest; in 1956 they were suddenly confronted with the possibility that their own security might depend on the policies of an Arab statesman. The newcomers to international policies in the Middle East – the United States and Russia – were both aware that population, development, and resources made Egypt the key to the Middle East. They regarded Arab nationalism as too strong a force to overcome, and therefore competed with each other for the maximum influence with an Egyptian government which, whatever its limitations from their point of view, was the best they could hope for.

The political cost of the expedition was great, particularly in Britain. In France the adventure accorded well with the strong wave of nationalism which the Algerian war had provoked, and which had engulfed even the left-wing government of Mollet. In Britain in contrast the attack on Egypt divided the nation more deeply than any event since Munich. The division cut across party lines and the opposition was on moral as well as practical grounds. The British government deliberately did not consult the other members of the Commonwealth, and the opposition of the Asian members threatened to pull that association asunder. France, with Britain in support, was forced to use the veto in the Security Council to defeat a resolution calling for a cease-fire, thereby exposing the two countries, as we have seen, to overwhelming defeat in the General Assembly. It was widely felt that British and French action had weakened the moral case of the west in confronting Soviet action in Hungary; and it certainly severed the North Atlantic alliance at a time when it should have been at its strongest.

The expedition was halted before it had occupied the whole of the canal zone – as it could easily have done in a very short time – even though the public opinion polls began to show increasing support for the government in Britain, the parliamentary threat to the government dwindled, and there were no very damaging resignations.[33] As the British government regained its strength in terms of opinion, however, the financial position of the country deteriorated rapidly and bankruptcy was in sight. With the United States frigid and the Soviet Union threatening, with the Commonwealth as divided as public opinion at home, the threat of the collapse of the pound was the key factor deciding the government to order a cease-fire, against the reluctance of its ally. For Eden this was to prove the tragic end to a career in which he had established a reputation for skilful and patient negotiation. His health had been precarious even before the strain of the Suez crisis imposed a heavier burden. On 23 November he left for three weeks' holiday in Jamaica, and on 9 January he resigned his office.

Meanwhile in the United States the policy of the adminis-

[33] Gaitskell as Leader of the Opposition had tried to persuade Conservative members of Parliament to withdraw their support from the government, but without success. Only two junior ministers resigned.

tration had come under heavy attack. It was recognized that
Dulles and Eisenhower had been strongly opposed to the use
of force – the president in particular having attached the
greatest moral importance to the preservation of law and order
in international affairs, rather than the settlement of a dispute
by war. But the administration was attacked for having
deserted its European allies; and it was rightly pointed out
that Dulles had been unable to provide convincing alternative
means to enforce his own views about the canal. Nor did
American policy gain in flexibility towards its ally when Dulles
entered hospital and the State Department came under the
temporary direction of Herbert Hoover, Junior.

The prestige of the Egyptian government now stood high,
both in the Middle East and internationally. The cease-fire
with Britain and France removed the stigma of defeat by the
Israelis, and a successful blow for independence and Arab
greatness had been struck. In world politics the image of Egypt
as the victim of aggression was made more impressive by the
votes which had been taken in the United Nations. The
liquidation of the Suez affair therefore was advantageous to
Egypt except in one respect. Anglo-French forces were evacuated, and Egypt's moral prestige was enhanced by its readiness
to accept a United Nations expeditionary force. Under continuing pressure from the United Nations and the United States
Israeli forces also withdrew, not only from Sinai but from the
Gaza strip – formerly part of Palestine, and the base for
fedayeen raids. In return the Israeli government received an
assurance of a not very precise kind from the United States of
freedom of navigation in the Gulf of Aqaba. Having taken its
stand on principles of law and order the American government
could scarcely refuse such an undertaking: on the other hand
it wanted to avoid taking a strong stand against Egypt now
that it found itself a competitor with the Soviet Union for the
favour of the Arab states. In characteristic language the
president said on 20 February 1957:

We should not assume that if Israel withdraws, Egypt will prevent
Israeli shipping from using the Suez Canal or the Gulf of Aqaba.
If, unhappily, Egypt does hereafter violate the Armistice Agreement
or other international obligations, then this should be dealt with
firmly by the society of nations.[34]

[34] *US Policy in the Middle East*, p. 307.

In practice this principle was no easier to enforce in the canal than it had been before. The Egyptian government contended that its exclusion of Israeli shipping was consistent with the Constantinople convention. The result was that when the canal was reopened in the spring of 1957 its use by all nations except Israel was resumed, the only difference being that dues were paid to the Egyptian nationalized authority and the canal was managed by Egyptians.

For Israel the gain of free navigation of the Gulf of Aqaba was substantial, and it made possible the development of the port of Elath. In addition, although Egypt was able to reoccupy Gaza, the Israeli army had once again, as in 1948–9, demonstrated its capabilities, and thereby ruled out the possibility of Egyptian attack until the military or the political balance should have undergone substantial change.

For Britain, and to a lesser extent for France, the failure of the Suez expedition was a humiliation and a turning-point, in spite of the fact that the creation of the United Nations expeditionary force provided a cover under which their forces could retire with honour. While British and French ships cleared the wreckage from the entry to the Suez canal at Port Said, the Egyptian government would not allow them to work for the United Nations in clearing the canal itself, although there were obvious practical reasons for their doing so.

The French government had regained none of its influence in the Middle East, nor secured any advantage in its conflict with the Algerian nationalists. The British government found its Middle Eastern position abruptly curtailed. It was made obvious that British use of bases in the Middle East was dependent on the goodwill of the host governments, and this had not been forthcoming. Not only did Jordan's adherence to the Baghdad pact become a dream of the past, but the Anglo-Jordanian treaty was denounced by the government of Jordan, and even Nuri al-Said announced that he could not attend meetings of the Baghdad pact if Britain did so. The British Middle East Office remained in existence, and was able to keep open personal lines of contact even when public relations were severed, but its activity was limited. The era of British dominance in the Middle East had been brought to an end, and was seen to have ended.

The future remained problematical. One of the starting-points of the Suez crisis was, as we have seen, Nasser's adoption of neutralism, but the crisis itself and its liquidation seemed to transform the Middle East into the very storm centre of the cold war. The neutralism which was so attractive to the Arab states was regarded by many people in the United States (and Britain) as a 'vacuum' which must be filled by the west rather than the Soviet Union. And in spite of the prestige which Egypt had won for itself, nothing had happened to solve the problem of leadership in the Middle East, or to remove the rivalries between Arab states. It was one thing for Arab governments to support Nasser in confrontation with Britain and France, and quite another for them to have to deal with the threat which domestic support for Nasser represented to their own régimes. While, therefore, 'neutralism', 'anti-imperialism', and 'Arab unity' were powerful forces of upheaval in every country, the attractiveness of great power support, for its own sake or as a safeguard against rivals, continued to be a countervailing factor.

Meanwhile President Eisenhower wished to ensure that the United States would be able to intervene immediately and effectively in any future Middle Eastern crisis. In a special message to Congress on 5 January 1957 he therefore sought legislation empowering the administration to give economic and military aid to any nation in the Middle East that asked for it, and to use American armed forces 'to secure and protect the territorial integrity and political independence of such nations, requesting such aid against overt armed aggression from any nation controlled by International Communism'.[35] While it sought Congressional support for what came to be known as 'the Eisenhower doctrine', the administration was subjected to vigorous attacks from its political opponents, who, as we have seen, had throughout been critical of the way in which the United States had treated its allies. In the course of defending the administration's proposals, Dulles remarked that if American troops had to intervene in the Middle East they would naturally feel happier if they were not standing shoulder to shoulder with British and French, and this added further to the bitterness felt in London and Paris towards the United States.

[35] *US Policy in the Middle East*, p. 20.

At the same time the enthusiasm and admiration expressed towards the United States in the Middle East began to evaporate. During the Suez crisis it had been rightly supposed that American policy sprang from a fundamental respect for law and order in international affairs and a rejection of the arbitrary use of force, and that more importance was attached to these principles than to the maintenance of an alliance. As soon as the crisis was over this goodwill evaporated, in spite of all that bound the Arab states to America rather than to Russia. The only way in which the United States could intervene against the Soviet Union was by the exertion of its power; whether, as in 1957, by cutting off economic aid, or by movement of its fleet and the landing of troops; and this was something that alienated leaders and governments, both for its own sake and because the Soviet Union was able to take on the guise of protector of Arab independence.

The result was that only Lebanon signed a formal agreement with the United States implying acceptance of the Eisenhower doctrine, although Iraq issued a joint statement with the United States asserting an identity of views on the threat of communism and the need to co-operate in defence against it. Eisenhower's representative, Richards, travelled across the whole area from Tunisia to Afghanistan in the summer of 1957, but received a cool welcome in the Middle East, and did not visit Egypt, Jordan, or Syria. On the other hand Saudi Arabia, Iraq, and Jordan all accepted military aid from the United States, and it appeared that Jordan might become dependent on American support, as it previously had been on British.

The success of Nasser and the setback administered to Britain encouraged and strengthened those Jordanians who favoured a policy of more 'positive' neutralism, to secure the possible advantages of a closer relation with the Soviet Union. In April 1957 this led to a government crisis, demonstrations and rioting, and a declaration of martial law. (It remains uncertain whether the king took swift action against an actual threat to his régime or took the initiative against a potential threat.) The intervention of other Arab states appeared possible, and units of the Sixth Fleet were moved to the eastern Mediterranean with troops ready to be parachuted into Jordan, while the American government declared that it regarded 'the independence and integrity of Jordan as vital'. All this was done with a careful avoidance of any mention of the Eisenhower doctrine by either side, but the reality of American financial and military support was there all the same.

In the atmosphere of crisis which the American assumption of Middle Eastern responsibilities had created, a worse threat appeared to materialize in Syria. Throughout 1955 Syria had entered into an increasingly close relation with the Soviet Union, had received a steady and substantial flow of arms, and had sent its officers for training in the Soviet bloc. This was a development which alarmed Nuri al-Said as well as the British and Americans, and in the spring of 1956 a plot was hatched by the Iraqis, to which the British and Americans were party, to effect a change of government in Syria. The plot never came to fruition. Instead the Suez crisis brought firm support from Syria for Nasser, and, without direct orders from the government, Syrian officers blew up the oil pipeline that crossed their country. The subsequent American intervention in Middle Eastern affairs, including the Eisenhower doctrine and support from Lebanon and Jordan, brought vigorous opposition from the Syrian government.

In August 1957 it appeared, at least in America, that the worst fears of the American government of a communist take-over in Syria were justified. The Syrian defence minister signed an economic and military agreement with the Soviet Union; three American diplomats were expelled, the chief of staff retired in favour of an officer supposedly of strong Soviet sympathies and other officers were purged. The American reaction has been well described:

It was a situation in which the United States could be said to have been mesmerized by a monster of its own creation. The danger of a Soviet take-over had been so explicitly heralded, a battle-drill of such precision had been prepared, resources of such magnitude had been deployed to guard against a surprise attack that, now that the enemy appeared to have struck, action could no longer be avoided.[36]

There was little that the American government could do; but rather than stand idly by it sent Loy Henderson (who had helped draft the Truman doctrine and who had been in Iran

[36] Seale, *Struggle for Syria*, p. 292.

at the time of Musaddiq) to concert with the kings of Jordan and Iraq, and the Turkish prime minister in Ankara, and to visit President Shamun in Beirut. Soon afterwards the Turkish government carried out manoeuvres on the Syrian frontier; and the Soviet government played its now favourite role of coming to the (verbal) protection of Syria. In this way, as we shall see, Syrian politics made their contribution to a fresh round of 'summitry' between America and Russia, and even to the Sino-Soviet split.

But such summitry did not determine Syria's future. That lay with its active politicians and army officers, an important number of whom, particularly the Baath leaders, were increasingly anxious about the fragmentation of Syrian political life and the dangers to the army of its involvement in politics. The way out appeared to be to take to its furthest conclusion the alliance with Egypt which had begun in opposition to the Baghdad pact and been cemented by the Suez affair. In January 1958 a group of officers left for Cairo and proposed to Nasser a union between the two countries. To such a union Nasser had never aspired; but in offering leadership to the Arab world in the expulsion of imperialism he had already drawn Egypt out of its aloofness to Arab Asia; now he could only choose between going farther, or spurning those who had accepted his leadership. Forced to accept union, he insisted that it be on his own terms, a fusion and not a federation, and thereby condemned the Baath party, the chief initiators of the move, to virtual political suicide. On 1 February 1958 the United Arab Republic was proclaimed at a joint meeting of the parliaments of the two countries.

The creation of the UAR brought a retaliatory move of an insubstantial kind when Iraq and Jordan joined in a short-lived Arab Federation, lasting a few months. Meanwhile Yemen was affiliated to the UAR. But few years were to pass before the union demonstrated the obstacles which any such arrangement was likely to encounter. Flexible and adroit as he was in international politics, Nasser did not find it easy to share power and jobs in such a way as to strengthen union with Syria. He imposed policies which were harmful to its business and commercial classes, and he rode roughshod over the Syrian army. The result was that in the summer of 1961 the union was broken by a fresh Syrian army coup.

The tensions of these years had their disruptive effect in Lebanon too. The empiricism and practicality which normally characterize Lebanese politics had been strained to breaking point by the pro-western policy of Shamun. Opposition to his government increased when it was rumoured at the beginning of 1958 that he intended to try to revise the constitution in order to stand for election for a second term – a rumour which was only denied after some months. By this time, at the end of May 1958, a stalemate seemed to have been reached. Neither the government nor the opposition had the strength or the will to dispose of the other. The government had sought the arbitration of the Arab League, but this had proved unavailing. It had also indicated to the British and American governments that it hoped for their support if necessary. At the same time it accused the government of the United Arab Republic of intervention in support of the Lebanese opposition, and brought this complaint before the United Nations. In consequence an Observation Group was sent by the United Nations to Lebanon, and the secretary-general visited both Lebanon and Egypt. Their reports on the supposed infiltration were to be largely negative.

At this point, however, a fresh eruption of far greater apparent inflammability occurred. On 14 July 1958 a successful rebellion was carried out in Iraq. The efficient system of intelligence and internal security which, together with political acumen, had kept Nuri al-Said in control for so long at last broke down, and army officers who were being directed to the Syrian frontier of the United Arab Republic overthrew the government with great violence. The king and his family were killed, together with Nuri al-Said, whose body was dragged through the streets of Baghdad. It soon became known that a new government had been formed under Brigadier Kassem, although its precise nature was difficult to determine.

This threatened to set the whole Middle East on fire, supposing that the revolt should spread to Jordan or Lebanon. The reaction of President Shamun was to appeal under the terms of the Eisenhower doctrine for support from the United States, and within hours American troops, carrier-borne by the Sixth Fleet, were finding space for themselves between the ice-cream merchants and the sunbathers on the beaches of Beirut. In the Security Council the American delegate proposed that a United Nations expeditionary force should be sent to Lebanon: but it did so on 15 July, just as the interim report of the Observation Group was circulated, claiming complete success in its supervision of the frontier and denying that there was any large-scale infiltration across it. The United States, in disembarking marines while urging United Nations action, with an apparent disregard of what the Observation Group had reported, was heavily criticized, in spite of its insistence that it was responding to an appeal from the Lebanese government. Two days later a similar appeal came from Husain of Jordan, and the British paratroops stationed themselves on the airfield of Amman.

From this point of maximum tension the Middle East quietly subsided. The alarm which the Iraqi revolution had provoked in the west stemmed from the possibility that it would be exploited by communists or supporters of Nasser. At first Kassem did not dare dispense with the support of these forces; but he had no intention of sacrificing Iraq's independence, and there was no immediate possibility of Iraq joining the UAR. There was as well a greater danger, which was that the Iraqi communists would win control from Kassem, and thereby secure a base from which to threaten the UAR. Nasser consequently tightened up control of the communists in Egypt and Syria; he outmanoeuvred the Baath party in Syria to obviate the danger of a nationalist alignment with Iraq; and he pressed ahead with an economic plan for the UAR. Of this last action the most immediate success came with the signature, in October 1958, of an agreement with the Russian government to finance part of the building of the Aswan dam.

Now that British and American intervention in the Middle East was more hotly resented than ever before, and the governments in question had no wish to incur the cost and the odium involved longer than was necessary, an atmosphere for compromise and common action was provided: the United Nations was the forum for it. In August first the United States and then the Sudan introduced resolutions aimed at providing 'plans for peace' and agreement on basic principles of conduct between the Arab governments. The Sudanese resolution won unanimous acceptance in the Assembly, and Hammarskjöld made a fresh journey to the Middle East to secure its implementation.

In September a change of government was achieved in Lebanon when General Shihab replaced Shamun, and the apparatus of crisis was dismantled piece by piece. American forces left by the end of October: in mid-November the Lebanese government withdrew the complaint it had lodged with the Security Council of interference by the UAR, and three weeks later the United Nations Observation Group came to an end. Similarly British troops were withdrawn from Jordan by the beginning of November.

The Soviet Union meanwhile had not given up the interest it had begun to show in the Middle East in 1955. It made no attempt to intervene directly; nor apparently did it try to take advantage of the overthrow of Nuri al-Said through the medium of the Iraqi communists. Its position of strength in Syria was, as we have seen, cut back by the formation of the UAR. On the other hand the Iraqi revolution brought to an end the Baghdad pact, the rump of which moved its headquarters to Ankara and, embracing now only Britain, Turkey, Pakistan, and Iran, with the support of the United States, was renamed the Central Treaty Organization. At the same time the prestige which the Soviet Union had acquired during the Suez crisis was enhanced in October 1957 by the successful launching of the first Sputnik, or earth satellite – to the observable discomfiture of the United States. Unable, or unwilling, to interfere directly in the Middle East, but enjoying this new prestige, Khrushchev sought to make the most of his position by proposing, on 19 July 1958, an immediate meeting of the Soviet Union, the United States, the United Kingdom, France, and India, joined by the secretary-general of the United Nations, to settle the outstanding problems of the Middle East. Cautiously, Britain and the United States took up his proposal, but diverted it to a meeting within the framework of the United Nations. Unwittingly they had thus entered on the long road that led to the abortive summit conference of 1960. Khrushchev accepted their modification of his proposal: but, presumably because of opposition from the Chinese, then began to sidestep. Fortunately for the Middle East, the appeasement of the area did not have to wait for a summit conference to occur.

After 1958 direct intervention in the affairs of the Middle East was seen on the one hand to be fraught with risks, and on the other to be of dubious value. Landing troops in Lebanon and Jordan the Americans and the British were fortunate enough to safeguard or at least to be in attendance at political stabilization without being involved in actual conflict and without being confronted by any rival intervention. As the later experience of the Egyptians in the Yemen and the Americans in Vietnam was to show, such a happy outcome could not be regarded as an automatic result of intervention. The Soviet Union for its part readily gave diplomatic support to Kassem's revolution in Iraq, supposing this to be consistent with their alliance with Nasser. Instead they found themselves engaged, as their great power rivals had been for several years, in another Arab dispute. Kassem's independence and un-predictability were in no way welcome to Nasser, and the Russian offer to finance the Aswan Dam was in part intended to balance the support given to Kassem in order to retain the alliance with Egypt. While the risks and hazards of interven-tion were thus apparent, the dangers of non-intervention appeared less. The danger of a communist take-over in Syria, whether real or imaginary, had been averted or had passed as a result of the actions of the Syrians themselves: and even the overthrow of Nuri al-Said had not been followed by a régime hostile to British and American interests.

The diminution of the British position in the Middle East consequent on the Iraqi revolution coincided with the tempor-ary settlement of the Cyprus problem. Britain had governed Cyprus on trust for Turkey from 1878 to 1914, when it was annexed, and as late as 1958 Selwyn Lloyd had spoken of the necessity for Britain to maintain sovereignty over Cyprus because of its treaty obligations to the Arab states, as well as to NATO, Greece, and Turkey. Meanwhile support had grown amongst the Greek population of the island for Enosis, or union with Greece – a movement already in existence before 1914, but achieving full momentum only in the 1950s. Under the leadership, both spiritual and political, of Archbishop Makarios, it then took advantage of a unique political organization in the form of the Greek Orthodox Church, associated with a guerrilla and terrorist organization under 'Dighenis' (whose real name was General Grivas). From 1951 Enosis had the support, cautious at first but outspoken by 1954, of the Greek govern-ment.

The British government, in spite of warnings, allowed itself to be taken by surprise by the rapid growth of the Enosis movement. But Britain was not alone in being opposed to Enosis. Some 18 per cent of the island's population of 550,000 were Muslim and Turkish-speaking, and these Turkish Cypriots were prepared to resist with every means the possibility of union with Greece. They had the support of the Turkish government, which was anxiously concerned about the future of an island only fifty miles from the Anatolian mainland.

The twofold obstacle to settlement – British interest in the maintenance of a base, and Greek-Turkish hostility – endured until 1959. For five years Cyprus was the scene of terrorism on the part of the Greek Cypriots, met by military counter-measures and the deportation (from March 1956 to March 1957) of Makarios and the bishop of Kyrenia to the Seychelles Islands. Then at the end of 1958 the possibility of a settlement suddenly emerged. The tenacity with which the British had insisted on the retention of Cyprus as a base disappeared. Its inadequacy had been demonstrated during the Suez crisis, for its harbours were neither large nor deep enough to marshal a seaborne force; and its value was diminished by events in the Middle East itself. Meanwhile negotiations were begun between the governments of Greece and Turkey, and on 11 February 1959 it was announced from Zurich, where the prime ministers and foreign ministers had been meeting, that agreement had been reached.

The terms of settlement between the Cypriots and the British provided for relative stability. Cyprus became an independent republic (which later joined the Commonwealth) and Britain retained sovereignty over two bases on the island. The dispute between Greek and Turkish Cypriots proved more lasting. A somewhat *simpliste* constitutional arrangement provided for a Greek president and Turkish vice-president, a government divided between Greeks and Turks in the proportion one to three, and a legislative assembly elected separately from the two communities in the same proportion. A device of this sort was inadequate to remove the antagonism between the two communities – fostered by the free play of political forces once British rule was removed. Five years after the settlement the conflict broke into the open again and British troops, followed by those of the United Nations, returned to the island. Cyprus became a minor pivot on which turned major issues of Mediterranean, especially Turkish, politics.

In the Arab Middle East British troops also made a fresh sortie in 1961 – but one that should be regarded as an exception rather than a pattern for the future. In 1899 Britain had made an arrangement with the ruling family of Kuwait under which it took responsibility for defence and foreign policy. In 1961 it was possible to remodel this arrangement; by that time Kuwait had become rich from oil and had acquired political stability through the growth of a stable middle class and the intelligent expenditure of oil revenue. The new agreement in consequence gave Kuwait its full independence while at the same time promising British assistance (in a form not defined) if it were requested by the Kuwait government.

Within two weeks of the signature of the agreement in June 1961 the attitude of the Iraqi government, whose president, Kassem, described Kuwait as 'part of the province of Basra', led the Kuwaitis to appeal for British help. A British force was landed to take up defensive positions in the fierce heat of the desert. On all grounds the expedition could be regarded as a success. British forces regained their lost morale after the Suez expedition by the efficiency with which they conducted their landing; and within four months they were able to withdraw. Whether or not Iraq had seriously intended an attack, none now occurred, and the independence of Kuwait became something in which the Arab states themselves would have an interest, rather than risking foreign intervention again. This was particularly true since Iraqi interests in Kuwait were balanced by those of Saudi Arabia, as was shown by the small force sent to Kuwait, side by side with the British, although there were no diplomatic relations between the two governments.

Arab reluctance to see a repetition of the Kuwait expedition was matched by British awareness of the extent to which their strategic reserve had been committed in a relatively minor operation. For the United Kingdom Kuwait would continue to be of major importance not only for the oil it produced but because it was part of the sterling area and thereby made a decisive contribution to the balance of payments. Military measures were not necessarily appropriate to the defence of an interest of this sort.

Short of the very unlikely event of direct military attack by the Soviet Union, and unless war was renewed between Arabs and Israelis, the possibility of intervention by Britain and America was thus seriously diminished. But the two powers retained bases in the area which continued to be of major importance to them as world powers. Both rented bases in Libya; the British retained a major base at Aden to which the Royal Air Force attached particular importance, and a smaller base at Bahrain, where the United States also maintained a small military establishment. These were flanked by the British base in Cyprus and American bases in Turkey. In addition, the British were still in treaty relationship with the shaikhdoms of the Persian Gulf – having signed treaties with the shaikhs in the full confidence of the nineteenth-century undertaking to protect them in perpetuity. At a time when the shaikhdoms were of importance to Britain because of the route to India, and could be defended from the sea, the British little foresaw that they would acquire immense wealth, and that the land frontiers would become of crucial importance because of the oil beneath them.

It did not follow that as the British had given up or lost their allies and their bases in the Middle East, they could continue to do so until they had withdrawn altogether. The shaikhdoms of the Persian Gulf lacked the political and social development which assured the stability of Kuwait and, isolated from the central focus of Middle Eastern politics, they would not benefit from the balance between Arab states which promised to safeguard Kuwait.[37] The importance of Aden as a major base changed as the self-imposed task of Middle East policeman appeared less profitable to the British, but, as the last remaining base in the area, it was not easy to give up. British interests in the Indian Ocean and South East Asia called for the maintenance of a secure route across the Middle East, and Aden was important, in spite of being remote from the two most direct lines of communication.[38] Moreover the American government, because of the importance of a new 'northern tier' in South East Asia and because of its own interests in

[37] See Elizabeth Monroe, 'Kuwait and Aden', *Middle East Journal*, Winter 1964.
[38] The northern route was over Turkey and Persia. The southern route over Egypt and the Sudan was closed as long as these two countries refused overflying rights.

the Middle East, exerted no pressure on the British to leave Aden.

This was a political situation which Nasser could exploit to the full, encouraging at one and the same time opposition to the British base and rejection of Arab conservatism. In addition, having landed troops in Yemen in 1964 in support of a republican uprising which had begun two years earlier, he welcomed a diversion which would distract attention from the extent of his military commitment and its lack of success in the harsh conditions of guerrilla warfare in Yemen.[39] In these conditions even those Adenis who welcomed the retention of the British base were politically vulnerable, and, as terrorism increased, in danger of their lives.

The labour government brought to power under the premiership of Harold Wilson in October 1964 carried out a fresh examination of British foreign and defence policy. The results were embodied in the 1966 Defence White Paper, and they included the decision to withdraw from the Aden base, while retaining that at Bahrain. This change of policy did not, however, promise any great relief to the discomfiture which resulted from the remnants of British power in the Middle East. Nasser claimed loudly and convincingly, in the Arab world, to have levered the British out of Aden; at the same time he took steps to consolidate the Egyptian position in the Yemen and subject the British base at Bahrain to the same irritation he had helped create elsewhere. Meanwhile those régimes which had until now combined stability with traditionalism, led by the shah of Iran and Faisal of Arabia, sponsored an Islamic pact as a counter to the ideology of Nasser's Arab socialism. But they had no reason to regard Britain or America as firm allies in this cause; while the British and American governments had long since learned the dangers of taking sides – especially the conservative side – in Arab quarrels.

[39] By 1964 some 40,000 troops were engaged in support of the republicans in the Yemen. The royalist forces received support, although not from land forces, from Saudi Arabia.

11

EUROPE, NATO, AND DE GAULLE

THE FRENCH refusal to ratify the EDC treaty had appeared to inflict a fatal blow on the development of European institutions as a whole and on the movement towards European unity. However, such a view underestimated the strength and persistence of those who had committed themselves to the cause of European union. Amongst such men the most important single figure was Jean Monnet, the principal architect of the Schuman plan and president of the High Authority of the ECSC. In November 1954 he announced his intention not to seek re-election at the end of his term of office in February 1955, in order to be free to campaign actively for the establishment of a United States of Europe. In the event his retirement from office was delayed by the difficulty of finding a successor; but this did not prevent his working actively with the governments of the Benelux countries and with those most interested in European unity to achieve a fresh start or a relaunching of Europe as they understood it.

The first step in this movement was taken at the conference of foreign ministers of the Six which was held at Messina at the beginning of June 1955. It was known that the French government, in spite of the fact that Edgar Faure had now replaced Mendès France as prime minister, was hesitant about a further essay into supranationality, and that the German government was alarmed about the extent of control and direction which appeared to be an essential part of new European institutions. None the less the Messina conference, as an intergovernmental body, took and retained the initiative, and a committee was set up under the chairmanship of Spaak to draw up treaties which would permit the implementation of proposals for integration of trade and energy.

The Intergovernmental Committee thus set up began its work in July 1955, and by November it was ready to draft its final report. During this time its meetings were attended by a British *representative* – a term carefully chosen to indicate that

Britain was not committed to the principles accepted at the Messina conference, but at the same time was more actively interested than would appear if it merely sent an observer. From the first, however, it was apparent that there was a fundamental difference between the British position and that of the Six, in that the former sought a free trade area, whose members would be free to fix their own external tariffs, while the latter wanted to establish a customs union with a common external tariff. In addition the British would have liked to make the maximum possible use of the existing OEEC institutions and adhere to the method and spirit of OEEC arrangements, while the Six believed in the necessity of establishing new institutions outside the framework of OEEC. Because of these differences the British ceased to participate in the committee's discussions in November 1955.

There were at the same time differences amongst the Six, of which the most important separated France from the others. The French wished to proceed slowly, with a maximum transitional period and with the maximum possible number of escape clauses; while all accepted the central proposition that the freeing of trade should be accompanied by the 'harmonization' of economic and social policies, the French were most anxious that trade liberalization should not move too far ahead of harmonization. At the same time the French looked for a higher external tariff than the other five. All these differences were obviously related to the comparatively weak trading position which France was in at this time, particularly in relation to Germany.

With the completion of the work of the Intergovernmental Committee its report – known as the Spaak report – became the subject of discussions between foreign ministers, which began in Venice in May 1956 and ended with the formulation of two treaties, one setting up a European Common Market and the other a European Atomic Energy Community by March 1957. During this time no other European country joined the discussions – although it would have been open to them to do so, if they accepted the Spaak report. The British government proposed that it should once again send a representative to participate in discussions; but as it made clear that its objectives were different from those of the Spaak report, its proposal was rejected.

The success of the negotiations, and the fact that the treaties which resulted from them were signed, and ratified by the governments of the Six during the summer of 1957, is attributable in part to the skill with which the Spaak report had been devised – as was evident by the fact that the treaties followed its main outlines very closely. In Germany the Adenauer government remained committed to European unity, in spite of the reservations of Erhard about the possible *dirigisme* of a customs union; in France the elections of January 1956 brought to power a relatively stable government under Mollet, who was outstanding amongst French statesmen for his commitment to European union. Moreover the negotiations were carried on during the period of the Suez crisis, which enhanced the feelings of those who sought a strong Europe independent of the United States.

As we have seen, the French government was more alarmed at the possible consequences of the rapid establishment of a customs union than were its partners. As a result important concessions were made to the French position. The transitional period during which a customs union would be established was to be of 12–15 years' duration, rather than the 10 years which the other members regarded as adequate. It was moreover to be phased, with careful safeguards that a substantial measure of harmonization had been achieved in the first stage before entering on to the second, so that no one country (and particularly France) should be competing on unfavourable terms because of longer paid holidays or a shorter working week. Most important of the concessions which were made to the French view was that relating to overseas territories. The negotiations were taking place at the moment when the French government was developing the legal framework within which the African colonies could achieve practical independence; but it wished to retain French links with the colonies, and was aware of the need for capital to finance economic development. On the other hand it was clear that even when the colonies were fully independent they could not easily be admitted as equal partners into a European Economic Community. To meet this difficulty the French proposed, and their partners accepted, an arrangement whereby the French overseas territories would have the right of entry for their products into the Economic Community on the same terms as France, and that in return they would extend the same tariff treatment to all members of the Six – although they would not be bound to the same external tariff as the Six themselves. More than this, the Community would set up a Development Fund to which all members of the Community would contribute for investment in the colonies or former colonies of the Six – of which the French were the most important part.

The caution which the French government showed and its firmness in insisting on these concessions inevitably created a certain amount of antagonism amongst the other members, especially with Germany. The arrangements for the overseas territories were particularly unattractive. They brought no marked trading advantages, and even disrupted the pattern of trade in some respects; for example Brazil would now compete unfavourably with the French African territories, and it was likely that German exports to Brazil would therefore suffer, with no corresponding increase in German exports to French Africa. There was no obvious gain for Germany in being able to contribute to a Development Fund; and a considerable disadvantage in linking Germany to the imperial position of France, with all the odium which that incurred amongst the Afro-Asian bloc. That these provisions were accepted, therefore, indicates the momentum which the relaunching of Europe had acquired. Monnet was able to argue the political necessity in his own country that provision for the overseas territories be included in the treaty; and although the convention which resulted was agreed initially for a period of only five years his insistence won the agreement of his partners.

The signature of the Rome treaties in March 1957 and their subsequent ratification meant that once again the federalist current in Europe had made an important surge forward, and that Britain was isolated from its most powerful and closest continental neighbours. The British government did not at this stage seriously entertain the possibility of joining the Six. To do so would have created unacceptable difficulties in relations with the Commonwealth. Macmillan as chancellor of the exchequer said in the House on 26 November 1956:

> I do not believe that this House would ever agree to our entering arrangements which, as a matter of principle, would prevent our treating the great range of imports from the Commonwealth at least as favourably as those from the European countries.

At least as important as this reservation, however, was no doubt the failure of the British government to assess or to forecast the strength of the European movement. Now as in 1950 there was considerable scepticism as to the chance of success of a European Economic Community. The disparity between the strengths of the French and German economies at this time suggested that it would be impossible to move forward to a customs union between the two; more than that, there were serious doubts as to the political stability of France itself, and its ability to solve its colonial problems, particularly that of Algeria.

The British government consequently sought actively to promote a free trade area in Europe, through OEEC, which would provide for an all-round reduction of tariffs between the EEC, the United Kingdom, and any other members of OEEC that wished to join. As a result of British initiative OEEC had set up a working party to explore the possibility of a free trade area in July 1956; it published its report in January 1957, and at the same time the British government published a White Paper which followed closely the main lines of the OEEC report. From the first, however, obvious difficulties appeared in the attempt to run negotiations for a free trade area side by side with those for the formulation and implementation of the treaties of Rome. As we have seen, the French government had fought hard within the Six for the harmonization of economic and social policies, without which, they believed, they could not accept free trade; it was improbable therefore that they would wish to extend the advantages of free trade to other countries outside the Six, which had entered into no similar commitments. The British might argue that the wider scope of a free trade area was preferable to the small customs union which the Six were setting up; but behind the British insistence on freedom for members of the free trade area to fix their own external tariffs lay the contention of the White Paper that 'it is essential that the United Kingdom should be able to continue the preferential arrangements which have been built up over the last twenty-five years'.

A further sharp dividing line was evident between Britain and the Six in the free-trade negotiations. The British advocated an industrial free trade area, and were not prepared to consider free trade in agricultural products. Inevitably agricultural questions had caused difficulty within the Six, but they had been overcome or circumvented. At this time the German and French positions on agriculture were similar, and it was generally accepted that special provision would have to be made for agricultural products. It was possible, therefore, in the treaty of Rome to provide for a common organization of the agricultural market, without specifying closely what form such organization would take. Problems which were postponed in this way increased over the next few years, since the devaluation of the French franc created an important price difference between German and French agricultural products. None the less the Rome treaty embraced agriculture as well as industry, and the British proposals for an industrial free trade area could scarcely be attractive to countries which were in practice being asked to open their frontiers to British industrial products without having a corresponding outlet for their own agricultural produce.

In retrospect, the British pursuit of a free trade area appears singularly unpromising. In spite of that the Council of OEEC expressed its determination to secure a free trade area, and in November 1957 set up an intergovernmental committee under the chairmanship of Maudling (who had been made paymaster-general in the British government) to negotiate towards this end. Throughout the next year – during which the Rome treaties came into effect on 1 January 1958 and de Gaulle came to power in May 1958 – the Maudling committee and its experts pursued solutions to the complex problems which the proposal of a free trade area implied – the products that should be included, control over the origins of goods entering into trade within the area, co-ordination of commercial policy, and the extent of tariff autonomy. In spite of this the basic differences between the French and the British positions remained, and by the end of 1958 it was clear that negotiations had broken down.

Inevitably a certain amount of bad feeling had been created in the process. It was not that the British view of the need to reduce barriers generally in Europe rather than form a tight customs union had no support amongst the Six; on the contrary it was very attractive to those who had anxieties about the *dirigisme* of the French or who were reluctant to accept the political implications of the Rome treaties. But in pressing the OEEC discussions at the same time as those for the Rome treaties, it gave the impression of trying to impede the movement towards the common market in order to benefit its own alternative arrangement. The British government emphasized the dangers of dividing Europe. Sir David Eccles, as president of the Board of Trade, stressed the dangers of creating the common market without the complement of the free trade area when he addressed the British Chamber of Commerce in Paris on 7 June 1957. 'Western Europe', he said, 'which over the centuries has suffered so often the agonies of division, and has all the time dreamed the same dreams of unity, might fly apart again.'[1] Those outside Britain might conclude that a simple alternative was open to Britain if it wished to preserve the unity of Europe, but that rather than adopt this alternative the British preferred to break the unity or at least reduce the momentum which the Six had achieved.

This impression was heightened by the proposal which the British government first put forward at the NATO Council meeting in December 1956, and developed at the Consultative Assembly of the Council of Europe in May. The British proposal, which was hopefully entitled the 'Grand Design', was that the existing European Assemblies, and those proposed for Euratom and the common market, should be merged, with parliamentarians from the NATO countries, into a single assembly. The assembly would normally work in commissions, whose membership would be the same as the existing assemblies. Such a proposal was scarcely welcome to the neutral states of Europe, whose membership of the Council of Europe or OEEC was acceptable precisely because these institutions were separate from WEU and NATO. More important, the British proposal once again raised the alarm of the Six, to whom it appeared an attempt to submerge the European Community in a wider organization which imposed little obligation on its members, and a means by which Britain might hope to influence the development of the European Community while remaining outside it.

These developments set one of the patterns of relationships in the western world over the next few years, and their slow unfolding came to a climax with Britain's abortive attempt

---

[1] *The Times*, 8 June 1957.

to join the EEC in 1962–3. But there were other alignments being made or remade at the same time. The crises of October 1956 over Suez and Hungary had an important effect, as we have seen, in increasing the incentive to union in Europe; they even affected, although not radically, the relationship between Britain and the Six. They had a far more fundamental effect on the North Atlantic alliance and on relations between Britain, France, and America.

Shaken by its ineffectiveness in Hungary and alarmed by the divisions which had revealed themselves over Suez, the North Atlantic alliance sought to repair the damage which these two crises had done to its cohesion. When the Council met in December 1956 it accepted a report from a committee composed of the foreign ministers of Italy, Norway, and Canada – the Martino–Langer–Pearson report – which sought to extend and improve the machinery for political consultation between members. By accepting the report the members of the alliance undertook to inform the Council of any development which significantly affected the alliance, 'not merely as a formality but as a preliminary to effective political consultation'. It was also agreed that members should not 'without adequate advance consultation adopt firm policies or make major political announcements on matters which significantly affect the alliance or any of its members'; and it was proposed that there should be more frequent meetings of foreign ministers within the NATO framework. Dulles expressed reservations on behalf of the United States, emphasizing particularly that the United States could not be expected to co-ordinate its policies with its allies, for example if it went to the defence of Formosa, and doubts about the value of foreign ministers' meetings were expressed by the French. But in general the need for political consultation was accepted.

It was more difficult to carry such resolutions into any effective practice. We have already noticed the alarms provoked by the British proposal for a Grand Design. More significant was the fact that for France the most important problem needing solution was that of Algeria, where rebellion had been in progress since 1954. From the French point of view the Algerian war was a matter of internal politics; but it had motivated the French participation in the Suez expedition; it weakened the alliance militarily since French troops were sent in increasing numbers to North Africa; and it was thought to evoke against the alliance as a whole the antipathy of the emerging nations. But the French government saw no reason to make the Algerian question a matter of consultation with its allies; rather it expected the support of the alliance for its own policies. At the eastern end of the Mediterranean the Cyprus question was rendered insoluble in part as a result of antagonism between the Greek and Turkish communities and in part by British resistance to the Greek demand for Enosis; but fresh proposals in the spring of 1957 that the secretary-general of NATO might intervene, or that a solution might be sought within NATO were rejected by the Greek government.

A more striking demonstration of the independent policies of at least one of the NATO members was given when the British government published its White Paper on defence in April 1957. The motive behind the reappraisal of British defence was partly strategic, and partly financial, as was frankly stated in the White Paper itself. It was pointed out that defence had absorbed 10 per cent of the British gross national product as well as an undue proportion of the energies of scientists and skilled engineers; while at the same time the maintenance of large forces abroad had placed a grave strain on the balance of payments. Yet this expenditure had failed to provide adequate defence against nuclear attack; such defence was indeed impossible. 'It must frankly be recognized', the White Paper[2] said, 'that there is at present no means of providing adequate protection for the people of this country against the consequences of an attack with nuclear weapons.' It followed, therefore, that Britain must help prevent war by the development of 'an appreciable element of nuclear deterrent power of her own'.

Concentration of limited resources in the nuclear deterrent must inevitably, on the assumptions of the White Paper, be accompanied by cuts elsewhere. Reductions in British forces on the Continent had already been discussed at the NATO Council in December 1956 and in the Council of WEU. Now the White Paper indicated that 13,000 men would be withdrawn from the Rhine army during the next year, and further cuts were foreseen thereafter; at the same time the aircraft of the

[2] Cmnd. 124.

Second Tactical Air Force and of the bomber force in England assigned to NATO would be halved. These reductions would permit the ending of conscription by 1960.

From a formal point of view the British government had kept to its commitments by bringing its defence reappraisal before NATO and by seeking the authorization of the WEU Council for reduction of its troops in Europe, as the WEU agreement of 1954 required. In spite of that, the decisions were arrived at on an entirely national basis in accordance with a national interpretation of British needs. On the continent of Europe an exaggerated interpretation was given of the extent to which Britain was withdrawing once again from its European commitments; in Germany feeling was heightened by the fact that the British government was engaged in heated argument with the German government about the sharing of the support costs of the British army in Germany between the two countries. In the Assembly of WEU a majority – although not an absolute majority as the WEU agreement required – of votes were cast in favour of a motion objecting to the Council's approval of the cuts in British forces in Europe.

Meanwhile the whole presupposition of military defence in Europe became a matter of debate and discussion within the countries of the western alliance during the course of 1957 and 1958. For those responsible for the direction of NATO, the Hungarian crisis had shown up weaknesses in the alliance; but there were others who saw it as an example of the kind of disorder in central Europe which would lead to serious conflict, the more so once tactical atomic weapons were introduced into NATO forces. As a result political leaders and eminent men explored publicly the possibility of some kind of 'disengagement' in Europe, of the sort which had been aired in previous years without attracting great public attention. In the spring of 1957 Gaitskell delivered a series of lectures at Harvard (later published under the title *The Challenge of Co-existence*) in which he proposed the evacuation of central Europe and the creation, by stages, of a disengaged zone which would cover the whole of Germany, Poland, Czechoslovakia, and Hungary, possibly also Rumania and Bulgaria. His ideas were taken up by the British Labour party, and restated by Denis Healey in a pamphlet *A Neutral Belt in Europe* published in January 1958. In Germany the SDP campaigned in 1957 for a reunited Germany and the

15*

replacement of existing military alliances by a collective security system. At the end of 1957 George Kennan, who had been a State Department specialist on Russian affairs and ambassador in Moscow, as well as the author of the articles in *Foreign Affairs* which defined the policy of containment, took up the idea of disengagement in the Reith lectures, broadcast by the BBC, which evoked quite unforeseen attention and interest throughout the world.[3] He went much farther than previous commentators had done by proposing the withdrawal of United States troops from Europe – partly on the grounds that then and only then, under pressure of necessity, Europe would look to its own defence.

Behind all these proposals for disengagement lay the idea that Russian domination of eastern Europe, and the confrontation of east and west on the north–south dividing line of Europe could not last indefinitely. As Kennan said, in characteristic language: 'The state of the satellite area today, and particularly of Poland, is neither fish nor fowl, neither complete Stalinist domination nor real independence. Things cannot be expected to remain this way for long (p. 35).' The fact that the forces of the two sides in the cold war faced each other across a line which ran through an area likely to produce the kind of up-heaval which had been seen in east Germany in 1953 and in Hungary in 1956 was a source of constant danger. Moreover the line left Berlin as an outpost in the east; and Kennan spoke of 'the extremely precarious and unsound arrangements which now govern the status of Berlin'. In this situation, it was argued by those who favoured disengagement, the west must for once take the initiative and not be caught unprepared by events; they must accept the risks and the disturbance of their own position which disengagement implied, to guard against future dangers and as the only, but none the less effective, means of persuading or (as it was sometimes argued) making it possible for Russian troops to be withdrawn from eastern Europe.

These proposals for disengagement never entered into serious negotiations between east and west. In 1955 the proposal which Eden had put forward for a demilitarized zone between east and west had got as far as the directive to the foreign ministers; but it was linked in Eden's concept with a reunified Germany,

[3] They were published under the title, *Russia, the Atom and the West* (1958).

and when it was revived by the Russians in May 1958 the British government insisted that the proposal did not constitute a suggestion for a neutral zone, as the Russians seemed to think. The Polish foreign minister put forward a plan for the elimination of nuclear weapons in central Europe, and this too was reflected in the Russian proposals of May 1958; but it met with no response from the western governments at the moment when they saw the possibility of compensating for the numerical weakness of their forces in Germany by equipping them with tactical atomic weapons. The British Labour party had no means of achieving power before the election of 1959 (and did not do so then), while the German social democrats suffered defeat in the election of 1957. In the United States not only did Kennan's ideas meet with no favour with the Eisenhower administration, but Kennan's erstwhile political chief, Acheson, wrote an article in *Foreign Affairs* to combat his ideas. Whether profitable negotiations would have been possible along the lines proposed by Gaitskell or Kennan therefore remains unknowable; on the face of it the incentive for the Russians to withdraw their troops from eastern Europe at the risk of seeing the collapse of communist régimes there appears slight, and the logic of those who argued otherwise incomplete.[4] The debate itself may, on the contrary, have persuaded Khrushchev that something was to be gained by bringing pressure to bear on Berlin; but when he did so, talk of disengagement virtually disappeared.

Even before then, the attempt which was being made to give the alliance greater political cohesion was matched by measures designed to increase its military strength. Since 1954 NATO strategy had been based on the assumption that tactical atomic weapons could be used in forward defence. It had consequently been possible to reduce the number of divisions which were deemed necessary, and at the same time to maintain the expectation that NATO would be strong enough to act as a shield against Russian attack rather than merely to act (as some had advocated) as a 'tripwire' which would bring the

---

[4] For example Kennan, continuing the passage already quoted: 'There must either be further violent efforts by people in that area to take things into their own hands and to achieve independence by their own means, or there must be the beginning of some process of real adjustment to the fact of Soviet domination. . . . I can conceive of no escape from this dilemma that would not involve the early departure of Soviet troops from the satellite countries' (pp. 35–36).

massive forces of nuclear retaliation into action. Even so, NATO troops on the ground in Europe fell short of the target of thirty divisions in 1954, or twenty-eight in 1957. The British were withdrawing troops; French troops were still in Algeria; in July 1957 the first three German divisions were placed under the command of SACEUR, compared with the twelve which were foreseen when German rearmament was first proposed.

The development of atomic and nuclear weapons and the possibility of delivering them by rockets and even by cannon created a new series of problems within the alliance. In its early stages these problems were not acute. The United States undertook to provide NATO forces in Europe with weapons capable of atomic delivery, and secured the agreement of the NATO Council for the stockpiling of atomic warheads under United States control in Europe. Should war break out the stockpiles would then be issued under the dual control of the United States and the governments whose forces were to use them. In 1957 the United States also offered to supply guided missiles to its allies; its offer was taken up by the British (who negotiated an agreement at the Bermuda conference in March); by Greece and Turkey, and by Norway and Denmark. By the end of 1957 the problem had become more acute. In October 1957 the Soviet Union successfully launched its first vehicle into space, and thereby struck the United States first with a sense of incredulity and then with a sense of imperative need to develop its missile strength lest it be overtaken by the Soviet Union in the race for nuclear pre-eminence. As intercontinental missiles were not yet available, this meant the establishment of intermediate missiles with nuclear warheads on the territories of its allies – or those that were willing to receive them.

In this way the problem of nuclear weapons within the western alliance became increasingly complex. When the alliance was signed the United States alone possessed atomic capability; now this monopoly was shared with the British. American legislation in the shape of the MacMahon Act was designed to limit the spread of nuclear weapons to other powers, but was incapable of preventing the development of other atomic and nuclear capabilities by a state which was sufficiently advanced and willing to devote resources to the task. Even when the Act was amended in 1958, it allowed the exchange of information only with those countries who had already reached an advanced stage in nuclear development – particularly Britain but not France. On the other hand, while in 1949 other national atomic capabilities would have contributed significantly to the strength of the alliance, the scale of development, the diversification of weapons, and of means of delivery was such that second-range powers like Britain and France could not add significantly to the destructive power at the disposal of the United States. None the less two national nuclear forces existed within the alliance and a third was in preparation; yet no plan had been devised or was foreseeable whereby these forces could be brought under the control of the alliance. Moreover the United States depended on its allies both for the deployment of tactical weapons in the field and for the installation of nuclear missiles close enough to the Soviet Union to fill the gap between manned bombers and the development of intercontinental missiles. For such weapons a system of dual control was developed, such that they could only be fired as a result of the decision both of the United States and of the host country. Such a system was probably as good as any that could be devised; but the emotions which were aroused by the proliferation of atomic and nuclear weapons, and the obvious predominance of the United States as the common partner in all such dual arrangements, meant that the problem of control would continue to worry the alliance and, at least until 1965, defy solution.

Meanwhile the major allies in the western alliance sought to repair the damage which had been done to their relationship by the Suez expedition. At the end of February 1957 Mollet travelled to Washington for discussions with Eisenhower, at the end of which they were able to publish a communiqué which avoided direct reference to their differences over the Middle East and concentrated on the points of agreement between them. By this time ill health had brought Eden's retirement as prime minister of Britain (on 9 January) and he had been succeeded by Macmillan, the first object of whose policy was to re-establish relations with the United States. In March he had discussions with Mollet, and then went to Bermuda for talks with Eisenhower, on the latter's suggestion. Great progress was made in setting the Anglo-American relationship on its earlier footing, by these two men, who had worked together some fourteen years earlier in North Africa. The United States agreed to participate in the military committee of the Baghdad pact; and an agreement in principle was worked out for the supply of guided missiles by the United States to Great Britain. Six months later, from 23 to 25 October, Eisenhower and Macmillan, with their foreign ministers, had further talks in Washington, at the end of which they said in their official communiqué:[5] 'We have met together as trusted friends of many years who have come to head the Governments of our respective countries. These two countries have close and historic ties, just as each has intimate and unbreakable ties with other free countries.' As a more tangible indication of the harmony of their views, it was announced that the president would request Congress to amend the Atomic Energy Act 'as may be necessary and desirable to permit of close and fruitful collaboration of scientists and engineers of Great Britain and the United States and other friendly countries'.

In this way much had been done to restore the 'special relationship' between Britain and the United States, which persistently recurred as a factor in international politics in spite of the prognostications of political scientists who predicted its termination and in spite of differences and tensions which threatened to disrupt it permanently. For France in contrast it was more difficult to restore full relations with the United States or with other members of the alliance, because of the full-scale war which was now going on in Algeria.

We have already seen how the concept of French 'Union' which had been invented with the foundation of the Fourth Republic had fallen by the wayside as a result of the unwillingness of the French colonies to continue in a quasi-federal association with France. Meanwhile in North Africa two of the French protectorates had found their way to independence with little bloodshed, but equally with little assistance from France. In Tunisia, negotiations which had begun between the French government and the Neo-Destour party in 1949 were broken off two years later and the Tunisian ministers arrested and exiled to the south. After three years of revolt and repression Mendès France, in the short period of office which ended

[5] RIIA *Documents, 1957*, p. 400.

the war in Indo-China and the impasse over EDC, entered into successful negotiations with the Tunisians which resulted in internal autonomy, soon to be followed by independence. Habib Bourguiba returned from exile to become prime minister under the bey and then, in 1957, president. In Morocco the sultan, Mohammed V, led the nationalist *Istiqlal* movement, and as a result he was deposed and taken into exile in 1953. However this only served to increase his prestige in his own country, where there was no rival movement of any strength and where the leader whom the French had put in Mohammed's place, el Glaoui, made his submission to the sultan in 1955. There was then no course for the French government to follow but to bring Mohammed back and negotiate Morocco's independence with him.

The whole experience of France's relations with these two North African protectorates had revealed the difficulty which the government encountered in dealing with right-wing opinion in its own country, and even more with the army and the administration in North Africa. In Paris the settlers and their friends formed a powerful parliamentary lobby; from Paris the French government had little power to ensure that its own civil servants and officers carried out its policies. The arrest and removal of Mohammed V was a striking example of this; it was neither commanded nor authorized by Bidault, the minister responsible, although he accepted responsibility and justified the action afterwards.

These difficulties were present in even stronger form in Algeria, where they were enhanced by the almost universal assumption in France that Algerian independence was inconceivable. Unlike Morocco and Tunisia, which were French protectorates, Algeria had been governed as part of France. This had meant that Algerians, whose forbears for ten centuries had known no unified independent state, had been profoundly influenced by French culture and, in the case of Ferhat Abbas and Messali Hadj, had married French wives; while Frenchmen, both settlers whose ancestors had made their home in Algeria since the 1830s and the inhabitants of metropolitan France, regarded the union of France and Algeria as indissoluble. Mendès France negotiated internal autonomy for Tunisia against the opposition of the right; but confronted with revolt in Algeria he said: 'One does not compromise when it comes to defending peace at home and the unity and integrity of the Republic. The Algerian départements are part of the French Republic. They have been French for a long time, and they are irrevocably French.'[6] Nevertheless the actual government of Algeria, where a population of a million Frenchmen lived side by side with 8–9 million Muslims, was complex, and designed to ensure the dominance of the French minority. Executive power was vested in a governor-general, appointed by and responsible to the French government. The Algerian statute provided for an Algerian assembly, of which half was to be elected by the French in Algeria, but which never achieved any effective existence. Algeria elected deputies to the French National Assembly; but it was impossible to give representation in proportion to population without producing a situation where Algeria ruled France; and the elections were always controlled by the French minority.

In these circumstances the first reaction of the French government to the revolt which broke out in 1954 was to try to apply the Algerian statute and give life to the institutions it had sought to create. In doing so, they were unaware that in the years since the war a nationalist movement had grown up whose demand could only be for independence. Even had the FLN (*Front de la libération nationale*) sought autonomy within a French framework (which it did not), it could only have done so on terms of equality between French and Muslim populations in Algeria and proportional representation between Algeria and metropolitan France. It was thus impossible for any French government to win support in the French Assembly for concessions to the FLN which would make negotiation possible. Moreover the French settlers, dependent as they were on the French government at home, had no respect for its authority; while the French administration in Algeria had acquired effective autonomy to act on its own initiative rather than on orders from Paris.

Events in the rest of the former French empire only strengthened the FLN's resolve. Algeria's neighbours, Tunisia and Morocco, were now sovereign states, although still dependent on French financial and defence support. They trod an uneasy path between support for the FLN and the maintenance of

[6] Speech in the National Assembly, 12 Nov. 1954; quoted by Dorothy Pickles *Algeria and France* (1964), p. 33.

their relations with France. In Black Africa growing nationalism was met by speedy and effective reforms; in June 1956 Gaston Deferre as minister for Overseas France carried through a *loi-cadre* which provided for assemblies elected by universal suffrage with very wide powers over their own affairs, and with something very close to responsible African government.

But in Algeria deadlock had been reached. The exploit of the local French authorities in removing Mohammed V was capped by the arrest of Ben Bella and four other FLN leaders who were flying from Rabat to Tunis in a Moroccan aircraft provided by the sultan of Morocco but piloted by a Frenchman who landed it at Algiers, thereby presenting the premier, Mollet, with a *fait accompli*. But neither side could achieve military victory. The FLN could not drive out the French army but neither could the army achieve lasting 'pacification'. Both sides therefore resorted to harsh extremities: the FLN to terrorism, and the French to torture to extract information. Most important, the French army in Algeria came to acquire a personality and independence of its own. It was led by officers many of whom had scarcely visited metropolitan France since the beginning of the Indo-China war, and who before that had been put in the position of having to decide whether their loyalty was to the Vichy government or to de Gaulle. These were men toughened by the exigencies of war and confident of a mission which they believed to be political and social as well as military, who had little respect for coalition governments in Paris and ceased to regard themselves as necessarily subject to their authority.

Unable to achieve victory in Algeria or to carry the struggle into France, the FLN sought support for its cause in the world arena. Their friends brought the Algerian case before the United Nations, as similar action had previously been taken on behalf of Tunisia and Morocco; the French delegation sought to avoid discussion of what it regarded as domestic issues, justified its record when it was obliged to do so; and on one occasion walked out in reaction to a resolution hostile to France.

In NATO, as in the United Nations, the French government expected to receive the support of its allies without question; but this they were extremely loath to give. In varying degrees sympathetic to French difficulties in Algeria, they were aware of the extent to which competition for the goodwill of the new states had become part of rivalry in the cold war. They had

454 A HISTORY OF WAR AND PEACE

no wish to be associated with the 'imperialism' of France in Algeria and they had good reason to establish friendly relations with Tunisia and Morocco (where the United States had successfully negotiated the right to maintain air bases).

These complex events came to a head in the spring of 1958. In France a new bill had been introduced at the end of 1957 to give Algeria something less than independence; but on 8 February French military aircraft, without direction from the French government in Paris, bombed the Tunisian village of Sakiet. Bourguiba sought to use this incident to press France towards a settlement, and proposed the good offices of Britain and the United States as well as the North African countries. An Anglo-American mission travelled to Tunis to assist in restoring Franco-Tunisian relations; it won little sympathy with the French. In April the French government fell, and nearly a month passed before Pflimlin succeeded as prime minister.

The result was that in Algeria the settlers and the army now united in opposition to a government which they regarded as unstable and ineffective, which threatened to make concessions to the FLN and to allow the internationalization of the conflict. An insurrection was carried out against no effective opposition in Algiers, and a Committee of Public Safety set up. But there was no one amongst the insurrectionaries who had the authority or the will to take power in France; instead they looked to de Gaulle as the one man who could lead an effective French government and settle the Algerian question. In France itself various politicians had for some time been in touch with de Gaulle, and with the whole security of France threatened by military insurrection or communist exploitation of the crisis, de Gaulle alone appeared capable of safeguarding the Republic. For de Gaulle himself the moment had come, after twelve years of waiting, when he could once again assume responsibility for the destiny of France. He was asked by the president to form a government and was invested by the Assembly on 1 June 1958.

De Gaulle inherited the problem of Algeria and that of the French empire; he inherited also a political system notorious for the instability and ineffectiveness of its governments. It took him four years and the utmost use of skilful politics and of his own authority to resolve the problem of Algeria. Those who had brought him to power from North Africa profoundly miscalculated his attitude to the FLN. We have already seen that de Gaulle recognized nationalism as the only strong and irresistible force in politics, and that the whole experience of the war showed how little importance he attached to ideology. He estimated, therefore, that it would be impossible in the long run to subdue the Algerians against their will, just as he had said that it would be impossible for the Soviet Union to maintain indefinitely its rule over eastern Europe. In trying to achieve the impossible – if indeed it should prove to be the case that the Algerians rejected association with France – France would only weaken itself more and more, and thus be incapable of playing its proper part in European and world politics, indeed would be incapable of achieving the greatness which was an indispensable part of its nature. The logical outcome of the argument was independence for Algeria; but it was only with infinite care in making grand speeches which did not reveal his full thoughts and intentions that de Gaulle moved towards this position. In doing so he succeeded in what had been impossible for the governments of the Fourth Republic, namely in maintaining his authority over the settlers, the administration, and the army in Algeria. To this end it was of great importance that in 1958 he had come to power legally, and achieved a constitutional succession, ratified by referendum, from the Fourth to the Fifth Republics. His legal authority was thus indisputable and he added to it in January 1961 by a referendum in which the French people declared their acceptance of 'self-determination' as the basis for settlement in Algeria. From this position of strength he was able to force down a second revolt on the part of the army in Algeria – even though the frustrations and emotions of those who thought themselves betrayed found their way into the terrorist but ineffective OAS (*Organisation de l'Armée secrète*) and into attempts to assassinate de Gaulle.

Negotiations began in secret between the French government and the GPRA (*Gouvernement provisoire de la République algérienne*) in October 1961. They were carried on in the town of Évian, and the bitterness engendered by the war was demonstrated by the death by bombing of the mayor, innocent host to the discussions. However, agreement was reached and signed in March 1962. The war which had sapped French energy over eight years and changed the structure of government in France itself was brought to an end. Algeria became an independent state, while certain French rights, including the exploitation of oil in the Sahara and the use of the naval base of Mers el Kebir, were safeguarded.

Having acquired a stable authority in France surpassing that of any previous government for nearly a century, de Gaulle used his position to give an entirely new direction to French foreign policy, and indeed to introduce a new style into international politics. Only when the Algerian problem was settled was he fully free to do so; but already the elements of the attitude were evident. On 24 September 1958 de Gaulle sent letters, which have never been published, to Eisenhower and Macmillan proposing important changes in the political direction of NATO, in which he is reported to have advocated a three-power directorate of NATO, the three powers being Britain, France, and the United States, which, having themselves world-wide responsibilities, could extend the purview of NATO to cover the whole world. Whatever reply was given, it was obviously not one which acceded to de Gaulle's proposals.

Even had his suggestions been accepted, he would have remained unconvinced of the principles on which the North Atlantic alliance was founded. Believing in nationalism as the strongest force in politics, de Gaulle considered the nation state as the only form of political organization which could be regarded as stable and effective. Authority was only possible within the nation state, and in the last resort nations would act in their own interests. Some states were naturally bound together in an alliance – provided the limitations of any alliance were recognized. Only in face of an actual threat from the Soviet Union were the United States and the European countries bound together in any natural form of alliance; to suppose otherwise was to court the risk of American withdrawal from the continent of Europe, leaving the European countries denuded of defence forces and lowered in morale. Within Europe co-operation was indispensable, and could most effectively be achieved, in spite of past conflicts, between Germany and France; but to pursue the political unity of Europe, to hope for integration rather than co-operation, was to chase a chimera. It was possible that Britain might abandon its traditional attitude to external relations as Germany had abandoned its aggressiveness; but proof had to be given of Britain's intention to do so. Most defective of all the new political organizations was the United Nations organization, which was furthest removed from reality in giving equal voice to states regardless of their power and in creating words without authority.

On 13 March 1959 the French Mediterranean fleet was withdrawn from NATO command, in war as well as peace, and in June the French government announced that it could not permit nuclear stockpiling on its territory unless it were allowed to participate in control of nuclear weapons. In response the supreme commander decided to withdraw nine American fighter and fighter bomber squadrons from bases in eastern France and to redeploy them in Britain and western Germany. Meanwhile the French pressed ahead with the development of atomic and nuclear weapons, and of aeroplanes to deliver them. This was not a new venture – the government of the Fourth Republic had initiated the development of nuclear capability; but it was taken up by de Gaulle as a central part of foreign and defence policy. Above all de Gaulle attached prime importance to the nuclear striking force as indispensable to French defence and to France's status as a great power. Undoubtedly he would have welcomed co-operation with Britain and the United States in the development of nuclear weapons; but they were intended as an instrument of national policy, and de Gaulle remained opposed to any attempt to create a system of direction or control based on the alliance. On 13 February 1960 the first French atomic device was exploded in the Sahara; by 1964 France had developed an atomic capability based on a bomber force, which depended for refuelling on planes purchased from the United States.

British policy towards Europe did not change as a result of de Gaulle's accession to power. The attempt to build a free trade area in Europe, based on OEEC and including the EEC as well as the other western European states, reached a dead end in 1959. In 1960 OEEC was succeeded by the Organization for Economic Co-operation and Development – no longer a European grouping but 'a rich man's club', of which Japan and the United States became members.

In the course of the discussions surrounding the Maudling

committee, however, it was evident that there was still a close similarity of view between Britain and the Scandinavian countries. Out of this harmony of view, and resulting from the impossibility of reaching a settlement for Europe as a whole, developed the proposal for a free trade area between the countries other than the Six. In July 1959 ministers from seven countries – those of Scandinavia, Austria, Portugal, Switzerland, and Britain – met at Stockholm and devised a convention to establish a European Free Trade Area, whose members would carry out tariff reductions between themselves to keep up with those provided for in the Rome treaty for the Six.

The motives behind the formation of EFTA were various. It had obvious economic advantages for its members, and there was little difficulty in agreeing on the details of the convention, which affected industrial goods, with a special Anglo-Danish concession on bacon and blue cheese. (Canned fish was counted as an industrial product; it was more difficult to decide whether frozen fish fillets should be classed with fresh or canned fish.) But it was also assumed that the formation of EFTA would facilitate negotiations with the Six. It was argued that EFTA would demonstrate that a free trade area as distinct from a customs union was a practical possibility, and the creation of EFTA would result in the establishment of a free market which would be attractive to the Six and so make them more eager to build a bridge between the Six and the Seven. In the event these arguments proved fallacious. Although the Six had indeed argued the difficulties of a free trade area, they had chosen a customs union not because it was more practical but because it was what they wanted; and in so far as EFTA was attractive to the Six, it was so to those who most wanted to keep the union as open to the rest of Europe as possible, rather than to the French, who all along had insisted that a country must accept commitments to the Economic Community before it could benefit from the freeing of trade.

The Conservative government in Britain under the premiership of Harold Macmillan was re-elected in October 1959 – the Conservatives achieving the unusual feat of increasing their majority for the second time. It was in a strong position to review Britain's place in the world and envisage radical changes. As the new decade opened the most outstanding development in

Europe appeared to be not the successful launching of EFTA but the progress made by the common market, while outside Europe that most traditional of British associations, the Commonwealth, seemed subject to increasing divergences amongst its members.

This was a period of successful decolonization on the part of the British government. For five years since 1954 they had sought to maintain order in Cyprus against the insistent demands of the Greek Cypriots for union with Greece and the growing enmity between Greeks and Turks in the island. In February 1959 an agreement between the Greek and Turkish governments was the prelude to British withdrawal from the whole of the island, with the exception of two sovereign bases – and the accession, in March 1961, of Cyprus to membership of the Commonwealth. In British Africa the years 1952–6 had been dominated by the conflict with the Mau Mau in Kenya; in 1957 the independence of Ghana initiated transfer of power to African states, and the new Macmillan government set in motion the steps which would bring African majority rule, and independence, to the states of east Africa.

For many people, particularly in the Labour party, the increased diversity of the Commonwealth made it of greater value as a bridge between the rich and the poor countries of the world and between white and black races. But for the Conservative government the contrast between the rapidly growing economic and political unity of the common market and the fissiparous Commonwealth was striking. In the summer of 1960 the direction in which the government was turning became evident when the cabinet was reconstructed. Heath was taken from the ministry of labour and appointed Lord Privy Seal with special responsibility for European questions; Sandys and Soames, both strong Europeans, were appointed to Commonwealth Relations and Agriculture respectively. Support for a European policy spread amongst the more politically aware of the public; the quality weekly *The Economist* urged such a policy (although Beaverbrook's *Daily Express* prepared to mount a campaign against it ending, when negotiations broke down, with the headline 'Hallelujah'), while less-interested sections of the population began to assume that entry to the common market was only a matter of time.

At the beginning of 1961 another essential element of Britain's external relations added to the forces leading towards Europe. The American elections of November 1960 resulted in an extremely narrow victory – but victory none the less – for John F. Kennedy, and in January his administration took office. There was no reason to expect that the son of a former American ambassador to London would regard the special relationship of Britain and America as more important than America's relations with Europe; and it soon became clear to the British government that their relations with the United States would be diminished if they became outsiders on the fringe of a strong political and economic community in Europe. Gone were the days when Ernest Bevin had seen Britain as a link between Europe and America, which would disappear if Britain were integrated into Europe. Now the American administration made it clear to Macmillan that if Europe were dividing into the Six of the Common Market and the Seven of EFTA, American policy would be on the side of the Six.

The irony of the situation as far as the British were concerned was that for the first time since 1945 there existed on the continent of Europe a strong and decisive political force (other than the communists) opposed to European union, but that the success of the common market in keeping up with its own time-table of tariff reductions and providing rapid growth for its members, the diminishing asset of the Commonwealth, and the attitude of the United States together persuaded the government that it should take the jump into Europe at which successive governments had baulked for so long.

In the judgement of Macmillan and his colleagues, supported by a special committee of civil servants under the chairmanship of Sir Frank Lee, it was now more than ever the case that Britain could not afford to remain outside Europe. The decision was taken to seek entry to the common market, and was announced to the House of Commons on 31 July 1961.

The subsequent negotiations which opened between Britain and the Six in October faced real and substantial difficulties. Britain was trying to enter a Community already in being, not acting as a founder. It had special Commonwealth interests, wider and more diversified than those which the French had overcome (and more complicated, from its own point of view, because of the rejection by Ghana of association with the 'neo-colonialism' of the common market). It was sensitive, as every democratic country is, to the demands of its agriculturalists, and it was more difficult to safeguard their interests because of the differences between the British system of cheap food based on subsidies and the Continental practice of tariffs.

In spite of the difficulties, negotiations made substantial progress. By the beginning of August 1962 agreement had been reached on some of the most important questions in the relationship of the Commonwealth to the common market – as a result of the readiness of the British to sacrifice the system of imperial preference for industrial goods. Macmillan and de Gaulle had met with cordiality and goodwill in June. But as the holiday season approached, an all-night sitting failed to solve the problem of temperate foodstuffs from the old members of the Commonwealth, and the negotiations were adjourned for three months.

In the meanwhile Macmillan made sure of his own political base. A Commonwealth conference meeting in September made clear that Britain's membership of the common market, harmful as it was to the economic interests of some countries and difficult as were the adjustments it called for, would be accepted by the other members – who indeed had little alternative. The following month the Conservative party conference raised scarcely a murmur in opposition to a more radical change of policy than any previous government of the century had made between elections.

Meanwhile the position of France under de Gaulle's leadership had grown even stronger. In March 1962 the Algerian war had come to an end with the signature of the Évian agreements. In September de Gaulle visited Germany, and received an overwhelmingly enthusiastic welcome from the people – to which he responded. Preparations were put in hand for the signature of a Franco-German treaty. The French economy had entered a period of rapid growth, benefiting from the investment and reconstruction of the Fourth Republic.

In such a position of strength de Gaulle might have concluded that British entry to the common market represented no serious threat to French leadership of Europe. The British were unlikely to press for close political integration, and would not be strong enough to break or to rival the new Franco-German coalition. But Britain could not be considered in isolation; for de Gaulle it was always one member of an 'Anglo-Saxon' partnership, and the possibility of British adherence to the treaty of Rome could not be dissociated from the question of Europe's relations with the United States.

On 4 July 1962 President Kennedy made a stirring speech at Philadelphia in which his views of what this relationship should be were clearly expressed. His words fortified the British government in the course in which they were engaged, and won warm approval throughout Europe – except in Gaullist France. He spoke of the interest which the United States had shown in the development of European Union, regarding united Europe 'not as a rival but as a partner'. He went on:

I will say here and now on this day of independence that the United States will be ready for a 'Declaration of Interdependence', that we will be prepared to discuss with a United Europe the ways and means of forming a concrete Atlantic partnership, a mutually beneficial partnership between the new union now emerging in Europe and the old American Union founded here 175 years ago.[7]

There then followed, in the autumn of 1962, a series of events which were to be decisive in the formulation of de Gaulle's policy. Some years earlier the American government had initiated development projects for various kinds of missiles, including Polaris, to be fired from submarines, and Skybolt, to be launched from an aircraft. The British had likewise begun the development of an air-to-ground missile, but had abandoned it because of the expense involved. Instead they had made an agreement with the United States for the supply of Skybolt. From the start it was clear that, other things being equal, a missile fired from a stationary submarine was preferable to one fired from an aircraft travelling little below the speed of sound; and by the end of 1962 it was clear that Polaris was successful. Thereupon Skybolt became a luxury toy, and one which the Kennedy administration could not afford in any circumstances, least of all when one of its domestic objectives was to hold down the budget and initiate tax reform. Had Skybolt failed it would have presented no problem; in fact it succeeded, within its limitations; once successful it would make increasing demands on the defence budget, the more so since it would be the favoured child of the air force and its lobby in Congress.

[7] *DAFR, 1962*, p. 226.

In these circumstances the Kennedy administration decided
to cancel Skybolt. In doing so they provoked domestic opposition, but to no greater extent than they had anticipated. In
Britain in contrast the cancellation threatened to be the straw
to break the political camel's back. The prime minister had
engaged in political manoeuvring of great skill in persuading
his own party to accept on the one hand decolonization in
Africa and the introduction of African majority rule, and on the
other Britain's entry into Europe. Subtly and carefully he had
persuaded the conservative party to yield, in the face of change,
their most cherished positions of imperialism and independence.
The cancellation of Skybolt meant that, in addition, Britain was
threatened with the loss of the independent deterrent, so that
the country would be manifestly dependent on the United
States and the Conservative government would be prey to the
ridicule of the Labour party.

The American government entirely underestimated the
nature and extent of the crisis it had provoked in London. It
expected that the British would want an alternative to Skybolt,
but at the beginning of November saw this as a technical
problem for which a solution could fairly easily be found.[8] In
the following weeks the British government made its position
clear; but as it did so the American administration took
cognizance of the political problem in a fresh dimension. Up to
this time the relationship between the NATO alliance and the
British and American independent deterrents had grown in a
haphazard way. It was Kennedy's intention to grapple with
this problem, but to do so after the negotiations for Britain's
entry into the common market were complete; then, he thought,
it would be possible to give practical implementation to his
ideas of 'interdependence' between a strong united Europe and
the United States. Instead the Skybolt affair gave the question
of the proliferation of nuclear weapons immediate practical
and political importance; in this dimension, as well as in
British politics, the replacement of Skybolt was more than a
technical matter.

Between Britain and the United States, each headed by
politicians of great skill, it was possible to devise a compromise
solution. To meet the requirement of de Gaulle's policies as well
would have been squaring the circle. That this was so rapidly

[8] See a report by Henry Brandon, *Sunday Times*, 8 Dec. 1963.

became evident at the two meetings which Macmillan had in mid-December; the former with de Gaulle at Rambouillet on 15 and 16 December 1962, the second with Kennedy at Nassau on the following two days. At Rambouillet there was little discussion. The barrier of silence could only have been effectively broken had Macmillan been willing to show that he attached more importance to co-operation with France in nuclear matters than with the United States; but for Macmillan to do so would have meant the reversal of British wartime and post-war foreign policy, and the exchange of a first-class nuclear power for a minor partner just developing a nuclear force. In contrast at Nassau Macmillan and Kennedy agreed on the supply of Polaris missiles to the British within the framework of NATO. The agreement read:

> The President and the Prime Minister agreed that the US will make available on a continuing basis Polaris missiles (less warheads) for British submarines. The US will also study the feasibility of making available certain support facilities for such submarines. The UK Government will construct the submarines in which these weapons will be placed and they will also provide the nuclear warheads for the Polaris missiles. . . . These forces, and at least equal US forces, would be made available for inclusion in a NATO multilateral nuclear force. The Prime Minister made it clear that except where Her Majesty's Government may decide that supreme national interests are at stake, these British forces will be used for the purposes of international defense of the Western Alliance in all circumstances.[9]

The extent of the compromise this represented was clear from the way it was described and justified in the two countries, for in Britain it was represented as the retention and safeguarding of the independent deterrent, in the United States as the beginning of a NATO nuclear force.

The offer of Polaris missiles was not made to Britain alone, but to France as well; and de Gaulle gave the offer serious attention. It rapidly became clear, however, how much importance the United States attached to the control of nuclear weapons within NATO, and in France this was interpreted as the continuance of American surveillance over the minor nuclear powers. On these terms de Gaulle had no wish to be admitted into the nuclear club; and the fact of British willingness to accept the Nassau agreement confirmed his never changing view that Britain would place its own interests, and its own subservience to the United States, before the interests of Europe and an alliance with France. The only course open for France was, therefore, to consolidate and cement its reconciliation with Germany, and from the strength of that position to exclude Britain, the 'Trojan horse'[10] of the Anglo-American alliance, from Europe. This intention de Gaulle made clear to the world in a press conference on 14 January 1963; on 22 January Adenauer – in spite of the pressure brought on him not to accept Gaullist policy towards Britain and America – signed the Franco-German treaty; and on 29 January the French foreign minister moved the indefinite adjournment of the Brussels negotiations.

De Gaulle's veto on British entry into the common market and the Franco-German treaty had implications for the common market itself almost as important as the effect on relations with Britain. The manner in which the veto had been imposed was clearly contrary to the spirit of the Community, while the anti-Americanism which inspired it was not shared by the other members. Franco-German co-operation was indispensable to the success of the Community; but Franco-German hegemony could only be a danger to the balance of the Community as a whole. The question at issue over the next few years would therefore be whether the momentum of the Community would carry it forward to closer union, or whether the strength of Gaullism in France would prove a barrier to further progress.

That the Community had its own momentum there could be no doubt. Industrialists and governments in the common market countries made their future plans on the assumption that the Community's timetable would continue to be carried out – not least the French government planned on this assumption. The pressure towards agreement within the Community increased when the Community had to negotiate with outsiders. Britain's application, abortive though it was, had had this effect; negotiations in 1964 for a further reduction of tariffs under GATT – the Kennedy round – produced a similar result.

[10] The phrase is attributed to Peyrefitte, Minister of Information. See Nora Beloff, *The General says No*, for one account of these events.

The institutions of the Community had brought together a body of men with an obvious interest in further progress. Discussions as to whether the Community's Commission constituted a 'supranational' body had ceased to be of great importance beside the evidence of the practical achievement of the Commission in its relations with the Council of Ministers, national governments, and national interests. It practised the art of the possible, using to the full its resources of technical knowledge and planning capacity, its direct relationship with the Community Assembly and with the press, and its machinery for the consultation of national interest groups to keep up a movement towards closer union. Group politics, of the kind so familiar in nation states, now existed at Brussels.

The first years of the Community's life had been relatively easy; much of the movement forward followed from the implementation of the treaty, and involved no sacrifices or major decisions on the part of its members in addition to those they had already made. Progress was also made easier by the fact that this was a period of economic growth – whether as a result of the Community or, as de Gaulle believed to be the case with France, because of the scale of investment in previous years. By 1964, however, greater momentum would be required to achieve the same degree of progress, for progress, if it was to be achieved at all, must now go beyond the bounds of a customs union to economic and political union.

The context in which these important developments might take place was that of agriculture. A customs union which excluded agriculture was scarcely practicable, and the treaty of Rome had provided for the harmonization of agricultural policies. But it had recognized that this could not be done simply by the progressive elimination of quota and tariff barriers. The inflexibilities of agriculture and the strength of farmers in national politics were such that harmonization could only be achieved if the Community were to take over some of the functions of national government. If this could be done, the prize would be great. Not only would a step be taken towards closer economic union, but the Community institutions would have acquired impressive added powers. The progress made would have been the more substantial since the treaty of Rome in any case provided for the introduction of majority voting in the Council of Ministers at the beginning of 1966.

The Commission had already been concerned with the problem of agriculture at the time of the negotiations with Britain in 1962, and after the veto of January 1963 it sought to demonstrate the vitality of the Community by further progress in this direction. It proposed the establishment of a European fund which would be used as compensation for the losses which member countries would incur as a result of harmonization of agriculture and, following an established Community practice, it secured the agreement in principle of the Council of Ministers to a single price for certain agricultural products, wheat chief amongst them. The European Agricultural Guidance and Guarantee Fund was to be raised by means of a levy on those who bought agricultural products cheaply outside the Community; and it would be used both to compensate those farmers, like the Germans, who suffered from a reduction in the price of their products, and to counter the effects of inflation in a country like France where agricultural prices would rise.

A programme of this sort would have been difficult to bring to fruition in the best of circumstances. Price fixing in agriculture is a hazardous task, and governments become increasingly sensitive to the reactions of farmers as elections approach – as they did in Germany in September and France in December 1965. But the decisive factor was the degree of will within the Community and amongst its members, and in this respect the key lay, as always, with France. Of all the six members of the Community, France stood to gain most from an agreement on agriculture. Its agricultural productivity was rising sharply, rural depopulation was accompanied by increased output, and it was in a strong position to take advantage of an enlarged market. On the other hand Gaullist France was most opposed to the movement towards economic and political union. It was the hope of the Europeans that the advantages to France – particularly to de Gaulle now that his leadership began to seem less indispensable to the French – would be sufficient to bring agreement on agriculture, and that the momentum towards union would thus be resumed.

Their hopes were ill founded. Whatever the advantages of an expanded agricultural market to France they were insufficient to induce de Gaulle to accept political union in Europe. The Commission and the other five Community members were moreover in a weak tactical position: agreements had been reached on agriculture as early as 1962, but only in mid-1965 did they link them to political union. At the end of June negotiations reached deadlock, and on 6 July France withdrew its ambassador from the Community, paralysing its activities.

Little indeed was left of Kennedy's 'Grand Design' for Europe and the Atlantic. At one of his periodic press conferences on 8 September 1965 de Gaulle refused any concessions to the common market unless France were given assurances that there would be no moves to further political integration in Europe. He spoke instead of closer ties which were being and should be developed between France and eastern Europe, and of a Greater Europe, from the Atlantic to the Urals, where co-operation would be developed between nation states. His vehemence towards the common market was matched by the terms in which he described France's membership of NATO – 'subordination which is described as integration' – and promised that this would be brought to an end by the time France's commitments expired – 'that is in 1969 at the latest'.

In December de Gaulle won re-election to the presidency by popular vote for the first time, although he had to enter a second ballot, having failed to establish an absolute majority at the first. Destructive as his policies were to European and Atlantic union, they offered little in their place. The alliance with Germany had not flourished, and could scarcely do so in view of the divergent interests of the two countries. De Gaulle's concept of Europe was fundamentally anti-American; but the German Federal Republic was dependent on the United States for the pursuit of its most essential foreign policy objectives with regard to the German Democratic Republic and Berlin. French policy was to develop trade and diplomatic contact with the countries of eastern Europe, while Germany still adhered to the Hallstein doctrine of not establishing diplomatic relations with countries (other than the Soviet Union) which recognized the German Democratic Republic. France had developed an independent nuclear deterrent, believed in its credibility, and was opposed to the Germans acquiring a similar capability; while the Erhard government, while recognizing the impracticability (and illegality under the terms of WEU) of its own manufacture of nuclear weapons, sought greater participation in nuclear affairs.

12

NEW BALANCE AND FRESH CONFLICT

THE early days of the movement to European union coincided with the Berlin crisis and the opening of the cold war. The uncertainties of a decade later resulting from de Gaulle's return to power and the European policy of the British were set against a background of comparable crisis – although the outcome was very different.

The first crisis again arose over Berlin, and was initiated by Khrushchev in November 1958. The motives for his action remain uncertain. Since the days of the Berlin blockade in 1948–9 the position of Berlin itself had not changed substantially. The city was divided; western forces were present in west Berlin by right of occupation and communication was still possible between the two halves of the city. On the other hand conditions in Germany and in the attitudes of the occupying powers had changed in a way that might have appeared decisive. The German Federal Republic was in almost every respect an outstandingly successful nation state. It enjoyed political stability, its government having been confirmed in office in 1953 and being able to look forward with reasonable confidence – justified in the event – to electoral victories in 1957 and 1961. It had pursued a consistent foreign policy which had won the respect of its former enemies in the west and had been rewarded with success in such long-standing questions as the Saar as well as in new designs for European unity. It was economically prosperous, with a high standard of living, and able to support a modern army as an almost equal partner in the North Atlantic alliance.

The GDR was in most respects very different. It too was stable politically, in communist terms. Its government was kept in power by the presence of Russian armed forces; but Ulbricht had survived both Stalinist purges and destalinization more effectively than any of his east European counterparts. But its economy had failed to prosper, collectivization had kept agricultural production at a low level, and the labour force was

469

constantly depleted by the flight of refugees to the west through Berlin.

While the GDR was thus in a sense an incubus within the communist system, the Soviet Union itself had grown greatly in power, and in particular in the achievement of nuclear capability. It had also, as we have seen, changed its policy towards Germany in a way in which the western powers had not. It now promoted the GDR and pressed for a confederation between the two German states as a prelude to reunification, while the western powers continued to insist on German elections as the necessary first step to unification. The Soviet Union urged the neutralization of Germany: the west clung to Germany's right to be a member of NATO. It may have been too that the Russian leadership felt very confident of some great achievement in Germany and Europe which would quite eclipse the experience of the Hungarian revolution, already fading into the past. Indeed that revolution had itself shown how ineffective the nuclear deterrent was as anything less than an ultimate weapon – in spite of which the British government had decided in 1957 to base its defence policy on nuclear weapons. At the same time the disengagement debate of 1957–8 had brought out the attractiveness in the west of some sort of withdrawal from the centre of Europe. Any or all of these considerations, together possibly with the wish for self-vindication *vis-à-vis* China, must have encouraged Khrushchev to probe the western position at Berlin and so, at the very time when he was denouncing Chinese nuclear irresponsibility, to run the risks involved in such a confrontation.

The prelude to the crisis in Germany – it may be that the tension in the Middle East and over Quemoy should also be seen as a prelude – was the exchange of notes by the two German governments, each with the support of its allies. The GDR pressed for a peace treaty, accompanied by discussions between the two German states on unification, which, it said, 'cannot be a matter for foreign powers; . . . it is the innate right of the German people themselves'; and on 27 October Ulbricht argued that the whole of Berlin lay within the territory of the GDR, and that the authority of the western occupying powers no longer had any legal basis. A speech by Khrushchev can, however, be taken as the formal opening of the crisis. On 10 November 1958 he addressed a Polish delegation led by

Gomulka in Moscow. He repeated the familiar arguments about a German peace treaty and the 'unification of the two German states'; but he then went on to denounce the western position in Berlin. He argued that the action of the western powers in western Germany had destroyed the Potsdam agreement, and continued:

What then is left of the Potsdam Agreement? One thing, in effect: The so-called four-power status of Berlin, that is, a position in which the three western powers . . . have the possibility of lording it in Western Berlin, turning that part of the city, which is the capital of the German Democratic Republic, into some kind of state within a state and, profiting by this, conducting subversive activities from Western Berlin against the German Democratic Republic, against the Soviet Union and the other Warsaw Treaty countries. On top of all this, they have the right of unrestricted communication between Berlin and Western Germany through the air space, by the railways, highways and waterways of the German Democratic Republic. . . . The time has obviously arrived for the signatories of the Potsdam Agreement to renounce the remnants of the occupation regime in Berlin and thereby make it possible to create a normal situation in the capital of the German Democratic Republic. The Soviet Union, for its part, would hand over to the sovereign German Democratic Republic the functions in Berlin that are still exercised by Soviet agencies.[1]

These ideas were developed and extended further, and on 27 November a note[2] was delivered to the governments of America, Britain, France, and the German Federal Republic in which the Soviet government reaffirmed its view of the 'patently absurd situation' of Berlin and said that it regarded as null and void agreements on the status of Berlin entered into in 1944 and 1945. It also suggested the possibility of Berlin being a 'free city', saying that it 'finds it possible for the question of West Berlin to be settled for the time being by making West Berlin an independent political entity – a free city – without any state, including either of the existing German states, interfering in its life', and suggesting that the United Nations might be associated with this free city.

In addition the note contained an ultimatum, for it made clear that the Soviet government would allow a period of six months in which a change of status of west Berlin could be

[1] *Soviet News*, 11 Nov. 1958.   [2] RIIA *Documents, 1958*, p. 146.

made. The ultimatum was not clear-cut; the Soviet government said that 'it regards this period as quite adequate for finding a sound basis for a solution', and it also said that 'if the above period is not used for reaching an appropriate agreement, the Soviet Union will effect the planned measures by agreement with the German Democratic Republic'.[3] Soon afterwards, this was extended to a threat to make a separate peace treaty with the GDR if no agreement was reached.

In reply the western powers reaffirmed their right to be in Berlin, which they said derived from the unconditional surrender of Germany, and could not be unilaterally abrogated; right of access, they said, followed from this. But in fact they were faced with a grave predicament. Their position in Berlin was fragile. Its military defence was dependent on nuclear weapons. At the same time it appeared – and was – very easy for Khrushchev to implement his threat to transfer control of the access to Berlin to the GDR. If this were done it would undermine the whole western policy towards Germany, since they would be forced to recognize the east German authorities if they were to retain access to Berlin. More than that, it would remove one of the slender pillars on which their position in Berlin rested. The nearer that the GDR approached to full sovereignty – which would be achieved if a peace treaty were actually signed – the more anomalous would western troops in Berlin and the right of communication appear. The supreme anomaly of a divided Germany, one-half of it under a government uncceptable to a majority of the people, would be eclipsed by the consequent anomaly of a western presence in Berlin. Moreover this could apparently be achieved without any dramatic coup, merely by the handing over of authority from the Soviet Union to the GDR, behind the shield of a Russian guarantee that an attack on the GDR would be an attack on itself. Nor did Khrushchev's speech or the note of 27 November offer any substantial possibility of a new agreement which would preserve any part of the western position intact. Even the proposal for a 'free city' was described as a solution 'for the time being' when it spoke of 'unhindered communications between the Free City and the outside world'. Its rather ambiguous reference to guarantees was linked to west

Berlin's undertaking 'not to permit on its territory any hostile subversive activity directed against the GDR or any other state'.

The Soviet government enjoyed an additional advantage, in that the crisis had been provoked at a time when the American government was entering a period of considerable weakness. The Khrushchev ultimatum would expire just as the long-drawn-out process of an American presidential election – to replace a president who, by the terms of the constitution, could not be re-elected – was getting under way. Secretary Dulles, who had dominated and directed American foreign policy since January 1953, was a sick man. In February 1959 he went into hospital and his duties were taken over by his under-secretary, Christian Herter; in April he resigned and Herter replaced him; a month later he died. On the other hand there was one clear limitation on Khrushchev's freedom of action: he was aware of the dangers of nuclear war, and equally aware that if the western powers were pressed too far, and were determined to defend their position, the risk of such war would be grave. These circumstances explain the drawn-out moves in the Berlin crisis over the succeeding years. On the one hand the vacillation of western policy concealed a fundamental determination to stand firm; on the other the toughness of Khrushchev's speeches and notes always left an escape route open should he meet with adamant resistance from the west.

When the western powers replied to Khrushchev's note of 27 November a month after receiving it they insisted that Berlin was not a problem to be considered by itself, and indicated their willingness to discuss the whole question of German unification and a peace treaty. To this Khrushchev had no objection; on the contrary he immediately proposed the holding of a summit conference to make this possible; but his interpretation of a peace treaty was quite different from that of the west; for him this would be a peace treaty with the two German states. At the same time the government of the GDR provided an additional element in the discussions in a note to the Soviet government, when it spoke of a confederation between the two German states, and referred for the first time (although obliquely) to the possibility of a separate peace treaty between itself and the Soviet Union.

At the beginning of the new year the crisis softened in certain respects, without any change which might contribute towards an eventual solution. While Khrushchev now became explicit in saying that the Soviet Union would sign a separate peace treaty with the GDR if no agreement was reached, he also spoke of the Soviet government's continued support for the 1956 Anglo-French plan for graduated reduction of forces. In January Mikoyan went to the United States 'on holiday', and engaged in trade talks with Eisenhower, Dulles, and Dillon, as well as addressing some 1,100 business men at a meeting of the Economic Club. On 10 January a fresh Soviet note proposing a peace conference in Prague or Warsaw, and accompanied by a Soviet draft of a German peace treaty, was sent to the western powers, who in return proposed a foreign ministers' conference, with the participation of the German Federal Republic and the GDR. On 24 January, on his return from the United States, Mikoyan said:

> We have not issued any ultimatums to anyone and have not threatened anyone. . . . The fact of fixing a date for the conclusion of the talks is not terrifying in itself. Talks cannot go on for ever. The main thing in our proposal is not the date for ending the talks, but the talks themselves, the necessity of their being held.[4]

In these circumstances (and with the effective elimination of Dulles by illness), Macmillan decided to go to Moscow for what he called 'reconnaissance, but I learn that has some sinister significance translated into Russian'. His proposal of a visit was accepted by the Russians and he arrived in Moscow, accompanied by Selwyn Lloyd, on 21 February. To the press and the public of the world Khrushchev's attitude during the visit remained puzzling; he described the idea of a foreign ministers' meeting as 'absurd', and proposed an Anglo-Soviet non-aggression treaty; he suddenly proposed accompanying his British guests to Kiev, and as suddenly cancelled his proposal, pleading toothache; but on their return they were met at the airport by Mikoyan. In total, however, the visit resulted in – or at least was accompanied by – an improvement in the tone of the relationship. On 2 March the Soviet reply to the western government's suggestion of a foreign ministers' conference spoke of a 'possible dangerous course of events' which could be averted by a summit meeting, but that if the west

---

[4]*Soviet News*, 28 Jan. 1959.

were not ready for a conference the Soviet Union considers that 'a conference of Foreign Ministers of the USSR, Great Britain, France, Poland, and Czechoslovakia should be summoned', together with the participation of the two German governments, as the British proposed. The communiqué[5] which was put out at the end of the Macmillan visit stressed the importance of 'achieving agreement to stop nuclear weapons tests under an effective system of international inspection and control' – and the discussions which had taken place on this topic may well have paved the way, as Macmillan later claimed, for a test-ban treaty in 1963. On Berlin they stated their disagreement, but recognized the importance of early negotiations.

Tension and relaxation continued through the spring months. United States aircraft were 'buzzed' in the air corridor to Berlin on the grounds that they had no right to fly above 10,000 feet; the United States government said they had the right, but would not exercise it for the moment. Negotiations went forward for a foreign ministers' conference, and this eventually met on 16 May. It was, however, abortive. It began with a dispute as to an appropriate arrangement for the seats of the German representatives; it then moved to the more substantial matter of a western proposed 'package plan' for reunification and security; and the Soviet Union proposed that troops should stay for a further twelve months in Berlin, while an all-German committee, with equal representation from east and west, should consider reunification and a peace treaty – if by then no agreement was reached, the Soviet Union would sign a peace treaty with the GDR. Between these two positions no reconciliation proved possible, and the conference, having dispersed once from 23 May to 13 July, finally broke up. However, Khrushchev's original six-month period for a solution of the crisis was now past and almost forgotten; and conversations continued; on 3 August it was announced that Khrushchev had accepted an invitation to visit the United States in the summer, and Eisenhower had accepted a similar invitation to the Soviet Union in the autumn.

In this way the apparent harmonizing of views between the two sides, and the impression of *détente* between the United States and the Soviet Union continued to increase. At the beginning of September the Soviet Union succeeded in sending

[5] RIIA, *Documents, 1959*, p. 11.

a rocket to hit the moon; the four powers announced the setting up of a ten-power Disarmament Commission which would report to the United Nations Commission; and on 15 September Khrushchev arrived in the United States for a two-week visit. He travelled across the continent, and for much of the time showed all the skill and enjoyment of an American politician seeking election or nomination. He was repeatedly questioned about the meaning of his statement that the Soviet Union would bury the United States, and in reply stressed the theme of competitive coexistence. In New York he said:

> I want to concentrate not on what disunites us, but . . . what, on the contrary, are the major points that unite us. . . . If you like capitalism, and I am sure that you do, God's with you. Continue in your efforts. But take care. A new system has emerged, a system that . . . has started to tread on your heels. And if – if at any time you start lagging behind, then we will certainly surpass you.[6]

He was given a standing ovation after this speech; at other times he broke out of the police cordons to shake hands with the crowd. He amused the world by being shocked at the making of the film *Can-Can* and protesting when he was not allowed to visit Disneyland because the police could not guarantee his security; only once or twice did he show Khrushchevian anger, saying that 'If you want an arms race, we accept the challenge . . . it took me 12 hours to get here; it will take me only $10\frac{1}{2}$ hours to get back.'

Khrushchev not only displayed himself to the American public. He addressed the United Nations Assembly, and met Eisenhower informally at the latter's mountain lodge at Camp David. On the former occasion the world hung on his words, expecting dramatic new proposals towards disarmament; in the event he suggested a three-stage plan towards general and complete disarmament which provided no obvious solution to the old problem of how this might be achieved. As an interim programme he suggested the disarmament of central Europe – the establishment of a denuclearized zone, withdrawal of all foreign troops from territories of European states, liquidation of military bases, and the conclusion of a non-aggression pact between the NATO and Warsaw treaty states – in which there was nothing new.

[6] *New York Times*, 18 Sept. 1959.

The meeting of Eisenhower and Khrushchev at Camp David was potentially of considerable importance and significance; but its actual outcome was limited. Eisenhower went some way towards the Soviet position when he said, in his press conference afterwards, 'we agreed, in addition to what we said in the communiqué, that these negotiations [over Berlin] should not be prolonged indefinitely but there could be no fixed time limit on them'. The communiqué itself had spoken of general disarmament, the reopening of conversations on Berlin, and the development of trade.

Throughout these exchanges the attitude of the British and American governments had been very similar. But the Berlin crisis had touched the interests and evoked the fears of other parties. First amongst these were the two German governments themselves. The Ulbricht régime stood to gain greatly from a settlement of Berlin and Germany along the lines proposed by the Soviet Union; the prolongation of the crisis with its accompanying uncertainty only exaggerated still further the basic difficulties of eastern Germany. Kept in power by its own coercive force and that of the Russians, the government of the GDR could not hope to enlist the support or co-operation of its people; but when it sought to increase efficiency by greater direction and control it was open to the inhabitants to leave, in spite of the risks and the hardships which this involved; and the most important escape route which they could take was through Berlin. Thus in 1957 some 260,000 refugees arrived in west Berlin or west Germany from the east; in 1958 there were 204,000. In the summer of 1958 the government engaged in a more rigorous campaign against independent doctors, as a result of which the refugee numbers rose in the months of July and August to 19,000 and 21,500 respectively – including a large number of doctors. In the spring of 1960 the government intensified its programme of farm collectivization and in the month of April 1960 some 17,000 refugees left, the highest monthly total for eighteen months. It was obvious, therefore, that the Ulbricht government would want above all to seal Berlin off from the west and to 'normalize' the situation in the sense of closing the frontiers of east Germany as those of other east European states were closed.

In the west the government of the German Federal Republic could not but be alarmed about the possibilities of some agreement between the United States and the Soviet Union which would sacrifice its interests or weaken its defensive position. In the immediate event their policy won support from de Gaulle, who viewed the readiness of Macmillan and Eisenhower to negotiate with the Russians with considerable scepticism. No doubt de Gaulle would have been more hesitant in his relations with west Germany had the objective of reunification been nearer to achievement; but for the time being an effective alliance between the two continental European powers was possible – and was soon to be more fully developed in a Franco-German treaty.

The opposition of a Franco-German point of view to the tentative negotiations of Macmillan and Eisenhower was evident as soon as Macmillan visited the European capitals on his way home from Moscow in the spring of 1959. It increased during the summer, and was heightened still further by the Camp David conversations. Adenauer's anxiety, and the difficulty of his position, were enhanced by covert overtures on the part of the Russian ambassador in Bonn to the SPD. De Gaulle for his part outlined on 21 October 1959 three conditions which should be fulfilled before a summit conference took place: there should be a more prolonged period of *détente* in which advantage could be taken of the contacts which existed between the Soviet Union and the western powers; there should be serious and intensive discussion between the western powers themselves as to their strategy and intentions at a summit meeting; and there should be personal contact between himself and Khrushchev. 'Happily', he said, 'this third preliminary condition seems likely to be fulfilled', as Khrushchev had agreed to come to France.

None the less the three western powers met in December 1959, and agreed to invite Khrushchev to a summit meeting in Paris in April 1960 – after an exchange of letters the date of 16 May was finally agreed. Meanwhile de Gaulle's Republic became increasingly prominent in world affairs. In February it became an atomic power; at the end of March Khrushchev visited France, and a few days after his departure de Gaulle made a state visit to Britain; in April he visited Canada and the United States. Adenauer for his part went to Washington in March for conversations with Herter and Eisenhower, and spoke of the possibility of a plebiscite in west Berlin, thereby indicating his almost desperate anxiety to prevent the United States making concessions to Berlin in response to Russian threats which he, like de Gaulle, believed to be unreal.

More important however was the fact that, as the proposed summit meeting drew nearer, the American government was forced to examine the hard core of its policy over Berlin – and did so in the face of the pressure coming from Adenauer and de Gaulle. As soon as this was done it was obvious that it had not moved any distance towards accepting the demands and proposals which Khrushchev had been putting forward since 1958, even though it had gone so far in an effort to create an atmosphere of harmony in relations with the Soviet Union. In consequence, in April 1960 both Herter and Dillon (who had succeeded Herter as under-secretary when he replaced Dulles) made speeches in which they reaffirmed a policy towards Germany which had been glossed over for some months, although never abandoned. They denounced the idea of a separate peace treaty, which Dillon said would be 'skating on very thin ice', and reiterated instead the need for a peace treaty with an all-German government formed after plebiscites in the whole country. Dillon said that while the United States government was willing to discuss measures to reduce tension over Berlin, they would not accept any arrangement 'which might become a first step towards the abandonment of Berlin'.[7]

The summit conference at which these speeches were angled never took place. On 5 May Khrushchev announced that an American reconnaissance plane had been shot down by a rocket over the Soviet Union. The United States said that a National Aeronautics and Space Administration weather research aircraft was missing after getting into difficulty over the north Turkey area. On 7 May Khrushchev gave a fuller report, as he was able to do since the pilot of the plane had been interrogated and the plane itself examined. Both interrogation and examination showed that the plane had taken off from Peshawar to fly across the Soviet Union and land in Norway, taking photographs on the way. Thereupon the State Department admitted that a U2 plane had flown such a mission to 'obtain information now concealed behind the iron curtain', and that similar flights had been going on for four years. On 9 May

[7] *DAFR, 1960*, p. 107.

Herter said that: 'the Government of the United States would be derelict to its responsibility . . . if it did not, in the absence of Soviet cooperation, take such measures as are possible unilaterally to lessen and overcome the danger of surprise attack'.[8] On 11 May Eisenhower gave a press conference in confirmation of the State Department view.

Khrushchev denounced the 'spy flights' of the United States with the utmost vigour, and made it abundantly clear that the summit conference could not go on unless the United States gave a full apology. He demanded that those responsible be punished; gave warnings to Turkey, Pakistan, and Norway, where the U2 bases were situated, and called for a meeting of the Security Council. After a brief meeting on the morning of 16 May the summit conference of 1960 was at an end.

The relationship between the U2 incident and the summit conference is not clear. It is generally assumed, however, that Khrushchev had reached the conclusion that he would gain nothing from the meeting, and that it had better therefore not take place. It is suggested that he believed his varied diplomacy since November 1958 to have softened Eisenhower to the point where important concessions would be made, and then to have realized at the last minute that this was not so. However that may be, it was noticeable that Khrushchev appeared careful not to make a full breach in relations with the west. He proposed that the conference be postponed for six to eight months and that Eisenhower's visit should also be postponed, although in six months' time a new American president would have been elected, to take office in January 1961.

By this time a fresh challenge to the American position and a new source of potential danger to the world had emerged in the Caribbean, only some 150 miles from the coast of Florida. On 2 December 1956 Fidel Castro had landed in the Oriente province of Cuba with 82 men, of whom a mere 12 survived to escape into the hills. For three years this handful of men increased in numbers, acquired arms, and gathered increasing popular support in opposition to the dictatorial régime of Batista. Having at first scoffed at a handful of revolutionaries, the government now had to face an ever growing threat to its authority; and could think of no way of doing so other than to increase the degree of terror and dictatorship, thereby divesting itself of the support which moderate men and men of property will usually give to legal authority. On 1 January 1959 Batista decided that his own life was more important than his régime, and fled to the Dominican Republic; Castro proclaimed Urrutia president, and made a triumphal entry into Havana. Urrutia established a government under the premiership of Cardona; but on 16 February Castro replaced Cardona and thus assumed a formal position appropriate to the power and leadership which he held.

During the revolution Castro had given no indication that he was other than a radical reformer, and claimed to owe allegiance to Montesquieu as much as to Marx. Nor did this change as he assumed power, and in consequence he received warm support in the United States, where the majority of the people had felt increasing discomfort at the association of their government with Batista's police dictatorship. In mid-April 1959 Castro paid an unofficial visit to the United States; he spoke of good relations and good understanding, said that Cuba would adhere to the pan-American defence pact, and stated that his government would not confiscate foreign property, but would on the contrary encourage private investment. He had a ticker-tape parade through New York, and addressed a crowd of some 30,000 in Central Park, expressing pleasure and confidence that the 'rich nation of the world has understood our cause'.

In May 1959, however, relations between Cuba and the United States began to deteriorate as the Castro government showed itself to be increasingly extreme in its internal policies and to align itself more and more with the Soviet bloc. The fundamental reasons for this change are still obscure. It may be that the deterioration had the same degree of inevitability as the rupture between church and state in France during the revolution. The extent of American property ownership in Cuba, and the importance of the United States as the chief importer of Cuban sugar were such that if Castro were determined to break Cuban dependence on America he could scarcely avoid alienating the United States and establishing links with the Soviet Union; and once this process had started, action and counteraction could rapidly escalate. It may have been that after three years of revolutionary war Castro was carried away by the emotions of nationalism or by the calculation that external tension would add to his internal authority; or it may be that he had hitherto been brilliantly successful in concealing his attachment to the Soviet bloc and minimizing the importance of his brother Raúl's membership of the communist party.

Whatever the explanation, the events were characterized by clumsy economic warfare between Cuba and the United States, a growing association between Cuba and the Soviet bloc, and the imprisonment and execution by Castro of his opponents, thereby provoking them into counter-action which in 1961 the United States found itself supporting. At the beginning of June 1959 an agrarian reform law was passed, which provided for the expropriation of American-owned sugar mills and plantations; it evoked the protest of the United States government, which did not dispute the right of the Cuban government to nationalize private property, but insisted on proper compensation. During the autumn of 1959 and the following spring mass trials occurred instead of the promised elections (which Castro now described as 'unnecessary'); meanwhile private planes from bases in Florida raided the sugar plantations and damaged the crop. In February 1960 Mikoyan visited Cuba and agreed to purchase sugar, as well as offering a loan and Soviet technical assistance; in June Jiménez (director of the Agriarian Reform Institute) visited the Soviet bloc, and negotiated an agreement with the Soviet Union for the supply of oil. At the end of June and the beginning of July 1960 the Texaco, Esso, and Shell oil companies were nationalized after they had refused to refine Russian oil. The United States had continued to protest against nationalization without compensation; on 5 July 1960 a Cuban law provided for the nationalization of all United States property in Cuba when it was deemed necessary in the national interest; on the same day Eisenhower signed a bill giving him discretionary authority to determine Cuba's sugar quota, and immediately cut the quota by 700,000 tons from 3·12 million; thereupon Khrushchev announced that he would buy Cuban sugar.

By this time the *détente* which had characterized Soviet-American relations had ended; and the summit conference had proved abortive. Eisenhower and Khrushchev, who so recently had sat talking cosily at Camp David, exchanged long-range shots in speeches and press conferences. On 9 July 1960 Khrushchev said:

... we shall do everything to support Cuba and her courageous people in their struggle for freedom and national independence which they have won under the leadership of their national leader Fidel Castro. ... Figuratively speaking, if need be, Soviet artillery-men can support the Cuban people with their rocket fire, should the aggressive forces in the Pentagon dare to start intervention against Cuba.[9]

On the same day Eisenhower stated that the United States would never permit the establishment of a régime dominated by international communism in the western hemisphere, and then on the 14 July – following a Khrushchev press conference on the 12th – that the principles of the Monroe doctrine were as valid today as in 1823.

It was, however, Eisenhower's successor in the presidency who had to conduct the trial of strength of which these initial exchanges were the preliminaries. When the new president took office in January 1961 he was aware of the dangers which confronted his own country and the peace of the world, and at the same time had far-reaching ideas of the course which he wanted world politics to follow. It was the more galling that amongst his first actions should be one of fiasco.

While running for the presidency John Kennedy had reproached the Republican administration for its inaction with regard to Cuba. In office he took over plans prepared by his predecessors by which the United States allowed, materially assisted, and shielded an invasion of Cuba by a small force of Cuban exiles. The expedition was organized by a Cuban National Revolutionary Council with headquarters in New York, whose director was Cardona, whom Castro had made premier after the revolution. The small force landed on 17 April 1961 at the Bay of Pigs; within a very short time it was overpowered by Cuban forces.

It was clear that those who had planned and supported the expedition were sadly misinformed by their intelligence services. Such a venture could only be successful if the Cuban army defected or if there were a massive popular uprising in its

[9] RIIA *Documents, 1960*, p. 564.

support. Neither occurred, and as a result the opposition to Castro was seriously weakened, while the United States opened itself to all the odium of having sponsored an invasion of Cuba without the credit or advantages of a successful operation. By this time Cuban delegations were being fêted in Moscow, and throughout the world left-wing forces, communist and non-communist, were ready to rally enthusiastically to the cause of Castro, victim of the great-power antagonism of the United States.

At this time, however, the problem of Cuba seemed less threatening than the Berlin question and, hanging over Berlin, the danger of nuclear weapons. It was this that led Kennedy to take up the loose strands left after the abortive summit conference of 1960 and seek a meeting with Khrushchev, in circumstances that would avoid the searchlight publicity of earlier occasions. Their meeting took place in Vienna at the beginning of June 1961; it was of signal importance in the development of Kennedy's views and policies. On the subject of Laos they made some progress and reached an agreement of intention. But the president came away from his meeting more rather than less convinced of the danger that Khrushchev would under-estimate American determination to defend Berlin. In a broadcast[10] on 6 June he said:

Our most somber talks were on the subject of Germany and Berlin. I made it clear to Mr Khrushchev that the security of Western Europe and therefore our own security are deeply involved in our presence and our access rights to West Berlin, that those rights are based on law and not on sufferance, and that we are determined to maintain those rights at any risk, and thus meet our obligation to the people of West Berlin and their right to choose their own future.

But his anxieties that he had failed to convince Khrushchev were borne out by Khrushchev's own account of the meeting, eight days after Kennedy's, in which he said that 'the conclusion of a peace treaty with Germany cannot be postponed any longer, and a peace settlement in Europe must be attained this year'. He continued:

[10] RIIA, *Documents, 1961*, p. 281.

The question that remains now is not whether to sign a peace treaty or not, but whether the treaty will be signed with the two existing German states – the German Democratic Republic and the Federal Republic of Germany – or with one of the German states, whether all countries that fought against Germany will take part in the peace settlement or only a part of them.[11]

Through the summer months the temperature of the crisis over Berlin increased. The Soviet position remained substantially as before, and as it had been set out in a memorandum given to Kennedy in Vienna: that peace treaties should be signed, Berlin made a 'free demilitarized city', and access to it negotiated with the government of the GDR. The western powers reaffirmed that their position in Berlin derived from the defeat of Germany. Both sides took defence measures which in the classical days of great-power diplomacy might have been seen as moves towards war. On the Soviet side it was announced that the government had decided to 'suspend the unilateral reduction of forces' and increase defence expenditure. Marshal Koniev was brought from retirement to head the Soviet forces in east Germany. On the western side General Maxwell Taylor was appointed to a panel of experts to advise on the defence of west Berlin, and General Clay was sent there as Kennedy's special representative. In August Vice-President Johnson visited Berlin and distributed the symbols of American wealth, fountain pens and chocolate bars, to its people. At the same time the Soviet Union resumed the testing of nuclear weapons on a grand scale. Most important, the United States government steadily increased its forces in western Europe.

The effect of the crisis on the GDR was serious as it led to a fresh increase in the flow of refugees to the west as its citizens rushed to take what they thought must be their last chance to escape – for they least of all had confidence in Berlin as a 'free city'. Figures issued by the German Federal Republic showed nearly 200,000 refugees in 1960 compared with 140,000 in 1959; and in the first six months of 1961 the figure exceeded 100,000. To this exodus the government had a simple if risky response – in August they sealed off the border between east and west Berlin, and between west Berlin and the surrounding territory. Henceforth a concrete wall would sever all connexion

[11] Ibid. p. 286.

for Germans between the two halves of the city, until in 1964 a minimal concession could be agreed between the two German governments to allow Christmas visits.

The construction of the wall itself heightened the tension in Berlin. There were those who argued that the western powers should forcibly dismantle it, and could do so with impunity. In fact no such action was taken; although when the GDR proclaimed a 100-metre 'no man's land' on each side they did not hesitate to patrol the 'forbidden' area on their own side of the wall. Nor did they hesitate to counter moves made by the Soviet forces in Berlin, so that for sixteen hours in October 1961 American and Soviet tanks faced each other across the border at 'checkpoint Charlie'.

The Berlin crisis subsided as it had begun, through the initiative of Khrushchev. Like the previous crisis of 1948–9 its permanent effect was to divide east from west Berlin – the division now being made more impenetrable than ever before. But communication between the great powers remained open. The softness of Khrushchev's position was evident when he addressed the 22nd congress of the CPSU in October 1961 and said:

The Soviet government still insists that the German question be settled as promptly as possible and is against endlessly deferring its settlement. The question of a time limit for the signing of a German peace treaty will not be so important if the Western powers show a readiness to settle the German problem; we shall not in that case absolutely insist on signing the peace treaty before December 31, 1961. The main thing is to settle the question; to do away with the vestiges of the second world war, to sign a German peace treaty.[12]

Negotiations punctuated by tension during the next eighteen months neither provoked conflict nor provided a settlement. In June of 1963 both Kennedy and Khrushchev visited Berlin. The restraint and control which characterized Kennedy's contact with a popular audience, whether directly or by radio and television, broke down as he told the people of west Berlin: 'Ich bin ein Berliner'; that he should do so was as clear an indication that the immediate crisis was past as the general terms in which Khrushchev outlined the conditions which were necessary for a solution of the German problem.

Khrushchev's motives in initiating and maintaining the

[12] Gruliow, *Current Soviet Policies*, iv (1962), p. 51.

Berlin crisis remain indeterminate. The tension it created may have served the internal purposes of his own dictatorial régime; the stand he took may have been intended as demonstrative argument in the Sino-Soviet dispute; he may have hoped for easy success. He met with resistance from the government of western Germany and from its erstwhile occupants. In speech and attitude the most adamant was de Gaulle, who maintained that negotiation could serve no useful purpose. He argued that the crisis had been created by Khrushchev and could be dismantled at his wish; negotiation in these circumstances could only consist of concessions to Khrushchev's demands. De Gaulle was strongly supported by Adenauer, in contrast to the British, who placed most emphasis on the need to neglect no opportunity of negotiation. In action, however, the decisive moves were taken by the United States; for while there was the maximum discussion and consultation within the framework of NATO, and while Britain and France participated in the increase of military strength in western Europe, there was no doubt that the decisive element in the confrontation was American.

The determination of the western powers to stand their ground showed the weakness of the Soviet position. Faced with opposition the Soviet government ran the risk of military conflict, and the very strength of the Soviet military position on the ground in Berlin increased the danger that the United States would use nuclear weapons. In addition, Khrushchev's position was weak in relation to the government of the GDR. Whatever advantage tension may have had in the Soviet Union or in the Sino-Soviet dispute, its effect in east Germany was to increase the flow of refugees and thus make it imperative for the Ulbricht government to put a barrier against further flight. To this extent Khrushchev lost his freedom of manoeuvre in an area where he appeared diplomatically as well as militarily strong. Whether the initiative for the building of the wall came from the GDR or from the Soviet Union, it was an action forced on Khrushchev by the interests of the GDR. It must therefore have been evident how dangerous were Khrushchev's proposals for the settlement of Berlin to the Soviet Union itself, since they would increase the independence of the government of the GDR and enable it to force the hand of the Soviet government, at the same time as the tension over Berlin was also increased.

The result was that Khrushchev, having made forward moves over Berlin for nearly three years, was forced to withdraw – and had the political courage and control over his country that made withdrawal possible. Few months were to pass before he had taken up a second forward position, not this time within the bounds of the Soviet empire, but in the exposed outpost of Cuba.

Whatever course relations between the United States and Cuba might have followed without the Bay of Pigs disaster, it was scarcely possible that they would improve for some time after it. The collapse of that venture had left Castro in a strong position; the opposition to his régime had thrown away its strength in premature and ill-judged action; the United States, having decided against rescuing the Cuban expedition by the use of its own forces, was scarcely likely to initiate an invasion when events had regained their calm.

It might have been expected, therefore, that Castro's government would draw the maximum material advantage from its links with the Soviet Union, and the maximum prestige from its example to 'popular' movements the world over. Instead it entered into agreements with the Soviet Union by which the latter provided arms and technicians to constitute a highly effective defence force, and then established its own missile bases with offensive capability. Neither government attempted to conceal that agreements had been reached for the supply of arms. The establishment of Soviet missile bases was not openly stated; but in that sunlit island nothing could be concealed from the photo-reconnaissance of American planes – more effective intelligence sources in this instance than agents.

The result was that in October 1962 the United States government, having watched with restraint the increase of Cuban military strength, and having been told repeatedly by the Soviet government that arms sent to Cuba were purely defensive, was confronted with the imminent arrival and installation of Soviet missiles capable of reaching, with nuclear warheads, the cities of the western United States. It took care it had made no mistake in its observation of what was happening; then, on 22 October, President Kennedy announced in a television broadcast that United States forces would institute a naval blockade of Cuba, would intercept vessels to ascertain whether they were carrying offensive weapons, and would maintain the blockade until the missiles already landed were taken away.

His speech[13] combined unmistakable firmness of purpose with moderation and restraint. The 'strict military quarantine' was linked with a declaration of policy: 'to regard any nuclear missile launched from Cuba against any nation in the Western Hemisphere as an attack by the Soviet Union on the United States, requiring a full retaliatory response upon the Soviet Union'. But at the same time he made clear that the blockade would not deny Cuba the necessities of life, as the Berlin blockade had done; and the speech ended:

I call upon Chairman Khrushchev to halt and eliminate this clandestine, reckless, and provocative threat to world peace and to stable relations between our two nations. I call upon him further to abandon this course of world domination and to join in an historic effort to end the perilous arms race and transform the history of man.

In this way the challenge facing the United States was interpreted as coming directly from the Soviet Union, with Cuba playing a subordinate role. The immediate confrontation with the Soviet Union was isolated from any other conflict; no mention was made of United States relations with Cuba; no attempt was made, beyond the reference to Berlin quoted above, to refer to other disputes, far less to the Chinese attack on India, which had increased in intensity and was before the General Assembly at this time. Kennedy made it clear that in this matter the United States would act alone. His government called for the Security Council to meet, and proposed United Nations supervision of the dismantling of missiles. The Council of the Organization of American States was also summoned. The NATO Council had been kept informed of developments, and Dean Acheson was sent to the European capitals to explain American action. But the ultimate responsibility and the intention of the United States to act alone were never in doubt.

Although the blockade was instituted, no Soviet ships were boarded, as those carrying missiles were diverted away from the blockade. A Soviet tanker was stopped and then allowed to proceed, and a Lebanese freighter under Soviet charter was boarded. The risk of local clashes was thus minimized. Communication was maintained between the two governments through the secretary-general of the United Nations, who proposed – ineffectively – that the blockade be suspended while talks were held. On 26 October Tass announced in Moscow that Khrushchev had written to Kennedy and U Thant proposing that the Soviet Union dismantle the Cuban missiles in return for the removal of American missiles from Turkey; but Kennedy replied without accepting the offer. On 28 October Khrushchev agreed unconditionally to the removal of the missiles from Cuba.

A bare account of the Cuban crisis gives little indication of its intensity, or of its importance in international affairs. Kennedy and his advisers showed supreme competence – no less so because they were working from a position of strength. They confined the crisis to Cuba, and took the minimum action necessary to achieve their ends, while mobilizing their maximum strength and the maximum degree of flexibility in its use should it prove necessary. They took every care to ensure that their intentions were clearly known to the Soviet Union, to the extent, as we have seen, that they allowed the first Soviet ship, seen to be a tanker, to pass without examination on board rather than risk a heightening of the crisis through misunderstanding. They controlled the release of news and comment in the national press, so that independent and irresponsible expressions of opinion would not distort the judgement of the Soviet leaders.

The care which they exercised would have been unavailing had it not been matched by caution on the side of the Soviet government and, in the last resort, the willingness of Khrushchev to admit defeat and withdraw rather than enter into conflict. With the Soviet people he could claim to be the saviour of peace by so doing; but he could not conceal from Castro that he had pushed Cuba into a position of vulnerability, only to withdraw in his own interests; nor could he deprive Kennedy of his prestige in the world at large, or shield himself from the accusations of the Chinese that he was cowardly in the face of American pressure.

Kennedy made no attempt to exploit his success. Adamant in his refusal to trade American missiles in Turkey for Soviet missiles in Cuba, he none the less made it as easy as possible for Khrushchev to withdraw; once he had done so he guarded against any danger of the intoxication of victory amongst his own people, and he made no attempt to exploit victory in other areas of the cold war.

In consequence the most serious crisis to have occurred between two nuclear powers was distinguished by the degree of communication and understanding between the leaders on each side while the crisis was in progress. As a result of this communication each was able to recognize the legitimate interests of the other – Khrushchev that America could not tolerate a threat to its existence, Kennedy that Khrushchev could admit defeat but not accept humiliation; and both accepted that the danger of nuclear war was a first and predominant concern, establishing a special relationship between them. The opening paragraphs of Khrushchev's letter of 28 October to Kennedy were singularly free of communist jargon when he wrote:

I have received your message of 27 October. I express my satisfaction and thank you for the sense of proportion you have displayed and for realization of the responsibility which now devolves on you for the preservation of the peace of the world.

I regard with great understanding your concern, and the concern of the United States people in connection with the fact that the weapons you describe as offensive are formidable weapons indeed. Both you and we understand what kind of weapons these are.[14]

A new balance and a new understanding had been established in the world, shortly to be symbolized by the construction of a direct telephone line between the White House and the Kremlin. One year later the two nuclear world powers signed a test-ban treaty and the Soviet Union, initiator and beneficiary of the greatest territorial changes of the post-war world, came to play the role of a mediator in international disputes appropriate to a *status quo* power.

As it did so the impact of communist China on world politics became the pre-eminent concern of the United States as well as the Soviet Union, and contributed to the incipient understanding between them. As we have seen, the first episodes in communist China's relations with the external world were the

[14] Ibid. pp. 397–8.

violence of the Korean war, a conflict not of its own choosing, and the conquest of Tibet, which in the Chinese view was no more than the re-establishment of rule over its own territory. No doubt this would have been accompanied by the final elimination of Chiang Kai-shek and his forces from Formosa, had that not been prevented by the interposition of the American fleet.

With the conclusion of the Korean war there followed a period in which China assiduously cultivated the goodwill of neighbouring states. In the pursuit of this line of diplomacy India proved an invaluable ally. In spite of Chinese action in Tibet, the whole approach of India to problems of foreign policy was one that facilitated China's new attempt to pose as an advocate of peace and a leading power in the representation and support of the peoples of Asia.[15] In pursuit of its policy of non-alignment, India had hitherto been given little opportunity to be more than a commentator on European and Atlantic affairs, or a mediator, as in Korea. The emergence of a neighbouring communist state, and one to which the United States showed its hostility, provided an opportunity for Nehru to demonstrate the principles of Indian foreign policy in practice and to achieve a cordiality of relationship with an Asian communist power of a kind which had eluded the United States in its conduct of the cold war – and which (although the fact was given less prominence in the Indian view) had also eluded India in its relations with Pakistan.

This was the background to the signature by Chou En-lai and Nehru of the declaration of five principles – the Panch Sheela – which was attached to a trade agreement relative to Tibet signed on 29 April 1954. The five principles governing the conduct of relations between the two states pledged both to non-aggression and non-interference in each other's internal affairs. Idealistic as they were, they nevertheless became a theme in international relations in Asia in succeeding years, constantly referred to in speeches and statements, and attached in varying forms to international agreements. In November 1956 Chou En-lai visited North Vietnam, Cambodia, India, Burma, and Pakistan, as well as the Soviet Union, Poland, and Hungary. Speaking to the Indian parliament he referred to the

---

[15] See Guy Wint, *Communist China's Crusade* (1965).

now famous five principles and paid tribute to India's contribution to peace – its contribution to the restoration of peace in Korea and Indo-China, its part in the Bandung conference, its policy on disarmament and the banning of weapons of mass destruction. Solidarity between India and China, he said, with their billion population would become a 'gigantic moral and material force in stabilizing the situation in Asia and Africa'.

Within a year there began to occur Chinese incursions into what was regarded by the Indian government as Indian territory in the area of Ladakh. In 1958 the Indian government discovered that the Chinese were building a road across their territory, and when they sent a patrol to investigate it was taken into custody. In reply to an Indian protest the Chinese government claimed that the territory was its own, and reported the release of the patrol.

This was the beginning of a tougher line in Chinese foreign policy associated with a change of power in the leadership. But news of the frontier incidents was not given to the Indian parliament or to the world until the summer of 1959. By that time there was clear evidence of intensive Chinese military activity in Tibet and of fresh incursions into the disputed frontier areas of India. Chinese rule had not been readily acceptable to the Tibetans; it had been most vigorously resisted by the Khampa tribesmen in the east of the country. Their resistance might not have spread to the rest of the country had the Chinese been content to exercise the loose supervision which had characterized their predecessors' rule; but to do so would have been out of keeping with communist authoritarianism. Consequently widespread fighting broke out between the Tibetans and the Chinese forces, which ruthlessly broke the revolt. Streams of refugees fled into India, and on 31 March the Dalai Lama sought political asylum there.

Giving a press conference on 20 June, the Dalai Lama spoke of the 'inhuman persecution' which the Tibetans had suffered and of a 'reign of terror which finds few parallels in the history of Tibet'. He went on:

Forced labor and compulsory exactions, systematic persecution of the people, plunder and confiscation of property belonging to individuals and monasteries, and the execution of leading men in Tibet – these are the glorious achievements of Chinese rule in Tibet.[16]

16 RIIA, *Documents, 1959*, p. 188.

The Indian government gave asylum to the Dalai Lama, and defended itself vigorously against charges made by the communist government of having aided the revolt. On 27 April Nehru said to the Lok Sabha:

Tragedy had been and is being enacted in Tibet, passions have been let loose, charges made and language used which cannot but worsen the situation and our relations with our northern neighbour. I am sure that the House will agree with me that in considering matters of such high import, we should exercise restraint and wisdom and use language which is moderate and precise. . . . We have fortunately kept out of the cold war and I hope that on this, as on any other occasion, we shall not use the language of the cold war.[17]

This attitude did not immediately change when fresh Chinese incursions were made into Indian territory at two points, at Longju in the North-East Frontier Agency and in the Ladakh area of Kashmir. The former incident Nehru described as a 'clear case of aggression'. Even so, he declined to take the case of Tibet to the United Nations, as the Dalai Lama requested, so that on 9 September the latter himself sent a telegram to the secretary-general, reminding Hammarskjöld that the General Assembly had adjourned discussion of the Tibetan question in 1950. He said that since then aggression by Chinese forces had not terminated; on the contrary, it had been substantially extended. He also said that Tibet was a sovereign state before the invasion in 1950, and accused the Chinese of attempting the 'total extermination of the Tibetan race, ruthless attempts to destroy Tibetan religion and culture, of large scale round ups of men, women and children for forced labour and of razing monasteries to the ground'. In response to his appeal the Irish Republic and Malaya sponsored a resolution at the fourteenth session of the General Assembly deploring the events in Tibet and calling for a restoration of civil rights. This provoked a debate on whether the resolution should be placed on the agenda, then on the resolution itself, which was carried 45–9–26.

Meanwhile the government of India had issued a White Paper on the frontier incidents; it proved to be the first of a series which came out over the ensuing years. There was room for discussion, since the areas in question were claimed by India and China as their territory. In the Ladakh district the

[17] Ibid. pp. 181–2.

border had not until now had any great practical significance, since it ran through barren territory; in the north-east the boundary had been established in an agreement between Sir Henry McMahon, representing the British government, and the Tibetan government in a convention of 1914. The line thus drawn was named after its British progenitor; it had not been recognized *de jure* by any Chinese government; but it had not previously been challenged – least of all when Chou En-lai and Nehru were agreeing on the five principles.

From the end of 1959 until 1962 there was no substantial change in the situation, in spite of published words and a meeting between Nehru and Chou En-lai. In the spring of 1962 China brought to a successful conclusion negotiations with Pakistan settling border questions between them. This brought vigorous protests from the government of India, since the only frontier of Pakistan with China was in Kashmir – the agreement[18] covered the border between Sinkiang 'and the contiguous areas, the defense of which is under the actual control of Pakistan'. The Indian government spoke of grave consequences, and said that 'it would never agree to any arrangements, provisional or otherwise, between the governments of China and Pakistan regarding territory which constitutes an inalienable part of the Indian Union'.

Then in October 1962 the conflict between China and India passed through an entirely new phase as Chinese troops made a fresh sortie in the Ladakh area, and in the North East Frontier Agency advanced about 100 miles against slender opposition, coming within striking distance of the Assam plains. There they halted, and the Chinese government proclaimed a cease-fire; after which the troops were withdrawn back to the disputed areas.

The new attack differed both in its scale and in its impact on the Indian government. In November 1959 Nehru had scorned any idea of abandoning the policy of non-alignment. Now he sought military aid, and such aid was forthcoming from the western powers. Throughout the earlier part of the dispute the Soviet Union had maintained a cautious neutrality between India and China, and as recently as the summer of 1962 had made an agreement with the Indian government for

---

[18] *American Journal of International Law*, vol. 57 (1963), p. 713.

the delivery of Soviet MIG fighters to the Indian air force and the building of a factory under licence in India. Under the stress of attack, however, India received help from Britain and the United States, and to a lesser degree from France, Australia, Canada, and New Zealand. American help was particularly important, since it included a substantial airlift of Indian troops and supplies in American planes flown from European bases for the purpose.[19]

In December 1962 Mrs Bandanaraike, prime minister of Ceylon, called a conference of South Asian powers, which met at Colombo, to mediate in the conflict; but as Chinese troops had withdrawn from their advanced positions, and as nothing had happened to remove the basic differences between India and China, the conference achieved little.

For China the question of Tibet was one of internal rather than foreign policy, and the Chinese government consistently maintained that the barren lands it claimed from India were also part of China. Even so, China's aggression against India remains difficult to explain. Military aggression was accompanied by diplomatic isolation, since China was able to make treaties not only with Pakistan but with India's other neighbours, Afghanistan, Nepal, and Burma. Moreover China had gained the prestige that always goes, in an imperfect world, with success, however brutal. Military observers might explain that the defeat of the Indian army was due to its lack of acclimatization; but their reasoning made little impact outside a small circle. With the decline in Nehru's health and his death in 1964 the claim of India to leadership in Asia was diminished still further. Within India the Chinese attack had inevitably had an extremely adverse effect on the Communist party of India; even so the continued inadequacies of Indian economic and social life offered plentiful ground for a renewed development of communism.

Chinese policy in Asia can be explained as the determination to act as a great power, and to shape the world in accordance

---

[19] The attack caused a flurry within the Commonwealth when Nkrumah expressed regret at the message of sympathy sent by Macmillan to Nehru, suggesting that he refrain 'from any action that may aggravate the unfortunate situation'. He received a brusque reply. Turkey would have sent aid to India but for Pakistani protests.

with the ideology of Chinese nationalism – albeit with a cautious regard for the practical interests of national security. Nowhere were these aspirations more apparent than within the communist world, where the Chinese made their bid for leadership by posing as fearless exponents of revolution against the conservative *status quo* attitude of the Russians. The dispute between the Russians and the Chinese took the form of a long-term debate in which the 21st party congress of the CPSU, a meeting of the Warsaw treaty powers in 1959, and the Rumanian party congress in June 1960 provided the first great concentration in the exchange of arguments. In the autumn of 1959 Khrushchev flew to Peking for the tenth anniversary of the Chinese revolution – having come directly from meeting Eisenhower in the United States, and changing aeroplanes in Moscow on the way; most important, a meeting of 81 communist parties was summoned in Moscow at the end of 1960, and produced an agreed declaration only at the end of some three weeks' meeting.

In these years the Sino-Soviet dispute centred in the question of the inevitability of war, and the fate of communist society should war break out. We have already seen how Khrushchev had put forward a revaluation of the question of war at the 20th party congress in 1956. He accepted that war was a risk as long as imperialism existed, for the reasons which Lenin had expounded in his thesis on imperialism; but he argued that since Lenin's time conditions in the world had changed, so that war was no longer 'fatalistically inevitable'. The key to the changed conditions was in the success of socialism, and the strength of the socialist part of the world. As he then said:

> In these circumstances, of course, the Leninist thesis remains valid: As long as imperialism exists, the economic base giving rise to wars will also remain. That is why we must display the greatest vigilance. As long as capitalism survives in the world, reactionary forces, representing the interests of the capitalist monopolies, will continue their drive toward military gambles and aggression and may try to unleash war. But war is not a fatalistic inevitability. Today there are mighty social and political forces possessing formidable means to prevent the imperialists from unleashing war and, if they try to start it, to give a smashing rebuff to the aggressors and frustrate their adventurist plans.[20]

[20] Gruliow, *Current Soviet Policies*, ii (1957), p. 37.

498   A HISTORY OF WAR AND PEACE

At the same time Khrushchev had argued that it was now possible for communist parties to come to power in certain countries without violent revolution. Once again, it was the success of 'Lenin and the Bolshevik Party' in the Soviet Union which had first made this possible, and the steadily increased strength of the 'socialist camp' provided conditions which did not exist when Lenin wrote. As a result:

in present-day conditions the working class in many capitalist countries has a genuine opportunity to unite the overwhelming majority of the people under its leadership and to ensure that the basic means of production are placed in the hands of the people. . . .

The winning of a firm parliamentary majority based on the mass revolutionary movement of the proletariat and of the working people would create conditions for the working class of many capitalist and former colonial countries to make fundamental social changes.[21]

The conclusions which Khrushchev drew from these theses were that it was possible to achieve peaceful coexistence with the capitalist world, and co-operation with neutralist countries. He denied that the imperialist camp was a single implacable bloc, and maintained that certain outstanding statesmen – notably Eisenhower and Macmillan, until the failure of the summit conference of 1960 – understood the necessity and desirability of coexistence.

The Chinese communists refused to accept Khrushchev's interpretation of the world or the conclusions which he drew from it, and they argued vehemently and continuously against him. They contended that Lenin's analysis of imperialism was as applicable in their own time as when it was written, and that the danger of war consequent on the imperialist system was as great as ever. They denied that the development of atomic and nuclear weapons had made any difference in this respect, and that nuclear war would destroy humanity. In *Long Live Leninism*, published in 1960, it was said:

Marxist-Leninists have always maintained that in world history it is not technique but man, the masses of people, that determine the fate of mankind. . . . If the US or other imperialists refuse to reach an agreement on the banning of atomic and nuclear weapons and should dare to fly in the face of the will of all humanity by

[21] Ibid. p. 38.

launching a war using atomic and nuclear weapons, the result will . . . certainly not be the annihilation of mankind. . . . Should the imperialists impose such sacrifices on the peoples of various countries, we believe that, just as the experience of the Russian revolution and the Chinese revolution shows, those sacrifices would be repaid.[22]

The Chinese rejected the Soviet view of the United States, saying that 'US imperialism holds nothing but venom for the peace efforts of the socialist camp headed by the Soviet Union'.[23] It followed that for them coexistence was impossible and undesirable. While Kuusinen said: 'All of us remember full well the moving demonstrations of friendship by masses of people during Nikita Khrushchev's stay in the United States of America, India, Indonesia, Burma, Afghanistan and France on his great mission of goodwill',[24] Liu Chang-sheng replied:

We should make it clear to the people that they should not be intimidated by the cold war waged by imperialism, that they should resolutely oppose its cold war policy, expose its ugly face and wage a head-on struggle against it. Only thus can the cold war be prevented from developing into a hot one.[25]

The climax of this first period of the dispute was the Moscow conference of November 1960. The increasing bitterness of the exchanges rose to a crescendo, and such evidence as exists indicates that it did not diminish at the conference itself – indeed the fact that the existence of the conference was not disclosed until it was over and a final declaration could be issued suggests that it was feared no agreement might be reached. The statement which eventually emerged from the conference, agreed by the 81 parties represented (including the Chinese), was for the greater part a victory for the Soviet point of view, although it contained important concessions to the Chinese. The strength of the socialist camp was affirmed as the decisive factor in world society, and the central thesis of the Soviet Union on war and coexistence was restated. 'War is not fatally inevitable,' it was said; and further:

The democratic and peace forces today have no task more pressing than that of safeguarding humanity against a global thermo-

---

[22] Quoted in G. F. Hudson and others, *The Sino-Soviet Dispute* (London, China Quarterly, 1961), pp. 92–93.
[23] Editorial in *People's Daily*, quoted ibid. p. 112.
[24] RIIA, *Documents, 1960*, p. 210.   [25] *Peking Review*, no. 24, 1960.

nuclear disaster. The unprecedented destructive power of modern means of warfare demands that the main actions of the anti-war and peace-loving forces be directed towards preventing war.

Equally, the policy of coexistence was described as meeting the basic interests of all peoples. At the same time the United States was denounced, and described as the source of possible war. 'The peoples of all countries know that the danger of a new world war still persists. US imperialism is the main force of aggression and war.'[26] The statement was ambiguous on the question of the 'national-liberation movement', subscribing to the Chinese view that 'national bourgeoisies' would at first participate in the struggle against imperialism, but then rapidly turn round to a readiness to compromise with imperialism and feudalism. Nothing was said about the way in which communist parties should obtain power in emerging countries.

The Moscow conference, however, was far from settling the Sino-Soviet dispute. Khrushchev gave a long report on the conference, in which he cited the estimates of British and American scientists of the scale of nuclear destruction (their figures related to their own countries, but the implication for the Soviet Union was made clear). At the same time he was more explicit than the Moscow statement in expressing support for 'national-liberation wars', as in Vietnam, Algeria, and Cuba, saying that the attitude of Marxists was 'most favourable' to them, in contrast to 'local wars', like the Suez expedition, which must be prevented lest they develop into thermonuclear war.[27] The Chinese Communist party resolution on the conference, in contrast, laid great emphasis on the conflict with the United States, 'the biggest international exploiter, the world gendarme, the chief bulwark of world reaction and modern colonialism and the main force of aggression and war of our time'.[28] It did not depart from the theses accepted at Moscow, but the way in which they were reported showed clearly that the Chinese communists remained unconvinced and unregenerate. Later events showed that the conference was indeed to be no more than a pause in the increasing feud between the two great communist powers.

The terms of the debate were public to the world – indeed it

---

[26] Quoted in Hudson, *Sino-Soviet Dispute*, pp. 187–9.
[27] Ibid. pp. 211–13.   [28] Ibid. p. 222.

was part of its essential character that it was conducted both
obliquely and openly, with neither side (at this stage) explicitly
naming its opponent. But the underlying causes of the dispute
and of the various stages of its development remain a matter of
conjecture. Undoubtedly the Chinese gained great confidence
from the fact that they had carried out their own revolution
without help from and against the advice of the Soviet Union.
Mao Tse-tung had applied Marxist-Leninism to Chinese
conditions, and his success had proved him right. It was the
peasantry which had brought him to power, and he now
surveyed the world to identify its 'peasantry'. He believed he
had found it in the colonial peoples, and was as convinced of
the correctness of his analysis as he had previously been in his
own country. The Russian Bolsheviks had won power in their
own country against a 'feudal' autocratic government, and
their successors might well be ignorant of the real nature of
the 'national bourgeoisie', but the Chinese experience had been
quite different; as a number of *Red Flag* pointed out:

> Comrade Mao Tse-tung . . . always reminded us that we must
> not fall into this trap laid by Chiang Kai-shek. In circumstances
> where the Chiang Kai-shek reactionaries continuously strengthened
> their counter-revolutionary state machine, would it have been pos-
> sible to win democracy peacefully? Would it have been possible to
> win political power peacefully? Obviously not.

When the same article reminded its readers that 'Mao Tse-tung
penetratingly pointed out that the Chiang Kai-shek reactionaries were nothing but paper tigers'[29], it invited Khrushchev's
scorn; but it was a powerful incitement to the Chinese communist leaders, who as late as 1948 had believed themselves
to be fighting against a tough and obdurate foe, only to be
faced with his collapse within a matter of months.

There is some evidence that when the Chinese communists
came to power they decided to make a formal alliance with the
Soviet Union only after a hard-fought debate in the politburo.
But they had made such an alliance, and it is possible that they
were willing to accord primacy to the Soviet Union in the
struggle against the imperialists, on the assumption that they
were themselves recognized both as a great power and as equal
in importance to the Soviet Union in discussions of communist

[29] Ibid. pp. 165, 166.

17

strategy. The alliance was followed by a great influx of Russian military and technical advisers into China, and it is reasonable to suppose that they gave rise to friction, as had similar emissaries in Yugoslavia. At the same time an event of greater importance had been initiated by the North Korean invasion of the south. The Chinese were presumably not party to this attack; but as United Nations forces pushed north up the peninsula, it fell to the Chinese to intervene to protect their own frontier. The war meant heavy costs for them in money and equipment, and it is supposed that they received Russian aid in this, although it is not known to what extent. Whatever the cost, they had taken the leading and most dangerous position in the conflict with the imperialist camp. Soon afterwards, their international prestige and importance had increased still further by the part they played in the Geneva conference on Indo-China and in the Bandung conference in 1955.

By this time Stalin had died. His successors, seeking to improve on his shortcomings in so many things, endeavoured to set relations with China on a more satisfactory footing. Chou En-lai (not Mao Tse-tung) went to Moscow for Stalin's funeral, and was accorded the place of honour in the communist protocol system, while the Chinese People's Republic was given primacy over the other people's democracies in public references. Substantial economic aid was now offered to China, and in October 1954 Khrushchev and Mikoyan visited Peking to set the seal on agreements for the construction of plants and the granting of credits. Aid which had been promised to China in 1950 was stepped up, and the Russians undertook to design and construct more than 100 industrial plants, in addition to 50 already promised.[30] In May 1957 Khrushchev claimed that Russian technicians were building more modern plants in China than existed in Russia.

One may assume that Sino-Soviet relations improved markedly in this period; but this was not to last. It may be that the Chinese view of the relationship was carried into practice in the events of October 1956 when, as we have seen, they intervened actively in European events, while the Soviet government retained the leadership of the socialist camp, taking action in Poland and Hungary which accorded with the

[30] David Floyd, *Mao against Khrushchev* (1964).

University of Winnipeg
CheckOut Receipt

03/12/01
11:39 am

Item: A history of war and peace, 1939-1945.
Due Date: 02-01-02

Have a great day!

Chinese prescription. But this was not true of the other events of that year. The Chinese were not consulted before the 20th party congress, in spite of the fact that Khrushchev claimed in his speech to be making a doctrinal revision on behalf of the communist world as a whole; nor were Khrushchev's moves to achieve reconciliation with Tito acceptable to the Chinese. At this time and throughout the early stages of the dispute the Chinese probably sought two objectives which, except in October 1956, could not both be achieved at the same time. They insisted throughout the public debate on the importance of socialist unity, and in these years they seem to have accepted Soviet leadership; but at the same time they were convinced of the correctness of their own view, and would accept unity only if the Soviet Union took the lead in expressing and putting into practice a Chinese view.

In fact, however, unity of view between Chinese and Russians was unlikely, because of the widely differing circumstances defining each country's position in the world system of international relations. The Chinese expected to play a leading role as a great power in Asia. In this respect they entered into a Chinese inheritance when they came to power. At the same time they remained isolated from the greater part of the machinery and processes of international intercourse. They were not recognized by the United States or many of its allies, and they were not represented at the United Nations. They could support the 'national liberation movement' with greater force of words, and even action, than the Soviet Union precisely because their doing so did not yet run counter to other objectives of diplomacy, whether in Europe or in the Commonwealth.

Possibly of greatest importance, China was not a nuclear power, and was not assisted by the Soviet Union to become one. We have seen that after Stalin's death the Soviet Union increased its aid to China; but it was not prepared to do so to the extent of sharing nuclear weapons or knowledge and equipment to make them. Perhaps as a substitute, the Russians proposed in 1958 the establishment of a joint fleet, but this was rejected, as they themselves in the next year turned down a Chinese request for a sample atomic bomb and details of its manufacture. This in itself was likely to create a barrier to the unity of the two powers and to provide the Chinese with an irremovable grievance. It also made a fundamental difference in their outlook on world affairs, if it was indeed the case that the Chinese government wanted nuclear weapons, while the Soviet government had reached the conclusion that nuclear weapons constituted the greatest danger in international relations. In a sense the possession of nuclear weapons made aggressive diplomacy more dangerous for the Soviet Union, since the higher the stakes were raised, the greater would be the risk on the one hand of the actual use of nuclear weapons and on the other of having to back down ignominiously. The risks of nuclear war were such that the Soviet Union would have a genuine interest in some form of arms control, while the Chinese could participate in disarmament discussions only as a non-nuclear power.

The divergences over nuclear weapons enhanced still further the fundamental differences between the two in their attitudes to the United States. For the Chinese communists the United States was the one implacable foe. It was the American government which had given help to Chiang Kai-shek, which had been the important enemy in the Korean war, which alone ensured the continued survival of Chiang Kai-shek on Formosa, made possible the insults offered by Nationalist occupation of Quemoy and Matsu, and had threatened to intervene in Indo-China. The United States kept Nationalist China in the United Nations and maintained an embargo on trade which it constantly pressed its allies to extend. For the Soviet Union, on the other hand, the United States was a rival to be respected and feared, whose ultimate collapse as a capitalist power was assured but which in the short run could not be seriously weakened except by nuclear war disastrous for both. Forty years had passed since the United States had taken even a minor part in the Russian civil war, and Russian territory was not in question – as in the Chinese communist view the Chinese territory of Formosa was. There even existed between the Soviet Union and the United States, as the two greatest rivals in the world system, and as the two powers with devastating nuclear capability, a special relationship which the Chinese could not easily destroy.

These were divergences which arose from the differences in the political and military position of the two countries in the world. But they formed the material for an ideological dispute.

Internal differences between the two countries were added to them, particularly when in the late summer of 1958 China embarked on the organization of rural communes, and claimed to be overtaking the Soviet Union by the speed with which it was advancing towards a socialist society (a claim which the Russian leaders ridiculed). As a result, an ideological rift of unprecedented importance and duration appeared in the communist world. Hitherto the success of Russian control over the international communist movement and over the governments of eastern Europe had suppressed divergences as quickly as they had arisen – with the single loss of Yugoslavia. Henceforward differences between the Soviet Union and China, which to the outside observer appear inevitable because of the strong contrast in the political circumstances of the two countries, would make ideological unity impossible to achieve, and would make it inevitable that the disputes within and between other communist parties as to the correct (and politically more advantageous) line to follow would flourish.

New alignments and new conflicts in international politics were even more important. The emergence of China had its effect on the cold war between India and Pakistan. Since the 1950s Pakistan had been a firm ally of the United States, ideologically opposed to communism and ready to accept economic and military aid. But the United States had never supported Pakistani action against India and was not prepared to support the Pakistani case on Kashmir. With the decline of anti-neutralism in America and the appearance of a Chinese threat to India, American relations with Pakistan's rival became closer. At the same time Ayub Khan's foreign minister, Zulficar Ali Bhutto, argued that the weaker partner in an alliance with America strengthened its position not by unswerving loyalty but by the pursuit of an independent policy, as a means of bidding up the price which the Americans would pay.

The result was a rapprochement between Pakistan and China, of which the settlement of the Sinkiang frontier was one indication. In March 1965 Ayub Khan visited Peking and addressed a mass meeting, speaking of Pakistan and China's 'common determination to eradicate the last vestiges of imperialism and colonialism'.[31] In the company of Chou En-lai he

[31] *New York Times*, 6 Mar. 1965.

listened to the attacks made by the mayor of Peking on United States policy in Vietnam, although in his own speech he spoke moderately of the need for negotiations.

Ayub's visit to Peking coincided with an increasingly tense phase in Pakistan's relations with India. One of the long-standing territorial disputes, concerning the area of the Rann of Kutch, erupted without leading to actual conflict. In May there was rioting in Srinagar following the detention of Shaikh Mohammad Abdullah, leader of the Kashmiri Muslims, and by August fighting was reported between Pakistani 'infiltrators' and the Indian army along the cease-fire line in Kashmir. In September 1965 there was a three-weeks' war between the two countries, each side using considerable forces of tanks and air-craft while at the same time avoiding any serious extension of the war, for example to east Pakistan. The war came to an end when both sides accepted United Nations terms for a cease-fire.

The war brought no substantial change in the Kashmir situation. Neither side was prepared to face the exhaustion and waste of a full-scale war, and forces were too evenly matched for either to win a quick victory. But the fighting demonstrated the new pattern of world politics. The American and the Soviet governments joined in urging a cease-fire, while the Chinese government gave full support to Pakistan. In the midst of the fighting the Chinese foreign minister, Chen Yi, stopped in Pakistan on his way to visit Mali; while Chou En-lai spoke of India as an outright aggressor which could not have acted without the consent and support of the United States. The Chinese also created a diversion by accusing the Indians of aggression against China and demanding the withdrawal of Indian troops from a disrupted area along the Sikkim boundary. The response of the Soviet government was to avoid offering similar support to India, and to condemn Chinese readiness to add fuel to the flames. When the fierce nationalism released by the war on both sides had subsided it was Kosygin who invited Ayub and Lal Bahadur Shastri, prime minister of India, to Tashkent to seek a peaceful settlement – a meeting which ended in the sudden death of Shastri.

Significant as were these alignments, they were overshadow-ed by the unrelieved hostility between China and the United

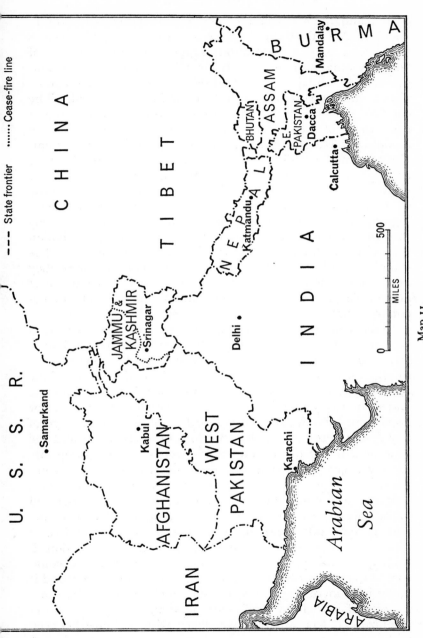

--- State frontier   ······ Cease-fire line

U. S. S. R.

CHINA

Samarkand

TIBET

JAMMU &
KASHMIR
Srinagar

AFGHANISTAN

Kabul

WEST
PAKISTAN

IRAN

NEPAL

Katmandu

BHUTAN

ASSAM

BURMA

Mandalay

E.
PAKISTAN
Dacca

Calcutta

Delhi

INDIA

Karachi

Arabian
Sea

ARABIA

500

0

MILES

Map II.

States, and the involvement of the United States in war in
Vietnam. After the Geneva conference of 1954 the United States
had given economic and military support to the government of
South Vietnam in an endeavour to establish a stable and
prosperous country which would be as strong a frontier against
the communist world as was the German Federal Republic. The
conditions of South East Asia were however totally different
from those of western Europe. There was no easy way of
founding stable government, far less democratic government.
Until November 1963 Ngo Dinh Diem, first as prime minister
and then as president, succeeded in remaining in power, and
elections were held in South Vietnam – not in the whole of the
country as the Geneva agreement had specified, and not meeting any western standards of free choice. When he was overthrown there followed a succession of governments, civilian
and military. None of them was based on a common understanding within the ruling families of Vietnam, nor were they
able to establish a consensus in a society which under the most
favourable circumstances would have faced difficulty in becoming a nation.

In the meantime North Vietnam was organized as a communist state and achieved the unity of a nationalist-revolutionary
communist society. It commanded considerable support in the
south, where communists had every incentive to continue
armed opposition to the government. They had experience of
and weapons for guerrilla warfare and neither experience of nor
opportunity for democratic political activity. The absence of
any firmly based national institutions of government and the
conditions of life in the countryside were entirely appropriate
to the pattern of guerrilla warfare devised by the Chinese communists. Above all they could expect support from the north.

While the United States was aware of the problems involved
in the reform of South Vietnam, it was confident that economic
and military aid would suffice to subdue the communists. It
attached importance to doing so, since it believed that if
communist subversion were not stopped in Vietnam it would
spread to the rest of South East Asia. But as the years passed it
found itself increasingly in a situation of classical imperialism –
in spite of its belief in self-determination, in a period of decolonization. Repeatedly it was faced with a choice between
withdrawal, and an extension of its commitment; and with

every increased commitment withdrawal became more difficult. It began by providing military and economic aid to a Vietnamese government, and then took over many of the functions of government, and would not permit a government unprepared to continue the war to come to power.

Apart from the relationship of the United States to the Vietnamese government there were no political changes in the situation; but guerrilla war grew in intensity, and the United States increased its own participation, the scale of its attacks, and the weapons used. In August 1964 United States planes bombed North Vietnamese bases in retaliation against an attack by torpedo boats on American warships. At the United Nations Adlai Stevenson described this as 'a single action designed to make unmistakably clear that the United States cannot be diverted by military attack from its obligations to help its friends establish and protect their independence'.[32] At this time President Johnson sought and was given Congressional support for 'all necessary action to protect our armed forces and to assist nations covered by the SEATO'. Far from being a single action, the air attack proved to be the prelude to massive air attacks on North Vietnam in 1965. Of even greater significance was the American realization that air attacks and advice to Vietnamese armies were ineffective substitutes for land forces. In the summer of 1965 the fiction that American troops were not in Vietnam was abandoned, and from then until the end of the year their numbers increased rapidly from some 50,000 to 200,000 men.

Military victory eluded the South Vietnamese and the Americans as North Vietnam increased its own military commitment – although its forces in the south were still estimated at less than 20,000 at the end of 1965. Nor did there appear to be any political reason for an end to the war. The North Vietnamese were engaged in a war of liberation which they were confident they would win; the South Vietnamese government was committed to resistance. China gave unqualified support to North Vietnam – although its practical assistance was limited to economic aid and the supply of weapons; in September 1965 Lin Piao, the minister of defence, described Vietnam as the focus of a world-wide military struggle in which the 'rural areas of the world' – Asia, Africa, and Latin America – could be won by

[32] *New York Times*, 6 Aug. 1964.

the proletarian revolutionary movement, thereby encircling the 'cities' of Europe and North America.

Both the difficulties and the possibilities of United States action in the 'rural area' of Latin America were demonstrated when a force of some 10,000 marines was sent to the Dominican Republic in May 1965, at the same time as the war in Vietnam was going through a fresh phase of 'escalation'. Governed until 1961 by Trujillo, who made himself notorious as a Latin American dictator, the Dominican Republic had failed since his overthrow to combine stability with progressive government. Juan Bosch, elected president in 1962, had been overthrown and forced into exile the following year, and the revolution of May 1965 had as its aim the return of Bosch and the re-establishment of the constitution. The American government believed that the revolutionary movement was infiltrated with communists and 'Castroites', and was alarmed at the possibility of the Cuban pattern being repeated in the Caribbean.

To counter this possibility it showed no hesitation in landing marines to prevent the revolutionaries taking control. It also brought together the Organization of American States, and secured the establishment of a peace commission and an OAS force; but there was no doubt that its own unilateral action had been effective in preventing Bosch's return to power. The political problem of establishing a government which would be progressive and anti-communist remained unsolved.

The political cost of the Dominican operation to the United States was great. In the OAS it won a bare two-thirds vote necessary for the establishment of an inter-American force and it made itself vulnerable to charges of imperialism and the ruthless use of military force. In spite of this the geographical situation of the Caribbean insulated American action from world politics. This could not be the case in Vietnam. At the end of 1965 the war there had not yet broken the new balance established between the United States and the Soviet Union, as the latter gave limited aid to North Vietnam, notably in the supply of ground-to-air missiles. But it prevented the development of a special relationship between the two nuclear powers at the same time as it opened the danger of war between the United States and China.

13

AFRICA: A NEW CONTINENT

SPEAKING TO the parliament of the Union of South Africa on
3 February 1960 Harold Macmillan said:

> Ever since the break up of the Roman Empire one of the constant
> facts of political life in Europe has been the emergence of indepen-
> dent nations. . . . Fifteen years ago this movement spread through
> Asia. Many countries there, of different races and civilisations,
> pressed their claim to an independent national life. Today the same
> thing is happening in Africa. The most striking of all the impressions
> I have formed since I left London a month ago is of the strength
> of this African national consciousness. In different places it may take
> different forms. But it is happening everywhere. The wind of change
> is blowing through the continent.[1]

His speech was in every way significant. The nationalism of
which he spoke was indeed evident in every part of Africa. It
expressed itself in the growing organization of political parties
and the demands for independence amongst political leaders,
and was evident in riots and disorders which broke out in
protest to imperial rule – the most serious of them the Mau Mau
movement in Kenya. It received support and encouragement
from the newly independent states of Asia, and each African
state in turn, having achieved independence, used the forum of
the United Nations to support the demands of those still under
foreign rule.

Yet even as he spoke Macmillan was aware that Britain was
in danger of being left behind by the speed with which Belgium
and France were transferring power to African governments. In
Europe the surge of nationalism beat for a century against the
ramparts of empire – Russian, Austro-Hungarian, and Turkish;
in Asia the old imperial powers, France and Holland, exhausted
by defeat and occupation, had tried to restore their dominion
over South East Asia. In Africa south of the Sahara African

---

[1] P. N. S. Mansergh, *Documents and Speeches on Commonwealth Affairs, 1952–62* (1963),
p. 347.

nationalism met with no opposition from the imperialist powers except Portugal, which experienced the direct challenge of colonial insurgence for the first time. Outside the Portuguese colonies African nationalism encountered resistance from the nationalism of European settlers in Africa, determined to maintain a position of privilege and domination – a force which in South Africa was strong, well organized, and successful and in Southern Rhodesia ensured at least a delay in the movement to African-majority rule.

It was not by accident that Macmillan made his speech in the centre of white African nationalism. The most significant transfer of power in the continent occurred in the British territories of Kenya, Nyasaland, and Northern Rhodesia, where the British government succeeded in framing and securing acceptance of new constitutions providing for majority African rule before giving independence. There were good reasons for expecting that such an operation would encounter far graver difficulties than in fact proved the case. Kenya passed through a period of extreme tension as the Mau Mau movement terrorized the European population by murdering men, women, and children in isolated farmsteads. Born of resentment of European dominance, the movement drew also on primitive emotions amongst the Kikuyu tribe and thrived on secret oath-taking and the threat of the supernatural, which disgusted many Kikuyu as much as it did Europeans. The effect was to create the atmosphere of violence and rebellion which renders negotiations for the sharing and transfer of power most difficult; and to discredit African political leaders – notably Jomo Kenyatta, who in April 1953 was sentenced to seven years' imprisonment for managing Mau Mau.

In Rhodesia and Nyasaland the way ahead appeared difficult because the European settlers, especially those of Southern Rhodesia, had taken the initiative to secure the construction of a union which would gain independence from Britain while the European minority were still dominant. The idea of such a union was not new, but it had been rejected before the second world war because the prosperity of Southern Rhodesia would, it was thought, make it too weighty a partner. The development of copper mines in Northern Rhodesia restored the balance, and at least this obstacle to federation was removed. The Rhodesians increased their pressure and at first won the sympathetic support of the Labour government, to be followed after 1951 by practical constitution making by the conservatives, and legislative enactment in July 1953. The advantages of federation to the Europeans in Rhodesia were evident, and it had convincing support in a (European) referendum. The motives of the British government were less clear. Much was said about the economic advantages of federation, although no detailed assessment was made of what these would be in practice, there was much talk of multi-racial partnership without any careful examination of the disparate ratios of European to African populations and European to African voters. African opinion expressed itself as strongly opposed to federation, which was seen as a means of prolonging white supremacy; and it had the support of students of Africa in Britain. (It would have taken exceptional prescience to foresee that the day would come when, if the federation still existed, it might be used as a lever to secure an African majority in Southern Rhodesia.)

The Mau Mau movement in Kenya and federation in Central Africa in quite different ways complicated the task of decolonization facing the British government. But when the Macmillan government was re-elected in 1959 it decided that the policy which its opponents had initiated in India in 1947, and which it had followed in Ghana and Malaya, would be extended to the rest of Africa, and that it would not use force to defend the interests of the European minorities against African demands for majority rule.

In spite of the difficulties which might be expected in Rhodesia and Kenya, the overrriding consideration for the Conservative government was to avoid a clash with African nationalism in which they would lack moral support from their own people and physical force to maintain order. They therefore arranged a series of constitutional conferences which extended the franchise in the Rhodesias, Kenya, and Nyasaland so that Africans were assured of an eventual majority. Their success in doing so was due to the balance of forces within each territory – such that the Europeans accepted an extension of the African franchise while the Africans accepted less than their total demands – and every effort was made to maintain a balance between Africans, as inter-tribal and inter-party rivalries emerged with the prospect of independence. For one of the liberal European leaders in Kenya the only alternative to the new constitutions – and then to independence – 'was to shoot Africans with bullets for the next ten years'.[2]

In this way the independent African states of Malawi, Zambia, and Kenya came to replace the old Northern Rhodesia, Nyasaland, and Kenya. On the way the Central African Federation disappeared. The British government avoided an overt reversal of the policy which had brought the federation into existence ten years previously, but it admitted the right of the members to secede, as did Malawi and Zambia. But in Southern Rhodesia progress stopped short. There a new constitution was introduced in 1961 which did not provide for African-majority rule – on the contrary, it provided the framework within which European nationalism could maintain power. In March 1962 a new Rhodesia Front was formed as an alliance of the nationalist, white supremacist sections of the country and, under the leadership of Winston Field, it defeated the United Federal party. In April 1964 Field resigned the premiership because of his reluctance to move towards a unilateral declaration of independence, and he was succeeded by the deputy prime minister, Ian Smith.

The relationship of Southern Rhodesia to Britain was more distant than that of the northern territories. Constitutionally it had enjoyed self-government since 1923. Geographically and in outlook it was closer to South Africa. The view which Rhodesians took of the experience of African rule did nothing to encourage them to hasten their own surrender of power – whether they took their examples from Ghana, where opposition leaders were imprisoned, from the disorder of the Congo, or from Kenya and Zambia, where many Europeans uprooted themselves – some of them travelling south – after independence. South Africa in contrast remained a successful state, in spite of the anathema poured on it from the rest of the world. By the moderate use of police terror the Nationalist government was able to remain in power; the country was prosperous (in spite of the low price of gold), and English and Afrikaners enjoyed a high standard of living.

In these circumstances the Smith government saw the alternatives before them as being to take their independence, and

---

[2] Michael Blundell, *So Rough a Wind* (1964), p. 281.

thus ensure their own dominance, or to submit to fresh constitution-making in London, when they would follow the pattern of their northern neighbour, exchanging the almost complete control over their own affairs which they already enjoyed for 'independence' under African rule. 'UDI' – a unilateral declaration of independence – became the dominant slogan of Rhodesian politics; and on 13 November 1965 Ian Smith (having two days previously sent a letter of loyalty to the Queen) declared Rhodesia an independent country.

The British government had used every means of warning and persuasion to prevent such a decisive step being taken. When they were unsuccessful they declared the Smith government to be illegal, and used financial and economic sanctions in an effort to coerce the Rhodesians into a different course of action. They steered a delicate course between the demands of the new African states for the use of force against the Smith government, the danger of their own slender majority at home, and the dependence of Rhodesia's neighbour, Zambia, on trade with and through Rhodesia, until an alternative could be provided.

In no other part of Africa south of the Sahara (except in the special case of the Congo) did the problems of mixed European and African communities complicate the transfer of power. The French fought a bitter war to maintain the union of Algeria with France, but even as they did so they prepared the way for the independence of their black African colonies. The transformation which this implied for the French concept of empire is examined in the next chapter.

In one great area of Africa the experience of decolonization was totally different. This was in the Belgian Congo – a territory whose history in colonial days had followed a pattern distinctive from that of British and French territories. It came under Belgian rule as a result of the initiative of King Leopold, and the government took no formal responsibility for the colony until 1908. Thereafter Belgian administration was as efficient and as humanitarian as any other colonial rule; but it advanced education by small degrees at the bottom and scarcely at all at the top, it prevented the development of African political organization, and did everything possible to isolate the Congo from the rest of Africa and from Europe.

Such isolation proved impossible to maintain as nationalism spread through Africa and neighbouring states – the French Congo across the river and Northern Rhodesia – moved towards independence under African rule. The Belgians themselves were sensitive to these changes and took steps to reform their administration of the Congo. Their doing so – as Tocqueville would have advised them – only increased African awareness of their own grievances. A dramatic demonstration of such discontent was given in riots in Leopoldville in January 1959, resulting in the death, according to the official record, of forty-nine Africans.

The practical difficulties in the way of handing over government to the Congolese at this point were immense. The Congo is now the largest African state, with the exception of the Sudan, although its population is only one-third that of Nigeria; it is geographically diverse, and its physical diversity is surpassed by the complexity of tribal groupings amongst its inhabitants. The task of government in any but the most static conditions would therefore be very great. For this task the Congolese had had little preparation. An insignificant number had received higher education,[3] scarcely any had participated in administration under Belgian rule, political organizations were not given recognition until August 1959 (although they had come into existence during the previous decade), and there was no experience of elections. Above all, nationalism existed as a force opposed to Belgian rule and as an expression of discontent; as a force making for the political unity of this vast and complex area it was very weak indeed.

These considerations neither deterred the Congolese leaders from pressing for self-government nor induced the Belgians (whose forbears had been so reluctant to involve themselves in the colonial adventures of their king) to hold on to power in the Congo at the risk of increasing unrest and disorder. In January 1960 a round-table conference was summoned in Brussels; the Congolese, for all their inexperience, achieved a unity in their negotiating position which won the acceptance of all their demands, and it was agreed that the Congo should

[3] By the end of the academic year 1959–60, 20 Congolese had graduated from the University of Lovanium (near Leopoldville), 2 from Elisabethville, and 4 from universities in Belgium. See the excellent account by Catherine Hoskyns, *The Congo since Independence, January 1960–December 1961* (1965).

become independent on 30 June 1960. A bare six months remained to elaborate the details of a constitutional and financial settlement and to hold elections for provincial and national assemblies. Even had unlimited time been available, constitutional arrangements would not have guaranteed a solution to political conflicts. As it was two uneasy divisions of power were made which were to prove the breaking points of the future: independence was to be handed over to a central Congo government, although provincial assemblies and governments would be established at the same time; and there was to be a prime minister and a head of state – the former invested and the other elected by the National Assembly.

The pressure on these weak points came from political forces within the country. The strongest of them was the independent interests of one of the provinces, Katanga, which, with only one eighth of the population of the Congo, produces more than half its wealth, as the result of the development of its mineral resources by foreign companies. At the time of independence the strongest political party in Katanga, the Conakat (*Confédération des Associations du Katanga*) was led by Moïse Tshombe, a man of forceful personality ready to ally himself with the foreign economic interests of his province against the central government, who had already secured a modification of the constitutional law in the Belgian parliament to give his party monopoly of power in Katanga. Separatist movements appeared in Kasai and in other provinces after independence; but none of them was so strong nor rested on such a firm base of economic wealth as that of Katanga. Meanwhile at the centre there existed differences of view as to the extent to which the central government should coerce the provinces; and these differences were represented by Patrice Lumumba and Joseph Kasavubu, the first prime minister and head of state respectively. It was Patrice Lumumba who had founded the only truly national political party, the *Mouvement national congolais*, in 1958 and who expressed the need for national unity with all the fiery appeal and the intolerance of a Robespierre.

The events which precipitated political conflict in the Congo also made it a matter of international concern. Within a week of independence the Congolese *Force Publique* – originally created by the Belgians to maintain order – mutinied against its Belgian officers. The Belgian government tried to persuade the Congolese government to agree to the use of Belgian troops to prevent the mutiny spreading and becoming a massacre; but it was only Tshombe who requested Belgian intervention. Belgian paratroops were landed none the less; Tshombe declared the secession of Katanga from the Congo. Lumumba and Kasavubu sought assistance from the United Nations – whose Security Council had recommended the Congo for membership on 7 July. They first asked for technical assistance to reorganize the administration and the security forces; then on 13 July they appealed for military assistance because Belgian intervention constituted an aggression and provided cover for the secession of Katanga. The secretary-general thereupon used his powers under Article 99 of the Charter to call an urgent meeting of the Security Council.

At this time the United Nations seemed a tower of strength in international affairs, and it owed much of its prestige to the achievement of Dag Hammarskjöld in establishing its anthority independently of the national interests of its members. None of the great powers of the world had any wish to involve themselves directly in the Congo, and the African states were intent on showing their ability to work through the United Nations in the solution of a predominantly African problem. A vital link between the southern African states and the old powers of Europe and America was provided by Tunisia, as a member of the Security Council – in the whole of Africa Tunisia had always been closest to Europe, and it was now represented at the United Nations by Mongi Slim, a statesman of Greek ancestry and outstanding skill and integrity.

From this consensus in the councils of the world there emerged two resolutions of the Security Council in July and a third in August 1960, which were unopposed.[4] These resolutions called for the withdrawal of Belgian troops, and provided for the dispatch of a United Nations force; the third of them was particularly concerned with the problem of Katanga, where United Nations forces had not yet been admitted.

The problem of the Congo was too great and too manifold for this unity to endure. The United Nations force was representative of a high degree of human civilization – it owed allegiance to an international organization, and its initial directives

[4] Resolutions of 14 July (China, France, and UK abstained), 22 July (unanimous), and 9 August (France and Italy abstained).

were that it was not sent to fight, but to maintain order. But the country to which it was sent was at this time characterized by the archaism of European mercenary soldiers and the primitivism of a backward African society. The dominant issue with which it was confronted was the secession of Katanga, in which classical problems of self-determination, of unity versus separatism, were inextricably mingled with the material interests of foreign enterprises intent on safeguarding their profits. In civilized societies law and order form a framework which is identifiable and can be upheld; in a revolutionary situation where there is a conflict of powers law dissolves into politics, and neither action nor inaction is possible without taking sides.

The core of the problem lay in the secession of Katanga, and the fact that the continued independence of that province was made possible by the wealth of its mineral enterprises and the presence of Belgian troops – while, conversely, Belgian troops enjoyed a privileged and protected position because of Katangese secession. The ending of the secession rapidly became a great cause for the 'left' in the Congo, in international politics, and in countries where opinions could be freely expressed. On the other side Tshombe and Katanga won the support of the 'right' – not only of those whose material interests were closely concerned, but of those who wanted the retention of a European presence in Africa and those who saw Tshombe as a man of practical good sense, uninfluenced by the heady ideologies of African socialism.

In the Congo Patrice Lumumba was most resolute in his hostility to Katanga and ceased to have any use for a United Nations force when it was not prepared to subdue the Tshombe régime by force. Outside the Congo he won political support from Ghana, Guinea, and Mali amongst the African states, and his cause was adopted by the Soviet Union, which intensified its criticisms of the United Nations and its attacks on the secretary-general. He also asked for and was given practical aid by the Soviet Union, which provided a few transport aircraft and lorries to move troops for an attack on Katanga. As he prepared for an actual attack on Katanga his political support narrowed sharply. The Ghanaians warned him of the unlikelihood of an attack succeeding and were concerned about the abandonment of neutralism implicit in the acceptance of Russian military aid. The African states could scarcely give aid to Lumumba after having committed their forces to the United Nations, which was too important for them for a breach to be acceptable.

Lumumba's attack on Katanga began at the end of August 1960 as delegates from the African states were engaged in a pan-African conference in Leopoldville; it quickly degenerated into tribal war. Then, on 5 September, Kasavubu announced that he had dismissed Lumumba and was asking Joseph Ileo to form a new government. The United Nations command saw the possibility that Lumumba might attack the capital rather than accept his dismissal, and decided that it was justified in acting to prevent civil war breaking out. It therefore closed airports to all but United Nations traffic and took over the radio station – actions which could be fully justified as designed for the maintenance of order, but which were clearly against Lumumba. Inevitably there was much argument as to the constitutionality of Kasavubu's action; on 14 September this argument was cut short when Colonel Joseph Mobutu announced that he was taking power with the support of the army. His action also ended direct Soviet intervention in the Congo, for shortly after taking power he closed the Soviet embassy, and the Soviet planes were then flown home by their crews. At the same time the Soviet Union, by directing its attacks against the United Nations and the secretary-general, isolated itself increasingly from African opinion outside the Congo, and suffered a marked diplomatic defeat in the Security Council and the Assembly.

Lumumba meanwhile continued to live in the prime minister's residence, guarded by the Congolese army, in the sense that he could not escape, and by the United Nations in that the Congolese could not arrest him. In this situation he was beyond reproach, and it was inevitable that his prestige should increase. His supporters planned his return to power, and organized his escape from his residence – but his freedom was shortlived, and he was arrested on 1 December 1960, four days after his escape. This sequence of events only increased the activity of his supporters, so that Kasavubu and Mobutu became convinced that Lumumba would only cease to be a danger to their government if he was transferred to Katanga. The transfer was made on 17 January, and Lumumba was not seen alive again. On 13 February the Katangese minister of the interior announced that Lumumba had been killed by villagers while trying to escape; it was generally assumed, however, that the Katangese were responsible for his murder, and that it had occurred sometime before the announcement was made. Whatever the facts of his death, Patrice Lumumba had achieved martyrdom. A postal clerk until shortly before independence, intolerant, suspicious, and headstrong, taken over as a hero by the Soviet Union and communists throughout the world, he none the less had captured the imagination of many amongst those who sought independence and dignity for Africans and African states.

With Lumumba's death the aims of the United Nations in the Congo seemed as far from achievement as ever. The one outstanding success had been the negotiation between Hammarskjöld and Tshombe in August, which had led to the establishment of a United Nations force in Katanga. But this was a force which had neither mandate nor strength to end Katangese secession, and was indeed in danger of becoming a hostage. Outside Katanga, parliamentary government had broken down. In Stanleyville Antoine Gizenga led Lumumba's followers in opposition to the uneasy alliance of Kasavubu and Mobutu in Leopoldville. Meanwhile in New York the pressure of the Afro-Asians in the United Nations for more decisive action against Katanga increased steadily and won support from the United States – but not from Britain or France.

By the end of 1961 the situation had changed decisively in favour of the central Congo and the United Nations. Three factors served to bring this change about. In successive resolutions in February and November 1961 the Security Council greatly strengthened the mandate of the United Nations force in the Congo, authorizing the secretary-general 'to take vigorous action, including the use of a requisite measure of force, if necessary, for the immediate apprehension . . . of all foreign military and para-military personnel'.[5] The forces at the disposal of the United Nations were increased. And at the beginning of August parliamentary government was reestablished under the premiership of Cyrille Adoula.

But nothing happened to bring negotiations between the central government and Katanga to a successful conclusion, so

[5] Resolution of 24 Nov. 1961, quoted by Hoskyns (*Congo since Independence*, p. 445).

that the United Nations could only establish its authority by force. It did so at the cost of one unsuccessful operation in September, which led indirectly to the death of the secretary-general. Any military operation by the United Nations had to achieve rapid victory with the minimum of bloodshed. A thin and artificial dividing line had been drawn between action to apprehend foreign military advisers and mercenaries, and political action against Katangese secession. Because of the support which Tshombe enjoyed, especially in Britain, France, and Belgium, the United Nations could not afford to be unsuccessful, and it could not even afford a major military showdown. In this situation, when the operation of mid-September failed (for reasons which are still unclear), Hammarskjöld sought to achieve a settlement with Tshombe by flying across the Congo by night to meet him at Ndola in Northern Rhodesia. A few miles from the airport his plane crashed and he was killed.

Inevitably it was supposed by many that his death had been contrived, although subsequent evidence was entirely on the side of an accident. A cease-fire was agreed in Katanga of an uneasy kind. Tshombe did nothing to remove his foreign advisers, and fresh arms continued to enter Katanga; while in New York U Thant of Burma was appointed acting secretary-general and the Security Council gave its November mandate to the United Nations force. The next clash came in the following month, and on this occasion the United Nations demonstrated its superiority sufficiently for Tshombe to capitulate – or at least to resort to political rather than military manoeuvring. Early in the morning of 23 December 1961 he signed a declaration, at Kitona, renouncing Katanga's secession and accepting the political unity of the Congo. In January 1962 Gizenga, who had joined Adoula's government in August only to break away again in October, was arrested, and the Stanleyville secession thereby ended as well.

Tshombe showed no disposition to honour the Kitona agreements. Throughout 1962 the Union Minière continued to pay royalties, export, and special taxes to the Katanga government, so that he had no difficulty in retaining mercenary soldiers. He used delay and evasion to prevent the extension of central government rule to Katanga, while adding to the strength of the Katangese forces. It appeared that he had only to bide his time for United Nations forces to withdraw through lack of finance or disagreement amongst its members, thereby removing the one serious challenge to his position.

His optimistic calculations were unfounded. In spite of the sympathy which Tshombe had enjoyed, especially in Belgium and in Britain, the strongest interest of the European powers and the United States, quite apart from the attitude of the African states, was in the ending of the Congo affair to minimize the danger of disorder and intervention by one or other side in the cold war, and no one now thought that Katangese independence (or rebellion) provided a basis for such stability – even though the British government continued to oppose coercion by the United Nations, whether by economic sanctions or military force. At the end of the year fresh fighting broke out between Katangese forces and United Nations troops, ending in the flight of Tshombe to Salisbury in Southern Rhodesia and an easy victory over the Katangese gendarmerie. On 15 January Tshombe once again announced that he was ready to end the secession of Katanga.

The Congo crisis had an important impact on the politics of the new African states and the position of Africa in world politics. It reduced the United Nations from the position of strength which it had acquired under Hammarskjöld's leadership to near bankruptcy, and showed the limitations of its authority when strong national interests or viewpoints were affronted. The cost and the frustrations of the exercise were a major discouragement to the great powers to involve themselves in African affairs. In the succeeding years there were isolated examples of military intervention by Belgian and American paratroopers in the Congo, by British troops in Uganda, Kenya, and Tanganyika, at the request of their governments, by French troops in the Gabon to maintain a government of their own liking. But the African states were fortunate in coming to independence when the exaggerated fears of communism which characterized the Dulles era had passed,[6] and when military bases were regarded as useless or a lost cause. The closest association of an imperial power with its ex-colonies was that of France with the poorer states of central and west

[6] In spite of the fact that Christian Herter regarded Ghana as a near-communist state.

Africa – refusing to pay its contribution to the United Nations Congo force, de Gaulle's government gave substantial aid to the francophone states, including direct contribution to their budgets.

African governments for their part wanted above all to maintain their independence and assert their own personality – in spite of their acknowledged dependence on outside aid for their economic development. Having achieved freedom from imperial rule they were extremely sensitive to any indication of American interest in their welfare as a defence against communism – justifiably, since they took swift action against the possibility of communist take-over. The Guinean government of Sekou Touré, choosing independence rather than membership of de Gaulle's newly fashioned Community in 1958, had turned to the Soviet Union and eastern Europe for a replacement of the aid – personal and financial – which de Gaulle had ruthlessly cut off; but in December 1961 it had expelled the Soviet ambassador on the grounds that the communists were planning to take power. In April 1964 a radical revolution with obvious and avowed communist sympathies in Zanzibar was followed by union with Tanganyika, in the establishment of the more moderate state of Tanzania. [7]

Associated with African neutralism was the strong desire for unity expressed by the new states. Pan-Africanism was an ideal that had developed in the days of colonial rule – particularly, as is so often the case with nationalist movements, among those of African descent in the West Indies and the United States. With independence the ideal remained; but it received very little practical implementation. Movements for independence had developed within the framework of imperial rule, and for all the accusations of 'Balkanization' levelled against the imperial powers, the boundaries of the new states remained those of the old colonies, with minor exceptions. In central Africa the proposed federation aroused antipathy amongst Africans, and no union other than that of Tanzania was formed; in west Africa the union of Mali was shortlived

---

[7] In January 1966 a report that the army had taken power in Upper Volta to thwart those who wanted to hand the country over to the Chinese communists suggested that here as elsewhere a communist threat, real or imaginary, could serve as a useful pretext.

and that of Ghana, Guinea, and Mali had little practical significance.

As the Congo crisis divided the great powers of the world, so it did the African states, bringing to the fore differences between the radicals and the reformers, between those who supported African union and those who argued, with Yusse Sule: 'Pan-Africanism is the only solution to our problems in Africa . . . But we must not be sentimental; we must be realistic . . . the idea of forming a Union of African States is premature'.[8] For two years the different camps were identified by the cities in which they met: the moderate Brazzaville group, which later grew into the Monrovia group, supporting mediation in the Congo and an inter-state economic secretariat; and the Casablanca powers, dominated by Ghana and the UAR, supporting Lumumba and African union.[9]

With the diminution of the Congo crisis unity was restored. In May 1963 thirty-one African states met at Addis Ababa.[10] Under the leadership of Emperor Hailé Selassié they drafted and signed the Charter of the Organization of African Unity.

[8] Nigerian delegate to the second Conference of Independent African States, Addis Ababa 1960, quoted by Colin Legum, *Pan-Africanism* (1962), p. 172.
[9] Their meeting took place at Casablanca because Morocco, which politically was closer to the Brazzaville group, sought support for its claims against Mauritania.
[10] Morocco did not attend because of its quarrel with Mauritania.

14

THE WARP AND WEFT OF
INTERNATIONAL RELATIONS

F R O M P L A T O onwards political theorists have likened political society to fabric, held together by the different strands of its weave. International politics in the twentieth century remained, as they always have been, substantially different from those of a national community; for governments retained ultimate control over their own countries, were independent of each other, and subjected to no overriding authority. They could only act within the limitations imposed by the resources of power at their command and they were restrained or pushed by public opinion, to the extent that it could express itself; but they remained sovereign independent governments.

Even so the twenty years following the end of the second world war were characterized by the growth of international institutions, some embracing almost all nations of the world, some only a few states, commanding respect and support from their members, acquiring, as all institutions do, their own internal loyalty and cohesion and exercising limited authority. To this extent international politics came to be more than the relations between nation states, and it is possible to discern the warp and weft of an international society.

THE UNITED NATIONS

The first world war ended with a sense of revulsion against the system of nation states and the diplomacy by which relations between them had been governed, and this was naturally accompanied by strong support for the creation of an international institution which would bring law, order, and organization into international as well as national life. During the second world war the general climate of opinion was different. There were few people who attributed this war to 'international anarchy'; even when emotions cooled it seemed to be much more the result of wilful aggression organized and directed by the leaders of a few countries. Nevertheless, as one commentator has pointed out, the hold of the nation state which 'shelters so much that civilized man rightly prizes' had been shaken by the second cataclysm of the century as by the first.[1] In Europe it seemed to have failed in its basic purpose of providing security; in Germany the exaltation of the nation state was part of the disease of Nazism; in the world in general it had been shown how frail were the restraints and customs which preserved normal intercourse between men. Even so the starting-point was different from that of twenty years previously, because it was necessary now to take account of the experience of an international institution, the League of Nations, as well. This experience had not been a happy one. Whether through faults in its constitution or lack of resolution in its members it had failed to contribute significantly to the security of the world or even to the conduct of international affairs. More important perhaps from a practical point of view was the fact that the League had failed to secure the adherence of one of the three leading powers of the wartime alliance – the United States – and in a sudden access of fervour for the principles of collective security had expelled another, the Soviet Union.

No doubt it is this that explains the curiously ambivalent attitude of the three great powers to the League of Nations. In a very real sense they were standing on the shoulders of their predecessors. For all the criticism heaped on Woodrow Wilson for his single-minded determination to include the Covenant of the League in the treaty of Versailles, this constituted the first and therefore the revolutionary step in the creation of the first such international organization, at the brief moment when it was possible to do so. Twenty-five years later the failure of the League and its alienation from two of the great powers meant that its name could hardly be mentioned. Moreover the precise diagnosis of the ills of international society was sufficiently different for the constitution of the new organization to show important variations of emphasis. But the broad design was the same; and the construction was made easier by the fact that no new ground needed to be broken. To quote again the same authority: 'at San Francisco, as at Dumbarton Oaks, the delegates paid the League a much more profound tribute

[1] H. G. Nicholas, *The United Nations as a Political Institution* (1959), p. 1.

than any formal eulogy could have expressed: they copied it'.[2]

The acceptability of some form of international security organization was in the first place tempered by hesitance on the part of the governments of the United States and the Soviet Union as to the extent of the commitment which they were prepared to accept in the politics of the post-war world. In the United States President Roosevelt himself does not seem to have doubted the desirability of such an institution, much as he wished to avoid the unenviable position which Wilson had created for himself by accepting an agreement which his country would reject. For this reason he took care to enlist the support of prominent Congressmen, particularly in the Republican party. In the end the decision was probably taken from the fact that American involvement in world affairs now seemed inescapable, and once that was accepted the general outline of an international organization, with its emphasis on some notion of lawful behaviour and its spreading of responsibilities for the enforcement of such behaviour, commended itself naturally to American thinking. It is less easy to guess at the reasoning which lay behind Stalin's acceptance of an international organization; but from the diplomacy which accompanied its establishment it is clear that he hoped for the maximum security for the Soviet Union with the minimum infringement of its position or its sphere of interest.

The Charter of the new organization which, because it was to be built on the basis of the wartime coalition, was called the United Nations organization, was devised at two conferences. The first was at Dumbarton Oaks in Washington, from August to October 1944 – as we have seen, this was in fact a relay conference between Britain, the United States, and the Soviet Union first, then with China replacing the Soviet Union. It produced a draft Charter, called 'Proposals for the Establishment of a General International Organization', which the second conference at San Francisco could discuss and vote on clause by clause.[3] This second conference was attended by the foreign ministers of all the members of the wartime United Nations (except Poland, since the identity of the Polish government was

[2] Ibid. p. 14.
[3] The four Dumbarton Oaks powers, with the addition of France, acted as sponsoring powers for the conference.

in dispute between the big three). Between the two conferences the most difficult question of all, that of voting procedure, was the subject of discussion, and spurious agreement, at the Yalta conference.

The striking feature of these discussions was the wide area of agreement, contrasted with the fact that on the vital point of voting the San Francisco conference nearly broke down altogether, and had to be saved by the intervention of Harry Hopkins with Stalin. The great powers agreed that none of them wished to create a supranational organization – and when the Charter finally emerged this was written into Article 2(1). They accepted that the main responsibility for the maintenance of peace rested with the great powers, and they agreed that they were not prepared to be obliged to undertake enforcement action without having voted for it. This was not only seen as a safeguard for national rights, but was also designed to ensure that action would be effective, and would not be entered upon unless it was certain to be carried through with full support from the great powers.

In the course of the negotiations it became clear, however, that the Soviet Union looked for a far more extensive veto, and that it wanted not only to prevent action to which one of the great powers was opposed, but also to safeguard its interests in the pacific settlement of disputes. At Yalta the United States and Britain had persuaded the Soviet Union to accept a formula which excluded the use of the veto (or any other vote) by a party to a dispute when the Security Council was seeking pacific settlement rather than enforcement action. In the end this formula was embodied in the Charter (Article 27) but this was only achieved after the Soviet Union had once again argued at San Francisco for an interpretation of the Yalta formula which would give a much fuller veto; the main contention in this argument being that as soon as the UN organization took up a question, it initiated a 'chain of events' which was likely to lead to enforcement in the end, and that the veto was therefore indispensable at the beginning. Inevitably the smaller powers – and particularly those of medium size like Australia – found this privileged position accorded to the great powers unsatisfactory; but they had little choice but to accept it if the organization was going to come into existence at all. However, the experience of the UN soon showed that the Soviet

Union had not departed from its interpretation of the veto power, which it used with a frequency and a scope which the other members of the organization had never intended.

Another of the points which had been at issue at Yalta was membership of the organization. It was agreed that this should be accorded in the first place to members of the wartime coalition, defined as governments which had declared war on the Axis by 1 March 1945. But at Dumbarton Oaks the United States, supported by Britain, had urged the inclusion of states which had been invited to the United Nations economic conferences and which were assisting the belligerents. Stalin countered this by requesting that all sixteen of the constituent republics of the Soviet Union should become members. Churchill and Roosevelt found this excessive, but they agreed to accept the representation of two Soviet Socialist Republics in addition to the Soviet Union – an agreement given effect at San Francisco. There was no obvious justification for such an arrangement, except that it might alleviate Stalin's sense of isolation – and might make it possible for India to be represented before the achievement of independence, which Churchill saw as more distant than was in fact to be the case. Once the wartime alliance had ceased to be an appropriate criterion for membership, however, there was no other which was obviously appropriate. It was possible to argue that there should be no bar to membership, since the organization claimed to be universal and was the stronger the more justified this claim could be made to be. On the other hand the Charter opens with a declaration of principles to which signatories subscribe, and once the organization was established it could be argued that a candidate for membership must not only accept these principles, but must be considered by the existing members to justify its acceptance by acting accordingly. However, Article 4 of the Charter provides that 'membership in the United Nations is open to all other peace loving states which accept the obligations contained in the present Charter and, in the judgment of the Organization, are able and willing to carry out these obligations'. As the words 'peace loving' are (to say the least) imprecise, and as the organization never achieved unanimity, the implementation of this article would depend on the way in which votes on new members were taken. This was provided for in the remainder of Article 4, which made it depend on 'a decision of the General Assembly upon the recommendation of the Security Council'; and such a recommendation was itself dependent on the unanimity of the great powers. It is not surprising, therefore, that as the divisions of the cold war found their way into the UN, each side should support the admission of countries which it hoped would be at least on balance on its side, and oppose the admission of others; and the shortage of communist or near-communist governments in the world placed the Soviet Union on the defensive. Consequently only 11 new members were admitted before 1955 when 16 countries were given membership under a 'package deal' agreed essentially between the United States and the Soviet Union. Once this point had been passed, however, and as each side in the cold war wished to gain the favour of newly independent states, the question of membership became less vexed; and as the organization grew numerically additional members in any case made less impact on it. The great powers in their wartime discussions, and great and small powers alike thereafter, had succeeded in establishing a world-wide organization designed 'to achieve international peace and security' (Article 1).

In all this the experience of the UN was markedly different from that of the League. The weakness of the League derived from the fact that Britain and France were the only great powers which were members from beginning to end, that the United States never wished to join, and that Germany, Italy, and Japan left the League when it did not suit their purposes. The UN in contrast has kept the membership of the great powers – perhaps because the Soviet Union's absence from the Security Council's meeting on the Korean war was seen to carry its own penalty; and the smaller powers have never been discouraged from seeking membership by the wrangling which their application has provoked within the organization. Great and small powers alike have absented themselves from certain meetings or have refused to participate in the work of some of the specialized agencies,[4] but until 1965 this was not followed by complete withdrawal. The outstanding exception to all this was the case of China, which was a founder member of the UN and a permanent member of the Security Council, but as the communist government was not recognized

[4] France – Algeria; South Africa – South West Africa; Portugal; Soviet Union.

by the United States or by many of its allies, China continued to be represented by the Nationalist government. By 1965 it was evident that as a result of this anomaly communist China had an interest in remaining outside the UN, and exercised an attraction to others, of which the first was Indonesia.

It was not in this wide membership, open to great and small powers alike, however, that the central hopes for the organization were placed. The driving force for its establishment lay in the desire to achieve peace and security, and this it was thought could only be achieved by the actions of the great powers. The core of the organization as far as peace and security were concerned was thus to be the Security Council. Of this body the five great or presumed-to-be-great powers, the United States, the Soviet Union, France, Britain, and China, were made permanent members; six other seats were to be filled by members for two-year periods. And it was here that the privileged voting power of the great powers was situated, decisions on all matters other than procedural matters being made 'by an affirmative vote of seven members including the concurring votes of the permanent members; provided that, in decisions under Chapter VI, and under paragraph 3 of Article 52,[5] a party to a dispute shall abstain from voting'.

This concession to the realities of national interest apart, everything was done to make the Security Council a close-knit and efficient organization to go quickly into action to preserve the peace. It was to be 'so organized as to be able to function continuously' and thus avoid the delays which had characterized the procedure of the League; it was to be assisted by a Military Staff Committee, and to have at its call from members, in accordance with a special agreement, 'armed forces, assistance, and facilities, including rights of passage, necessary for the purpose of maintaining international peace and security'. In addition, it was to be primarily responsible for action undertaken to achieve the pacific settlement of disputes. It was to call on parties to a dispute to submit to such procedures as arbitration and judicial settlement – which, as members of the organization, they were committed to resort to in any case – to investigate and to recommend, and to propose reference to the International Court where appropriate. It was in the pursuit of these objectives that the exception to the veto rule was made,

[5] Both references are to the Pacific Settlement of Disputes.

parties to a dispute being obliged to abstain from voting.

Given the applicability of the veto in all other non-procedural decisions of the Security Council, one could well ask what were the circumstances in which the Council might be able to act. The concentration of directive power in the Council, the attempt to create an efficient close-knit body able to avoid the delays and inaction of the League Council, derived from the belief that the war just ended was the result of deliberate planned aggression rather than accidents or miscalculation. But it was obvious that the Security Council could not act against one of its own members as long as the veto was applicable to enforcement measures; it could act against small powers; and it could also act against the former enemies, who were not members of the organization at its inception and could not, without revision of the Charter, become permanent members of the Security Council.

It is not surprising, therefore, that the Security Council acted only once in a way similar to that which had been envisaged for it – in calling for resistance to the attack of North Korea on South Korea – and this was only possible through the unforeseeable absence of the Soviet Union from the Council. Even so, the military direction of the operation against North Korea could not be in the hands of the Council, where disagreement amongst the permanent members had made impossible any effective action on the part of the Military Staff Committee[6] or any agreement on the contribution of armed forces for UN use. Instead, the United States was responsible for actual military direction of the operation, although it reported to the United Nations. But the Soviet Union soon realized the obvious error of absence from the Security Council, and its delegate in August assumed his rightful place as chairman, thereby destroying the fortuitous unanimity of the great powers present and voting.

The impact of these events on the shape and future of the UN might have been different had the veto power been used only in this comparatively extreme case. In fact it had been used consistently and repeatedly by the Soviet Union before that time. In the absence of the documents it is impossible to know how Russian policy on the UN, and to particular issues which were brought before it, was framed. We have supposed

[6] The committee was set up on 4 February 1946 and has never been formally dissolved.

that the original Russian adhesion to the organization derived in part from a desire for security against Germany, and in part from a desire not to isolate itself from its wartime allies. But in the years immediately after the war Germany was not a threat to the Soviet Union; and after 1947 good relations with the western powers ceased to be an object of policy. Moreover, in spite of its three-seat representation in the Assembly, Russia found itself in a permanent minority on all the issues to which it attached most importance. It seems likely that Stalin at least considered withdrawing from the UN – the World Peace Council was acclaimed as surpassing the UN (although this may have been no more than propaganda for its own sake) – and it has been suggested that the Russian absence from the crucial Security Council meetings in June 1950 originated from a planned face-saving withdrawal from the organization as a whole.[7] Whatever the motives for Soviet action, the form which that action often took was the use of the veto – most notably on the Greek question and the admission of new members.

In this way the activity of the Security Council had been gravely impaired long before the Korean question showed the risks attendant on the veto power by the way in which those risks were avoided in that particular case. The result was that the distinction which the Charter drew between the work of the Security Council and that of the Assembly very quickly began to be blurred. As we have seen, the Security Council was given the directing role in enforcement, and the major role with regard to pacific settlement of disputes. The Assembly was denied any competence in a dispute with which the Council was charged, and it was assumed that the Council would deal with urgent and important matters, leaving the less serious matters to the Assembly. But the ineffectiveness of the Security Council led inevitably to important questions like the Greek question, Korean independence, and most notably the Palestine question being referred to the Assembly. Procedural means were soon found to circumvent the exclusion of a question from the Assembly's agenda while it was under discussion by the Council by presenting it under a different and distinct form. Similarly, when Britain decided to refer the Palestine question to the UN, the Assembly was called into special session to discuss

[7] See A. Dallin, *The Soviet Union at the United Nations* (1962), ch. 3.

the future of the mandate, as was constitutionally correct in view of the responsibility of the Trusteeship Council to the Assembly. But a question of major importance for security had been taken to the Assembly, not the Security Council.

To counter the growing ineffectiveness of the Council the American government proposed that its work should be done by a committee of the Assembly, and so in November 1947 an Interim Committee (which came to be known as the 'Little Assembly') was created, to be summoned whenever the Assembly itself was not in session to handle any matter referred to it by the Assembly. In the event it had little practical importance, partly because the Assembly itself met so often and for such long periods that there was no place for an Interim Committee. But in 1950 a further step was taken, again as the result of the initiative of the American government, in the passing of the 'Uniting for Peace' resolution. This grew directly out of the experience of the opening of the Korean war, and was designed to avert the risks which it had revealed. The resolution was passed by the Assembly on 2 November 1950 by 52–5–2.[8] The opposing votes were those of the Soviet bloc, and the Soviet Union afterwards always maintained that the resolution was illegal. Under its terms the Assembly can be summoned at twenty-four hours' notice by a vote of seven members of the Security Council or by a majority of the Assembly itself. Once assembled it has the power to recommend action to maintain or restore international peace and security, 'including in the case of a breach of the peace or act of aggression the use of armed force when necessary'.

The importance of these provisions is obvious. Ironically, the resolution was first given effect against the action of two of its principal supporters, when the Assembly called for a cease-fire in the Middle East in October 1956. But quite apart from this particular instance, it is clear that it constituted an actual revision of the Charter, although legally it did not take that form. Moreover the terms of the Uniting for Peace resolution went further. It provided for the setting up of a Peace Observation Commission 'to observe and report situations anywhere in the world likely to endanger international peace'; and it called on member states to provide forces ready for use by the UN. There was a direct relation between these provisions and

[8]Argentina and India abstained: the Lebanon was absent.

the circumstances of the Korean war, for it was widely recognized that the effectiveness of UN action owed much to the presence in Korea of a UN mission, and to the fact that American troops were stationed in Japan, and American naval and air forces in the area, so that they could go into action immediately. But these two parts of the resolution had little practical effect. The Peace Observation Commission was set up and used once, in the Balkans in 1952; and while some nations are at present earmarking national contingents for UN service, this has occurred as a development quite separate from the resolution, although this has not prevented the Assembly from authorizing UN police forces in the Middle East and in West Irian.

Fortunately for the survival of the organization, as its internal balance shifted away from the Security Council, the Assembly showed that it had acquired a life of its own as a political institution. This was attested to by the evident desirability of membership, on which we have already commented. It was shown further in the emergence of 'blocs', particularly in the Assembly. One has only to name these blocs – the Afro-Asian, the Arabs, the Latin Americans, the communists, the British Commonwealth, the western Europeans – to see how much, with the exception of the communists, they overlap each other, and how fluid they are likely to be in their actual voting. But they exist, and are recognized by the Charter's references to 'equitable geographical representation'. Their importance has sometimes been exaggerated, and their activities have sometimes been deplored, possibly because the most enthusiastic supporters of the United Nations nurture a liberal view according to which political parties are the natural proponents of expediency and opportunism to the detriment of conscience and disinterestedness. But a cooler appraisal of politics shows that political combinations must and do occur in any organization which succeeds in being more than an ineffective bystander, and the existence of bloc voting in the UN is a measure of the importance which its members attach to it.

For many governments the importance of the UN is enhanced by the fact that membership gives them a stature in world politics which they could not possibly achieve except in an institution which accords them a vote equal to that of the Soviet Union and the United States, even though their population would not fill a fair-sized town in either of those countries; while one or two others achieve an influence in the UN more nearly in proportion to what seems their due by their size and population, but which they are denied in the world of power politics.[9] Not only can the delegations of such countries vote, but they can suppose that in doing so they are taking part in the formulation and enunciation of a 'moral law of the world', and in voicing the moral instincts of the peoples of the world against the corruption of power. Sometimes their claim to be doing so must seem bogus – at least when set against the record of law and morality practised within their own states – but at others, as when the small powers insist on the need for disarmament and the perils of nuclear weapons, it is not. And bogus or not, it makes membership of the UN worthwhile.

In this way the General Assembly developed into something similar to the image that had been invoked at San Francisco, of a 'town forum of the world'. But like a town forum – and unlike what most of the delegates at San Francisco had imagined – the meetings were often noisy, vehement, and fruitless rather than restrained and constructive. Certainly it reflected the dominant concern of a large number of the newer members with the question of colonial rule and its termination.

The San Francisco conference brought out an inevitable conflict of interest between powers with and those without imperial responsibilities; the conflict was resolved by a compromise which provided a firm starting point for those who wished to subject colonial rule to international scrutiny. The territories which had previously been governed under League of Nations mandates were, provided the mandatory powers agreed, placed under the supervision of a Trusteeship Council. Under the Charter this Council is composed of the permanent members of the Security Council, all the trustee powers, and other members elected by the General Assembly in such number as to produce equality between the administering and non-administering powers.

The Trusteeship Council was given no power other than that which follows from the possibility of bringing facts to light and maintaining a constant supervision and intermittent moral

[9] On the other hand China, the country with the world's greatest population, continued to be represented by the Nationalist government; Indonesia, with some 80 million inhabitants, left the UN in 1965 but rejoined in 1966.

pressure. Moreover the territories which came under its aegis – Samoa, the Cameroons, Ruanda-Urundi – did not become focal points of international interest. One territory, South West Africa, might well have developed into such a focal point, but the government of South Africa incorporated this former League of Nations mandated area into its own territory, and refused to admit that the Trusteeship Council had any competence in the matter. Finding UN criticism of its apartheid policy and its incorporation of South West Africa equally unacceptable, it withdrew from the Assembly from 1955 to 1958, when a more flexible policy brought a return to the UN and the visit of a UN Good Offices Committee to Pretoria.

It was other provisions of the Charter, therefore, which gave the greatest opportunity to bring the question of colonial rule into public debate. Most important of these was Chapter XI, the Declaration Regarding Non-Self-Governing Territories. In this chapter the signatories to the Charter who were responsible for 'non-self-governing territories' undertook certain obligations as a 'sacred trust', including the development of self-government, the furthering of international peace and security, and the promotion of 'constructive measures of development'. In addition they undertook (in Article 73e) 'to transmit regularly to the Secretary-General for information purposes . . . statistical and other information of a technical nature relating to economics, social and educational conditions in the territories for which they are . . . responsible'.

The obligations implied in such words were not by themselves very great; but they were extended as soon as the UN began its work. Australia, Belgium, Denmark, France, the Netherlands, New Zealand, Britain, and the United States submitted information about the territories under their government, although Spain and Portugal did not. In December 1946 an Ad Hoc Committee of the General Assembly was set up to consider such information, and this was followed by the establishment of a Special Committee, which was then renewed for successive periods of three years. In varying degrees the colonial powers argued that Article 73(e) did not require them to submit political information, and that the information they did provide for the secretary-general was intended for documentation only, not for discussion and decision.

In contrast, the opponents of colonialism maintained that the distinction between the Trust Territories and colonies was an accident of history, and that the colonial powers were thus accountable to the UN. They further insisted that self-government was the only form of good government; so that colonial rule should not be judged by the welfare of the people, but by the speed with which it was moving towards its own dissolution. It followed from this that comparisons between non-self governing territories and neighbouring independent states were irrelevant, and an Assembly resolution of December 1950 prevented the secretariat from making such comparisons.

The division in this debate was determined by the steady inflow of new members of the UN, amongst whom a large majority either had recently gained their independence, or had an interest in 'anti-colonialism'. But by the time this had happened the number of powers interested in the retention of colonial rule in any substantial form had greatly diminished, so that in November 1961 an Assembly resolution calling for a rapid end to colonialism was carried by 97 to nil, with Britain, France, Portugal, South Africa, and Spain abstaining. Similarly, the anti-colonialist members of the Assembly sought the right for the Assembly to determine whether a country could be regarded as 'non-self-governing', and to establish that the transmission of information was not optional but obligatory, and it finally succeeded in securing an Assembly resolution to that effect – by which time it was directed primarily against Portugal.

Article 73, or Chapter XI, was not the only lever in the Charter which could be wielded by those interested in the plight of subject peoples. Article 11(2) gives the Assembly the power to 'discuss any questions relating to the maintenance of international peace and security', and this has been taken as sufficient to justify the discussion by the Assembly of matters which sovereign powers have claimed come within their domestic jurisdiction and are therefore expressly excluded from the competence of the UN by Article 2(7). In this way the Indian government brought the treatment of Indian subjects in South Africa before the Assembly, and later the racial policies of that government as a whole were the subject of debate. The claim that colonial questions were the concern of the Assembly could be made even more plausibly when independence movements engaged in war or terrorism, as was the case in Algeria and Cyprus.

In certain specific cases the UN has contributed directly to the movement towards self-government. In 1949 the Assembly resolved that Libya should gain its independence by 1952 and Somaliland no later than 1960, and thereby gave obvious encouragement to nationalism in neighbouring territories. It played an important part through its Good Offices Committee in the transition of Indonesia to independence. The Trusteeship Council and the Committee on Information have provided information and understanding as well as political argument, and the resources of the UN have been drawn on for the supervision of plebiscites in Eritrea, British Togoland, and the British Cameroons.

There can be no doubt that the constant debate of the colonial question in the Assembly has also influenced the course of events. Much as the legality of such discussion may be questioned by a government such as that of Portugal, the Assembly has acted in this respect, as we have suggested, as a forum for one of the outstanding political issues of the period. By so doing it has contributed to public opinion in democratic countries with colonial responsibilities and made colonial governments more hesitant to use force in 'police actions'. At the same time it has encouraged those who struggled in whatever way for independence, and made it easier for them to keep up the momentum of revolt. Its influence should, however, be seen as one contributory factor amongst many. The nationalism which has spread from Europe to Asia and to Africa has had a catalytic effect on the demographic strength of colonial peoples, and together nationalism and population growth have constituted a force of overwhelming dimensions. At the same time it must be seen that the General Assembly has, like all assemblies, acted as a moderating influence. Its moral and suasive power, such as it is, can only be captured by the mobilization of a majority, so that extremist resolutions have consistently failed, to be replaced by others of more moderate aim and language which can command widespread support.

There were other ways in which the UN had, by 1960, established for itself an authority quite different from what might have been foreseen in 1945. This it had done in part by its very existence, and by bringing together delegations of nation states who became familiar with each other – in spite of the frequency with which national delegations change – and were able to engage in a form of day-to-day diplomacy, of lobbying, bargaining in corridors, and discreet agreement which was unknown to traditional diplomatic procedure conducted by telegrams and ambassadors.

More important than this, however, was the fact that the organization had begun to acquire an executive – and a centre of direction – not, as had been intended, in the Security Council, but in the secretary-general. His office gradually acquired an importance and authority which the Charter had scarcely envisaged, even though it contained the germ of his power. Article 99 of the Charter stated that 'The Secretary-General may bring to the attention of the Security Council any matter which in his opinion may threaten the maintenance of international peace and security'. It thereby gave the secretary-general more decisive power than had been wielded by his predecessor under the League. Thereafter the election of the first secretary-general, Trygve Lie (a former foreign minister of Norway), was quickly followed by a further extension of the secretary's powers. Lie established the right of the secretary-general to intervene in the proceedings both of the Security Council and the General Assembly. In addition, he began to campaign actively for what he regarded as the interests of the UN and of world peace. He did so at a time when the organization was burdened with responsibilities almost too heavy for so young an institution, and at a time when any attempt to assert the authority of the secretary-general would inevitably bring opposition from whichever party felt its interests to be adversely affected.

It was characteristic of Trygve Lie (who had belonged to the Norwegian government in exile during the war and helped transfer the Norwegian fleet to Britain) that he should abjure neutrality. He was opposed to the establishment of the UN in Switzerland, and later wrote:

Personally I had never . . . regarded a neutral country as the ideal site for an active, 'trouble shooting' world organization. . . . World peace, and the world I wished to live in, could not be won or assured by the type of thinking which made neutrality its first concern during the last World War.[10]

It followed that the UN should play an active role in world

[10] *In the Cause of Peace* (1954), p. 59.

affairs, and that the secretary-general should provide leadership for it to do so. But by trying to make the UN an 'active, trouble-shooting world organization' he inevitably encountered at times the apathy and at times the opposition of members who would gladly support the general principles of the organization but were less ready to accept their application in areas where their national interests were involved. To Trygve Lie it appeared proper that once the UN had agreed on the partition of Palestine, it should provide the force necessary to ensure that its decision was carried into effect; but he found no support for such action from those who had voted for the resolution. When the United States suddenly reversed its policy and proposed a new trusteeship, he went so far as to propose that he and the American delegate, Warren Austin, should resign in protest against the bad faith of the American government in going back on a UN decision, and thereby making its work impossible. More dramatically, he reacted with great vigour at the news of the invasion of South Korea, and regarded this as a situation which he should bring to the attention of the Security Council under Article 99 – although the action of the American delegate made it unnecessary for him to do so.

His unqualified and active support for UN action in Korea evoked bitter hostility from the Soviet Union, and this was to be of crucial importance, since his term of office came to an end in February 1951. The Soviet Union had supported his candidature in 1946 and had supported his initial actions to strengthen his office; now Vyshinsky said: 'He is unobjective, two faced, and we will have no truck with him.' The result was deadlock, since the United States took up an opposite position, and would consider no alternative to the Secretaryship other than the reappointment of Lie. From this situation an escape was found – setting a precedent for future deadlocks in the organization – by an extension of Lie's term of office. This was done against the vote of the Soviet Union – but such a vote did not constitute a veto. Not surprisingly the Soviet Union and its satellites did not abandon their opposition to Lie, and from the day of his extension in office on 2 February 1951 they boycotted him officially and socially, neither submitting credentials to the secretary-general nor inviting Lie and his wife to dinner parties, even when they invited the secretariat. But this did not shield the secretariat from the fury of those in Senator McCarthy's

America who were alarmed at the possibility of communist infiltration into government. For many such people the UN appeared a natural bolt-hole for 'disloyal' Americans, and UN employees were brought before a sub-committee of the Senate Judiciary Committee – where several of them pleaded the Fifth Amendment of the constitution. For all Lie's efforts to protect his staff, and to act consistently with the principle that 'the Secretary-General and the staff shall not seek or receive instructions from any government or from any other authority external to the Organization' (Article 100), he was obliged to accept a certain number of dismissals and a consequent lowering of morale.

In this atmosphere Lie announced his intention to resign on 10 November 1952. But although he did so in the maelstrom of the Korean war and the loyalty issue, and although he had acquired a certain reputation for exuberant combativeness rather than measured and cautious diplomatic activity, he left the office of secretary-general considerably stronger than it had been under the Charter. He had enhanced the powers and prestige of the office within the UN itself. He had also travelled across the world – to the Middle East, Latin America, and to the European capitals – and engaged in peace-keeping or peace-seeking diplomacy directly with governments.

At the same time the UN had developed other resources for conciliation and interposition wherever conflicts might occur in the world. It had dispatched a Commission of Investigation concerning Greek Frontier Incidents. There had been a Security Council Committee of Good Offices on the Indonesian question and a UN Commission on India and Pakistan. The Security Council had also established a Truce Commission for Palestine – a Commission which was headed at first by Count Folke Bernadotte, until he was murdered on 16 September 1948 by Jewish terrorists who were immediately disowned by the Israeli government.

Nearly five months passed after Lie's announcement of his intention to resign before the permanent members of the Security Council could agree on a successor. On 31 March 1953 their choice fell on a man who in a short time was to capture the imagination of the world, and who, when he died in an aeroplane accident in September 1961, left behind him a collection of sombre yet hopeful recollections which far transcended his political office.[11] But when he was elected he was scarcely known – even though he was a minister without portfolio in the Swedish government[12] – and he was appointed on the assumption that he would be quieter and less forceful in his conduct of his office than his predecessor.

Soon after his appointment, as we have seen, the influx of new members into the UN began to change the character of the organization. This was particularly true after 1955, when competition between the cold war powers for the support of the 'uncommitted' nations made the UN an important forum. The conversations and bargains which could then be effected in the corridors of the UN buildings acquired an enhanced significance, and at the same time the secretary-general could hope to find a larger group of middle nations who would support a UN policy on any single issue which came up.

However, this was perhaps less important than the attention which Hammarskjöld himself gave to his office. He was a man of deep and subtle thought, who trod the paths of diplomacy with immense care and self-control, but who developed a clear view of the office he filled and the way it should be used. His concept of the secretariat he explained in a lecture given to the University of Oxford on 30 May 1961, which justifies quotation at length:

To sum up, the Charter laid down these essential legal principles for an international civil service:

It was to be an international body, recruited primarily for efficiency, competence, and integrity, but on as wide a geographical basis as possible;

It was to be headed by a Secretary-General who carried constitutionally the responsibility to the other principal organs for the Secretariat's work;

And finally, Article 98 entitled the General Assembly and the Security Council to entrust the Secretary-General with tasks going beyond the *verba formalia* of Article 97 – with its emphasis on the administrative function – thus opening the door to a measure of political responsibility which is distinct from the authority explicitly accorded to the Secretary-General under Article 99 but in keeping with the spirit of that Article.

[11] Dag Hammarskjöld, *Markings* (1964).
[12] The announcement of his appointment described him incorrectly as director-general of the Swedish Foreign Ministry.

This last-mentioned development concerning the Secretary-General, with its obvious consequences for the Secretariat as such, takes us beyond the concept of a non-political civil service into an area where the official, in the exercise of his functions, may be forced to take stands of a politically controversial nature. It does this, however, on an international basis and, thus, without departing from the basic concept of 'neutrality'; in fact, Article 98, as well as Article 99, would be unthinkable without the complement of Article 100 strictly observed both in letter and spirit.[13]

The occasions on which the secretary-general could play the role so carefully described in this passage were numerous. In 1954 he flew to China to talk to Chou En-lai, and endeavoured to secure the release of eleven American airmen captured in Korea; this and his subsequent diplomacy can be assumed to have been responsible for their release a few months later. In 1956 he made an extensive visit to the Middle East, with authority from the Security Council; but his attempt to ease the task and strengthen the authority of the UN Truce Supervision Organization (which had remained since the time of the Arab-Israeli armistice) was thwarted by the outbreak of the Suez crisis. This crisis itself then thrust upon him the task of organizing the United Nations expeditionary force and negotiating with Nasser the terms under which the force would enter Egypt, as well as arrangements for clearing the canal. In 1958 he enlarged the UN Observation Group in the Lebanon, in spite of the fact that the Soviet Union vetoed the Security Council resolution giving him authority to do so. Equally important, he established a UN Office in Jordan. In 1959, after the Security Council had dispatched a sub-committee to Laos, which reported that there was no evidence of aggression across the Laotian border, he flew there himself, and on his return left behind a senior UN officer, who later became 'Special Consultant to the Secretary-General'.

The development of the secretary-general's office in this distinctive way was possible only because of the readiness of the Security Council and the General Assembly to give him definite but loosely defined authority. Thus the resolution on the Lebanon empowered him: 'to take such measures . . . as he may consider necessary', and later the Arab governments sponsored a resolution authorizing him to make 'such practical arrange-

---

[13] *The International Civil Servant in Law and in Fact* (1961), pp. 13–14.

ments as would adequately help in upholding the purposes and principles of the Charter in relation to Lebanon and Jordan in the present circumstances. . . '. The secretary-general's office thus acquired a strength and authority which was based on the fine sense of Dag Hammarskjöld, the consensus of the Security Council and the Assembly, the willingness of member governments to resort to the United Nations, and the availability of UN officers to establish a 'UN presence' wherever it might be needed, in Vientiane or Amman. It is understandable, therefore, that in July 1960, when the government of the Congo appealed for UN military aid, the organization and its executive should appear strong enough to meet this new crisis. Certainly the secretary-general proved strong enough, thanks to the support he received in the Assembly, to ride out a fresh storm of criticism of his office from the Soviet Union when in September 1960 Khrushchev told the Assembly that the post should be abolished and replaced by a collective executive of three (a 'troika') representing the communist, the western, and the neutral states respectively.

But as events turned out the issues to be decided in the Congo, particularly with regard to the secession of Katanga, taxed the 'neutral' political authority of the secretary-general's office to breaking point and destroyed the consensus of the organization. Hammarskjöld himself met his death, presumably by accident, on 18 September 1961. This placed an immeasurable strain on the UN, the more so since its finance, and particularly the financing of its special peace-keeping operations, depended on the consensus and support of member governments. In the years following the Congo operation the organization had still to demonstrate its powers of recovery.

The impact of the UN on the course of international events must remain a matter for individual assessment. We have seen how it acted swiftly to counter aggression in Korea: but the United States and its allies might well have acted similarly without the UN. It was powerless to take action against Soviet forces in Hungary or to give any effective response to Imre Nagy's appeal for recognition of his country's neutrality; it could not even break down the Kadar government's refusal to admit the secretary-general or his officers. A special committee of the Assembly investigated the Hungarian revolt as well as it could by questioning refugees, and submitted a report which evoked widespread and renewed condemnation of Soviet action. It scored an outstanding success in the creation of the United Nations expeditionary force at the time of the Suez crisis, for it thereby made it possible for British and French troops to withdraw with less loss of prestige, and it established a semi-permanent armed force interposed between two sides in a minor cold war. In the colonial sphere, Assembly debates made it impossible for imperial 'police actions' to escape the focus of the world's attention.

DISARMAMENT

The constant preoccupation of European political theory has been the justification of power and its use. No such body of theory has been written about the relations between states, but the activities of the UN, however arbitrary they sometimes appear, may have made a practical contribution to an extension of this inquiry into the international field. However that may be, the UN and its members achieved little success in the actual diminution, under agreement, of the armed force wielded by nation states. The Charter gave special responsibility in this respect to the General Assembly when it said, in Article 11: 'The General Assembly may consider . . . the principles governing disarmament and the regulation of armaments, and may make recommendations with regard to such principles to the Members or to the Security Council or to both.' Moreover the new organization met in 1946 with the knowledge that the problem of armaments had been given a new dimension by the invention and explosion of the atom bomb. The UN was thus continuously seized with the problem of disarmament, even though discussion on disarmament also went on outside its aegis; but the results achieved were slight.

In 1946 the United States possessed a monopoly of atomic weapons. Impressed by the danger which the new bomb meant for the world, it proposed to the newly constituted UN Atomic Energy Commission that it should set up an International Atomic Development Authority which would control the production and use of atomic fuel. Bernard Baruch, speaking for the United States, offered the UN a choice between 'world peace or world destruction', and undertook on behalf of his government to surrender the American stockpile and technical knowledge to such an authority once it was established. He insisted, however, that the authority should have enforcement powers, free of the possibility of veto.

On this rock the 'Baruch plan' foundered, since it was unacceptable to the Soviet Union; it is in any case a matter for speculation how long the United States readiness to surrender its monopoly of atomic power would have lasted in the conditions of the cold war. In 1947, following resolutions passed by the General Assembly, the Security Council set up a Commission for Conventional Armaments. For five years the two Commissions worked parallel to each other, but neither was more effective than the other. In 1952 an Assembly resolution merged the two together in a single Disarmament Commission.

The UN retained its interest in disarmament discussions even when, as was later the case, they were conducted outside its aegis. But the decisions on which any progress must depend were those of national governments, and for them disarmament was always subordinate to armament and strategy. The dropping of the first atomic bomb had revealed a new threat to mankind: but it also opened up vast new possibilities of weapons development. Government energies and expenditure were in consequence devoted to the construction of a hydrogen bomb to succeed the atomic weapons, and to the development of bigger bombs, smaller bombs, and cleaner bombs – and then to their production as economically as possible. The dramatic landmarks in this progress were the explosion of the first Russian atomic weapon in September 1949, the American hydrogen bomb in November 1952, and its Russian successor in August 1953. The British followed with a hydrogen bomb exploded at Christmas Island in May 1957 and the French successfully tested a nuclear device in February 1960. Meanwhile strategy had come to take account of the formidable possibilities of the new weapons. The period when they were thought of merely as larger versions of high explosive weapons was past, and as technological progress forged ahead, strategic planning sought to keep abreast of the changed scale of warfare.

In this environment, and while the cold war went through a period of maximum tension, it was unlikely that disarmament discussions would make rapid progress. The western powers – and they were able to command a majority in the Security Council and the General Assembly – insisted on the importance of disclosure of armaments, followed by international inspection to verify disclosures made, and the implementation of agreements. The Soviet Union in contrast proposed that there should first be a convention prohibiting atomic weapons, then great power reduction of armaments by one-third: only thereafter should states be required to submit information about their armaments and armed forces, and an international control organization be set up.

Following the establishment of the Disarmament Commission in 1952 the British and French governments sought to narrow the gap between these extreme positions by working out a programme of balanced disarmament by stages. Their intention was to take account of the disparate proportions of atomic to conventional armaments in the American and Russian armouries, to devise a plan which would achieve a 'balanced' reduction of both, and to achieve this by such stages that at no point in time would either side be vulnerable.

The Anglo-French proposal was accepted by the government of the United States but was initially rejected by that of the Soviet Union. Then, on 10 May 1955, the Soviet position changed, and the Russians put forward a new disarmament plan which closely approximated to the Anglo-French proposals. Their motivation for doing so remains difficult to establish. But while the western governments welcomed the change in the Russian position, they did not proceed to explore the possibilities it opened up. The date of the Soviet proposals was that on which the western powers formally proposed a meeting of heads of state. The disarmament suggestions were therefore taken, as a result of western insistence, away from the Sub-committee of the Disarmament Commission to the summit meeting. There they were given priority by the Soviet Union: but the western powers insisted on tackling first the question of European security, and above all Germany. Eisenhower proposed 'open skies' to guard against surprise attack, but the main body of disarmament discussion as it had proceeded up to that point received scant attention.

In the interval between the ending of the conference and the resumption of the work of the Sub-Committee on 29 August it appeared that the gap between east and west had narrowed further, as both sides were now prepared to accept some form of international control, while agreeing that complete control of national armament was impossible to achieve. In fact, however, nothing had been gained, for the United States now backed away altogether from substantial disarmament questions. Its government realized that the effect of the Soviet proposals would be to stabilize conventional force levels at a time when German rearmament had just become a practical possibility, and when new threats were appearing in the Middle East. As Harold E. Stassen said to the Disarmament Sub-Committee on 6 September: 'The United States does now place a reservation upon all of its pre-Geneva substantive positions taken in this Sub-Committee or in the Disarmament Commission or in the United Nations on these questions in relationship to levels of armament.'[14]

The Disarmament Sub-Committee continued its meetings through the next two years, but while the gap between specific disarmament proposals sometimes appeared to grow narrower, fundamental differences remained. The western governments had shown at Geneva that, however much attention they might give to plans for disarmament, they were unlikely to accept practical progress on any large scale while political and security questions – particularly Russian domination of eastern Europe and east Germany – were unsettled. And while the Soviet Union proceeded rapidly with the development of nuclear rocketry, evidenced by nuclear explosions (unannounced, but detected in the west) and the first Sputnik, it was improbable that sufficient confidence would be established to make arms control possible. During most of this period the Soviet Union was able to make the running in the disarmament debate by pressing proposals which it presumably knew the west would be unlikely to accept, as well as by reducing the size of its armed forces consequent on the development of nuclear weapons. But in August 1957, when the western powers proposed a new plan for 'partial' disarmament, it was rejected out of hand by the Soviet Union, although it secured an overwhelming majority in the General Assembly.

On 6 September 1957 the Disarmament Sub-Committee adjourned *sine die*. In November 1958 it was replaced by a commission which included 'all the members of the United Nations'. This highly unsuitable body for disarmament discussions met only once – to approve the proposal emanating

[14] US Bureau of Public Affairs, *Documents on Disarmament, 1945–59* (1960), i. 513.

from the four-power foreign ministers' conference of August 1959 to set up a ten-power disarmament committee, based on 'parity' of communist and non-communist members.[15]

In addition, as we have seen, disarmament had formed the main plank of Khrushchev's speech to the UN in September 1959. It was hoped that significant progress might be made at the summit meeting of May 1960. When this proved abortive discussions were resumed in the Ten-Power Committee on 7 June 1960, only to be brought to an end by the Soviet Union three weeks later.

Much less dramatically, a small beginning had taken place in 1958 towards agreement on arms production, although not on actual disarmament. In that year the western powers abandoned their previous insistence that a possible ban on the testing of nuclear weapons be discussed only in the context of general disarmament, and as a result a conference of experts from Britain, the Soviet Union, and the United States met in Geneva to discuss the technical feasibility of detecting tests. Meanwhile the Soviet Union had announced that it would unilaterally give up nuclear testing – an announcement which was, however, greeted with scepticism in America, since it followed hard on the successful completion of a series of tests in Russia. The British too were just embarking on a short series of tests which they declined to cancel. Despite this, a fresh conference on the banning of tests opened in Geneva on 31 October 1958 and from then until September 1961 (when a new Soviet series was carried out) there were no further tests in the atmosphere or large tests underground. On 29 March 1960, at Camp David, Khrushchev and Eisenhower agreed to a voluntary moratorium on underground testing 'under the threshold' (i.e. not susceptible of detection, or of distinction from earthquakes, by seismology). More significant, the negotiations in Geneva finally led, in August 1963, to the signing of a test-ban treaty between Britain, the United States, and the Soviet Union. But by that time France had joined the nuclear powers, and China was to explode an atomic device little more than a year later. Neither of these two newcomers to the nuclear club was willing to subscribe to the test-ban treaty.

[15] Its members were: United States, Britain, France, Canada, and Italy; the Soviet Union, Poland, Czechoslovakia, Rumania, and Bulgaria.

ECONOMIC AND SOCIAL AGENCIES

The scourge of war impressed on the statesmen of the western world the need to relieve human suffering and to provide international institutions for economic recovery and development in the post-war world. These humanitarian aims were indissolubly linked with the desire so to order the economic affairs of the world as to remove the heavy burden of depression and unemployment, and with it one of the root causes of war. The Soviet Union did not share these objectives. While it was prepared to join in the establishment of the UN, it saw this as an institution to give security by political rather than economic means. Its own economy was so closely controlled that it was unwilling either to contribute to or to receive from international economic institutions. Its participation in the economic and social institutions of the UN consequently was minimal.

The basic construction of the UN included as one of its essential parts the Economic and Social Council, parallel to the Trusteeship Council and responsible to the Assembly. The power given to the Economic and Social Council under Article 62 of the Charter was to

make and initiate studies and reports with respect to international economic, social, cultural, educational, health and related matters and . . . make recommendations with respect to any such matters to the General Assembly, and to the specialized agencies concerned.

In practice much of the Council's work has been carried out through its regional commissions – the Economic Commission for Europe, which was set up in 1942; for Latin America, for Asia and the Far East, and for Africa. Undoubtedly the most important function of the commissions has been to provide information. They have depended on governments for the supply of information – and the unwillingness of the Soviet Union and the eastern European countries to provide this has been a severe limitation, although ECE has published annual surveys of east-west trade. Equally, their recommendations can only be given effect by the action of national governments. But they have provided, in annual reports, special surveys, and statistical material, a mass of documentation for use both in universities and by governments, on a scale never previously achieved.

Under the aegis of the Economic and Social Council were brought the International Labour Organization, which had survived intact from the League of Nations, and such agencies as the Universal Postal Union and the World Meteorological Organization. During the war new agencies were established – the United Nations Relief and Rehabilitation Administration, whose work was brought to an end in 1947, and the Food and Agriculture Organization; with the establishment of the UN itself the list was lengthened still further. Here again the attitude of the Soviet Union was in marked contrast to that of the western powers. In the days of the League of Nations Litvinov had poured scorn on members' preoccupation with drugs, refugees, and signals while collective security was whittled away.[16] This attitude did not change substantially after the war. No objection was made to such harmless bodies as the Postal Union and the World Meteorological Organization, but the other 'non-political' specialized agencies the Soviet Union refused to join – although in some cases policy changed after the death of Stalin. The agencies, like the Economic Commissions, extended their membership outside the UN itself, and the Soviet Union could use this as a reason for not participating – although it is scarcely likely to have been an actual deterrent.

The most important of the specialized agencies in which the Soviet Union has never participated are those concerned with international trade and finance. Partly as a result these have developed into institutions with only a loose connexion with the UN, so that their development requires separate treatment.

In the absence of the active participation of the Soviet Union, it was inevitable that the discussions of post-war economic policies and institutions should be dominated by Britain and the United States. Between these two powers there were important differences of outlook, and a disparity of resources which increased in scale as the war went on. In economics as in politics the United States abandoned the isolationism which had led to its withdrawal from the World Economic Conference in 1934, and here too the end of isolation was accompanied by a marked desire and intention to construct a world based on sound financial and economic principles. Such principles were, however, conceived (especially by Cordell Hull) with a degree

---

[16] See Dallin, *The Soviet Union at the United Nations*, p. 61.

of simplicity and clarity of outlook only possible in a country endowed with an abundance of natural resources and industrial skills, and an apparently unshakeable position in world finance; and they showed an optimistic detachment from Congressional politics and the protectionism which resulted therefrom.

The central American theme was that trade must be liberalized universally, and that this would lead to world prosperity. They were not opposed to the formation of customs unions, with free internal trade and a common external tariff, although these were less desirable than world-wide reduction of tariffs; but they were opposed to discriminatory tariffs. But the British government inherited a discriminatory tariff in the form of Commonwealth preference, which for political reasons could not easily be abandoned. In addition, it maintained that the liberalization of trade was not enough by itself. It would indeed have its own attendant risks of a very grave order unless it were accompanied by policies designed to safeguard countries like Britain from foreign depression and slump.

These differences of view had become very clear in wartime discussions between the two governments, particularly in the preparation of the Atlantic Charter and the Lend-Lease agreement. Keynes, as principal British negotiator, remarked that the difficulties in which Britain would find itself after the war would necessitate bilateral arrangements and discrimination against the United States. This provoked great concern among the Americans, and the under-secretary of state, Sumner Welles, reported:

I said that if the British and the United States governments could not agree to do everything within their power to further, after the termination of the present war, a restoration of free and liberal trade policies, they might as well throw in the sponge and realize that one of the greatest factors in creating the present tragic situation in the world was going to be permitted to continue unchecked in the postwar world.[17]

This strength of feeling in the American administration led to its insistence that some undertaking on post-war economic policy be included in the Lend-Lease agreement, but the British view was respected and the relevant article in the Mutual

[17] Quoted by Gardner, *Sterling-Dollar Diplomacy* (1956), p. 45.

Aid Agreement of 23 February 1942 – the famous Article VII – represented an amalgamation of the two countries' views. It provided that the final conditions for Lend-Lease

shall include provision for agreed action . . . directed to the expansion . . . of production, employment, and the exchange and consumption of goods, which are the material foundations of the liberty and welfare of all peoples; to the limitation of all forms of discriminatory treatment in international commerce, and to the reduction of tariffs and other trade barriers.[18]

In addition to this Churchill asked for and received an assurance from the president that the article did not call for the immediate dismantling of imperial preference. This assurance he expressed in his own words in the House of Commons on 21 April 1944 when he said he had 'obtained from the President a definite assurance that we were no more committed to the abolition of Imperial Preference than the American Government were committed to the abolition of their high protective tariffs'.[19]

Even so, Article VII provoked considerable differences of interpretation in the years that followed. In the United States the view was generally taken that while a concession had been made to existing British obligations, the principle of multilateralism had been accepted and should be pursued as one of the objectives of post-war economic policy; in Britain the supporters of imperial preference regarded it as having a political importance which outweighed economic considerations, and always argued that it should not and had not been bartered away by Article VII. These differences did not prevent the British and American governments continuing their study of the long-term problems of the international economy as soon as the Lend-Lease agreement was signed, and, in spite of divergences of national interest, experts and governments alike succeeded in seeing the problem before them as a whole. They recognized that any plans to stabilize the post-war international economy must cover exchange stability and balance-of-payments problems; long-term investment; the reduction of trade barriers; measures to secure full employment; price control for primary products.

The first two of these objectives were the principal concern of

[18] Cmd. 6391. [19] Quoted by Gardner, p. 65.

the conference which met in July 1944 at Bretton Woods in New Hampshire. The conference had been preceded by a series of discussions in which the principal participants had been Harry Dexter White of the United States Treasury and John Maynard Keynes, who had been called into government service from Cambridge at the beginning of the war. Each of these men had devised a plan which came to bear his name, and which, once published, was taken up with an excessive national enthusiasm on each side of the Atlantic. Both plans were concerned with establishing the means to maintain equilibrium in normal conditions rather than with correcting the gross imbalance which resulted from the war. But the Keynes plan was the more far-reaching and imaginative of the two – too much so for the conference, where the balance was finally struck on the side of caution rather than adventure. Even so, the departure undertaken at Bretton Woods was striking.

It was seen that international monetary stability depended on each country having access at known rates to other currencies as part of its general liquidity position. At the same time availability of other currencies would be coupled with the obligation to maintain exchange rates with a sense of responsibility towards the international economy as a whole; so that each country would eschew competitive devaluations, multiple exchange rates, and anomalous cross exchange rates, while retaining an acceptable means of adjusting its exchange rate other than being forced to deflate or inflate in order to keep the exchange rate constant. To achieve these ends the conference established the International Monetary Fund, and it also secured the adhesion of the signatories to the agreement, who thereby became members of the Fund, to certain principles of conduct.

The resources of the Fund were provided by a quota contribution from each member; of this quota part was subscribed in gold or US dollars, the proportion being 25 per cent of the quota, or 10 per cent of the member's holdings of gold and US dollars, whichever was the less; the rest in the member's own currency. In addition, each member of the IMF agreed with the Fund a suitable gold par value for its currency, and undertook to keep its exchange value within 1 per cent of the par value. This part of the agreement thus rules out the possibility of all but the smallest day-to-day changes in the exchange rate, and it also disallows multiple exchange rates (i.e. different rates according to the purpose for which the currency is going to be used) and disorderly cross rates (e.g. when the sterling-dollar rate of £1 = $4; but lira-sterling and lira-dollar rates are such that the cross rate in Italy is £1 = $2.60). Adjustments of exchange rates were of course provided for; but under the agreement they were to be taken with the consent of the Fund, in such a way that the Fund would act both as umpire and adviser in the movement of national exchange rates.

The Fund was also given the role of banker, in order to provide members with additional liquidity in other members' currency. It was in this respect more than any other that the agreement fell short of the proposals which Keynes had devised; for these could have established a new international paper currency (called 'Bancor') and permitted very extensive overdraft facilities for members with the Fund. In contrast to this the IMF agreement made it possible for each member to purchase another's currency, not to borrow it,[20] within certain strict limits. The limits were obviously designed to prevent the exhaustion of one currency and the glut of another, and were based on the assumption that a country needing to purchase another currency outside these limits should adopt some more fundamental means of readjustment to an equilibrium position. But the Fund also foresaw the possibility of one currency being in demand from several or all of the other members, and it made special provision to meet this contingency of a 'scarce currency'. It provided for the Fund to buy the scarce currency with gold, or to borrow it; and it further provided that once the Fund formally declared a currency to be scarce, the members should have the right to impose restrictions on the freedom of exchange operations in the scarce currency. The importance of these provisions was considerable; for what they did was to recognize that the problem of a scarce currency was one which concerned the creditor country as well as its debtors; this was a significant advance in international economic doctrine.

The IMF was one of two institutions established at Bretton Woods. The second was the International Bank for Reconstruction and Development (the World Bank or IBRD), de-

---

[20] This is the terminology of the Fund. In fact 'purchase' in this case is more accurately described as short-term borrowing within set limits. The difference between this and the extensive credit envisaged by Keynes is no less important.

signed to meet the problem of long-term investment. It too had been prepared in discussions between White and Keynes during the war, but it had provoked fewer tangled questions and attracted less public attention. It was easy to see that it would have a vital role beside the Fund. If successful it would provide the means by which growth and development of national economies could be promoted. This was considered the more important at Bretton Woods by those who thought that the United States, having replaced Britain as the great creditor nation, would not undertake international lending as Britain had done, or at least would not be able to absorb the servicing of loans which it did make in large-scale imports – again as the British economy had been singularly suited to do.

The structure of the Bank was and is comparatively simple. All the founder members of the Fund were members of the Bank, and subscribed a quota to its capital, which in most cases was the same as the quota to the Fund (but was larger in the case of the United States). The total capital amounted initially to $10 billion. However, each member only paid up 2 per cent of its quota in gold or United States dollars and a further 18 per cent in its own currency. The remaining 80 per cent was not called up and was not available for lending, but was intended as a reserve to meet the Bank's obligations. Once established it became the task of the Bank to decide which requests for loans it would favour and which projects best merited its support. In doing so over the ensuing years it very quickly assumed a specialized function which came naturally to it, providing finance for construction and development projects which were insufficiently attractive to private investment but which might play a key role in providing the infrastructure for a growing economy. Its assessment of projects of this kind required careful survey; and from this emerged a new role for the Bank almost as important as its primary function – the provision of survey statistics and advice for developing countries. It also increased its capital resources by a series of bond issues, beginning in the United States in 1947. In this way, and by means of advice and guarantee, it increased the flow of private capital into developing countries.

The world into which the IMF and the IBRD emerged proved very different from that which had been envisaged at Bretton Woods. The objective of a single world-wide economic community based on multilateral trade and convertibility of currencies was unrealizable as long as political divisions remained as sharp as they became after 1945. The table entitled 'Agencies in Relationship with the UN' published annually in the *Statesman's Year-Book* shows the extent of the membership of the Fund and Bank: it also shows the absence of the communist bloc. Within the western world, moreover, the imbalance of trade was far greater than had been recognized at Bretton Woods, even though that conference had sought to take account of immediate post-war problems by providing for a transitional period in the operation of the Fund.

This imbalance was the inevitable consequence of the disruption caused by the conflict which had just ended. Before the war Europe had always had a deficit in its merchandise balance of accounts, but this was more than offset by a surplus on the 'invisible' items of the balance of payments – interest on loans, shipping, and banking services. After the war the deficit on merchandise was increased. This was partly the result of lower production, particularly of consumer goods during the period of reconstruction, but it was also due to the severance of trade with eastern Europe and the loss of American markets during the war. At the same time the pre-war surplus on the invisible items was replaced by a deficit, because of the sale of overseas investments, the loss of shipping in the war, and the maintenance after the war of a continuing high level of military expenditure abroad. As a result European imports from the United States were seven times its exports to the United States, and there existed an apparently permanent 'dollar problem'.

These difficulties were given sharp prominence in the experience of the American loan to Britain, which was negotiated at the end of 1945. The British government, conscious of the long burden of the war which it had borne, hoped for generous aid in meeting its post-war commitments. It had been shaken by the abrupt ending of Lend-Lease as soon as the war ended; for although the long-term settlement of Lend-Lease represented a minimal burden[21] the immediate problem was to maintain a very high level of overseas military expenditure, which was no longer underpinned by Lend-Lease, before there had been time to recover a strong trading position. The American government

[21] The main part of the bill, amounting to $20 billion was wiped out; the remainder, some $650 million, was repayable at an effective rate of interest of 1·6 per cent.

in contrast was impressed by its own generosity in the Lend-Lease settlement, and took the view that if it was now to give further financial aid it must be in return for the adoption by Britain of sound financial practices – and if possible with the ending of discrimination against the United States.

The arduous negotiations to resolve these differences were brought to a hasty conclusion on 6 December 1945, for the British government felt unable to enter the Bretton Woods agreement without first securing the American loan, and this it had to do by the last day of 1945 if it was to become a founder member. The agreement provided for a loan to Britain of $3.75 billion at 2 per cent, with repayments beginning on 31 December 1951. (The British had hoped for an interest-free loan.) The issue of imperial preference was left untouched, but on the other hand the agreement required that sterling for current transactions should be made convertible a year after the loan came into force, and that there should be no quantitative restrictions against American imports after the end of 1946. In addition, an imprecise arrangement was made for the liquidation of sterling balances – that is to say of British indebtedness in countries like India and Egypt, where the conduct of the war had made necessary extensive and exceptional purchase of local goods and services.

In this way Britain was being pushed towards the convertibility and non-discrimination which were the presuppositions of the Bretton Woods system more rapidly than any other part of the world. But for convertibility and non-discrimination to be practicable, it was necessary for Britain to improve substantially its balance of trade and payments. There were serious obstacles in the way of such an improvement which were outside Britain's control or could not easily be changed – the terms of trade, which moved against Britain, the exceptionally severe winter of 1946–7, and the continuance of overseas military commitments. Further, it had not succeeded in reducing sterling balances; on the contrary, in the summer of 1947 these stood higher than ever. As a result Britain had failed to achieve the balance of payments position which would make convertibility practicable, least of all in a world where convertibility was the exception. Meanwhile the American loan was being run down far more quickly than had been foreseen, as a result of the rise in American prices consequent on the ending of controls.

The full extent of this weakness did not appear to be realized by the British government, and on 15 July 1947 the pound sterling became convertible, with some expressions of pride and confidence on the part of the government and the press.[22] The result was an immediate and heavy drain on dollar reserves, which could only be maintained by drawing on the American loan to the point where it was almost exhausted. Hasty negotiations with the United States were begun, and on 20 August convertibility was suspended. At the same time the British and American governments reached an agreement for a more flexible interpretation of non-discrimination which permitted the purchase of higher priced goods in soft currencies – although in practice the requirement of non-discrimination had been less important, since so often goods were bought from the United States because they were simply not available elsewhere.

The whole experience of the Anglo-American loan, apart from its effect on Anglo-American relations, revealed the extent of the dollar problem, and showed an imbalance between the United States and Europe which the newly established IMF was too fine an instrument to correct. It had also been assumed when the Bretton Woods system was established that it would be supported by a similar organization to develop and promote world trade. In the event the success in this field was very limited. British and American negotiators had agreed on 'Proposals for Consideration by an International Conference on Trade and Employment' in the autumn of 1945, and these proposals were taken up by a UN Preparatory Committee representing nineteen countries in October 1946. Once again important differences appeared between America and Britain, on whose agreement the success of the whole venture depended. The American view laid most emphasis on multilateral trade – 'that international trade should be abundant, that it should be multilateral, that it should be non-discriminatory'.[23] The British view in contrast laid great stress on the maintenance of full employment. The difference between the two views showed a difference of national interest and of national attitudes to

[22] The confidence shown by the British government is explained partly by the fact that by separate agreements with various countries sterling had begun to be increasingly convertible over a period before 15 July without causing any serious drain on reserves. For a full discussion of the crisis see Gardner, *Sterling-Dollar Diplomacy*, pp. 313 ff.
[23] Clair Wilcox, head of the American delegation (quoted ibid. p. 270).

economic problems. The Americans saw a growth in trade as an infallible stimulus to economic growth in general; the British lived under the memory of the slump of 1929, and (supported by several other countries, for example Australia and New Zealand) believed that multilateral trade unaccompanied by an obligation to pursue sound employment policies would simply mean the free export of economic depressions. The Americans saw the freeing of trade as the removal of restrictions, which could be undertaken with no greater requirement than goodwill and determination; while a successful employment policy required dubious manipulation of the country's economy. The British for their part also insisted that any country which experienced a chronic surplus in its balance of payments should take responsibility for curing the disequilibrium which such a surplus indicated. Alongside these differences of view about the general issues of trade and employment there were also inevitable differences about the kind of restrictions which in the past had been imposed on trade. For the United States the worst offenders in this respect were discriminatory tariffs and particularly the British system of imperial preference; the British naturally found these more easily defensible than the high level of protection maintained by America.

In conditions either of wartime co-operation or of great international prosperity it might have been possible to reconcile these differences, even at the risk of producing a compromise so watery as to be of little immediate use. But these conditions did not exist in the two years after the war. With the experience of the loan before their eyes the British became chary of another advance towards multilateralism; and although the American administration offered tariff reductions up to 50 per cent, the British remained suspicious that such reductions would not survive once their impact was conveyed from American business into Congress. They therefore – Labour government and Conservative opposition alike – refused to be persuaded away from imperial preference. At the same time the smaller developing powers also expressed strong reservations about multilateralism, which they regarded as too strong medicine for their growing economies. In consequence, although the Charter of an International Trade Organization was drawn up at Geneva in the spring of 1947 and then again at Havana in the following winter, and was signed on 23 March 1948, it was never ratified, and the organization never came into existence.

The long negotiations did, however, have some permanent result. In addition to drafting a Charter for ITO the Geneva Conference produced a General Agreement on Tariffs and Trade, which was eventually signed by 37 countries. The agreement took over many of the provisions which were included in the ITO Charter, and it also provided the machinery for tariff reduction by a process of bargaining. Following the same principles as the ITO, the GATT proscribed quantitative restrictions, except in certain specified conditions. These exceptions included 'restrictions to safeguard the balance of payments' (similar to those provided in IMF), together with protection of agriculture and the development of under-developed countries. Tariffs, in contrast, were not proscribed but were to be reduced. The first round in this process took place at the Geneva conference itself, and resulted in substantial reductions.[24] Further rounds of bargaining took place in the ensuing years, at Annecy in 1949, at Torquay in 1950–1, and at Geneva in 1956. In addition, the GATT acquired its own small staff of experts in Geneva. Thus even allowing for the fact that some of the tariff reductions were for show, being on items in which there was comparatively little trade, the achievement was substantial; and although no permanent organization came into existence of the kind envisaged in the ITO Charter, the GATT did provide a machinery for the bargaining of tariff reduction where none had existed before.

By this time too the IMF had demonstrated its effectiveness in the provision of short-term international credit. From 1956, and even more after 1958 when the scarcity of dollars ceased to dominate international payments, the problem disappeared and the Fund was seen to work more closely in accordance with the expectations with which it had been founded. In March 1961 Portugal became the seventieth member of the Fund–although membership still did not extend to the Soviet bloc. Convertibility had become customary rather than being

[24] The American tariff was brought to its lowest level since the Underwood Tariff of 1913, concessions being made on import items worth $1,766·5 million in 1939. In return the US received concessions on export items worth $1,192 million in 1939. The gain was thus substantial but it was disappointing in the context of Geneva as it included very little diminution of imperial preference (see ibid. p. 360).

the exception, and the dollar had ceased to be virtually the only currency in demand in the Fund.[25] The Fund had moreover developed its own customary procedure, which its *Annual Report* for 1961 described in these terms:

Members are given the overwhelming benefit of the doubt in relation to requests for transactions within the 'gold tranche', that is, the portion of the quota which can be regarded as equivalent to the gold subscription. The Fund's attitude to requests for transactions within the 'first credit tranche', that is, transactions which bring the Fund's holdings of a member's currency above 100 per cent but not above 125 per cent of quota, is a liberal one, provided that the member itself is also making reasonable efforts to solve its problems. Requests for transactions beyond these limits require substantial justification. They are likely to be favorably received when the drawings or stand-by arrangements are intended to support a sound program aimed at establishing or maintaining the enduring stability of the member's currency at a realistic rate of exchange. . . . These policies and procedures have worked well and have now stood the test of repeated application: experience has shown that they enable the Fund to conduct its operations with flexibility and dispatch, and that they serve the interest of the countries receiving assistance.

As a result the Fund made a major contribution to relieving national crises in balances of payments which otherwise would have had to be met by exchange and trade restrictions or by deflationary measures detrimental to economic growth and full employment. It established a code of behaviour and standards of consultation and consideration of the interests of other states which could be maintained because of the assistance available. The cushion it provided against temporary difficulties made it easier to maintain the standards of behaviour, involving consideration for other nations' economies as well as one's own, which were laid down in the original agreement. It also made its contribution to the problems of developing countries through the advice it was able to give, sometimes in conjunction with other members of the UN 'family', on monetary and exchange problems.

[25] From the beginning of the Fund to 30 April 1958, 91·7 per cent of all purchase had been in US dollars. In the financial year 1960–1 the proportion fell to 34·6 per cent, and in the second half of the year to 25·6 per cent. Purchases were made instead of Deutsche marks, Netherlands guilders, French francs, Italian lire, Argentine pesos and Danish krone (IMF, *Annual Report, 1961*).

The success of the Fund by the end of the 1950s did not mean that problems of international liquidity had disappeared, and as the new decade opened fresh expedients were sought to provide greater liquidity and to refurbish the machinery of international payments. But within its limitations its achievement was indisputable.

Meanwhile the main body of the UN had taken important steps forward in providing for the development of the economically backward areas of the world. The Economic and Social Council set up a Technical Assistance Committee, and from 1949 member governments made voluntary contributions to an Expanded Programme of Technical Assistance. The programme was run through the specialized agencies, the directors of which, together with the secretary-general of the UN, formed a Technical Assistance Board. The income for the programme was derived from the developing countries as well as from the advanced countries of the west. At first the Soviet bloc made no contributions to the programme. Then in 1953 a change of policy brought a pledge from the Soviet Union of $1 million (compared to $12·8 million from the United States) in a total budget of $22·4 million.[26]

In 1957 the possibilities and importance of technical assistance appeared increasingly important, and at the end of that year an Assembly resolution was passed establishing a new UN body, the Special Fund for Economic Development.[27] It was intended that the Special Fund should work through the existing agencies to 'provide systematic and substantial assistance in fields essential to the integrated technical, economic and social development of the less developed countries'. In practice it was able to do this by providing assistance in research, education, and training, and also by resource and feasibility surveys. It was envisaged that its income should amount to $100 million, but in its initial years it fell short of half that figure. Again contributions came from developing and from developed nations, and a sample of pledges of contributions on 1 December 1960 is given on p. 566.

[26] In contrast the USSR, the Ukraine, and Byelorussia withdrew from the World Health Organization in 1949.
[27] For the relation of this Fund to the proposal for SUNFED – the Special United Nations Fund for Economic Development – see Andrew Shonfield, *The Attack on World Poverty* (1960), pp. 93 ff.

19

Special Fund Pledges, 1960 $ *US*

Byelorussia	50,000
Iran	125,000
Nepal	2,000
Ukraine	125,000
USSR	1,000,000
United Kingdom	5,000,000
United States	18,200,000

The growth of technical assistance gave a new dimension to the role of world economic institutions, surpassing the emphasis on financial stability and liberalization of trade which had dominated the minds of western statesmen at the end of the war. As we have seen, the Bank alone amongst the Bretton Woods institutions provided for development as well as reconstruction; and as it gave increasing importance to its development function it none the less did so with the care and caution appropriate to a Bank. It was represented at meetings of the Technical Assistance Board (as was the IMF) but it remained aloof from the activities of the UN 'family'. In 1960 it sought to achieve greater flexibility in its operations by providing a special fund for projects of a slightly more adventurous kind administered by a new International Development Association; but the criticism could still be brought against it of venturing too little and providing insufficient support to the specialized agencies.

The Bretton Woods institutions and the UN programme of technical assistance were all intended to have world-wide scope. In the conditions of the cold war other institutions had grown up in Europe, and aid to underdeveloped countries as an instrument of national policy had developed on a greater scale than UN technical assistance. Before going on to survey these developments, however, we must consider briefly the institutions and groupings which survived from the days before 1945.

COMMONWEALTH AND STERLING AREA

The most virile of these was the British Commonwealth. Before the war this title referred to the collectivity of the Dominions – Canada, Australia, New Zealand, and South Africa[28] – in all

---

[28] Eire was in a special relationship to Britain, and this remains true today, although the relationship changed when Eire formally became a Republic in 1949. It is in some respects closer, in others more distant than that of members of the Commonwealth.

of which at that time European, especially British, settlers were dominant. The title was sometimes extended to cover the colonies as well: but Churchill at least was clear as well as eloquent when he referred to 'the British Commonwealth and Empire'. It is significant that his most famous use of this phrase was when he said: 'Let us therefore brace ourselves to our duty and so bear ourselves that if the British Commonwealth and Empire lasts for a thousand years, men will still say "This was their finest hour".' His appeal evoked a warm response in the old Dominions. Independently, they had declared war on Germany in 1939 and now they gave every support to Britain while it stood alone in Europe against Hitler. Commonwealth forces played an important part in all the main theatres of war, and co-operation was based on continuous consultation between Commonwealth governments. Outside the Dominions the war had the effect rather of stimulating nationalist feeling. In India an attempt by the Cripps mission to negotiate independence broke down on the British insistence that they retain direction of the war; subsequently the communal feelings of the Congress and the Muslim League grew rapidly in strength.

After the war a decisive turning-point in the development of the Commonwealth came with the grant of independence to India and Pakistan. By the speed and determination with which the British government gave independence it prevented the accumulation of bitterness, while the new Indian and Pakistani governments decided to seek membership of the Commonwealth – a decision of historic importance, taken after long consideration. In this way some 400 million people joined the Commonwealth who were not of British or European descent. Immediately thereafter both countries became republics, and thereby demonstrated that it was possible to remain in the Commonwealth without accepting the monarchy.

Twenty years later the relationship between these two countries exemplified the weakness as well as the strength of the Commonwealth. The experience of partition created deep and lasting bitterness in the relations between the two countries. Territorial disputes and ideological differences kept these emotions alive through subsequent years, until they were unleashed once again when war broke out between the two states in the autumn of 1965. Whether in the meantime membership of the Commonwealth provided any appeasement of the differences between India and Pakistan must remain an open question. The reaction of Britain and the other Commonwealth countries to the new conflict was to turn to the UN rather than the Commonwealth as a mediating agency; and in January 1966 President Ayub and Premier Shastri met in Tashkent, not in London or Colombo.

Burma and Ceylon became independent at the same time as India and Pakistan. Burma decided not to join the Commonwealth. But the example set by India, Pakistan, and Ceylon was followed by the colonies of Britain as they achieved full self-government. Inevitably a group of nations of such diversity only remained a group because they were loosely associated. Already in 1950 Nehru had said:

We are all members of the Commonwealth – that rather strange and odd collection of nations which seems to prosper most in adversity. Somehow it has found some kind of invisible link by seeing that practically there is no link and by giving complete independence and freedom to every part of it. . . . The Commonwealth has grown and changed repeatedly, and, while member nations of this Commonwealth sometimes disagree, sometimes have interests conflicting with each other, sometimes pull in different directions, nevertheless, the basic fact remains that they meet as friends, try to understand each other and try, as far as possible, to find a common way of working.[29]

The Commonwealth had no permanent institutions. It did not develop a Commonwealth Appeal Court, as some Commonwealth citizens would have wished (following an earlier precedent of appeals to the Judicial Committee of the Privy Council); only in 1965 was it decided to establish a Commonwealth Secretariat. On the other hand meetings of Commonwealth prime ministers took place approximately every other year, interspersed with occasional meetings of finance ministers. Such meetings did not seek to arbitrate in disputes between members – such as the differences between India and Pakistan. They were designed to provide information, understanding, and co-operation.

The very informality of such meetings and the freedom which

[29] Delhi, 27 Dec. 1950, quoted by Ingram, *The Commonwealth Challenge* (1962).

they left to their participants meant that for many years the Commonwealth relieved tension and created no new strains – with one important exception. Then in 1961 the Union of South Africa became a republic, and in the same year intended seeking readmission to the Commonwealth with its new status. It became increasingly obvious however that its domestic racial policies were deeply objectionable to the other members, especially to the Asians and Africans: and as a result the government withdrew its request and left the Commonwealth. Four years later Rhodesia's unilateral declaration of independence renewed the tension of race relations.

The members of the Commonwealth enjoyed full independence and equality with each other; none the less Britain remained at the centre and played an irreplaceable role. This was evident in the existence in Britain of a department of state, the Commonwealth Relations Office, which was unparalleled in any of the other member countries, and was indicated by the fact that the Commonwealth prime ministers' conferences always met in London (although finance ministers also met elsewhere) and until 1965 were serviced by the British cabinet secretariat. More substantially important, the possibility of British admission to the European common market appeared to carry far deeper implications for the future of the Commonwealth than any comparable move on the part of one of the other members would have done.

British attitudes towards the Commonwealth have remained those of pride and a sense of greatness – sentiments which have compensated for and sometimes concealed a loss of power in international relations. Among the other members of the Commonwealth the association has been valued and retained for varying reasons. For some, Commonwealth preference has been of major importance; in the old Commonwealth the member which has benefited most from this tariff advantage, New Zealand, was also a country with deep ties of sentiment to Britain. Access on advantageous terms to the British market has been valuable to some of the new Commonwealth countries; in addition, the Commonwealth connexion has increased attractiveness to capital, both private and government. The Commonwealth provides for economies in diplomatic representation, and it offers easily available training for diplomats and government officers of all sorts. Commonwealth students have found it relatively easy to study in Britain,[30] and as university fees were kept below an economic figure, students benefited from a concealed subsidy, in addition to any scholarship or grant they might be receiving. Technical advice, an accumulation of knowledge, and the machinery for co-operation were also available in the Commonwealth, whether in the Commonwealth Bureau of Dairy Science and Technology or the Commonwealth Parliamentary Association; and while these resources might be found elsewhere, outside the Commonwealth, there was no incentive to scrap what already existed.

In all these ways, then, the Commonwealth represented practical advantages and ties of sentiment in varying degrees to its members; it imposed minimal obligations and exacted no diminution of independence.

Closely associated with the Commonwealth, yet distinct from it, was the sterling area.[31] This characteristically British institution had achieved a separate and distinctive existence when Britain left the gold standard in 1931, and a large number of countries decided to follow Britain by stabilizing their currencies in terms of sterling. The relationship remained a loose one, however; various motives persuaded the countries of the Commonwealth and Empire, Middle Eastern countries under British influence, and many of the smaller European countries to belong to the Bloc, as it was then called. And as sterling was freely convertible into other currencies there was no barrier at all between the Bloc and outside countries. But the war brought a marked change. The sterling area diminished in size and came to include only the British Commonwealth (except Canada), Eire, Egypt, the Sudan, Iraq, and Iceland; and instead of being a loose association of convenience it became an organization for economic warfare, whose object was to make the most strategic use of foreign exchange, especially dollars.

As we have seen, it was impossible when the war ended to return to the free system which had preceded it. Convertibility was inadmissible as long as reserves of dollars and gold plus current dollar earnings were much less than potential demand

[30] The Robbins report found that 10 per cent of students in higher education in Britain in 1961–2 were from overseas, and that 60 per cent of overseas students were from Commonwealth countries.

[31] For a fuller account see W. M. Scammell, *International Monetary Policy* (1961) on which this section has drawn heavily.

for dollars from the sterling area. More than that, the United Kingdom's external liabilities were now so much in excess of reserves that it could neither meet these liabilities by increased production nor allow them to be converted into other currencies, especially dollars. To meet this contingency the accounts of other sterling area countries, and countries outside the sterling area, were blocked, and released only in gradual stages. At the same time the range of convertibility was slowly extended, as we have seen, by bilateral agreements, leading up to the convertibility of sterling on 15 July 1947. This had to be abandoned five weeks later, and the sterling area then became once again one within which there was (with the exception of the blocked accounts of sterling balances) free exchange, but from which exchange into other currencies was limited and controlled. Inevitably this affected the pattern of trade, which operated within a system of internal multilateralism bounded by external limited convertibility. This was essentially the condition of the sterling area from this time until the introduction of non-resident convertibility in December 1958.

THE FRENCH UNION AND THE COMMUNITY

As we have seen, the development of the French empire was very different from that of the British. In the constitutions of both the Fourth and the Fifth Republics an attempt was made to transform the empire, first into 'L'Union française', then into 'La Communauté'. In fact, however, the institutions which were thereby established never achieved decisive importance but were eclipsed by conflict, as in Indo-China, or by swift moves to independence. Traditionally the objectives of French colonial policy had been towards integration and assimilation. Within certain strict limits this policy had achieved success. The overseas territories of France in the West Indies and the Indian Ocean and Algeria sent deputies to sit in the French parliament. In Africa a strong political party, under the leadership of Houphouët-Boigny, accepted the principle of federation and urged its implementation. Houphouët-Boigny himself sat in the French cabinet and participated in the drafting of the constitution of the Fifth Republic; he supported federation as a way of preventing the 'balkanization' of Africa and stated that he had no use for a Community which did not have closer bonds than the British Commonwealth.

The limits which circumscribed this success were, however, immovable. Integration might be a successful policy for small communities like West Indian islands; but it could only be applied to a country like Algeria, with some 9 million inhabitants, a million of them Muslims, if the Algerians were given less than full political rights. The experience of England and Ireland in the nineteenth century had shown the difficulty of ruling two communities of different race and culture in a single union. Federation gained its supporters amongst some Africans; but for most federation was far less attractive than independence. In no part of the world had France succeeded in establishing colonies dominated by a French population – having been outmanoeuvred by the British in India and Canada – and even had it done so, the experience of the British colonies in the nineteenth century suggests that federation would have had a limited appeal. To the Syrians and Lebanese, and to the peoples of Indo-China, struggling against a France reluctant to concede self-government, it meant even less.

The pace of change accelerated rapidly after 1956. By that time French colonies and protectorates in the Middle East and Indo-China, Tunis and Morocco had all achieved independence; and a war of independence was being fought in Algeria. In June 1956 the French Assembly passed a *loi-cadre* providing fundamental political reforms in its African colonies, including universal suffrage on a common roll for the election of territorial assemblies to which African governments would be responsible. The implementation of this law was started by the government of the Fourth Republic. At the same sime, in 1957, the Rome treaty brought the French (and Belgian) African colonies into association with the European members of the common market. Then in 1958 de Gaulle took office in France and initiated the drafting of a new constitution, in which the 'French Union' became the 'Community'. Chapter XII of this new constitution proved to be a lengthy and sometimes obscure definition of the Community, defining its competence in foreign policy, defence, and economic matters, and establishing an Executive Council, a Senate, and a Court of Arbitration. In addition, the president was to be elected by an electoral college drawn from the overseas territories as well as from local government bodies in France.

The constitution was submitted to referendum in France and

in the territories which were to form the Community, thereby giving them the opportunity to choose immediate independence rather than membership. If they opted to belong to the Community they could look forward to independence in the future, as this was specifically provided for in Article 86 of the constitution. This fact, together with the economic advantages to be gained, persuaded an overwhelming majority to vote for the constitution on 28 September 1958, with the single outstanding exception of Guinea under the leadership of Sékou Touré. Guinea thus became independent, but the reaction of the French government was immediately to withdraw all support, both its contribution to the finances of Guinea and all its civil servants. It indicated to Britain and the United States that it would not welcome their substitution for France's role and refused to sponsor Guinea's membership of the United Nations. The Republic of Guinea thereupon sought and received aid from the Soviet bloc and from China.

After this the movement to independence proceeded with far greater speed than the framers of the constitution had expected. Those states which had favoured federation, the Ivory Coast chief among them, led the way as the Community fell short of their conception of a federation. An attempt to retain the links between the constituent parts of French West Africa had only partial and temporary success: former French Sudan and Senegal formed a federation named Mali, but two months after independence in June 1960 it broke apart, the former Sudan retaining the name of Mali.

In spite of the speed with which the movement to independence proceeded, it was accepted by the French government, which negotiated agreements with each of the territories concerned. Thus the experience of Guinea was not repeated, and the links with France remained.

The Community came to be described as a 'Commonwealth based on treaties'[32] and its institutions were reformed, as they had come to play a role similar to that of Commonwealth conferences; while *Le Monde* on 22 March 1960 foresaw the possible creation of 'un grand ministère de la Communauté, sorte de Commonwealth Relations Office'.

The treaties on which the Community came to be based were

---

[32] *Guardian*, 1 Apr. 1960.

19*

concerned primarily with defence and with economics. In the
latter respect they were of great importance. Both directly and
indirectly – by the provision of civil servants – France sub-
sidized the budgets of the new states. It also provided substantial
sums for capital investment, and at the same time, by a system
of *surprix*, ensured a market for agricultural products at prices
higher than those prevailing in the world. Moreover the
association established between the French and Belgian African
colonies and the European common market was modified in
accordance with the changed status of the African countries,
without diminishing the advantage accruing to them. The new
relationship was embodied in a convention of association,
agreed and initialed on 20 December 1962. It provided for a
common EEC tariff, subject to progressive reductions, on
imports from the eighteen African states; the African states in
turn undertook progressive reductions of tariffs to each other
and to the EEC countries, with safeguards for developing
industries. Equally important, the African countries were to
benefit almost exclusively from the European Development
Fund for overseas countries and territories.

THE ORGANIZATION OF AMERICAN STATES

The United States came into existence as a result of a war of
independence from imperial rule; in the succeeding century
and a half it did not acquire an empire of its own. It fought a
war against Spain which resulted in the loss to Spain of its last
colonies; but Cuba gained its independence in 1902; the
Philippines became independent, as we have seen, in 1946;
Puerto Rico became a Commonwealth in 1952 and in the
following year was judged by the United Nations to have full
internal self-government in voluntary association with the
United States.[33] After the second world war the United States
became the trustee power for the Japanese Pacific islands (the
Marshalls, Carolines, and Marianas) under the special provisions relating to strategic areas.

But while never acquiring a formal empire, the United States
had played an active role of intervention in the affairs of Central
and South America. From the time of the Monroe doctrine in

[33] Nevertheless a small group of Puerto Rican terrorists attempted to assassinate
Truman on 1 November 1950, and fired shots, wounding five Congressmen, in
the House of Representatives on 1 March 1954.

1823 through the period of the 'Roosevelt corollary' of 1904 the United States had asserted its hegemony over Latin America. In 1895 Lord Salisbury had contested its right to such hegemony: but in doing so he succeeded only in giving a useful definition of it. He said:

The Government of the United States is not entitled to affirm as a universal proposition, with reference to a number of independent states for whose conduct it assumes no responsibility, that its interests are necessarily concerned in whatever may befall those States simply because they are situated in the Western Hemisphere.[34]

Forty years later Franklin Roosevelt substituted a 'good neighbour' policy for the previous interventionism of the United States; and during the war the Latin American states either joined the conflict on the side of the United States, or showed a benevolent neutrality. With the conclusion of the war it was to be expected that a fresh approach would be made to the problem of relations between the American states, both because of the new spirit then prevailing and because the United States did not want its special relationship with Latin America to disappear into the generality of the UN.

The negotiation of a new treaty between the American states began at Chapultepec in Mexico in the spring of 1945, was carried further in Petropolis, Brazil, in August 1947, and brought to a successful conclusion at Bogotá, Colombia, in 1948. The circumstances of the negotiations illustrated the difficulties which they faced. They were prolonged by the antipathy of the United States towards the Perón government in Argentina; in 1947 Nicaragua was excluded from the Petropolis conference on the ground that its government had come to power as the result of a coup d'état and Ecuador withdrew from the conference in mid-course when its government was overthrown; the Bogotá conference had to be suspended as the result of an outburst of violence following the assassination of the Liberal party candidate for the presidency. None the less the negotiations produced results. On 30 August the Petropolis conference unanimously adopted a mutual security pact, known as the 'Rio Pact', of which Article 3 was the core. It read:

[34] Quoted in Dexter Perkins, *A History of the Monroe Doctrine* (1960), p. 178.

The High Contracting Parties agree that an armed attack by any state against an American State shall be considered as an attack against all American States, and, consequently, each one of the said Contracting Parties undertakes to assist in meeting the attack in the exercise of the inherent right of individual or collective self-defense recognized by Article 51 of the Charter of the United Nations.[35]

The Bogotá conference ended on 1 May 1948 after reaching agreement on a 'Charter of the Organization of American States'. This Charter reaffirmed the provisions for mutual security already provided for in the Rio Pact. It also provided procedures for the pacific settlement of inter-American disputes, ruling that these procedures were to be followed before a dispute was referred to the Security Council, and established the institutions of the OAS. These consisted of an Inter-American conference, to meet every five years and decide general action and policy; a consultative meeting of foreign ministers to act on urgent matters; and a Council of the organization – the working body concerned with day-to-day administration. By the Charter the OAS thus became the successor to the pre-war Pan American Union, and took over from that union its technical and information offices for the promotion of economic, social, cultural, and juridical relations among American nations.

The establishment of the OAS did not by itself go very far towards solving the political and economic problems of the Americas. These problems may be described as those of internal political stability, of economic progress, and of relations between states. The problems which militated against internal political stability are too complex and diverse to be fully explored here. They ranged from the racial and cultural diversity of a country like Peru, inhabited by Amazon tribes, mountain Indians, and descendants of the Spaniards, to the rigidity of police dictatorship as in the Dominican Republic under Trujillo. Economic problems stemmed above all from the lack of native capital, and the development of indigenous resources by foreign – especially United States – owned enterprises. The problem of international relations was twofold: the states of South and Central America were often divided from each other by petty squabbles and personal rivalries and showed little sign of achieving the Indo-American union which Haya

[35] *Decade of American Foreign Policy, 1941–9* (1950), p. 422.

de la Torre had foreseen when he founded the APRA[36] movement in 1924; at the same time these states were inevitably
dominated by the 'colossus of the north'.

For the United States the motives and fears which had
inspired the Monroe doctrine took on a new importance with
the development of the cold war. In earlier days the United
States government had not hesitated to intervene in order to
maintain its own interests in the southern hemisphere; the
threat which it now faced was that one of the endemic outbursts
of violence in a Latin American country would bring to power
a communist government, with the full support behind it of
the Soviet Union and the communist world.

In 1954 this threat appeared imminent as a result of the
growth of communist strength in Guatemala. In January 1953
the Communist party, having just regained legal existence as
the Guatemalan Workers' party, won twenty-eight out of
thirty-two seats contested in legislative elections. It was strong
enough to appeal to the people as the most effective challenge
to privilege, while the president, Arbenz, was forced to rely
increasingly on the communists if he was to carry out reforms.
In February 1954 his government expropriated the United
Fruit Company's banana plantations and distributed the land
to the peasants. In April Guatemala withdrew from the OAS; in
May the State Department announced that an important supply
of arms from Stettin had landed there.

Consistent with the normal pattern of Latin American politics, the policies and actions of the Arbenz régime had led to the
departure of an important number of opponents to the neighbouring countries of Honduras and Nicaragua, and in Honduras
an army was organized under Colonel Castillo Armas ready to
invade Guatemala. The United States signed military agreements with Honduras and Nicaragua in April and May, and
provided these two countries with arms. On 18 June 1954
Castillo's forces invaded Guatemala from Honduras; the
Arbenz government appealed to the Security Council to take
action under Articles 34, 35, and 39 'to prevent the disruption
of the peace and international security in this part of Central
America and to put a stop to the aggression in progress in
Guatemala'.

The full extent of United States support for Castillo is

[36] *Alianza Popular Revolucionaria Americana.*

difficult to establish; but its diplomatic manoeuvres were necessarily open for all to see. Secretary Dulles had already ruffled the sensibilities of his European allies by asking seafaring nations not only to participate in an embargo on arms shipments but to give permission to the United States to stop and search merchant vessels – a request which brought a particularly stiff answer from the British government. The fact that these events most unfortunately coincided with the Geneva foreign ministers' conference added further to the tensions of Anglo-American relations. Then, in reaction to Guatemala's appeal to the UN, the United States supported a resolution, proposed in the Security Council by Brazil and Colombia, referring the complaint to the OAS. The chairmanship of the Security Council was held at this time by Cabot Lodge, but this did not prevent him acting in the interests of his own country. Blandly he described the 'delicate balance' which the UN Charter established between regional and universal organizations, and said that 'to place one against another in a controversy . . . may be fatal to them both'. On 25 June the Council agreed not to place Guatemala's complaint on its agenda until a report had been received from a fact-finding mission of the OAS; but the voting showed how far the United States had had to rely on the support of old friends and allies rather than the merits of the case – Brazil, Colombia, Turkey, and China joined with the United States to give a majority of one over the Soviet Union, Denmark, New Zealand, and Lebanon, with Britain and France abstaining. By the time the OAS mission reached Guatemala the Arbenz government had collapsed. It was succeeded by a government under Castillo, and American objectives had been achieved – the threat of a communist Guatemala had been removed, and the affair insulated from outside interference.

It could well be argued, however, that the threat had grown to such proportions because of the failure of long-term policies in Latin America, and of personnel to implement them. In this respect the Guatemalan affair brought no significant change. For the United States the OAS continued to be a means to the achievement of political stability and the exclusion of foreign political interests from the Americas; the Latin American states wanted to make it into a means for promoting economic development and welfare; but the United States was not prepared to provide either the capital or the leadership to make this possible. At the Bogotá conference in 1948 Secretary Marshall, having so recently promoted an imaginative plan for European recovery, outlined the policy of the next decade when he told the Latin American governments:

My Government is prepared to increase the scale of assistance it has been giving to the economic development of the American republics. But it is beyond the capacity of the United States Government itself to finance more than a small proportion of the vast economic development needed. The capital required through the years must come from private sources, both domestic and foreign.[37]

In successive conferences the Latin American governments urged the need for an 'economic charter' and sought promises of an increased capital flow and arrangements for the control of commodity prices – particularly coffee, on which Brazil, Colombia, El Salvador, and Costa Rica depend heavily for their economic viability – but these pleas met with little or no response.

The turning-point in American policy however came in 1958, when Vice-President Nixon made a goodwill mission in the company of his wife to Uruguay, Argentina, Paraguay, Bolivia, Peru, Ecuador, Colombia, and Venezuela. He found that his goodwill was not always reciprocated, and in Lima and Caracas he was met with violent protests, demonstrations, and personal abuse. The immediate reaction of the American government followed nineteenth-century tradition, and four companies of marines and paratroopers were sent to Caribbean bases, but the long-term reaction was more constructive. Correspondence between President Kubitschek of Brazil and Eisenhower prepared the way for a conference of twenty Latin American governments, together with that of the United States, in Washington in September 1958. Reversing its previous policies, the United States agreed that an inter-American economic development institution should be established, and the way was opened for an entirely new approach to the economic problems of the region.

The momentum to continue along this road might not have been maintained had it not been for events in Cuba. But the success of the Castro revolution suggested to the government

[37] J. W. Gantenbein, ed., *The Evolution of Our Latin American Policy* (1950), p. 280.

of the United States there was an imperative need to tackle the fundamental economic and social problems of Latin America; and the ineffectiveness of the political machinery of the OAS to provide any counter to Castro indicated how hollow it might become when serious issues were at stake. The new initiative taken by the Republican administration was accordingly carried forward by the Democratic government, and the personal association of Douglas Dillon, as under secretary to the treasury under Eisenhower and secretary under Kennedy, was maintained. In a speech to the Latin American diplomatic corps in Washington on 13 March 1961 Kennedy sought to put his own imagination and vigour behind the new programme when he said:

I have called on all people of the hemisphere to join in a new Alliance for Progress – *Alianza para el Progreso* – a vast co-operative effort, unparalleled in magnitude and nobility of purpose, to satisfy the basic needs of the American people for homes, work and land, health and schools – *techo, trabajo y tierra, salud y escuela.*[38]

In August 1961, when the Inter-American Economic and Social Council met at Punta del Este, Uruguay and all the American states except Cuba agreed to establish the Alliance for Progress. As its name implied, it was to be a co-operative effort in which each of the Latin American countries would collaborate to improve education, carry out land reform, revise tax structure and tax administration, while the United States provided the material and financial support for economic development. Events were to prove that such a programme needed more than brave words to bring it to success; but the changing character of the OAS from the days before Nixon's visit to South America was plain to see.

EUROPEAN INSTITUTIONS
The sense of grievance felt by the countries of Latin America towards the United States derived in part from an awareness of the imaginative and constructive energy, as well as the material resources, which their northern neighbour devoted to western Europe after the war. For while in the southern hemisphere the United States had developed its policies at a safe and cautious pace, its attitude to western Europe had under-

[38] *DFAR, 1961*, p. 397.

gone a complete transformation since the days of Coolidge's refusal to countenance any revision of war debts, or their being linked to reparations payments.

No doubt the contrast was in part due to the immediate and obvious threat of communism, in part to the dramatic quality of the crisis of trade and payments in Europe at the end of the war. At the beginning of 1947 such trade as was possible in Europe was the result of a series of bilateral agreements which permitted the expenditure by one country of a certain amount of the other's currency, beyond which all purchases had to be made in dollars or gold. The objective of aid which the United States was prepared to give under the Marshall plan was therefore twofold: to raise productivity, sometimes by such a basic method as the provision of food; and to establish a system of payments which would generalize the purchasing power of each country. This could be done only by co-operative effort, and co-operative effort on this scale could only be achieved through the creation of new institutions.

The United States set up a new branch of its executive government to administer Marshall aid, called the European Co-operation Administration. It was naturally centred on Washington, but was supported by missions in each of the countries receiving Marshall aid. In the early years these missions were appropriately so named, and were spurred on by a sense of purposeful reconstruction. They also represented the beginning of a new problem in American administration, where the proliferation of American establishments abroad constituted a constant threat to the control and authority of the ambassador as his country's chief representative. In Europe itself the institutional development was even more significant. The acceptance by the European countries of the initial Marshall offer was followed by the setting up of a Committee for European Economic Co-operation, and this was succeeded in 1948 by the OEEC. The directing body of the OEEC was a Council, which was strictly intergovernmental in character. Decisions were reached by agreement, and where a vote was taken it had to be unanimous. On the other hand the objectives of the organization were essentially those of co-operation to promote increases in production and develop multilateral trade by the removal of restrictions on trade and payments. At the same time it was to 'continue the study of Customs Unions or analogous arrangements such as free trade areas, the formation of which might constitute one of the methods of achieving those objectives'. These aims could not be pursued without an exchange of information which would have been inconceivable before the war. Moreover the Council, which met every two months with ministerial representation and more often with deputies, was supported by a permanent secretariat which was continuously engaged in studying the European economy and implementing the decisions of the Council. This gave the organization its own identity, and was of crucial importance in ensuring that co-operation was not something confined to speeches and declarations of intention made at ministerial conferences.

The first task of the CEEC and the OEEC was to secure from member governments an analysis of their anticipated investment and trade over the next four years, and then in conjunction with the ECA, to devise an estimate of need in terms of United States aid. The ECA for its part insisted on the OEEC taking responsibility for the division of aid amongst its members – a task which was undertaken in the first place by a committee of four making recommendations to the Council as a whole. As a result of this activity nearly $6,000 billion was distributed in aid over the first fifteen months. A high proportion of this amount was at first spent on foodstuffs, raw materials, and semi-finished goods; but by the last quarter of the period the proportions had changed markedly in favour of investment goods. The impact of American aid in the provision of investment goods was often very great indeed, since tools and machinery which could not be manufactured readily in Europe provided the missing link in a whole investment programme. But it was in this field that the degree of co-operation within OEEC was least. It had been hoped that there would be considerable co-ordination of investment programmes between the member countries; in fact there was little, and as the opportunity for profitable investment was so vast, this probably did not make very much difference in the long run.

It was therefore rather in the field of trade and monetary arrangements that the main work of the OEEC was done. In this area it had two main achievements to its credit. It promoted the liberalization of trade by securing agreement amongst all members for the removal of quantitative restrictions; and it set up a system of payments which developed intra-European multilateral convertibility. Without OEEC this rapid development could not have been achieved, and would have been subject to the much more tedious process of unco-ordinated bilateral negotiation. As it was, the increase in productivity which Marshall aid made possible was accompanied *pari passu* by an increase in trade.

The removal of quantitative restrictions on imports was brought about by resolution of the Council. Thus in November 1950 it was agreed to eliminate quotas on 50 per cent of the imports traded on private account by 15 December 1949; and by the end of 1950 67 per cent of intra-European trade had been freed from quantitative restrictions. To facilitate payments between member countries, on the other hand, new institutional arrangements were made by the setting up of the European Payments Union. This was only achieved after prolonged bargaining and often acrimonious discussion. A first step was taken with an agreement on Multilateral Monetary Compensation signed in November 1947; and this was followed by two further payments agreements of a year's duration. The essence of these arrangements was that dollar aid was used not only to cover deficits with the dollar area, but to cover one European country's deficit with another, and thus avoid the necessity of restricting imports from that country. That an agreement of this kind should be difficult to negotiate in detail followed inevitably from the varied trading positions of each of the members; as, for example, Belgium was a strong creditor *vis-à-vis* its European partners, but a debtor *vis-à-vis* the United States; Britain was a creditor in relation to France but not Belgium, and so on. Meanwhile the ECA continued to press for more fully multilateral trade and payments in Europe. This it did partly with the general intention of promoting economic union, but also because as long as trade was not multilateral there would be a tendency to look to the United States, and dollar aid, for what, under normal conditions, could be procured in Europe. It was this pressure, together with the improved productivity of Europe, which made possible the signature in September 1950 of the EPU agreement. The agreement was retroactive, and the EPU's operations were thus counted as having started from 1 July 1950.

Essentially the operations of the EPU were very simple. It

offset the debts and credits of its members against each other in such a way that at the end of each accounting period of a month each country had either a debt or a credit with the union. In this way a credit with any one country would automatically be used to settle debts with any other. A formula was included in the agreement for the settlement of accounts between each country and the union. Under this formula part of a debt with the union could be allowed to accumulate as debt up to a certain amount set by the country's 'quota' (which had been determined as a percentage of its trade at the beginning of the union), part was settled in gold. The same was true of the union's obligations to its creditors. Like its predecessors the union was dependent on American dollar support, although to a lesser extent. The detailed operation of the settlement formula made it possible for the union's payments of gold to exceed its receipts; and to cover this eventuality it was provided through ECA with liquid resources up to $350 million.

Membership of EPU obviously created special difficulties for Britain, as the leading member of the sterling area. At the time when EPU was negotiated these difficulties gave rise to strong foreboding in Britain, no doubt because of the second grave financial crisis which it had experienced in 1949, which had been met by the unwelcome expedient of devaluation. It was natural that in these circumstances there should be considerable anxiety that the effect of the EPU agreement, supported as it was by American dollars, would be to strengthen the European currency area at the expense of sterling, so that the use of sterling as an international currency would be curtailed. To counter this apparent danger the British negotiated the insertion of an optional clause in the EPU agreement which enabled countries who made bilateral agreements with Britain (or indeed between each other) to advance credits to each other as an alternative to EPU credits. In the event the anxiety about sterling proved exaggerated, and the effect of the agreement, together with the optional clause, was to extend the use of sterling, and thereby place added responsibilities on Britain to maintain the stability of its currency. From an overall point of view, however, Britain's membership of EPU was of immense advantage, since it linked the two currency areas together, and thereby created an area of multilateral settlement covering some 40 per cent of the world's commodity trade, or 60 per cent counting the countries with which Britain had bilateral agreements establishing transferable accounts.[39]

By any measure the success of Marshall aid, and the stimulus which it had given to European co-operation, was plain for all to see. There was a rapid increase in European production and productivity. Industrial output for the OEEC area as a whole in the second half of 1950 was 25 per cent above 1938; steel production was 65 per cent greater at the end of 1950 than in 1947; agricultural production had increased 33 per cent over the same period. The dollar gap was reduced from 8.5 billion in 1947 to 1 billion in 1950; and at the beginning of 1951 Britain was the first of the OEEC countries to suspend Marshall aid. No doubt in the normal course of events American aid to Europe would have come to an end at this time and ECA wound up with the formula 'mission accomplished'. But the outbreak of the Korean war changed all this. While Europe no longer needed American economic support to stimulate and underpin its economic recovery it found American aid indispensable for the accomplishment of its rearmament programme. The United States for its part was ready to continue its support of Europe, not only for the general reasons of support for what it regarded as part of western civilization, but more specifically to provide defence against an apparent military threat.

This resulted in a modification of the institutions concerned with American support for western Europe. The ECA was abolished by the Mutual Security Act of 1951, and its functions handed over to the Mutual Security Agency, working under a director in the Executive Office of the President. Henceforward the MSA was responsible for economic and technical aid which came under the heading of 'defence support'. OEEC on the other hand remained in existence. Military planning for European defence was undertaken by NATO, but the initial intention of the organization to provide for economic co-operation was quickly abandoned. OEEC remained in existence but, partly because of the membership of neutral nations

[39] Transferable accounts had been established from the beginning of 1947 in preparation for convertibility. They enabled a number of non-sterling countries (some of which later became members of EPU) to transfer sterling between themselves and the sterling area for current transactions without reference to the Bank of England.

(Sweden, Switzerland, and Austria), did not assume any important new commitments as a result of European rearmament. It made possible the exchange of information and views about the inflationary effect of rearmament, and it continued the process of trade liberalization which had been its greatest contribution to economic recovery. It might have become much less important as a result of the creation within Europe of the new institutions of the six countries of 'Little Europe', were it not that the British government was intent on keeping OEEC alive, not only for its own sake but as a counterweight to the smaller institutions, of which Britain was not a member.

Equally important was the fact that EPU remained in existence. Its operations were modified slightly to deal with the changed conditions of the developing area. Over the long period its successful functioning depended on a fairly stable balance amongst its members. In practice – as might be expected – this did not exist; notably Belgium was a chronic creditor, while western Germany passed in 1951 from being a persistent debtor to a strong creditor. However, this was accompanied by a general improvement in European productivity and the level of reserves, with the result that by 1955 OEEC made preparations for the ending of EPU by working out a European Monetary Agreement, signed by its members. In the event convertibility was not reached until 1958, and on 27 December EPU was closed. The EMA then came into effect, setting up a European Fund – in effect a loan fund – and a Multilateral System of Settlements. At least in the early years these operated in a much more restricted sphere than had EPU, and were principally advantageous in assisting the less developed western European countries, notably Greece and Turkey.

OEEC was of great importance in providing for the recovery of European trade. Far greater innovations in the field of political institutions were made in the attempt to promote closer political unity in Europe, and particularly in the institutions of the six countries which accepted the federalist approach to union.

After OEEC the first of the European institutions to be created was the Council of Europe. In its practical achievements it was the least important; but it served as a meeting ground where a European outlook could be fostered and where plans for further union could be formulated and discussed. The Council is made up of two political bodies: a Consultative Assembly and a Committee of Ministers. The Assembly at its inception had 135 members drawn from the fifteen countries belonging to the Council, chosen either by their government or by their national parliament. As we have seen, those who were most committed to the principle of European union would have liked to give the Assembly legislative powers; but the opposition to such integration – led here as in every other European and Atlantic institution by Britain – was strong enough to prevent this happening, and to retain power in the hands of the Committee of Ministers, who are representatives of national governments. A particular limitation placed on the Assembly was that it was not allowed to discuss questions of defence – although Churchill ignored this proscription in 1950, and thereafter the Committee of Ministers informed the Assembly that it had no objection to the Assembly discussing the 'political aspects of European security'.

The result of the lack of power given to the Assembly has been to make it move at the pace of its slowest members, and to deny it any supranational attributes. Its most important tangible achievement has been to pass a series of conventions which have been accepted by most or all of the member governments. The most important of these, and the one which most excited the imagination, was a European Convention on Human Rights – a proclamation of human freedom and individual dignity in the face of past Nazi tyranny and the present menace of communism. The Council sought to improve on a similar United Nations convention by establishing a Commission and a Court to provide machinery for the enforcement of the Convention, but to do so would mean giving an effective right of appeal against national sovereignty, and it is not surprising that such an attempt met with little success. Other conventions, of no great political importance, established equivalence of diplomas leading to admission to universities, and of periods of university study; and there was a convention on extradition.

In its organization and procedures the Council succeeded in establishing its European character, to the extent that members came to be grouped according to party allegiance, both for an equitable distribution of posts within the Assembly, and later in debate. And the very existence of the Council has been a testimony to the European spirit.

Beyond that, events have so shaped themselves that there has in practice been little scope for the Council's activity. During the first sessions of the Consultative Assembly the federalists in the European movement tried to strengthen the Council to become a European government, but the resistance of Britain, the Scandinavian and the neutral powers made this impossible. Instead they helped create the climate of opinion which welcomed the setting up of the ECSC, with its membership limited to 'the Six' – France, Germany, Italy, Belgium, Holland, and Luxembourg. Thereafter it attempted, partly on its own initiative, partly in taking up the proposals put forward by Eden and named after him,[40] to bring about a close association between the Six and the other members. But in practice the Six had embarked on a venture whose very nature was to separate them from the rest of Europe, and there was no way of avoiding this fact. In the field of economics there was little activity that did not fall within the domain of either ECSC (and later EEC and Euratom) on the one hand and OEEC on the other; defence issues, even when no longer excluded from its purview, were largely handled by NATO and WEU; and in many other matters the Council found that it lacked the universalism which made the UN, however defective, a more appropriate organization.

The ECSC has proved a quite different kind of institution. As we have seen, there were specific reasons deriving from French policy towards Germany, added to the general movement towards a more federal Europe, which gave this new organization its supranational characteristics. The treaty of 18 April 1951 setting up ECSC[41] gave these supranational functions to a High Authority, whose functions were to implement the treaty, to make appropriate regulations to carry out its

[40] The Eden plan, which was presented in March 1952, proposed that the Committee of Ministers and the Consultative Assembly should fulfil the functions of ministerial committee and assembly for all the European institutions. When they were acting as part of ECSC, they would be attended only by the representatives of the Six; otherwise they would have full attendance; but they would remain the same institutions. The principles of the plan were accepted by the Committee of Ministers and the Consultative Assembly in May 1952, but it was never put into practice.

[41] *European Yearbook, 1951*, i. 361 ff.

intentions, and to levy a tax to finance its operations. Its status and authority were moreover explicitly described in the treaty in these words:

> The members of the High Authority shall exercise their functions in complete independence, in the general interest of the Community. In the fulfilment of their duties, they shall neither solicit nor accept instructions from any government or from any organization. They will abstain from all conduct incompatible with the supranational character of their functions.
>
> Each member state undertakes to respect this supranational character and not to seek to influence the members of the High Authority in the execution of their duties.

It had been the original intention of the French government to set up no other executive body than the High Authority, but in the course of negotiating the treaty it bowed to the reservations of the Belgian and Dutch governments in this respect, and agreed to the establishment of a Council of Ministers, which lacks the power of initiative but in certain instances checks the actions of the High Authority.

The High Authority was thus explicitly relieved of any responsibility to national governments. Eight of its members are chosen by the member states acting together, and the ninth co-opted by them; once appointed they cannot be dismissed by national governments, although any one may refuse to renew a member of the High Authority when his term of office expires. It followed logically from this that there should be some body to which the High Authority would be responsible. Under the treaty this body was to be the Assembly of the Community, chosen by national parliaments from amongst their own members; and it was given the power to dismiss the High Authority as a whole by a vote of censure. In addition, the treaty set up a Court to hear appeals from industrial concerns and member governments against decisions by the High Authority. Later Euratom and the EEC were established with parallel institutions, and it was then possible to merge the Assemblies and Courts of all three communities into a Common Assembly and Court of Justice.

Five years passed between the original proposal of the Schuman plan and the Messina conference, which led to the signature of the Rome treaties on 1 January 1957. These treaties set up two new communities, Euratom and the EEC. The text of the treaties shows the institutions of the new organizations to be significantly different from those of the ECSC. This is explained partly by the fact that the Messina conference took up the threads which had been dropped by the defeat of EDC; but also by the much wider range of economic activity which was placed within the purview of the EEC (although not Euratom).

The essential difference was that while ECSC concentrated the power to implement the treaty in the hands of the High Authority, subject to check by the Council of Ministers, EEC and Euratom gave the power of decision to its Council of Ministers. Each of the two new communities set up a Commission, which is the rough equivalent of the High Authority; they gave the Commission the sole power to initiate proposals for the implementation of the treaties, and the function of putting such proposals into practice once they had been accepted; but their acceptance depended on a vote in the Council of Ministers. In both cases the rules for voting are complex. There are five different voting procedures: in three cases members have 1 vote each; in the other two votes are weighted, 4 each to France, Germany and Italy, 2 each to Belgium and the Netherlands and 1 to Luxembourg. In this way it is possible on some votes to protect every member's interests by requiring unanimity, on others to protect the rights of the small states against the large, on others to prevent the possibility of the three largest being overruled by a combination of the smallest. At the same time it is recognized that the Community cannot develop unless its interests are protected against the veto of one or two of its members; and for this reason the treaty is designed to lessen the veto power of members as the Community passes out of the transitional phase into full operation.

The distribution of power within any set of institutions is never measured by the terms of a constitution alone, and it follows that the degree of supranationality must be assessed in terms of activity as well as treaty arrangements. When this is done there can be no doubt that ECSC has achieved a high degree of supranationality, albeit in a limited sphere. This has been possible in the first place because of the economic success of the Community. By the end of the transitional period in

February 1958 the Community had abolished customs dues, quantitative restrictions, discrimination by price and by transport charges, and currency restrictions on payments for trade in coal, coke, iron ore, steel, and scrap. The result of this was a very rapid increase in the first three years, maintained at a slower pace thereafter, of trade within the Community in everything except coal. It has also established its credit, and can raise loans and relend to aid investment. It is not surprising that this development has met with little opposition from member governments. The High Authority has used the supranational authority given to it by the treaty; in doing so it has not needed to make any proposals which involve member states in more than they had already undertaken by the treaty itself, and it has worked within the framework of expanding production and an expanding market. At the same time the limitations on the power of the High Authority have been shown in its experience with the coal industry. As this industry began to encounter strong foreign competition from imported coal, and more important, from oil, the problem it had to face was to reduce rather than expand production and to concentrate production in the most efficient pits. In these circumstances the High Authority found itself in conflict with national governments, which naturally sought to protect the interests of their own industries (and voters) rather than those of the Community as a whole; and in this confrontation the Authority found itself unable, either by the text of the treaty or in practice, to overrule member governments.

It is equally to be expected that in its earliest years the EEC would go little distance towards extended supranationality. Whereas the ECSC treaty had embodied most of the important policy decisions in its limited sphere, the Rome treaties left many of these decisions still to be taken, even though the broad lines of development were laid down. It therefore followed that such decisions would be taken by national governments agreeing together rather than by supranational decisions. In spite of this the establishment of EEC (and to a lesser extent Euratom, whose range of action has been much less complex) must be counted as a marked advance towards supranationality. Under its aegis negotiations between governments ceased to be merely bargaining between rival powers – although when economic interests and votes were in question, particularly in agriculture, this inevitably played a large part – but were also directed towards the achievement of agreed aims to the establishment of a Community. The Commission itself is a sufficiently real entity for the member governments to have accredited permanent representatives, with the rank of ambassador, to it; and in several fields special committees have been set up with representation from the Commission and from national ministries. As a result, discussions between governments, and between governments and the Commission became 'more than purely international negotiation, for the Commission is there in a leading role not just as a broker but to represent the interests of the whole against the parts'.[42] The extent to which the European institutions had acquired a life of their own must also be measured in the way in which political parties and pressure groups – the life-blood which animates political institutions – have been formed on a European basis, so that members of the European Assembly meet as liberals or socialists rather than as nationals, and pressure groups think it worth paying for offices and activities in Brussels as well as their national capitals.

Thus while EEC obviously falls short of full supranationalism, it has succeeded in establishing that there is a whole whose interests are as worth pursuing as those of each of its parts. It has also shown a clear path towards closer union in Europe; most clearly in the agreement that the European Assembly should prepare plans for its own direct election, in place of selection by national parliaments. How fast this process would have proceeded had not de Gaulle come to power in France and rejuvenated French nationalism it is impossible to say.

The economic aspects of the European Communities are of equal importance. Academic economists have long discussed the varying merits of a general development towards free trade, and of the establishment of a customs union with complete internal free trade but protected by tariffs from the outside world. The initial policy of the American government, during and after the war, was designed to promote universal free trade; its promotion of European recovery by the Marshall plan, and even more the constant support which it gave to the union of Europe have meant a partial abandonment of that policy. The ECSC has succeeded in establishing a common market between the six member countries in coal and steel. Under EEC agree-

[42] U. W. Kitzinger, *The Challenge of the Common Market* (1961), p. 59.

ments the reduction of tariffs within the Community proceeded more quickly than the Rome treaty required, so that from 1 January 1961 industrial tariffs within the community stood at only 70 per cent of their 1957 level and quantitative restrictions had virtually disappeared.[43] Associated with this reduction of internal tariffs there has been a very marked increase in trade within the Community, and an unusually fast growth rate – although opinions necessarily differ as to the extent to which this is attributable to the existence of the Community.

But while the Community is undeniably a customs union, it is not one which has set up high industrial tariffs to the rest of the world. As signatories of GATT, each of the member countries had already assumed an obligation in respect of customs unions, namely that the external tariff of such a union should not be higher or more restrictive than national tariffs prior to the union. In drawing up a common external tariff the Community has kept to this obligation, although it has neces- sarily meant that a high tariff country like France must reduce tariffs and the low tariff members increase them; moreover in the first stages of harmonizing national tariffs with the agreed new external tariff the Community has proceeded more quickly than it had originally agreed; and it has acted on the assumption that as the process of harmonization goes on, it will have to provide for a lower external tariff to keep up with agreed tariff reductions under GATT.

When the Rome treaties were negotiated most of the signa- tories had some kind of colonial responsibilities. By far the largest were those of France, whose extensive colonies in Africa were still on the way to independence, and whose Algerian departments were still administered as part of France. It would obviously have been impossible to ignore this relationship in framing the treaty, since France would act as a trade bridge between its own empire and the European customs union. Moreover the French government made it a condition of its going forward with the European common market that some arrangement should be made for the overseas burden which it

[43] For agriculture the Rome treaty laid down general objectives of increased productivity, safeguards for the agricultural population, market stability, regular supplies, and fair prices for the consumer. The attainment of these objectives, and the assignment of priority to them, was to prove a more complex task than the reduction of industrial tariffs.

had assumed of financing the development of its African territories amongst the other members of the Community.

As a result, as we have seen, the Rome treaty set up an Association of the overseas territories with the EEC. Under the terms of the Association the members of EEC (that is to say the six European countries) agreed to extend the same tariff reductions and elimination of quantitative restrictions as to each other; while the overseas associates for their part undertook to extend to all members of EEC the same treatment in regard to tariffs as they accorded to the country with which they had special relations. More important, the treaty set up a Development Fund of $581¼ million to which each of the EEC members contributed in agreed proportions.[44] Of this the major part ($511¼ million) was allocated to French overseas territories.

Before the treaty could be put into effect the political framework within which it was conceived changed fundamentally, as the territories concerned achieved their independence. But having been brought into the Community as colonies, they had no wish (with the exception of Guinea) to achieve independence at the expense of severing their links with EEC, especially with the Development Fund; nor did France have any intention of abandoning its civilizing mission by cutting itself off from its former colonies – once it had learned the lesson of Guinea. On the other hand the Association perpetuated a division, most obviously in Africa, which derived from the days of colonial rule; and this was something which carried economic disadvantages (for example in maintaining economic barriers between former British and former French territories), even though these might not outweigh the attractiveness of the Development Fund.

We see, then, that the western world was extremely fertile in the development of new institutions and institutional arrangements for political and economic development. In this respect the Soviet bloc was less creative. In January 1949 Comecon was established in Moscow, having as its first members Poland, Czechoslovakia, Hungary, Rumania, and Bulgaria, as well as the Soviet Union, and was later joined by east Germany,

[44] France and Germany $200 million each, Belgium and the Netherlands $70 million each, Italy $40 million, Luxemburg $1¼ million (cf. Kitzinger, *Challenge of the Common Market*).

Albania, North Korea and North Vietnam. But there was no room for such a body to perform a role of voluntary co-operation in the centrally-directed system of the Stalinist world. Just as the Cominform served as an instrument for the exclusion of Yugoslavia, so Comecon provided the framework for an economic boycott of Tito. But the decisive relationships within the Soviet bloc were bilateral, between the Soviet Union and its satellite. Even when, in 1950, the rouble became the standard currency for international transactions within the bloc, the main result was to enable the Soviet Union to determine the rates of exchange, and thereby increase its advantage in trade with the satellites. The pattern of trade and the structure of the economies of the eastern European countries underwent fundamental revision as a result of Stalinist control. A very high proportion of trade now took place within the bloc rather than with western countries.[45] But this trade did not follow from a planned development of the region as a whole. On the contrary, the economy of each country was given a markedly autarkic direction, wasteful of economic resources.

After the death of Stalin political control over the countries of eastern Europe was loosened, and at the same time Comecon was given fresh importance and vitality as an organ by which economic co-operation could be achieved. Its organization was developed, regular meetings were held, and member countries were represented by ministers or deputy ministers. But it was impossible for Comecon to develop as an autonomous body, given the Soviet system. The increased freedom of the satellites did not disappear after 1956, but it was essentially freedom within certain limits for national governments to take their own road to socialism; so that, for example, Polish agriculture was not subjected to collectivization. Within this system of 'polycentrism' there would inevitably arise conflicts of interest between the Soviet Union on the one hand and its satellites on the other, and to a lesser extent (on the economic plane) between the satellites themselves – tensions which increased when China could act as a sounding board for the demands of the satellites. Comecon provided part of the framework within which these conflicts could be reconciled or fought out.

[45] Thus the trade of Bulgaria and Czechoslovakia with other bloc countries, as a percentage of their total trade, rose from 12 and 11 per cent (1937) to 92 and 60 per cent (1951) respectively (see Brzezinski, *The Soviet Bloc*, pp. 174 ff.).

AID: ECONOMIC, TECHNICAL, AND MILITARY

The purpose of this chapter has so far been to examine the political and economic links between nations which have survived or developed into institutional form. Taking a broader view, one can see that one of the outstanding characteristics of the period with which we are concerned was a rapidly growing awareness of the immense gulf which separated the rich from the poor nations in the world – and with this awareness an implicit assumption that such wide diversity of wealth was in some way unacceptable. Nowhere did this assumption receive better expression than in President Kennedy's inaugural address of January 1961, when he said:

> To those people in the huts and villages of half the globe struggling to break the bonds of mass misery, we pledge our best efforts to help them help themselves, for whatever period is required – not because the Communists may be doing it, not because we seek their votes, but because it is right. If a free society cannot help the many who are poor, it cannot save the few who are rich.[46]

At the same time governments used their economic resources in an attempt to further their political interests to an extent unparalleled in previous history. The use of wealth to establish alliances or extend political influence was not new;[47] but the scale on which this was done had changed completely.

We have already seen how the institutions of the UN were organized to promote economic stability and development, and we have indicated briefly the relationship established between the old imperial countries of Europe and their former colonial empires. We must now turn to the development of aid given by nation states to the poorer countries of the world. The pattern of such aid is a complex one, because of the diverse motives which inspired it. The political motives for aid led a country like China to provide assistance to new African states while struggling to maintain the rate of economic development at home; with similar motives the United States government channelled apparently disproportionately large amounts of economic and military assistance to South Korea and Formosa, while Israel sought to counter and encircle Arab influence by

---

[46] RIIA, *Documents, 1961*, pp. 1–2.
[47] See for example H. Feis, *Europe the World's Banker* (1931), for an account of such activity before 1914.

THE WARP AND WEFT OF INTERNATIONAL RELATIONS 597

economic interest in Africa. At the same time the mid-west of the United States, traditionally the home of isolationism, but an area which had a long record of sending missionaries to China and Africa, now produced a young generation of idealists prepared to teach Asians to drive tractors and to study soil in a laboratory; while in England a few people who in 1942 had established a characteristically *ad hoc* body called the Oxford Committee for Famine Relief saw it develop into a secular fund-raising and fund-distributing organization seldom if ever equalled. Yet these efforts, important as they were in a national context or in comparison with what had gone before, were puny indeed compared with the forces of growth to which they sought to provide a corrective; for it was characteristic of the rich countries that their populations increased, if at all, relatively slowly but that their capital accumulation proceeded ever more rapidly; while in the poor countries population growth was not only unchecked but actually increased by improvements in medicine and hygiene, and capital had not yet accumulated to the point where it could provide both a higher standard of living and a surplus for new investment. The consequence was that for all the wealth expended, for example by the United States on defence and foreign aid, the gap between its per capita income compared with that of a country like India became greater, not less.

On 20 January 1949 Harry Truman gave his inaugural address on assuming office as president of the United States. In it he outlined four points which would guide his policy, of which three were immediately forgotten, and the fourth was seized upon by the public and the press and achieved a status of its own as Point Four. The emphasis given to Point Four was appropriate. The first three points were general and predictable – support of the United Nations, promotion of world economic recovery, and 'strengthening of the freedom-loving nations against the danger of aggression'. Point Four in contrast drew attention to the low standard of living of the majority of the people of the world, compared with the fact that the advanced nations had the technical means to improve their lot. The most valuable assistance that could be given, therefore, was in the provision of technical knowledge to help others to help themselves, together with capital assistance on a limited

20

scale to enable underdeveloped countries to take advantage of
newly acquired skills. As Truman said in his speech:

For the first time in history humanity possesses the knowledge and
the skill to relieve the suffering of these people.

The United States is pre-eminent among nations in the development of industrial and scientific techniques. The material resources
which we can afford to use for the assistance of other people are
limited. But our imponderable resources in technical knowledge are
constantly growing and are inexhaustible.[48]

In this as in so many of the decisions which he took Truman was
guided by his awareness of historical development. Commenting
on the Point Four programme in his memoirs he said:

I knew from my study of American history that this country was
developed by the investment of foreign capital by the British, the
Dutch, the Germans, and the French. These countries invested
immense sums in the development of our railroads, mines, oil lands,
and the livestock industry. . . . The first packing house west of the
Mississippi River was built by a Frenchman, a count in Napoleon's
army. . . .

It seemed to me that if we could encourage stabilized governments
in underdeveloped countries in Africa, South America, and Asia,
we could encourage the use for the development of those areas of
some of the capital which had accumulated in the United States.[49]

Six months later Truman sought an appropriation from Congress to implement his proposal, but a further year passed,
and it was not until June 1950 that legislation was passed in
the Act for International Development. Appropriations for
technical assistance were then made, to the value of $34.5 mil-
lion; this was $10 million less than the President had asked for
and the sum was further reduced, when it was embodied in the
budget for 1951–2, to slightly less than $30 million, of which
$12 million was a contribution to UN Technical Assistance.

Truman's initiative was followed in January 1950 by an
equally important proposal from the Australian government. At
the meeting of the Commonwealth foreign ministers in Colombo
– a conference which Ernest Bevin, now a sick man, attended as
one of his last great acts as foreign secretary – Percy Spender,
the Australian minister for external affairs, proposed that

[48] *Memoirs*, ii. 227.   [49] Ibid. p. 231.

economic assistance should be given to the countries of South East Asia, firstly to relieve starvation, secondly to provide technical assistance and training, and thirdly to provide capital equipment. The proposal was made within the framework of the Commonwealth partly because three-quarters of the people in South and South East Asia lived in countries belonging to the Commonwealth, which thus provided a tradition of flexible consultation and co-operation. Moreover governments like that of Australia were aware that in so far as there was a threat of communism from the widespread existence of poverty, it was likely to receive less attention in this area from the United States, simply because of the predominance of Commonwealth interests.

In this way the Colombo plan was born. However, its name was from the first misleading and became even more so. Although the original proposal had been made at a Commonwealth conference in Colombo, membership of the plan was quickly taken up – as had always been hoped – by the South and South East Asian countries that were outside the Commonwealth; and it was joined by two important donor countries, the United States and Japan.[50] But there has been very little plan – least of all any kind of governmental co-operation like that undertaken in Europe by OEEC. A Consultative Committee has met for three weeks every year – attended in the first two weeks by officials and in the last week by ministers – but the main object of the meetings has been to provide discussion of national plans and progress rather than to plan for the region as a whole. The plan has facilitated the supply of finance for capital development, since capital coming from the donor countries often provided a small direct contribution, and has served the additional purpose of giving a project a cachet which attracts other money. The most distinctive feature of the Colombo plan, however, has been the provision of technical training. In this it has achieved genuine co-operation in that the flow of training is not solely from the developed countries to the underdeveloped. Thus during the first ten years of the

[50] The original members of 'The Colombo Plan for Co-operative Development in South and South-East Asia' were: Australia, Canada, Ceylon, India, New Zealand, Pakistan and the United Kingdom. Malaya and British Borneo, Cambodia, Laos, Vietnam, and the United States joined in 1951; Burma and Nepal in 1952; Indonesia in 1953; Japan, the Philippine Republic, and Thailand in 1954.

20*

plan India was the fifth largest supplier of technical training in the area, and this has included the training of a few Australians, New Zealanders, and Japanese. The extent of this kind of training has been increased by American 'third-country' programmes, where the training has been offered by an Asian country, particularly Thailand and the Philippines, while the United States has borne the expense.

In June 1950 the Korean war changed the pattern and direction of American aid. Europe now received military assistance under the Mutual Security Programme in far larger measure than economic aid. At the same time aid to Africa and Asia was increased: Europe remained the largest recipient, although account must be taken of the fact that increasing military support was given to France for the conduct of the war in Indo-China. Until 1960 the American government did not disclose figures for military aid; when it did so it transpired that France had received nearly one-third of the total of $13.7 billion given to Europe. The leading recipients of military aid in the period 1950–9 were as follows:

	$ million
France	4,502
Taiwan	2,057
Italy	1,993
Turkey	1,717
South Korea	1,292
Netherlands	1,238
Belgium	1,214
Britain	1,077

Source: New York Times, 24 Feb. 1960.

Moreover legislation providing for aid began to make clear that it was given as part of cold war operations. After 8 January 1952 military and defence support under the Mutual Security Act was made dependent on a full contribution on the part of the recipient country to 'its own defensive strength and the defensive strength of the free world'; and under the same act technical assistance to non-NATO countries depended on their agreement 'to take such action as may be mutually agreed upon to eliminate causes of international tension'. The natural accompaniment of this mobilizing of economic and military resources was an attempt to deny the sinews of war – and cold war – to the communist world. Thus in 1948 the Economic Co-operation Act had encouraged trade between western and eastern Europe, except for the export from the west of certain items of definite strategic importance; but in October 1951 Congress passed the 'Battle Act' which forbade assistance to countries which failed to plan an embargo on the export to the communist world not only of military materials but of a list of commodities which might be used in war production. In practice the act was extremely difficult to apply. It made sweeping denunciation of trade which the United States could easily do without, but which other countries could only abandon at a considerable loss to themselves – a greater loss than to communist countries, as far as these could be calculated; and of necessity it had to give the executive branch of government the task of making exceptions 'when unusual circumstances indicate that the cessation of aid would clearly be detrimental to the security of the United States'.[51]

The development of aid as a weapon in the cold war became more pronounced after the success of the Republicans in the presidential elections of 1952 and the appointment of John Foster Dulles as secretary of state. Coming to office under the impact of the Korean war, Dulles sought to extend containment across the world, to safeguard all the frontiers with the Soviet Union against communist expansion; and the most fruitful way of doing this in his view was by forming defence pacts. He was in consequence critical of countries which were unwilling to join such pacts, and both he and Congress preferred to concentrate military aid and economic support on those countries ready to show their commitment to the western side by joining a pact with the United States, while offering very much more slender aid to countries which chose to remain 'neutral' or 'non-aligned'. Under this general direction the countries which benefited most were those in key areas of the cold war in Asia, particularly South Korea, Formosa, and South Vietnam.

The pattern of aid associated with this phase of American foreign policy is evident in the tables provided by the International Co-operation Administration for the House Appropriations Committee (see p. 602). The figures cover defence

[51] Mutual Defense Assistance Control Act of 1951 (see H. B. Price, *The Marshall Plan and its Meaning* (1955), pp. 169–70).

support but not direct military aid; money provided for specific development projects, the 'special assistance programme' for countries not qualifying for defence support; and technical assistance given under the Point Four programme. Assistance in one form or another thus went to some fifty-four countries in addition to west Berlin; but at the same time the disproportion between the aid given to Korea and to India is evident.

United States Economic Aid, 1956–8

	Year ended 30 June 1956	*Year ended 30 June 1957*	*Year ended 30 June 1958 est.*
Afghanistan	18,300,000	14,391,000	5,800,000
Argentina	84,000	—	350,000
Bolivia	25,400,000	23,300,000	20,100,000
Brazil	3,604,000	4,512,000	4,700,000
Burma	—	—	12,700,000
Cambodia	45,100,000	34,500,000	26,000,000
Ceylon	5,000,000	6,083,000	1,400,000
Chile	2,174,000	2,456,000	2,500,000
Colombia	1,323,000	1,156,000	1,290,000
Costa Rica	907,000	994,000	1,050,000
Cuba	471,000	569,000	570,000
Dominican Republic	265,000	156,000	190,000
Ecuador	1,660,000	1,809,000	1,880,000
Egypt	2,623,000	686,000	—
El Salvador	934,000	1,069,000	1,000,000
Ethiopia	2,923,000	9,600,000	Classified
Ghana	—	360,000	500,000
Greece	26,800,000	25,700,000	15,700,000
Guatemala	18,176,000	17,518,000	12,400,000
Haiti	6,361,000	2,126,000	Classified
Honduras	1,156,000	1,324,000	1,350,000
Iceland	—	8,462,000	5,100,000
India	60,400,000	68,700,000	81,300,000
Indonesia	11,100,000	11,700,000	21,300,000
Iran	65,500,000	51,600,000	26,600,000
Iraq	2,277,000	3,640,000	2,200,000
Israel	23,984,000	26,847,000	9,000,000
Japan	900,000	2,300,000	2,500,000
Jordan	7,500,000	21,200,000	31,700,000
Korea	326,900,000	305,700,000	220,600,000
Laos	48,700,000	49,500,000	Classified

	Year ended *30 June 1956*	*Year ended* *30 June 1957*	*Year ended* *30 June 1958 est.*
Lebanon	7,800,000	12,100,000	2,700,000
Liberia	1,782,000	1,716,000	2,000,000
Libya	7,520,000	19,280,000	12,400,000
Mexico	705,000	888,000	680,000
Morocco	—	20,067,000	Classified
Nepal	1,958,000	4,347,000	4,065,000
Nicaragua	756,000	681,000	900,000
Pakistan	106,700,000	98,700,000	55,800,000
Panama	1,096,000	1,023,000	1,170,000
Paraguay	1,801,000	1,530,000	1,480,000
Peru	2,819,000	2,594,000	2,850,000
Philippines	29,100,000	33,900,000	19,000,000
Saudi Arabia	—	22,000	25,000,000
Somalia	60,000	1,387,000	650,000
Spain	58,426,000	69,999,000	56,150,000
Taiwan	73,300,000	83,700,000	60,000,000
Thailand	34,500,000	34,500,000	24,000,000
Tunisia	—	8,489,000	Classified
Turkey	107,800,000	58,800,000	74,500,000
Uruguay	154,000	254,000	200,000
Venezuela	150,000	135,000	170,000
Vietnam	195,700,000	59,400,000	179,200,000
West Berlin	17,178,000	11,406,000	11,170,000
Yugoslavia	29,803,000	14,992,000	11,750,000

Source: New York Times, 24 May 1958.

In addition to military assistance and economic aid enumerated in the tables above, the United States contributed to the agencies of the UN; the Export-Import Bank made loans to be spent on United States goods and services – amounting to $1.1 billion in the year ended June 1957; while surplus agricultural produce was sold to the value of $1.5 billion, mainly in foreign currencies which were then used to defray American costs in the countries concerned, and to make further loans.

In most important respects Soviet assistance to underdeveloped countries differed from that of the western powers. It was on a much smaller scale, and it was given in the form of credits rather than direct aid. Credits were opened with the Soviet bloc countries as well as the Soviet Union, in a way that was obviously planned and directed along the same lines as Soviet bloc trade.[52] The terms of the credit were such as to emphasize the difference between Soviet credit and that offered by the western international agencies – interest was charged at the low rate of 2·5 per cent.

The goods supplied have been principally of two sorts – industrial equipment and arms. The sacrifice involved for the Soviet Union is obviously very different between these two. Lagging behind the United States in its own capital equipment and faced with competing claims from developing countries in eastern Europe and from China, it has provided a steel mill for India and hydro-electric plants to Afghanistan at the cost of other possibilities. On the other hand its arms deliveries have generally been supplied out of obsolescent equipment at the sacrifice of little more than its scrap value.

The Soviet bloc has gone farther than the United States in the concentration of its assistance – although it has generally concentrated on politically sensitive countries rather than those allied to the Soviet Union. Entering into competition with the United States in offering assistance to developing countries at a time when Dulles was still constructing an alliance system, the Soviet Union made much propaganda value of the fact that it did not attach 'strings' to aid. In a formal sense this has generally been true; in practice the terms of credit have obviously imposed limitations by restricting the range of possible purchases, fixing prices, and creating a future dependence for supplies and spares. In addition, assistance has, as we have seen, generally been made available to countries prepared at least to support Soviet foreign policy.

We have already suggested that the humanitarian objectives of aid to underdeveloped and poverty-stricken countries fell short of achievement, in the sense that the disparity between the rich and the poor nations went on increasing and that the scale of world poverty and hunger was scarcely diminished. The success of aid as a means to promote national interests was also qualified. The foreign policies and alignments of countries receiving aid did not necessarily bear a close relationship to the provenance of aid they received – even when such aid came

[52] At the same time China has opened lines of credit independently of the Soviet Union in the first instance for Cambodia, Ceylon, Nepal, and Egypt.

predominantly from one side in the east-west conflict; and the receipt of aid sometimes provoked a stronger reaction of nationalist independence than of political connexion with the donor country. To some extent aid from outside helped the governments of developing countries to stay in power; but there was no guarantee that it would do so, as the examples of Iraq and Cuba showed.

Soviet Bloc Aid Programme, 1954 to mid–1959* (US $ million)

Recipient	Total	Economic	Military	Economic deliveries	Military deliveries
Afghanistan	160	130	30	40	30
Argentina	110	110	—	5	—
Burma	42	42	—	10	—
Ceylon	50	50	—	5	—
Egypt	700	300	400	50	400
Syria	318	168	150	25	150
India	650	650	—	150	—
Iraq	238	138	100	—	100
Ethiopia	100	100	—	—	—
Yemen	50	50	20	—	20
Indonesia	240	140	100	25	100
Yugoslavia	200	200	—	100	—
Finland	120	120	—	20	—
Iceland	25	25	—	5	—
Total	3,003	2,203	800	425	800

*Based on official announcements of the governments, documents, and the press.

Source: J. S. Berliner, *Soviet Economic Aid* (1960).

Part of the underlying assumption of aid as an instrument of national policy in the western countries, particularly in the United States, was that it would promote stability. Even this assumption was only partially justified. Where military and defence support aid was given, it might disturb an existing balance of power and promote international tension, as was the case with American aid to Pakistan.

Similarly, in internal politics and economic development the receipt of aid often promoted instability rather than smooth unruffled development towards a higher standard of living –

as indeed the developed societies of the west might have expected from their own history. And many communities had been hamstrung in their economic development by corruption, nepotism, and extortion by moneylenders and landlords; the injection of economic aid did not automatically eliminate faults of this sort – it sometimes allowed their development on a grander scale. The countries of western Europe, for all their wealth and education, struggled with their own problems of stability and development; it is scant wonder that a country like Turkey or Iran, receiving aid from a variety of national and international donors, should have difficulty in translating the advice of their own and imported experts into a constructive national economic policy. In spite of these facts, the scale of western aid was largely maintained into the 1960s. The British and even more the French government saw a direct advantage in maintaining the old imperial connexion; the German government saw advantages to be gained in European politics through an acceptance of the French view of European aid to Africa; Israel more than any other country developed aid as part of its foreign policy. In the United States the very large aid programme ran the gauntlet of Congressional legislation, through committees and sub-committees of House and Senate, and the administration found increasing difficulty in justifying expenditure on the grounds that it furthered the interests of American foreign policy.

Some 150 years before the development of aid programmes Alexander Hamilton had warned his countrymen:

It is not here meant to recommend a policy absolutely selfish or interested in nations; but to show, that a policy regulated by their own interest, as far as justice and good faith permit, is, and ought to be, their prevailing one; and that either to ascribe to them a different principle of action, or to deduce from the supposition of it arguments for a self-denying and self-sacrificing gratitude, on the part of a nation which may have received from another good offices, is to misrepresent or misconceive what usually are, and ought to be, the springs of national conduct.[53]

At least to Hamilton, then, it would have come as no surprise to discover that the recipients of aid were more often ready to use it as a lever to induce more than they were to align their domestic and foreign policies with those of the United States.

[53] *Pacificus Letters*, no. 4 (*Works* (New York, 1903), iv. 465).

Documentary Sources

Churchill, W. S. *Into battle; speeches compiled by Randolph S. Churchill.* London, 1941.

— *The sinews of peace; post-war speeches,* ed. by Randolph S. Churchill. London, 1948.

Documents on American foreign relations, 1938/9– . Vols i–xiii sponsored by the World Peace Foundation, vols xiv– by the Council on Foreign Relations. Boston.

Great Britain, Foreign Office, and USA, Dept of State. *Documents on German foreign policy, 1918–1945, from the archives of the German Foreign Ministry,* series D (1937–45). London, 1949–56.

Gruliow, L., ed. *Current Soviet policies* [i]–iv, *the documentary record of the 19th-22nd Communist Party Congress . . . from the translations of the Current Digest of the Soviet Press.* New York, Praeger, 1953– .

Holborn, Louise W., ed. *War and peace aims of the United Nations,* i: *1939–42.* Boston, World Peace Foundation, 1943.

Hurewitz, J. C. *Diplomacy in the Near and Middle East; a documentary record,* ii: *1914–56.* Princeton, NJ, Van Nostrand, 1956.

RIIA. *Documents on international affairs, 1928–* . London, OUP, 1929– .

Rosenman, S. I., ed. *The public papers and addresses of Franklin D. Roosevelt,* vol. iv. New York, Random House, 1941.

USA, Dept of State. *American foreign policy, 1950–5; basic documents.* 1957. 2 vols.

— — *American foreign policy: current documents, 1956.* 1959.

— — *Papers relating to the foreign relations of the United States, diplomatic papers:*
(a) *The conferences at Malta and Yalta, 1945.* 1955.
(b) *The conference of Berlin, the Potsdam conference, 1945.* 1960.
(c) *The conferences at Cairo and Tehran, 1943.* 1961.

— — *Peace and war: US foreign policy 1931–41.* 1943.

— — *United States policy in the Middle East, Sept. 1956–June 1947; documents.* Aug. 1957.

— — *United States relations with China, with special reference to the period 1944–9.* 1949.

— Senate, Committee on Foreign Relations and State Dept. *A decade of American foreign policy: basic documents, 1941–9.* 1950.

USSR, Ministry of Foreign Affairs. *Correspondence between the Chairman of the Council of Ministers of the USSR and the Presidents of the USA and the Prime Ministers of Great Britain during the Great Patriotic War of 1941–5,* i: *Correspondence with Winston S. Churchill and Clement R. Attlee.* London, Lawrence & Wishart, 1958.

Select Bibliography

1. From War in Europe to World War

Beloff, Max. *The foreign policy of Soviet Russia*, ii: *1936–41*. London, OUP for RIIA, 1949.

Berlin, Isaiah. *Mr Churchill in 1940*. London, Murray, 1949[?].

Bryant, Arthur. *The turn of the tide, based on the diaries and autobiographical notes of Field Marshal the Viscount Alanbrooke*. London, Collins, 1957.

— *Triumph in the west, 1943–6, based on the diaries and autobiographical notes of Field Marshal the Viscount Alanbrooke*. London, Collins, 1959.

Bullock, A. L. C. *Hitler; a study in tyranny*. London, Odhams, 1964.

Butler, J. R. M., ed. *Grand strategy*, ii: *September 1939–June 1941*, by J. R. M. Butler; iii: *June 1941–August 1942*, pt 1 by J. M. A. Gwyer, pt 2 by J. R. M. Butler.

Butow, R. J. C. *Tojo and the coming of the war*. Princeton UP, 1961.

Churchill, Winston. *The Second World War*, i: *The gathering storm;* ii: *Their finest hour;* iii: *The grand alliance*. London, Cassell, 1949–54.

Deakin, F. W. D. *The brutal friendship: Mussolini, Hitler and the fall of Italian fascism*. London, Weidenfeld & Nicolson, 1962.

Deutscher, Isaac. *Stalin*. London, OUP, 1949.

Eden, Anthony. *The Eden memoirs, 1960–5*, ii: *The reckoning*. London, Cassell, 1965.

Feis, Herbert. *The road to Pearl Harbor; the coming of the war between the United States and Japan*. Princeton, NJ, Van Nostrand, 1950.

De Gaulle, Charles. *Mémoires de guerre*, i: *L'Appel*. Paris, Plon, 1954. Eng. tr. *War memoirs*, i: *The call to honour, 1940–2*. London, Collins, 1955.

Hull, Cordell. *The memoirs of Cordell Hull*. New York, Macmillan, 1948.

Jones, F. C. *Japan's new order in East Asia; its rise and fall, 1937–45*. London, OUP for RIIA, 1954.

Langer, W. L. *Our Vichy gamble*. New York, Knopf, 1947.

— and S. E. Gleason. *The challenge to isolation, 1937–40*. New York, Harper, 1952.

— *The undeclared war*. New York, Harper, 1953.

Leahy, W. D. *I was there*. London, Gollancz, 1950.

Sherwood, R. E. *The White House papers of Harry L. Hopkins*. London, Eyre & Spottiswoode, 1949. 2 vols.

Spears, E. L. *Assignment to catastrophe*, ii: *The Fall of France, June 1940*. London, Heinemann, 1954.

Storry, Richard. *The double patriots; a study of Japanese nationalism.* London, Chatto & Windus, 1957.

Tanner, V. A. *The winter war; Finland against Russia, 1939–40.* Stanford UP, 1957.

USA, Dept of State. *Nazi-Soviet relations, 1939–41: documents from the archives of the German Foreign Office,* ed. R. J. Sontag and J. S. Beddie. Washington, 1948.

Weygand, Maxime. *Memoirs, iii: Recalled to service.* London, Heinemann, 1952.

Woodward, E. L. *British foreign policy.* London, HMSO, 1962.

2. Wartime Diplomacy between the Great Powers

With a few obvious exceptions, the bibliography for Chapter 1 is equally relevant to Chapter 2.

Byrnes, James. *Speaking frankly.* New York, Heinemann, 1947.

Churchill, Winston. *The Second World War,* iv: *The hinge of fate;* v: *Closing the ring;* vi: *Triumph and tragedy.* London, Cassell, 1951–4.

De Gaulle, Charles. *Mémoires de guerre,* ii: *L'unité;* iii: *Le salut.* Paris, Plon, 1956–9. Eng. tr. *War memoirs,* ii: *Unity;* iii: *Salvation.* London, Collins, 1959–60.

Djilas, Milovan. *Conversations with Stalin.* London, Hart-Davis, 1962.

Feis, Herbert. *The China tangle; the American effort in China from Pearl Harbor to the Marshall mission.* Princeton UP, 1953.

— *Churchill, Roosevelt, Stalin: the War they waged and the peace they sought.* Princeton UP, 1957.

— *Between war and peace; the Potsdam conference.* Princeton UP, 1960.

Forrestal, James. *The Forrestal diaries,* ed. by W. Millis. New York, Viking Press, 1951.

Leonhard, Wolfgang. *Child of the revolution,* tr. by C. M. Woodhouse. London, Collins, 1957.

RIIA. *Survey of international affairs 1939–46: America, Britain, and Russia, 1941–6,* by W. H. McNeill. London, 1953.

Stettinius, E. R. *Roosevelt and the Russians.* New York, Doubleday, 1949.

Truman, H. S. *The Truman memoirs,* i: *Year of decisions.* New York, Doubleday, 1955.

Butler, J. R. M., ed. *Grand strategy,* v: *August 1943–September 1944,* by John Ehrman; vi: *October 1944–August 1945,* by John Ehrman. London, HMSO, 1956.

610   A HISTORY OF WAR AND PEACE

3. From War to Cold War

Bell, Coral. *Negotiation from strength; a study in the politics of power.* London, Chatto & Windus, 1962.

— *The debatable alliance; an essay in Anglo-American relations.* London, OUP for RIIA, 1964.

Clay, L. du B. *Decision in Germany.* London, Heinemann, 1950.

Grosser, Alfred. *Western Germany,* tr. by Richard Rees. London, Allen & Unwin, 1955.

— *La politique extérieure de la quatrième république.* Paris, Eds du Seuil, 1965.

Kennan, George. *American diplomacy 1900–50.* Chicago UP, 1951. (Includes the *Foreign Affairs* articles.)

Lippmann, Walter. *The cold war.* New York, Harper, 1947.

Nicholas, H. G. *Britain and the United States.* London, Chatto & Windus, 1963.

Price, H. B. *The Marshall plan and its meaning.* Ithaca, NJ, Cornell UP, 1955.

RIIA. *Survey of international affairs, 1939–46: Four-power control in Germany and Austria, 1945–6,* by Michael Balfour and John Mair. London, OUP, 1956.

Seton-Watson, Hugh. *Neither war nor peace.* London, Methuen, 1960.

— *The east European revolution.* London, Methuen, 1956.

Truman, H. S. *Memoirs,* ii: *Years of trial and hope.* New York, Doubleday, 1956.

Windsor, Philip. *City on leave: a history of Berlin 1945–62.* London, Chatto & Windus, 1963.

4. Confrontation

The bibliography for Chapter 3 is equally relevant. In addition:

Dedijer, Vladimir. *Tito speaks.* London, Weidenfeld & Nicolson, 1953.

Ripka, H. *Le coup de Prague.* Paris, Plon, 1949. Eng. tr. *Czechoslovakia enslaved.* New York, Macmillan, 1950.

RIIA. *The Soviet-Yugoslav dispute.* London, 1948.

— *Defence in the cold war.* London, 1950.

— *Atlantic alliance: NATO's role in the free world.* London, 1952.

— *Britain in western Europe; WEU and the Atlantic alliance.* London, 1956.

Ulam, A. B. *Titoism and the Cominform.* Cambridge, Mass., Harvard UP, 1952.

5. Palestine, Israel, and the Arab States

The wartime memoirs cited for Chapters 1 & 2, especially those of Churchill and de Gaulle, are valuable for the history of the Middle East.

Berger, Morroe. *The Arab world today.* New York, Doubleday, 1962.

Berque, Jacques. *The Arabs, their history and future,* tr. by Jean Stewart. London, Faber, 1964.

Crossman, R. H. S. *Palestine mission, a personal record.* London, Hamilton, 1947.

Hourani, Albert. *Syria and Lebanon: a political essay.* London, OUP for RIIA, 1946.

Khadduri, Majid. *Independent Iraq, 1932–58; a study in Iraqi politics.* 2nd ed. London, OUP for RIIA, 1960.

Kirk, G. E. *A short history of the Middle East.* 7th ed. London, Methuen, 1964. (See also under RIIA.)

Lacouture, Jean and Simone. *Egypt in transition.* London, Methuen, 1958.

Laqueur, W. Z. *Communism and nationalism in the Middle East.* London, Routledge & Kegan Paul, 1956.

Lewis, Geoffrey. *Turkey.* 3rd ed. London, Benn, 1965.

Longrigg, S. H. *Oil in the Middle East; its discovery and development.* 2nd ed. London, OUP for RIIA, 1961.

Marlowe, John (pseud.). *The seat of Pilate.* London, Cresset Press, 1959.

Monroe, Elizabeth. *Britain's moment in the Middle East.* London, Chatto & Windus, 1963.

RIIA. *Survey of international affairs 1939–46: The Middle East in the war, 1945–50* by G. E. Kirk. London, OUP for RIIA, 1952.

— *The Middle East; a political and economic survey.* 3rd ed., ed. Sir Reader Bullard. London, OUP for RIIA, 1958.

Salibi, K. S. *The modern history of Lebanon.* London, Weidenfeld & Nicolson, 1965.

Seale, Patrick. *The struggle for Syria; a study of post-war Arab politics, 1945–58.* London, OUP for RIIA, 1965.

Sykes, Christopher. *Cross-roads to Israel.* London, Collins, 1965.

Weizmann, Chaim. *Trial and error.* London, Hamilton, 1949.

6. China, Japan, and Colonization in Asia

The wartime memoirs cited for Chapters 1 & 2 are valuable for this chapter.

Ball, W. M. *Nationalism and communism in east Asia.* Melbourne UP, 1952.

Beloff, Max. *Soviet policy in the Far East, 1944–51.* London, OUP for RIIA, 1953.

Feis, Herbert. *The China tangle; the American effort in China from Pearl Harbor to the Marshall mission.* Princeton UP, 1953.

Fifield, R. H. *The diplomacy of South East Asia, 1945–58.* New York, Harper, 1958.

Gullick, J. M. *Malaya.* London, Benn, 1964.

Kahin, G. M. *Nationalism and revolution in Indonesia.* London, OUP, 1952.

— ed. *Governments and politics of South East Asia.* 2nd ed. Cornell UP, 1964.

Kennedy, M. D. *A short history of communism in Asia.* London, Weidenfeld & Nicolson, 1957.

Lancaster, Donald. *The emancipation of French Indochina.* London, OUP for RIIA, 1961.

Luard, Evan. *Britain and China.* London, Chatto & Windus, 1962.

Mansergh, P. N. S., ed. *Documents and speeches on Commonwealth affairs 1952–62.* London, OUP for RIIA, 1963.

Moon, Penderel. *Divide and quit.* London, Chatto & Windus, 1961.

Pye, L. W. *Guerrilla communism in Malaya.* Princeton UP, 1956.

Rose, Saul, ed. *Politics in southern Asia.* London, Macmillan, 1963.

RIIA. *Survey of international affairs 1939–46: The Far East, 1942–6,* by F. C. Jones and others. London, OUP for RIIA, 1955.

Spear, Percival. *India, Pakistan and the west.* 3rd ed. London, OUP, 1956.

Stephens, Ian. *Pakistan.* London, Benn, 1963 and Penguin Books, 1964.

Storry, G. R. *A history of modern Japan.* London, Cassell, 1962.

7. The Far East: Korea and After

Refer also to the bibliography for Chapter 6.

Eden, Anthony. *The Eden memoirs,* iii: *Full circle.* London, Cassell, 1960.

Honey, P. J. *North Vietnam today.* New York, Praeger, 1962.

Lyon, Peter. *Neutralism.* Leicester UP, 1963.

Modelski, George, ed. *SEATO; six studies.* Melbourne UP, 1962.

Navarre, Henri. *Agonie de l'Indochine.* Paris, Plon, 1956.

Rees, David. *Korea, the limited war.* London, Macmillan, 1964.

RIIA. *Collective defence in South East Asia; the Manila treaty and its implications.* London, 1956.

8. Atlantic Alliance and European Union

Ball, Mary M. *NATO and the European movement.* London, Stevens, 1959.

Beloff, Max. *Europe and the Europeans.* London, Chatto & Windus, 1957.
— *New dimensions in foreign policy: a study in British administrative experience, 1947–59.* London, Allen & Unwin, 1961.
— *The United States and the unity of Europe.* London, Faber, 1963.
Buchan, Alastair. *NATO in the 1960s.* London, Chatto & Windus, 1960.
Diebold, William. *The Schuman plan.* New York, Praeger, 1959.
Freymond, Jacques. *The Saar conflict, 1945–55.* London, Stevens, 1960.
Haas, E. B. *The uniting of Europe.* London, Stevens, 1958.
Lerner, Daniel, ed. *France defeats EDC.* London, Thames & Hudson, 1957.
Mulley, F. W. *The politics of western defence.* London, Thames & Hudson, 1962.
North Atlantic Treaty Organization. *NATO, the first five years, 1949–54,* by Hastings Ismay. Paris, 1954.
Zurcher, A. J. *The struggle to unite Europe, 1940–58.* New York UP, 1958.

9. The Soviet World and its External Relations

Brzezinski, Z. K. *The Soviet bloc; unity and conflict.* New York, Praeger, 1960.
Dallin, D. J. *Soviet foreign policy after Stalin.* London, Methuen, 1962.
Djilas, Milovan. *The new class.* New York, Praeger, 1957.
Kaser, Michael. *Comecon; integration problems of the planned economies.* London, OUP for RIIA, 1965.
Laqueur, Walter and Leo Labedz, eds. *Polycentrism: the new factor in international communism.* New York, Praeger, 1962.
Leonhard, W. *The Kremlin since Stalin.* London, OUP, 1960.
Lowenthal, Richard. *World communism; the disintegration of secular faith.* London, OUP, 1964.
Mackintosh, J. M. *The strategy and tactics of Soviet foreign policy.* London, OUP, 1962.
Nollau, Gunther. *International communism and world revolution.* London, Hollis & Carter, 1961.
Seton-Watson, Hugh. *The pattern of communist revolution; a historical analysis.* London, Methuen, 1953. (Rev. American ed. *From Lenin to Khrushchev.* New York, Praeger, 1960.)
Wolfe, Bertram. *Khrushchev and Stalin's ghost; text, background and meaning of Khrushchev's secret report to the twentieth congress.* London, Atlantic Press, 1957.

Zinner, P. E.   *National communism and popular revolt in Eastern Europe.*
New York, Columbia UP, 1956.

10. Abadan, Suez, and Cold War in the Middle East

Avery, Peter.   *Modern Iran.*   London, Benn, 1965.

Bromberger, Merry and Serge.   *The secrets of Suez,* tr. by J. Cameron.
London, Pan Books, 1957.

Burns, E. L. M.   *Between Arab and Israeli.*   London, Harrap, 1962.

Campbell, J. C.   *Defense of the Middle East.*   Rev. ed.   New York,
Harper, 1960.

Childers, E. B.   *The road to Suez; a study of western-Arab relations.*
London, Macgibbon & Kee, 1962.

Dayan, Moshe.   *Diary of the Sinai campaign.*   London, Weidenfeld,
1966.

Eden, Anthony.   *The Eden memoirs,* iii: *Full circle.*   London,
Cassell, 1960.

Eisenhower, Dwight.   *The White House Years,* ii: *Waging peace,*
1956-61.   New York, Doubleday, 1961.

Finer, Hermann.   *Dulles over Suez.*   Chicago, Quadrangle Books,
1964.

Ford, A. W.   *The Anglo-Iranian oil dispute of 1951-2.*   Berkeley,
California UP, 1954.

Hourani, Albert.   'The Middle East and the crisis of 1956', in
Oxford University, St Antony's College, *Middle Eastern Affairs,*
No. 1, 1958.

Kerr, Malcolm.   *The Arab cold war, 1958-64; a study of ideology in*
politics.   London, OUP for RIIA, 1965.

Laqueur, W. Z.   *The Soviet Union and the Middle East.*   London,
Routledge, 1959.

Mansfield, Peter.   *Nasser's Egypt.*   Harmondsworth, Penguin
Books, 1965.

Nasser, Gamal Abdel.   *The Philosophy of the Revolution.*   Cairo,
Dar al-Maaref, 1955 [?].

Rondot, Pierre.   *The changing patterns in the Middle East,* tr. by
Mary Dilke.   London, Chatto & Windus, 1961.

Thomas, Hugh.   'The Suez Report', *Sunday Times,* 4, 11, and 18
Sept. 1966.

11. Europe, NATO, and De Gaulle

For books on North Africa see the bibliography for Chapter 13.

Beloff, Nora.   *The General says no; Britain's exclusion from Europe.*
Harmondsworth, Penguin Books, 1963.

Buchan, Alastair.   *NATO in the 1960s.*   Rev. ed.   London,
Chatto & Windus, 1963.

Camps, Miriam. *Britain and the European community, 1955–63.* London, OUP, 1964.
— *What kind of Europe?; the community after the veto.* London, OUP for RIIA, 1965.
Economist Intelligence Unit. *The Commonwealth and Europe.* London, 1960.
Gaitskell, Hugh. *The challenge of coexistence.* London, Methuen, 1957.
Howard, Michael. *Disengagement in Europe.* Harmondsworth, Penguin Books, 1958.
Kennan, George. *Russia, the atom and the west.* London, OUP, 1958.
Kitzinger, U. W. *The challenge of the common market.* Oxford, Blackwell, 1961.

12. New Balance and Fresh Conflict
Crankshaw, Edward. *The new cold war.* Harmondsworth, Penguin Books, 1963.
Draper, Theodore. *Castro's revolution; myths and realities.* New York, Praeger, 1962.
FitzGerald, C. P. *The Chinese view of their place in the world.* London, OUP for RIIA, 1964.
Floyd, David. *Mao against Khrushchev; a short history of the Sino-Soviet conflict.* New York, Praeger, 1963.
Hudson, G. F. and others. The Sino-Soviet dispute, documented and analysed. London, *China Quarterly*, [1961].
Hughes, T. J. and Evan Luard. *The economic development of communist China, 1949–60.* London, OUP for RIIA, 1965.
Schlesinger, Arthur. *A thousand days.* London, Deutsch, 1965.
Sorensen, T. C. *Kennedy.* London, Hodder & Stoughton, 1965.
Windsor, Philip. *City on leave; a history of Berlin, 1945–62.* London, Chatto & Windus, 1963.
Wint, Guy. *Communist China's crusade; Mao's road to power and the new campaign for world revolution.* London, Pall Mall Press, 1965.

13. Africa; a New Continent
Austin, Dennis. *Politics in Ghana, 1946–60.* London, OUP for RIIA, 1964.
Barbour, Nevill. *Morocco.* London, Thames & Hudson, 1965.
Behr, Edward. *The Algerian problem.* London, Hodder & Stoughton, 1961.
Bennett, George and C. G. Rosberg. *The Kenyatta election: Kenya, 1960–1.* London, OUP, 1961.
Blundell, Michael. *So rough a wind; the Kenya memoirs.* London, Weidenfeld & Nicolson, 1964.

Brzezinski, Z. K., ed.   *Africa and the communist world.*   Stanford UP, 1963.

Dumont, René.   *L'Afrique noire est mal partie.*   Paris, Ed. du Seuil, 1962.

Hodgkin, T. L.   *Nationalism in colonial Africa.*   London, Muller, 1956.

Hoskyns, Catherine.   *The Congo since independence, January 1960–December 1961.*   London, OUP for RIIA, 1965.

Julien, C.-A.   *L'Afrique du nord en marche.*   Paris, Juillard, 1953.

Micaud, Charles, ed.   *Tunisia.*   London, Pall Mall Press, 1964.

RIIA.   *A survey of North West Africa (the Maghrib),* ed. by Nevill Barbour.   London, OUP for RIIA. 1959.

Segal, Ronald, ed.   *Political Africa.*   London, Stevens, 1961.

— *African profiles.*   Harmondsworth, Penguin Books, 1962.

Thompson, Virginia M. and R. Adloff.   *French West Africa.*   London, Allen & Unwin, 1958.

Welensky, Roy.   *Welensky's 4000 days.*   London, Collins, 1964.

14. The Warp and Weft of International Relations

See bibliography for Chapters 8 and 11 for books on European institutions.

Boyd, Andrew.   *United Nations, piety, myth and truth.*   Rev. ed.   Harmondsworth, Penguin Books, 1964.

Burns, A. L. and Nina Heathcote.   *Peacekeeping by UN forces.*   London, Pall Mall, 1963.

Cheever, D. S. and H. F. Haviland.   *Organizing for peace.*   London, Stevens, 1954.

Claude, I. L.   *Swords into plowshares.*   New York, Random House, 1956.

Dallin, Alexander.   *The Soviet Union at the United Nations; an inquiry into Soviet motives and objectives.*   London, Methuen, 1962.

Hammarskjöld, Dag.   *The international civil servant in law and in fact.*   Oxford, Clarendon Press, 1961.

— *Markings,* tr. by Leif Sjöberg and W. H. Auden.   London, Faber, 1964.

Lie, Trygve.   *In the cause of peace; seven years with the United Nations.*   New York, Macmillan, 1954.

Nicholas, H. G.   *The United Nations as a political institution.*   2nd ed.   London, OUP, 1962.

United Nations Year Book.

Bull, Hedley.   *The control of the arms race.*   London, Weidenfeld & Nicolson, 1961.

Noel-Baker, Philip.   *The arms race.*   London, Calder, 1960.

Black, Eugene. *The diplomacy of economic development.* New York, Atheneum, 1963.

Gardner, R. N. *Sterling-dollar diplomacy; Anglo-American collaboration in reconstruction of multilateral trade.* Oxford, Clarendon Press, 1956.

Scammell, William M. *International monetary policy.* 2nd ed. London, Macmillan, 1961.

Shonfield, Andrew. *The attack on world poverty.* London, Chatto & Windus, 1960.

Ingram, Derek. *The Commonwealth challenge.* London, Allen & Unwin, 1962.

Mansergh, P. N. S., ed. *Documents and speeches on Commonwealth affairs, 1952–62.* London, OUP for RIIA, 1963.

Pickles, Dorothy. *The government of France.* London, OUP, 1964.

— *The fifth French republic; institutions and politics.* 2nd ed. London, Methuen, 1962.

Williams, Philip. *Crisis and compromise: politics in the fourth republic.* London, Longmans, 1964.

— and Martin Harrison. *De Gaulle's republic.* 2nd ed. London, Longmans, 1961.

American Assembly, 16th, New York, Oct. 1959. *The United States and Latin America.* New York, Columbia University, 1959.

Pendle, George. *A history of Latin America.* Harmondsworth, Penguin Books, 1963.

Perkins, Dexter. *A history of the Monroe Doctrine.* London, Longmans, 1966.

Brzezinski, Z. K. *The Soviet bloc: unity and conflict.* Harvard UP, 1960.

Kaser, Michael. *Comecon; integration problems of the planned economies.* London, OUP for RIIA, 1965.

INDEX

Abbas, Ferhat, 451.

Abdul Rahman, Tunku, 218 f.

Abu Dhabi, 400.

Acheson, Dean, 117; defines US defence perimeter (Jan ' 1950), 197–8, 200; and Hiss, 198; proposes German rearmament, 292–3; reject's Kennan's disengagement thesis, 447; and US action towards Cuba, 489.

Addis Ababa, conference of African states, 525.

Aden, 260, 434 f.

Adenauer, Konrad: and Schuman plan, 118; western European policy of, 279, 287, 469; and rearmament, 293, 296 f., 335; and Saar question, 311 f.; and re-unification, 326–7, 331; establishes diplomatic relations with USSR (1955), 347–8, 350; and Berlin crisis, 478–9, 487; visit to Washington (Mar. 1959), 478–9

Adoula, Cyrille, 521 f.

Afghanistan, 259 n, 425, 496, 604.

Albania, 121.

Aleutian islands, 197.

Algeria, 455–6; see also under France.

Ali Mahir, 152, 383.

Alliance for Progress, 580.

Amery, Julian, 301.

Aqaba, Gulf of, 422–3.

Arab League, 163.

Arab states: nationalism and search for unity, 141, 159–60, 162–3; foreign intervention creates artificial divisions, 141; oil, 141, 160, 162; attitudes to Israel, 161, 176; inter-Arab rivalries, 389–91.

Britain: influence and power (pre-1939), 141–2, 157–8; support for Arab nationalism, 142;—for Arab unity, 148; decline of position (post-1945), 157–9;—attempt to revive, 163–5; effect of Suez invasion on position, 423.

France: influence (pre-1939), 141–2; and Algeria, 400; and Suez, 423.

USSR: limited interest in Stalinist period, 157, 393; Khrushchev's revision, 393–4.

USA: 2nd world war and extension of interest, 157, 392; ambivalence in policy, 387–8, 392–3; oil interests of, 392.

Arbenz, Guzmán, 577.

Arcadia conference (Dec. 1941), 30–33

d'Argenlieu, Adm. Thierry, 214.

Argentina, 75, 575, 579.

Aswan dam, 158, 399, 401–3, 406, 429, 431.

Atlantic Charter (Aug. 1941), 24–25, 31.

Attlee, Clement: prime minister (July 1945), 49, 77; wartime experience of Russians, 107; and Palestine question, 168; visits Truman during Korean war (Dec. 1950), 233.

Australia: and Japanese plans for Asia, 13; and Far Eastern Commission 179 f.; and Allied Council for Japan, 181; provides occupation troops for Japan, 181; and ANZUS pact, 241; and Manila Treaty, 255; supports Britain in Suez crisis, 410–11; assists India, 496; and Security Council veto, 529; reports on non-self-governing territories, 538; and Colombo plan, 599, 600.

Austria: Stalin proposes restoration as independent state (1941), 48; at foreign ministers' conference (Oct. 1943), 48; Russian claim to reparations, 48; Potsdam agreement, 80–81, 102; election (1945), 97–98, 103; Anglo-American reluctance to assume responsibility for occupation, 101; four-power occupation agreed, 101–2; Allied Council for, 102; Soviet recognition of, 102–3; Soviet economic policies, 104; neutrality, 261, 343; and Warsaw Treaty, 338, 342; State Treaty, 342–3; and EFTA, 458.

Hitler, *cont.*
Britain, 11; and invasion of Russia, 20–21; and Matsuoka, 27; declaration of war on US, 27; and Italian surrender, 44–45; rejection of Balkan strategy, 45; plot of July 1944, 60; prestige in Middle East, 143–4.

Ho Chi Minh (*ps.*): recognition by communist China, 195, 215;—by USSR, 215; and independence of Indo-China, 213–15.

Hoffmann, Johannes, 311–12.

Honduras, 577.

Hong Kong, 194.

Hoover, Herbert, Jr, 422.

Hopkins, Harry: Roosevelt's aide, 12; visits Stalin (1941), 24; visits London (Apr. 1942), 33; Moscow visits (1941), 24;—(May 1945), 67, 76, 529; at Yalta, 70 n.

Houphouët-Boigny, F., 571.

Hull, Cordell: Jap. policy, 15; Hull–Nomura talks, 23, 25–26; and de Gaulle, 31, 53–54; views of postwar world, 46–48.

Hungary: Vienna award (Aug. 1940), 19; and Germany in 2nd world war, 20, 27; elections (1945), 97–98; peace treaty, 99–101; Ferenc Nagy govt, 113, 122; and Marshall offer, 114–15; purge (1949), 322; and Warsaw treaty, 338; and new Soviet policy (1956), 356; rising (1956), 362–7;—impact of, 366–7, 373, 443, 445; 'Hungarian road to socialism', 368; disengagement debate (1957–8), 445–6.

Hurley, P. J., 188, 189, 190.

Husain, King, 391 n., 401, 429.

Ibn Saud, King, 144, 391.

Iceland, 138.

Ileo, Joseph, 520.

India: Japanese plans for, 13; and British Middle East policy, 163–4; and UN Palestine resolution, 170; and Japan, 182, 241; and Tibet, 196–7, 493–4; independence, 201, 202–4; nationalist movement in, 201–2; importance in world politics, 204, 239;—in British Asian policy, 240, 245–6; and Indonesian independence, 207–10; and Korea,

India, *cont.*
237; membership of Vietnam commission, 251; and SEATO, 257; and Bandung conference, 259–61; neutralism of, 261;—Dulles's antipathy to, 246; conflict with China, 492–6; and Sino-Pakistan agreement, 496; war with Pakistan, 505–7; and Indians in S. Africa, and Commonwealth 567–8; and Colombo plan, 599 n.; and US aid, 602; and Soviet aid, 604.

Indo-China: Japanese plans for, 13; occupation, 15, 23, 201; Chinese recognition of Ho Chi Minh govt, 195, 215; under French Empire and Union, 212; Japanese surrender, 213; Ho Chi Minh govt, 213; French war, 214–15, 246–7; Bao Dai govt, 215; at Geneva conference (1954), 247–51; Geneva agreement, 251–2, 337, 497; effect of war on European politics, 299, 302, 312; *see also* Cambodia; Laos; Vietnam.

Indonesia: establishment of republic, 201, 206; conflict with Holland, 206–9; Linggadjati agreement (Nov. 1946), 206; Renville agreement, 207; attempted communist coups (1946, 1948), 206, 209; independence agreement, 210; importance in world politics, 210–11; and US, 211; increase in communist strength (1952), 353; and USSR, 211, 353–4; and UN 532; and Colombo plan, 599 n.

Indus river, 204

International Bank for Reconstruction and Development (World Bank), 557–8, 566.

International Development Association, 566.

International Monetary Fund, 556–8, 563, 566.

International Trade Organization, 561–3.

Iran: occupation by Britain and USSR, 104, 151; Azerbaijan crisis (1946), 104–6, 393; German influence in, 151; abdication of Riza Shah, 151; and Bandung conference, 259 n.; nationalization of AIOC, 376–81;—settle-